*Indigenous South Americans
of the Past and Present*

INDIGENOUS SOUTH AMERICANS

of the

PAST AND PRESENT

An Ecological Perspective

David J. Wilson

SOUTHERN METHODIST UNIVERSITY

WESTVIEW PRESS
A Member of the Perseus Books Group

Copyright © 1999 by Westview Press, A Member of the Perseus Books Group

Published in 1999 in the United States of America by Westview Press, 5500 Central Avenue, Boulder, Colorado 80301-2877, and in the United Kingdom by Westview Press, 12 Hid's Copse Road, Cumnor Hill, Oxford OX2 9JJ

Book design by Jane Raese

Library of Congress Cataloging-in-Publication Data
Wilson, David J. (David John), 1941–
   Indigenous South Americans of the past and present : an ecological
perspective / David J. Wilson.
        p.   cm.
   Includes bibliographical references and index.
   ISBN 0-8133-3609-0 (hc). — 0-8133-3610-4 (pb)
   1. Indians of South America—Social life and customs.   2. Indians
of South America—Antiquities.   3. Ethnology—South America.
4. Human ecology—South America.   5. Archaeology—South America.
6. South America—Antiquities.   7. South America—Social life and
customs.   I. Title.
F2230.1.S7W55   1999
980'.01—dc21   98-41779
                                                                CIP

The paper used in this publication meets the requirements of the American National Standard for Permanence of Paper for Printed Library Materials Z39.48-1984.

10   9   8   7   6   5   4   3   2   1

Contents

Tables and Figures

Preface

THIS IS AN AGE WHEN ANTHROPOLOGY, like other disciplines, has become more and more specialized. Many of its practitioners in the two main subfields—archaeology and ethnology—are increasingly unable or unwilling to inform themselves about, or even be interested in, the research and publications of their colleagues in other subfields. In fact, archaeologists and ethnologists working in one part of a continent may not have the time or interest to keep up with the research and literature of their colleagues who work elsewhere on that continent. Perhaps even more characteristic of this age, however, is the increasing theoretical fragmentation of the discipline. Many researchers still would classify themselves as adhering to a consistent overarching theoretical structure—for example, ecological anthropology—that requires them to be informed about recent sociocultural phenomena, if they are archaeologists, or about the ancient prehistoric past, if they are sociocultural anthropologists. Nevertheless, there now seem to be almost as many isolated theoretical perspectives as there are faculty in each department. Among these (often mutually exclusive) perspectives, anthropologists may describe themselves as symbolists, interpretivists, structuralists, cognitivists, feminists, medical anthropologists, cultural ecologists, cultural materialists, and so on—that is, if they care to classify themselves as theoretically oriented at all, since some (postmodernists, for example) would prefer unabashedly to be characterized as atheoretical, if not totally antitheoretical.

This book, as suggested by its title, *Indigenous South Americans of the Past and Present*, in several ways runs counter to these trends. First, it deals with an entire continent rather than focusing on just one of its geographic areas, giving more or less equal weight to the eastern lowlands—the vast area to the east of the Andes that constitutes Venezuela, the Guianas, Brazil, Paraguay, Uruguay, and Argentina—as it does to the Andes—the narrow mountainous and Pacific littoral area that constitutes much of Colombia, Ecuador, Peru, Bolivia, and Chile. Second, the book focuses as much or more on recent indigenous groups as it does on the prehistoric past. Indeed, in some geographic areas (e.g., Tierra del Fuego, the Sierra Nevada de Santa Marta, and the Central Andes) both archaeological and

recent sociocultural data are provided that document an essentially unbroken sequence of indigenous adaptation in those areas. Third, as suggested by the subti-
tle, *An Ecological Perspective*, the book follows the theoretical lead of Julian
Steward and his adherents in arguing that cultures—ancient or modern—must
be understood as much by reference to the physical environment, which provides
a critical part of their adaptive context, as by reference to their many sociocultural features.

The last book to deal with the archaeology, ethnology, and environments of
indigenous South Americans in terms of such a theoretical structure was *Native
Peoples of South America*, which was published forty years ago by Julian Steward
and his colleague Louis Faron. Thus, professors searching for a text in courses
where the South American anthropological and environmental data are brought
together in dealing with both ancient and recent adaptive systems may have encountered the same problem that I have increasingly faced in the past several
years. It has been difficult, if not impossible, to find a single publication that
would form the main text of such a course. Although used copies of Steward and
Faron were available until rather recently, it is no longer possible to find enough
of these copies for courses that have enrollments of at least ten to fifteen students. Moreover, Steward and Faron's book has become outdated in at least two
significant ways. First, with the recent development of ecological anthropology,
Steward's theory of cultural ecology has become less and less acceptable. Cultural
ecology, when judged especially by the work of its adherents who acknowledge
an intellectual debt to Steward, tends to focus on the material infrastructure of
adaptive systems—including the physical environment, subsistence, and demography—while paying little, if any, attention to such features as ritual and cosmology. Second, with the increase in archaeological and ethnological research since
the 1950s, there is no question that we know far more today about indigenous
South Americans than was known at the time Steward edited the seven-volume
Handbook of South American Indians in the late 1940s, on which his and Faron's
book was based.

Indeed, the vastly greater knowledge we have at the end of the twentieth century means that a single monograph must, of necessity, deal with a relatively restricted number of exemplary cases of indigenous adaptation to the continent
over the thirteen thousand or so years since the first-known human arrivals
there. This book nevertheless deals with at least several cases of each of the four
main levels of sociopolitical integration—bands, villages, chiefdoms, and
states—that have existed during that vast amount of time. Following the introductory chapter, Chapter 2 begins the substantive part of the book. In it, I outline the intellectual background, beginning with Steward's cultural ecology, of a
new theoretical structure—the systems-hierarchical evolutionary paradigm—
that grows not only out of Steward's thinking, but also out of that of Roy Rappaport, Kent Flannery, Jeffrey Parsons, Elman Service, Betty Meggers, Gerardo
Reichel-Dolmatoff, and Marvin Harris, among a number of other researchers. I
then discuss in detail the main elements of the paradigm, showing how it incorporates the best features of previous theories but throws out some of their other,

more problematic, features. I apply the paradigm consistently throughout the rest of the book, both in presenting the data and theories on indigenous human adaptation to the continent and in critiquing and/or refining the theories of other researchers.

Given the twin issues of a lack of dialogue between the two main subfields of anthropology and the increasing theoretical fragmentation of our discipline, the reader quickly sees that I lay out my theory and apply it consistently with no less a goal than demonstrating its reasonableness in bringing the discipline back together. I also imply, at the least, that no other theory (including the highly polemical theory of cultural materialism espoused by Harris) can do this as well as the systems-hierarchical paradigm. Although I make no excuse for my missionary zeal in attempting to reawaken interest in the creation of a grand unifying theory for anthropology, I must nevertheless beg the reader's indulgence while the enterprise is being carried out. By the last chapter of the book, I think it will be clear in any case that I consider the paradigm to be a "work in progress" rather than some sort of fait accompli. Indeed, it is one that I will continue to tinker with and that I suspect will receive much constructive criticism from others.

The next two chapters discuss a variety of topics that provide the necessary background in appreciating the almost incredible variability that has characterized indigenous adaptations from place to place across the continent through thirteen thousand years. Chapter 3 addresses the geological and biological evolution of South America, describing in detail the eight main environmental zones of the continent. Although the indigenous people of the continent fade momentarily into the background in this chapter, the inclusion here of such a detailed overview of the physical environment—both abiotic and biotic—needs little or no justification in light of the ecological and evolutionary underpinning of the paradigm developed and used throughout this book. Chapter 4 relates subsistence types (e.g., hunting-gathering, slash and burn, irrigation agriculture) to their appropriate environmental contexts and these two aspects of indigenous adaptive systems, in turn, to the maximum level of sociopolitical integration that could be achieved in these contexts. The remainder of the chapter provides a detailed overview of the principal flora and fauna of the continent, including a treatment of the main plant and animal resources utilized by indigenous groups that, I think, no earlier anthropological book on the continent has done—this treatment is based on reference to the principal cultigens in *Lost Crops of the Incas* (National Research Council), hallucinogenic substances in *Plants of the Gods* (Schultes and Hoffman), and medicinal herbs in *Healers of the Andes* (Bastien). For most people who have not traveled to South America, it, like any continent outside the purview of daily routine, is replete with exotic floral domesticates (the few faunal ones, such as llamas, alpacas, and guinea pigs, will be familiar to all, of course). These plants need to be discussed in some detail not only because they show the genius of human adaptation, but also because they help explain the variability that characterizes adaptive systems across the continent as well as the achievement of such complex prehistoric societies as the Inca.

Chapters 5 through 9 deal with the different exemplary adaptive systems and theoretical arguments on which I have chosen to focus. These chapters proceed geographically from south to north—and around the continent in roughly counterclockwise fashion in order of evolutionary scale from band through village, chiefdom, and state societies—and include several groups, related sites, and topics. Chapter 5, on bands, begins by redressing Steward's "bands as marginals" argument and then deals with the Ona and the Yahgan of Tierra del Fuego, based on Martín Gusinde's monumental studies in the early twentieth century; the Nukak of eastern Colombia, based on Gustavo Politis's recent study in the 1990s; and the Paleoindian sites of Fell's Cave, Monte Verde, Pikimachay, Tibitó, Taima-Taima, Caverna da Pedra Pintada, and Pedra Furada, based on archaeological research carried out between the 1930s and the mid-1990s. Parenthetically, it should be noted that neither Gusinde's two uniquely masterful studies nor that of Politis has yet been translated from Spanish to English, so the overviews of the Ona, the Yahgan, and the Nukak included in this book make the data available for the first time in reasonable detail to those who do not read Spanish fluently.

Chapter 6, on villages and chiefdoms of the Amazon, begins by constructing a model of human adaptation to the Amazon *terra firme* and *várzea* niches, based on the work of Emilio Moran and that of Betty Meggers. It then redresses features of Donald Lathrap's "displaced-persons theory"—from the *várzea* to the *terra firme*—and Robert Carneiro's Kuikuru arguments, which formed the basis for the latter researcher's well-known theory of circumscription and warfare in the origins of the state. Next the chapter deals with the Mundurucú of the south-central Amazon, based on Robert and Yolanda Murphy's studies; the Yanomamö of the northern Amazon, based on Napoleon Chagnon's long-term research; the Shuar-Jívaro of eastern Ecuador, based on Michael Harner's research; the Desana of eastern Colombia, based on Gerardo Reichel-Dolmatoff's work; and the Omagua of the Amazon *várzea*, based on Spanish ethnohistorical documents. The chapter ends by taking a critical look at Anna Roosevelt's ecologically based "complexity in the Amazon" argument and Pierre Clastres's strongly contrasting political argument (in *Society Against the State*) about why no complexity ever occurred on the *terra firme*.

Chapter 7, on villages and chiefdoms of the northwest, deals first with the Kogi of the Sierra Nevada de Santa Marta, based on Gerardo Reichel-Dolmatoff's work; and their Tairona predecessors, based on ethnohistorical documents and Alvaro Soto Holguin's archaeological excavations at Buritaca and nearby sites. It ends with an overview of arguments made by Donald Lathrap, Jorge Marcos, and James Zeidler about Real Alto site, on the southwest coast of Ecuador, in relation to the rise of societal complexity in the Central Andes (not to mention Mesoamerica) and to the Bororo of central Brazil, a discussion I have based on Claude Lévi-Strauss's elegant work *Tristes Tropiques*.

Chapter 8, on contemporary central Andean groups, begins by discussing models of human adaptation to the sierra environment. It then goes on to deal with the Q'eros Quechua of southeastern Peru, based on Steven Webster's work; and the Kallawayas of Ayllu Kaata, northwestern Bolivia, based on Joseph Bastien's research.

Chapter 9, on the rise of prehispanic Central Andean states, deals first with models of human adaptation to the coast environment, where the first state formation in South America occurred. It then critiques Michael Moseley's "maritime hypothesis" of Andean state origins and Robert Carneiro's "coercive theory" of state origins, based on my own research on the Peruvian coast. The chapter ends with detailed overviews of the Chavín culture, the first widespread cult phenomenon in the Peruvian Andes; the Moche polity, the first large-scale, or regional, state in the Central Andes; and the Inca empire, the largest imperial polity ever to exist anywhere in South America.

Chapter 10 brings the discussion back full circle to the paradigm I develop in Chapter 2—first, by summarizing briefly and explicitly its main features, and, second, by critiquing several other paradigmatic approaches/models in light of it. The final section—organized in four parts that include band, village, chiefdom, and state adaptive systems—summarizes some of the main theoretical conclusions that can be drawn from a consideration of the materials and arguments presented in Chapters 3 through 9.

Over the four years it took me to write this book, I attempted to present both the theoretical arguments and the data on each indigenous group or site as lucidly and interestingly as possible. For the reader unfamiliar with certain anthropological, ecological, and South American terms that are consistently used in the text, a glossary is provided following Chapter 10. Coupled with this, I have produced a series of more than 120 accompanying illustrations that should make clear to any reader—whether lay, academic colleague, or student—not only the reasoning behind the theoretical discussions, but also as many details as possible of the environment and culture (from infrastructure to cosmology) of each indigenous group whose adaptive system is discussed. In this regard, I believe that the first two chapters of the book draw the reader almost inevitably into a consideration of the interesting data with which it deals (ranging from Ona gender relations and warfare, through the magical-hostile world of Mundurucú and Shuar-Jívaro headtaking, to the imperial Inca system), and of how these data relate to the construction and development of the systems-hierarchical evolutionary paradigm. Ultimately, my goal is twofold: to present South American–specific anthropological data and to imply how data and theories of a more universal, worldwide nature might be addressed in a paradigmatic context of the kind employed in this book.

Finally, on a more personal note, I have spent over half my life residing, traveling, and carrying out research in South America. Throughout this book, I have attempted to convey my deep interest in the continent and its indigenous peoples, and I hope that this book will encourage others to read and learn more about the continent and travel or do research there. However, from both a theoretical and empirical perspective, I also argue that all features of indigenous adaptive systems—from subsistence to cosmology—must be understood as potentially related to one another in the functioning, maintenance, and evolution of these systems. From the standpoint of science, this means that all of these features should be included in anthropological investigations, but from a broader humanistic perspective, this argument also implies that respect should be accorded indigenous religions, cosmologies, and cultures in general—however much the forces of change exerted by the outside world continue ever more strongly to affect them.

David J. Wilson

Acknowledgments

THIS BOOK BUILDS FIRST AND FOREMOST on the work and writings of Julian Steward, whom I count among the anthropological researchers and theoreticians who have most inspired me in my own work. Among his many contributions to the science of anthropology, Steward provided the first convincing demonstration of the active dynamic that exists between human cultural systems and the environmental context to which they adapt. I also owe a debt to the thinking and polemical argumentation of Marvin Harris, whose publications, especially *Cannibals and Kings* and *Cultural Materialism*, constitute, in my opinion, the most important contribution by any single anthropologist toward the full development of the implications of Steward's original cultural ecological arguments.

Adding to Steward's and Harris's contributions, specifically in taking them in the more reasonable direction of an ecological anthropology that transcends the limitations inherent in the infrastructural determinism of Steward's cultural ecology and Harris's cultural materialism, are Kent Flannery and the late Roy Rappaport. In their publications and in several seminars at the University of Michigan, they provided direction and inspiration that I expect to last at least the rest of my active career. Although I have been influenced strongly by a number of their publications, Flannery's paper "The Cultural Evolution of Civilizations" and Rappaport's book *Pigs for the Ancestors* clearly brought about the most insight into the ultimate potential of an all-inclusive systems approach that at once embraces both the concrete/material and the abstract/mental features of human adaptive systems—thereby, for example, bridging the divisive gap between those researchers who would prefer to focus only on the countable, siftable, weighable phenomena of this world and those who react to such "vulgar" procedures by focusing on their bipolar opposite, namely, what the materialists might view as the "touchy-feely" abstractions of symbols and meaning systems. As I attempt to demonstrate in this book, both of these theoretical stances must be included in the building of a comprehensive approach to understanding the origins, functioning, and evolution of human adaptive systems.

I must also credit two other individuals for their pathbreaking application of the principles of ecological anthropology to several South American cases and hence for leading the way. They are Betty Meggers, who has published the most persuasive account of the potentials and limitations of the Amazon Basin for human adaptive systems in her book *Amazonia*, and the late Gerardo Reichel-Dolmatoff, whose elegant arguments about the adaptive relationship between ideology and the rest of the human ecosystem are contained in his numerous writings on Colombia, especially *Amazonian Cosmos* and "Cosmology as Ecological Analysis."

In my own work in South America, I have been influenced in particular by two researchers: Gordon Willey and Jeffrey Parsons. Their archaeological investigations in both Peru and Mexico represent the successful result of Steward's original urging that, if we are to understand the nature and evolution of recent and ancient subsistence-settlement systems, we must carry out settlement pattern studies of those systems. As will be clear shortly, I am also indebted to Jeffrey Parsons and Kent Flannery for introducing me to the writings and thinking of Elman Service and for insisting that heuristic models of sociopolitical systems—including those dealing with (1) levels of sociopolitical integration and (2) systemic functioning—are a necessary feature of the cross-cultural evolutionary approach originally advocated by Steward.

For a sabbatical leave in 1994 to begin researching and writing this book, I thank the Department of Anthropology and the dean of Dedman College at Southern Methodist University. This is the appropriate place to thank Southern Methodist University for its forward-looking policy of providing all of its faculty, including myself, with a powerful new generation of personal computers capable, to give just one example, of permitting me to use the latest versions of Adobe Illustrator (from 4.0 through 7.0) to prepare all of the graphics that accompany the text. In fact, I think most students and colleagues who visit my office think that SMU provided special glue as well to keep me virtually attached to the computer.

John Phinney, a colleague in anthropology and the Institute for the Study of Earth and Man librarian at SMU, over the past decade has consistently brought to my attention new acquisitions on South America and has offered much encouragement over the several years it took for this book to take shape. I should also note that, on the death of Steward, Southern Methodist University acquired his library. Thus, in doing research in the literature for several sections of this book—such as Robert Murphy's 1958 publication on Mundurucú religion in the chapter for the Amazon—I often was using materials from Steward's personal library. Already following in his theoretical footsteps, I thus had the occasional, more concrete experience of following in his reading of the South American literature as well.

For careful editorial work in checking the quantitative figures in several chapters relating the English system of measurement to the metric system, I owe a debt to Michael Bletzer, who caught several errors before they escaped my computer to achieve more enduring published form. For information and materials that helped in the preparation of the chapter on band-level societies, I wish to thank David Meltzer, for revised dates on the phases at Pedra Furada site, Brazil; and Lewis Binford, for access to his copies of Gusinde's monumental studies of the Yahgan-Yámana and the Ona-Selk'nam of Tierra del Fuego, carried out in the 1920s not too many years before the complete demise of both of these peoples. Lew also provided me with papers and a book published in Colombia by Politis, a student of one of his own former students, Luis Borrero, on important recent studies carried out by Politis and his colleagues of the Nukak Makú, a group of rain-forest foragers still living in the eastern part of that country.

Having been trained at Michigan by earlier students of Binford, I have had the considerable pleasure over the past few years of becoming associated with him as a colleague. As is well known among anthropologists, he is the intellectual progenitor of what many consider to be the most influential approach in the latter half of the twentieth century to the development of anthropological archaeology as a science. Lew has a habit (which I suspect many of his colleagues over the years have experienced) of walking into one's office in the morning and asking, "Well, what special theoretical insights have you come up with today?" Putting the most favorable light on it that I can muster from my point of view, I must admit that he has always asked the question too early in the day's work to get any sort of coherent answer out of me. However, should he read these pages, I hope that he will find at least a few such insights here—most of them achieved after a few cups of coffee a little later in the day.

My love and thanks go to my wife, Paula, who has contributed in many ways to this book. She is a former student herself at Florida Atlantic University of Gerald Weiss, South Americanist anthropologist and researcher on the Campa of eastern Peru, and at Florida International University of Janet Chernela, another South Americanist anthropologist and researcher on the Wanano of eastern Colombia. Paula has mentioned materials to read, argued points, suggested refinements of sections, and in general encouraged me ceaselessly throughout the sometimes daunting experience of writing a book that deals with indigenous South Americans across the entire continent. There is no place better than this to express my love and admiration for my two sons, Jon and Chris, who help in enterprises such as this one simply by being here—on the scene, so to speak! To my seven feline "offspring"—Megan, Shayna, Lexie, Josie, Casey, Sebastian, and Isabella—I owe not a little of the sanity I have retained after the occasional vexing day at the office.

I also thank Karl Yambert, senior editor; Elizabeth Lawrence, project editor; Jan Kristiansson, copy editor; and all of their associates at Westview Press for wisely and firmly guiding this book from manuscript through to its final form. Over several years of continuing enthusiasm and unflagging support for this book, Karl has kept me on track and determined, in spite of occasional adversities, to develop it properly and see it through to publication. I also owe a debt of gratitude to two of the three reviewers, who kindly chose not to remain anonymous so as to permit further dialogue with me regarding their suggestions for improvements to the manuscript. They are Joseph Bastien (University of Texas–

Arlington) and Betty Meggers (Smithsonian Institution). I have not followed all of their suggestions, but those that were incorporated have undoubtedly improved the final version—so I must thank them for their contributions, just as I thank all of the researchers whose work has been incorporated here, while at the same time absolving all from any egregious and overlooked errors, which are entirely my responsibility.

Finally, I express my gratitude to several dozens of students in my undergraduate and graduate courses with whom I have discussed much of the materials dealt with in this book. Over the past several years, these discussions have frequently helped me refine still undeveloped arguments and, just as often, have resulted in suggestions by the students themselves about the proper and logical way to view, analyze, and relate the various data discussed here. There are too many to name them all, but I hope that a few who chance to read the pages that follow will find familiar signs along the way of the mutual enterprise we all engaged in as we discussed the indigenous groups of South America.

D.J.W.

CHAPTER I

Introduction

SOMETIME FIFTEEN TO twenty thousand years ago, the first human settlers of the Americas crossed the land bridge between the Old and New Worlds and, through countless generations, eventually made their way south across the Isthmus of Panama to the continent of South America. As their ancestors to the north had done, the first inhabitants of the southern New World became expert collectors and hunters of the wild flora and fauna that flourished in astonishing diversity across the length and breadth of this vast area. Although the earliest date of their arrival in South America is still the subject of research and much debate, we now know with some certainty that by thirteen thousand years ago the Paleoindians, as they generally are called by anthropologists, had extended their occupation of the continent as far south as the Chilean site of Monte Verde, located some 5,500 kilometers south of the isthmus. By about eleven thousand years ago, they had reached the southernmost tip of the continent, judging from archaeological finds at sites such as Palli Aike and Fell's Cave in Chile.

In what in general human evolutionary terms was but a brief flash of time—from thirteen thousand years ago to the beginning of the European conquest in A.D. 1532—the descendants of the Paleoindians adapted to every possible inhabitable environment throughout the continent—including the frigid straits and coniferous forests of the far south, the grassy pampas of modern-day Argentina, the rugged seasonally arid Brazilian uplands south of the Amazon River, the vast green sweep of the Amazon rain forest itself, and the awesome Andes mountain chain perched high over the western edge of the continent along its entire 7,700-kilometer length.

The types of human adaptive systems, or "levels of sociocultural integration," as anthropologist Julian H. Steward (1955:5) calls them, one would have encountered just prior to A.D. 1532 in this great diversity of environments included all of those found in other parts of the preindustrial world: migratory gatherer-hunter band groups still exploiting wild flora and fauna as had their Paleoindian ancestors; sedentary and semisedentary tribal villagers focused on small-scale agriculture, or horticulture; societies of incipient sociopolitical complexity, called chiefdoms, relying on relatively more intensive and productive agricultural systems; and, finally, societies at the maximum, or state, level of preindustrial complexity based on even more intensive food-producing systems involving irrigation agriculture.

SOUTH AMERICAN INDIGENOUS GROUPS

The mention here of just a few of these groups by name (some sounding like so many poetic tongue twisters), as well as one or two features of their fame, makes clear not only that any attempt at comprehensive anthropological treatment of indigenous South Americans faces challenges, but also that at least some are known even to the beginning scholar focused on this continent (see Figure 1.1). At the level of hunter-gatherers there were (or are)

- the Yahgan (Yámana) canoe people and the Ona (Selk'nam) guanaco hunters of Tierra del Fuego, located at the southern tip of the continent, both groups adapted to one of the most challenging environments anywhere in the world;
- the Chono and Alacaluf (Halakwulup) canoe people of the towering forests and deep fjords of the rainy Chilean archipelago;
- the Puelche and Tehuelche of the dry, grassy southern pampas of Argentina, who used multiple leather thongs with attached pouches containing stones (more succinctly called *bolas*) to bring down the ñandú, or South American ostrich, of this area; and
- the Sirionó, who until very recently roamed the humid jungles of eastern lowland Bolivia practicing a mix of horticulture and hunting-gathering that permitted the continuance of their essentially mobile lifestyle.

All of these groups are now either totally extinct as populations or have lost most, or all, of their traditional lifeways as they were assimilated into nearby Latin American culture.

At the autonomous village level there are (or were)

- the Bororo of central Brazil, whose complex on-the-ground village layouts represent one of the most interesting and complicated South American social organizations;
- the Sherente of central Brazil, who, like many other South American groups from the Amazon area to the Andes, live in opposing but complementary societal halves called moieties;
- the Tupinambá of the eastern Amazon Basin, now extinct, but infamous in early colonial times as cannibals who cooked their human victims in large pots;
- the Kayapó of the southern Amazon Basin, a fiercely independent and, to intruding Brazilian settlers at least, warlike people whose cause recently was taken up by anthropologist Darrell Posey and rock star Sting;

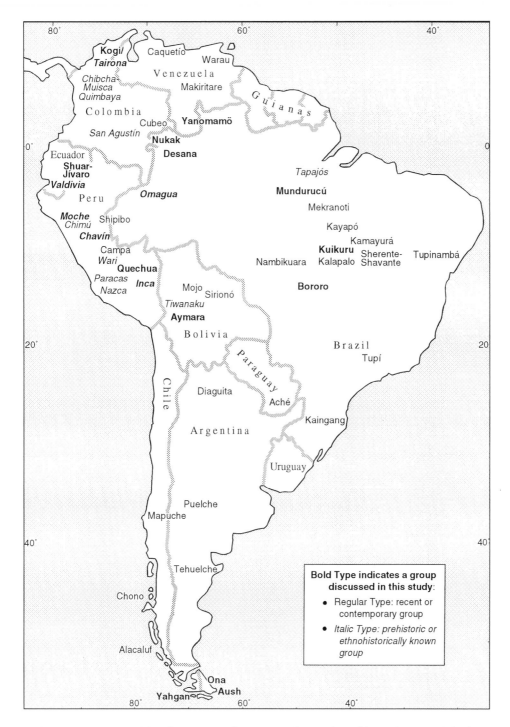

FIGURE 1.1   Map of South America showing modern political boundaries and the location of selected indigenous groups past and present.

- the Mundurucú of the upper Tapajós River, in the southern part of the Amazon, known for their matrilocal marriage rule, the social solidarity of the women, and the long-distance raiding expeditions against unrelated groups carried out by the men, who, upon bringing human captives and trophy heads back to the settlements, returned in an exalted spiritual state that disallowed sexual relations for several years;
- the Yanomamö "fierce people" of northernmost Brazil and southeastern Venezuela, whose shamans, like many of those from Tierra del Fuego to the jungles of Venezuela, "throw" magical darts (called *hekura,* in Yanomamö) around their environment to cause any number of ills and, not surprisingly, the corresponding need for shamans in other villages to suck these darts out of the body in attempts to cure the intended victims; and
- the Shuar-Jívaro, of eastern Ecuador, who attacked nearby neighbors, including even their own kin, and until just recently shrank the heads of human victims killed on raiding expeditions to gain control over the soul power (called *muisak*) of the killed warriors.

Among the many groups at a village level of complexity outside the Amazon are

- the Kogi of the Sierra de Santa Marta, northern Colombia, a still unassimilated people who recently invited outsiders from BBC television in for a brief stay in their mountain fastness to deliver, as our "elder brothers," a message aimed at averting further ecological disasters in what they see as the dying "civilized" world of we "younger brothers";
- the Colorados, who live in rain forests on the western slopes of the Ecuadorian Andes and are so named because of the men's custom of dyeing their hair with a red paste made from the achiote plant;
- the Aymara and the Quechua, who live in the hundreds of thousands across the high grasslands, or *puna,* and adjacent deep valleys of the Andean countries of Bolivia, Peru, and Ecuador, and who, although partly assimilated into national economies, still maintain egalitarian village adaptations that date back several thousand years; and
- the Mapuche of central Chile, who were famous in the early colonial period for their fierce resistance to the European encroachment and who still maintain many aspects of their traditional way of life.

Whereas some of the band and village groups mentioned here have survived and many others are extinct, all of the indigenous Contact-period cultures at the levels of chiefdoms and states are now extinct, most of them having met with this fate either during the Conquest or within a century or so after the arrival of the Old World outsiders. This occurred not least because these cultures occupied some of the most productive environments, to which, not surprisingly, the intruders were attracted for their own use. Nevertheless, we are speaking here of the extinction of these cultures as sociopolitical entities, or polities, and not as peoples, since in many cases at least some fraction of their populations survived the shock of intrusive cultures and diseases.

Among the best-known Contact-period societies at the chiefdom level were

- the Tapajós of the lower Amazon River, who were made famous by the accounts of Francisco de Orellana both for their great numbers and sociopolitical complexity and for the fact that their war leaders appeared to be women (hence the name *Amazons,* from Greek mythology, given to the river);
- the Omagua of the upper Amazon River, whose settlements, like those of their downstream neighbors, appear to have extended for "leagues" along the main river channel and were based on the high productivity of the nutrient-rich waters of the main channel of the river;
- the Tairona, whose prehispanic chiefdom-level societies are ancestral to the village-level Kogi (which, as will be seen in a later chapter, raises the issue of societal *de*volution in the face of the European intrusion);
- the Muisca, or Chibcha, of the central Colombian plateau around the modern city of Bogotá, famous, like other Colombian indigenous groups, for their exquisite gold-and-copper alloy artifacts made by the "lost wax" technique;
- the San Agustín culture, southern Colombia, well known for its production of large, free-standing stone statues; and
- the Valdivia and Jama-Coaque complexes of coastal Ecuador, famous for their elegant modeled pottery figures and vessels as well as for the possible signs (of interest to diffusionist scholars) of influences from various far-flung places, including Polynesia and west-central Mexico.

The ancient states of the Central Andes, beginning with the most recent at pre-1532 and going back to about A.D. 450, include

- the Inca, whose imperial organization and highway system extended along the Andean mountain chain from what is now central Chile to the southern extreme of modern Colombia, a larger area by far than that occupied by any other polity in prehispanic South America;
- the Chimú of the Peruvian north coast, famous for their huge mud city of Chan Chán, one of the largest of such centers anywhere in the world;
- the Lupaqa and Pacaxes kingdoms of the Bolivian and Peruvian *altiplano,* or "high plain," around Lake Titicaca, famous among modern-day travelers to the area for their beautifully constructed stone burial towers, called *chullpas* here and elsewhere in the Andes;
- the Wari of the central Peruvian highlands, the probable creators of the first extensive state, or empire, in this part of South America and whose ancient capital lies near the modern city of Ayacucho;

- the Tiwanaku of the Lake Titicaca region, known both for their giant carved stone statues with "weeping" eyes and for the highly productive ridged fields they constructed along the shore of the lake;
- the Nazca of the Peruvian south coast, known by almost anyone who has read about South America as the creators of an extensive (and still mysterious) series of lines and drawings etched out on nearby desert plains, or pampas; and
- the Moche of the Peruvian north coast, well known for one of the most elegant pottery styles ever produced in South America and, more recently, made famous around the world by the archaeological rescue from the hands of would-be tomb robbers of fabulous royal graves containing gold and silver artifacts and hundreds of other luxury goods.

SCOPE OF THIS BOOK

Nearly fifty years ago, fresh from the editorship of the seven-volume *Handbook of South American Indians*, Julian Steward joined with a coauthor, Louis Faron, to write a book entitled *Native Peoples of South America*, with the goal of providing a much-needed overview of the disparate sets of anthropological data included in the volumes. Considering the potential interest of indigenous South American cultures of the past and present to anthropologists and other students of human adaptation and evolution, it may seem surprising that the volumes of the *Handbook*, published between 1946 and 1950 by the Bureau of American Ethnology, represented the first attempt ever to synthesize scientifically everything then known about the great diversity of indigenous groups that had been for so many thousands of years established on the southern continent of the New World.

As stated by Steward and Faron in the preface to their 1959 book, "scores of explorers, Spanish administrators, missionaries, and historians," not to mention a few early ethnographers, had described the cultures and achievements of indigenous South Americans, often at some length, but no one had ever before attempted a synthesis aimed at bringing together the ethnographic and archaeological data. Moreover, Steward went one important step further than the multiauthor seven-volume work could go—namely, he examined these data in light of the theoretical context of his (then-new) *cultural ecological* perspective on human adaptive systems, which, among other things, attempted to point out the intimate relationship that occurs between human cultures at all levels of sociopolitical integration and their subsistence environments.

In light of the tremendous increase in our knowledge of past and present indigenous South Americans in the years since Steward and Faron's pathbreaking book was published, as well as advances in the sophistication of ecologically based theories about human adaptive systems, it is surprising that no book aimed at synthesizing the ethnographic and archaeological data on a continentwide level within a singular, coherent theoretical framework has been published since then. Meggers's (1992b) *Prehistoric America*, which makes reference to ethnographic data, is an exception at the much broader hemispherical level, but for

South America in particular in the years since Steward and Faron's book appeared, archaeologists have written and edited books on prehistoric topics (e.g., Gordon Willey's [1971] *An Introduction to American Archaeology: South America* and Jesse Jennings's [1978] *Ancient South Americans*) while ethnologists have written and edited books on recent or contemporaneous topics (e.g., Patricia Lyon's [1974] *Native South Americans* and Daniel Gross's [1973] *Peoples and Cultures of Native South America*).

In fairness to South Americanist scholars, however, this lack surely is due in large part to the very volume of the data and the increasing challenge to any single individual since Steward to bring them adequately together. Thus, at a point now over forty years later, any attempt at a meaningful synthesis must of necessity limit itself to exemplary case studies of a broad cross-section of the groups and environments mentioned earlier in this Introduction, since with all the data now available it would be quite impossible to equal Steward and Faron's feat at anything other than encyclopedic length.

Rationale: Ethnology and Archaeology

In spite of this constraint, the underlying rationale of this book is that there is a need for an updated, continentwide treatment of indigenous South American cultures that includes consistent reference to the sociocultural and archaeological information we now have at hand for the groups that have inhabited the different geographic areas of the continent. Following the theoretical lead of Steward and several other anthropological scholars, I argue that data from both recent and ancient adaptations in each major area provide the strongest, if not the only reasonable, basis for understanding continuity and change in that area. In a very real sense, then, this book takes the not unreasonable view that we can permit ourselves to be as interested in the recent as we are in the ancient.

But readers familiar with the science of prehistory will know that, even though it is possible for archaeologists to determine with some accuracy the material features of ancient cultural systems—such as the artifacts, subsistence (food) items, dwellings, monuments, and sites—it is not particularly easy to dig up or detect the nonmaterial features, such as social organization and ideology. Nevertheless, while ethnologists are very good at determining all of the features of the traditional adaptive systems they study, including kinship and beliefs, it is often very difficult or impossible for them to know the time depth of features of the material culture without reference to archaeological data. The point, succinctly put, is that each of these two subfields of anthropology—ethnology and archaeology—has its strengths as well as its limitations. Each therefore needs the data and perspectives gained by the other, at least if the anthropologist is interested in achieving the most complete perspective possible on continuity and change over long time periods and hence in contributing to the development of overarching anthropological knowledge and theory.

Moreover, given the evidence of continuity in some adaptations over time, the data we have on the recent groups in a particular geographic area of the continent (e.g., origin myths, gender relations, group size, subsistence practices, settlement patterns, and intergroup conflict for the Ona-Selk'nam and the Yahgan-Yámana of Tierra del Fuego) may well enhance our understanding of their ancestors in reference to the much more limited material data available to us from the dim past (e.g., the faunal remains and projectile points from Fell's Cave near the Strait of Magellan). Even though carrying out such a procedure clearly requires something akin to a leap of faith, it is a plausible one, nonetheless—especially if we can determine (as can be done, for example, for the far southern tip of the continent) that the earliest and latest peoples in an area are characterized by the same basic adaptive system, or, to use Steward's term again, the same *level of sociopolitical integration*.

General Theoretical Questions

At the same time, as the reader probably already has inferred, when we can make a case for long-term continuity—such as thirteen thousand years—the question arises, "Why did some human adaptive systems, or groups, exhibit essentially no change over such a long period of time?" (We return to this question in terms of theory in Chapter 2 and in terms of the data on groups of a particular geographic area in other chapters.) Yet as we see in the case of the Fell's Cave data (Chapter 5), there is plenty of evidence for change over time in the fauna hunted and the tool types employed to hunt these fauna (e.g., forms and materials used). We thus can characterize areas featuring such essential sociopolitical continuity as places where "the more things changed, the more they stayed the same," a characteristic also known in the jargon of systems theory as *dynamic homeostasis*, or long-term equilibrium.

If we have constructed a reasonable model or set of models for determining differing levels of sociopolitical integration—as is done in Chapter 2—then another evolutionary phenomenon arises when we leave the data for one geographic area aside and go on to each of the next major areas. It is possible to ascertain that human adaptive systems in other areas are characterized by relatively more complexity, based on a whole series of criteria including the nature of the environment, the subsistence system, population size, the domestic or household economy, the political system, and leadership, ritual, and ideology. For example, comparison of adaptive systems of the far south to those of the Amazon Basin shows that by the Contact period people in the former area relied on mobile hunting-gathering strategies involving small groups of about twenty-five people and small, nonpermanent camps with insubstantial architecture; whereas people in the latter area generally relied on slash-and-burn horticulture that involved larger groups of one hundred or more persons and larger, more permanent villages with architecture that lasted at least several years. Thus, the second major theoretical question that occurs as we begin to compare areas is, "Why did the groups in some geographic areas appear to be more complex than those in other areas or, at the very least, rather uniformly different, according to our set of criteria?"

Finally, in reference to some of the archaeological sequences we will examine, a third evolutionary phenomenon arises that again involves the need to compare and contrast different levels of sociopolitical integration. That is, it is possible to ascertain that people living in certain areas of South America—as a matter of fact, nearly *all* areas except for the extreme south of the continent—exhibit substantial evolutionary change over time. If we recall the earlier mention in this Introduction of selected South American groups, it should be clear that the first inhabitants of the Central Andes were adapted at the level of migratory band societies, that later inhabitants developed an indigenous agriculture and settled down into larger village societies, and that, ultimately, by the end of the sequence the extensive Inca empire had developed. The third question of theoretical importance thus is, "Why did the noncomplex earlier groups of certain areas evolve, or develop, into relatively quite complex (or at least very different) groups?" In contrast to systems where "change leads to no change" (i.e., the far south), those systems where "change leads to more change" are often called *deviation-amplifying* in the jargon of systems theory.

We can also introduce another interesting phenomenon here, specifically with reference to the Central Andes, where it is possible to make a case that some of the features of later cultures originated in earlier, less complex cultures in the sequence and hence that this changing sequence exhibits at least some continuity. Put another way, although we have plenty of evidence for sociopolitical evolution in this particular geographic area, there is nonetheless an ongoing Central Andean way of life, or tradition. Here, then, we can turn on its head our earlier characterization of the far south by asserting that in the Central Andes "the more things stayed the same, the more they changed."

On the basis of the preceding paragraphs, three questions of theoretical importance arise at the most general level as we examine the data on indigenous South Americans:

1. Why did the human adaptive systems of some geographic areas exhibit essential continuity, or dynamic equilibrium, over the long sequence of their occupation of those areas?
2. Why did the adaptive systems of other areas exhibit more complex levels of sociopolitical integration than the areas of lowest productivity?
3. Why did the systems of yet other areas exhibit substantial evolutionary change, or deviation amplification, over the long sequence of occupation?

Before we can begin to pose answers to these three questions, we need to have at hand an explicit set of models that structure our thinking and analysis along lines similar to those of Steward in his cross-cultural approach to understanding the relationship between cultures and their environments. This goal is carried out in Chapter 2.

CHAPTER 2

Theoretical Approach

As IMPLIED IN the Introduction, a primary goal of this book is to present the data on recent and ancient South Americans within the context of a consistent and explicit theoretical framework. In spite of the initial difficulties that readers new to anthropology might have in grappling with theory—in all its seemingly complicated and arcane aspects—it is critically necessary, first, in understanding the nature and implications of arguments made by various scientific researchers and, second, in enabling the construction of cross-culturally valid hypotheses based on questions such as those posed in the last chapter. As I hope this discussion and the rest of the book demonstrate, more often than not theory aids immeasurably in making clear why particular kinds of data are interesting and relevant. In addition, a theoretical construct makes clear what data are irrelevant. For example, in a book of this kind it is unnecessary to present the exact details of how hammocks are constructed by a particular Amazonian group (i.e., what kind of material is used, how it is twined, and how it is woven) unless the relevance of such detail is made clear in light of a general theory about human adaptive systems.

Yet as any reader of the South American anthropological literature will know, some earlier books on the indigenous peoples of this continent have dealt as much with the (rather numbing) details of material culture as with the presentation of data that we might view today as having more central adaptive significance. Fortunately for the reader interested in South American indigenous groups, many of the features of material culture (e.g., the use of hallucinogenic drugs to acquire soul power and the taking and shrinking of *tsantsas*, or human trophy heads, among the Shuar-Jívaro) are of great importance in determining the nature of the adaptation and must be discussed in light of the theoretical framework to be presented here (e.g., in the Jívaro case, with respect to subsistence, population numbers, settlement size and spacing, social organization, warfare, and ideology). Once this framework is more or less firmly grasped, there should be no end to the kinds of interesting questions and hypotheses that will then arise as the reader investigates South American groups not dealt with in this book or groups elsewhere in the world. This sort of goal is precisely what Julian Steward (1955) had in mind in proposing his cultural ecological theory, which can be characterized as an attempt to understand on a cross-cultural basis all levels of sociopolitical integration wherever and whenever they occurred in the world.

HISTORICAL BACKGROUND

To enhance understanding of the theoretical approach presented in the next section, let us first examine its historical underpinnings in the earlier cultural ecological theory of Steward and the later cultural materialist theory of Marvin Harris. Then, to place the implications of Steward's and Harris's materialist work in sharper perspective, we look briefly at the approach to South American indigenous cultures recently taken by Lawrence Sullivan in *Icanchu's Drum,* a monumental study of religion that is as far from Steward and Harris as it seems possible to get. This section ends with a discussion of the ecological theories of Roy Rappaport and Kent Flannery to show how their work can be viewed as a means of bridging the rather wide gap between the approach of the "vulgar" materialists and that of (what might be termed by some scholars as) the "touchy-feely" mentalists at the other end of the continuum.

That is, I intend here to lay the groundwork for a theoretical model that combines the best elements of current theories that approach anthropological data from several perspectives. Moreover, as we see in later chapters, the model not only provides a structured point of reference in understanding the complicated multivariate arguments of certain researchers, but, when the need occasionally arises, also serves as a sort of "battlement" from which to venture forth and engage in (polemical) sorties with other theoretical perspectives.

Steward's Cultural Ecology

Arguably, Steward's (in Steward and Faron 1959:45) greatest contribution to our understanding of the nature of indigenous adaptations on the continent was his simple but profound assertion that "there is a considerable correspondence in South America between environment and cultural types." Although he did not see environment as being the only important feature of human adaptive systems, after Steward published his arguments (see Steward 1955, 1977; Steward and Faron 1959) it became reasonable to examine the distributions of different levels of sociopolitical integration in relation to the distributions of major environmental types. Specifically, he noted that at Contact period there was a surprisingly close correspondence between the following societal levels and environments: the great irrigation-based states and the Central Andean area of the continent (including the high sierra itself as well as the valleys of the adjacent Pacific coast), chiefdom societies and the broken highlands of the northwestern part of the continent, village slash-and-burn farmers and the rain forests of the Amazon Basin, and nomadic hunter-gatherers and the least productive, or "marginal," southern areas of the continent.

Thus, anyone after Steward who looked around the continent and saw no "rhyme or reason" in the distributions of these different societal levels would be forgetting his most compelling argument about why certain types arose where they did. But Steward did not stop with this simple assertion. As shown in Figure 2.1, which is a graphic depiction of his and Faron's (1959) textual argument in *Native Peoples of South America*, one could understand the variability in the geographic distribution of these four main societal levels in terms of a hierarchically layered cultural "cake" characterized by an implicit and, at first glance, eminently reasonable causal chain. For example, when thinking in terms of a linear, or sequential, order of causation (i.e., a → b → c, etc.) at the "economically marginal" southern tip of the continent, one noted a close correspondence between the nature of the Fuegian environment and subsistence productivity (i.e., low-productivity gathering-hunting), between subsistence productivity and population size/density (i.e., low), between population size/density and the maximum community size (i.e., fewer than fifty persons per local group), between community size and the settlement patterns (i.e., dispersed camps), and between these patterns and the sociocultural type (i.e., bands). In fairness to his theoretical position, however, I want to point out that Steward was not quite as linear in his thinking as this causal chain implies, since, once it was in place, he saw a more complicated series of feedback relationships occurring among these variables.

In any event, although this sort of linear reasoning makes good sense in answering the simple question of why only band societies might be able to adapt to the far south, Steward's model does not provide a completely adequate framework for our understanding of these groups. For example, in its focus on what Steward called the "cultural core" (that is, every cultural variable, or feature, shown between the environment and the sociocultural type in Figure 2.1), his model excludes an explicit place in the chain for such important political, economic, and ideological features as trade, war, leadership, ritual, religion, and mental phenomena in general. And worse yet from the point of view of this book, wherever trade, war, and leadership might lie in this model, there is no question that Steward (and later materialists) saw "mind" as an epiphenomenon—in other words, as lying so remotely above material-world, or core, phenomena that it was essentially irrelevant in understanding human adaptive systems.

But in spite of the ever-enduring and greatly divisive debate over the causal priority of mind versus the material world, it is at least reasonable to see "cause" as coming from the top down as well as from the bottom up. Bluntly stated, today we can assert that if one wants to achieve an understanding of how societies function and why they are the way they are (or were the way they were), then one has to study higher-level, ideological phenomena as well. Otherwise, as in the case of a study of the Kofyar by Robert Netting (1968), himself a disciple of Steward, one sees a focus only on the material core of this traditional Nigerian village society, with no mention of ritual and ideology and their possible role in the functioning of the Kofyar adaptive system.

Another problem with Steward's theoretical modeling was how he defined states, chiefdoms, village societies, and bands. In essence, he defined states by a

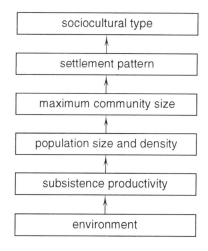

FIGURE 2.1   The bottom-up cultural ecological model proposed by Steward and Faron (1959).

whole series of "positive" features they possessed that the other three kinds of societies did not have—for example, in the Inca case, including dozens of crops, extensive agricultural terracing, irrigation, high numbers of people, food surpluses, craft production, and political hierarchy. Then, in relation to states, Steward defined chiefdoms by positive features (war, priests, temples, societal divisions) as well as by negative ones (less political integration, less areal extent). He defined village societies, in turn, by a few positive features in relation to the two more complex levels (simple farming, kinship, shamans) as well as by quite a lot more negative ones (bare subsistence, little technological skill, no full-time specialists, no temples, no priests, no ethical system). Finally, although Steward described bands positively as being nomadic and having gathering-hunting subsistence, he defined them negatively as lacking almost everything that characterized the other, more complex levels of sociopolitical integration.

As should immediately be clear, this sort of argument is at best naïve and at worst, from today's perspective, culturally biased and racist. Furthermore, it is a progressivist argument, since it makes states appear to be at the pinnacle of human endeavor (a highly Western notion) and bands as representing a sort of bargain basement of human achievement. At appropriate points later in this book, we turn Steward's argument on its head in asserting that bands in South America, until their recent extinction, clearly had the edge in the sweepstakes of societal equilibrium and longevity. States, from this point of view, turn out to be the most unsuccessful societies in the longer-term sweepstakes, since they were relatively quite short-lived and their systems were highly volatile. Village societies and chiefdoms would, of course, fall somewhere in between bands and states in this regard.

In spite of the problems associated with Steward's approach, the lasting contributions of his work are twofold. First, he insisted that human social systems must be understood first and foremost as adaptations to their local environments, and he proposed his cultural ecological model (as shown in Figure 2.1) as a structured way of achieving this understanding. Second, he insisted that making relative sense of cross-cultural differences requires models that aid us in distinguishing among several levels of sociopolitical integration (i.e., bands, villages, chiefdoms, civilizations). Indeed, those who follow the spirit of Steward's contributions would consider it highly inappropriate to react to the use of such models, as some researchers still do today (e.g., Bawden 1989; Leonard and Jones 1987), by rejecting them altogether based on their presumed lack of generality or usefulness. This is pretty much akin to throwing the baby out with the bath water. In a very real sense, then, I am attempting here to clean up Steward's theoretical "babies" by removing some of their attendant problems and updating them in light of current theory.

Harris's Cultural Materialism

Let us turn now to the theories of Harris, the most distinguished recent advocate of the Stewardian materialist approach. In a series of books, especially *The Rise of Anthropological Theory* (1968), *Cannibals and Kings* (1977), and *Cultural Materialism* (1979), Harris's cultural materialist theories have probably become more publicly known than the theories of any other anthropologist in the twentieth century. Following the lead of Steward's culture core concept, Harris insists that the key to understanding all cultures—not just the four traditional types we have discussed earlier but modern industrialized ones as well—is via an examination of the processes occurring at the level of societal infrastructure. Using terms proposed by Karl Marx (whom he [1979:x] sees as "the Darwin of the social sciences"), Harris argues in all of his works that the mode of production and the mode of reproduction—that is, subsistence and demography—constitute independent infrastructural variables affecting all the other higher-order, dependent variables of a society (e.g., ritual and ideology). Naturally, then, the proper study of any human adaptive system must begin first and foremost with an examination of the "true" causal variables that form the material basis for the rest of the system.

However, Harris differs from Steward in several important respects. First, in contrast to Steward's layer-cake, bottom-up causal model, Harris is a systems theorist, arguing that the form and functioning of societies are the causal result of the complex mutual interaction of five groups of variables at three basic hierarchical levels. As shown in my graphic depiction of his (textual) model in Figure 2.2, at the level of the societal structure these variables include the *domestic economy*, or the organization of the (lower-order) infrastructure at the settlement and household levels; and the *political economy*, or the organization of the (lower-order) infrastructure within and between bands, villages, chiefdoms, and states. In other words, although Harris views structural variables as derived from the infrastructure, he also sees them as organizing and regulating it. Hence his infrastructurally deterministic, bottom-up causal chain is more a statement about the origins of structure (and superstructure) than it is a denial that the higher-order variables are necessary for the regulation and maintenance of the infrastructural level.

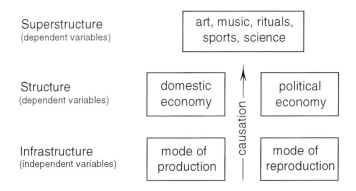

FIGURE 2.2   The infrastructurally deterministic model proposed by Harris (1979).

Second, unlike Steward, Harris sees the importance of including superstructural phenomena at the highest level of his model. Again, as with the level of structure, he views the superstructure as consisting of dependent variables whose adaptive origin lies in the infrastructure. Nevertheless, he fully appreciates the important role that such behavioral phenomena as ritual have in regulating any or all of the lower-order variables. For example, in his analysis of the function of *ahimsa*, or cow love, in India, Harris convincingly shows how an entire human ecosystem—including agricultural production and numbers of people and cattle—is articulated in light of religion and ritual. People are informed by their religious concept of cow love in making practical decisions and carrying out down-to-earth behaviors that have a decidedly concrete effect on the material world—including the number of cattle, the ratio of male to female cattle (i.e., the bovine sex ratio), the use of oxen in agriculture, and, ultimately, the very survival of the human and cattle populations.

But although Harris views the superstructure as important in relation to the regulatory roles of religion and ritual, he steadfastly denies that it can actually bring about any lasting changes in the infrastructure. In other words, as a dependent variable, superstructure has its origins in the lowest level and can react to changes in that level but has little or no causal effect on the infrastructure. One way to be convinced that Harris is correct in this assertion is to consider the following hypothetical example: A small group of people from a state society, with essentially total knowledge of all its systemic features, is dropped down on some tiny, uninhabited, and relatively underproductive desert island. These people would surely fail in any attempt to create and maintain a state society because neither mind nor the behavioral actions derived therefrom could possibly produce a complex society in such an underproductive environment. It follows that if the people in our example were able to survive by creating a hunting-gathering economy, then this different infrastructure would in short order bring about a total revamping of their "civilized" superstructure—ultimately creating a belief system and rituals that were totally appropriate to the newly established subsistence focus on foraging.

However, at least two possible reasons not to be convinced by Harris come to mind as well. The first is based on the idea that if such higher-order phenomena as rituals and ideology are critically necessary in the proper functioning and maintenance of a human adaptive system, then it is equally plausible in a theoretical sense that they can have negative, even disastrous, effects on that system. These system-destroying phenomena could occur for any number of reasons—including (1) highly sanctified (antisystemic) policy "misdeeds" emanating from a priestly recalcitrance at the highest levels of a society, with ultimately devastating effects on the infrastructural variables; (2) a revolutionary change in the infrastructure that made a slow-to-react, essentially unchanged superstructure inappropriate under the new circumstances and thus unable to maintain the system; or (3) an evolutionary, complexifying (and counterintuitive) change in the infrastructure that left ideology and other higher-order regulatory institutions far behind, and, as a result of a lack of orderly controls and maintenance, caused the society to collapse or reorganize at a much less complex level. The second reason not to be convinced by Harris's argument about superstructure as a totally dependent variable can be understood in relation to the desert island example. Although, following Harris, the superstructure of the pioneering population clearly would change to fit the new subsistence system, this population was dropped onto the island with a particular cultural background and mind-set that surely would affect the nature of the newly created infrastructure.

In the end, then, as with all classic issues (e.g., nurture versus nature or, in this case, mind versus matter), the solution may lie in theoretical compromise, that is, in a middle-ground argument that includes the point of view of both sides. We thus can agree with Harris that, in the absence of the proper infrastructure (i.e., productive land and crops), a complex society cannot be created simply by force of mind, but we can disagree with his assertion of materialist determinism by affirming that what is in people's minds at the point they create a pioneering adaptive system will probably have a substantial effect on its features once it is in place. Nevertheless, Harris's contribution to our understanding of the nature of human adaptive systems remains clear. In his five-part, three-level model he has given us the most explicit systems framework produced by any social scientist to date. Although the framework itself needs some revamping (e.g., with respect to the issue of causation) and some revising (e.g., some critical variables are explicitly missing from his model), in a very real sense he has kept Steward's theoretical baby alive and well. He has also cleaned it up a bit in the process, namely, by adding some of the features that were lacking in his predecessor's cultural ecological model.

Sullivan's Critique

One South Americanist scholar who disagrees fundamentally with the approach taken by some of the cultural ecologists/materialists is Lawrence Sullivan (1988). In the introduction to *Icanchu's Drum*, Sullivan points out that systematic studies of South American indigenous peoples fall into three different groups, none of which, in his opinion, has yet won the day over its competitors. The first group focuses its study primarily on human *mentalité*—or mind, language, and symbolic codes that order the universe—as the most important causal force in shaping human social systems. The second group stresses the long history of human existence on the continent, focusing on the material remains—such as art, architecture, settlements, cultivars, artifacts—left by the succession of indigenous inhabitants from the remote past to the present. The third group, an apparent offshoot of the second group and quite akin to the Stewardian cultural ecologists, stresses the primacy of the ecological (i.e., environmental) base of human social systems, focusing on climate, soil, calories, flora, and fauna.

In his own approach to understanding South American indigenous cultures, Sullivan presents the full range of religious beliefs associated with the histories of groups and the life processes that they, like all humans, experience—from cosmogonies (myths of origin), through cosmologies (beliefs about the meaning of the world), to terminologies (beliefs about the meaning of death, or the terminus of life). Sullivan clearly realizes that outstanding contributions have been made by ecologically oriented scholars who are able to transcend the inherent limitations of a narrowly constructed (Stewardian) cultural ecology—for example, as represented in the work of Gerardo Reichel-Dolmatoff (e.g., 1950, 1971, 1976, 1996). This scholar, as we see at several points later in this book, ably brings together the best features of all three approaches, showing how the religion and ritual of certain indigenous groups of Colombia are intimately (and adaptively) related to a host of variables at the level of infrastructure. Yet in light of Sullivan's presentation of continentwide cosmogonies, cosmologies, and terminologies, it also becomes clear that a major part of South American belief systems has more to do with imposing human orders of meaning on existence than it does with the day-to-day grind of making a living in a particular environment.

The lesson to be learned from Sullivan's study is that we should proceed with some caution as we attempt to construct an adequate theoretical approach to understanding the totality of each human adaptive system, including religious beliefs. As we discuss the various groups, there are many examples of religious and ritual systems whose features include adaptively oriented beliefs and practices—that is, ideologies and behaviors directly related to survival in the physical and social environments. At the same time, however, we must be aware that some other features of the societal superstructure may well be adaptively neutral. To argue otherwise—namely, that all aspects of religion and ritual are intimately related to survival in the material world—is to run the risk, as Sullivan well realizes in his study, of reducing the meaning and function of religion strictly to the level of the (vulgar) material world. In other words, such an argument would be base and reductionist.

Yet one of the main contributions of ecological anthropology has been the convincing demonstration that religion and ritual are not so totally remote from the material world that they are irrelevant in its functioning. Indeed, a variety of ecological studies has shown that ritual is an important higher-order feature in the functioning and maintenance of all traditional human adaptive systems. We need go no further than Harris's ecological study of the function of Indian cow love to be convinced of this.

Rappaport's Ecological Anthropology

In the publications on his work among the Tsembaga Maring, a tribal village people of highland New Guinea, Rappaport (1968) showed how one could understand their adaptive system not only in light of a number of variables at all levels of society, but also in relation to a complicated ritual cycle called *kaiko*. Like other highland New Guinea peoples, the Maring are slash-and-burn horticulturists who rely on small-scale farming of root crops for carbohydrates and on pig husbandry for their principal source of protein. They live in politically autonomous, egalitarian villages of fewer than two hundred people. Presumably, as population numbers rose in earlier times and settlements began to encroach on each other's land, village groups adapted to such pressures by developing an ongoing cyclical pattern of hostile skirmishes and raids followed by periods of peace and festivals. The *kaiko*, in turn, arose over time as an adaptive response to the need for regulation and control over what had become a complex local and regional system.

An abbreviated version of Rappaport's graphic model of the functioning of this system at the local level is shown in Figure 2.3. The model presents an argument that is rather sharply different from the theoretical approach taken by Steward. For example, it includes not only a specific hierarchical level for ritual as the principal regulatory institution governing the entire local adaptive system, but also an even higher (more abstract) level for the ideological system, or cognized model, which in turn governs every level, including ritual, below it. Moreover, in what can be viewed in terms of our earlier discussion as constituting a significant counterargument to the cultural materialist position of Harris, Rappaport is more concerned to show the (top-down) causal effects of the cognized model and ritual level on intergroup behavior and the local ecosystem than he is the bottom-up effects of infrastructure. To describe the beliefs characterizing the highest-order, most abstract level of any human adaptive system, Rappaport uses the term *ultimate sacred postulates*, or what for the purposes of this book I occasionally abbreviate as USPs—a shorthand term for all aspects of a societal ideology, including those with critical control functions over the adaptive system.

With regard to the local ecosystemic processes depicted in Rappaport's model, a whole host of features, or variables, with complex interrelationships is shown as characterizing the Tsembaga Maring system. These variable features include the numbers of pigs and humans, pig husbandry, fights over invasions of gardens by pigs, and the amount of land under cultivation. In the unabbreviated original model, Rappaport shows a similar set of complex feedback relationships for a number of other variables at the three higher levels in the model. Even in the simplified version shown here, arguments about such relatively noncomplex human adaptive systems as village-level societies can become quite complicated. If in the end one nevertheless feels enlightened about the possible true nature of a

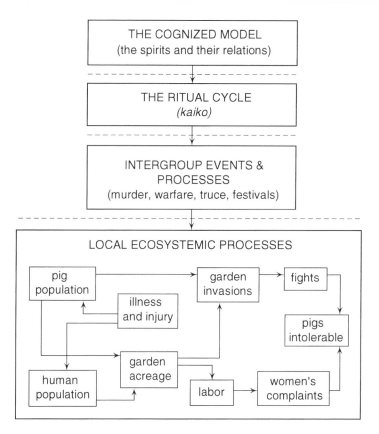

FIGURE 2.3   The case-specific systems model (abbreviated version) proposed by Rappaport for the Tsembaga Maring. Redrawn and adapted from Rappaport (1971).

system—i.e., how it may really function—then such complicated arguments are invaluable.

We can now make explicit some of the more important assumptions and analytical procedures that are necessary to achieve the insights and contributions of Rappaport's study: First, it assumes that the world of a particular cultural group is knowable (not to mention orderly enough to be knowable) by an outside scientific observer. Second, his work assumes that the proper study of the group includes the retrieval of data on a variety of discrete aspects, or variables, of that group's lifestyle—including the environment in which it makes its living, the subsistence system, the numbers of people (and in this case, pigs), the local economy, political relations between local groups, and ritual and belief systems. Third, it assumes that all of these discrete variables can be viewed by the observer as hierarchically organized in terms of several systemic levels, ranging from the most concrete (and material) at the bottom to the most abstract (yet still materially important) at the top. Fourth, the study assumes that the system functions and is maintained as a result of the interaction of variables at all of these levels, implying that a failure to study one or more levels (e.g., ritual and ideology) will result in a failure to understand the system in its entirety. Fifth, Rappaport assumes that it is up to the observer to study every possible (adaptive) feature of the system at all levels and to propose hypotheses about the often complex interrelationships among suites of variables.

In sum, Rappaport's contribution to the theoretical approach being built here clearly includes the argument that cultural groups must be studied as systems that consist of a hierarchical arrangement of socioenvironmental levels, from the most concrete at the base to the most abstract at the top. If this is the proper way to proceed, then if we wish to understand a given human adaptive system, we must address data at all levels—quantitatively, at the levels of the countable, siftable, and weighable phenomena of the material world, and qualitatively, at the more abstract levels of ritual and ideological phenomena. An equally important contribution of Rappaport's work is the use of a graphic model as an aid in making clear what are often highly complicated textual arguments about systemic (feedback) relationships. To be convinced that such a model is useful, the reader may consider the difficulty of getting a quick handle on the (textually presented) theories of Steward and Harris without the accompanying graphics as an aid in understanding, and critiquing, these scholars' theoretical approaches.

One other implication of Rappaport's approach to the study of human adaptive systems must be made explicit at this point: The ecological study of such systems does not merely entail a consideration of just those variables, such as soils, plants, subsistence, calories, and population numbers, that are commonly viewed as ecological (or, to use Harris's [1974:5] phrase, all the "guts, wind, sex, and energy" types of variables). In the case of human populations specifically, such a study also includes variables such as political relations, ritual, religion, and USPs, as we have seen. Ecology, after all, is the study of organisms in their home (the root *eco* comes from the Greek word *oikos*, meaning "house" or "place to live"; see Odum 1971). As the work of both Harris and Rappaport teaches us, all of the higher-order variables in human societies are equally relevant insofar as they are instrumental in organizing, regulating, and maintaining people in the social and physical setting that is their home.

Flannery's General Systems Model

The theoretical approach taken in this book also owes much to the work of Flannery, especially with respect to selected features it incorporates from his model for the operation of control hierarchies, shown in simplified graphic form in Figure 2.4. Although this model is at first glance (and probably the second as well) somewhat intimidating in terms of its systemic abstractions, what we are looking at here is a general systems model that attempts to go beyond the limitations of Harris's and Rappaport's models. As we have seen, the principal drawback of Harris's cultural materialist model is its insistence on one-way infrastructural causation, in spite of its theoretical utility in pointing to a general (and finite) set of systemic variables and levels. For our purposes, Rappaport's model is limited only in that it was developed strictly for the Tsembaga Maring case rather than being

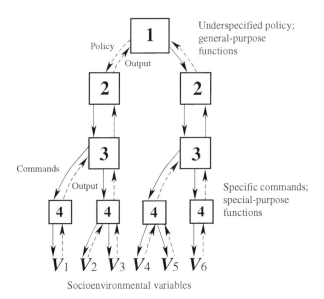

FIGURE 2.4   The control hierarchy of an adaptive system model proposed by Flannery. Redrawn and adapted from Flannery (1972).

presented in a generalized form that might be of utility in the development of a more universalistic approach to understanding human adaptive systems.

Flannery's model redresses each of these limitations, specifically in the reasonableness of its argument about causation and in its generalizing approach to the control hierarchies of all adaptive systems. First, it argues that all human adaptive systems are characterized by a hierarchical arrangement of variables that include control functions (e.g., leadership, ritual, ideology) at the top and output functions (e.g., subsistence production, population levels) at the bottom. Second, it argues that the higher-order variables affect lower-order ones in terms of policy, whereas the lower-order variables affect higher-order ones in terms of output. Put another way, the lower-level variables (e.g., the agricultural system of a chiefdom society) need the upper-level ones for direction and regulation as much as the upper-level variables (e.g., chiefly decisionmaking and ritual) need the lower-level ones for systemic relevance and a support base. If this is true of all types of human adaptive systems, which Flannery argues is indeed the case, then each level in the system has causal importance in determining the nature and functioning of the others. One other useful argument of the model with respect to causation is that it suggests examples of a number of different "socioenvironmental" variables that could be instrumental in changing or maintaining a human adaptive system. For example, in the case of the formation of a state, or civilization, these could include any combination, or all, of the following variables: irrigation, population growth, environmental circumscription, interregional trade and symbiosis, warfare and conquest, and religion.

A couple of difficulties presented by the model must be pointed out here as well. First, as the reader new to this sort of theorizing might already have concluded, in comparison to the models of Harris and Rappaport this one is rather too abstract to be useful as an actual working model, or "heuristic device"—in other words, one that does what such devices are supposed to do, which is to orient the user specifically with respect to *which* variables are at *what* levels. Instead, the model describes the levels of the control hierarchy in terms of numbers, and the user of such a model might well wish to know just what a "1" is in relation to a "2" and so on. The second drawback is the assertion that all causal variables in societal change (or maintenance) can be viewed as peripheral to the control hierarchy of a society, that is, placed at the bottom of the control hierarchy, as the socioenvironmental variables are shown in Figure 2.4. This assertion makes the major causes in systemic change (or maintenance) appear to be essentially external to the system itself (i.e., located at the boundaries of the system or beyond). We might postulate, instead, that such factors might be internal or, as is far more likely to be the case, both internal and external to the boundaries of a particular adaptive system (the reader will appreciate the added complexity here in attempts to describe/explain causation in certain cases).

This issue is, of course, ultimately an empirical one. In other words, it is one to be resolved by problem-oriented research and relatively good data sets. Recalling the earlier statement that we do not want to throw out any theoretical babies with the dirty bath water, our task now is to outline precisely how we can bring together the best elements of the foregoing principal theories. Clearly, the result should meet the rigorous requirements set out here as we carried out the easy part of this enterprise, namely, the critique of earlier theories. Once the critique is done, the task is to revise theoretical structures, so that we can move on in a reasonably enlightened way to utilize them.

PERSPECTIVE OF THIS BOOK

Let us now proceed to a presentation of the three principal theoretical structures that provide the framework within which we study, compare, contrast, and, ultimately, attempt to make adaptive and evolutionary sense of the indigenous South American groups to be discussed in this book. These structures are (1) a systems-hierarchical model that incorporates selected features of the theories of Steward, Harris, Rappaport, and Flannery about human adaptive systems; (2) a proposed revision and elaboration of Elman Service's (1962) band/tribe/chiefdom/state model that includes a variety of defining criteria for each level of integration ranging as completely as possible from concrete/material to abstract/mental phenomena; and (3) a series of statements about population as a critical variable that not only will aid in making sense of the differing levels of sociopolitical integration found across the South American continent at Contact period, but also suggest a probable reason that sociocultural evolution beyond a band level occurred everywhere it did.

The Systems-Hierarchical Model

The general thrust of the theoreticians followed in this book has been the assertion that an adequate model of human adaptive groups must be at once systemic and hierarchical, hence the name *systems-hierarchical model* that I give to it here. Since in later chapters the model is applied to selected systems characterizing the four principal levels of sociopolitical integration, at this point it is premature to show how the model can be used in understanding South American indigenous groups and the arguments of researchers about them. Nevertheless, I hope that I have given enough preliminary rationale for accepting the approach as a valid one in the study of human adaptive systems.

To use an example closer to home, we may assert that any attempt to explain and describe human organizations, which consist of *Homo hierarchus* individuals in groups, usually includes a chart indicating the following chain of control and systemic functioning: Beginning at the top, the chain runs from a group charter (e.g., the U.S. Constitution) and related ideologies/beliefs all expressing a host of ultimate sacred postulates (e.g., the U.S. Bill of Rights and "In God We Trust"); down through the different levels of political leadership that lie below it (e.g., the executive, legislative, and judicial branches of the U.S. federal government); and, finally, on down to the level of collective or individual actions and behaviors of a variety of kinds. Since even models of nonhuman ecosystems are often shown hierarchically organized (e.g., trophic levels), surely in dealing with any human adaptive system, one must take its hierarchical nature into account when proposing the structure of a theoretical model. This includes both ancient and recent preindustrial societies at all levels of integration, from bands to states.

The model graphically represented in Figure 2.5 obviously owes a significant debt to Harris's cultural materialist strategy in asserting that to be useful, a working heuristic for structuring our thinking and arguments about human adaptive systems must include an explicit, or named, set of variables and hierarchical levels. Thus, among the features of Harris's model included in the systems-hierarchical strategy are the mode of production, the mode of reproduction, domestic and political economy, and the three hierarchical levels of infrastructure, structure, and superstructure. In contrast to Harris's model, however, the superstructure has been further divided into its more abstract mental aspect (ideology, USPs) and its more concrete behavioral aspect (ritual and leadership). Since in my opinion Harris trivializes his own version of superstructure by adding such potentially irrelevant phenomena as sports and advertising to it, I have included here only those most general ideological and behavioral phenomena that may be viewed as centrally important in the regulation and control of societal systems.

Turning to the levels of structure and infrastructure, I have added to Harris's basic model social organization as a centrally adaptive and regulatory feature of all societies, and following Steward's arguments about the adaptive significance of settlement pattern, I have added it as a variable at the level of the infrastructure. In addition, again following Steward's arguments, I have added the physical

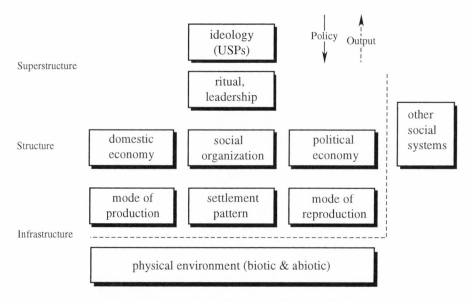

FIGURE 2.5   The systems-hierarchical model of human adaptive systems.

environment at the bottom of the systems-hierarchical model to make it clear that we must take relevant aspects of the biotic and abiotic environment into account as we carry out analyses of societies at all levels of sociopolitical integration. That is, the viewpoint taken here is that states, just as much as bands, are supported and affected by their environment.

I have occasionally encountered students (not to mention colleagues) who seem to think that, whereas bands must certainly be understood as intimately related to the environment within which they hunt and collect (e.g., Colin Turnbull [1961] asserts that for the BamButi of Africa, their religion *was* the environment), states somehow have reached a plateau of "complexity" where they have risen above such vulgar considerations. But state societies, as Flannery (1972) teaches us, usually are based on a relatively limited spectrum of cultivars and corresponding subsistence strategies—such as monocropping—and therefore are far more likely than band societies to experience systemic collapse as the result of either human-induced problems (e.g., salinization) or environmental perturbations (e.g., droughts), if not a combination of both. Moreover, it is the very sociopolitical complexity of states that makes their functioning in terms of information flow so potentially counterintuitive and subject to breakdown (recall our earlier argument about system-destroying misdeeds), and they fall apart rather more easily—and thus may be more ephemeral—than less complex societies.

In addition to making the physical environment a specific feature of the model (and textual arguments), the systems-hierarchical approach follows Flannery in asserting that human adaptive systems exist within both a physical milieu and a social one. Thus, other social systems are included as a critical causal feature in this model of a local adaptive system. However, lest it be thought that only peripheral, or external, phenomena (e.g., warfare and trade with outside groups) are viewed as causal in the model, all of Flannery's other socioenvironmental variables are viewed as internal to the system (e.g., physical circumscription under environment, irrigation under mode of production, and population growth, maintenance, or decline under mode of reproduction). Hence, causation involving intervariable relationships is considered potentially complicated—that is, it includes variables both internal and external to the local, bounded human adaptive system. Finally, and again following Flannery, causation among the various levels of a human adaptive system is viewed in the model as a two-way street, as being both top down and bottom up. Unlike his general systems model, however, no specific causal arrows are indicated, since, among other things, this makes our model look *too* counterintuitive. Instead, the two kinds of causation in his model, policy and output, are shown at the upper right as a reminder about the two-way nature of the relationships among all variables and hierarchical levels in an adaptive system.

As we see later in dealing with actual theoretical arguments, the specific placement of causal arrows on the model is an empirical question—that is, a function of a researcher's arguments about a set of interrelationships among variables in a given adaptive system under study. Using the model, a researcher can present these arguments rather precisely in a graphic form that indicates not only what complicated multivariate causes are being invoked but also what the researcher's particular theoretical perspective is—for example, either totally top down or bottom up and hence, in light of our earlier arguments in this chapter, potentially one-sided and unrealistic.

The Principal Variables of the Model

Having provided an overview of the basic arguments represented in the systems-hierarchical strategy, following the lead of Harris (1979), I want to list the ten principal variable groups indicated in the graphic model, accompanied by a brief definition of the group and a listing of some of the subsystem variables that may be seen as included within it.

Ideology   The higher-order and more abstract features of the superstructure that promote and maintain a society, inform its members about appropriate behaviors, and reinforce those behaviors that are necessary for systemic survival.

Cosmogony: myths of origin
Cosmology: myths about the meaning, nature, and structure of existence
Cognized environment, including spirits/ghosts
Ultimate sacred postulates/laws/rules

Ritual and Leadership   The more concrete aspects of the superstructure involving centralized collective or individual behaviors at the level of policy that maintain, regulate, and change the system.

Shamanic and priestly activities
Public ceremonies
Individual leadership of subsistence activities
Leadership of societal activities: for example, in peace, war
Policy decisions by individuals, headmen, chiefs, rulers

Domestic Economy   The organization of the modes of reproduction and production at the structural level of the household and the local settlement.

Division of labor
Age and sex roles
Household activities
Reciprocity: generalized
Settlement-level group activities
Clothing and related technology
Property rights and inheritance
Rules of behavior, laws

Social Organization   The central adaptive institutions at the level of structure that involve rules, patterns, and behaviors related to kinship and marriage and their role in organizing the domestic economy, the political economy, and the infrastructure.

Kinship systems
Social structure: moieties, sibs, clans, ramages, classes
Marriage rules: exogamy, endogamy
Postmarital residence rules: matrilocality, patrilocality, neolocality
Gender relations
Socialization, enculturation, education

Political Economy   The organization of the infrastructure and the local adaptive system in general in relation to other social systems.

Trade, tribute, storage, redistribution
Reciprocity: balanced, negative
Territoriality and boundary demarcation
Warfare, military organization
Alliance formation: for example, feasting and other joint meetings
Artistic canons of architecture, pottery, and other societal artifacts

Mode of Production   The behaviors and technology involved in the production and consumption of the energy base, whose productive potential (or carrying capacity) is determined by the nature of both the subsistence system and the relevant environment.

Subsistence system: for example, hunting, gathering, horticulture, irrigation
Technology of subsistence: for example, artifacts/tools, canals, terracing

Settlement Pattern   The number, density, permanence, size, and function of settlements across the landscape within the area occupied by the adaptive system.

Community (within-site) features
Duration of occupation of sites
Site size, density, and spacing
Hierarchy of site size and function

Mode of Reproduction   The population size and density of an adaptive system within the area it occupies and the behaviors involved in regulating population numbers and densities.

Population size: growth, maintenance, decline
Sex ratio (number of males divided by number of females)
Fertility, natality, mortality
Infant care and medical control of fertility, health, life span
Population controls: sexual abstinence, abortion, infanticide, prolonged lactation

Physical Environment (Biotic and Abiotic)   The relevant features of the abiotic and biotic environment that provide for the survival of the human population, including both energy resources and those features that relate to systemic maintenance, in the form of settlement spacing and defense, with respect to other adaptive systems.

Biotope
Geographic features: topography, soil types, vegetation, oceans, rivers, streams, lakes
Precipitation patterns, elevation, and latitude
Nature of plant and animal resources
Nature of other abiotic and biotic resources: for example, availability of stone and wood for tool making and architecture, clays and tempers for pottery making, and other needed or desired materials
Limiting factors and natural hazards

Other Social Systems   The aspects of neighboring systems that affect the local adaptive system in terms of its own regulation, functioning, and survival.

Level of sociopolitical integration
Proximity of the system(s)
Nature of geographic and/or political boundaries of the system(s)

Political stance of the system(s): for example, cooperative, neutral, hostile
Trade items/resources

With some fifty-one subvariables subsumed under the ten basic variable groups, it may come as a relief to the reader to know that no model purporting to show causal relationships could easily and convincingly deal with more than just a few of them at once, nor do I have any intention of attempting a practical application of such an unwieldy beast. In this regard, it would probably not be wrong to assert that most arguments in anthropology about why things are the way they are and why they function the way they do are limited to fewer than ten systemic variables. This does not mean that the theoretical discussion to this point cannot be taken to its logical end—namely, at least in showing the systems-hierarchical model and the fifty-one subvariables that have been listed under the ten principal variable groups (Figure 2.6). If we wish to gain an adequate understanding of the overall nature and functioning of a given adaptive system, then, at the least, none of the ten main variable groups can be ignored or left aside in our analysis. That is certainly the case for the research studies we consider in later chapters.

Levels of Sociopolitical Integration

In addition to the model of human adaptive systems discussed previously, we also require some means of broadly modeling the levels of sociopolitical integration of South American indigenous groups. Such a model is important not least because it gives us a parsimonious way of describing the overall nature of a group without immediately having to characterize it in detail. For example, if we say that band societies were adapted to Tierra del Fuego or that state societies arose in the Central Andes, then, following what Steward teaches us about the relationship between environment and human subsistence-settlement systems, at least two principal aspects of the adaptation immediately are apparent to us: the general level of sociopolitical integration and the nature of the environment in relation to that level.

In light of the immediate mental connection one makes between a level and an environment, however, if I were to say that, while carrying out an archaeological research project, I have found evidence of an ancient state society in Tierra del Fuego, most Stewardian-oriented scholars would probably be quite skeptical (as is the way of most scientists). Their skepticism would be a response to the word *state*, which invokes a number of related criteria—including a relatively much more productive environment, a correspondingly productive subsistence system based on agriculture, high population numbers, monumental architecture, and so on. Most everyone knows that Tierra del Fuego was relatively quite low in environmental productivity and that only a hunting-gathering subsistence base was present in this area in prehistoric times, not to mention that no one in recent centuries has reported seeing prehistoric monumental architecture anywhere in the area.

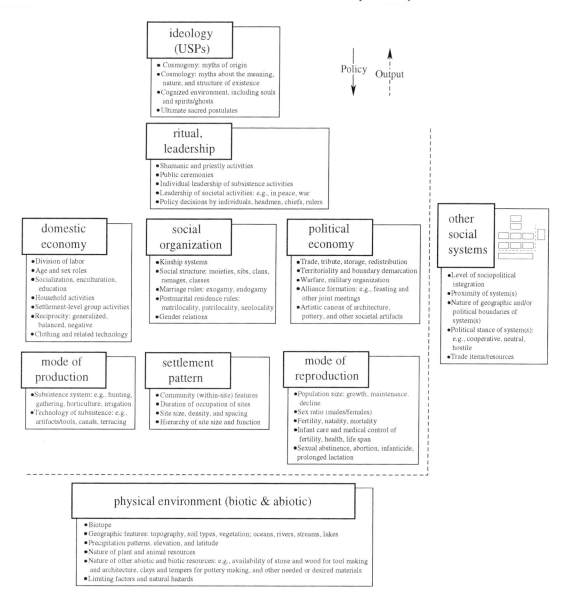

ideology (USPs)
- Cosmogony: myths of origin
- Cosmology: myths about the meaning, nature, and structure of existence
- Cognized environment, including souls and spirits/ghosts
- Ultimate sacred postulates

Policy ↓ Output ↑

ritual, leadership
- Shamanic and priestly activities
- Public ceremonies
- Individual leadership of subsistence activities
- Leadership of societal activities: e.g., in peace, war
- Policy decisions by individuals, headmen, chiefs, rulers

domestic economy
- Division of labor
- Age and sex roles
- Socialization, enculturation, education
- Household activities
- Settlement-level group activities
- Reciprocity: generalized, balanced, negative
- Clothing and related technology

social organization
- Kinship systems
- Social structure: moieties, sibs, clans, ramages, classes
- Marriage rules: exogamy, endogamy
- Postmarital residence rules: matrilocality, patrilocality, neolocality
- Gender relations

political economy
- Trade, tribute, storage, redistribution
- Territoriality and boundary demarcation
- Warfare, military organization
- Alliance formation: e.g., feasting and other joint meetings
- Artistic canons of architecture, pottery, and other societal artifacts

other social systems
- Level of sociopolitical integration
- Proximity of system(s)
- Nature of geographic and/or political boundaries of system(s)
- Political stance of system(s): e.g., cooperative, neutral, hostile
- Trade items/resources

mode of production
- Subsistence system: e.g., hunting, gathering, horticulture, irrigation
- Technology of subsistence: e.g., artifacts/tools, canals, terracing

settlement pattern
- Community (within-site) features
- Duration of occupation of sites
- Site size, density, and spacing
- Hierarchy of site size and function

mode of reproduction
- Population size: growth, maintenance, decline
- Sex ratio (males/females)
- Fertility, natality, mortality
- Infant care and medical control of fertility, health, life span
- Sexual abstinence, abortion, infanticide, prolonged lactation

physical environment (biotic & abiotic)
- Biotope
- Geographic features: topography, soil types, vegetation; oceans, rivers, streams, lakes
- Precipitation patterns, elevation, and latitude
- Nature of plant and animal resources
- Nature of other abiotic and biotic resources: e.g., availability of stone and wood for tool making and architecture, clays and tempers for pottery making, and other needed or desired materials
- Limiting factors and natural hazards

FIGURE 2.6   The complete systems-hierarchical model of human adaptive systems, with ten principal variables and fifty-one subvariables.

Such a twofold mental association between a level of integration and an environment may at first glance seem trivial, but there are scholars (e.g., working in the Amazon) who have made just such an association that many others find highly unlikely. So, armed with a knowledge of environments and the requisite model of levels of sociopolitical integration, not only can we do better science as we proceed, but we should also experience a bit of (scientific) entertainment along the way as we look at the "holes" in some arguments. Of course, my point here is a serious one: Without theoretical models and the Stewardian cross-cultural perspective we are going to take, nothing would make much sense, and we would end up not very enlightened by the exercise. Even more seriously, however, there has been much criticism (e.g., Bawden 1989; Leonard and Jones 1987) of the use of what is seen as evolutionary "stage" terminology (e.g., bands → tribes → chiefdoms → states). This has occurred not only because such terminology is viewed as progressivist, but also because invoking a limited set of types seems to imply that we take highly disparate data sets and try to cram them into what essentially have become rigid pigeonholes, or, to paraphrase one researcher, ideal types akin to platonic forms that do not actually exist in the real world.

It is not my intent to go deeply into this (no-win and never-ending) argument here. Instead, I want to make two points. First, all sciences need some sort of scale for assessing the differences among a set of phenomena that may be seen as ordered along a continuum. A good example comes from psychology, where levels of maturation based on an extensive series of developmental criteria including age are described in terms of infant, child, adolescent, young adult, and so on—however arbitrary the age distinction between levels may be, since we all recognize that some people mature earlier and some later. But such levels are a necessary part of the science of psychology and are in universal use in most societies as well. Second, although such models can indeed be a bit rigid, we can make them as broad as possible by, for example, establishing a whole series of criteria for defining the four principal levels of sociopolitical integration to be used. That is precisely what we do here.

The model presented in Figure 2.7 is based on similar models proposed by Service, Jeffrey Parsons, and Flannery and represents my attempt over some years of teaching undergraduate and graduate courses to construct a heuristic that broadly defines and distinguishes each of the four levels of sociopolitical integration. Rather than recounting the details of Figure 2.7, I wish to make a few general orienting and explanatory statements. First, the left side of the figure lists a series of behavioral criteria ordered from the most abstract societal features (at the top) to the most concrete, or material (at the bottom). The societal features presented in each column under the four levels of integration are general characterizations in light of the variables contained in the systems-hierarchical model. Second, instead of using the problematical term *tribe*, I follow Harris in preferring the term *village* or *village society*. Among other things, tribe has been applied indiscriminately to a number of societies that are/were organized at an adaptive level that might more adequately be called "bands" or "chiefdoms" (using our terminology). Worse yet, many of these tribes are seen as having chiefs rather than *headmen* (or *headwomen*), the term preferred by evolutionary ecologists. As a matter of fact, *chiefs* is a term usually restricted by such scholars to the leaders of chiefdoms. Third, the two kinds of egalitarian society, bands and villages, and the two kinds of stratified society, chiefdoms and states, are separated by broken lines, whereas the two overarching societal types (egalitarian and stratified) are separated by a solid line between the columns. The broken lines indicate that

BEHAVIORAL CRITERION	EGALITARIAN		STRATIFIED	
	BAND	**VILLAGE**	**CHIEFDOM**	**STATE**
RITUAL AND RELIGION	ad hoc, shamans	ceremonies, ritual cycles, shamans	full-time priestly specialists	hierarchy of priests
POLITICAL ORGANIZATION	ephemeral	headman	chief	ruler
ECONOMIC ORGANIZATION	reciprocal, face to face	reciprocal, face to face	central focus, redistributive	highly central, tribute
SOCIAL ORGANIZATION	egalitarian	egalitarian	ranked descent	class society
SOCIAL STRUCTURE	kinship based (achieved status)	kinship based (achieved status)	elite/commoners (ascribed status)	socioeconomic (ascribed status)
MODE OF PRODUCTION	gathering-hunting	small-scale farming	larger scale (localized)	intensive agriculture
SETTLEMENT PATTERN	seasonal camps, impermanent	more permanent settlements	two levels of site size and function	three or more levels of site size and function
MODE OF REPRODUCTION	low density (<1 person/km²)	low density (<1–1+ p/km²)	moderate density (1–10s p/km²)	high density (10s–100s p/km²)
POPULATION SIZE	25–50 (micro-) 500 (macro-)	~100–1000+	several 1000s to ~25,000	~25,000 to several millions
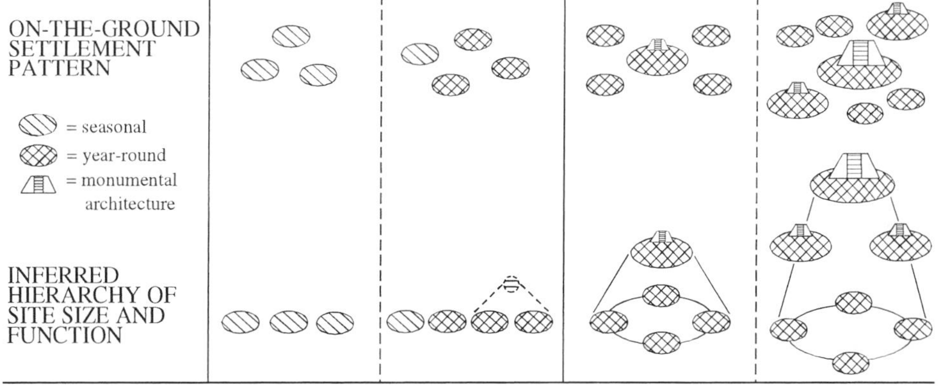 ON-THE-GROUND SETTLEMENT PATTERN				
INFERRED HIERARCHY OF SITE SIZE AND FUNCTION				

⬭ = seasonal
⬮ = year-round
△ = monumental architecture

FIGURE 2.7   Levels of sociopolitical integration.

the difference between each group under the overarching headings is more one of degree; the solid lines suggest that the difference between egalitarian and stratified societies is more one of kind. Fourth, the bottom of the figure contains a summary form of what the four kinds of societies should look like on the ground in relation to each other; using the data on the kinds of sites we find archaeologically or (in the case of bands and village societies) study ethnographically, we can make inferences about the hierarchy of site size and function.

Band societies in general consist of small groups of twenty-five to fifty people who temporarily (e.g., seasonally) occupy encampments and then move on to another site as they carry out their foraging activities. The three-site settlement pattern (used as a hypothetical example) may thus represent the same small group of persons moving from one site to the next on a seasonal basis. Although bands, like all human societies, are composed of *Homo hierarchus* individuals, leaders come and go depending on the activity being undertaken. For example, a woman with expertise in gathering and a keen memory of the location of certain plants may lead a small group on a subsistence foray, someone else may lead in other kinds of activities in which she or he has greater expertise and knowledge, and in still other situations activities may be carried out by group consensus without any apparent leaders at all.

Village societies, in contrast, have a relatively more productive and localized subsistence system based on a continuously available resource (e.g., small-scale farming or fishing) that provides a context for year-round permanence of settlements. Note, however, that not all village societies are shown as being sedentary year-round. Some may instead fission into smaller band groups on a seasonal basis, for example, as in several Amazon cases (note that this immediately raises the question of what to call these groupings—bands or villages—the answer to which probably depends on what part of their seasonal cycle is under investigation). One other feature of village societies is that they occasionally become hierarchical, as autonomous villages unite under military leaders to carry out attacks in response to pressure exerted by some other nearby group. Both the Yanomamö and Shuar-Jívaro cases provide examples of this sort of ephemeral hierarchy, as is discussed in Chapter 6. This phenomenon is shown on the figure as a set of broken lines leading up to a circle that represents the "stratification" resulting from temporary military leadership of groups that are normally egalitarian and autonomous at the village or local household level.

Unlike band and village societies, which are organized at the level of the camp or village settlement, chiefdoms and states are characterized by subsistence-settlement systems linked in enduring networks of a political, economic, and religious nature. Among the on-the-ground data that an archaeologist would find enabling the hypothesis that such a network existed are similar pottery, architectural, and iconographic diagnostics indicating contemporaneity and linkage among sites; relatively high numbers and densities of sites and, hence, population; a principal, or primary, site whose size and architectural complexity are greater than those of any other sites in the hypothesized system; and several or many widely distributed second-tier sites that function as intermediate nodes in the maintenance and regulation of the system. In relation to states, a chiefdom is defined by the smaller overall size of the system, the relatively small size of the central site, the presence of smaller-scale monumental architecture on this site, and a two-level hierarchy of site size and function. A state, in turn, may be defined as having more of everything that defines a chiefdom: more sites, more architectural monumentality, and more levels in the hierarchy of site size and function. It usually also has more political and economic clout in imposing its policies on the population, so that there may be greater uniformity of pottery, architectural, and iconographic diagnostics from site to site in the system.

The Role of Population

The Introduction began with a brief overview of the data we now have at hand that permit a comparison of the earliest human systems in South America with those existing at the time of the Conquest and occupation of the continent by Europeans. As mentioned there, we know that only band societies were present some twelve to thirteen thousand years ago and that by the mid-sixteenth century the full range of sociopolitical levels was established across the continent. We also know that, although the first humans to arrive must have been very few in number (i.e., in the few hundreds or thousands), by A.D. 1532 indigenous South Americans numbered in the many millions (Steward and Faron [1959] estimate the total continental population to be just over 10 million in A.D. 1500). Thus, we may postulate that humans must have adapted to the environments of South America in such a way that everywhere outside the areas of most limited productivity the following processes occurred: groups put their expert (lay botanical) knowledge of the environment to work in order to modify and intensify subsistence productivity, cultivars and farming developed in certain favorable settings and spread to other areas through a slow process of human-directed adaptation, population numbers rose as a function of changes in sociocultural practices and subsistence, and the problems and challenges deriving from these infrastructural changes were solved by modification of aspects of all the other levels of the societal system, so that village, chiefdom, and state societies arose in the appropriate settings.

This scenario may seem plausible in its apparent argument for a two-way causal relationship between higher-order and lower-order societal levels (i.e., mind ⇔ matter), not to mention careful in avoiding the one-sided determinism of the cultural materialist viewpoint. Unfortunately, however democratic in terms of causation this scenario may appear at first glance, it is actually as one-sided and top down as the cultural materialist perspective is one-sidedly bottom up. It makes the whole process of sociocultural evolution on the continent appear to have been entirely the result of human intent. In other words, behavior was guided by mind, so that human populations could better themselves and achieve the complexity they somehow knew would help them reach the plateau of a "civilized" existence.

At that point in time and until quite a long time afterward, no one had any inkling of what a chiefdom or a state was and could not possibly have been aiming in that direction. Furthermore, if we assume that, similar to recent descendants today, band societies liked their lives the way they were—namely, in a *state of nature*, to use the Hobbesian term—then they would have wished for societal equilibrium or no evolution at all out of the band level of integration! The question thus arises as to whether we have achieved theoretical deadlock here. That is, having earlier argued against the unreasonableness of (materialist) infrastructural determinism and now against the equally unreasonable idea of societal self-betterment via some form of mental urge to get civilized, have we left ourselves with no resolution to the dilemma of fundamental causation?

Surprisingly, given the earlier discussion of cultural materialism in this chapter, a resolution of this problem comes from none other than Harris (e.g., 1979), the supposed infrastructural determinist himself. I have seen no one make a better case for a fundamental cause that not only gets the evolutionary sequence going, but also probably existed before the time Amerindians got to Beringia and certainly continued (continues) to be present throughout the prehistoric (and historic) sequence—that is, *population growth and pressure*. But in the sense Harris describes it, this continual trend is as much a psychological problem and controlled by mind as it is an inexorable infrastructural force in societal evolution. (Perhaps we can even out-finesse the materialist here in showing that he is actually a two-way causalist "lamb" unfairly garbed by the mentalist opposition in materialist "wolf" clothing.) One has only to read the doom-and-gloom reports of the Club of Rome (see Meadows et al. 1972; Meadows, Meadows, and Randers 1992) on world population tendencies to know that anytime the population is growing, it is doing so at exponential rates no matter how slow the doubling time may be (doubling time = 70 ÷ the growth rate; i.e., a population starting at 100 persons and growing at 2 percent per year will double in thirty-five years, the resulting 200 doubling to 400 in thirty-five more years, and so on). Since humans and other populations find their very success in growth and adaptive expansion into other ecological niches, the real question becomes, "How do we as a species keep population growth more or less in check?"

Given this tendency and knowing what we know about the dynamic homeostasis that, for example, characterized Tierra del Fuego populations, how could these people have been so successful in maintaining equilibrium for more than ten thousand years? The answer Harris proposes is a simple nonmathematical one, yet powerfully compelling in its logic: The only way such populations could have maintained equilibrium was to keep their numbers in check via ideologies, mental intent, and behavioral practices that involved sexual abstinence, abortion, and infanticide (a fourth practice, discussed in later chapters, is prolonged lactation). Since most women can have at least four children with their spousal partners during a lifetime, implying a doubling of population each human generation, all traditional societies (in the absence of effective contraceptive devices) have to practice one or more of these three psychologically stressful practices. Abstinence is not much fun given the highly sexed nature of our species; abortion is stressful, especially in a physical sense to the mother; and infanticide is something mothers in traditional societies might rather avoid doing. Therefore, it is easy to see that human groups would intensify subsistence whenever they could in appropriate environmental contexts not only to ease these psychological stresses, but also to reduce the pressures of nutritional stress brought about by their inability, in the nearly universal absence of effective contraceptive devices, to keep population from growing.

However, this argument for population growth and pressure throughout human prehistory and history is not without its attendant controversy. Figure 2.8 summarizes in graphic form the main features of (1) an older nonpopulation pressure model, which stands rather firmly against such an argument; and (2) a newer

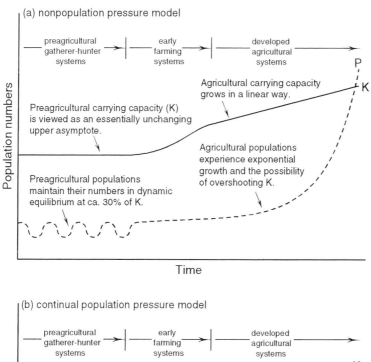

(a) nonpopulation pressure model

preagricultural gatherer-hunter systems → early farming systems → developed agricultural systems

P

Agricultural carrying capacity grows in a linear way.

K

Preagricultural carrying capacity (K) is viewed as an essentially unchanging upper asymptote.

Agricultural populations experience exponential growth and the possibility of overshooting K.

Preagricultural populations maintain their numbers in dynamic equilibrium at ca. 30% of K.

Population numbers

Time

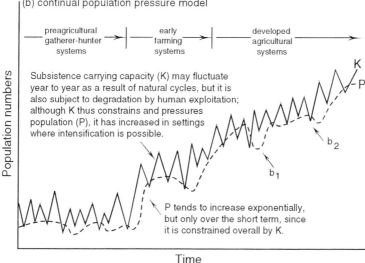

(b) continual population pressure model

preagricultural gatherer-hunter systems → early farming systems → developed agricultural systems

K
P

Subsistence carrying capacity (K) may fluctuate year to year as a result of natural cycles, but it is also subject to degradation by human exploitation; although K thus constrains and pressures population (P), it has increased in settings where intensification is possible.

b_2

b_1

P tends to increase exponentially, but only over the short term, since it is constrained overall by K.

Population numbers

Time

FIGURE 2.8   Two models of the growth of human adaptive systems: (a) a nonpopulation pressure model (an older view) and (b) a continual population pressure model (a view followed in this book).

model, followed in this book, of continual population pressure, which has been proposed by Harris as well as anthropologist Mark Cohen (1977).

The Older Model

Several important features of the older nonpopulation pressure model (Figure 2.8a) should be pointed out here. First, it makes a critical distinction between preagricultural and agricultural systems. At the preagricultural stage, it argues that human adaptive systems tended to maintain their population numbers in dynamic equilibrium at levels representing about 30 percent of the estimated carrying capacity of a subsistence-environmental context. With the development of agriculture, populations began to grow exponentially—which is not an unreasonable assertion given recent population trends in historic times as well as in later prehistoric times after the rise of chiefdoms and states. At the same time, adherents of the more general features of the model argue either (1) that after rising to new levels agricultural carrying capacity remained a straight-line asymptote, just as in the preagricultural stage; or (2) that, as shown in Figure 2.8a, agricultural carrying capacity has grown only linearly as populations grow exponentially. Whichever of these two views one accepts, the dilemma of population overshoot—or a rise in numbers beyond the carrying capacity of an adaptive system—thus becomes highly probable.

The view taken here is that the older model has a number of unacceptable weaknesses. Among them are the following: (1) it ignores the near certainty of substantial growth in overall population numbers at continentwide levels, no matter how slowly this occurred, in earlier preagricultural times (e.g., how better to explain the expansion of Paleoindians into South America?); (2) it cannot easily explain why populations, once agriculture had been developed, ever began to grow in the first place; (3) given the lack of a material explanation for population growth in this theory, its adherents have argued that the answer lies not in the realm of the material infrastructure but rather in changes in ideology or social organization (here we may note that such changes, however plausible, cannot easily be tested, if at all, given the limitations of the material record in archaeology); and (4) it is essentially a nonparsimonious theory since it requires a special and distinct argument for the preagricultural stage and one for the agricultural stage.

The Newer Model

The model employed in this book is shown in Figure 2.8b. In contrast to the older model, it argues first that carrying capacity—in other words, the productivity of a subsistence-environmental context as measured in terms of human population numbers—is a fluctuating phenomenon both for preagricultural and agricultural systems. It may vary not only seasonally in a more predictable way, but also yearly in far more complex and unpredictable ways as a function of such environmental variables as rainfall, sunlight, frost, length of the growing season, soil productivity, and environmental hazards. Equally importantly, however, both Harris (1977) and Cohen (1977) argue that human exploitation of the environment may itself ultimately result in a degradation of its subsistence productivity, either through normal day-to-day practices in some egalitarian societies or through attempts to intensify production in some stratified ones. In the Amazon Basin, for example, it is arguably the case (see Chapter 6) that the Yanomamö reduce the hunting carrying capacity of their local environment and must therefore move settlements. And, as we imply in dealing with northern Colombia (Chapter 7), the intensification that occurred with the rise of prehistoric Tairona chiefdom societies may well have been partly responsible for the eroded landscape that provides the subsistence setting for their recent descendants, the Kogi. Second, for the reasons mentioned earlier in discussion of Harris's theory, the model followed here argues that populations always tend to rise at least against the lean-period, or bottleneck, carrying capacity of their subsistence system.

Because of this continual linkage between the two variables—carrying capacity and human numbers—population is continually constrained and potentially pressured by subsistence-environmental productivity. Nevertheless, in spite of this, it has risen substantially in contexts where intensification was possible (and carrying capacity was thus raised)—namely, through human ingenuity as an adaptive response to the pressure resulting from population growth in relation to the constraints of subsistence systems.

In light of Harris's and Cohen's arguments, a theoretical example of population overshoot of carrying capacity accompanied by environmental degradation and a correspondingly severe reduction in population numbers is shown at point b_1 in the continual population pressure model of Figure 2.8. And in light of the unpredictable fluctuations of natural cycles in the subsistence-environmental context and the tendency for population to grow, an example of a less severe constraint on population is shown at point b_2 in the same model. (I characterize this latter case as a "zap point," i.e., one where the human adaptive system gets a stern reminder in the form of severe nutritional stress that population growth must be continually checked through some form of cultural regulation.)

In sum, the challenges posed by the continual population pressure model are twofold: first, with regard to the carrying capacity variable, one must demonstrate fluctuations due either to cycles in the natural environment or to temporary human overexploitation of resources; and, second, one must show that populations tend to rise. As already suggested, it is possible to meet the first challenge in at least some of the cases examined in later chapters. However, as we see in the case of most band- and village-level societies, it is possible to demonstrate the close relationship between both variables primarily by reference to the behaviors that keep population numbers and densities regulated. Such features include sexual abstinence, abortion, and infanticide, as mentioned earlier, as well as prolonged lactation, shamanism, sorcery, and warfare, as we see in later chapters.

In addition, the religious and ritual systems of many adaptive systems have features that indicate anxiety or concern about critical limiting factors in the productivity of their subsistence-environmental context—in other words, features that support the theoretical assertion of a close relationship between population numbers and carrying capacity in spite of the absence of data showing the precise dynamics of the carrying capacity curve. The essentially universal presence in lowland South American societies of one or more of these higher-order regulatory features indicates that the general model is at least valid as applied to this area of the continent. Although the data are scantier for highland South America, the model is also likely to be valid for the remaining areas of the continent. In all such cases, we thus find cultural corroboration of the operation of the ecological "law of the minimum," or Liebig's law—by which population numbers in relation to resources are understood not by reference to the most plentiful resource or to the years of most abundant productivity, but rather by reference to that necessary resource that is available in the least quantities (e.g., protein, in the case of Amazonian groups) or to the lean year in which all resources experience a severe downturn in productivity (e.g., the recent Kogi adaptation of the northern Andes of Colombia and ancient maritime groups of coastal Peru).

CHAPTER 3

An Overview
of South American
Environments

Fₒₗₗₒᴡɪɴɢ ᴛʜᴇ ᴛʜᴇᴏʀᴇᴛɪᴄᴀʟ ʟᴇᴀᴅ of Steward outlined earlier, this chapter deals with the great diversity of environmental zones found across the continent and discusses how, in view of the potentials and limitations of these zones, we can lay the groundwork for understanding the different kinds of indigenous subsistence adaptations found in each of them (Chapter 4). In terms of the systems-hierarchical model, the data and arguments presented in this chapter and the following one permit the construction of an effective basis for connecting environment and mode of production, the two most basic variables of the societal infrastructure, to demography and every other sociopolitical feature of indigenous band, village, chiefdom, and state societies throughout South America.

Fundamental in any attempt to understand South American environments are the geologic processes that gave rise to the continent and, during some hundreds of millions of years, have continued to have significant evolutionary impact on both the abiotic (inorganic) and biotic (organic) features that characterize it. The first section therefore begins with current theories of plate tectonics, going on to discuss the implications of tectonic processes for human adaptation to the continent. The second section, which owes much to classic accounts by Carl Sauer (1963) and by Jean Dorst (1967) on South American environments, paints in broad strokes the features of the eight main environmental zones of South America while at the same time setting up the logical underpinning for arguments about the differing subsistence productivities of the eight zones. (Additional environmental details are presented in later chapters when they are relevant to discussing some of the arguments in the anthropological literature about the potentials and limitations of certain environments for indigenous sociocultural evolution.)

CONTINENT FORMATION

Based on current theories of global tectonic processes, the origins of the South American continent go back some 200 million years to the point when the original supercontinent of Pangaea began to break apart as the various plates started their slow but inexorable movement across the earth's surface (see James 1973; Russo and Silver 1995). By about 180 million years ago two continental land masses had formed, with Laurasia in the north and Gondwanaland in the south. In the next 120 million years a number of smaller island continents began to form, a process that effectively isolated the floral and faunal populations of each. Among them was the continent of South America, separated now by open sea from its former geographic partners—and thus providing an excellent example of the evolutionary divergence, or the increased diversity of species, that occurs in the absence of larger numbers of competitors for the various ecological niches in an isolated setting.

Like Australia, South America's particular biological characteristic prior to the breakup of the supercontinent was the presence of larger numbers of marsupial species than placental ones, the exact reverse of the situation in North America at this time. However, as opposed to the herbivorous marsupials found in Australia, most of those of South America were able to occupy a meat-eating niche left open by the absence of suitable placentals to fill it. Thus, for example, evolutionary processes in South America produced a marsupial saber-toothed form quite similar to the placental saber-toothed cat, called *Smilodon*, of North America.

Meanwhile, seafloor spreading out of the Mid-Atlantic Ridge was forcing the heavier continental plate of South America westward while the same process out of the East Pacific Rise was forcing the lighter oceanic Nazca Plate eastward (see Figure 3.1a). As a result, some 175 million years ago a violent collision began to occur between these two plates that even today significantly affects the western edge of the South American continent. Prior to the collision, the continent had high mountain ranges along its eastern edge (the Brazilian side) and no mountains along its western edge (the Andean side), which is the geographic opposite of the situation today. Figure 3.1b shows the tectonic processes that have shaped the continent since the collision between the Nazca and the South American Plates began. The lighter Nazca Plate has been permanently forced under the heavier continental plate as a result of the collision. In the process, the deep Nazca submarine trench has been formed along the subduction zone where the Nazca Plate is forced down under the continental plate. Some 15,000 meters of vertical relief separate the bottom of the trench from the high snowcapped peaks of the adjacent Andes Mountains less than 100 kilometers away. This is one of the greatest elevation differences over such a short distance anywhere in the world.

Tectonic processes have also shaped the southern and northern edges of the continent. A recently proposed theory argues that the eastward-flowing mantle under the Nazca Plate is blocked by the subducted portion of the plate and is forced to flow around this obstruction to the south and the north (Figure 3.1b).

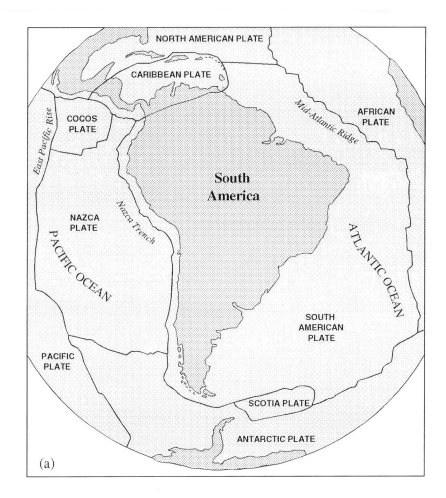

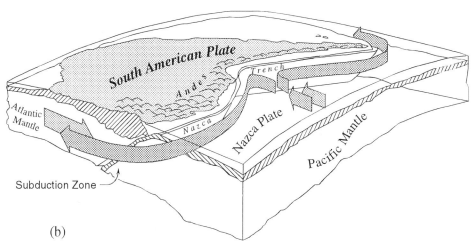

FIGURE 3.1   Plate tectonics showing (a) the plates of South America and the surrounding area of the globe and (b) the tectonic processes that shape the continent. Redrawn and adapted from Russo and Silver (1995).

The evidence of mantle flow around the northern and southern edges of the continent shows up in the configuration of South America at these extreme points: the southern tip, at Tierra del Fuego, is being pushed back to the east while the same process is occurring along the northern edge with respect to the part of the continent that makes up the Caribbean Plate.

As indicated in the figure, the other geologic process that has been occurring since the collision began is the formation of the Andes Mountain chain, which has been forced up along the entire western edge of the continent just as the Nazca Trench has been forced down. This area is an active part of the Pacific *rim of fire*, a term that describes not only the intense volcanism that has accompanied mountain building here but also the severity of the earthquakes that continually occur all along this coastal region. In the classic account of the *Beagle* voyage in the 1830s, Charles Darwin (1962 [1860]) tells of his experience with one of these earthquakes and the accompanying tidal wave, both of which wreaked tremendous damage on a port town along the coast of northern Chile. He also became aware of how over vast amounts of time such geological processes were instrumental in mountain building when he found marine fossils in rock formations located in the high Andes. These, he reasoned, could only have been built over countless millions of years given the slow rate at which geological processes move the land up.

A more recent example of the destructive force of tectonic processes is the earthquake that occurred in northern Peru on Sunday, May 31, 1970. With the epicenter located 25 kilometers out to sea from the modern fishing port of Chimbote, the quake jarred loose an estimated 50 million cubic meters of ice and rock from nearby Huascarán peak in the Andes. Sweeping down the lower slopes of the peak at a velocity of 320 kilometers per hour, the huge avalanche jumped a 300-meter-high cliff and in seconds covered nearly all of the small town of Yungay with four meters of debris mixed with massive boulders. Unfortunately, it was a busy market day and an estimated fifteen thousand people were killed. Those few who escaped the avalanche had the good fortune to be within running distance of a nearby hill on which the town cemetery and a large statue of Christ were located. Elsewhere in the region the earthquake killed an additional fifty-five thousand people and destroyed 180,000 buildings, all in the space of just a few minutes (see Bode 1989).

A more subtle but equally life-extinguishing disaster occurred in South America a little more than 2.5 million years ago when the Panamanian land bridge rose up from the sea to join the formerly isolated continent with North America. Unlike the faunal populations of the southern continent, which had existed in essentially noncompetitive isolation for tens of millions of years, those of North America were the successful evolutionary result of a long series of competitive encounters with Eurasian-African species as North America was intermittently connected via the Beringia land bridge to the Old World. With more brain power characterizing the North American placentals as a result of natural selection for those creatures best able to compete, most of the South American marsupials had little chance for survival as the onslaught began.

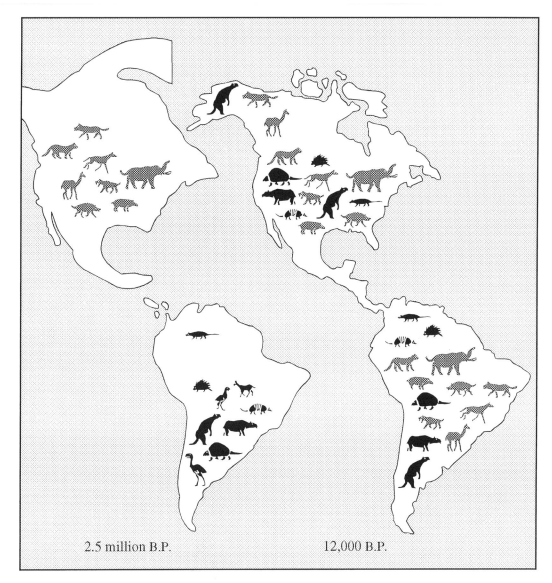

2.5 million B.P.   12,000 B.P.

FIGURE 3.2   The Great American Interchange: maps showing the distribution of selected faunal species in North and South America before and after the closing of the water gap between the two continents. Redrawn and adapted from Lewin (1982).

Figure 3.2 shows the kinds of species found in North and South America both before and after the rise of the Panamanian bridge. The great evolutionist George Gaylord Simpson (1967) describes what happened after the bridge rose as "The Great American Interchange" (see also Lewin 1982)—a two-way migration between both continents that led to a broader distribution of some species and to the extinction of many of the forms that had existed in South America prior to the rise of the bridge. In the section on Paleoindian bands in Chapter 5, we return to a consideration of some of the resulting late Pleistocene faunal species that were hunted by the first human inhabitants of the continent.

In sum, the distinctive shape of South America, its geomorphologic makeup, and its evolutionary history must all be understood as resulting from long-term tectonic and organic processes that began some 200 million years ago. One example of how all of the geologic and biological variables taken together are critical for understanding human cultural development is mentioned by Harris (1977) in *Cannibals and Kings*. There he argues that the Old World and the New World had distinct developmental trajectories because no species suitable for domestication as draft animals were present anywhere in the New World. That they were present in the Old World explains why the wheel and all other related complex technology, including military machines such as ships and guns, were invented there—ultimately leading to the "conquest" of the New World by the Old rather than the reverse. The point is that both biological and cultural evolution must work with the materials that are immediately at hand. This, of course, sets up a context characterized both by potentials for development and by corresponding limitations.

ENVIRONMENTAL ZONES

The differences in faunal populations between South and North America as well as the impact the rise of the Panamanian land bridge had on each notwithstanding, there are strong geographic similarities between the two continents. Four similarities merit mention here. First, as noted by Sauer (1963), the continents are similar in overall shape (any reader disinclined to stare at maps for long periods of time may not have noticed this similarity). Each is triangular, with its broadest portion in the north and an acute tip at its southern end. Second, each continent has its current great mountain ranges located along its western edge, immediately adjacent to the Pacific Ocean (the reason for which has been discussed in the preceding section). Third, both continents have ancient, wide, and heavily eroded highlands along their eastern edges—which, in the case of South America, is pertinent to our examination of some of the limiting factors characterizing human adaptations to the Brazilian Highlands and the Amazon Basin in this chapter and in Chapter 6. Fourth, each of the two continents has vast plains extending between its western mountains and its eastern highlands that have been subject over millions of years to aggradation, or buildup, as erosional material worked its way down from the higher lands to the east and the west.

Here the similarity ends, however, and the remainder of this section provides a general description of each of the eight main environmental zones found across the South American continent (Figure 3.3). These zones are described in an order that proceeds in counterclockwise direction from south to north (which is also the order in which the chapters of this book are organized). They comprise Patagonia, the Pampas, the Gran Chaco, the Brazilian Highlands, the Amazon Basin, the Orinoco Basin, the Caribbean littoral, and the Andes.

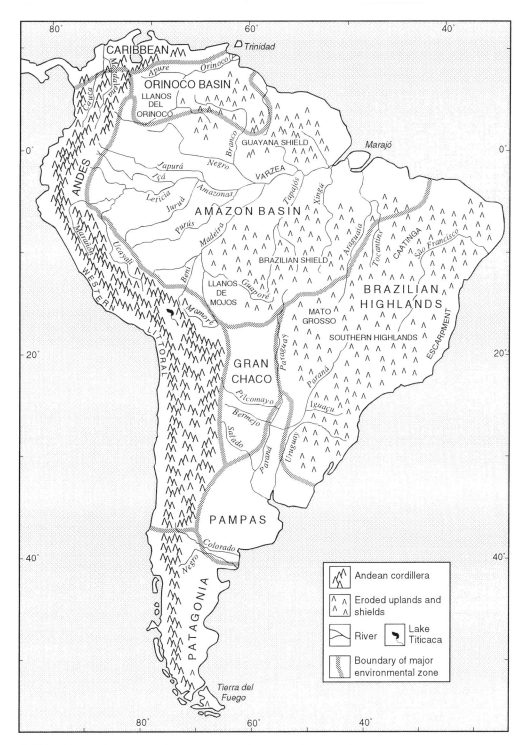

FIGURE 3.3   The principal environmental zones and geographic features of South America.

Patagonia

This zone (Figure 3.3) includes within it the southernmost land anywhere in the world to which human populations were able to adapt until recent historic times (the only land lying farther south is Antarctica). It is thus reasonable to lump the entire southern tip of the continent into one environmental zone called *Patagonia*, a geographic term that comes from the Spanish and means "land of big feet" (European explorers found large footprints of indigenous people on sandy beaches here). In many respects the western and eastern halves of Patagonia could hardly be more different from each other.

If the southernmost geographic position of Patagonia leads one to expect severe climatic extremes, it is in the western half where such extremes are more apparent. Here, mountain-building processes combined with glaciation have created a complex mingling of thousands of islands and deeply cut fjords, the latter headed by low-lying glaciers that reach down out of the adjacent Andes. Heavily moisture-laden air masses arriving in counterclockwise direction out of the southwest hit against the Andean barrier, creating, in combination with the high southern latitudes (ranging from about 37° to 55° S. lat.), one of the colder and more humid environments in the world. The ocean in this area, especially farther south, is extremely turbulent, since currents from the Pacific and the Atlantic sides meet in head-on collision as they cut across the narrow opening in the southern tip, through the Strait of Magellan, or are forced around the tip itself, at Cape Horn.

Tides along the Chilean archipelago, which constitutes the maritime edge of the western half of Patagonia, are the highest in the world—reaching above 15 meters in some places. Although winds on the exposed, western side of the islands are fierce, the islands themselves provide some protection on their leeward side. This, in combination with extensive mudflats that teem with marine life when exposed at low tide, made the area highly suitable for low-density human fishing and gathering populations in the prehistoric and more recent past. From an outsider's perspective, however, the area has its intimidating features as well. These include dense forests that are nearly impossible to walk through (Charles Darwin [1962 (1860)] notes this feature on his trip through here on the English ship the *Beagle*) and rainfall that at 50° S. latitude, for example, ranges between 610 and 860 centimeters annually.

The eastern half of Patagonia stands in sharp geographic contrast to the western half. Because rainfall in the southern latitudes of the continent comes primarily from the southwest, or out of the south Pacific ocean, the height of the Andes here is sufficient to block most of it from ever striking the eastern part of Patagonia. Lying in the rain shadow of the Andes, the eastern half is thus far drier than the western half and consists of vast plateaus covered with low steppe vegetation averaging about 1 meter in height.

Two animals common to the steppes are the rhea, or ñandú, and the guanaco (*Lama guanicoe*). Guanacos were particularly useful to the indigenous inhabitants of the Patagonian steppe, providing them with meat, hides, and wool and thus filling a role quite similar to that of the bison for indigenous groups of the North American plains. Characterized by strong dominance hierarchies, guanacos generally live in small family groups consisting of one adult male, up to ten females, and a number of offspring. When winter snows at higher elevations make it impossible to graze there, larger multifamily aggregations gather in open areas on lower-lying ground.

As discussed in Chapter 5, this dynamic aspect of guanaco group size and location during the year was especially true for the colder climes of the eastern part of Tierra del Fuego, the large island that forms the southern tip of continent and is separated from the mainland by the Strait of Magellan. It is relevant to note here that Tierra del Fuego (whose name, "Land of Fire," comes from the fires built in oceanside camps by the native inhabitants) is a copy in miniature of the eastern and western halves of Patagonia described previously. That is, the western half is mountainous, filled with dense forests, very humid, and primarily suitable for a maritime, or ocean-oriented, adaptation by human groups. The eastern half is flatter and drier, with extensive grasslands that provide, as mentioned, a favorable habitat for guanacos and a terrestrially oriented hunting-gathering adaptation.

Some of the principal climatic and geographic features of Patagonia are summarized in the maps shown in Figure 3.4. Although different in terms of rainfall, soil types, and basic vegetation environments, both the western and eastern halves have climates that are far colder than anywhere else in South America except for the high Andes. Temperatures are somewhat more moderate near the oceans along the western and eastern edges, but the map showing frost-free period in Figure 3.4 indicates that less than eight months of the year are free of below-freezing temperatures throughout most of Patagonia. With respect to temperatures in general, however, it is fair to say that this zone is less frigid on average than comparable (continental) climes in northern North America. The problem is that it really never warms up a great deal, creating an environment that is cool, at best, in summer and cold in winter.

The Pampas

Consisting of flatter terrain covered by tall perennial grasses, the Pampas (from the Andean Quechua word meaning "plain") extend over most of the area of the modern republic of Argentina between the Río Negro, in the south, and the vast Río de la Plata gulf formed by the Paraná, Paraguay, and Uruguay Rivers, in the north. Although the landscape rises some 500 meters in elevation from the Atlantic coastline inland to the Andean boundary of the Pampas on the west, this elevation difference is not enough to create a significant gradient. Thus, few rivers are able to form in spite of a rainfall regime, at least in the eastern part of the Pampas, that is distributed throughout the year.

There is no hard-and-fast dividing line between the southern part of the Pampas and the Patagonian environmental zone, since the one gradually merges into the other. But in general the Pampas have a much milder climate and more rainfall than the Patagonian steppes, so they produce a richer grassy vegetation and,

48

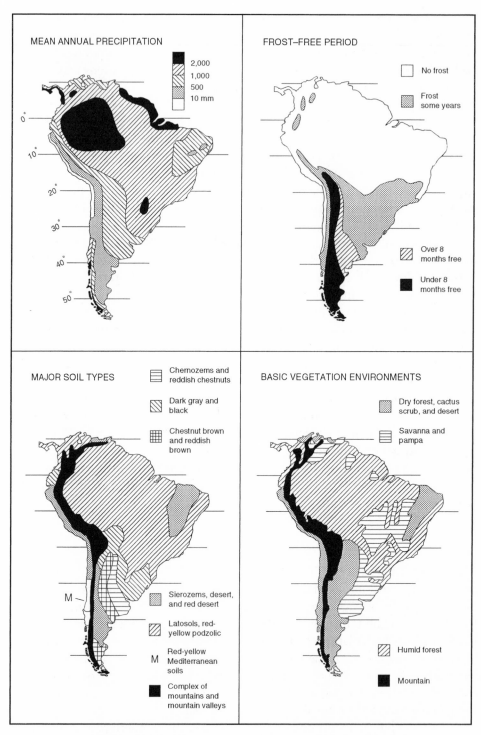

FIGURE 3.4   Maps showing the mean annual precipitation, frost-free period, major soil types, and basic vegetation environments of South America.

presumably, had somewhat higher productivity for migratory band subsistence systems. Forming a sort of northern boundary of the Pampas is the vast *pantanal*, a marshy area that lies adjacent to the Río Paraná and the lower reaches of the Paraguay and the Uruguay Rivers.

Although one of South America's most productive zones today, in part for agricultural crops but even more so for cattle ranching, the Pampas did not in prehispanic times have a subsistence productivity capable of supporting sedentary agricultural societies—in spite of a climate that is milder and rainier compared to Patagonia. Given the much higher subsistence productivity in the industrial age, the major factor limiting productivity and population numbers/densities in ancient times was probably the lack of steel-plow technology to cut through the thick sod formed by pampean grasses and their root systems. (The same argument presumably is also true for the plains of North America.)

As in the case of Patagonia, guanacos and the ñandú formed the basis of hunting-gathering subsistence economies across most of the Pampas. The latter is similar in its habits to the guanaco. The ñandú lives in small, polygynous family groups consisting of a single male, up to six females, and their offspring. In both Patagonia and the Pampas the two species live in proximity to each other, and the ñandú's extreme sensitivity to predation provides a convenient alarm system to the guanaco groups.

The Gran Chaco

Proceeding north from the southern tip of the continent, this is the third and final environmental zone that can be characterized as putting severe constraints on the size and complexity of prehispanic and recent indigenous adaptive systems. Geologically, the Gran Chaco consists of a series of plateaus that descend dramatically from the slopes of the Andes out toward the Paraguay and Paraná Rivers lying along its eastern edge. Although rainfall increases in the direction of these two rivers, the entire Chaco area is characterized by distinct dry and wet seasons and by a lower water table—factors that, taken together, are favorable for the growth of extensive thickets of cactus and scattered stands of thorny, xerophytic vegetation (*Prosopis* sp.).

Along the Ríos Pilcomayo and Bermejo, the two main streams that cross the Chaco, there are low-lying areas that flood during the rainy season and create extensive swampy areas. In other places both these and the lesser rivers of the Chaco disappear underground in sandy terrain. Given the difficulties of survival for groups other than migratory bands in this hostile environment, the only significant modern penetration of the area has been a railroad line that connects southeastern Bolivia to southern Brazil.

The Brazilian Highlands

As indicated in Figure 3.3, the Brazilian Highlands occupy one of the largest areas of any of the eight environmental zones. Encompassing a wide range of latitudes and extending broadly across the eastern half of the continent, this zone cannot be described in simple, overarching terms. Nevertheless, the entire area constitutes the subtropical part of the Brazilian shield, a highly eroded remnant of the mountains that existed in the eastern part of the continent millions of years ago. With a geologic substratum consisting of schists, micaschists, and granites, soils in general are thin and poor in nutrients. Subsistence productivity is therefore low. Slash-and-burn agriculture was possible throughout most of the zone, however, and the highlands can therefore be rather sharply distinguished in terms of productivity from Patagonia, the Pampas, and the Gran Chaco to the south, where, as mentioned, only hunting and gathering was possible. This zone has three main subareas: the *caatinga*, the southern highlands, and the coastal escarpment.

The Caatinga

Formed from the indigenous words *caa*, meaning "forests," and *tinga*, meaning "white," and also called the *sertão*, the *caatinga* is the driest area anywhere in Brazil. Only 100 to 175 centimeters of rainfall occur annually, and the dry season lasts from four to seven months, during which rainfall averages far less (50 centimeters). Although during most years precipitation is nevertheless adequate for small-scale agriculture, the *caatinga* region is notorious for the severity of its unpredictable drought, or *secca*, years. Given the pronounced dry season in all years, most plant species here are xerophytic. When the leaves of the scrub forest oak fall during the dry time of the year, the tree takes on the uniformly grayish-white color that gives rise to the subarea's name. The scarcity of wildlife further limits the productivity of human adaptive systems focused on hunting. For example, the capybara, the largest rodent in South America, exists in small numbers; several species of armadillos are present in desert areas; and a few species of monkeys are found in areas where rainfall is somewhat greater.

The Southern Highlands

This second subarea can be further subdivided into two smaller areas. The first is a forested area in the east that receives far more rainfall than the *caatinga*, although subsistence productivity is generally limited by the impoverished nature of the soils (nevertheless, the coffee plant does well in modern times on the red soils found in parts of this area). The second is the Mato Grosso region to the northwest, a vast sandstone plateau whose soil cover consists of heavily eroded, and therefore nutrient-poor, lateritic clays. Soils that are lateritic (from the Latin for "brick") in general contain an abundance of iron and aluminum oxides and lack silica and kaolin, the latter two having been leached out. When left exposed to the sun too long, for example, as a result of extensive clear-cutting of the forest, these soils harden irreversibly to a bricklike state from which the regeneration of the natural vegetation becomes impossible. Slash-and-burn, or shifting, cultivation, in contrast, usually does not bring about these irreversible processes, since plots are small and used only for a limited number of years.

The Coastal Escarpment

Immediately adjacent to the Atlantic coastline, the Brazilian Highlands plunge abruptly down some 800 meters to form the coastal escarpment. This third principal subarea of the highlands overlooks the ocean all along the coast south of Natal, located at the easternmost tip of the continent at roughly 5° south latitude, to Porto Alegre, at 30° south latitude. The narrow coastal strip, like the humid forests of the southern highlands, is more heavily watered than either the *caatinga* or the Mato Grosso areas, with an average of 180 centimeters of rain per year and no dry season. However, the soils of this area suffer from the same great antiquity and lack of nutrients that characterize the rest of the highlands zone.

The Amazon Basin

Encompassing 6 million square kilometers, the Amazon Basin covers a larger area than any other environmental zone in South America except the Andes. As shown in the maps of Figure 3.4, however, this huge zone is far more homogeneous in terms of frost (none ever occurs), major soil types (mostly latosols), and basic vegetation environments (humid forest) than, for example, the Brazilian Highlands. The only major climatological variable across this largest single expanse of tropical rain forest in the world is rainfall, which occurs in average annual amounts exceeding 200 centimeters in the west-central sector and along a thin strip of coastline near the mouth of the Amazon River. Although the areas of lesser precipitation range between 100 and 200 centimeters per year, which is no more than the average annual rainfall in the southern part of the adjacent Brazilian Highlands, almost no area of the Amazon has the lengthy and pronounced dry season that is present in the *caatinga* and the Mato Grosso regions. The principal exception is a transitional zone consisting of a patchy mosaic of forests and grassy savannas along the southeastern boundary of the basin in the region of the upper Tapajós and upper Araguaia Rivers.

The boundary of the Amazon Basin indicated in Figure 3.3 has been delineated by Betty Meggers (1996) as including an area of essentially tropical rain forest that has the following characteristics: elevations of less than 1,525 meters above sea level, little seasonal variation in the length of the day as a result of the equatorial location, equally little variation in the intensity of insolation, constantly warm temperatures that exceed 20° C and usually vary no more than 2–3° C, rainfall occurring at least 130 or more days a year, and a relative humidity that constantly exceeds 80 percent.

Aside from the heavy rainfall, a critical limiting factor in a major portion of the basin is the great antiquity of the Brazilian and Guyana Shields, both of which have been heavily eroded over the past tens of millions of years. Soils throughout the Amazon range from poor to only moderately productive, since the consistently high temperatures (of both soil and air) do not permit the formation of the well-developed layer of humus that is found in temperate zones. (I have more to say about these limiting factors and their implications for sociopolitical complexity in dealing with indigenous adaptations to the Amazon in Chapter 6.) All areas of land that are not inundated during the annual flood stage of the rivers are classified as belonging to the *terra firme* (from the Portuguese for "solid land"), which makes up an estimated 98 percent of the basin. Here, as in the case of the Brazilian Highlands, the primary subsistence-settlement adaptation in ancient and recent times has been based on slash-and-burn agriculture.

With high rainfall occurring nearly everywhere, it is not surprising that numerous rivers are found throughout the Amazon Basin. But in spite of the rainfall, the maximum flood of the main channel is only 15 meters in the rainier upper reaches of the river and 6 meters in the somewhat drier lower reaches. This is because the rainy seasons to the north and south of the equator occur at different times of the year—that of the north during the Northern Hemisphere's summer, June to August, and that of the south during the austral summer, October to April. A critical feature of the terrain in this regard is the significant lack of any gradient. For example, in the nearly 3,000 kilometers that separate the Peruvian border from the mouth of the Amazon, the river falls only 65 meters. Thus, the flow of the river is as much due to the pressure created by the constant heavy amounts of rainfall as it is to gravity.

The rivers of the basin are categorized as belonging to one of three basic types that range from poor to excellent in terms of their productivity and hence their suitability for an abundance of aquatic life. These categories are blackwater, clearwater, and whitewater rivers. Since both the blackwater and the clearwater rivers flow into the Amazon off the ancient, nutrient-poor shields lying to the north and south, they carry little silt and are at the lower end of the productivity spectrum.

Blackwater rivers are so named because of the color they acquire as a result of their low banks, the proximity of seasonally inundated forest (*igapó*), and the constantly decaying litter that falls into them, releasing acids and consuming precious oxygen. Biotic productivity in blackwater rivers—which include the Río Negro and several tributaries of the Tapajós—is the lowest of any of the three types. Clearwater rivers have higher banks and less vegetal material falling into them, so they are less acidic and provide more favorable habitats for aquatic life. The biotic productivity of these rivers—which include the Tapajós itself—is thus higher.

Whitewater rivers are by definition any streams that descend from the Andes—including the Japurá, the Içá, the Leticia, the Juruá, the Purús, and the Madeira. They bring down tremendous loads of silts and dissolved nutrients, which not only give them their characteristic color but also make their waters highly productive and abundant in aquatic species such as turtles, manatees, and many species of fish. During flood stage they also deposit nutrient-rich silts on the riverbanks, providing continuously higher year-to-year yields from slash-and-burn agriculture. This unique levee-bank niche, called the *várzea*, constitutes the single most productive ecosystem in the entire basin. Although limited in size to only 120,000 square kilometers, or about 2 percent of the basin, the *várzea* provided the context for the development of stratified societies (see Chapter 6).

The highly uniform conditions of constant warmth combined with high rainfall and humidity have created a luxuriant growth of vegetation unequaled elsewhere in South America or most other places in the world. Rising to heights of nearly 90 meters, the highest trees have adapted to the limitations of this environment by forming canopies that permit very little sunlight or rain to penetrate directly to the ground level far below. In the dim light below the canopy, the understory of the forest is often rather sparsely vegetated—contrary to what one might expect to see in a tropical "jungle" area.

Since much of the rainfall nonetheless hits the ground indirectly, tropical trees have adapted to the dangers of leaching by developing shallow root systems that, aided by a great variety of leaf-munching insects and other detritovores, quickly recycle much of the nutrients lost in the form of leaf fall. The net result is that most nutrients are locked up in the vegetal biomass itself and thus are not available to form a humus layer on the ground. There has also been selection for wide dispersal of the individuals of each species, an adaptation to the dangers of the rapid spread of plant-specific diseases in such a setting. Nevertheless, over a given small area of forest one finds an almost unbelievable variety of species distributed in apparently total disorder. For example, in an area of 3 acres naturalist Dorst once counted 654 trees belonging to sixty different species.

As with plants, the number and diversity of animal species are greater than in other environmental zones of South America. Except for a few social animals, such as monkeys (*Platyrhinians*) and peccaries (*Tayassu* sp.), however, most species have adapted to this setting through wide dispersal of individuals. In general, mammalian fauna are scarce compared to other parts of South America such as Patagonia, and all fauna combined constitute a small fraction—on the order of substantially less than 1 percent—of the total organic biomass. Included among these fauna are the tree sloth, a few deer species, two species of peccary, the tapir, the great anteater, rodents such as the capybara, and several species of monkeys.

Feeding on these animals is a variety of reptilian predators, including crocodiles, caimans, the giant anaconda, and the bushmaster. Feline predators include the ocelot, the jaguarundi, the puma, and the jaguar, this last not only being the largest of the felines in South America, but also, fearing neither humans nor other creatures, one of the fiercest and most deadly. Other than the crocodilians and the anaconda, among the most infamous of the predators inhabiting the rivers and streams are the deadly piranhas, aggressive swimmers capable of reducing a 45-kilogram capybara to a skeleton in less than one minute. Another river inhabitant is the candiru, a tiny fish with backward-pointing spines that has the rather nasty habit of swimming up bodily orifices such as the urethra.

Just three of the many classic naturalist studies that have been written on the Amazon Basin are: Alfred Russell Wallace's *A Narrative of Travels on the Amazon and Rio Negro*, first published in 1853; Henry Walter Bates's *The Naturalist on the River Amazons*, first published in 1863; and Alex Shoumatoff's *The Rivers Amazon*. This last book, published in 1978, is a latter-day version of the two nineteenth-century classics. Of the many contributions made by the two earlier scholars, one stands above all the others: When confronted with the incredible diversity of faunal and floral species in the basin, both Bates and Wallace (the latter a codiscoverer, with Charles Darwin, of the theory of natural selection as a primary mechanism of biological evolution) were highly adept at documenting important evidence for the speciation brought about by evolutionary forces. All three of these writers brilliantly capture the essence of this complex ecosystem.

The Orinoco Basin

The Orinoco River Basin is a low-lying area that is sharply delimited everywhere by mountain ranges, with the exception of its delta in the northeast. These mountains include the Venezuelan coastal range on the north, the Colombian Andes on the west, and the Guyana Shield on the east. In places, the demarcation between the lower basin itself and the surrounding ranges is an abrupt, dramatic one. This is the case, for example, in the southeast where the high flat-topped mesas of the Guyana Shield terminate in cliffs as high as 1,500 meters. From one of these cliffs plunges Angel Falls, at 1,000 meters the highest waterfall in the world.

Like the Brazilian Highlands, the Orinoco Basin has distinct dry and wet seasons, although even during the dry season some rain falls. The climate is thus favorable for the formation of vast grassy savannas, or llanos, especially in the western sector. The flora and fauna of the basin include many of the species found in the adjacent Amazon. Among these are numerous types of fish and the manatee, an aquatic mammal, as well as several terrestrial species, including deer, peccaries, and armadillos.

The Orinoco River itself originates in the Parima Mountains, in Yanomamö territory, and runs for slightly over 2,000 kilometers. The principal woody vegetation of the basin occurs in the form of gallery forests confined to the sides of the river and its tributaries. Since the Orinoco flows off the northwestern edge of the Guyana Shield, it does not bring down much silt or dissolved nutrients from its highland sources. Thus, the amount of alluvial land is scarce along most parts of the river, not to mention its tributaries as well. With a limited niche for agriculture, yet vast areas of grassy llanos, the Orinoco Basin can be generally characterized as a context appropriate for migratory hunting-gathering groups.

The Caribbean Littoral

Although including outlier ranges of the Andes, the Caribbean littoral zone is unique enough that it can be distinguished as a separate zone from the Andes—not least because a good part of it consists of a low-lying coastal shelf adjacent to the Caribbean Sea. Its eastern and western sectors are rather distinct.

The Eastern Sector

Immediately to the southwest of the great Gulf of Venezuela and Lake Maracaibo is a narrow branch of the Andes that runs along the Caribbean coastline for nearly 1,000 kilometers, to a point very near the mouth of the Orinoco River. Although the peaks of this mountain chain do not reach the heights of those in the main Andes farther south, this is a distinctly vertical environment with elevations ranging as high as 4,900 meters in its western part. Toward its eastern end, the chain drops in elevation to about 2,100 meters, not far from the mouth of the Orinoco and the Island of Trinidad (see Figure 3.3). The entire coastal shelf in this area is semiarid, with low amounts of rainfall ranging between 25 and 30 centimeters and few permanent streams. The vegetation of the coast consists of desert-adapted xerophytic plants, whereas that of the mountains closely resembles the Ecuadorian Andes, which lie far southwest. For example, up to about 3,000 meters is a temperate zone where potatoes and cereal grasses are grown, with humid upland *páramo* and herbaceous vegetation lying above this elevation.

The Western Sector

From the same point southwest of Lake Maracaibo where the Venezuelan cordillera begins, another range extends some 500 kilometers out to the north, becoming the northernmost extension of the Andes Mountains. As this range approaches the Caribbean coast, it splits into two parts. One heads to Punta Gallinas, itself the northernmost extension of the continental landmass. The other extends out to the west along the coastline and terminates in the fabled Sierra Nevada de Santa Marta, a huge triangular-shaped massif that rises dramatically up from the coastal plain to twin snowcapped peaks 5,790 meters above sea level. Lying just 42 kilometers inland, this is the highest coastal mountain in the world. Although much of the Caribbean environmental zone in general was limited in prehispanic times to slash-and-burn agriculture and hence to low-density egalitarian adaptive systems, the extensive exploitation of multiple environmental zones along the north flanks of the Sierra Nevada de Santa Marta provided the infrastructural base for the rise of societies comparable in complexity to those of the *várzea* niche in the Amazon Basin (see Chapter 7).

To the west of the Sierra Nevada de Santa Marta lies the mouth of the Río Magdalena and, beyond it, a wide coastal plain that extends to the Isthmus of Panama. Both the Magdalena mouth and the coastal plain receive far heavier precipitation than the coastal sector to the east of Lake Maracaibo, with rainfall reaching above 500 centimeters throughout most of the area. Around the mouth of the Magdalena itself lie vast marshes (called *ciénagas*) that are periodically inundated by the river during its flood stage. Elsewhere to the east are areas with some of the most luxuriant rain forest found anywhere in South America.

The Andes

Relative to all other areas of the continent, the Andes zone is by far the most complex environmentally. First, as shown in Figure 3.3, it runs continuously all the way from 10° north of the equator to about 55° south of it, a distance of 7,700 kilometers. Thus, the lower level of permanent snow and the different inhabitable microenvironments that lie vertically stacked below the snow all vary as a function of proximity to the equator. In other words, these microenvironments rise in elevation approaching the equator and drop lower and lower at greater distances from it.

Second, the Andes Mountains vary climatically from east to west—with three principal subzones: (1) the Andes chain itself; (2) the Pacific littoral, or coastal shelf, which lies to the west of the Andes; and (3) the humid tropical *montaña*, which lies along the eastern slopes of the Andes and overlooks six of the environmental zones discussed earlier. Just as the climate of the Andean chain varies in terms of distance from the equator, so is there a great deal of variability from north to south in the other two subzones, especially along the Pacific littoral.

Third, the width of the Andes varies from place to place along the western edge of the continent. Current theories about plate tectonics suggest that the pressure exerted by mantle flow on the Nazca Plate is greatest in the central midsection of the continent, where, as shown in Figure 3.3, a great bend has been created at a point roughly coincident with the modern political boundary between Peru and Chile (see also Figure 1.1). Here also, the Andes are at their widest, creating the largest expanse of high intercordillera flatland anywhere along their length.

Fourth, the cordilleras, or chains, that make up the Andes vary in number and width from north to south. Where these cordilleras are narrow and plunge deeply down into low intervening, subtropical or tropical valleys—in Colombia, for example—there occur some of the most compact and complex juxtapositions of microenvironments found anywhere in the world, providing both opportunities and limitations for human adaptive systems.

Fifth, rainfall and the direction from which it comes vary from area to area in the Andes. Proceeding from north to south, the following generalizations can be made: (1) in the northern Andes of Colombia and Ecuador rain strikes the Andes from both the Pacific side, on the west, and the Amazon Basin side, on the east, creating a situation of relatively ample rainfall in the intervening mountains themselves; (2) in the Central Andes of Peru and Bolivia, where all of the precipitation comes out of the Amazon, the intervening mountains are only moderately well watered and become increasingly dry toward their western edge; (3) in the Andes of northern Chile very little rainfall comes from the east out of the Gran Chaco and northern Pampas, and, as with Peru to the north, no rainfall at all strikes the western littoral north of about 30° south latitude, so this area is extremely dry; (4) farther south all rainfall strikes the Andes out of the west from the south Pacific Ocean, and the intervening mountains are increasingly dry toward their eastern edge (i.e., toward the Pampas side). Since the boundaries of the modern Andean nations of Colombia, Ecuador, Peru, Bolivia, and Chile coincide fairly well with major changes in one or more of these five geographic variables, it is reasonable to proceed on this basis from north to south in describing this environmental zone.

The Colombian Andes

In the far north the Andes are divided into three main cordilleras, with the Cauca and the Magdalena River valleys running from south to north through them. In light of the tropical latitudes of this area and the deeply downcut nature of the two valleys, in a narrow space of less than 300 kilometers from east to west the terrain alternates continuously between higher alpine climates and humid tropics. The widest and most productive region occurs in the easternmost cordillera on the high plateau of Bogotá, a cold humid environment that lies at about 3,000 meters above sea level. This is the *páramo* region, and it provides a context suitable both for the pasturing of animals and the cultivation of the potato (*Solanum tuberosum*), a native Andean crop introduced in prehispanic times from the Central Andes farther to the south.

Located nearby are deeper valleys, where at 2,500 meters and below the climate is more temperate and suitable for maize cultivation. In general, although this part of the Andes was relatively productive for prehispanic agriculture, the highly broken terrain kept population groupings relatively localized and small and therefore constrained in terms of sociopolitical complexity. The far western edge of Colombia is one of the rainiest parts of South America, and its tropical rain forest and mangrove swamps are similar to the far eastern area of the Amazon Basin.

The Ecuadorian Andes

South into Ecuador the Andes reach their narrowest point anywhere along the western edge of the continent, forming two closely spaced cordilleras that lie about 100 kilometers apart. Twenty volcanoes are scattered along these two mountain chains, including Cotopaxi, which, rising to 5,943 meters, is the highest active volcano in the world. Lying between the two chains is a series of basins at elevations averaging about 3,000 meters. These highland basins constitute the classic example of the Andean *páramo* environment.

In spite of the equatorial latitude, at this elevation ambient temperatures in the *páramo* are low and abundant rainfall occurs throughout the year. Temperatures can vary substantially on a daily basis, however, ranging between –2 °C at night to 12 °C in the daytime. The characteristic weather of the *páramo* is a cold, penetrating drizzle much of the time, and few indigenous Andean animals except for the woolly tapir, the spectacled bear (*ucumari*), and several bird species were adapted to these rigorous conditions prior to the arrival of human groups on the scene. Nevertheless, the black, acidic soils of the *páramo* are relatively productive for agriculture.

With neither rain forests nor absolute deserts characterizing the northern, central, and far southern parts of coastal Ecuador, they are transitional between the wetter Colombian coast to the north and the drier Peruvian coast to the south. There is abundant rainfall throughout the year along this broad coastal shelf and on the adjacent western side of the Andes, with dense tropical vegetation found nearly everywhere. In the midst of these humid tropical lands, along the southwest coast to the west of the Bay of Guayaquil lies a section of coast that is anomalously dry. This subtropical area is the northern outlier of the unique conditions of aridity created by the Peru Coastal Current as it sweeps along the Peruvian coast and hits the southwest coast of Ecuador before heading out to the west into the open Pacific Ocean and past the Galápagos Islands.

The Peruvian Sierra

Two main cordilleras form the Andes of Peru, just as in Ecuador, but here the distance widens to double that of the *páramo*. High grasslands are present here, but in contrast to Ecuador there is a stronger seasonal difference in precipitation. The rainy season occurs normally between December and March, followed by an eight-month period during which there is little rain (although most rainfall occurs during the Southern Hemisphere's summer, the people of this part of the Andes consider it to be winter, since, in spite of the warmer temperatures, it is the time of inclement weather). With elevations averaging 3,500 meters or more above sea level and a lengthy dry season, conditions are favorable for the widespread growth of a short, spiny-tipped grass known as ichu but little else in the way of native vegetation (see also Figure 3.4). This cold, dry, tundralike environment, known as the *puna*, is not a single continuous environment. Areas of *puna* alternate with areas of low hills and deeply downcut river valleys that together form a complex mosaic of vertically stacked microenvironments ranging between elevations of 2,000 and 4,500 meters. Added to this broken topography is a series of large basins situated at temperate elevations that include, from north to south, the Cajamarca, Callejón de Huaylas, Jauja-Huancayo, Ayacucho, and Cuzco Basins.

The Peruvian sierra provides a far more extensive, and therefore ultimately more productive, setting than the northern Andes for a combination of subsistence strategies that since about 1800 B.C. has included (1) at higher elevations, a pastoralist adaptation focused on llamas *(Lama glama)* and alpacas *(Lama pacos)*, the Andean camelid domesticates, and the cultivation of various tubers, including potatoes; (2) at middle elevations, the cultivation of quinua *(Chenopodium quinoa)*, a high-protein indigenous cereal grass, and maize, a probable introduction from Mesoamerica; and (3) at lower elevations, the cultivation of various indigenous fruit-bearing trees and coca *(Erythroxylon coca)*. With the development of agriculture as well as subsistence strategies involving the exploitation of multiple environmental levels, the sierra in prehispanic times was characterized by denser populations and more sociopolitical complexity than either the Ecuadorian or the Colombian Andes.

The Western Littoral of Peru and Chile

Nothing could provide a greater contrast with the relatively well-watered Andean sierra than the littorals of Peru and northern Chile, which together form the largest continuous area of desert anywhere in the New World. Sandwiched narrowly between the Pacific Ocean and the Andes Mountains, which lie less than 50 kilometers inland from the sea, the coast desert runs for over 3,500 kilometers between 3° and 30° south latitude and encompasses central and northern Chile as well as the entire Peruvian littoral. Considering its tropical location, the coastal desert should be characterized by the same lush vegetation that is found along the western side of the continent north of the equator. A complex set of oceanographic, geographic, and meteorological factors—including the Peru Coastal Current, the configuration of the western coastline, the flow of air masses in this part of the south Pacific Ocean, and the barrier to Amazonian-derived precipitation created by the high Andes—helps explain why this is not the case.

Flowing in a counterclockwise direction, the Peru Coastal Current strikes the western side of South America at 38° south latitude, running like a 160-kilometer-wide "river" all along the littoral before heading out to sea just north of the westernmost protrusion of the continent at Cabo Blanco, Peru. As the current collides with the northwest-trending coastline and adjacent marine shelf, it "sets out" to the west-northwest from the edge of the continent and brings about a displacement of waters at the ocean's surface, which, in turn, causes an upwelling of colder marine waters from the depths of the Nazca Trench to replace the surface waters. Because of this, average ambient temperatures along the littoral are 20°C, or some 4°C cooler than normal for these latitudes, and temperatures at the surface of the ocean are even colder, averaging nearly 20°C below normal.

As the prevailing southwesterly air masses come into contact with the current, they are sharply cooled immediately above the surface of the ocean, which brings about an inversion of temperatures that traps cold air *below* a layer of warm air. From May to October, these conditions produce a thick cloud bank along a 500-kilometer stretch of the central and north Peruvian coasts that warms up as it hits the land and thus never condenses enough to produce anything more than a slight drizzle of moisture called *garúa*. (This inclement season of cooler foggy weather occurs during the austral winter, so inhabitants of the coast have their winter while the nearby Andean people are experiencing "summer.") The net effect is that, aside from the *garúa* drizzle, the littorals of Peru and northern Chile normally have no source of rainfall from weather that originates in the south Pacific.

The humid easterlies out of the Amazon cool down sufficiently upon striking the eastern cordillera of the Andes that most precipitation occurs here. The small amount remaining strikes the western cordillera but never reaches farther to the west below an elevation of 3,000 meters above sea level. The entire western side of the Andes from this elevation on down to the coastline itself thus receives no rainfall from Amazonian sources. In light of the desertic conditions created by multiple oceanographic, geographic, and meteorological conditions, the western littoral would be essentially uninhabitable if not for the handful of rivers in northern Chile and some fifty rivers in Peru that have developed along the western side of the continental divide as a function of rainfall and snowmelt in the high Andes.

The Peruvian and Ecuadorian Montaña

The entire eastern side of the Andes from Ecuador through southern Peru receives heavy rainfall from the prevailing easterlies coming out of the Amazon Basin. In the northern Andes closer to the equator, tropical temperatures are present up to elevations of 1,500 meters above sea level. As the humid air from the basin rises higher on the eastern side of the mountains, it condenses further and even more rainfall occurs here than in the Amazon proper. Most of the slopes lying between 1,500 and 3,000 meters are thus heavily shrouded in perpetual mist. This is the "cloud forest," or as it is called in Spanish, *la ceja de la montaña* ("eyebrow of the montane jungle"). Above 3,000 meters lies a more temperate environment that grades into *puna* at elevations above 4,000 meters, depending on the distance from the equator. With spectacularly deep canyons (called *pongos*, from the Quechua word for "door") eroded into the sides of the Andes by the heavy rainfall and rivers with nearly unnavigable rapids running through these narrow canyons, this is one of the most challenging environments for human adaptation anywhere in South America. Nevertheless, several of the most famous archaeological sites of the continent are found here—including the Inca site of Machu Picchu.

The Bolivian and Chilean Andes

Continuing to the south along the eastern side of the Andes, decreasing amounts of rainfall occur as the chain reaches higher latitudes. These eastern slopes, called *yungas* in Bolivia, nonetheless include the full Andean contingent of vertically stacked microenvironments—ranging all the way from lower tropical elevations, up through more temperate climes, and on to the higher *puna*. To the west of the *yungas* region is one of the widest and most extensive areas of high plains in the Andes, the *altiplano* of Bolivia, which averages some 4,000 meters in elevation and extends across relatively colder latitudes between 15° and 22° south latitude. Decreasing amounts of rainfall occur here from north to south, so that at its southernmost extreme in southern Bolivia and northern Chile the *altiplano* becomes a cold, high-altitude desert.

In the northernmost part of the *altiplano* is Lake Titicaca, a body of water that covers an area 175 kilometers long by 55 kilometers wide. With relatively cool water temperatures ranging between 10° and 12°C, the lake nevertheless temporizes the adjacent land to the point that even some lower-altitude crops, such as quinua and barley, can be grown here in addition to the tubers that normally are cultivated at such elevations throughout the Andes. The vast *altiplano* that surrounds the lake and extends farther to the north and south was capable of the same agricultural productivity that characterizes other major basins to the north in Peru, and it became the scene of societal developments that were among the most complex in the prehispanic sequence of the Central Andes.

CHAPTER 4

Subsistence and Sociocultural Development

THE ENVIRONMENTAL DATA discussed to this point support two principal arguments about traditional indigenous adaptations of the past and present to the environmental zones of South America. First, the subsistence productivity of each of the eight zones can be described as having both potentials and limitations deriving from the zone's geographic features. Second, each zone can be compared and contrasted with the others in having an overall productivity that is less than, the same as, or more than that of the others.

In the first and second sections of this chapter we now proceed to the more general concern of relating subsistence productivity in the different environmental zones to the different levels of sociopolitical integration found in those zones. In the first section similar zones are grouped together along a continuum consisting of four types of subsistence productivity: (1) low, (2) moderately low, (3) moderately high, and (4) high. Each of the subsistence productivity types is discussed with regard to the kinds of faunal and floral subsistence resources that characterize it. The second section then discusses the close correspondence between the productivity of these resources and the societal level(s) found within the zone. Reinforcing an earlier argument, we see that there is a predictable relationship between environment and subsistence, on the one hand, and the kinds of societies that arose across the continent through thirteen thousand years of indigenous adaptation to it, on the other.

The third section presents an overview of the cultivated plants of the Andes and adjacent western littoral, dealing with a selected group of the important cultivars found in this huge geographic area that stretches from Venezuela in the far north to central Chile in the south. The cultivars of the Amazon Basin are not dealt with here primarily because the majority of them are well known outside of South America—which is not to imply that we yet know very much about the great numbers of wild plants that are collected and used by indigenous Amazonian groups, including shamans. Although many of the indigenous cultivars of the Andes are also well known (e.g., potatoes, peanuts, manioc), some of the Andean crops discussed here (e.g., mashua, maca, and oca) are unknown even though they have been important mainstays of indigenous subsistence systems of western South America.

The data on Andean plant domesticates provide some of the necessary background for the fourth section, which deals with the origins of agriculture in South America but focuses particularly on the Andes, to date the best-known area of the continent in relation to this problem. Among other things, this discussion supports the argument that a primary reason indigenous groups in certain areas evolved beyond an egalitarian band level of sociopolitical integration surely had to do, first, with the subsistence potential of their environmental setting for such a development and, second, with the universal human ability to bring about evolutionary changes in subsistence productivity via artificial selection in plants and animals.

The fifth section deals briefly with the preservation of Andean cultivars in the later, ceramic period of coastal Peru, pausing to consider not only the excellence of this preservation, but also how some of the domesticated plants were depicted by descendants of the creators of these plants on pottery of the south Peruvian coast. The sixth section describes the principal hallucinogenic plants used by indigenous peoples in both the Amazon and the Andes and their general role in ritual and religious activities. Here we may note that it is the rain-forest environment that has a far greater variety of such plants than anywhere else on the continent including the Andes. The final section rounds out the discussion in this chapter of plants of economic utility (third section) and those with psychoactive properties (sixth section) by focusing on the use of medicinal herbs by the Kallawaya, of northwestern Bolivia, who have long been famous throughout the Andes for their expert knowledge of the healing properties of wild plants.

SUBSISTENCE PRODUCTIVITY

Low Productivity Areas

As should be clear from the preceding chapter, Patagonia, the Pampas, and the Gran Chaco all have the lowest productivity for traditional indigenous subsistence systems of prehispanic and recent times. Although the introduction of Old World domesticates (e.g., sheep in Tierra del Fuego, wheat in the Pampas) and technology (e.g., the steel plow in the Pampas) has made portions of these environments substantially more productive in modern times—and therefore capable of sustaining nation-states—in general no agriculture was practiced here during some ten thousand or so years of prehispanic human occupation. Instead, subsistence-settlement systems throughout the central and southern part of the continent involved a nonsedentary, or migratory, hunting and gathering adaptive strategy.

As shown in Figure 4.1, the resources exploited by the indigenous inhabitants included a wide range of wild flora and fauna. In Patagonia, subsistence was primarily focused on marine and terrestrial fauna—fish, shellfish, sea birds, whales (beached), and the guanaco; a secondary focus was on wild flora, including several species of edible berries. In the Pampas, subsistence centered around a variety of terrestrial fauna, including the guanaco, the ñandú, the armadillo, and the tuco-tuco (a small rodent). Plant resources in the xerophytic thickets of the Gran Chaco included the algarroba bean (*Prosopis* sp., a legume similar to mesquite beans), while faunal resources included the ñandú and the peccary, the latter being a small wild pig similar to the North American javelina.

Outside of these three environmental zones, elsewhere in the South American lowlands to the east of the Andes there are isolated settings of relatively limited extent that are generally unsuitable for agriculture. These include the central Brazilian coast, several areas in the central and northern Amazon, the llanos of Venezuela, and parts of the Caribbean coast. In spite of the nearby presence of horticultural systems based on slash and burn, the adaptive systems of these areas consist of migratory gathering and hunting. Nevertheless, as we see in Chapter 5, the Nukak of eastern Colombia practice some horticulture, although their primary focus on hunting and plant gathering requires them to maintain a mobile lifestyle that limits population numbers and overall sociopolitical complexity to a band level of integration.

Moderately Low Productivity Areas

All of the remaining environmental zones of the continent east of the Andes— including the Brazilian Highlands, the Amazon Basin, and the Orinoco Basin— have been appropriate contexts for the development of a mixed subsistence strategy that includes slash-and-burn horticulture as well as gathering and hunting. The Chilean coast, located in the southeastern part of the Andes chain, is also characterized by the same productivity level. Although far more sedentary than groups in the low productivity zones, the people of moderately low productivity areas nonetheless are forced by the constraints of the environment and their slash-and-burn subsistence system to move at fairly frequent intervals to new terrain at various distances away from their old settlements.

It will be recalled that the soils of these zones in general are relatively nutrient-poor and that most of the nutrients are found in the vegetal biomass itself. In slash-and-burn agriculture, small sections of the forest are cut down, left to dry for several weeks or months, and then burned. This process releases the majority of nutrients from the cut vegetation directly onto the soil, providing a sort of quick fix to otherwise poor soils. But, as discussed in greater detail in Chapter 6, there is a limit of only several years (three, on average) before these nutrients are used up, and hence a move is required to new areas, where the whole process is repeated. Obviously, this limitation has implications for the overall density and numbers of the human populations inhabiting these zones. Another limitation of this type of

64

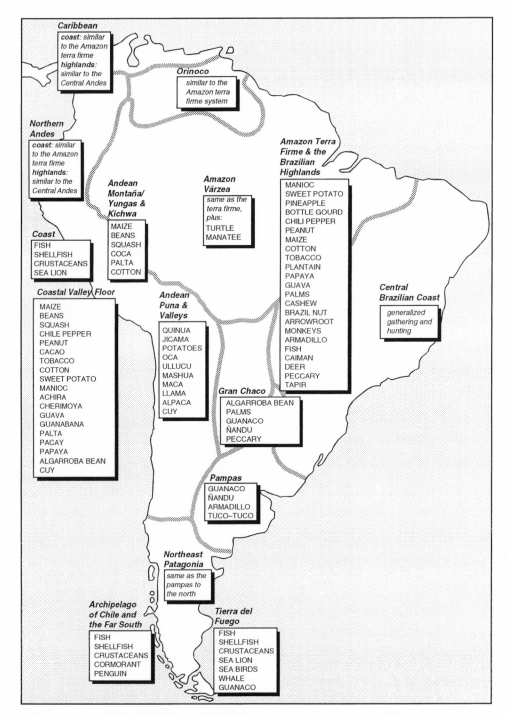

Caribbean
coast: similar to the Amazon terra firme
highlands: similar to the Central Andes

Orinoco
similar to the Amazon terra firme system

Northern Andes
coast: similar to the Amazon terra firme
highlands: similar to the Central Andes

Amazon Terra Firme & the Brazilian Highlands
MANIOC
SWEET POTATO
PINEAPPLE
BOTTLE GOURD
CHILI PEPPER
PEANUT
MAIZE
COTTON
TOBACCO
PLANTAIN
PAPAYA
GUAVA
PALMS
CASHEW
BRAZIL NUT
ARROWROOT
MONKEYS
ARMADILLO
FISH
CAIMAN
DEER
PECCARY
TAPIR

Andean Montaña/ Yungas & Kichwa
MAIZE
BEANS
SQUASH
COCA
PALTA
COTTON

Amazon Várzea
same as the terra firme, plus:
TURTLE
MANATEE

Coast
FISH
SHELLFISH
CRUSTACEANS
SEA LION

Central Brazilian Coast
generalized gathering and hunting

Coastal Valley Floor
MAIZE
BEANS
SQUASH
CHILE PEPPER
PEANUT
CACAO
TOBACCO
COTTON
SWEET POTATO
MANIOC
ACHIRA
CHERIMOYA
GUAVA
GUANABANA
PALTA
PACAY
PAPAYA
ALGARROBA BEAN
CUY

Andean Puna & Valleys
QUINUA
JICAMA
POTATOES
OCA
ULLUCU
MASHUA
MACA
LLAMA
ALPACA
CUY

Gran Chaco
ALGARROBA BEAN
PALMS
GUANACO
ÑANDU
PECCARY

Pampas
GUANACO
ÑANDU
ARMADILLO
TUCO–TUCO

Northeast Patagonia
same as the pampas to the north

Archipelago of Chile and the Far South
FISH
SHELLFISH
CRUSTACEANS
CORMORANT
PENGUIN

Tierra del Fuego
FISH
SHELLFISH
CRUSTACEANS
SEA LION
SEA BIRDS
WHALE
GUANACO

FIGURE 4.1   Selected subsistence resources in the principal environmental zones of South America. Based on Steward and Faron (1959) and Pearsall (1992).

agriculture in a tropical forest setting is that the cultivars employed are generally rich in carbohydrates but poor in protein, the two basic elements of an adequate diet other than minerals and vitamins. Since protein therefore has to come mostly from hunting, the low animal biomass of the tropical rain forest poses an additional limiting factor. Besides the constraints posed by the biotic and abiotic environment, however, there are other variables at work in the adaptive systems of these areas. For example, a hostile political environment—itself an integral part of indigenous adaptations—can affect the distribution of settlements as well as the frequency and distance of moves to new settlement locations.

Figure 4.1 shows the principal subsistence resources that are characteristic of most parts of the Brazilian Highlands and the Amazon Basin. Among them is a great variety of cultivars, including manioc (*Manihot* sp.), sweet potato (*Ipomoea batatas*), pineapple (*Ananas comosus*), chili pepper (*Capsicum* sp.), peanut (*Arachis hypogaea*), maize (*Zea mays*), bottle gourd (*Lagenaria siceraria*), tobacco (*Nicotiana* sp.), plantain (*Musa paradisiaca*, a form of banana that is a European introduction), as well as a number of wild plants, including palms (*Acrocomia* sp.), cashew nut (*Anacardium occidentale*), Brazil nut (*Bertholletia excelsa*), and arrowroot (*Tacca leotopetaloides*). Animal species hunted or trapped include monkeys, armadillo, fish, caiman, deer, peccary, and tapir.

A comparison of the resources shown in Figure 4.1 for the Brazilian Highlands and the Amazon to those of the Andes demonstrates that the former compare quite favorably in number and variety to the latter. This favorable comparison notwithstanding, the slash-and-burn systems of the eastern tropical lowlands in general are lower in productivity per unit area than the intensive agricultural systems of the highlands and coast of the Central Andes.

Moderately High Productivity Areas

Intermediate in productivity between *terra firme* Amazonia and the Central Andes are the northern Andean highlands of Colombia as well as isolated areas elsewhere, including especially the Sierra Nevada de Santa Marta (in prehispanic times), the Amazon *várzea*, and possibly the Llanos de Mojos area of the southwestern Amazon. Subsistence resources vary in these areas according to the specific environment in which they are found, as shown in Figure 4.1, but all were contexts where stratified societies at a chiefdom level of sociopolitical integration arose in the prehispanic period.

High Productivity Areas

The highest productivity subsistence zones of the continent include the Andes of Ecuador, Peru, and northern Bolivia as well as the coastal valleys of Peru. As mentioned earlier, a great number of domesticated and wild flora were (and still are) utilized here in combination with intensive irrigation agriculture in the better-watered areas to produce the maximum productivity and sociopolitical complexity of any subsistence-settlement systems of prehispanic South America. Domesticated plant resources of the coast include maize *(Zea mays)*, squash *(Cucurbita)*, and beans *(Phaseolus vulgaris)*—the "holy American triad," which provides all the protein necessary for an adequate diet—as well as chili pepper *(Capsicum* sp.), peanut *(Arachis hypogaea)*, cacao *(Theobroma cacao)*, sweet potato *(Solanum tuberosum)*, manioc *(Manihot esculenta)*, avocado *(Persea americana*, or palta, as it is called in South America), papaya *(Carica candicans)*, cotton *(Gossypium barbadense)*, tobacco, and a host of other foods, such as achira *(Canna edulis)*, cherimoya *(Annona cherimola)*, guava *(Psidiumgua java)*, guanábana *(Annona muricata)*, and pacay *(Inga feuillei)*, that are generally unknown outside of South America. Plant resources of the Andean sierra include maize, beans, squash, coca *(Erythroxylon coca)*, palta, cotton, potatoes, and other native tubers such as oca *(Oxalis tuberosa)*, ulluco *(Ullucus tuberosus)*, mashua *(Tropaeolum tuberosum)*, and maca *(Lepidium meyenii)*. Prehispanic domesticated animal resources of the Andean coast and highlands were more limited, but they nevertheless formed a critically important part of the diet in both areas. They include the alpaca, llama, and guinea pig, or cuy *(Cavia porcellus)*.

PRODUCTIVITY AND
SOCIOPOLITICAL INTEGRATION

The two maps shown in Figure 4.2 provide a summary of the main arguments of this chapter: (1) significant differences exist among the eight environmental zones of the continent, (2) similar zones can be grouped into larger areas on the basis of their overall subsistence productivity, (3) these subsistence productivity areas can be compared and contrasted in terms of their potentials and limitations (no environment is without both!), and (4) there is a close association between each major subsistence productivity area (or in some cases, sections of an area) and the level of sociopolitical integration of the human adaptive systems that are found in it. Although the terminology used by Steward and Faron (1959) to characterize the indigenous subsistence areas is somewhat different from that employed in this book, a comparison of the sets of terms used in the maps of Figure 4.2 (both of which are redrawn from their book) with those employed in this book (see Figure 2.7) indicates that no critical substantive differences exist between them. For example, the band level is equivalent to hunter-gatherer band societies, the village level is equivalent to farming-pastoralist societies and tropical forest village societies, and the chiefdom and state levels are the same as the terms used by Steward and Faron.

The map in Figure 4.2b shows the distribution of the different levels of sociopolitical integration at the very end of the prehispanic sequence, just prior to the arrival of Europeans on the South American scene. In contrast, as becomes clear in Chapter 5, a map for the time of the earliest extensive human occupation of the continent would show only band societies everywhere. As a matter of fact, based on current evidence this early band society map would be a valid representation of sociopolitical integration across the continent for an immense pe-

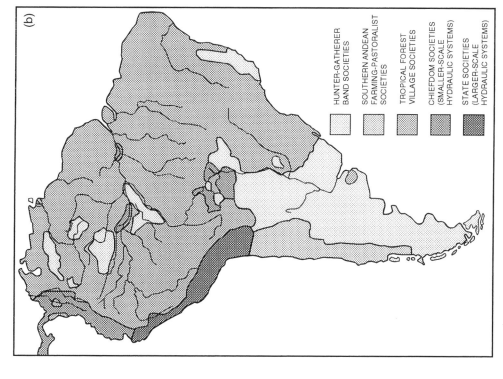

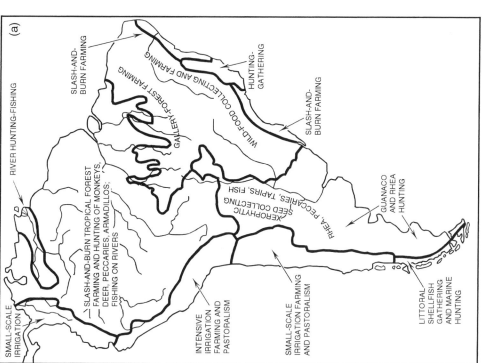

FIGURE 4.2 Maps of (a) the major indigenous subsistence areas of South America and (b) the distribution of prehispanic and traditional cultural types in relation to these areas. Based on maps in Steward and Faron (1959).

riod of time lasting nearly ten thousand years, from about 13,000 to 3500 B.P. (before the present, or 11,000 to 2500 B.C.).

Sometime around 3300 B.C. in Ecuador and just after 2500 B.C. in Peru, village societies would have to be shown along with bands on a second "evolutionary" map, as people settled down in autonomous sedentary settlements in areas where processual changes in population, technology, and subsistence (including early agriculture) brought about this gradual adaptive change. Then, just after 2000 B.C., as more intensive agriculture developed in those areas where it was possible, chiefdoms arose and would have to be shown on yet a third evolutionary map, along with areas where band and village groups had reached a point of dynamic equilibrium, or homeostasis. Finally, in an even shorter time after this, or just after 350 B.C., the first states began to emerge in areas along the western littoral. Throughout the 1,880 years remaining in the prehispanic sequence, there would be continued evolutionary development to the point where we can represent sociopolitical systems of the continent using Figure 4.2b.

The preceding sections can be summarized by reiterating a critical point made earlier in this book: Without any reasonable doubt there exists an ecological-evolutionary underpinning—both in space (the different subsistence productivity zones) and in time (the evolutionary sequence just outlined)—to *where* and *when* the different levels of societal integration appeared in South America. Given this, we can now suggest reasonable answers (hypothetical, nonetheless) to the three questions posed in the Introduction.

Question 1: Why did the human adaptive systems of some geographic areas exhibit essential continuity, or dynamic equilibrium, over the long sequence of their occupation of those areas?

Hypothetical answer: These systems did so because the environments they occupied were low in subsistence productivity and because to survive over the long term, the people of each local area had to organize their system so that their hunting-gathering subsistence strategies and low population numbers were effectively regulated and maintained by a number of higher-order variables.

Question 2: Why did the adaptive systems of other areas exhibit more complex levels of sociopolitical integration than the areas of lowest productivity?

Hypothetical answer: These systems did so because they occurred in zones of greater environmental and hence subsistence productivity. This does not mean, however, that these systems were any more free than those of low productivity areas of the need to develop a series of higher-order cultural regulatory variables to maintain the adaptation within its longer-term limits.

Question 3: Why did the systems of yet other areas exhibit substantial evolutionary change, or deviation amplification, over the long sequence of occupation?

Hypothetical answer: These systems did so because the people lived in more productive environments that permitted intensification as an ultimate adaptive response to population growth and pressure and also because the people were forced by the inexorable nature of this fundamental process to adapt to it, in other words, to evolve culturally.

ANDEAN CULTIVARS

As noted in *Lost Crops of the Incas*, a 1989 study produced by the National Research Council, at the time of the arrival of the Spanish conquerors in the early sixteenth century the people of the Andes cultivated as many as seventy crop species—or nearly the same number as agriculturists in all of Europe and Asia. But because of the conquerors' lack of interest in many features of the complicated agricultural systems of indigenous Andean groups, they replaced many of these species with European plant domesticates. In the process, over the centuries some thirty native South American species fell into obscurity (except where they were cultivated in more remote areas of the Andes) and continue to be unknown to the outside world up to the present. Nevertheless, the Andean system of cultivars in its totality is estimated to have produced enough food to support some 15 million people, or not that many fewer people than the population living in the same area today.

Brief descriptions are presented in this section of ten root and tuber cultivars, three grains, two legumes, three members of the squash family, and six fruits. Only a few of these cultivated plants are familiar to someone who has not lived and traveled rather extensively in the Andes, since most of them are not available even in the most well-stocked markets of the Northern Hemisphere.

Roots and Tubers

Looking somewhat like a lily, achira (*Canna edulis*, Figure 4.3a) is closely related to the ornamental canna lilies grown in temperate and tropical regions outside South America. Cultivated extensively in the Andes, achira is especially important in the indigenous subsistence systems of Peru and southern Ecuador. Although it is cooked and eaten directly, more frequently the rhizomes of this starchy plant are shredded on grater boards so that the fibrous pulp can be separated from the starch and sold for use in the preparation of other foods. A highly adaptable plant, achira is especially important in providing a nutritional safety factor in situations where it survives when other crops fail. Although low in calcium and phosphorus, achira is high in potassium content, and the nutritious leaves and shoots provide at least 10 percent protein.

Ahipa (*Pachyrhizus ahipa*, Figure 4.3b) is a legume—that is, producing pods with seeds—but in the Andes it is grown for the underground tuber it produces. Although found today in only a few places, including valley floors in Peru and Bolivia lying between 1,500 and 3,000 meters elevation, ahipa once was cultivated as far south in the Andes as the Jujuy and Salta regions. It is fast maturing, unaffected by day length, has a strong resistance to pests and disease, and produces high yields. Characterized, like other legumes, by the presence of rhizobia bacteria in its root nodules that produce nitrogenous compounds to nourish it, ahipa not only can be cultivated in poor soils but also enriches them.

Arracacha (*Arracacia xanthorriza*, Figure 4.3c) produces a carrotlike root below ground and a celerylike stalk above; both parts of the plant are eaten. It is culti-

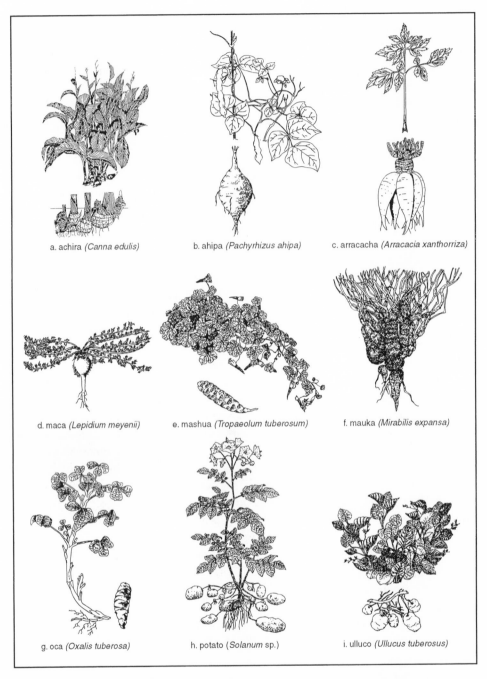

a. achira *(Canna edulis)* b. ahipa *(Pachyrhizus ahipa)* c. arracacha *(Arracacia xanthorriza)*

d. maca *(Lepidium meyenii)* e. mashua *(Tropaeolum tuberosum)* f. mauka *(Mirabilis expansa)*

g. oca *(Oxalis tuberosa)* h. potato *(Solanum* sp.) i. ulluco *(Ullucus tuberosus)*

FIGURE 4.3 Cultivated plants of the Andes (a–i: roots and tubers). Redrawn and adapted from figures in National Research Council (1989).

vated in the Andean sierra from Bolivia to Venezuela, usually in smaller house gardens rather than in the more extensive fields that lie farther away from settlements. It takes longer to mature than the potato but can be produced at roughly half the cost in energy. In Colombia and highland Peru, arracacha is popular as an ingredient in a typical Andean stew called *sancocho*. The bright yellow roots of this plant are rich in Vitamin A and contain a starch that is easily digested, while all of its parts have a high calcium content.

Maca (*Lepidium meyenii*, Figure 4.3d) is highly restricted in its cultivation in the Andes, being found primarily at elevations of up to 4,300 meters in the Lake Junín region of north-central Peru. It grows on extremely infertile, rocky ground at higher altitudes than any other crop in the world, in an area known for its high winds, intense sunlight, and nighttime cold. Since nothing else will grow in such a setting, however, maca makes agriculture possible where it otherwise would not be. It is especially valued by the indigenous Andean people of the Junín area, as it reputedly enhances the sexual potency and fertility of both humans and domesticated animals. In addition, maca is rich in both protein and starch as well as sugars and essential minerals—a nearly perfect plant by any standard.

After the potato, oca, and ulluco, mashua (*Tropaeolum tuberosum*, Figure 4.3e) is the most important root crop in the Andes. It is cultivated in small, terraced plots in cool and moist valleys from Argentina to Colombia, and researchers note that it grows especially well on ancient terraces. Like maca, mashua is a hardy, frost-resistant plant that produces high yields in poor soil at higher elevations, and, like manioc, it needs little attention, can be stored (growing) in the ground, and can be harvested when needed. Its tubers are roughly the size of small potatoes and when eaten raw have a sharp, peppery taste rather like that of radishes. Mashua tubers usually are boiled with meat in stews. Traditionally mashua is eaten by indigenous women and children throughout the Andes and is commonly grown because it is particularly easy and non–labor intensive to cultivate.

Although cultivated for centuries by indigenous Bolivians and Ecuadorians, mauka (*Mirabilis expansa*, Figure 4.3f) is the Andean crop most recently discovered by the outside world (in the 1970s, by a Bolivian scientist). It produces a great abundance of succulent stems that, for a tuberous plant, are unusually rich in protein (17 percent). Mauka also has the advantage of growing well in the chill, windy climate at high-Andean elevations where only a few other crops, such as maca and a few types of potato, can be cultivated. Mauka produces giant tubers that grow to the size of an average adult forearm. However, they contain a harsh chemical that burns the lips and tongue and can be made edible only by exposing them to the sun for some hours.

Oca (*Oxalis tuberosa*, Figure 4.3g) is of such importance in Andean agriculture that it is second to only one other root crop, the potato, in its contribution to the diet of the region. But, unlike the potato, which is fourth among all crops in worldwide production, oca has never been accepted in any area outside the Andes except Mexico, where it was introduced some two hundred years ago. Known for its shiny skin, which ranges in color from white to red, oca is yet another of the extremely hardy Andean cultivars that are tolerant of the extreme cold, high winds, and poor soils characteristic of elevations between 3,000 and 4,000 meters. Its nutrients include carbohydrates, calcium, and iron.

The potato (*Solanum* sp., Figure 4.3h), although known to everyone, was first domesticated in the Andes. Over the eight thousand or so years since it was first brought under cultivation, thousands of different types of potato developed as it was adapted to the great variety of microenvironments scattered all along the Andean chain. Very few, if any, of these types have the appearance of what passes for the potato elsewhere in the world: Andean potatoes are generally small and irregularly shaped (they would not be acceptable in modern packing plants, which require uniform size and shape), and they come in a great variety of brilliant colors, including black, red, brown, yellow, and purple. Unlike some other species of Andean roots and tubers, potatoes are not as tolerant of the most rigorous high-altitude conditions and do better in richer soils at more temperate elevations below 3,500 meters. As with other Andean tubers, such as maca, a means of storing potatoes over long periods of time extending to several years or more has been achieved by indigenous groups, which alternately squeeze the juice out with the bare feet in the daytime sun when the tubers are soft and then let them freeze overnight. Carried out over a several-day period, this process freeze-dries the potatoes and turns them into a storable form known everywhere in the Peruvian and Bolivian Andes as *chuño*.

Ulluco (*Ullucus tuberosus*, Figure 4.3i) is one of the premier crops of the high Andes, second only to the potato, and in some areas even exceeding it in production and consumption. Ulluco is yet another Andean plant by definition— that is, it is well adapted to producing moderate yields on the sometimes poorer soil of high altitudes and is resistant to pests and the frosts that can occur at night even during the summer growing season. Of all indigenous Andean crops, this is one of the few to be accepted by the European inhabitants of the area, to whom it is known as papa lisa. Although ulluco tubers can be freeze-dried like the potato, they will last for as long as a year if they are stored in the dark at the higher, cool elevations of the Andes. Ulluco is especially high in vitamin C, averaging around 23 milligrams per 100 grams of fresh weight. Anyone who has walked through an Andean market will have noted ulluco tubers in the vegetable stalls, since they come in an incredible variety of bright colors, including purple, pink, yellow, red, and red striped on white.

Although distantly related to the sunflower, yacón (*Polymnia sonchifolia*, Figure 4.4a), the last plant in this category, is grown for its edible tubers and not for the seeds it produces. Instead of storing carbohydrates in the form of starch, as with most other roots and tubers, this plant stores carbohydrates in the form of a fructose polymer—making it the Andean equivalent of the fructose-rich sugar beets grown elsewhere in the world. Unfortunately the human body does not have the necessary enzymes to process this polymer (inulin), which means that it passes through the digestive tract unmetabolized and provides few calories. Yacón is cultivated in the Andes from Venezuela to northwestern Argentina, and like other roots and tubers, it grows well even in poorer soils at high elevations.

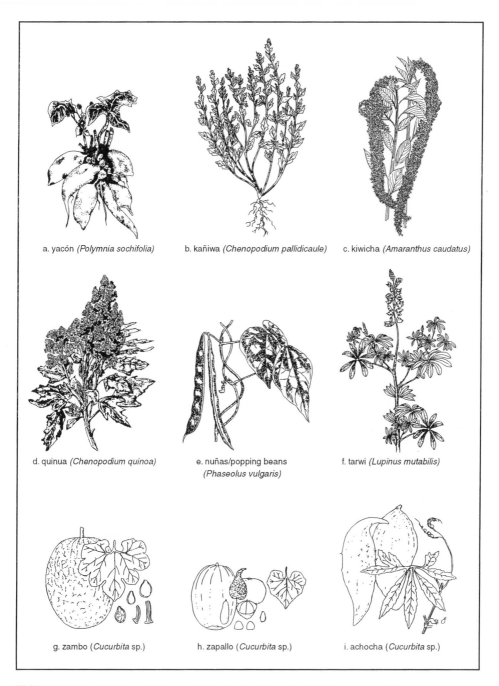

a. yacón *(Polymnia sochifolia)*   b. kañiwa *(Chenopodium pallidicaule)*   c. kiwicha *(Amaranthus caudatus)*

d. quinua *(Chenopodium quinoa)*   e. nuñas/popping beans   f. tarwi *(Lupinus mutabilis)*
                                       (Phaseolus vulgaris)

g. zambo (*Cucurbita* sp.)   h. zapallo (*Cucurbita* sp.)   i. achocha (*Cucurbita* sp.)

FIGURE 4.4   Cultivated plants of the Andes (a: tuber, b–d: grains, e–f: legumes, g–i: squashes). Redrawn and adapted from figures in National Research Council (1989).

Grains

Kañiwa (*Chenopodium pallidicaule*, Figure 4.4b) is one of the most important of all Andean cultivars. It is characterized by a hardiness that permits cultivation at higher elevations than any other Andean grain, and its seeds contain high amounts of protein (16 percent). Year-round temperatures in its native area on the Peruvian *puna* and Bolivian *altiplano* average less than 10°C, and frost occurs during at least nine months of the year, even during the height of the growing season. With such cold-hardiness, kañiwa therefore provides farmers with a safety net during the worst years when other crops are killed by abnormal frosts. Kañiwa is also resistant to water stress, salt, and pests. Like other Andean grains, it produces a cereal-like seed but, with its broad leaves, is not classified as a cereal. Kañiwa is not completely domesticated in the sense that it still grows like a weed and is able to reseed itself year after year.

Kiwicha (*Amaranthus caudatus*, Figure 4.4c) is little known outside its native area of the Andean sierra between Ecuador and northwestern Argentina. It is not only tolerant to heat, pests, and drought, but also can easily be grown outside the highlands. Each plant produces on the order of one hundred thousand tiny grains, each one of which is scarcely bigger than a poppy seed, but they can be heated and popped, boiled as porridge, or ground into flour for making thin cakes. The seeds produce more protein (13–18 percent) than any other major cereal in the world, and the amino acid balance of this protein approaches the ideal balance for the human diet.

The Incas considered quinua (*Chenopodium quinoa*, Figure 4.4d), the last of the Andean grains discussed here, so important to their societal well-being that in the Quechua language it was called *chisiya mama*, or "mother grain." Thus, it is not surprising that the present limits of cultivation of quinua coincide fairly well with the geographic extent of the Inca state in southern Colombia, Ecuador, Peru, Bolivia, northern Chile, and northwestern Argentina. Like kañiwa, its grains are rich in protein (averaging 16 percent but containing up to 23 percent, or twice the level of common cereal grains) and have an excellent balance of amino acids. Since it is exceptionally high in several amino acids—including lysine, cystine, and methionine—it is complementary to other Andean grains (some of which are very deficient in lysine) as well as to legumes such as the common bean (which is deficient in cystine and methionine). The consumption of plants like quinua, in synergistic combination with the others mentioned here, thus has provided an adequate plant protein substitute for any Andean diet that is low in animal protein.

Legumes

Nuñas (*Phaseolus vulgaris*, Figure 4.4e) is a form of common bean, although its beans are hard-shelled and popped in preparation for eating. It is cultivated above 2,500 meters in the area from Ecuador to southern Peru. Like other beans, it has nitrogen-fixing characteristics that aid in restoring soils when it is intercropped with nitrogen-removing plants such as maize. Since beans in general are high in protein and have long been a critical part of the Andean diet, this popping variety is particularly important to people who live at the highest altitudes where it is impossible to heat water to sufficient temperatures to cook other varieties of beans that cannot be popped.

Tarwi (*Lupinus mutabilis*, Figure 4.4f) is another Andean legume whose seeds have an extremely rich protein content that, like beans and peanuts, exceeds 40 percent (it ranges between 41 and 51 percent). It is cultivated throughout highland Bolivia, Peru, and Ecuador, and in many areas tarwi is a main staple in the diet, together with maize, potato, and quinua. As in the case of several of the roots and tubers mentioned earlier, it can be cultivated on very poor soils and is tolerant of frost, drought, and pests. The strong taproot of the plant loosens hard soils, and like all legumes, tarwi collects atmospheric nitrogen to restore depleted soils. Its seeds contain alkaloids, which make them bitter and unpalatable, so they are usually soaked in the running water of a stream for several days, after which they are cooked in soups and stews. Once the alkaloids have been washed out, the seed coats can be removed so that the seeds can be ground into a flour that consists of over 50 percent protein.

Vegetables

As with all the cucurbits (squashes, pumpkins, and gourds), zambo (*Cucurbita* sp., Figure 4.4g) is easily cultivated in soils of varying quality and moisture content. Given its wide distribution from Mexico to the Andean highlands, zambo may have originated in Mesoamerica and spread from there down to the south. In any event, it grows well throughout the Andes at elevations between 1,000 and 2,000 meters. If stored in a dry place, zambos will remain edible for as long as two years, and instead of gradually rotting over this time, their flesh stays fresh and sweet—a storage record unequaled by any other fruit in the world. The seeds are especially rich in oleic acid, the primary ingredient present in olive oil, and can be baked and eaten like peanuts.

The center of diversity of zapallo (*Cucurbita* sp., Figure 4.4h), also called winter squash, is the Andean sierra between southern Peru and northern Chile and Argentina, although during the period of the maximum expansion of the Inca state in the late 1400s and early 1500s this plant spread northward as far as Colombia. It is cultivated in the warmer parts of both the coast and highlands, although it is more tolerant of cool climates than other Andean squashes and can be grown in southern Chile as far south as the limits of agriculture. The fruits of the zapallo are sometimes huge, ranging in weight between 20 and 40 kilograms. Botanical experts claim that the zapallo is characterized by more variability of form than any other cultivar in the world, although the general form of the fruits is bulbous and cylindrical.

Achocha (*Cucurbita* sp., Figure 4.4i), the final vegetable plant discussed here, produces small fruits under 15 centimeters long. Although now cultivated as far north as Mexico, achocha is considered to be South American in origin and grows in profusion in mountainous Andean valleys up to 2,000 meters in elevation. It is more cold tolerant than any other of the family *Cucurbitaceae*. Immature achocha fruits can be eaten either raw or cooked while the seeds are still soft, and they look and taste like little cucumbers. Once mature, the fruits must be cooked, since the seeds become hardened and indigestible.

Fruits

Mora de Castilla (*Rubus glaucus*, Figure 4.5a) is a blackberry that grows wild and in gardens from the northern Andes to the southern highlands of Mesoamerica. The fruits are large, ranging up to 3 centimeters long. Although the mora de Castilla can be grown from seeds, it is usually propagated vegetatively utilizing tip layers or pieces of stems. Although this fruit is essentially unknown to the outside world, some experts consider it to be superior in flavor to cultivated blackberries and raspberries grown elsewhere in the world.

Ugni (*Myrtus ugni*, Figure 4.5b), found primarily in Chile, is yet another Andean food plant unknown outside South America. It grows wild in mountainous forest clearings in the far south of Chile. A bushy plant, it is drought and frost resistant, growing to a height of about 2 meters. The fruits range up to 1.5 centimeters in diameter and have a wild strawberry–like taste.

Capulí cherry (*Prunus capuli*, Figure 4.5c) is one of the most common fruit-bearing trees in the Andes from southern Peru to Venezuela. Since its name appears to be derived from the ancient Náhuatl language of Mexico, botanists think the plant might have been introduced to South America in post-Conquest times by the Spaniards. It thrives best in subtropical or warm temperate regions of the Andes, although it will grow at elevations between 2,200 and 3,100 meters at the equator.

Cherimoya (*Annona cherimola*, Figure 4.5d) is cultivated throughout the Andes from Venezuela to Chile. Its fruit has a distinctive shape that is reproduced in prehistoric pottery vessels dating back at least as early as A.D. 700 on the north coast of Peru. Probably then, and most certainly in modern times, the cherimoya fruit has been considered one of the most delicious of all fruits cultivated in the Andes. In the last few centuries its cultivation has spread elsewhere in the world. For example, the cherimoya is considered a premium fruit in markets of the United States, where it can sell for as much as $20 per kilogram. With a high sugar content, the cherimoya is a sweet fruit, and it also contains moderate quantities of calcium and phosphorus as well as thiamine, riboflavin, and niacin.

The pacay (*Inga* sp., Figure 4.5e) is one of the few legumes eaten as a fruit and not as a vegetable. Anyone who has walked through modern markets on the Andean coast or in the highlands has seen its characteristic green pods lying about on the ground, discarded by someone who cracked them open to pry out the white, sugar-rich pulp that lies nestled inside. These pods can also be seen—curled up and dry as a bone, but well preserved nonetheless—on the surface of many archaeological sites dating to the more recent times all along the coast of Peru. Although widely popular as a snack in the sierra and coast of Ecuador and

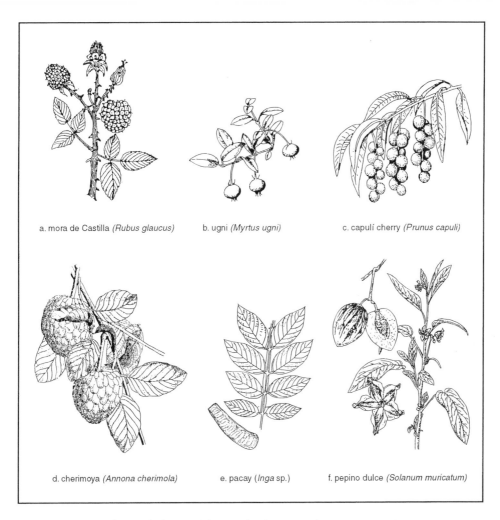

a. mora de Castilla *(Rubus glaucus)*   b. ugni *(Myrtus ugni)*   c. capulí cherry *(Prunus capuli)*

d. cherimoya *(Annona cherimola)*   e. pacay *(Inga* sp.)   f. pepino dulce *(Solanum muricatum)*

FIGURE 4.5   Cultivated plants of the Andes (a–f: fruits). Redrawn and adapted from figures in National Research Council (1989).

Peru, the white pulp of the pacay is not particularly nutritious, containing roughly 1 percent protein and 15 percent carbohydrates. But the species *Inga*, like several other plants mentioned here, are hardy and highly productive and can act as a safety net food during hard times. Pacay trees will grow on marginal soils away from the land used for other crops, but when planted in the midst of fields, they are excellent nitrogen fixers and can thus raise the fertility levels of land used for agriculture.

The final plant discussed here is called the pepino in English, but this is a misnomer, since *pepino* means cucumber in Spanish and the pepino dulce (*Solanum muricatum*, Figure 4.5f) is certainly not a cucumber. It is actually related to the tomato and grows on plants of similar size and shape. In any case, like the cherimoya, this is a "dessert" fruit. Its nutritional value lies principally in its very high vitamin C content (about 35 mg per 100 g), in addition to containing moderate amounts of vitamin A, 7 percent carbohydrates, and 92 percent water. (Henceforth, genus and species nomenclature is given only when plants or animals not yet mentioned are discussed; otherwise, to facilitate the reading of the text, only the common English or South American name is used.)

AGRICULTURAL ORIGINS

It is an established principle of botany that the identification of the area where a plant was domesticated involves knowing not only the present distribution of that plant, but also the area where the greatest number of varieties and related wild forms of the plant are found. An awareness of a cultivar's history of introduction to areas outside the continent of its origin is also, of course, critical in determining where the domestication process took place. For example, from history (not to mention archaeology) we know that the potato did not exist anywhere else in the world except South America prior to the arrival of the Spaniards on the western side of the continent in A.D. 1532. And since the greatest number of varieties of the potato as well as related wild forms (from which, it is supposed, these varieties were domesticated) is found in southern Peru and northern Bolivia, this is considered the most likely area where the domestication of the potato took place.

This section deals with four related aspects of the domestication process in South America. First, since aside from the llama, alpaca, and guinea pig this process overwhelmingly involved plants, an overview is presented of the timing, or chronology, of the appearance of some of the important cultivars. Here we see that ample grounds exist for arguing that indigenous groups began domesticating plants not too many thousands of years after their arrival in South America. Indeed, to leap briefly ahead to the data discussed in Chapter 5 on Monte Verde site, southern Chile, we find that equally convincing grounds exist for the argument that even when people first arrived on the continent, they began collecting an astonishing variety of staple and medicinal plants. This clearly suggests that the indigenous inhabitants of South America have been from the start "expert lay botanists who knew how to wring the most out of their environments"—to roughly paraphrase a statement made by Kent Flannery (1968) some years ago in a classic paper on preceramic hunter-gatherers and the origins of agriculture in the Valley of Oaxaca, Mexico.

The second part of this section discusses Donald Lathrap's elegant arguments about the probable role that house gardens had in the transitional process from merely collection of wild plants to their domestication and use in traditional horticultural and agricultural systems. The third deals with the recent arguments advanced by archaeological botanist Deborah Pearsall, as well as by Bruce Smith, of the Smithsonian Institution, on the coevolutionary origins of the Andean complex of domesticated plants and animals in corral enclosures. Finally, the fourth part outlines the main features of the early periods of Richard MacNeish's Ayacucho sequence, from ~9000 to 1750 B.C., as the slow process of transition from hunting-gathering to early agricultural subsistence-settlement systems took place.

The Chronology of South American Plant Domestication

By the time of the European arrival on the continent nearly five hundred years ago, three related but climatically and phytogeographically distinct agricultural systems had developed in South America: (1) *low-altitude systems,* below 1,000 meters in the Brazilian Highlands, the Amazon, the Orinoco, and the Caribbean, that were based on roots, maize, and beans; (2) *midaltitude systems* of the Andes, between 1,000 and 3,000 meters, that were based on maize and legumes such as peanuts and beans; and (3) *high-altitude systems* of the Andes, between 3,000 and 4,300 meters, that were based on the potato and many of the tubers and grains mentioned in the preceding section of this chapter.

Unfortunately for arguments about the timing of the origins of these crop groups—which were developed independently in each of the three altitudinally and geographically distinct areas—the vast bulk of the evidence for their earliest appearance is restricted to the area of the continent where the best preservation has occurred and the most archaeological work has taken place, namely, the desert coast of Peru (Figure 4.6). But given the logic of the botanical principles mentioned previously in identifying the origin areas of domestication, the coastal desert of the western littoral is the least likely place where this process took place. That is, there are no related wild forms of these cultivars growing there to-day, nor are these forms thought to have occurred there in the distant prehistoric past. Thus, in discussing the chronology of South American plant domestication, we are concentrating of necessity on the one area outside of Patagonia, the Pampas, and the Gran Chaco where we know domestication did not take place.

Moreover, the fact that most of the data come from the Peruvian coast means that the earliest *known* dates are probably quite a bit later than the actual dates of domestication of the crops in these three distinctive areas. The significant exception to this situation, in Peru at least, consists of the data on early cultivars from a number of dry cave sites located precisely in the area where the midaltitude and high-altitude cultivars were domesticated. Outside of the Peruvian coast and sierra, lesser amounts of evidence on early cultivars are available from sites in northwestern Argentina, northern Chile, coastal Ecuador, and the Caribbean zone of Colombia and Venezuela (Figure 4.6). For our purposes, then, it is more appropriate (and certainly less confusing) simply to list the early time periods and the crops that make their appearance during these periods, relying on the data from the dry cave sites and coastal contexts for the Andean area of Argentina and Chile as well as coastal and highland Peru and coastal Ecuador.

The Earlier Preceramic Period: ~8000–5000 B.C.

At Guitarrero Cave, located at midelevation (2,580 meters) in the Callejón de Huaylas (Figure 4.6), Thomas Lynch's (1980) excavations have produced remains of two tubers (oca and possibly ulluco), a legume (the common bean), an Andean fruit *(Solanum hispidum),* and chili pepper—all of which come from Stratigraphic Complex IIa, dating to 8000–7500 B.C., or the earliest part of this

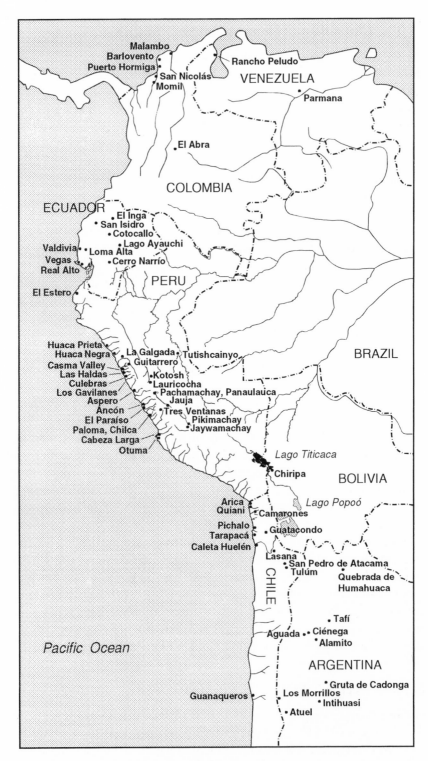

FIGURE 4.6   Sites of western South America with early plant remains. Redrawn and adapted from Pearsall (1992).

long time period. Oca, as mentioned earlier, is a high-elevation cultivar, and chili pepper is a low-elevation cultivar, whereas the rest are from the midelevation areas of the Callejón itself. Thus, already at this early time period, groups of the Callejón were in contact with the people and plants of other elevation zones. By 5000 B.C. lúcuma and lima bean were also present in the subsistence system of the inhabitants of the cave.

The Middle Preceramic Period: ~5000–4000 B.C.

Among the roots and tubers that make their appearance during this period in the broader geographic area between northern Argentina/Chile and coastal Ecuador are the potato and possibly oca, both of which are high-Andean crops. Quinua is the only one of the several Andean grains that appears in quantity this early, although maize is present, if insignificantly, in the archaeological record at sites such as Guitarrero Cave. Among the legumes are the common bean and lima bean. Other crops include squash, chili pepper, guava, and the bottle gourd (used as a container). It is interesting that most of the earliest finds in Peru for this period come not from the coast, but from the dry cave sites in the sierra, which further strengthens a sierra (and in some cases, *montaña*) origin for these crops.

The Later Preceramic Period: ~4000–1800 B.C.

A number of additional cultivars were added to Andean hunter-gatherer subsistence systems during this long period. Among the roots and tubers are manioc, achira, sweet potato, and jícama. Among the pulses, or legumes, are jack beans and peanut. Fruits include avocado (palta), pacay, and cherimoya. And now, along with bottle gourds, cotton is added to the complex of utilitarian, or industrial, crops. In addition to camelid wool, it will become a major source of fiber for weaving cloth as well as for twining in the production of nets and other utilitarian items. Finally, among several other cultivars introduced during the later preceramic is the coca plant. From this point on through to the present, coca leaves have been chewed along with lime, which releases narcotic alkaloids, as a means of coping with the physical stress that accompanies the work effort and foot travel of both men and women throughout the Andes and adjacent coast, but especially at the higher altitudes above 3,000 meters. The earliest utilitarian cultivar mentioned previously, the bottle gourd, became the receptacle in which the lime was carried and then, when needed, removed with a stick or spatula to add to the wad of coca leaves placed in the cheek.

In light of the very early development of the domesticated plants mentioned here, it must be emphasized that the hunter-gatherer groups developing these cultivars did not automatically become sedentary as a result of their development. Instead, human control over these plants became another one of the several strategies that provided the basis for the maintenance of a mobile, nonsedentary lifestyle. Thus, there is little or no evidence for a settling down into sedentary societies until the later preceramic period on the western coast, some-time between 2500 and 1800 B.C.

With regard to the domesticated plants characterizing the lowland complex, in the coastal area from Ecuador south to Peru, all of the following cultivars appeared between 3300 and about 1800 B.C.: manioc, sweet potato, achira, jack bean, palta, pacay, guanábana, cherimoya, pineapple, papaya, cotton, squash, and chili peppers. If we assume a lowland origin for all or most of them and a long process of domestication similar to that of the Andean midelevation and high-elevation complexes, it is probable that they were being developed by indigenous inhabitants of the eastern lowlands roughly at the same time the process began in the Andes.

The Role of House Gardens

In the case of both seed crops and roots and tubers, their wild progenitors may often (if not always) have come under the gradual control of humans as they colonized the open, disturbed areas around dwellings. Accustomed already to evaluating the potential utility of plants noticed in gathering activities carried out farther afield from their dwellings, indigenous groups would therefore quickly have made any useful intruders a regular part of their procurement activities. These plants also would have been especially attractive, since they were establishing themselves in the relatively more productive, nitrogen-rich soils found in the disturbed areas around human settlements. As mentioned earlier, Lathrap (1977) takes these speculative comments a step farther for the eastern tropical lowlands in arguing that it was in small house gardens where the process of domestication of a whole series of cultivars took place—including fruit trees, roots and tubers, and the cucurbits. He reasons that these gardens would have been a controlled environment, by definition, with neither too much nor too little sun. As mentioned in Chapter 3, in tropical rain forests scattered larger trees help protect the lower plants near ground level both from excessive insolation and excessive rainfall. Taller fruit-bearing trees in the house gardens would have served this function nicely.

In the course of his studies of the Shipibo, an indigenous group located in the eastern Peruvian Amazon, Lathrap counted between fifty and one hundred different cultivars in the small space of their house gardens. Among them were the calabash tree (*Crescentia cujete*); a variety of palms, including the peach palm (*Guilielma gasipaes*), whose hard wood is called chonta and used for making bows, and other palms whose fruits are harvested and whose leaves are used for thatching and matting; several fruit trees, including the avocado, pacay, guava, and lúcuma; and a variety of smaller plants, including cacao, two dye plants (*Genipa americana*, or genipe, and *Bixa orellana*, or achiote), the cashew bush, some twenty to thirty medicinal plants, the chili pepper, tobacco, and plants yielding fish poisons. The Shipibo garden also serves as an experimental plot, with new species of plants continually being brought in from the surrounding forest to be grown and evaluated for their use as potential cultivars. Lathrap mentions that several European introductions—including the mango tree, citrus fruits, and the plantain (the cooking banana)—all became a crucial part of the diet by virtue of their introduction into the subsistence system via the house garden.

The Shipibo and many other Amazonian groups distinguish conceptually between the house garden and their *chacras,* or fields, which lie at greater distance from the dwelling/household garden area and are used for growing the main staple crops, such as manioc. The former area is considered to be controlled, organized, and safe, whereas the *chacra* is seen as part of forest and therefore filled with dangerous, malevolent spirits. The house garden is included in that highly delimited area that the Shipibo and others can keep under the maximum possible human order. No unwanted vegetation from the dangerous outside world is let into this zone of imposed human order, resulting in an artificial floral environment that totally encases the dwelling.

Origins of the Andean Complex of Domesticates

Utilizing the data from Panaulauca Cave, a limestone rock shelter excavated in the 1970s by John Rick (1980), Deborah Pearsall (1992) has constructed a coevolutionary scenario for the origins of agriculture in the high Andes that is analogous to the model proposed by Lathrap for the moist tropical rain forests to the east. Panaulauca Cave lies at 4,150 meters in the Lake Junín region of the north-central Peruvian Andes (Figure 4.6) and has a record of human occupation dating from the present back to ~7700 B.C. The traditional recent subsistence-settlement system of this area is centered on the herding of llamas and alpacas and the cultivation of a variety of high-elevation cultivars that include potato, oca, mashua, ulluco, maca, quinua, kañiwa, and tarwi. Among the plant remains found in various stratigraphic levels of the rock shelter were maca and quinua, while among the faunal remains were camelid bones (it was not possible to identify whether they were alpacas or llamas, an exceptionally difficult task in light of the morphological similarities between these two related species).

After several thousands of years of hunting the guanaco, the wild ancestral form of the llama, people began to tend them in rock corral enclosures, according to Pearsall. This led to increased manipulation of the breeding processes and ultimately to the creation of semidomesticated forms. At the same time, plants such as maca and quinua might have become established in the manure-rich, disturbed habitat provided by the corral. For example, the wild ancestor of maca may well have been an opportunistic pioneering plant in this habitat, and the seeds of quinua became established by passing unharmed through the digestive tracts of the camelids that had grazed on them out on the high *puna* away from the corrals. As suggested by Lathrap's Shipibo study, these plants would have been noticed by people already accustomed for thousands of years to evaluating the potential utility of plants in their far-ranging foraging activities.

At some later point, people began planting the seeds and tuber cuttings in the more controlled environment of abandoned corrals to protect them from grazing animals, including the now semidomesticated camelids. Selection for increased seed or root size, and other diagnostic features that indicate a stage of early domestication distinguishing these plants from their wild progenitors, would be the next step in human control over these emerging cultivars. Therefore, over a period of some thousands of years sedentary subsistence-settlement systems based on agriculture and camelid herding evolved out of the migratory hunting-gathering systems that had characterized the earliest human occupation of the *puna*.

In a similar coevolutionary vein, Bruce Smith (1995) has recently suggested that five main species define high-altitude food production in the Andes: llama, alpaca, quinua, cuy, and potato. He argues that all five species were probably domesticated together in the Andes of southern Peru and northern Bolivia between 3000 and 2000 B.C., or near the end of the preceramic period. In addition to the high amounts of protein provided by quinua and the flesh of cuy and camelids, potatoes and other root crops rounded out the diet by providing rich sources of carbohydrates. Smith notes that both the guanaco and the vicuña—wild ancestors of the llama and the alpaca, respectively (see Figure 4.7)—were preadapted by nature to domestication. Both are highly gregarious social species that form herds characterized by strong male-led dominance hierarchies. Just as we must assume that early indigenous groups were expert lay botanists, so must they have been expert observers of the behavior of the animals they hunted. Given this knowledge, humans could easily have stepped in at the top of the dominance hierarchy, or pecking order, to manage and manipulate the breeding of the herds.

In a number of the Andean cave sites shown in Figure 4.6, the faunal materials from early stratigraphic levels indicate that by about 7000 B.C. indigenous groups were hunting guanaco and vicuña (*Lama vicugna*), along with deer. In the occupational layers of these caves dating to the period between 7000 and 2500 B.C., the number of camelid bones increases dramatically over time in relation to deer bones. For example, in some of the Peruvian cave deposits prior to 5000 B.C. camelid bones constitute 26 to 42 percent of all the animal bones, whereas after this point camelid bones make up 82 to 98 percent of the bones. The number of bones of newborn and younger animals also increases over time in the occupational layers. Clearly, the process of camelid domestication was occurring in the adaptive systems centered on these sites. A similar picture emerges from excavations at Chiripa site, located near Lake Titicaca in Bolivia (Figure 4.6), where by 1500 B.C. camelid bones account for 98 percent of animal bones in the excavated materials. All this suggests a stronger focus on the control and management of camelid herds.

At the same time that camelids and quinua were coming under the control of humans, in the synergistic camelid-grain combination mentioned in Pearsall's arguments, the guinea pig, or cuy (Figure 4.7), was being domesticated. These rodents are ideal for domestication as edible household animals: they are small, have a high reproductive rate, are not particularly intelligent to begin with, and can be fed discarded food scraps and grains such as quinua. Smith notes that cuys were an important part of hunter-gatherer diets in the far northern and southern parts of the Andes between 10,000 and 5500 B.C., at sites such as El Abra in the Colombian Andes (Figure 4.6). By 2500 B.C. at Pikimachay and Jaywamachay

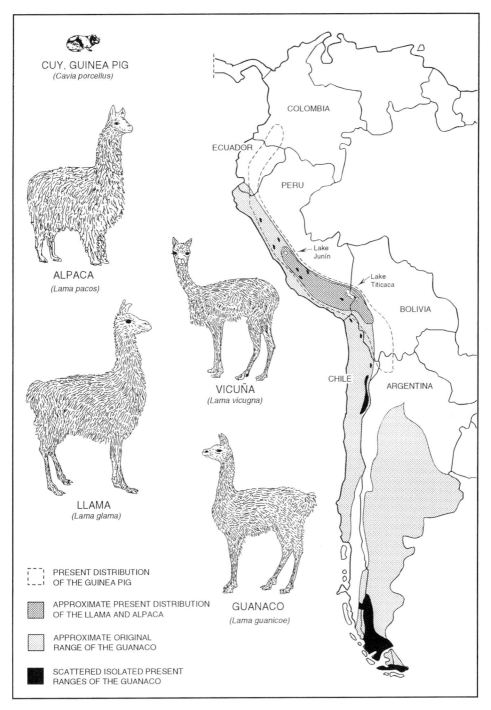

FIGURE 4.7   Drawings of the guinea pig and the Andean camelids, domesticated (alpaca, llama) and wild (vicuña, guanaco). Map indicates the approximate distributions of all of these species but the vicuña, either in prehistoric times (guanaco) or in the present (alpaca, llama, guinea pig). Redrawn and adapted from Franklin (1981) and Morales (1995).

Caves in the Ayacucho Basin (Figure 4.6), guinea pig bones increase significantly in the occupational layers.

The Early Ayacucho Sequence

Between 1969 and 1975 Richard MacNeish (1992) carried out an interdisciplinary project in the Ayacucho Basin, Peru, aimed at understanding the evolution of preceramic subsistence-settlement systems and the rise of agriculture in the Andes. As in the case of his well-known earlier project in the Tehuacán Valley, Mexico (see Byers and MacNeish 1966–1977), MacNeish chose the Ayacucho area for a regional study on agricultural origins because it had a wide variety of microenvironmental zones, wild plants suitable for domestication, a generally dry climate that promotes the preservation of millennia-old plant remains, and a number of dry cave sites that could be excavated in his attempt to establish a sequence that covered the period when the domestication of Andean plants and animals was occurring.

During the course of the research, regional settlement pattern fieldwork produced a sample of some six hundred prehispanic sites, fifteen of which were excavated stratigraphically, yielding a sequence of twenty-two phases and evidence of the early domestication of plants. Later, in Chapter 5, the data from Pikimachay Cave related to the pre–9000 B.P. time period is discussed. Here, we examine the data from the later phases between 9000 and 1750 B.P. (7000 B.C.–A.D. 250) as a means of providing an overview of the evolution of early agricultural systems out of the earlier hunter-gatherer systems in one of the few areas of South America where a problem-oriented project on agricultural origins has been successfully carried out. Such a broad processual perspective should flesh out some of the bare bones data discussed in the preceding sections of this chapter on the timing of the appearance of the various Andean cultivars.

As shown in Table 4.1, the relevant periods, or phases, dating between 9000 and 1750 B.P. from MacNeish's work in Ayacucho include Puente (9000–7100 B.P.), Jaywa (7100–5800 B.P.), Piki (5800–4400 B.P.), Chihua (4400–3100 B.P.), and Cachi (3100–1750 B.P.). The main features of each can be summarized briefly.

Puente Phase (9000–7100 B.P.)

This is the period immediately following the late-Pleistocene extinction of a number of animals that had earlier been hunted by Paleoindian groups in the Ayacucho Basin. A total of some sixteen discrete occupations was found, mostly concentrated in the humid woodlands located at intermediate elevations between the forest riverine and thorn forest scrub microenvironments, on the one hand, and the high *puna*, on the other. Except for one slightly more extensive occupation, the great majority of the sixteen occupations represent places that were seasonally occupied by small bands of fewer than fifty persons. Subsistence was focused on the hunting of deer and wild camelids, the occasional trapping of

TABLE 4.1 The Evolution of Subsistence-Settlement Systems from Hunting-Gathering to Early Agriculture in the Ayacucho Sequence, South Highlands of Peru, 9000–1750 B.C.

Phase Name (and Estimated Chronology B.C.)	Number of Occupations	General Features of the Subsistence-Settlement System	Subsistence Resources
Cachi (3100–1750)	50	First sedentary agricultural villages at lower elevation; temporary camps in the puna; llama corrals at some sites	Taro and chili peppers added; guinea pig domesticated as well as camelids, possibly
Chihua (4400–3100)	38	Population roughly the same, organized at a band level	New cultivars include beans, gourds, lúcuma, potatoes, maize, and possibly coca; guinea pig and llama bones common in the refuse
Piki (5800–4400)	40	Higher population; bands focused less on hunting than before and more on collecting; appearance of horticulture	Domesticated gourd, quinoa, and possibly squash; wild guinea pigs penned; bones of other wild fauna more limited in number than earlier
Jaywa (7100–5800)	20	Somewhat higher population; bands focused on hunting, trapping, and plant collection	Wild fauna: deer, camelids, guinea pigs; wild flora: achiote, berries, and grasses
Puente (9000–7100)	16	Small bands focused on hunting and collecting; metate and mano grinding stones for processing plant foods	Deer, guinea pigs, wild camelids; wild plants

SOURCE: MacNeish (1992).

wild guinea pigs, and the collection of wild plants. The presence of stone-grinding implements suggests that seed collecting was also a part of foraging activities (for other lithics of this phase, see Figure 5.16).

Jaywa Phase (7100–5800 B.P.)

MacNeish sees the following phase, Jaywa, as one of growing population, based on an increase in site numbers from sixteen to twenty, and of decreasing numbers of hunted animals. As the glaciers retreated in the higher *puna* after the late Pleistocene, and climatic conditions became warmer, so did the people of Mac-Neish's study area adapt their subsistence-settlement strategies accordingly. They gradually came to occupy a wider range of microenvironments than before and hence came into increasing interaction with the plants and animals of the lower, middle, and higher elevations in the Ayacucho Basin. Ample numbers of Jaywa phase sites are located in each of the three microenvironments. MacNeish believes that indigenous groups also were increasingly engaged in *scheduling* their seasonal round—that is, they were occupying different ecozones in an organized temporal sequence as they moved up and down in this complex vertical environment during the passage of the seasons.

With respect to faunal populations, the same animals are hunted and trapped as in the preceding phase, including deer, wild camelids, and guinea pigs. But there is now more evidence of the exploitation of a variety of plant foods, including achiote, berries, grass seeds, and unidentified fibrous plants. Stone technology remains the same for the most part as in Puente (see Figure 5.16). Overall, then, although this is a period where some change is occurring, the human adaptive systems of Ayacucho were essentially conservative: They were maintaining an equilibrium system characterized more by staying the same as before than by changing. At the same time, the minor adaptive shifts—the little adjustments—were sowing the seeds of the far more significant changes that would occur in succeeding periods.

Piki Phase (5800–4400 B.P.)

In light of the preceding developments, it comes as no surprise that substantial evolutionary changes characterize the Piki phase in the regional sequence. Foremost among these is the appearance of cultivars, although MacNeish notes that the evidence is meager. Nevertheless, the first cultivars in Ayacucho include domesticated bottle gourd, quinua, and possibly a species of squash. Grinding stones, or metates, become far more numerous in this phase than before, providing additional evidence of a substantial increase in the exploitation of plant foods. From the excavated evidence, MacNeish argues that plant foods were especially important in the diet during the wet season of the year, since a number of sites dated to this phase are located down in the lower-elevation riverine and thorn forest microenvironments where the greatest number and variety of such resources are available.

Along with the new cultivars, hundreds of bones of guinea pigs—far more than in any prior period—appear on the floors of some dwellings as well as in pits dug into the floors that probably served as hutches. However, since the cuy bones do not appear at all different from those of modern wild ones, MacNeish believes that Piki phase represents a transitional step from the trapping of wild guinea pigs to their actual domestication: namely, a taming of the animal to keep it more readily at hand for human consumption. The bones of other wild fauna, including camelids, are found in lesser quantities, a trend that runs somewhat counter to that noted for other areas of the Andes as the process of taming and eventual domestication of llamas and alpacas was beginning in those areas.

Finally, as indicated in Table 4.1, the number of sites—and presumably population numbers—now increases to at least double that of any preceding period while the number of hunted wild fauna continues to decrease. Both Mark Cohen (1977) and Marvin Harris (e.g., 1977, 1979) have argued that this is precisely the pressuresome situation within which the conditions are set for the adaptive shifts that lead to the beginnings of agriculture. This is not to suggest, however, that increasing human predation on the animal populations was the only reason for environmental degradation, since, as the pre-Puente phase sequence throughout South America indicates, the late Pleistocene was a period of severe environmental change that itself resulted in the extinction of a number of hunted fauna. But whatever the precise contribution of human and environmental factors, the net result seems to have set up conditions that were ripe for changes in the relationship between human adaptive systems and the plants and animals that would become domesticated during the period from 9000 to 1750 B.P. in Ayacucho.

In light of the uniform and extensive occupation of the main three altitudinal zones of the preceding Jaywa phase, MacNeish notes that very few sites were found in the middle-elevation humid forest zone and the upper-elevation *puna* zone. Given the temporary nature of the lower-zone encampments and their apparent wet-season time of occupation, he suggests that additional numbers of middle- and upper-zone sites probably existed beyond those few found by the survey teams. If so, then population had reached a point where it was not only double that of the preceding phase, but also substantially greater.

In sum, these data suggest to MacNeish that Piki can be characterized as being qualitatively different from any preceding phase, whereas Jaywa is merely quantitatively different from Puente phase. Another way to put this is that Piki is different in kind from Jaywa, whereas Jaywa is merely different in degree from Puente. Throughout the sequence to this point, however, the level of sociopolitical integration is still at a migratory band level. Thus, as mentioned in the discussion of the Jaywa data, these are systems characterized as much or more by conservatism in attempting to maintain the fundamental features of their lifestyle as by any revolutionary shifts in it. Although the Ayacucho people probably were attempting to maintain the status quo by changing only those features (i.e., increased exploitation and domestication of plants) that would permit them to stay the same (at a band level), nevertheless through their adaptive adjustments they had inadvertently opened the door to the far more sweeping evolutionary changes that were possible, once agriculture was developed, in the Andean setting.

Chihua Phase (4400–3100 B.P.)

During the Chihua phase, site numbers in the Ayacucho study region remained roughly the same as in the preceding period, or thirty sites as compared to forty in the Piki phase. Population numbers seem therefore to have reached an adaptive plateau at this point before rising substantially beyond this level, as we know they clearly did, in the later part of the prehispanic time period—for example, when the Ayacucho-centered Wari state developed in the Middle Horizon Period between about A.D. 600 and 1100. In spite of this temporary demographic stasis, substantial change continues to occur in the subsistence system of the region. For example, added now to gourd, quinua, and squash are common bean, achiote, calabash (tree gourds), lúcuma, and possibly coca, potato, and, near the end of the phase, maize.

Large numbers of guinea pig bones continue to be present, but MacNeish notes that their skulls are now different enough from those of wild cuys that the domestication process had arguably begun. Although there is still no evidence of the presence of domesticated camelids, a change occurs in the kinds of bones found (including the selective killing of male juveniles) that suggests either the taming of wild forms or, perhaps, enough control over breeding that semidomesticated llamas already were beginning to appear.

Cachi Phase (3100–1750 B.P.)

For the purposes of this chapter, this period represents the culmination of the evolutionary processes that appear to have been triggered by environmental and population changes some six thousand years earlier, not to mention enhanced and carried forward by the ability of humans to adapt to such fundamental changes by creating new subsistence-settlement strategies in environments where intensification is possible. Site numbers continue to rise, with a total of fifty occupations found in the region. But now, for the first time, a number of sedentary hamlets is established in the lower-valley zone, as suggested by the appearance of permanent rock-walled architecture at seven of the fifty sites.

As was the case in Jaywa phase—and probably Piki and Chihua as well—settlements are located in all of the main microenvironments of the region. Since the *puna* sites appear to be temporary and are found in association with camelid corrals, MacNeish argues that the adaptive strategy that developed in this period involved the occupation of permanent lower-elevation sites, but with a continuation of the mobile behavior that would permit control over the resources exploited at higher elevations as well. What we see occurring here, then, is the establishment of the classic vertical adaptation to the Andes involving a mixed strategy of sedentism and mobility, so that the people of one subsistence-settlement system can have access to the widest possible range of resources found in closely juxtaposed microenvironments.

LATER ANDEAN CULTIVARS

Given the extreme desertic conditions of the western littoral between northern Peru and central Chile as well as the excellent preservation of organic materials that occurs in this unique environment, it is worthwhile to provide more tangible evidence of this preservation in the form of a number of cultivars that date between the Early Horizon and Late Horizon Periods on the central and south coast of Peru (~900 B.C.–A.D. 1532). The selected group of cultivars depicted in Figure 4.8 are from controlled stratigraphic excavations and were originally illustrated in Margaret Towle's book *The Ethnobotany of Pre-Columbian Peru*, published in 1961. Since the excavations were carried out prior to the radiocarbon method of dating developed in the late 1940s, however, it is not possible to pinpoint their age in anything other than a general way based on the diagnostic features (e.g., ceramics) of the sites where they were found.

Although Towle describes the preservation of these and the other remains she looks at as being on the whole "fairly well preserved," this would appear to be something of an understatement. There are very few other environmental contexts in the world where such preservation can be found outside of dry cave sites.

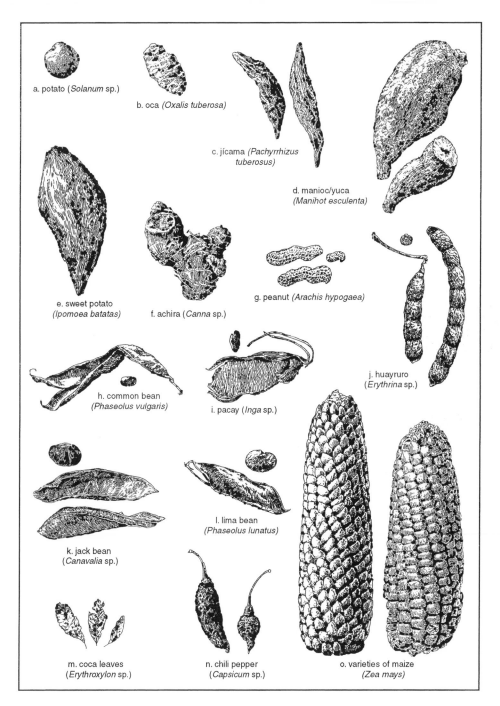

FIGURE 4.8 Selected preserved plant remains from coastal Peruvian sites dating between the Early Horizon and the Late Horizon, ~1000 B.C.–A.D. 1532. Redrawn and adapted from figures in Towle (1961).

All of the cultivars illustrated here come from subsurface contexts in open air sites, including Ancón (see Figure 4.6), Vista Alegre (Rímac Valley), and Pachacámac (Lurín Valley) located on the central coast of Peru and Paracas (Pisco Valley) and Cahuachi (Río Ingenio) located on the south coast.

The earliest materials shown in Figure 4.8 appear to be those from Paracas (jícama, Figure 4.8c) and Ancón (lima bean, Figure 4.8l; maize, Figure 4.8o), dating sometime after 900 B.C. In my own archaeological research on the north coast in 1979–1980 in the Santa Valley, we found fragments of small maize cobs on the surface of sites with associated pottery dating to this same time period, or between 900 and 350 B.C. Even though the remainder of the cultivars depicted in the figure date to later periods, it is still noteworthy that such fragile remains as coca leaves can be excavated totally intact with an appearance that is nearly the same as when they were originally harvested. For example, the well-preserved coca leaves shown in Figure 4.8m are from a *chuspa*, a small textile pouch used in the Andes as a container for coca, excavated from Middle Horizon Period (A.D. 700–1100) levels at Vista Alegre, Rímac Valley.

Aside from the preservation of actual remains, which provides a nearly perfect record of the morphological and genetic characteristics of ancient cultivars, there also are iconographic representations of these cultivars in the drawings painted on pottery vessels from a number of the prehistoric cultures of Peru. Those shown in Figure 4.9, for example, are from three different time periods dating between 900 B.C. and A.D. 1100 and two different areas, the north-central highlands and the south coast. The earliest depictions shown, of achira and chili pepper, date to the Early Horizon Chavín culture of the north-central part of Peru, whereas the others are from Nazca pottery of the Early Intermediate (~350 B.C.–A.D. 700) and Pacheco pottery of the Middle Horizon (~A.D. 700–1100), both of these latter two cultures/art styles located on the south coast.

A comparison of the cultivars depicted in Figure 4.9 with the more botanically "accurate" drawings in Figures 4.3, 4.4, and 4.5 indicates that the iconographic depictions are obviously rather abstract or stylized. Nevertheless, it is possible to identify fairly easily which cultivars are being shown (never mind that a very close comparison should also demonstrate that some of the identifications in Figure 4.9 are open to question). Perhaps the more important point to make here, however, is that the Chavín, Nazca, and Pacheco drawings come from people who in a very real sense were the descendants of the original expert lay botanists who had created the Andean group of cultivars over many thousands of years prior to the ceramic period—thus laying the groundwork for, among other things, the kind of sociocultural complexity that is accompanied by the creation of pottery and complex art styles.

HALLUCINOGENIC PLANTS

In the fascinating book *Plants of the Gods*, Richard Evans Schultes and Albert Hoffman (1992) point out that of all traditional societies in the world the indigenous groups of South America are second only to those of Mexico in the number

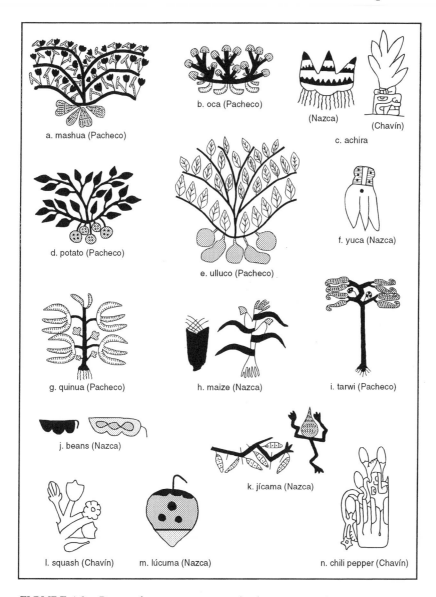

FIGURE 4.9   Pictorial representations of cultivars on prehistoric pottery of Peru, including Chavín (~1000–200 B.C.), Nazca (~0–A.D. 700), and Pacheco (~A.D. 700–1100) cultures. Redrawn and adapted from figures in Ravines (1978).

and diversity of hallucinogenic plants used in magic and ritual. It is therefore relevant to discuss the nature and importance in indigenous adaptive systems of several of the more extensively used hallucinogenic plants of the eastern tropical lowlands and the Andes.

First, it comes as something of a revelation to learn that of the 150 hallucinogenic plants currently known to ethnobotanists, fully 130 of them are from the

New World, whereas only 20 are known from the Old World. Given the equally diverse plant communities of both areas, not to mention the far greater time depth of the human occupation of the Old World, it is surprising that so many plants should be known and used by the indigenous inhabitants of the Americas. Schultes and Hoffman believe that this anomaly comes from the fact that the societies of the Old World for the most part evolved to "highly agricultural levels," whereas those of the New were, or still are, basically hunting societies. Since a hunter's success depends on "medicine power," which is often acquired by carrying out vision quests under the influence of psychoactive plants, these plants are thus far more important in the ritual and religion of indigenous New World societies.

Although this is an interesting hypothesis, this chapter should have already begun to make clear that hunter-gatherer subsistence systems on the South America continent are and have been based at least as much on plant foods and fishing as on animal foods, if not far more so—never mind that where protein is in relatively short supply compared to carbohydrates, drug use and ritual may well focus on the former food resource rather than on the latter (see Chapter 6). In any case, many or most of these groups still rely on hallucinogenic plants in carrying out traditional rituals. In contrast, many hunter-gatherer groups of the far south, although based heavily on guanaco hunting for their livelihood, did not take hallucinogenic drugs at all because none was available.

Moreover, as discussed in Chapter 6, horticulturist-hunter groups of the Amazon have other reasons for ingesting hallucinogens besides the enhancement of hunting prowess. In the case of the Jívaro of eastern Ecuador, this includes the acquisition of a "killer" soul—not only to stimulate a man's desire to go out and kill other people but also to make him succeed in the attempt. Finally, the highly developed agriculturists of the Andes employed plants with psychoactive powers in their own religious systems.

Although Schultes and Hoffman's well-taken question of why the use of hallucinogens was so prevalent in the New World is not yet answered, it seems that nearly *all* indigenous South Americans have used psychoactive plants wherever they are found in the local environment. To make the point another way, expert lay botanists would have rather quickly discovered the properties of all plants in their local environment—whether these properties were nutritional, mind altering, or even lethal! But even where such plants are unavailable, there are cases where a group has found out about their hallucinogenic powers from its neighbors and has devised a means of acquiring the plants.

Five principal genera of hallucinogenic South American plants are discussed here (with indigenous names given in parentheses). They include *Anadenanthera* sp. (yopo, huilca), *Banisteriopsis* sp. (ayahuasca, yajé, natemä, caapi), *Brugmansia* sp. (yas, huacachaca), *Trichocereus* sp. (San Pedro), and *Virola* sp. (ebene, epená, nyakwana). (The most commonly used name, whether a single indigenous one or the genus name, is employed here in accordance with the terms used in the Schultes and Hoffman book as well as in the anthropological literature.)

Yopo (Anadenanthera sp.)

Two species of *Anadenanthera* (Figure 4.10a) are used by indigenous South Americans to make hallucinogenic snuffs—one of them in the Orinoco and northern Amazon (*Anadenanthera peregrina*) and the other in northern Argentina and the southern Amazon (*Anadenanthera colubrina*). Although the distribution map in Figure 4.10a indicates that the present, or recent, use of yopo has been confined to these two areas of the eastern lowlands, it was probably also employed in prehispanic times in indigenous religion and ritual in the northern Colombian Andes, where it was obtained by Chibchan groups (near what is now Bogotá) through trade with people of the forests to the east.

Where still in use, yopo snuff, which is prepared from the seeds of the plant, may be taken daily by shamans to induce trances and visions that permit them to carry out a variety of magico-religious tasks. Among the Guahibo of eastern Colombia, for example, these tasks include communicating with the *hekura* spirits (about which I have more to say in Chapter 6), making prophesies and divinations, helping prevent sickness, improving the men's ability to hunt, and improving the alertness of the dogs in hunting and protecting the village. Quite a bit of variation exists in the preparation of yopo, but generally it involves toasting and grinding the seeds from the plant, after which lime from pulverized snails or the ashes of plants may be added to produce an alkaline admixture. In northern Argentina the Mashco people prepare a snuff from *Anadenanthera* seeds and also smoke them to produce similar hallucinogenic trances and visions.

Taking yopo produces a number of physical reactions, in addition to the hallucinogenic visions, including an initial loss of consciousness followed by a feeling of looseness in the limbs. A late-eighteenth-century report (Gumilla 1791) on its use in the Orinoco observes that the men who took it were thrown into a frenzy, whereupon they would injure themselves and, finally, seized with great rage, go out on raids against their enemies. In the Orinoco area today, many groups inhale powdered yopo from a small wooden tray into the nose through the thin leg bones of birds that have been tied together in the shape of the letter Y so that the powder enters both nostrils with equal force at the same time.

Ayahuasca (Banisteriopsis sp.)

One indication of how widely plants of the second genus, *Banisteriopsis* (Figure 4.10b), are used in indigenous religious systems is the many different names it has in the area of its distribution. Nevertheless, South Americanist scholars most frequently call it ayahuasca ("vine of the soul"), the Quechua language term for it. According to Schultes and Hoffman (1992), ayahuasca is generally considered by all who use it to free the soul (or one of them, at least, among groups where multiple souls exist) so that it can wander freely, releasing its owner from the constraints of daily life to discover "true reality." Many groups gather a number of different types of ayahuasca and mix it with various other psychoactive plants to produce an equally great variety of trance and vision experiences.

96

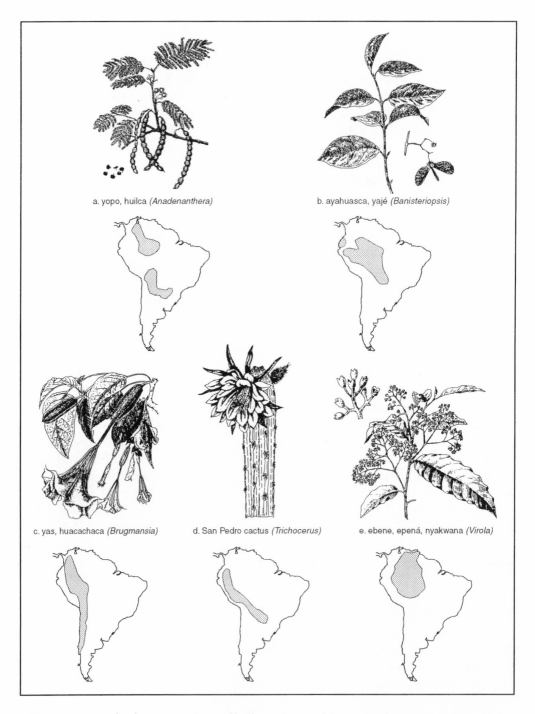

a. yopo, huilca *(Anadenanthera)*

b. ayahuasca, yajé *(Banisteriopsis)*

c. yas, huacachaca *(Brugmansia)*

d. San Pedro cactus *(Trichocerus)*

e. ebene, epená, nyakwana *(Virola)*

FIGURE 4.10   The five main genera of hallucinogenic plants utilized by indigenous South Americans and the distributions of these plants in relation to known use. Redrawn and adapted from figures in Schultes and Hoffman (1992).

Ayahuasca is gathered by scraping the bark from a rain-forest liana. Then, depending on the area, it is prepared either by boiling the bark for several hours to produce a thick, bitter liquid, which is then ingested in small doses, or by pulverizing it and adding it to cold water to be taken in larger doses (since it is less concentrated in this form). Its physical effects on the body usually include such unpleasant reactions as nausea, dizziness, and vomiting. Its psychotropic effects include euphoria and aggression, and everywhere it is taken, for reasons still unknown to scientists, it produces visions of jaguars and huge snakes, although these animals are certainly present in the environments included in the distribution map in Figure 4.10b.

With respect to the jaguar, probably the most dangerous and feared animal of the rain forest, shamans of the Yekuana, or Makiritare, of central Venezuela who take ayahuasca *become* the jaguar and are able to exercise the powers of a cat as they carry out curing or bewitching activities. And snakes seen by shamans in ayahuasca-induced visions among the Conibo-Shipibo of eastern Peru are acquired as powerful allies that defend them in supernatural battles against the hostile shamans of other, nearby groups. Above all, throughout the area of the plant's use it aids shamans in carrying out healing rituals in curing the ill. Once shamans take ayahuasca, they are able to summon healing spirits who respond to the entreaties to cure their patients. Schultes and Hoffman also point out that many who take it experience the sensation of flying and in so doing are able to carry out such feats as flying to the Milky Way to encounter heaven, flying about in the sky as a bird, or traveling in a supernatural canoe to retrieve souls.

Brugmansia sp.

Once thought to belong to the genus *Datura*, recent research has shown plants of the genus *Brugmansia* (Figure 4.10c), the third of the five hallucinogenic plants discussed here, to be different enough to warrant placing them in a distinct generic category—although both genuses nonetheless are quite similar in appearance. Schultes and Hoffman think that knowledge of the properties of *Datura* probably was brought by the first Paleoindians arriving in the New World, since many species of this genus exist in the Old World. Not only would this have aided them in recognizing related New World species of *Datura*, but also, once in South America, the strong similarity of the *Daturas* to the *Brugmansias* would have made it rather quickly clear that the latter plants had similar hallucinogenic properties.

Many species of *Brugmansia* exist along the western side of South America. For example, three are found at elevations above 1,800 meters in the Colombian Andes, where indigenous groups use the seeds as an additive to *chicha*, or maize beer. Crushed leaves and flowers are added to hot or cold water in preparing *Brugmansia* species as a form of tea. But however the plant is ingested, its effects always bring about a physically convulsive, or violent, phase. Those who take it first fall into a heavy stupor, with eyes vacant and nostrils dilated. This is followed by the violent phase, during which eyes roll, foam comes out of the mouth, and the body goes through a period of severe convulsions. The third phase is more peaceful, as the taker of this powerful hallucinogen falls into a sleep that lasts for several hours. After waking up, he may recount the details of visits made to the ancestors. Lingering longer than these first physical effects and the hallucinations, however, are some very unpleasant aftereffects that include, in more-or-less ascending order of seriousness, pronounced nausea, outbursts of violence, and temporary insanity.

Among the Jívaro a species of *Brugmansia* is added to parched maize and administered to recalcitrant children, who, while intoxicated, are lectured on behalf of the spirits as to how to behave properly. In Peru, where local species are called huacachaca, *Brugmansia* is taken to enable the finding of treasures in ancient tombs, or *huacas* (hence the meaning of huacachaca in Quechua, "plant of the tomb"). In the Colombian Andes the plants of this genus have just about as many uses as mentioned earlier for yopo—including its being given to patients to relieve rheumatism (its tropane alkaloids make it an effective medicine), to the men to make them better hunters, and to the dogs in helping them search for game.

San Pedro Cactus (Trichocereus sp.)

Although the use of most of the South American hallucinogenic plants may well go back to the time of the first Paleoindian inhabitants of the continent, San Pedro cactus (*Trichocereus* sp., Figure 4.10d), the fourth genus discussed here, is one of the few for which we have excellent evidence of its antiquity in prehistoric adaptive systems, even if this evidence is confined to more recent millennia. For example, judging from its depiction on various media including pottery, textiles, and stone in the Chavín art of Early Horizon Peru, San Pedro played an important role in the religious activities of this culture beginning as early as 900 B.C. (Figure 4.11).

The stems of this columnar cactus, which grows in desertic conditions both on the coast and in the highlands, are sliced into thin cuttings and boiled for some hours until a thick potion is produced. Upon ingesting the liquid, shamans at first experience drowsiness and dizziness, followed by a feeling of tranquillity and psychic detachment from the physical world. As the rituals associated with San Pedro proceed, the shamans are able to free themselves from the constraints of material reality to fly freely and ecstatically through the cosmos, communicating with the spirits.

San Pedro is widely sold in traditional markets throughout the coast of Peru, and it is used by *curanderos*, or curing shamans, in treating a variety of illnesses. Occasionally, to increase its potency and effectiveness, dust and powdered human bones from cemeteries are added to it. During a nighttime ritual a shaman sets up a *mesa*, or "table," of power objects placed on a cloth on the ground and ingests San Pedro to carry out a battle with the hostile forces that have brought about the illness. Sometimes the hallucinogenic potion is given to the patients themselves, whose reactions run the gamut from remaining calm and somnolent

FIGURE 4.11   A depiction of the principal Chavín deity, with anthropomorphic features including serpent hair, a snake belt, feline fangs, and taloned hands and feet. In its right hand the deity holds a piece of *Trichocereus*, or San Pedro cactus. Redrawn and adapted from Burger (1992).

to engaging in violent dancing and falling writhing upon the ground. San Pedro works other magico-religious wonders as well: For example, it is able to guard houses much as a guard dog does, whistling in ghostly fashion to scare away intruders on the owner's property.

Virola sp.

Virola (Figure 4.10e) is the fifth of South America's most widely used "sacred inebriants," as Schultes and Hoffman call them. Obtained from the bark of a tree, it is used by village groups throughout the rain forests of the eastern Amazon as well as in most of the Orinoco Basin area (Figure 4.10e). The Tukano of eastern Colombia have a myth that *Virola*, which they call viho, was received by humans at the beginning of the cosmos when the Sun's daughter, who had engaged in an incestuous act with him, scratched his penis, whereupon the sacred snuff powder issued forth with his semen. From that time until now it has been used only by the shamans to contact the snuff person, Viho-mahse, who from his home in the Milky Way guides human affairs and controls access by the shamans to all other spirits. *Virola*'s use is also restricted to the shamans among other nearby groups who employ it in rituals of curing, prophecy, and divination.

The methods of preparation vary from place to place. For example, among groups of eastern Colombia the soft, inner layer is scraped away from the bark, which must be collected in the early morning hours. After mixing the shavings with cold water for some minutes, the shaman boils down the resulting brownish liquid to a thick syrup, which is left to dry and finally pulverized into a powder that is combined with ashes from cacao bark. The Makú, a group of band societies of this same area, simply ingest the inner layer of the *Virola* bark directly without any preparation at all.

Elsewhere in the eastern lowlands, for example, in the Orinoco area, its use and the methods of preparation are somewhat distinct. Any male who has gone through the puberty rites that occur at ages thirteen to fourteen may use *Virola*, or ebene as it is called here. It is often used on a daily basis for communicating with the spirits, who may be summoned either to cure or to carry out some act of vengeance against a nearby enemy. The Waiká dry the inner bark shavings over a fire so that they may be stored for later use. Then, after a procedure of boiling, drying, and pulverizing very similar to that of groups in the Colombian Amazon, the snuff powder is mixed with the ashes from the bark of a rare, leguminous tree as well as with the aromatic leaves of third, nonhallucinogenic plant cultivated just for this purpose.

Schultes and Hoffman note that among some rain-forest groups this hallucinogen is taken in "frighteningly excessive amounts," involving various inhalations in rapid succession and from three to six teaspoons of snuff in each inhalation. Everywhere that *Virola* is dried into a powder, it is snuffed into the nostrils by one or another tubed instruments. For example, the Yanomamö take ebene by having another person blow it with substantial force through a long tube into their nostrils and sinuses. This causes the taker of the drug to reel backward with equal violence, whereupon the eyes begin to water and copious amounts of green mucous are discharged from the nostrils. With his eyes rolling from the effects of ebene and a dreamlike expression on his face, the taker enters a period of hyperactivity during which the *hekura* spirits are contacted. The session ends with a protracted period of stupor and inactivity.

KALLAWAYA MEDICINAL HERBS

At various points earlier in this chapter, I stressed that some thirteen thousand years of experience with the natural environment have given indigenous South Americans an exquisitely detailed knowledge of the nutritional and psychoactive properties of their continent's flora. Although during this immensely long period of time most groups have come to have an equally sophisticated knowledge of the healing properties of the wild plants found in their local area, nowhere is this more true than of the Kallawaya of northeastern Bolivia. For hundreds of years up until the beginning of the twentieth century, Kallawaya medicine men left their villages in the deep *yungas* valleys located near Lake Titicaca to travel the

Andes from Ecuador to northern Argentina, carrying with them a variety of herbal medicines, which they employed in healing the sick. Indeed, the name *Kallawaya* itself means "Land of the Medicine." Although the development of modern medicine has brought about a corresponding decline in indigenous confidence in traditional healing practices, Joseph Bastien's research (1987) makes it clear that the tradition is still vigorously alive and well in the Kallawaya area itself. Since his study of their adaptive system is dealt with in detail in Chapter 8, here we confine the discussion to a brief overview of Kallawaya concepts of illness before going on to discuss the properties and uses of nine exemplary herbs that are among the nearly two hundred plants the Kallawaya employ in the healing process.

Although Kallawaya healing derives from traditions dating well back into the prehispanic period prior to A.D. 1532, Kallawaya concepts of disease have been influenced since that time by European notions based on Greek humoral theory, or the idea that the world is made up of four primary elements (fire, earth, water, and air) and that the body is constituted by four basic fluids (blood, phlegm, yellow bile, and black bile). Diseases in the European-derived Kallawaya view are categorized into hot, cold, and cordial (this last being diseases that come and go). However, unlike the Greeks, who understood the body as analogous to systems of nature in that health involves symmetry and balance, the Kallawaya view the body as being in a pendulumlike state of continual flux between hot and cold and between wet and dry. Health, in this theory, involves attention to the hot/cold and wet/dry factors in properly maintaining the hydraulic dynamics of the body, or the cycles of fluids and food that, in turn, produce secondary fluids (e.g., mucus, sweat, urine, semen) and semifluids (e.g., feces), which become toxic to the body if they are not eliminated regularly.

The Kallawaya see the most important bodily fluids, or humors, as being air, blood, and fat. Air, which gives life-sustaining breath, is also associated with the wind, which in turn can cause respiratory illnesses. Blood (*yawar*) represents the life principle, and each person is thought to acquire by the age of seven all the blood he or she will ever have, save through the unlikely event of a blood transfusion. Thus, bodily or mental states such as weakness and depression are seen as being caused by the loss of blood at some point after this age. Fat (*wira*) is the energy principle and is viewed as being carried via the blood throughout the body. As we see in Chapter 8, the mountain on whose slopes the Kallawaya live is itself viewed as a giant living organism that must be fed fat by ritualists in order to remain viable. Indeed, anyone who is fat is considered healthy by Kallawaya standards (the men, especially, are attracted to fat women), whereas anyone who is thin is considered to be sickly. Diseases are caused anytime the cyclical flux of these humors in the body is thrown out of kilter thermodynamically. Hot diseases include fevers, toothache, and liver ailments; cold diseases include the common cold, any sort of cough, and rheumatism; and cordial diseases are ephemeral ones such as earaches, sore eyes, and bodily weakness, which pass relatively more quickly.

The diagnosis of the physical causes of disease is carried out on the patient by the medicine man feeling the pulse and examining the urine as well as in a divinatory way by dissecting guinea pigs (see also Morales 1995). Upon entering the home of the patient, the medicine man asks that a guinea pig be brought to him. He then rubs the guinea pig on the skin of the patient's forehead and over the heart before cutting open its belly to examine the heart, liver, and lungs. (Because the guinea pig was domesticated in the Andes to be eaten as a tasty source of protein, these divinatory procedures do not appear cruel to the Kallawaya or to other Andeans who employ guinea pig divination.) The patient's circulatory and respiratory systems are then compared by analogy to the corresponding parts of the guinea pig. If, for example, the guinea pig has a strongly beating heart, then fat and blood are being adequately pumped by the patient's heart throughout the body.

Although the Kallawaya live at elevations between 2,700 and 5,000 meters in the higher temperate and cold elevations of the Andes, many of the plants they use to make herbal medicines are found along the fringes of the rain forests that lie far below to the east. Bastien (1987:54) categorizes eighty-nine plants of the nearly two hundred in the Kallawaya pharmacopeia in terms of their therapeutical properties and relationship to three aspects of human physiology: (1) humors (blood, bile, urine, milk, phlegm, sweat), (2) processing organs (lungs, digestive tract, reproductive tract), and (3) the frame (muscles and bones, senses, nervous system). Some of the forty-seven therapeutic properties explicitly recognized by the Kallawaya medicine men are blood coagulants, bile purgatives, bile refrigerants, urinary diuretics, phlegm expectorants, sudorifics (sweat inducers), digestive tract purgatives, lineaments, and analgesics. Putting the case somewhat more simply, Bastien (1987:5) notes that the Kallawaya pharmacy "includes remedies that are nature's equivalent of aspirin, penicillin, and quinine and others that have yet to be discovered by modern medicine." One indication of the scientific foundation of Kallawaya healing practices—which are based not only on the observation of illnesses and the effect of herbal medicines on them, but also on the long-term development of a healing tradition—is that more than fifty species of plants used by the Kallawaya have been adopted by pharmaceutical companies in the capital city of La Paz.

Only nine plants are discussed here in order to give some idea of Kallawaya plant knowledge and the application of this knowledge in traditional curing practices. Following Bastien's lead, the plants are listed by their indigenous name, or names, with genus and species designations given in parentheses. Although some outside medicinal substances (e.g., alcohol) are employed, the main point of the following descriptions of plants and their uses is to indicate the pharmaceutical sophistication with which traditional Kallawaya medicine men approach the healing process. In this process they utilize herbal medicines whose proved efficacy results from the centuries-old application of scientific principles involving observation and cause and effect. A reader confronted more or less suddenly with the plants shown in Figure 4.12 might well consider how long it would take to acquire the knowledge to which the Kallawaya are privy by virtue of ongoing training and tradition. To encounter such knowledge in an indige-

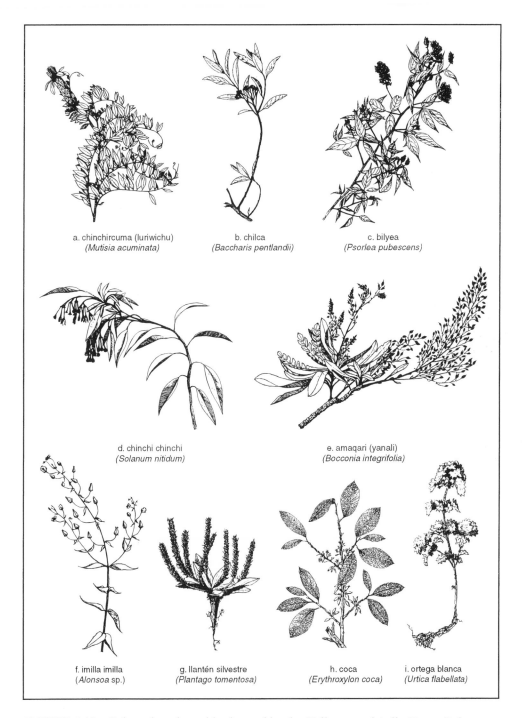

a. chinchircuma (luriwichu)
(*Mutisia acuminata*)

b. chilca
(*Baccharis pentlandii*)

c. bilyea
(*Psorlea pubescens*)

d. chinchi chinchi
(*Solanum nitidum*)

e. amaqari (yanali)
(*Bocconia integrifolia*)

f. imilla imilla
(*Alonsoa* sp.)

g. llantén silvestre
(*Plantago tomentosa*)

h. coca
(*Erythroxylon coca*)

i. ortega blanca
(*Urtica flabellata*)

FIGURE 4.12   Selected medicinal herbs used by the Kallawaya of Ayllu Kaata, Bolivia. All figures redrawn and adapted from Bastien (1987), except for Figure 4.12h, from Pulgar Vidal (1996).

nous context forces us to reconsider the Western notion that we alone represent any sort of unique repository of wisdom, medical or otherwise.

Chinchircuma/Luriwichu (Mutisia acuminata)

This is one of the plants (Figure 4.12a) found growing at the higher mountain elevations where the Kallawaya reside. It is a medium-sized bush common along the sides of Andean trails, and its bright reddish yellow flowers, the source of the herbal medicine it produces, attract hummingbirds, from which it gets its Aymara name, luriwichu. Chinchircuma is used in Kallawaya medicine for a variety of purposes. One of the men with whom Bastien carried out his research uses it as an inhibitor of heart palpitations and the pain that accompanies them. His prescription for preparing the drug was to mix one chinchircuma flower with three flowers of Spanish broom (*Spartium junceum*) in a cup of boiling water, to be ingested by the patient four times a day for the duration of the palpitations. He also prescribed this same herbal preparation for use in cases of breathing difficulty for patients with mucus-clogged bronchial passages. Another healer boiled 20 grams of chinchircuma flowers in unadulterated form to prepare a liquid that was administered to patients with heart problems, coughs, nervous disorders, and arthritis. Mixed with cow fat, the leaves of the chinchircuma plant are used to make a salve that is massaged on small children's legs to aid them in learning to walk. Although mentioned as early as the seventeenth century (e.g., Cobo 1979), chinchircuma, according to Bastien, has not yet been subjected to laboratory analysis to determine its active ingredients.

Chilca (Baccharis pentlandii)

This is another of the medicinal plants (Figure 4.12b) that grow wild at higher, cooler elevations in the Andes. From Bolivia to Ecuador, chilca is found along the banks of watercourses and in fallowed fields at elevations between 2,500 and 3,700 meters above sea level. The sticky resin produced from the crushed leaves of chilca is used to prepare a balm with analgesic qualities that aids healers in reducing the inflammation caused by bone fractures, muscle sprains, and rheumatism. As early as the seventeenth century, Cobo (1979) described its use in cases of pains of the loin and intestines, physical disabilities caused by malaria , and insomnia. No complete analysis of chilca's pharmaceutical constituents has been carried out, but Bastien suggests that its balsamic qualities probably are produced by compounds of benzoic and cinnamic acids. Although used primarily to prepare external poultices, chilca resins are also employed in preparing mates, or warm tealike infusions, that aid in curing diarrhea as well as acting as an abortefacient in terminating pregnancies. In this latter case, at least one Kallawaya healer told Bastien that he frowned on its use either in making a person sick or in taking a human life. Apparently not all medicine men feel this way, of course, or its efficacy as an abortefacient would not be known to traditional Kallawaya medicinal science.

Bilyea (Psorlea pubescens)

Aside from chilca, the other most commonly used herb of the Kallawaya healers is bilyea (Figure 4.12c). Because its pointed leaves grow in groups of three, it is often called trinitaria ("trinity") in Spanish. The plant grows to a height of about 2 meters and is found on hill slopes at elevations between 1,000 and 3,500 meters, in the lower regions of Kallawaya territory and beyond, toward the lowland rain forests. Bilyea is a legume, meaning that among its features are roots that are rich in nitrogen. The active pharmaceutical ingredients in the roots include the toxins vitexin and coumarin, the latter acting in the liver as an anticoagulant and hence as an inhibitor of heart attacks caused by blood clots. Since coumarin is also a known carcinogen, not to mention a potent toxin, its use is banned in the United States. Kallawaya herbalists, in any case, are well aware that the potency of bilyea plants varies as a function of soil nutrients and exposure to insolation, so they know where to look to find the most potent ones. Its principal internal use involves the preparation of mate (tea) made from crushed leaves whose properties aid in curing acid stomachs, intestinal irregularity, diarrhea, and worms, as well as in cleansing the urinary tract. Since bilyea is high in riboflavins, which are converted to coenzymes that work together with proteins to provide energy to the body, taking it in liquid form may well have positive nutritional effects. Its external uses include the preparation of poultices that act as astringents or balms and that stop the bleeding from wounds.

Chinchi Chinchi (Solanum nitidum)

This plant (Figure 4.12d) grows at high temperate and colder elevations and is especially plentiful around the marshy shores of Lake Titicaca at an elevation of 3,750 meters above sea level. Chinchi chinchi grows to about 2 meters in height and produces clusters of berries that are crushed in preparation for medicinal application. Since chinchi chinchi is a member of the nightshade family, or the *Solanaceae*, it has toxic properties that include the presence of gluco-alkaloids that are highly injurious to bodily tissues. Taken in sufficiently high doses, the plant thus becomes lethal, and it is not surprising that Kallawaya herbalists limit its use to external poultices that are prepared by boiling the berries in water and then applied to the skin to kill various parasites, including fleas and lice. Chinchi chinchi pastes are also used in treating two indigenous diseases. The first of these, called *chullpa* ("burial place"), is believed to result from some Kallawaya violating the grave of an ancestor and manifests itself in the form of osteomyelitis, or "inflamed muscles with slivers of bone protruding through the skin" (Bastien 1987:63). Kallawaya science thus has its limitations, and Bastien notes somewhat wryly that they have no idea that osteomyelitis results from a bacterial infection within the patient's bones. The second disease is called *orijado* and is a form of *susto* ("fright") in infants brought about because their mothers, while still pregnant, had chanced to gaze on a dead black dog. The symptoms in children suffering from *orijado* include listlessness and diarrhea, and they are treated by placement of the chinchi chinchi paste in a black cloth that is then tied around the child's midsection. Aymara mothers of the Titicaca region also apply the bitter paste to their breasts at the point they wish to wean nursing children, although Kallawaya healers frown on this practice because of the toxic nature of the alkaloids in the paste.

Amaqari/Yanali (Bocconia integrifolia)

The amaqari plant (Figure 4.12e) is found on the fringes of the Amazonian rain forests, and Kallawaya herbalists, during their travels, harvest its leaves and the clusters of berrylike fruits (yanali), which are dried, toasted, and ground into a fine powder to be used in preparing medicinal potions. Although the fruit and leaves are classified as hot, they are used in the treatment of cold diseases such as coughs, colds, and rheumatism. For example, in the case of coughs brought about by a bad cold, one-quarter teaspoon of amaqari powder is added to a cup of boiled water mixed with honey and is drunk immediately at the point the coughing begins. For other cold symptoms, the patient's chest is rubbed with a portion of freshly crushed moist berries mixed with camphor, alcohol, and a weed called waji. Since amaqari contains alkaloids, Bastien notes that it is efficacious in calming the pains brought about by rheumatism. Among the alkaloids present in genus *Bocconia* is boconine, which has highly potent anesthetic properties that also make it effective in the treatment of arthritis.

Imilla Imilla (Alonsoa sp.)

Since the blossoms of this small flowering plant (Figure 4.12f) are similar in appearance to the female reproductive organs, it is called imilla imilla ("maiden maiden") or warmi warmi ("woman woman") in Aymara. Applying the doctrine of signatures or in this case using the medicine produced from a plant to heal an organ that resembles a part of the plant, Kallawaya healers place branches of the imilla imilla plant in a cup of boiling water to administer to women with uterine ailments, including a delay in the menstrual cycle. Although imilla imilla's active ingredients are not known, Bastien notes they may well be beneficial in the treatment of uterine problems, irrespective of the fortuitous similarity between the blossoms and the female sexual anatomy.

Llantén Silvestre (Plantago tomentosa)

This is one of a number of medicinal plants that grow widely from Colombia to Bolivia and points south. Growing as a weed in moist fallowed fields, the rubbery lanceolate-shaped and potassium-rich leaves of llantén (Figure 4.12g) are used to treat a variety of ailments. In Colombia the leaves are used both externally and internally, including placing them on the forehead in the case of headaches and making a maté out of them that is drunk to stop internal bleeding. Crushed llantén leaves are used in Ecuador to relieve the pain and itching of insect bites and to heal cuts and sores. Kallawaya healers use llantén primarily in preparing infusions to treat internal problems such as kidney pain and swelling resulting from hard work, headaches, heart attacks, throat inflammations, acid stomach, and diarrhea. In the case of diarrhea, which can cause dehydration and death in infants, the curative is prepared by boiling the leaves in water together with a beaten egg, to which sugar is added after the liquid cools down. Potassium, sugar, boiled water, and other nutrients are precisely the ingredients, notes Bastien, that are used effectively around the world in applying oral rehydration therapy to heal infant patients suffering from severe diarrhea.

Coca (*Erythroxylon coca*)

Earlier in this chapter I briefly discussed the importance of coca chewing in providing relief to Andeans engaged in strenuous work and travel at high altitudes. The leaves of this plant (Figure 4.12h) also play an important role in ritual and in the traditional healing practices of most indigenous Andean people, including the Kallawaya. Coca grows in the lower *yungas* valleys at elevations between 700 and 1,900 meters, or well below the altitudinal range of the Kallawaya and other high-Andean settlements, but because of its overriding importance in traditional culture, people for centuries have found ways to obtain it—by traveling directly down into the *yungas,* as the Kallawaya do; by trading for it (in prehispanic times); or by purchasing it in markets (in the post-Conquest period). Although there exist roughly ninety species of the genus *Erythroxylon* throughout tropical and subtropical South America, the two principal species of coca are *E. coca* and *E. novogranatense.*

Studies (cited in Bastien 1987) have shown that coca leaves are highly nutritional in that they contain enough carbohydrates, protein, calcium, and iron so that 100 grams would satisfy the recommended daily allowance for the average person (the required weekly intake would thus be 700 grams, or 0.7 kilogram). However, nowhere in the Andes where coca is grown and chewed do people usually ingest more than one pound (450 grams) of coca a week, so although it is useful as a nutritional supplement, it is chewed not for this reason but for the release of the narcotic alkaloids that relieve fatigue, hunger, and altitude sickness (hypoxia). Indeed, as we see in discussing the Kogi in Chapter 7, in some parts of the Andes coca chewing is associated with poor nutrition in that it reduces hunger pangs and related fatigue in people whose diets are inadequate. Where diets are excessive in potato consumption, however, the higher metabolic rates of energy expenditure in the body brought about by coca chewing actually have been shown to be "salubrious to digestive processes and carbohydrate consumption" (Bastien 1987:57).

Aside from chewing the leaves, the Kallawaya also use them, either in maté form or in quids as a poultice, to treat a variety of the internal and external complaints patients bring to the medicine men. The treatments include (1) a mixture of 30 grams of leaves marinated for four days in cane alcohol, the traditional alcoholic drink of Central Andeans, which is used to treat stomach problems such as indigestion, colic, and dysentery; (2) the same mixture used to massage muscles that are sore from colds and work at high altitude and, to further the cure, placed in boiling water, the vapor of which is then inhaled (Bastien does not mention that any imbibing of this highly potent concoction [called *pusi tunqha* by the Aymara, or "forty proof"!] is done, just in case that might help in the cure as well); and (3) coca quids (presumably prepared beforehand by chewing them in the mouth) placed on the feet to relieve swelling and soreness, on body joints to treat rheumatism, and on the forehead to treat headaches.

Ortega Blanca (Urtica flabellata)

Aside from coca, this is the other plant among the nine discussed here that is familiar to non–South American readers, since ortega blanca (Figure 4.12i) is nothing more than the common nettle, whose prickly hairs inject a painful toxin into any hiker unwary enough to stray too close to the plant. This is precisely the feature of the plant that Kallawaya healers employ when placing it against an area of the body that is sore from rheumatism. By irritating the skin, the nettle hairs increase the flow of blood to the affected area. Although Bastien is uncertain of the exact therapeutic effect of the nettle stings, he notes that such a treatment is a good example of homeopathy, or "the administration of minute doses of drugs that are capable of producing in persons symptoms like those of the disease treated" (Bastien 1987:65). White nettle is also used by the Kallawaya healers to prepare a mate infusion for treating tuberculosis and irritations of the ovary and uterus. Other species, Bastien notes, are used in Colombia to act as a diuretic and in Ecuador to treat urinary tract pain, to act as a blood astringent, to stop menstrual flow, to treat diarrhea and hemorrhoids, and to reduce the symptoms of asthma. The important role of the nettle in traditional Kallawaya herbal medicines and in household remedies may be due to the presence of vitamin A, vitamin C, protein, chlorophyll, ammonia, carbonic acid, and formic acid in its leaves. Its nutritional qualities are helpful in treating tuberculosis, which can be precipitated by poor-quality nutrition, and in healing fractures by stimulating the flow of blood to the affected area.

CHAPTER 5

Band Societies
Present and Past

A̲ᴛ ᴇᴀʀʟɪᴇʀ ᴘᴏɪɴᴛs ɪɴ ᴛʜɪs ʙᴏᴏᴋ I have discussed two key issues in relation to the long-term continuity of band-level societies in some areas of the continent. First, in light of the remarkable cultural stability that characterized human groups from prehistoric to recent times in settings such as Tierra del Fuego, I
raised the general theoretical question of why some indigenous South American
peoples did not evolve out of the band level of sociopolitical integration while
the great majority of those in other environmental zones did. Second, in answering this question, I proposed the hypothesis that such cultural stability, or dynamic equilibrium, occurred in Patagonia because once agriculture was developed in the seven other environmental zones, Patagonia became, relatively
speaking, the lowest in subsistence productivity while remaining nonetheless a
highly suitable context for the continued maintenance of hunting-gathering
adaptive systems.

Since Patagonia permitted the fewest numbers and lowest densities of human
populations, it would logically have the most stable human adaptive systems anywhere on the continent. But as we see in the present chapter, this does not imply
that the peoples of Patagonia or band groups in other parts of South America (see
Figure 5.1) were less "capable" culturally or any less complex in some respects
(e.g., the ability of mind to come up with intricate cosmologies) than indigenous
South American cultures of other places and times. It does mean, however, that
the Patagonian and other groups formed highly stable, smaller-scale systems that
were less complex sociopolitically than the village, chiefdom, and state societies
that arose in the other seven environmental zones—a point that we have so far
addressed both in theory and in relation to critical features of the environments
and their corresponding subsistence systems, but not in relation to all the other
data on societies at each of the four levels of sociopolitical integration. These
other data, of course, form the principal focus of this and later chapters.

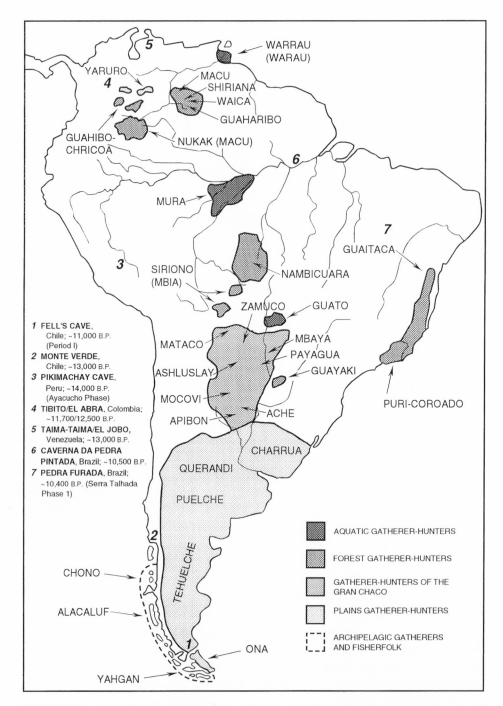

FIGURE 5.1   Map showing the location of recent band societies, the principal types of hunter-gatherer subsistence adaptations, and Paleoindian sites discussed in the text. Data on recent groups adapted from Steward and Faron (1959).

In a theoretical vein, let me reiterate here that such evolutionary issues could not be addressed at all had I not laid the groundwork by (1) discussing the four levels of sociopolitical integration—bands, villages, chiefdoms, and states—that permit the comparison of cultures through time and across geographic space; (2) presenting a systems-hierarchical model that argues, among many others of its features, for an intimate connection between environment and culture (hence, our use of the ecological term *human adaptive system*); and (3) outlining in some detail the main features of the eight environmental zones of the continent, a procedure that has permitted us to compare and contrast their productivity in light of the different subsistence systems that developed in them over a period of more than ten thousand years of human occupation.

Another possible reason for the nonevolution of Patagonian band societies, aside from our Stewardian insistence that sociopolitical complexity ultimately rests on the environmental and subsistence infrastructure, was their geographic remoteness from the developments based on agriculture that occurred elsewhere in South America beginning around 8000 B.C. This diffusionist issue, specifically as it was raised by Julian Steward (see Steward and Faron 1959), is addressed briefly as the first topic of this chapter. Following that, the next two sections discuss, first, the Ona (Ona-Selk'nam) and the Yahgan (Yahgan-Yámana) of Tierra del Fuego and, next, the Nukak of eastern Colombia.

The Ona and the Yahgan present highly interesting cases from an ecological standpoint. Although they lived in adjacent areas, their environments and subsistence adaptations were sharply distinct. Knowing this, no one who has followed the arguments of this book would be remiss in predicting that their cultures would therefore be distinct in significant other ways and that probably little interaction occurred between them—although they were located just a few tens of kilometers apart for a time period that most likely endured nearly as long as the human presence in Patagonia. The next section, on the Nukak, provides comparative data on a band group that lives far to the north in the rain forests of the northwestern Amazon Basin. Although they inhabit an environment that is quite distinct from that of Tierra del Fuego, a number of rather interesting parallels exist between the Nukak and the Fuegian groups—including the presence of territoriality and interband or interlineage boundaries.

Following the presentation of the data on these three recent/contemporary band groups, the final section leaps back into the most remote South American past: first, to outline briefly the climates, fauna, and flora of South America during the Paleoindian Period (~13,000–10,000 B.P.) and, second, to see what can be reconstructed of the adaptations of the earliest inhabitants of the continent by reference to seven widely spaced Paleoindian sites around the continent. As shown in Figure 5.1, these sites comprise Fell's Cave, southern Chile; Monte Verde site, south-central Chile; Pikimachay Cave, southern Peru; Tibitó site, central Colombia; Taima-Taima site, northern Venezuela; Caverna da Pedra Pintada site, along the Amazon River in Brazil; and Pedra Furada Rock Shelter, east-central Brazil. The Fell's Cave data provide support for the sociopolitical continuity I have argued for in Patagonia. More broadly, in briefly examining the data from all seven Paleoindian sites, we see that ample grounds exist for the assertion that there existed a great deal of cultural variability (e.g., lithic tool types and subsistence systems) from the very beginning among these roughly contemporaneous and far-flung sites. At the same time, in the case of certain sites (especially Pikimachay Cave and Pedra Furada Rock Shelter) we address the whirlwind of controversy and scientific skepticism that surrounds claims for the presence of humans in South America at any time much prior to thirteen thousand years B.P.

BAND-LEVEL MARGINALITY

Earlier I alluded to the fact that Steward exhibits a curious mixture of reasonableness and bias in his theoretical arguments about why band societies were the way they were. On the one hand, he and Faron (1959) argue, for example, that hunter-gatherers at the time of European contact were noncomplex because they lived in unproductive regions that were too cold, too arid, or too swampy for agriculture to be practiced. This explains why they had sparse populations, why their settlements were impermanent and small, why they produced few material artifacts, and so on. When taken in conjunction with the long time depth of the archaeological stratigraphy in sites like Fell's Cave, the requisites of adaptation to low-productivity environments explain why band groups endured in stable equilibrium over long periods of time. These views are the reasonable part of Steward's theory about the adaptive relationship between a culture and its environment, and accordingly, I have incorporated them in updated form in this book.

On the other hand, Steward (1963; Steward and Faron 1959) views band-level societies as cultural and geographic "marginals." For example, Steward and Faron (1959:374) state that "most of these societies were remote from the centers of inventiveness, and they received comparatively few of the traits found among the more complex cultures." Even sadder yet for the marginals, Steward and Faron (1959:391) see them as lacking in inventiveness and as having manufactures, or artifacts, that were "invented long ago and which, though also found among other Indians, were superseded by better techniques in most societies." Thus, presumably "worse" band-level cultural features, such as netting and twining, bark canoes, flint-and-iron pyrite firemaking, spear throwers and bolas, and percussion musical instruments, eventually got replaced elsewhere by their culturally "better" counterparts: heddle-loom weaving, dugout canoes, wooden fire drills, bows and arrows, and wind instruments. Following his bands-as-marginals argument, Steward characterizes them in the following nutshell: They were stably adapted but culturally stunted in their developmental growth both by their remoteness from where the evolutionary "action" was and by their lack of inventiveness, itself presumably caused by their living in such marginal environments.

Although theory in anthropology has come a long way since these views were written, and it is thus unfair to accuse Steward of theoretical naïveté, from the perspective of the theory espoused in this book we may nevertheless permit ourselves to argue that his viewpoint is progressivist. Namely, it expresses the conviction that cultures that grow up in environments where agriculture is possible, and that become characterized by all the material elements of such adaptations, are somehow "better" than those where only hunting-gathering subsistence is possible. Let me briefly outline the theoretical argument of this book again or, in this instance, my *counterargument* to Steward: All preindustrial peoples in South America, or elsewhere for that matter, were capable of adapting to appropriate environments in such a way that they evolved to more complex levels of sociopolitical integration; this was achieved principally through the domestication of a great variety of plants and animals. All indigenous South Americans not only were capable of such an "achievement" but also probably were *forced* into it by the tendency of their populations to grow. Where groups could adapt by intensifying—that is, by developing agriculture—they did so, although ultimately they had to control their numbers in one way or another. Where groups could not adapt by intensifying, they were faced very quickly after their arrival in an area with keeping their numbers rigorously tuned to the carrying capacity of their hunting-gathering subsistence system. If this argument is taken as valid, then bands are anything but marginals; instead, they represent the longest-term cultural "success story" in South America. As we see shortly, this latter case is highly characteristic of the Fuegian peoples.

If my counterargument to Steward is correct, then the general lack in Patagonia of any of the inventions—whether they be material artifacts or nonmaterial institutions—of other parts of South America simply means that they were irrelevant to the adaptive systems of that area. We can fairly conclude, then, that Steward's arguments are progressivist *and* antiecological in that he fails to realize the ultimate implications of his cultural ecology perspective. Putting the case in our own terms, he fails to see that the level of sociopolitical integration of a culture is far better understood with respect to the productivity of its subsistence system in a given type of environment and all the other related regulatory institutions and behaviors than it is with respect to the proximity of that culture to other systems or the inventiveness of the people who constitute those systems. Human adaptive systems, in my argument, thus consist of highly integrated sets of locally relevant behaviors, material items, and nonmaterial institutions, not of grab bags of unrelated features that diffuse willy-nilly across a landscape without respect to the nature of those local systems.

To drive home the point that the marginality issue unfortunately is still alive and well, I close this section by noting that a Ph.D. archaeologist and I were recently looking at one of the maps of South America on the wall outside my office. I mentioned to the person (not a colleague in my department) that it was possible to see a rhyme and reason to the distribution of peoples at different levels of sociopolitical integration across the continent, especially in light of Steward's persuasive arguments about the relationship between cultural adaptations and environments, and that this distribution probably had nothing to do with cultural genius or a lack thereof. Without saying too much about the arguments just made here, I also mentioned that as far as I knew Patagonia was universally characterized by migratory band societies—in other words, that no prehistoric village, chiefdom, or state societies were found anywhere in that environmental

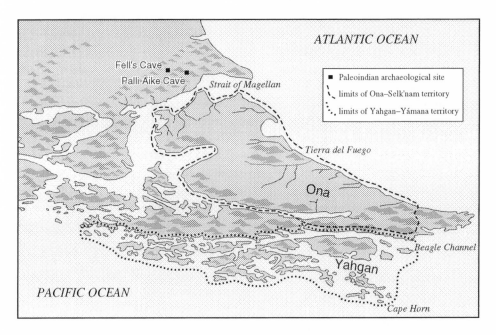

FIGURE 5.2   Perspective map of the southern tip of South America showing the location of the Ona-Selk'nam and the Yahgan-Yámana groups and the Paleoindian sites of Fell's Cave and Palli Aike Cave. Redrawn and adapted from Moore (1964).

zone. I then asked (as devil's advocate, admittedly) why that might be. Without hesitation, the person responded that the people of Patagonia simply were too far from where states were invented in the Central Andes for their characteristics to have had time to reach there. I rest my (ecological) case.

THE ONA AND YAHGAN

History tells us that the Ona were encountered by Europeans for the first time during Ferdinand Magellan's voyage in 1520 through the strait named after him and that the sight of numerous fires burning on the beaches at night gave rise to "Land of Fire," a name that would be subsequently associated with what was then (prior to the settlement of Antarctica) the southernmost inhabited part of the earth (Figure 5.2). The indigenous people of Tierra del Fuego did not become well known to the world, however, until Charles Darwin's (1962 [1860]) publication in 1839 of *The Voyage of the Beagle*. As anyone who has read this book knows, it includes an account of Darwin's encounters with South American geology, fauna, and flora, from Brazil to Peru, which became part of the background leading him to postulate natural selection as the principal mechanism of biological evolution. It also contains passages on how, upon encountering the Yahgan canoe people, this nineteenth-century European gentleman could scarcely believe that such "wretched savages" belonged to the human race. Nevertheless, the scientist in him was able to rise above narrower nineteenth-century English prejudices, permitting him to see that these people, so different from any indigenous peoples to the north (i.e., in the Andes and Brazil), must have come down from the north at some remote time in the past to adapt, and thus endure, in the Fuegian climate.

In 1875 Thomas Bridges, a Protestant missionary, came from England to bring Christianity to the Yahgan, establishing a small settlement at Ushuaia in the Beagle Channel. Although the Bridges family learned much about the Ona and Yahgan (e.g., see Bridges 1950), it was not until 1918–1920 that Martín Gusinde (1986, 1990) carried out a serious anthropological study of these peoples. This was fortunate for science, at least, since within three short decades after that the Ona and the Yahgan had disappeared from the earth—killed off by diseases introduced by the new settlers as well as, in the case of the Ona, by bounty hunters hired by the European ranchers now established on the main island. The ranchers wanted the land freed of its indigenous inhabitants in favor of the far more commercially valuable sheep.

Gusinde's Ona-Selk'nam Data

Physical Environment

Tierra del Fuego Island, the western part of which was the home of the Ona, is shown in the accompanying perspective map of the southern tip of South America (Figure 5.2). Of the total area of 48,000 square kilometers that the island covers, only about 35,000 square kilometers were suitable for a hunting-gathering existence. The Ona themselves recognized three principal zones within the habitable part of the island, each zone coinciding with three distinct cultural groups (Figure 5.3). The first of these was the northern plains zone, which was inhabited by the P'ámica Ona. It is a relatively flat area similar to the Patagonian pampas lying to the north, although there are scattered hills that in places rise to maximum elevations of about 300 meters above the plain. The sandy soils of the zone support low steppe vegetation (*Nothofagus antarctica,* or beech), and small rivers drain the inland area in all directions. Throughout this northern area, a rich diversity of bird life (ducks, swans, flamingos, and ansares) is present, but the mainstay of P'ámica Ona life was formed by the cururo (*Ctenomys magellanicus*), a type of wild rodent that was far more numerous here than the other animal important to Fuegian subsistence systems, the guanaco.

The second zone the Ona recognized was the southern plains and mountains, inhabited by the Hámška Ona. This zone has forests and dense swampy thickets in the north and high mountains rising to ~2,400 meters elevation in the south (these mountains were the main barrier between the Ona and the Yahgan). Although some foxes and sea lions were hunted, the principal faunal species in this zone was the guanaco. Not surprisingly, in light of the differences between the

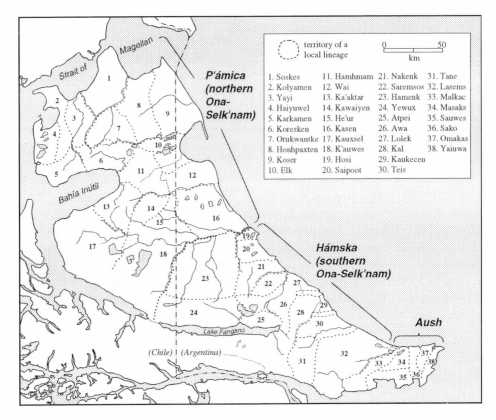

FIGURE 5.3   Map of Tierra del Fuego showing the distribution of the thirty-eight local lineage territories of the northern Ona-Selk'nam, the southern Ona-Selk'nam, and the Aush. Redrawn and adapted from Gusinde (1990).

northern plains and this southern zone, the Hámška Ona considered the guanaco a more noble animal to hunt and looked down on the P'ámica as mere "cururo eaters."

The third zone was the far southeastern part of the island (shown outside the Ona boundary, to the east, in Figure 5.3), which was inhabited by the Aush, or Wínteka. In contrast to the focus on terrestrial animals elsewhere on the island, Aush subsistence relied heavily on the hunting of marine mammals. The Aush language was only partly intelligible to the other inhabitants of the island, and Aush culture in general was far more distinct from the culture of either of the other two groups than the P'ámica Ona and Hámška Ona were from each other.

Mode of Production

Vegetation, except for beech trees, was sparse throughout Tierra del Fuego, and thus almost no plant foods were present in the diet of either the Hámška or the P'ámica. Indeed, Gusinde (1990:250) notes that the diet of both groups consisted "of meat and nothing more than meat." Guanacos, the principal animal hunted in the southern zone, according to Gusinde's (1990:12) account, are "curious creatures of little intelligence" and have highly predictable habits of movement. As a result, a group of Hámška Ona could lie in wait for them until they came down to lower elevations in the early morning and late afternoon hours to drink in the streams, where they could easily be surrounded and killed with bows and arrows. Occasionally when small herds were spotted that stayed in the same area for a few days, groups of three to eight men would surround them. But more often than not a man went out alone with his dogs to hunt guanaco, heading in a random direction until the dogs located the animals or their spoor and barked. Winter hunting was easier and more successful than that in other seasons, since the guanaco came down to the open areas at lower elevations to find food at this time. Occasionally when the men were off on a raid on another group, the women had to carry out the task of hunting guanaco, although Gusinde notes that in these cases the dogs did most of the work, including the kill, since the women never used any of the Ona weapons.

A guanaco kill was dressed down on the spot, with most of innards given to the dogs. If the hunter's camp was close, then the animal would be dragged back home; if not, it would be butchered on the spot into five pieces, which would be placed high up in the branches of a tree so that the foxes would not get them. The hide always was removed from the animal and taken back to camp. There was little worry about the safety of the meat left in the tree, however, as no one would think to take the meat from a kill he had not made. In this regard, guanaco-related USPs included "never wasting any meat" and "killing no more animals than were needed by immediate family members and nearby neighbors." Once the meat was brought back to camp, the hunter's wife carried out the distribution of the five main parts of the kill to the women of other nearby families. If two neighbors had both made kills, then almost no one ever made vulgar comparisons of the quantity and quality of what was reciprocally given.

Cururos, the principal animal hunted in the northern plains, are burrowing creatures. On the first day after finding a nest, the hunters would remove nearly all the dirt above it. On the second day, the men, boys, and sometimes the women would return and crush the animals in their nest. Hunters also ran after them and killed them with sticks if the animals were able to escape their human predators. Since the nests were nearly impossible to find under deep snow, cururos were primarily a summertime food, requiring the P'ámica to hunt marine mammals during the winter. Birds, trapped with rope snares, were important in the subsistence economy of the north.

Collecting in both the northern and southern areas was, according to Gusinde (1990:268ff.), "how the women looked for food." Plant foods included bayas (a berry from a variety of hyacinth), *Boopis australis* (a juicy root), mushrooms, and seeds. But as already indicated, plant foods were so infrequently found anywhere on Tierra del Fuego Island that they could not be counted on. Given the monotony of eating cururo or guanaco meat, however, the little amount of food pro-

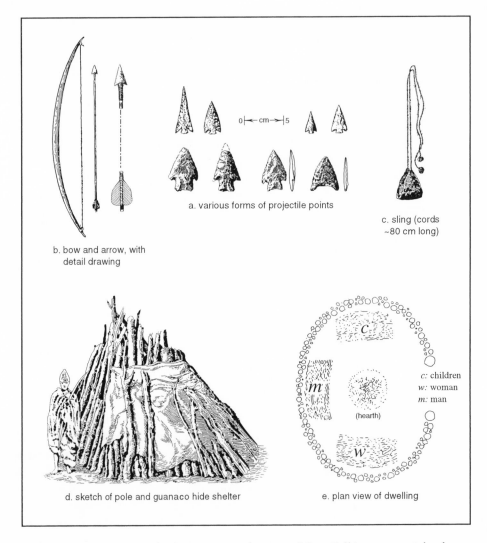

a. various forms of projectile points

b. bow and arrow, with detail drawing

c. sling (cords ~80 cm long)

d. sketch of pole and guanaco hide shelter

e. plan view of dwelling

c: children
w: woman
m: man

FIGURE 5.4   Drawings depicting various features of Ona-Selk'nam material culture. Redrawn and adapted from figures in Gusinde (1990).

vided by the women was considered very important nonetheless, as Gusinde notes. The women also gathered clams and small marine fish in pools along the beaches at low tide; bird eggs were gathered in the springtime.

Selected Ona artifacts are shown in the upper half of Figure 5.4. Not all of the men had the ability to make bows and arrows, but at least one member of a family usually knew how to do so. Gusinde (1990:216) calls the arrows, which were 60–80 centimeters long, "a small work of art." Projectile points were made from flint found in only a few places on the island, and Cabo San Pablo (the easternmost point in Lolek territory, or number 27 in Figure 5.3) was the best place. The flint from here and sea lion skins from the coast in general were obtained by trade among the various territorial groups. In the north slings (Figure 5.4c) frequently were used for hunting cururos and birds as well as in fighting.

Settlement Pattern

Since hunting provided the only form of subsistence, the settlement pattern necessarily consisted of continual migratory movements by small family groups across the island landscape. Therefore, as Gusinde notes, the land had to be very lightly populated by human groups, since if their numbers had been any higher, both the cururo and the guanaco would have been quickly used up and human survival on the island would have been impossible. Each hunter thus considered it necessary to have an extensive region at his disposal to maintain his family. The quest for food was a never-ending one, nonetheless, and Gusinde's Ona informants told him that the central feature of their adaptive system was the search for food, a search that was never far from their thoughts, since they knew they would go hungry and perish should they fail to find enough to eat.

At each campsite the men and the women worked together to put up the shelters (e.g., Figure 5.4d, e), a task that could be completed in about thirty minutes. Depending on the area, either cururo or guanaco skins were placed over pole frames and the gaps between the hides were filled with moss or other plants to keep the cold wind out. Inside the hut a fire was always kept going in a shallow hearth so that the cold air would not become intolerable. In the north the women had to carry the eight to twelve poles for constructing a hut from camp to camp, as wood was much scarcer than in the south. As many as fifteen guanaco skins were used in the south to cover the hut, with the leather being protected from moisture by the application of abundant amounts of guanaco grease and red-colored soil. The only time camps larger than one nuclear family were constructed was during the occasional men's initiation rite, the klóketen.

Mode of Reproduction

With about 35,000 square kilometers of land suitable for a hunting-gathering way of life, and with each ten-person family needing about 100 square kilometers to maintain itself, Gusinde estimates the total pre-Contact number of P'ámica, Hámška, and Aush to have been between thirty-five hundred and four thousand people—which is equivalent to a population density of between 0.10 and 0.11 person per square kilometer. But this is only an estimate, since by the time of Gusinde's arrival in 1918 only a few hundred Ona were left. On one occasion in 1919 at a ranch owned by the Bridges family, European observers counted a total of 216 Ona constituting twenty-seven families (or about 8 persons per family). These included 60 men (seventeen years of age or older), 58 women (seventeen years or older), 49 older children (eight to seventeen years), and 43 smaller children (under eight years). If we used these figures to form an admittedly crude population pyramid, we would see that this was a declining population but that there was rough parity between the sexes, since the adult sex ratio (SR) for this small population can be calculated at ~103, or very near the normal sex ratio of 105 for world populations (e.g., see Odum 1971; Clapham 1983).

Given human fecundity and the tendency of populations to grow, preindustrial groups must control their numbers by one or more of a variety of means—including abstinence, abortion, infanticide, and long lactation to suppress ovulation. Gusinde does not offer much data on such controls, although he does report that Ona mothers breast-fed their babies for about two years until the next child came along. Gusinde also reports that the Ona did not practice infanticide, since they told him that, loving children as they did, it was "unimaginable" to them. Moreover, fertility was great, as each woman mentioned having given birth to an average of seven children. The survivability of children was a problem, however, since on average only four offspring in each family survived the difficult life and rigors of the Fuegian climate.

Nevertheless, the Ona of the early twentieth century had an adequate diet. This is indicated in part by their long occupation of the island as well as by their being among the tallest of indigenous South Americans—with twenty-four men Gusinde measured averaging 173 centimeters and twenty-two women, 160 centimeters. In spite of their good health at the time of European Contact and their "burgeoning" numbers, ironically the Ona were soon to die out. Indeed, the Contact-period policy of having many children might be expected of a people who were suddenly confronted with many more guanacos per person than had ever been available before. They also were probably keenly aware of their dwindling numbers and thus desperate to check the decline.

Whatever the case, if each couple in the earlier pre-nineteenth-century period had an average of four children, the population would have been doubling each generation. If we assume a twenty-year generation, this is equivalent to a population growth rate of 3.5 percent ($70 \div x = 20$, where 70 is the "magic numerator," x is the growth rate, and 20 is the doubling time [DT]). To demonstrate that such a growth rate would have meant a population that was out of control (or, to use Gusinde's terms, killing off all the animals and dying out itself), let us assume that 100 people arrived on Tierra del Fuego in 9000 B.C. and that their numbers grew at 3.5 percent per annum. With the population doubling every generation, their numbers would have reached 3,200 persons a scant one hundred years later, at 8900 B.C., and already would have been pushing the low end of Gusinde's estimate for the *late* prehistoric maximum of 3,500 persons. Some 445 doubling times later (by A.D. 1900) the population would have reached 3200[445], or a number most likely exceeding every atom in the universe!

Clearly, as much as the Ona "loved children," they would have had to keep their growth rate as near to zero population growth after "8900 B.C." as they could, with no possibility of any out-migration for excess numbers, since we may presume that hunting-gathering subsistence adaptations to the north, on the mainland, were already "filled up" with people. Let us hypothetically conclude, then, that in addition to long lactation the Ona practiced other means of population control to regulate and maintain their beautifully stable adaptation—perhaps even including preferential female infanticide, a point we take up again.

Domestic Economy

Selected data in this category, especially including the division of labor and age and sex roles, are discussed elsewhere in this section. Nevertheless, several features including clothing, personal modesty, and body paint are of interest to mention. Gusinde notes that animal skins were used not so much to conserve body warmth as to keep the cold wind from directly striking the body. And the southern Ona, at least, wore their skins with the fur side out, the same as the guanaco. During the periods of most extreme cold in the winter when temperatures dropped well below freezing, guanaco fat was mixed with red-colored soil and applied to the skin to retain body heat. Younger men and all women and children kept the pubic area covered in any case, since it was considered bad form to do otherwise. Three colors of body paint—red, black, and white—were used. Women used red (from ochre) on the chest and face to decorate themselves, and the men used it for warfare; black (charcoal) was used only for funerals, mourning, and the *klóketen* festival; and white (from limestone, located at a single unidentified source on the island) was used for fine body painting.

Social Organization

As mentioned previously, the basic adaptive unit was the nuclear family. Although it is likely that the family structure of 1920—that is, with a mother, a father, and four or more children—had changed substantially from pre-Contact times, there are no data indicating precisely who each of the members of the "ten-person adaptive unit" were. One suspects, however, that among each family group were a few close relatives, including grandparents and unmarried sisters and brothers of the married couple. Monogamous unions prevailed, and there was no hierarchy in terms of birth or social position. Girls could marry only after first menses but usually waited until they were between fifteen and nineteen, whereas boys had to go through the *klóketen* initiation rite before they married and usually waited until they were about twenty.

   Although there are no data on longevity, we may presume that delaying marriage for women until several years after first menses would be one way to reduce the total number of children they would have during their childbearing years. There was a strong aversion to marrying anyone who lived nearby one's habitual area of occupation, the Ona men preferring to look for a spouse at some distance away from their home. The residence rule after marriage was a patrilocal one. The levirate was practiced, with a widow marrying the brother of her deceased husband and thus potentially extending her childbearing years.

Political Economy

As shown in Figure 5.3, the land occupied by the Ona and Aush was divided into thirty-eight named territories, each named for a respected headman (whether from the present or past, Gusinde does not state). For subsistence purposes, individuals and families were limited in their use of resources to the territory in which they lived. The boundaries of these territories, respected by all, were marked by large rocks, cliffs, natural mounds, watercourses, and lagoons. They remained fixed over the generations, and all persons were taught or reminded of their locations. Outsiders could not enter another group's territory without permission, violators either being openly attacked or, if not, ousted by later "vengeance assaults." Property within the territory consisted of the hunted animals found within it, and its 40 to 120 human inhabitants could hunt wherever they chose to do so. Boundaries, however, were open to any young man in search of a wife. Thus, local band exogamy could include marriage to a woman from another nearby territory. Aside from young men seeking wives, another exception to the need to honor boundaries and the animals within them was when a beached whale was discovered. No matter who had discovered it, the whale's flesh belonged to all who came to the beach, the reason being that no local group could possibly hope to exploit the whole animal before most of it rotted away.

Gusinde notes that the Ona were irritable and sensitive in their dealings with nearby groups and highly vengeful with respect to territorial rights. Warfare, or armed conflict, between the territorial groups was infrequent and small scale, involving groups of eight to forty men on each side. In addition to trespassing, the causes of war included witchcraft or sorcery by the shamans, or xon. In preparation for armed conflict, all of a local group's relatives and nearby friends in the territory were called upon. This larger group then manufactured large numbers of arrows, and stores of meat were amassed by the men to be eaten by the women and children during the period of hostilities. For battle, men colored themselves with a dry red powder, each man also painting a horizontal red line across his face and white dots on his nose and cheekbones. The men chose a headman, who wore a special fox headdress, to act as the leader during the hostilities. Following him, the raiders would take off to attack another group during the early dawn or late evening when there was little light. Once the fighting started between two groups, it was often without quarter. The combatants shot arrows at each other and engaged in hand-to-hand combat using fists and rocks. Women and children related to a lawbreaker were sometimes killed and captives were sometimes taken, but noncombatant deaths were rare and captives generally were set free, as killing and captive taking were not the purpose of war.

Gusinde stoutly denies that population control was its purpose either, since, although combatants were often killed, war did not result in significant numbers of deaths. But considering the data on territoriality, resource rights, and illegal entry as a cause of war, we may plausibly suggest that local territorial populations were pushing against the long-term, sustainable carrying capacity of their environments and that this was the reason for bounded territories and property rights to the resources within them. War in this case would thus have been related more to the exigencies of the overall adaptation, specifically at the level of infrastructure, than to some innate Ona tendency toward hostility.

Nevertheless, Gusinde describes Ona warfare as being fueled by "blood revenge" as well. In other words, Group A would attack Group B, not because someone from B had entered illegally into A's territory, but because Group B warriors recently had killed someone from A who entered B's territory to hunt without permission. Thus, to be truly ecological in light of the theory presented in this book, we must look at *cause* in terms both of (1) blood revenge at the political level and (2) populations that guarded their resources because their numbers were close to, or pushing against, the optimum levels that could be sustained by the hunted animals in their territory.

In any case, the Ona regulated their politics not only through war but through ritualized peacemaking as well. To end strife, both sides would agree to a meeting place where the two groups faced each other at roughly 150 meters apart. Then they would start approaching each other, making speeches, as first one side and then the other shot arrows at their (soon-to-be) former adversaries. To keep the arrows from penetrating the skin deeply, however, the barbed heads were removed and replaced by hide. After this a few days of "friendly" interaction would occur between the parties and their families, and all would then return home. In addition to war and peace, regulation of conflict between individuals at the local level occurred in the form of wrestling and arrow duels, neither one of which usually ever resulted in injury or death to the combatants.

Ritual and Leadership

Among both the P'ámica and the Hámška there were bewitching and curing shamans, called *xon*, who exercised considerable magical power and regulatory control over the populace. These men were in control of life and death, health and disease, good and bad weather, and war, not to mention the finding of beached whales to scavenge, so they were greatly respected and feared. In their role as bewitchers, the *xon* employed small darts called *kwáke*—considered to be small living objects—which they flung like an arrow shot from a bow either at nearby enemies or at the other main Ona group. As with many other lowland South American people who have such darts, the *kwáke* would enter the body and eventually sicken and kill the victim. The mission of the *xon* in their role as curers was therefore to find the offending object, coax it to the surface of the skin, suck it out, and, holding it up to the mouth with the hands, blow it to a safe point far away from anyone.

All the Ona had a soul, called a *kášpi*, but a shaman had three different aspects to this soul, called *wáiyuwen, há'hmen,* and *tšánem*, respectively. The first of these he sent out to do battle with the souls of other shamans. The second had a slightly more complicated but equally strategic, mission in war: Looking like an innocuous guanaco (or a soul in guanaco garb), it was sent out to gather intelligence about the whereabouts and battle plans of a hostile group. After the return of the *há'hmen*, the shaman went into a trance and upon awakening would advise the men about going out to raid depending on whether he thought they would win (the *xon*, according to Gusinde's Ona informants, were never wrong, and if the men did not heed the *xon*'s warnings about an impending loss, they usually were slain in battle). The third soul, the *tšánem*, was another manifestation of a *xon*'s power to kill: It took the form of a wisp of smoke that could not be distinguished from a normal one, and, once it got inside a person's body, that person was doomed to die irrespective of any curing *xon*'s efforts (a belief that would certainly provide him with a convenient excuse in the event of a family's ire at his patient's untimely demise).

Recall Gusinde's data indicating that each Ona family needed a large area of approximately 100 square kilometers—or an area of roughly 10 × 10 kilometers—to provide it with enough guanacos and cururos to survive. Perhaps one way the separation between the groups was maintained (I am speculating here), aside from actual warfare or the threat thereof, was the danger of getting too close to a group with a shaman inclined to fling darts around at nearby enemy intruders. Clearly the threat of such magical danger would have been effective in maintaining adequate distances among the various families. The magical powers of the *xon* and people's belief in them would thus have been caused by the very real infrastructural problem of maintaining optimally sized populations in each territory.

The *klóketen*, the men's initiation rite into adult male ceremonial life, was the other important ritual sustainer and regulator of Ona life. In the north it was carried out during the summer when hunting was better, whereas in the south it was carried out during the winter for the same reason. Various families would participate from throughout the P'ámica or the Hámška area, but there was little mixing between the two principal geographic groups. Gusinde witnessed a *klóketen* that was held in a particular clearing in the southern woods that met the standards of the proper place to hold one. To be suitable, the clearing had to have higher ground along one edge, where the Great Hut (Figure 5.5b, d) of the *klóketen* rite was placed. The Great Hut, or *hain*, had to be roughly two hundred steps away so that the huts of the women and children in the woods to the south were close enough to permit them to view the *klóketen* but not so close that the secret aspects of the ritual could be observed.

The Great Hut itself was larger and sturdier than a normal dwelling hut, measuring about 8 meters in diameter by 6 meters high. The structure was held up by seven posts, each one representing one of the seven men of the mythical past who had built the first *klóketen* hut. The candidates (Figure 5.5a) were prepared for their initiation ordeal by their mothers, who scrubbed them clean, smeared red earth mixed with guanaco fat all over them, and painted three wide white lines down their faces. A masked man, called a *so'orte* (Figure 5.5c), then came out of the *hain* to place hoods over the boys' heads so that they could not see, and he led them back to it. Once inside, several *so'ortes* grabbed the nude boys' genitals, yanking on them painfully for a period lasting some thirty minutes. Once this unpleasant ordeal was completed, the boys' hoods were removed and the *so'ortes* took their masks off as well, at which point the initiates became aware that their tormentors were not the bad spirits they had thought them to be but were none other than their own flesh and blood.

Then the initiates were told the origin myth about the relations between the sexes: In the beginning the women ran the men's lives and told them what to do.

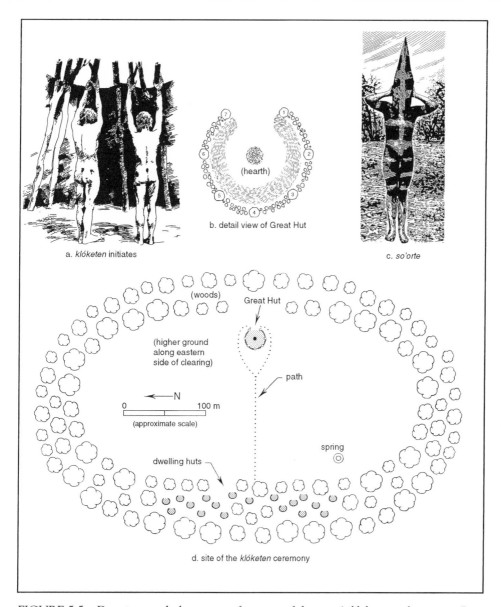

a. *klóketen* initiates

b. detail view of Great Hut

(hearth)

c. *so'orte*

(woods)   Great Hut

(higher ground
along eastern
side of clearing)

path

N

0   100 m

(approximate scale)

spring

dwelling huts

d. site of the *klóketen* ceremony

FIGURE 5.5   Drawings and plan views of aspects of the men's *klóketen* puberty rite. Redrawn and adapted from figures in Gusinde (1990).

The men stayed home to care for the children, maintain the hearths, and work the hides. Nevertheless, the men were stronger and the women knew this, so the women got together and created a secret society to maintain control over them. They constructed a *hain* at some distance from the dwellings and held their meetings there. Neither the men nor the prepubescent children could enter the *hain*. The women's days were spent in camp bossing their husbands around, whereas at night all the women slept in the *hain*. Even at this time, however, the men hunted the guanaco. One day Man-Sun (Kran), the best guanaco hunter of all, happened upon two young girls who were laughing about how the women always were dressing up as spirits and scaring the men, who naïvely thought they were real spirits. Man-Sun went back and told the men about this deceit, whereupon they rose up and killed all the women except for a few of the youngest girls. After that only the men could witness the *klóketen* rites and administer them. Once the initiates had heard the origin myth and the ceremony was complete, each initiate was taken out to spend time alone for several days in a remote part of the woods to toughen him up for the rigors of hunting and the dangers of warfare.

Ideology (USPs)

We have, of course, already touched on many aspects of ideology and the ultimate sacred postulates of Ona society, including the *klóketen* rite. Clearly, although this was an egalitarian society—that is, with more or less equal rights and respect shared by the men and women—there was inequality both in shamanism and the *klóketen*, since only the men could be shamans and only the men could participate in the secret ceremonial life of the Ona. Ideologically balancing out the actual domination of men, we may speculate, was the myth that women were once in control. Whatever the case, the origins of gender inequality may well have had to do with the fact that the men were overwhelmingly the primary providers of food. Moreover, with populations in each territory at their optimum size, the men were also the maintainers through war of local ecosystemic integrity in keeping intruders out.

We have also encountered Man-Sun, or Kran, who was a hero to the men in the *klóketen* myth because he had wrested control of ceremonial life away from the women. His female counterpart was Woman-Moon, who hated humans and killed children, especially if they looked at her. Further suggesting mythical support for the domination of the women by the men, the spots on the Moon were viewed as healed scars from the wounds caused by a fiery stick that Man-Sun had used to hit her. Every day Man-Sun chased Moon-Woman across the sky, and her phases were seen as a continual attempt to hide from him.

Two other spirits are of relevance here: Tšaskels, a giant who killed children and pregnant women, cutting away the skin of the women's pubic area to wear it as a trophy; and the *yoši*, who were male spirits with huge sexual appetites who took women off into the woods. In general, then, we see that in myth and ritual the Ona downplayed the importance of the female part of existence in favor of the male. In contrast, the Yahgan system was quite different in this regard, and it will come as no surprise that this was probably a function of a very different subsistence system characterized by an equally distinctive division of labor.

A Summary Model

The data on the Ona adaptive system discussed in the preceding sections are summarized in the systems-hierarchical model shown in Figure 5.6. This model is presented for some, rather than all, of the more than twenty cases discussed in

127

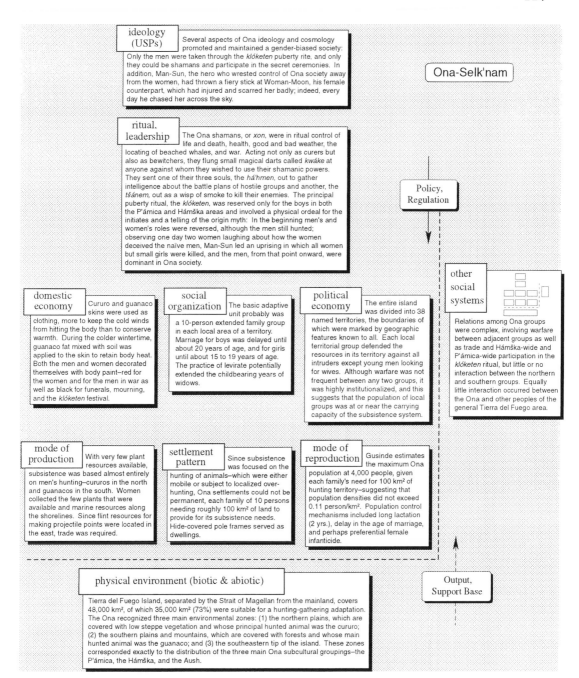

FIGURE 5.6 Systems-hierarchical model summarizing the principal features of the Ona-Selk'nam adaptive system. Based on textual data in Gusinde (1990).

Chapters 5 through 9—because showing a model for every case may be too much of a good thing. In addition, there are no "causal" arrows shown on the model because a few minutes' perusal of the figure should make obvious the systemic relationships among the ten variables, although it is worth pausing to consider the probable chain of cause and effect running between the (sub)system formed by the environment and subsistence, on the one hand, and the nature of gender relations as exemplified in the superstructure, on the other. Note also how the data at three different levels in the model—including methods of population control (mode of reproduction), warfare (political economy), and the shamanic use of magical darts and soul power (ritual and leadership)—must all be invoked in understanding/explaining how the Ona maintained and regulated their adaptive system—including, most importantly, their numbers in relation to the carrying capacity of their subsistence-environmental context.

Gusinde's Yahgan-Yámana Data

Physical Environment

The extreme southern tip of the continent is an archipelago (Figure 5.7) characterized by tortuous channels, a jumble of small islands, rough seas, chilling rains, dense fogs, and a climate governed by cold winds and frigid currents from Antarctica. Measuring 380 kilometers from east to west and an average of 75 kilometers north to south, the archipelago is separated from Tierra del Fuego Island (where the Ona lived) by high mountains along the northern edge of the Beagle Channel and from the western Chilean archipelago (where the Alacaluf lived) by extremely rough seas to the west of the Brecknock Peninsula. Two main environmental zones are present: the drier east, which is similar to the pampas of the continent and the main island to the north; and the rainier west, which is covered with stunted beech forests. With dense forests and rugged terrain on most of the islands, especially in the west, there was little place for the construction of huts except along the beaches. In the west as well, glacier-covered mountains line the Beagle Channel and chunks of ice that have broken off the glaciers lie scattered across the surface of the water.

In December, the warmest month, temperatures reach about 8°C, although in June, the coldest month, temperatures do not go much below 2°C. Thus, with temperatures staying within a fairly narrow range year-round, there is little seasonality in the Fuegian archipelago. Gusinde notes that in such an environment snow can occur in "summer" and warm days can occur in "winter." Rains in the west range between 300 and 400 centimeters per year, and a continual misty rain can occur here for days on end. The sun, not surprisingly, rarely peeks out from the clouds. For example, the members of one expedition, in June 1883, counted twenty-eight hours of sunlight in an entire month, or three full days of sunlight out of a total of thirty. Worse yet, there is substantial unpredictability of rainfall from year to year in that severe droughts can occur during some years (especially in the eastern zone), whereas during other years snow and cold temperatures of-

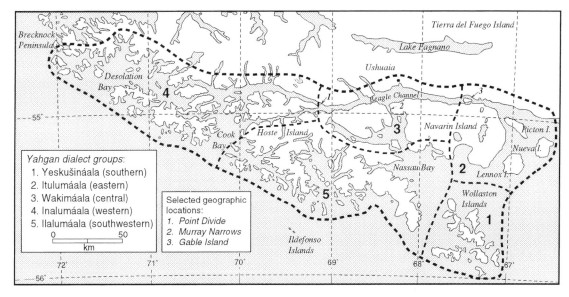

FIGURE 5.7   The five dialect (and geographic) districts of the territory recognized by the Yahgan-Yámana. Based on detailed textual description in Gusinde (1990).

ten last too long for even a short growing season. In sum, it can be said that, compared to more northern areas of the continent, the climate of the archipelago is relatively unfavorable at best.

Beech woods dominate the impoverished flora of the area, and at this far southern latitude the treeline lies at a very low elevation of 200–300 meters above sea level. In general, the terrestrial part of the archipelago is also poor in faunal species, although a variety of marine animals is present—including shellfish, crustaceans, otters, seals, elephant seals, sea lions, and at least five species of whales. Guanacos are present on Navarin Island, in the northeastern part of the archipelago, but they were few in number and therefore less important to the Yahgan living here than they were to the Ona to the north.

Mode of Production

Gusinde notes that the Yahgan were hunter-gatherers more than they were fisherfolk. They hunted sea mammals and birds along the shoreline, gathered shellfish and crustaceans, and scavenged the occasional whale that washed up onto the beaches. Indeed, only rarely did they penetrate the inland areas of the myriad islands of the archipelago. Even along the shorelines, however, there was little predictability in finding a food resource at any specific place, and families had to ply the coastline for some distances in their search for food. It is impossible, then, to discuss subsistence without mentioning that the Yahgan were canoe people, first and foremost, oriented toward the exploitation of marine resources found in the marine waters near the shoreline or on the immediately adjacent beaches.

The canoes were constructed of three long pieces of bark stripped from Antarctic beeches found well inland from the beaches. Gusinde describes them as being well made and graceful in appearance (see Figure 5.8), although they were small, relatively unwieldy, and fragile craft. Nevertheless, the Fuegians were able to paddle them across the rough open ocean to the Ildefonso Islands 50 kilometers to the south of the Hoste Island area, which is a testimony to the seaworthiness of the canoes and the skill of the paddlers. Although the man alone constructed the canoe, it was considered the sole property of his wife, who protected and cared for it. Moreover, she alone paddled it and was the sole decisionmaker as to the techniques used to propel it and the specifics of the course taken. The whole family traveled in the canoe—the woman sitting with her possessions in the back, the children in the middle, and her husband with his weapons in the prow.

As shown in Figure 5.8e, the tools used in subsistence included a variety of harpoons employed for different animals and conditions. For example, the large harpoon had a 20-meter cord attached to it and was used to hunt seals and elephant seals. Single-point spears were used for the land hunting of seals or for the killing of a beached whale, whereas multiple-point spears were used for lobsters and shellfish. The bow and arrow was an important weapon for all of the Yahgan, not just in the east where some guanaco hunting went on. Although the Yahgan made their own bows and arrows, in the east the Ona were often the source of these weapons through trade. The best source of the chert and quartz used for projectile points (Figure 5.8f) was found in the Cape Horn area, and these materials were traded for throughout the archipelago. Like the Ona, in bird hunting the Yahgan employed the sling (Figure 5.8d), which could fling a rock some 80 meters but was only roughly accurate at its optimum killing distance of 12 meters. However, the most indispensable tool, aside from the canoe, was the hafted shell scraper (Figure 5.8b), which was used by men and women alike in their respective tasks of butchering animals, debarking trees, working wood, and cutting skins.

Just as the women and men worked together to carry out subsistence efforts in the canoes, so did each gender play an equally important role in actual food getting. The men hunted the larger game, while, in addition to rowing the canoes, the women gathered mussels, sea urchins, and crabs and fished. In this last case, several women usually fished the same spot together, using baskets (Figure 5.8c) to gather smaller fish from the water and dump them into the canoe. The women and children also gathered bird eggs and mushrooms, of which a variety of sweet-tasting types were present. Among the foods the Yahgan would not eat were foxes and otters (both of which were hunted for pelts), cranes and owls (the meat was "too lean"), rats, bats, and any predatory birds that eat carrion—never mind that the Yahgan themselves ate carrion in the case of dead whales discovered on the beach. Indeed, Gusinde notes that sometimes they suffered terrible food poisoning from this practice, dying from the toxins created by the putrefaction of the whale meat.

Live whales occasionally were hunted, the men using harpoons and the women paddling the canoes in flotillas of as many as twenty families. But given the fragility of the bark canoes, this was a dangerous activity. Whales that had

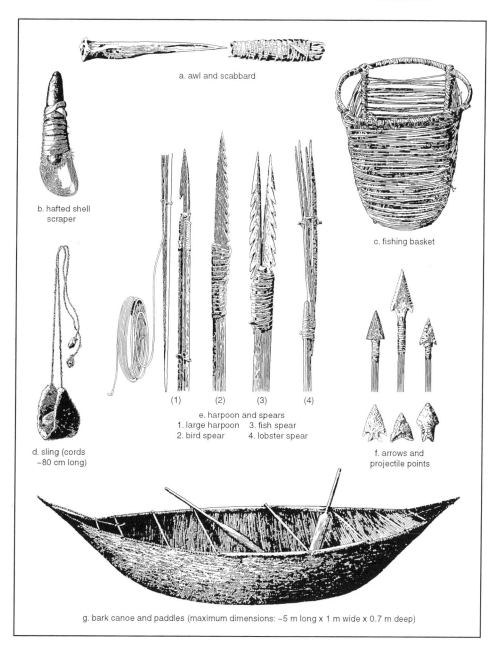

a. awl and scabbard

b. hafted shell scraper

c. fishing basket

d. sling (cords ~80 cm long)

(1)   (2)   (3)   (4)

e. harpoon and spears
1. large harpoon   3. fish spear
2. bird spear   4. lobster spear

f. arrows and projectile points

g. bark canoe and paddles (maximum dimensions: ~5 m long x 1 m wide x 0.7 m deep)

FIGURE 5.8   Drawings of various features of Yahgan-Yámana material culture. Redrawn and adapted from figures in Gusinde (1986).

not been sufficiently weakened could flail about, destroying the canoes and killing their occupants. As a result, whales usually were killed only after they had become beached or were scavenged after they had been dead for a time. The first person to touch such a whale "owned" it, but all of its parts were shared in an organized way with whomever came along. Every part of the whale to be thus consumed had a name, with fully twenty-two names used to describe everything from the tail to the lips. For example, the lips, which were considered an especially tasty treat, were called *kauwa*.

Settlement Pattern

Given the differences in climate between the western and eastern zones of the archipelago, distinct types of dwelling huts were found in the two zones. In the east conical huts were built of loosely piled logs and were purposefully left drafty so that the fierce winds would not blow them down and the smoke from the hearth could escape before asphyxiating the inhabitants. In the west domed huts were built of tightly positioned logs and branches, more snugly constructed to keep out the incessant rains and to permit the hearth fire to dry the humid air in the interior of the hut. But in both the east and the west huts were used at most for a week or two before the inhabitants moved on to search for food in another area. Multiple huts for various families were constructed only when girls' and boys' initiation rites were held, when a whale was found beached, or when a *yékamuš*, or shaman, prophesied a rigorous winter. Otherwise, the size of settlements was no larger than the one hut needed for the basic adaptive unit, a single nuclear family.

Mode of Reproduction

Prior to the years of Gusinde's research, estimates of the Yahgan population had varied between two thousand and three thousand persons, usually based on counts made in a small area and then extrapolated to the overall archipelago. In contrast, Gusinde arrived at his estimate via a different procedure: based on the length of coastline needed by each family's canoe (a figure he does not give us) and the entire length of the Fuegian coastline (not given either), he estimated that there was a total of 450 canoes in the archipelago. Assuming six persons per canoeing family (as was the case in 1918–1920), his total population estimate for the Yahgan was twenty-seven hundred persons, a figure that accords closely with the estimate of twenty-five hundred that he reports was made by Bridges in 1870.

Whereas the Ona were among the tallest of indigenous South Americans, the Yahgan were among the shortest—the men in a small sample taken by Gusinde measuring 160 centimeters (versus 173 centimeters for the Ona men) and the women measuring 145 centimeters (versus 160 centimeters for the Ona women). It is no wonder that the Yahgan men considered the Ona women to be giants and would not think of ever marrying them, nor would the Ona women "stoop so low" as to marry a Yahgan man. The differences in stature, although based on inadequate sample size, do square well with the other data indicating that almost no contact occurred between the two geographically contiguous groups.

Like the Ona, the Yahgan breast-fed their babies for a long period, or at least until the end of the child's second year. As for other possible means of regulating population, by the time Gusinde came to the area there were fewer than 100

Yahgan left, and thus he heard nothing about the practice of infanticide. But the Bridges family (see Bridges 1950) did find that this practice was occurring in the 1880s, noting that it was carried out in cases of deformed infants, desertion by a husband, and on the youngest daughter if all the previous children were daughters. In 1884 Bridges noted that of 1,000 Yahgan, the number of adult males was 277 and the number of adult females was 316 (reported in Gusinde 1986). Equivalent to a low sex ratio of 88 (SR = 277 ÷ 316 × 100), these numbers certainly contradict any argument that preferential female infanticide was being practiced at that time (see the Shuar-Jívaro, discussed in Chapter 6, who also have a similarly low sex ratio). By the decade prior to Gusinde's arrival, the Yahgan were having seven to ten children per family, although there was a "terrible" infant mortality at the time. For example, of the eleven children born to one family, only two had survived.

Whatever the case, Gusinde notes that overall Yahgan population densities were low and probably always had been so, since the environment and their subsistence adaptation would not permit any higher numbers of people. We may thus hypothesize that over the hundreds and thousands of years of their presence in the archipelago the Yahgan must have had to practice one or another form of population regulation. But Gusinde notes as well that children between the ages of two and ten years old were especially at risk in this difficult setting. In light of this, prior to the arrival of the European diseases in pre-Contact times high infant mortality may have been a major factor in the regulation of population numbers. In other words, the rigorous environment itself may have been regulatory in keeping Yahgan numbers adjusted to the carrying capacity of the subsistence-settlement system.

Domestic Economy

The Yahgan produced fire by striking extremely hard rock, usually flint, against iron pyrite (pre-Contact times) or a thick iron nail (post-Contact times). The sparks were aimed against soft tinder consisting of dry moss. The two rocks themselves (flint and iron pyrite) were considered to be a married couple: *wa*/flint (harder) was male, and *kipa*/pyrite (softer) was female. But given the humid environment and the difficulty of drying tinder and keeping it dry, fire was extremely problematic for the men to make. Instead, the Yahgan preferred to keep the hearth fires going permanently—either in the protected environment of the hut or on the rocks and sand placed for that purpose in the bottom of the canoe.

As for clothing, the Yahgan went essentially nude throughout their lives, although both men and women wore a pubic covering and some men wore a short cape made of sea lion skin. The only real gender distinction, other than anatomy, was in hair style—the men generally cutting their hair shorter than the women. Most Yahgan plastered themselves all over with fish oil, however, which helped against the cold and moisture. In fact, Gusinde notes that among the most difficult things he had to do was spend any amount of time at all inside the huts, since they usually reeked of rotten fish oil. Like the Ona, three colors of body paint were used: black (from charcoal), white (from lime rock whose source was the north middle shore of Navarin Island and thus had to be traded), and red (from ochre, which was plentiful in the west and was therefore traded in to eastern groups).

Social Organization

The nuclear family was the basis of social life. Marriage usually was monogamous, and there was basic gender equality, especially because of the equal importance of men's and women's subsistence contribution. Local groups of families were loosely linked by blood, so people searched for mates well outside this local grouping. As noted earlier, both the man and the woman worked together in subsistence, and neither a single man nor a single woman alone could do all that was needed to survive. Every person therefore was expected to marry, since it was the economic basis for survival. For this reason also, the sororate was practiced: It was a man's obligation to bring his sister-in-law to his hut when she was widowed lest she perish (one presumes that she could survive for a time if her children were older but as yet unmarried).

At menarche girls faces were painted in the recognition that they would soon marry (Figure 5.9), and at marriage both the man's and the woman's faces were painted with three parallel lines placed across the face below the eyes. These were worn for about a week, with the paint being renewed each morning. When a man was getting set to marry, he gave gifts to the woman's father (harpoons, skins, flint, or a new canoe) as a courtesy and expression of gratitude. Although Gusinde says that bride price did not exist, he notes that the woman's father seemed to expect something in return for giving up a daughter. This obviously indicates that unmarried girls were valued for their role in maintaining family life through their subsistence efforts in helping their mothers. After the marriage feast was held, either the man or the woman (usually the woman) would move to the hut of the spouse's parents in the camp. At the end of the week-long marriage ceremony and the departure of the invited guests, the new couple would then get into a canoe and go off to establish a life.

Political Economy

Just as the Ona were divided into bounded territorial units, the Yahgan were divided into what Gusinde calls five distinct "dialect" groups, which resulted in part from natural geographic divisions that cut across the Fuegian archipelago and in part from social divisions (see Figure 5.7). Environment played the primary role in creating these divisions, however, and there was far less sociocultural interaction among the dialect groups than among the local groups living within each dialect group. For example, the seas between the Wollaston Islands, where the Yeskušináala group lived, and the other Yahgan groups to the north and west were so rough that canoes could make it between them only one or two days per year! And as is often the case when there is little contact between

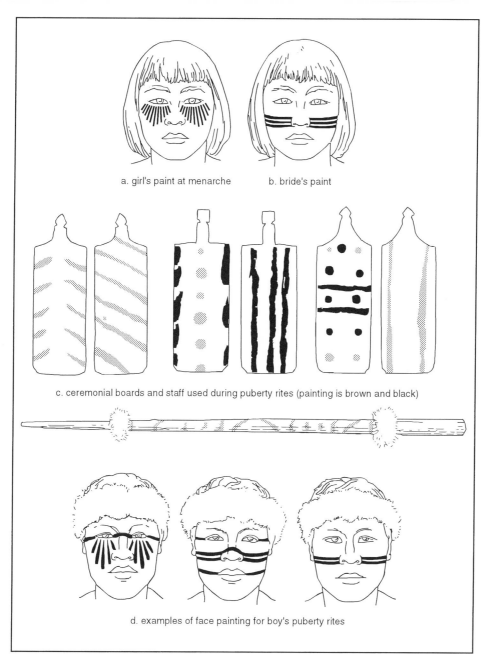

a. girl's paint at menarche   b. bride's paint

c. ceremonial boards and staff used during puberty rites (painting is brown and black)

d. examples of face painting for boy's puberty rites

FIGURE 5.9   Drawings of body painting and other art connected with the Yahgan-Yámana rites of passage. Redrawn and adapted from figures in Gusinde (1986).

groups, the Yeskušináala were seen as most dangerous and savage by the people of the other four groups. The Yeskušináala were indeed infamous for killing any outsiders, Yahgan or European, who were shipwrecked on or near their shores. There also were social reasons for the divisions between the central group, the

Wakimáala, and those to the east and west, which were seen as tainted by their occasional association with the Ona and the Alacaluf, respectively.

Moreover, the people of each geographic/dialect group knew exactly where the frontiers lay that separated their subsistence area from that of their neighbors. And although strangers from one side of a boundary could enter the other group's territory temporarily—as when a beached whale was found—anyone entering without permission for longer periods of time was considered an intruder. Within each of the five areas people could go wherever they wished, although the land/seascape was further divided, on the basis of the numerous bays and inlets, into local areas consisting of groups of families that considered themselves kindreds. These local areas, according to Bridges (1950), were called *ucur*, which meant "dwelling place" of any kind as well as "kinfolk."

Since the population was even more highly dispersed than that of the Ona, Gusinde notes that fights were infrequent. But the Yahgan had a highly developed sense of honor, which could cause conflict even at the most local level, and a keen sense of the boundedness of their five main territorial groupings, which could bring about conflict at a more general level. Interneighbor feuds based on honor were the most common, however, both between the men and between the women, who, according to Gusinde, fought each other like "wildcats." If someone from one local group killed a person from another group, then on occasion a flotilla of canoes from the group of the murdered person would converge on the other group. The two groups would meet in lines of canoes, with the women paddling and the men hitting each other with harpoons, lances, and sticks. If the avenging group got its hands on the murderer, he would be gravely wounded or killed outright.

Ritual and Leadership

The puberty rite, called *tšiéxaus*, was aimed at fostering in children all the precepts of the ideal Yahgan person, and Gusinde tells us that both sexes were required to go through the rite. In light of the equal roles played by men and women in subsistence, it comes as no surprise that both boys and girls were formally initiated into adulthood. The causal connection between participation in subsistence and rites of passage would perhaps not be so compelling if not for the contrasting data we have for the Ona, where, as we have seen, women were not integral participants in the primary subsistence quest and were not initiated into adulthood by any formal means. As noted earlier in this book, it was just this sort of cross-cultural comparison that Steward saw as the real strength of anthropology. It follows, then, that latter-day, infrastructurally oriented (Stewardian) cultural ecologists such as Robert Netting, who remove ritual from their consideration of cause and function in human adaptive systems, have little to tell us about the systemic intricacies of the Yahgan and Ona adaptations.

Interestingly, it takes Gusinde only some dozens of pages to describe the environment and the Yahgan subsistence system, but several hundred to describe such rituals as the *tšiéxaus*. This difference may be because he is a priest, but also because he believes that the *tšiéxaus* encapsulated all aspects of Yahgan life from the most spiritual to the most basic. It was only through an understanding of its details, he says, that an outsider could appreciate the humanity and ideological sophistication of a people whose daily life and physical appearance made them seem so savagely base. The occasion for holding a *tšiéxaus,* which required a gathering of many families, most often was afforded by the finding of a beached whale. Some fifty to eighty people (eight to ten families) would converge on the spot, usually the inner part of some bay at the edge of a cliff or deep woods so as to be hidden from any outside eyes. As with the Ona a Great Hut was built, although it appears to have been located at much less distance away from the dwelling huts. The interior was decorated with painted wooden tablets that measured about 20–45 centimeters long and 7–10 centimeters wide (Figure 5.9c). According to Gusinde, the painted decorations on the tablets were precisely that, *decorations,* in that no cosmological meaning of any kind was attached to the designs.

During the *tšiéxaus* several women would care for the smaller children, who were the only members of a group from whom the secrets of the initiation ritual were kept. Both the boys' and the girls' faces were painted (Figure 5.9a, d). At the start of the ceremonies the adult women and men filed into the Great Hut, seating themselves in a certain order and maintaining silence. With a leather skin thrown over the heads of the initiates, they were tied up and pushed forcibly into the Great Hut by people designated as "helpers." Once the adolescents were inside, the adults seated around the edge began to shout and moan, scaring the initiates a great deal. A man dressed as Yetáita, a bad spirit, then appeared to leap out of the fire at them, the boys being roughly handled and shaken, but not the girls.

Following this, as in the case of the Ona *klóketen,* the initiates were told all the teachings and myths of the Yahgan. Both the boys and girls were admonished to be obedient to tradition; to not be negligent or lazy or gluttonous; to respect their elders and not to interrupt them when they were speaking. The major themes were personal honor, self-control, altruism, and stoicism. Girls were told never to fight with their husband, to get up early, to be happy with each child, to be kind to visitors, and to be quiet if their husband had an affair with another woman. Boys were told to be good hunters, to share with all, to never kill anyone, to not torture animals, and to get up with the sun. Both boys and girls were then taken on practice subsistence forays to test their skill and mettle at all the necessary tasks they would have to carry out as adults. The *tšiéxaus* lasted until the initiates had learned their lessons or until the whale meat ran out, whichever came first.

So far I have described a society in which both genders apparently participated equally at all critical levels of the adaptive system, from subsistence to ritual. It is with the *kina* ritual, however, that some of these ideals of gender equality end. This ritual, a secret ceremony, was a further initiation of young men into Yahgan myth. A Great Hut was constructed, and inside, during the ritual, the young men were told the Yahgan origin myth: The women were once in control of Yahgan society. They built the canoes, and the men owned them; they sat in the prow, and the men sat in the back and paddled; the women had relative freedom, and the men took care of the children. In sex the women did not lie beneath the men, and in general the women dominated the men. Then the stronger men, realizing things were not right, for them at least, rose up and killed most of the women; the rest were turned into animals. Thus, the *kina* was an arrogant reminder of the men's feeling of superiority and of their domination and control. Tempering this male chauvinism, however, a few women were invited to the Great Hut of the *kina*, something that never occurred in the case of the Ona *klóketen*.

Yahgan shamans were called *yékamuš*, and like the Ona *xon*, they employed darts or little magical living objects called *yékuš* that were invisible to the shaman's adversaries and injured, weakened, and killed them. If a *yékamuš* did not throw the dart sufficiently far and it fell to the ground before hitting an adversary, then the shaman was considered weak. Whatever the case, it is hard to imagine that with plenty of dart-throwing shamans around, anyone would want to live too close to them. The ultimate effect of such practices and beliefs would have been the maintenance of population dispersal, and thus, as with the Ona shamans, the *yékamuš* were clearly a potent magical force in regulating the basic adaptation. However, unlike the Ona, where all the shamans were men, some Yahgan women were shamans. As curers, of course, the shamans attempted to suck out the offending *yékuš* darts that had made a person ill and, holding them up to the palm, blow them far out of harm's way.

Ideology (USPs)

The Yahgan recognized four seasons (although I argued earlier that it is hard to see much seasonality in an environment with such a narrow range of temperature throughout the year). They also recognized eight divisions of the year (e.g., *hakuérum*, "when bark is loose"; *éma*, "first bird's eggs"; *hánisluš*, "purple beech leaves"; *staiyákin*, "first snow"; and *lëmkúmëtši*, "sun goes to west," or the shortest day of the year). In astronomy, they viewed dense star groups as being "stands of beech trees" and recognized the Milky Way, solar halos, the phases of the moon, and the constellations Rigel and Betelgeuse (the latter probably more recognizable to most youths of the late twentieth century as a Michael Keaton movie). The Yahgan terms for the four cardinal directions were *ilu* or *ila*, for south; *itu* or *ita*, for east; *inga*, for north; and *inu*, for west (these roots are at the beginning of the names of several of the dialect groups in Figure 5.7). Like the Ona, the Yahgan believed in a supreme being (Temaukel, for the Ona; Watauineiwa, for the Yahgan).

THE NUKAK

The Nukak, who speak a language of Makú origin, are one of the last remaining indigenous groups of South America to enter into contact with Western society. One of the probable reasons they have survived far longer than the Ona and the

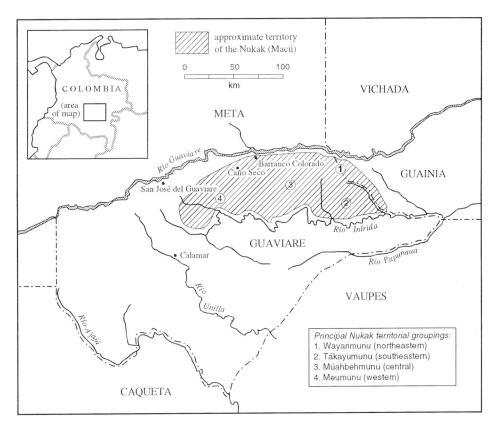

FIGURE 5.10   Map showing the location of the Nukak bands of the rain forest of east-central Colombia. Redrawn and adapted from figures and textual descriptions in Politis and Rodríguez (1994).

Yahgan is that they live in what was, until not many decades ago, a remote part of the northwestern Amazon Basin (Figure 5.10). Although undoubtedly affected by a brief intrusion from the outside world during the rubber boom of the early twentieth century, they lived a traditional hunting-fishing-gathering way of life, which probably has lasted for centuries, until the 1980s. This is not to say, however, that they were unaffected by the introduction of European diseases to this area of the northwest Amazon much prior to the 1980s. In addition, under the influence of recent *colonos*, or pioneering Colombian farmers, some of the Nukak have begun to adopt horticulture and South American cultivars into a way of life that nevertheless remains focused on hunting and gathering. In recent years representatives of the New Tribes Mission, a Florida-based missionary group, have established several base camps in the Nukak area and have begun making contacts that include the provision of medical treatment, the trading of traditional goods for metal items such as pots and machetes, and the studying of the Nukak language and culture.

The first significant contact by anthropologists occurred in 1990 when Gustavo Politis, an Argentinian, and his colleagues began a study of several Nukak bands, spending a number of weeks on several occasions traveling with them during the rainy season (and later during the dry season) as the Nukak carried out their daily lives and subsistence activities. During the fourth visit a young Spanish-speaking Nukak man named Monicaro helped them in the translation of Nukak to Spanish, so it appears likely that at least some of the earlier data from this project are more from visual observations than from detailed conversations by researchers fluent in Nukak. Nevertheless, Politis and his colleagues (Politis and Rodríguez 1994; Politis 1995) have already provided much valuable data on such aspects of Nukak culture as worldview and cosmology, in addition to a wealth of information on subsistence and settlement.

Politis's Nukak Data

Physical Environment

The extent of the area the Nukak occupy is not yet known with certainty, but it is estimated as measuring about 175 kilometers east-west by about 60 kilometers north-south, or encompassing some 10,000 square kilometers of jungle between the Guaviare and the Inírida Rivers (Figure 5.10). The climate is a rain-forest one, with temperatures averaging ~26°C and annual rainfall ranging between 2,500 and 3,000 millimeters. During the short dry season, which occurs in January and February, the rainfall drops to a relatively "scant" 50 millimeters per month, as opposed to the peak rainfall of 400 millimeters per month that occurs during the height of the rainy season between June and August.

Mode of Production

Nukak subsistence is based on the hunting and collecting of a variety of animal and plant species as well as on other wild resources, such as honey. Among the frequently hunted animals are five species of monkey as well as the white-lipped peccary, the land tortoise (*Testudo* spp.), and birds. Among the animals less frequently encountered are agoutis, caimans, armadillos, and collared peccaries. Of all these species, only monkeys and peccaries are found in groups that consist of a number of individual animals. Insect foods include the larva of the genus *Rynchophorus palmatarum*, or palm grub (mojojoy, in Nukak). A variety of useful plant species is found here as well, many with scientific and indigenous names that are unknown, except to botanists, in the outside world. These species include plants that are used as sources of *barbasco* (*Lonchocarpus* sp.), the fish poison, and *curare* (*Abuta* sp.), the poison used on blowgun darts to stun monkeys and other small game; several types of palms; and many fruit-bearing trees, such as *Iryanthera* sp. (corópanat, in Nukak).

During the fieldwork carried out by Politis and his colleagues, monkeys were hunted two out of every three days by small groups of men and older boys. Instead of walking through jungle thickets as they hunt, these groups generally use well-established paths as they search for troops of monkeys to kill. Three to four monkeys may be brought back to camp from a single hunt, at which point the task of preparing and cooking them falls to the women. From each hearth the cooked meat is distributed among the other families, except for the heads of the monkeys, which are kept by the family of the hunter. When herds of white-lipped peccaries are found, usually in swampy areas where they go to eat, hunting them is a communal task. All of the men and some of the women go out and surround the herd, the men throwing lances to kill as many animals as they can. Although Politis does not mention what the women do on such hunts, they probably do not help in bringing the meat back to camp, since he notes that the flesh of the peccary is taboo for them. In fact, even smelling the meat of this animal is considered disgusting to the women.

All the men, women, and children engage in the collection of wild plant species and a small number of what Politis terms *manipulated* plants. Although their diet is overwhelmingly based on the exploitation of wild plant and animal species, the Nukak cultivate these manipulated plants in two types of small *chacras,* or gardens: one in which recently acquired cultivars such as manioc, sugarcane, banana, chili pepper, and papaya are grown; and the other, in use probably for some centuries, in which a select group of traditional plants is grown. The latter, which are very small and found at a relatively great distance from camps, are used to cultivate chontaduro palms *(Bactris gasipaes)*, achiote, and plantains. Chontaduro, for example, is likely to have been a part of Nukak subsistence for a long time given its incorporation into origin myths. Other indications of the importance of these gardens is that the dead are buried here and interband rituals (called *bakuán*) are carried out here as well.

In the Nukak case we thus have a band-level society that, although migratory, has traditionally practiced a small amount of horticulture, which constitutes, according to charts provided by Politis, 13 percent or less of the diet. In carrying out basically wild food–focused subsistence efforts, the Nukak have engaged in behavior that has changed their environment into a human-made one—making it more favorable for the proliferation of certain useful wild species than for others. In constructing a campsite, the Nukak disturb the ground, leaving the seeds from plants they have collected and consumed in the disturbed soil. Since the area cleared for a campsite is not large enough (it ranges between 30 and 120 square meters) to disturb the canopy formed by the larger trees, the natural processes of secondary succession do not occur. Thus, the plants whose seeds are left as garbage thrive.

Over the years, with the construction of more and more campsites, the Nukak have created a jungle environment that is more an artifact of human occupation and less the pristine environment that would exist had humans never come here. We may thus have an example of what the transitional stage was like between essentially no cultivation at all and the early, more intensive horticultural experimentation that Donald Lathrap (1977) refers to in discussing house gardens as experimental jungle plots (see Chapter 4).

Settlement Pattern

In spite of the practice of some horticulture, the central feature of the Nukak adaptation is high mobility. During the rainy season, an average of five to six days is spent at a campsite, whereas during the dry season the average number of days is three. Camps are never occupied for more than twenty days. Moves between camps range between 1 and 20 kilometers, with an average travel distance of 4.5 kilometers. During each move the Nukak must carry all of their material items, including hammocks and steel pots, which are carried by the women; and blowguns, lances, and machetes, which are carried by the men, who hunt as the trek from one camp to the next is carried out. Politis argues that two principal factors govern the strategy of high mobility: first, the need to avoid overusing the resources in the area around a campsite; and second, a sophisticated policy of managing and using resources over a far wider area than that around a single campsite. Other factors play a role as well, however—including the death of someone, the accumulation of garbage and fecal material, and the need to engage in encounters with other bands to exchange information, carry out joint rituals, and meet future marriage partners.

I have already mentioned that the size of camps is small, generally consisting of two to six dwellings (see Figure 5.11). As the Nukak arrive at a new campsite, it is the men's task to begin the construction of the dwellings. First, they clean out the underbrush, leaving intact the larger trees, to which they attach a system of posts and beams. After this, the hammocks are slung from tree branches and posts in each dwelling. During the rainy season banana leaves are used to construct a roof over the family's dwelling area, keeping it and the hearth fire protected from the heavy rainfall. As shown in the figure, dwellings in rainy season camps are conjoined, all facing out into a small open space, which is used for various daily tasks and children's play.

Mode of Reproduction

Estimates by New Tribes missionaries of the total Nukak population range between seven hundred and one thousand people, which would suggest densities of about one person per 10 square kilometers, or 0.1 person per square kilometer. The Ona population density (based on an estimate of thirty-five hundred persons occupying 35,000 square kilometers) was the same. According to Politis, the number of people in each band ranges generally between ten and thirty persons, each family consisting of five or fewer persons, including occasional widows and orphans. Overall, in the bands studied by the anthropologists there were five adult males for every six adult females, which is equivalent to a sex ratio of ~83. This, as we have seen in the case of the Yahgan (SR = 88), appears to rule out preferential female infanticide as a means of population control. However, Politis and his colleagues provide no other data from which we could infer possible societal or environmental mechanisms of population regulation.

143

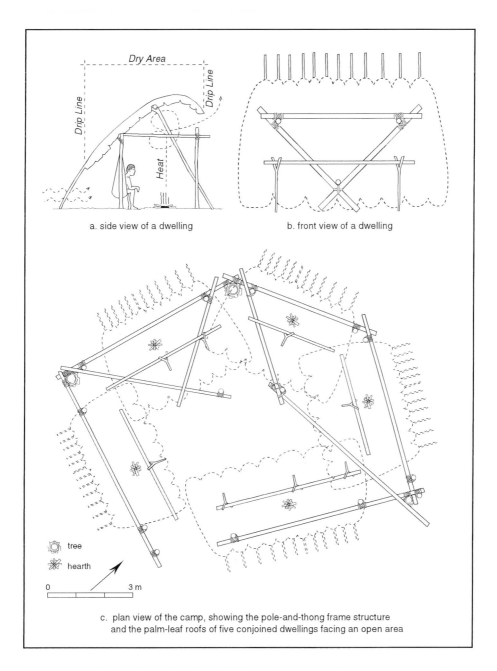

a. side view of a dwelling

b. front view of a dwelling

tree

hearth

0   3 m

c. plan view of the camp, showing the pole-and-thong frame structure
and the palm-leaf roofs of five conjoined dwellings facing an open area

FIGURE 5.11   Drawings depicting Nukak architecture and campsite construction
during the rainy season. Redrawn and adapted from figures in Politis and Rodríguez
(1994).

Domestic Economy

Two features of interest to note here are the Nukak practices of depilation and of body and face painting. Depilation is common, with the men, women, and children periodically removing all facial hair, including the eyebrows, with a particularly sticky resin. Both the men and the women also cut the hair on their heads very short, and both sexes use the red dye from the achiote plant to paint different geometric designs on their faces and bodies. Occasionally a resin is also smeared over these painted lines so that delicate little white feathers can be attached. It is also noteworthy that Nukak faces very rarely express displeasure or anger. They are a people who, as described by Politis and as seen in the stunning photographs of his book *Mundo de los Nukak* seem to exhibit continual happiness and an immense tranquillity.

Social Organization

Group size and composition are flexible, as intimated earlier, as the people from one band leave to join another and marriages occur. The fundamental unit, however, is a small group of ten to thirty people, organized in two to five families with close ties of kinship, that lives together over the longer term. Couples in general are monogamous, although Politis notes that one in five males has two wives. Marriage is exogamous to the local band unit and tends to be matrilocal, with the men going through a period during which they must demonstrate to their wife's group that they are competent providers of food. Patrilocal marriages also occur, so there is no single hard-and-fast residence rule.

Political Economy

Nukak bands tend to join with other nearby bands into larger, affiliated territorial groups in the context of which most, if not all, interband social interaction occurs—including marriage, rituals, and changes in each band's composition. As indicated on the map in Figure 5.10, these endogamous regional territorial groups are named and include the Wayarimunu, the Tákayumunu, the Múahbehmunu, and the Meumunu. (The placement of these groups on the map in Figure 5.10 is based on Politis's textual description. Note also the *-munu* suffix, probably meaning "people," attached to the name of each group, just as one finds the *-áala* suffix at the end of the five Yahgan geographic/dialect groups, as shown in Figure 5.7.)

As in the case of the Ona and the Yahgan of Tierra del Fuego, the fact that they name their territorial groups suggests that the Nukak view their world in terms of three geographic/social levels of inclusiveness: (1) the area habitually used by each band, (2) the named territorial area, and (3) the entire area they occupy in relation, or in contrast, to other indigenous peoples of this part of eastern Colombia. Politis notes that two other groups have been identified by another researcher, so if we assume that a total of six territorial groups exists here, then each territory extends over an area of some 1,600 square kilometers and includes an average maximum population of about 160 persons organized in eight to ten separate bands (as compared to the Ona case, where an average of one hundred persons lived in a named territory covering 1,300 square kilometers).

Not all of the Nukak spend their entire lives in each of these territories. On occasion groups of four or five men travel to a place in the eastern part of Nukak territory known as the Hill of the Blowguns (Cerro de las Cerbatanas). There they obtain cane for making blowguns, bringing the raw material back not only for themselves but also for their relatives. In addition, a band occasionally moves across territorial boundaries when it is displaced by tensions occurring between it and neighboring bands. It thus appears that the boundaries between territories are rather more flexible than were those of the Ona and the Yahgan.

Ritual and Leadership

Although Politis mentions Nukak ritual in passing, he does not give any specific details about it, nor does he say anything about the nature of leadership. Since Nukak band groups are multifamily—in contrast to the Ona and Yahgan case, where nuclear families formed the basic day-to-day adaptive unit—we may presume that some sort of informal ad hoc group leadership exists. It is possible, then, that a particularly astute hunter might lead such activities as peccary hunting and that an equally astute woman will lead groups of women who are engaged in collecting. This is speculation, however, and it may easily be the case that decisions are made through discussion among all of the adults and the achievement of pangroup consensus.

Ideology (USPs)

According to Politis, there are several animals for which there are specific gender-related taboos against eating and several whose flesh no one may consume. I have already mentioned that women may not eat the flesh of the peccary. They also may not eat caiman flesh, which does them harm, or the flesh of ducks, since it makes them skinny. No Nukak man or woman will eat the flesh of the tree sloth (*Bradypus* sp.), and any reader who has seen one will probably know why. Also, no one may eat deer, tapir, or jaguar flesh. The taboo related to these three animals has to do with the Nukak belief that in their bodies live the spirits of the dead who have gone to the lower world. These spirits go out at night in the forest looking for food and wearing the skins of deer, tapirs, and jaguars. Indeed, all taboo animals are nocturnal, and the nighttime is dominated by the spirits of the dead as well as by a class of spirits called *nemep*—never mind that, in spite of this belief, the Nukak hunt a certain species of small monkey at night.

As shown in Figure 5.12 (which is my graphic version based on Politis's textual description), the Nukak conceive of the world in three levels: a lower world, this world, and the upper world. The lower world is isolated from the earth. Living in it are other Nukak and animals, such as the tapir and the deer, each species hav-

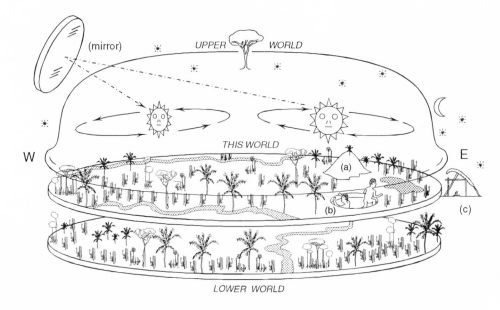

a. Cerro de las Cerbatanas (Blowgun Hill)
b. origin of the Nukak from the lower world via
a hole in the earth layer
c. camp in the east where the sun, moon, and
stars live and from which the sun rises

FIGURE 5.12   Model of the principal features of Nukak cosmology. Based on textual description in Politis (1995).

ing its own campsites and dwellings. From this lower world came the original Nukak, the ancestors of those now in this world, via a hole dug by a primeval woman with long fingernails, who, living up in this world and having heard a clamor, dug the hole to see what was going on down below. After the original inhabitants had climbed up out of the hole onto the earth, bringing the chontaduro palm up with them in baskets, the waters of a river or a flood covered up the hole. Those who could not get up to the earth layer in time had to stay below, living there forever. Those who had escaped through the hole in the earth saved themselves from the flood by climbing up the slopes of Cerro de las Cerbatanas.

The Nukak visualize the sky as being like a flat-bottomed plate with curving sides that is inverted over the earth, touching the earth plane at the edges of the horizon. Each morning, the sun, which is metaphorically seen as a Nukak person, goes out from its home in the east to distribute food, traveling just below the sky plane. Once it reaches the center of the sky at midday, however, it goes back to its home in the east. Thus, after midday what one sees in the western sky is not the actual sun at all; rather, it is the sun's reflection in a giant mirror (I have used artistic license in the figure) as it is returning to its home in the east. Near the road to the sky in the east is a campsite, just beyond a lake and very near the hole where the Nukak climbed up to this world, from which one can climb up to the sky world. Living there in the eastern camp are the sun itself, the moon, and some of the larger stars.

Every Nukak has three souls, each of which has a different destination when a person dies. The principal soul goes to the upper world, where the spirits of the ancestors dwell, and lives there forever in a place somewhat different from the earth layer. In the center of this sky world there is a single tree where birds and monkeys live. The second soul, like the souls of the largest trees in the forest, goes to live in the House of the Tapir (in the lower world?—Politis does not indicate its location), coming out only at night to eat fruits from the trees. This is the soul that uses the skins of the sacred animals for its nocturnal wanderings, and it can be very dangerous to the living. The fact that the spirits of dead humans use these skins means that the deer, tapir, and the jaguar are equivalent to humans. The third soul, or *nemep* (Politis does not give us the names of the other two souls), stays in the jungle of this world, living in various places, including the holes of tree trunks. A malign spirit of little intelligence, it looks like a large, clumsy monkey with enormous feet and comes out at night to look for food and to bother the Nukak. When one of these spirits is seen, people construct a fence of palm stalks and leaves around the campsite to protect themselves.

As Politis notes, the number three appears to have special significance for the Nukak in structuring their cosmology: the cosmos has three levels, each person has three souls, there are three major sacred animals, and each of these animals has three souls as well. In an apparent jab at the dyadic structuralism of Claude Lévi-Strauss, Politis suggests that the triadic emphasis in Nukak cosmology indicates the Nukak universe does not operate as a function of binary oppositions. Instead, the Nukak conceive of it in terms of a fundamental set of tripartite divisions that permit them to understand nature, live in their jungle world, and imagine a life after death.

THE PALEOINDIAN PERIOD

The preceding discussion of three of the recent South American band-level groups makes clear that these groups, in spite of their relatively limited and noncomplex material cultures, are anything but limited and noncomplex when it comes to the less tangible but equally critical behavioral and ideological features of their adaptations. As we have seen, among the latter are their intimate knowledge of their environment and how to use and maintain its resources, their creation of specific behaviors that maintain and regulate their adaptations (e.g., population controls, local-group exogamy in marriage, territorial boundaries, war, shamanistic magic, and rites of passage), and, finally, their development of sophisticated cosmologies that provide the overarching meaning and guidance to help them in various ways, from the practical to the abstract, to carry out their lives. Since we have found this to be true even for the Fuegian band societies—who lived in the harshest, most limiting, and challenging environment anywhere on the continent—we may safely assume that it is also true for every other recent band society across the continent.

The question then becomes whether we can assume such adaptive complexity even for the earliest period of human occupation in South America, the Paleoindian Period (~13,000–10,000 B.P.). Bluntly put, the position I take here is that indeed we can, especially given the evidence we have from several key Paleoindian archaeological sites and their distribution in a rather wide variety of paleoenvironments. In fact, the geographic variability of Paleoindian site locations alone suggests that, even over the shorter term of, say, just a few centuries, the earliest inhabitants were highly adaptable as they moved from north to south down the continent. That is, they were fully able to penetrate new kinds of environments and deal with the resources found there as they moved southward. This is evidenced not only by the variability among the environments where Paleoindian sites are found, but also by the material culture found at those sites (e.g., lithic industries). Following the tenets of the systems model outlined in Chapter 2, we thus may postulate that most, if not all, of the sophisticated behaviors already mentioned for recent bands were also characteristic of the earliest indigenous South Americans, either from the very start of their arrival or a few centuries thereafter.

The Paleoenvironment

Climate and Vegetation

Prior to the finding of sites of acceptable antiquity—that is, dating between about 13,000 and 10,000 B.P.—in the tropical and subtropical lowlands of South America to the east of the Andes, the most parsimonious model (e.g., see Lynch 1983) of the earliest human occupation of the continent was as follows: The Paleoindians of the southern continent, like their contemporaries in North America, were specialized hunters of the late Pleistocene megafauna and other gregarious animal species that inhabited grassy, open environments. Assuming that a barrier of tropical rain forest, to which it was presumed Paleoindians were not well adapted, lay all across the equatorial lowlands of the northwestern part of the continent, this model postulated that the easier—if not the only logical— route for them to take during the initial peopling of South America was down the Andes Mountains. Here, high open environments populated by herd animals would have been present in a nearly unbroken 5,500-kilometer chain from the Isthmus of Panama to Tierra del Fuego.

Several comments can be made on this model. First, studies of the late Pleistocene paleoclimate (see Whitmore and Prance 1987) show that the climate and vegetation zones of the Andean chain—which, as we have seen in Chapter 3 are related to elevation, latitude, and rainfall patterns affected by east-west position in the chain—were "compressed" during the period of advancing glaciers prior to 10,000 B.P. That is, the snowline was lower, and the warmer humid *páramo* environments of the north and the colder and drier *puna* environments to the south extended down to lower elevations. This compression presumably means that *páramo* and *puna* environments were at least as plentiful during the period between 13,000 and 10,000 B.P., if not more extensive and continuous than now. So the Andes did present an attractive environment for hunter-gatherers at this time.

Second, it is now clear that the vast tropical rain forests of the northeastern lowlands experienced episodes of substantial contraction and discontinuity as global temperatures fell, rainfall patterns changed, and drier conditions ensued in northeastern South America. Put another way, forests that today are essentially continuous, but not totally so, became in the late Pleistocene much smaller in extent as so-called refugia, or isolates composed of rain-forest flora and related fauna, separated by extensive open areas formed. At the same time, the appearance—however temporary in the long term—of open, grassy areas in the tropical northeast could have provided conditions favorable for some species of gregarious animals and the related type of human hunting adaptation outlined previously. Anyone "requiring" such conditions in the northeastern lowlands for their arguments about the initial peopling of South America obviously would be adhering to a model that argues a priori for specialized hunting Paleoindian groups rather than for the less specialized and much more adaptable groups I argue for in the introduction to this section.

Third, whether or not future research turns up Paleoindian sites in what were once grassy, open areas in the now heavily rain-forested northeast, the need for postulating open environments for such sites in the Amazon has become a moot point with the recent finding of Caverna da Pedra Pintada site. This site is located in what has always been gallery rain forest along the Amazon River, at least since humans first appear to have arrived on the South American continent. Furthermore, Monte Verde site—located neither in an open, grassy environment nor in a tropical rain forest, but in temperate, seasonally rainy forests just to the north of the Chilean archipelago—suggests that even greater variability was characteristic of Paleoindian adaptive systems.

Flora and Fauna

Judging from our knowledge of the diets of band groups in most, if not all, temperate, subtropical, and tropical environments of the continent, at least some Paleoindian diets in these areas probably included a substantial percentage of plant foods as well as the flesh of hunted animals. Unfortunately, with the significant exception of Monte Verde site, where conditions of preservation are excellent, plant remains generally have been entirely lacking or been problematic in the archaeological deposits dating between 13,000 and 10,000 B.P. Complicating matters further, as we have seen in the discussion of the Ona, Yahgan, and Nukak diets (the first being focused on guanaco or cururo, the second on shellfish and marine animals, and the third more evenly balanced between animal and plant foods), there is also substantial variability from environment to environment, and from group to group, in the percentages of these two kinds of foods. From this we may conclude that the nature of ancient and recent band diets in a given environment is much more a question of empirical data from appropriate recent

FIGURE 5.13   Late Pleistocene mammals hunted by Paleoindian bands
in South America. Redrawn and adapted from Lynch (1983).

groups or archaeological sites in that environment than it is one of extrapolation
from sites in other areas.

In any event, with the cautionary note in mind that plant foods could be and
probably were a part of many Paleoindian diets, let us briefly take a look at some
of the hunted (or possibly hunted) fauna that appear in archaeological contexts
around the continent. As shown in Figure 5.13, they include (1) the smaller paleolama and the larger camel, ancestral forms of later Andean camelids including
the guanaco and the vicuña (and their domesticated forms, the llama and the alpaca); (2) hippidium, the Pleistocene horse of the Americas; (3) mylodon, the
large ground sloth; (4) capybara; (5) toxodon, a large hippolike creature; (6)
megatherium, the giant sloth whose standing height was well over that of any
human hunter; (7) glyptodon, a giant armored creature related to the much
smaller armadillos of today; and (8) arctotherium, a form of Pleistocene bear.

By about 10,000 B.P. all of these forms had become extinct, with the exception
of the camelids and the capybara, which evolved into the descendant forms of
today. One hunted animal not shown in Figure 5.13 is the mastodon, the large
Pleistocene elephant that went extinct at about the same time. Judging from the

faunal remains at Paleoindian sites, elephants were hunted widely in South America, from Taima-Taima to Monte Verde; horses were hunted nearly everywhere in the Andes, with the apparent exception of Monte Verde; and camelids, not to mention deer (not shown), were hunted as well. The other species may have been hunted, since their remains frequently are found in archaeological contexts in cave sites, but the data are less good given the lack of convincing evidence of either butchering marks or unquestionable, direct association with human occupational features (e.g., hearths, dwellings).

Some of these creatures would have been formidable opponents for human hunters—or they look that way, at least, to us urbanites of the late twentieth century. In discussing whether animals such as the mastodon and the megatherium could be brought down by spear-wielding human hunters, I always take pains to point out the rite of passage to adulthood that until recently was customary among the BaMbuti hunter-gatherers of the Ituri rain forest, Africa. A young hunter smeared himself with elephant dung to hide his human odor, and with only a fire-hardened spear in hand, he waited in the bushes beside a trail until an elephant came along. When it did, he quickly jabbed the spear hard into the belly of the animal and then ran like Hades to get away from the wounded and terrified beast. Usually he would have to follow it for some distance before it finally died, but alone and relatively tiny against such an intelligent and dangerous adversary, he had succeeded in killing it to provide meat for his band. The ground and giant sloths, at least, were relatively more small-brained and slower than the elephant, and we know from the archaeological data that mastodons were hunted. We can thus probably assume that indigenous South Americans, descendants of the people to the north who had hunted large animals, were equally capable of such a feat with any of the larger animals shown in Figure 5.13, including megatherium.

Key Paleoindian Sites

Fell's Cave

This is not only the first site of Paleoindian date that was found in South America; it is also a testament to Junius Bird's (1988) scientific care in excavating it—Fell's Cave remains one of the hardy few whose data have survived the critical scrutiny of archaeologists over several generations to become hallmarks of the period. Junius and Peggy Bird first excavated Fell's Cave (Figure 5.14) and nearby Palli Aike in 1936–1937, a scant decade before the development of radiocarbon dating. Returning to both sites in 1969–1970, Junius Bird obtained samples for dating from various stratigraphic levels that placed the earliest occupation of Fell's Cave, or Period I, between 11,000 and 10,000 B.P., with subsequent levels representing a nearly unbroken sequence of human occupation that includes the most recent inhabitants of the area, the Ona and the Alacaluf.

Located in rolling hills composed of lava, conglomerate, and sandstone and covered by xeric grassland (under 200 millimeters mean annual rainfall), both

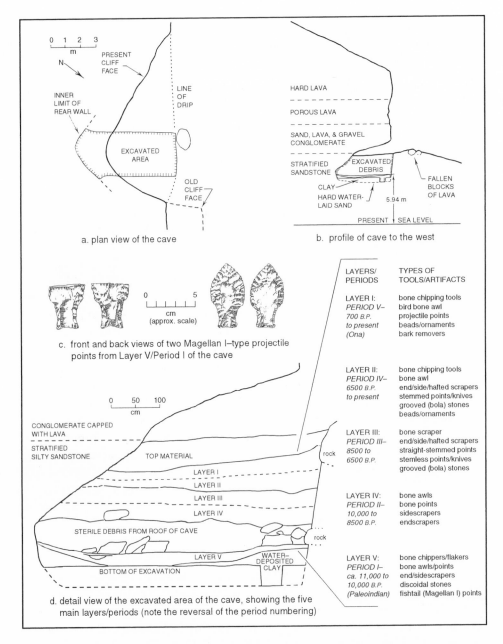

a. plan view of the cave

b. profile of cave to the west

c. front and back views of two Magellan I–type projectile points from Layer V/Period I of the cave

d. detail view of the excavated area of the cave, showing the five main layers/periods (note the reversal of the period numbering)

LAYERS/ PERIODS	TYPES OF TOOLS/ARTIFACTS
LAYER I: PERIOD V– 700 B.P. to present (Ona)	bone chipping tools bird bone awl projectile points beads/ornaments bark removers
LAYER II: PERIOD IV– 6500 B.P. to present	bone chipping tools bone awl end/side/hafted scrapers stemmed points/knives grooved (bola) stones beads/ornaments
LAYER III: PERIOD III– 8500 to 6500 B.P.	bone scraper end/side/hafted scrapers straight-stemmed points stemless points/knives grooved (bola) stones
LAYER IV: PERIOD II– 10,000 to 8500 B.P.	bone awls bone points sidescrapers endscrapers
LAYER V: PERIOD I– ca. 11,000 to 10,000 B.P. (Paleoindian)	bone chippers/flakers bone awls/points end/sidescrapers discoidal stones fishtail (Magellan I) points

FIGURE 5.14   Profile and plan views of Junius Bird's excavations at Fell's Cave. Redrawn and adapted from various figures in Bird (1988) and Willey (1971).

sites have witnessed significant environmental change over the past eleven thousand years. Beginning with Period I, mesic grassland (under 400 millimeters annual rainfall) began to give way to the xeric grassland of today as temperatures rose and rainfall decreased. As this occurred, there was a substantial reduction in the extent of grasslands in this area of southern Patagonia, and grazing animals hunted by the people camping here were correspondingly affected as well. Ground sloths and horses died out, and even the guanaco, which had survived the climatic change of the late Pleistocene, was present in much reduced numbers (Bird 1988). Around 8500 B.P. precipitation increased to modern levels of just above 200 millimeters per year, and both humans and guanacos became established in numbers that would continue nearly up to the present day.

Measuring about 8.5 meters deep and 11 meters wide, Fell's Cave lies in cliffs that are located along the Río Chico overlooking a small lake (Figure 5.14a, b). In spite of the changes in climate, the environment in Period I would have been treeless and windswept, much as it is now. Occupying the cave only temporarily at any one time, judging from the relative scarcity of midden debris, its inhabitants hunted the ground sloth and the native American horse, leaving barbless fishtail points (Figure 5.14c) and other stone and bone artifacts in the debris dating to this period. Cremation burial probably was practiced, since burned human bones were found by Bird. Four hearths containing the burned bones of horse, sloth, and guanaco were uncovered in the excavations as well. By Period II the horse and the sloth had disappeared from the record, and the cave's inhabitants appear to have begun to rely primarily on smaller game, including birds, foxes, and the occasional guanaco. Above this layer the bones of birds and foxes decrease in numbers, while those of the guanaco increase.

At the same time as the environment changed from Period I to Period II, fishtail points were replaced by bone points (Figure 5.14d). These points, in turn, were replaced by stemless points in Period III. Indeed, in viewing the published photographs of the stone and bone tool types characteristic of the various periods (Bird 1988), one is struck by the fact that a great deal of cultural evolutionary change occurs here over some eleven thousand years of occupation, right up to the artifacts characteristic of recent indigenous groups of the area (Bird calls them "Ona," although the cave sites are located in what was Alacaluf territory). Yet in spite of all the change in material culture, we are still dealing with migratory guanaco hunters throughout the sequence; in other words, the more things changed here, the more they stayed the same. To recall the argument stated in Chapter 2, Tierra del Fuego is thus an area representing the most stable of South American adaptive systems, or those that represent maximum homeostatic equilibrium.

Monte Verde Site

This site, which lies in temperate forests at the northern edge of the Chilean archipelago some 1,300 kilometers to the north of Fell's Cave, was discovered in 1976 by Tom Dillehay (1984, 1987) and Chilean colleagues of his while they were surveying the area. Monte Verde is located at the edge of a small watercourse called Chinchihuapi Creek, where, soon after the site was abandoned a little less than thirteen thousand years ago, a bog formed. Over the immense period of time since then, the bog has preserved a most astonishing assemblage of wooden structures and artifacts as well as a wealth of subsistence debris that includes the remains of several dozen plant species collected or traded in by the site's inhabitants from thirteen different nearby ecological zones and points as far away as the Pacific Ocean, lying over 30 kilometers away to the west (Figure 5.15a).

Dillehay estimates that over several seasons he and his colleagues excavated roughly four-fifths of the site, which ranges in depth from 5 to 15 centimeters. Ultimately they uncovered the well-preserved log foundations of a settlement consisting of ten to twelve conjoined dwellings (Figure 5.15c). Judging from the stubs of upright poles with fragments of attached hide found in the ground beside the dwellings, Dillehay suggests that they consisted of pole-frame structures that were draped with animal skins. Scattered about the interiors of most of the structures were twelve small hearths, or braziers; two larger hearths lay just outside the structures adjacent to the creek. Also found inside the dwellings were stone tools, grinding stones, carbon, several rough wooden mortars, and plant remains that include seeds, nuts, fruits, and berries.

Stone tools (Figure 5.15b) were found on the site, but the absence of much flaking debris suggests to the excavators that the production of lithic artifacts was not as important as other industries. Nevertheless, a variety of techniques of stone tool production and the use of widely scattered quarry sources both indicate some complexity in this aspect of the subsistence adaptation. Lithic tool types include (1) bifacially and unifacially flaked tools; (2) pecked-ground tools, such as two probable bola stones (Figure 5.15b depicts one of them); and (3) rocks straight from the creek bed that exhibit only minimal signs of modification from their use as tools. More numerous were tools made of wood, including a probable lance, a digging stick, and three hafted stone scrapers. In addition, piles of wood logs were found, which suggests they were stored temporarily for later use in construction or in the making of artifacts. Finally, aside from stone and wood tools, several mastodon-bone tools were recovered that had been fabricated from the remains of as many as seven individual mastodons found across the site.

Downstream 23 meters to the west of the conjoined dwellings, Dillehay and his colleagues excavated the packed sand-and-gravel foundation of a separate hut that, because of the shape of its plan, they designated the "wishbone structure" (Figure 5.15d). Here, again, were found the preserved stubs of upright wooden poles, in this case spaced at about 50-centimeter intervals around the edge of the structure. These probably supported a hide-covered frame. In the debris inside the enclosure attached to the front of the structure the excavators found stone tools, braziers, pieces of well-preserved animal hide, seeds, stalks of totora reed (*Scirpus* sp.), and chewed leaves of the boldo plant (*Pemus boldus*)—a plant whose leaves are still used by local Chilean residents of the Monte Verde area to brew a medicinal tea. Around the exterior of the structure were more hearths, stone tools, wood artifacts, and mastodon bones.

Because of the site's unique preservation and age, it is perhaps inevitable that Monte Verde would receive the criticism of what one might call the "Paleoindian Police," or PIP for short, a group of variable constituency that consists of researchers who have found and excavated contenders in the category of Paleoin-

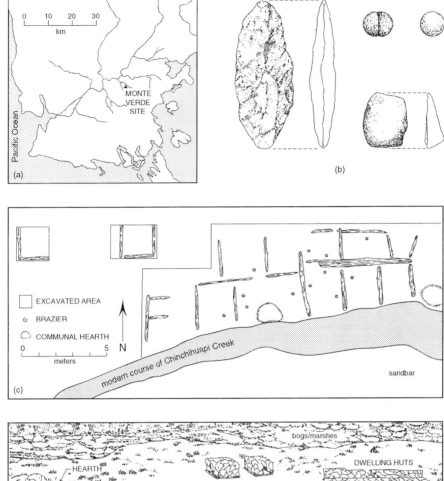

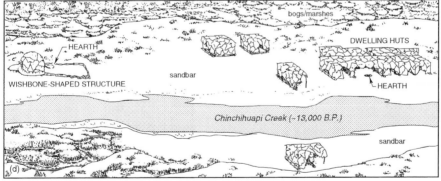

FIGURE 5.15   Monte Verde site showing (a) a location map, (b) a partial plan view, (c) a perspective reconstruction view, and (d) selected stone artifacts dating to Monte Verde V (~13,000 B.P.). Figures redrawn and adapted from Dillehay (1984).

dian Period sites and others who have not. Nevertheless, all of them make it their business to visit these sites and/or publish critiques on every aspect of their excavation, analysis, and interpretation. For example, in an article entitled "Glacial Age Man in South America?" Tom Lynch (1990) questions whether this is a human site at all. This analysis is, of course, what science is all about—in this case not accepting at face value the claims for the remarkable preservation of a band-level campsite dating back more than twelve thousand years (see also Gibbons 1997). Nevertheless, such group visits and published critiques do not, as a rule, characterize the sites of any later period in the prehistoric sequence. Perhaps this is because the earliest "this" or the earliest "that" still stirs some people's imaginations and critical faculties far more than do the later remains.

Pikimachay Cave

In light of the previous discussion, it is probably fitting that we go on to do a little PIP work ourselves, specifically with respect to the arguments made by Richard MacNeish about the earliest stratigraphic levels at Pikimachay. This site lies in a high-Andean setting 3,300 kilometers to the north of Monte Verde, at 2,750 meters above sea level in the Ayacucho Basin of southern Peru (Figure 5.1). Pikimachay (Flea Cave) and nearby Jaywamachay (Pepper Cave) were discovered and excavated by MacNeish (1971, 1992) during the Ayacucho project. In Chapter 4 I discussed the origins of agriculture in the later part of the Ayacucho sequence, from the Puente through the Cachi Phases between 9000 and 1750 B.P. Here it is the pre-Puente part of the Ayacucho sequence that interests us, specifically the data on the Paccaicasa and Ayacucho Phases from the first of these two cave sites.

Pikimachay lies a scant 13 kilometers from the modern town of Ayacucho on the eastern slopes of a hill composed of volcanic rock. The cave's mouth is about 12 meters high and 53 meters wide, with the distance from the mouth to the rear of the cave measuring a little over 24 meters—a snug site, to be sure, for a Paleoindian campsite. In 1969 and 1979 the excavators dug into the deepest level of the stratified deposits of the cave. Here, in the higher part of zone k (see Figure 5.16), several animal vertebrae and a possible ground sloth rib bone were discovered along with "four crude tools fashioned from volcanic tuff and a few flakes" struck from a green stone that is exotic to the cave (MacNeish 1971:39ff.). The tuff is not exotic, however, most probably having fallen from the roof of the cave. It is soft and crumbly, does not fracture conchoidally, and could not be used for anything other than the crudest "bashing" kinds of tasks—all in all, a most unlikely material for the production of Paleoindian stone tools, or tools of any other period for that matter. No date was obtained for this level.

In zone j, the next higher level (Figure 5.16), fragments of vertebrae and ribs of mylodon, or ground sloth, were found along with forty flakes and fourteen "stone tools," most of the former and all of the latter consisting of volcanic tuff. The Carbon-14 date obtained from one of the vertebrae is 19,600 ± 3,000 years B.P. Fossilized and burned animal bones as well as more supposed tools came from the next level up, zone i1—with one of the bones yielding a radiocarbon date of 16,050 ± 1,200 years B.P. Zone i, the highest stratum of the Paccaicasa Phase, contained yet more stone "artifacts" of volcanic tuff, more stone "flakes," and the bones of ground sloth and horse. The vast majority of the fifty tools of the Pac-

157

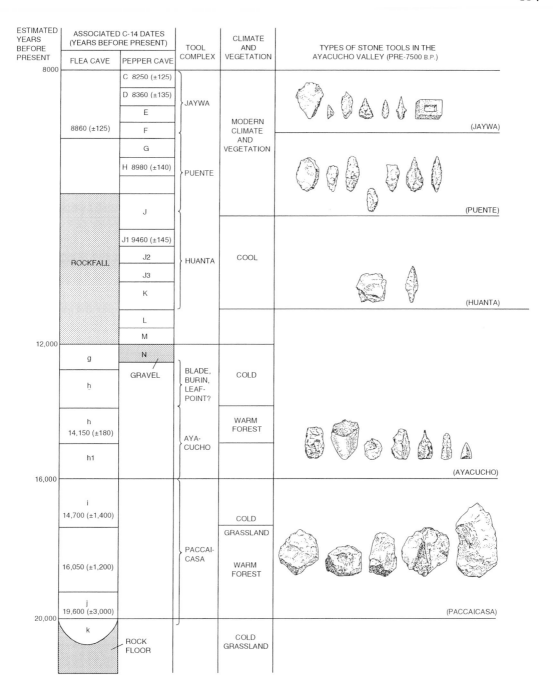

FIGURE 5.16 Chronology of the early Ayacucho sequence showing the periods and their characteristic stone tools, including the controversial "tools" dating to the Paccaicasa Period (~20,000–16,000 B.P.). Redrawn and adapted from MacNeish (1971).

caicasa complex are large and crude, most likely representing rocks that were shaped by natural processes as they fell from the cave ceiling and walls. The few remaining tools consist of rounded pebbles and fragments of basalt from outside the cave. If no human occupation occurred in the Paccaicasa stratum, however, the few possible candidates for tools may well have been brought in by later inhabitants and then displaced to lower strata by burrowing animals.

In sharp contrast to the lithic materials found in the Paccaicasa deposits, those of the Ayacucho deposits at Pikimachay (zone h1 and zone h in Figure 5.16) were made from chalcedony, chert, quartzite, and basalt—all of these being glasslike stones that fracture conchoidally and therefore that one would expect to be used in stone-tool production. Some 250 completed stone artifacts were found in zone h as well as over one thousand waste flakes. Tools were found that had been fashioned out of animal bone and deer antlers—including projectile points, punches, and fleshers. Among the animal remains were ground sloth, horse, deer, skunk, puma, and, possibly, camelids. With the date of ~13,000 B.P. at Monte Verde site, Chile, the radiocarbon date of 14,150 ± 180 years B.P. from a sloth humerus in zone h is acceptable, since earlier dates are plausible the farther north one goes— at least assuming, as most archaeologists do, that entry into North and South America was across the Beringia land bridge and from north to south.

Tibitó Site

Unfortunately for arguments that sites in the far northwest should be older than either Monte Verde or Pikimachay, the earliest C-14 date for a Paleoindian site in Colombia is 12,460 ± 160 years B.P., from unit C3 at El Abra rock shelter on the high plain of Bogotá. This does make it roughly contemporaneous with Monte Verde site. Nearby Tibitó, which dates about 700 years later, is an open air site that is similar in some respects to Monte Verde. However, since no dwellings or solid indications of plant remains were found here, it provides an idea of what a more typical, less well-preserved open air site is like (see Correal Urrego 1986).

Located immediately around the edges of a huge sandstone boulder, as shown in Figure 5.17, the site lies in a swampy flat that much earlier had been a lake bed. The partial remains of mastodon, horse, and deer were found in stratum 3A of deposit I at Tibitó, with organic materials from this stratum yielding a radiocarbon date of 11,740 ± 110 years B.P. Many of the bones of the animals are split and charred, and a few show cut marks. Other animal remains include smaller mammals such as armadillos, rabbits, and cuys. Found in direct association with the animal remains were a few stone tools, most of them of chert, that belong to the Abriense tool complex. Among the characteristics of this complex, selected examples of which are shown in Figure 5.17a, are unifacial edge retouch on cores and flakes, small size, and a rather rough and ready appearance. Abriense tools also are present in the Paleoindian levels at El Abra, the site at which they were first defined as an industry, and at Tequendama site, which lies about 25 kilometers to the southwest of El Abra and Tibitó (Figure 5.17). The earliest radiocar-

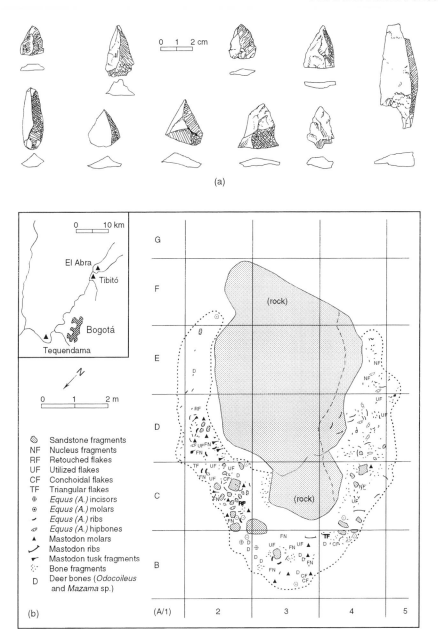

FIGURE 5.17 Selected Abriense lithic types (a) and a plan view of deposit 1 at the site of Tibitó, Colombia (b). Redrawn and adapted from figures in Correal Urrego (1986).

bon date at Tequendama is 10,920 ± 260 years B.P., placing it well within the Paleoindian occupation of the Colombian high plain and some 340 years later than Tibitó.

According to Alan Bryan (1987), Tibitó is neither a kill site (as argued by Gonzalo Correal Urrego, its excavator) nor a specialized butchering site (although most, if not all, of the remains shown in Figure 5.17b seem to indicate this). Rather, Tibitó is a habitually occupied campsite to which Paleoindian hunters and gatherers brought the remains of their kills and carried out other activities such as the processing of plant remains (no details are given on plants in either Correal Urrego 1986 or Bryan 1987). The presence of the several species of smaller animals such as guinea pigs certainly rules out Tibitó as a classic big-game kill site, unless the smaller animals were hunted or trapped nearby on the occasion of one or more mastodon kills. Also arguing against this as a kill site are the remains of several individual larger animals, suggesting many visits rather than just one or a few kill episodes. Nevertheless, the absence of hearths and dwellings suggests that it was indeed a special function site that did not involve longer-term stays during any given visit.

Taima-Taima Site

Located on the Venezuelan coastal plain some 900 kilometers to the northeast of the Colombian *altiplano* are three more sites of probable Paleoindian date: El Jobo, Muaco, and Taima-Taima (Figure 5.18d). Although dating between twelve thousand and fourteen thousand years ago, and thus roughly contemporaneous with the Colombian sites, these sites are characterized by a tool complex that is quite distinct from the Abriense complex. First defined in the 1950s by José Cruxent (see Rouse and Cruxent 1963) from surface collections made in the upper Río Pedregal valley, the El Jobo lithic complex is characterized by long, narrow bifacially flaked lanceolate projectile points as well as by other types of flake and chopper tools (Figure 5.18a, b). El Jobo projectile points were found in later excavations carried out by Cruxent and others at Muaco and Taima-Taima, both of which lie within 3 kilometers of each other about 10 kilometers to the east of the town of Coro and 70 kilometers to the northeast of El Jobo type site—so, like Abriense, the El Jobo complex is relatively widespread in its distribution.

Both Muaco and Taima-Taima are ancient water hole sites, where bones of late Pleistocene taxa such as mastodon and glyptodon are found in association with El Jobo projectile points. Unfortunately, although burned bone from Muaco has been dated between 14,000 and 16,000 B.P., various modern artifacts, including fragments of glass, were found associated with the ancient remains, probably as a result of displacement by waters of the spring here. Thus, even though the faunal assemblage from Muaco contained a mastodon bone that probably had been modified by humans, the site has not been generally accepted by the PIP. Because some of the archaeological deposits at Taima-Taima have possibly been disturbed by spring action, this site has had its critics—in spite of the fact that Cruxent found mastodon and glyptodon bones associated with El Jobo projectile points and other lithics in the basal gray sand stratum here, along with organic materials that produced fourteen radiocarbon dates ranging between 12,000 and 14,000 B.P. (Figure 5.18e).

More recently, in 1976 Cruxent joined Bryan and other archaeologists in carrying out additional excavations in the basal stratum at Taima-Taima (see Bryan et al. 1978). This time the excavations were more conclusive. Lying in the gray

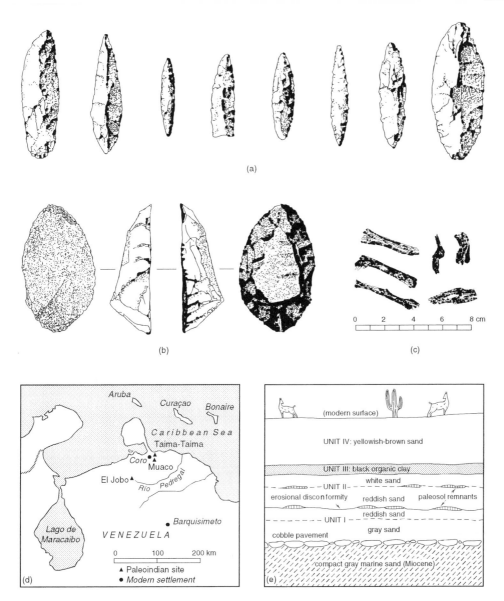

FIGURE 5.18   Selected El Jobo lithic types (a, b) and drawings from the Taima-Taima excavations, (c) sheared wood twig fragments hypothesized to be mastodon stomach contents, (d) a map showing the location of Taima-Taima and other nearby Paleoindian sites, and (e) a schematic profile of the stratigraphy. Redrawn and adapted from figures in Rouse and Cruxent (1963) and Bryan et al. (1978).

sand stratum just above a cobble pavement of Miocene age were the dismembered remains of a juvenile mastodon that exhibited several cut marks on its ribs and the left humerus. Flaked stone artifacts of El Jobo type were found in direct association with the mastodon bones, including one quartzite projectile point within 3 centimeters of the left ulna. Several rough stones, probably used in butchering the animal, were found nearby the skeleton and, in one case, jammed into the right acetabulum (hipbone socket). The nearby leg bones of an adult mastodon appear to have been used in the butchering process as well, since they had been crisscrossed everywhere with cut marks.

A "concentrated mass of small wood twig fragments," hypothesized by the excavators (Bryan et al. 1978:1277) to be the remains of masticated food from the mastodon's stomach, yielded four radiocarbon dates ranging between 12,980 ± 85 and 14,200 ± 300 years B.P. (Figure 5.18c). This suggests a minimum age of 13,000 B.P. for the Taima-Taima mastodon kill. Since the excavation of the stratigraphic levels lying above the basal gray sand unit turned up no signs of subsequent use of the site area by human groups, Bryan and his colleagues argue there is little likelihood that either the stone artifacts or the mastodon bones were moved down either by water action or by some other agent from the upper strata. Comparing El Jobo to Abriense, and by extension to other Paleoindian sites in South America, they also argue that the regional tool technologies are too different from each other to be seen as anything other than adaptations to different environments.

Caverna da Pedra Pintada

As should be clear from Chapter 3, the Amazonian rain forest is a difficult environment in which to find archaeological sites, especially early ones such as those discussed in this chapter. Flooding rivers, changing channels, and excessive rainfall all combine to damage or destroy the remains of human occupations, and the structures in these occupations usually are built entirely of organic materials that quickly rot away. In fact, from work along the Ucayali River in the upper Amazon region, Peru, Donald Lathrap (1970) once noted that almost the only material items that survive the rigors of the environment are the pottery vessels, pottery plates, and quartz and flint grater board teeth used by indigenous groups who cultivate and process bitter manioc (and not all Amazonian groups do this). Very few archaeologists have ever been attracted to this difficult environment—although Clifford Evans, Betty Meggers, Lathrap, and Anna Roosevelt, along with several Brazilian archaeologists such as Eurico Miller, have been significant exceptions to this rule.

In light of all these factors, it is little wonder that the Amazon would be left out of the picture in attempts to model the peopling of South America and the nature of Paleoindian adaptations. Although one suspects that almost anyone who ever thought about the problem would not a priori rule out a route of entry, or occupation, along either the eastern seaboard or inland in the Amazon Basin, aside from the site of Pedra Furada there has not been much hard evidence to back up such a suspicion. The recent find of Caverna da Pedra Pintada by Roosevelt and her colleagues (Roosevelt et al. 1996; see also Gibbons 1996), however, is now providing us with exactly that kind of evidence. Caverna da Pedra Pintada site is located along the north bank of the Amazon River nearly 400 kilometers up from its mouth, in 300-meter-high sandstone hills that lie near the modern town of Monte Alegre (Figure 5.19h). On the floodplain below grow

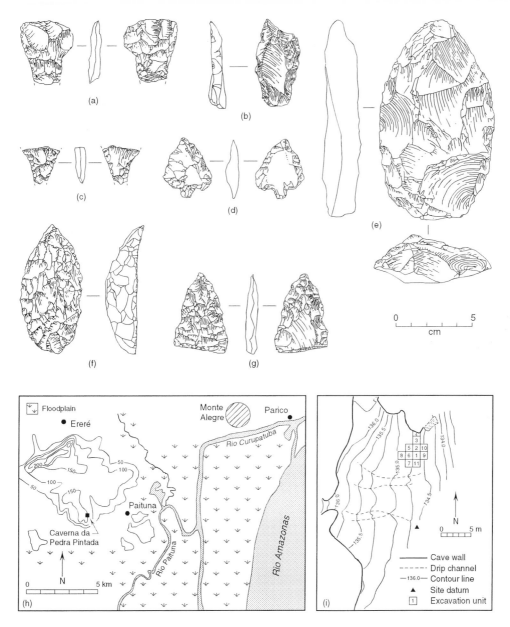

FIGURE 5.19 Paleoindian lithic artifacts from Caverna da Pedra Pintada site, Brazil (a–g); a map showing its location near the Amazon River (h); and a plan view of the main chamber (i). Redrawn and adapted from Roosevelt et al. (1996).

thick gallery forests in a humid climate that receives ~2,000 meters of rainfall annually. Many other caves and rock shelters are found in these hills, and a number of them contain rock paintings, but given the widespread opinion that such cave art would be fairly recent, no one had carried out stratigraphic excavations in the cave floor deposits. The cave itself (Figure 5.19i) lies on the southern slopes of the hills, about 130 meters above the flatter surrounding terrain and a short 3 kilometers from the *várzea*.

Focusing work in the deposits at the northern end of the cave, which auger cores had shown to consist of deep, well-preserved, and stratified midden debris, Roosevelt and her colleagues excavated eleven 1 × 1-meter squares to a maximum depth of 2.25 meters down to the bedrock lying below the floor of the cave. Some twenty archaeological strata were found, including 65 centimeters of post-Pleistocene, or recent, debris and 30 centimeters of late Pleistocene debris. The two principal strata of the Paleoindian midden contained, according to Roosevelt, four main periods of occupation judging from changes in lithic styles over time. From fifty-six carbonized plant specimens in these strata, a large suite of radiocarbon dates was obtained indicating that the first occupation of the cave occurred sometime around ~11,200 B.P. and ended some fourteen hundred years later at ~9800 B.P. (geomorphologist Vance Haynes [1997] has averaged the fourteen earliest dates out to 10,500 B.P. for the earliest occupation and thus disagrees with Roosevelt's estimate).

The lithics found in the Paleoindian strata included twenty-four complete tools and over thirty thousand waste flakes. Chalcedony, quartz crystal, and quartz breccia were used to manufacture the tools, and all are from sources outside the cave itself. Among the variety of tool types shown in Figure 5.19 are unifacial gravers (b), stemmed bifacial points with contracting stems (c), stemmed triangular bifacial points (d), endscrapers (e), limaces with graver tips (f), and fragments of bifaces (a, g). According to the excavators, a variety of techniques was used to make the tools, including heat treatment, percussion and pressure flaking, and bifacial and unifacial flaking. Most likely, the bifacial points were used either as knives or were hafted as points on spears, darts, or harpoons.

Given the faunal remains in the earlier strata, Paleoindian subsistence at the cave was focused primarily on fish from the nearby lakes, streams, and the main river; and secondarily on a variety of other aquatic and terrestrial animals, including tortoises and turtles, mussels, snakes, birds, and large land mammals weighing over 65 kilograms (these last are unidentified but are possibly ungulates). Plant remains in the Paleoindian deposits include a leguminous tree, called Jitaí, whose seeds are used today for making a sort of flour; four fruit-bearing trees, called achúa, pitomba, maruci da mata, and apiringa; three common varieties of palms, called sacurí, tucumã, and curuá; and, finally, Brazil nuts. The diet clearly was rich and varied and, unlike the Andean sites discussed earlier in this section, did not include any of the late Pleistocene megafauna.

The Paleoindian strata also contained "hundreds of lumps and drops of red paint," which indicates to the excavators that among the paintings on the walls of Caverna da Pedra Pintada are probably some that date to the period between 11,200/10,500 and 9800 B.P. Overall, then, the excavators argue for a mobile, broad-spectrum adaptation that included periodic visits to camp in the cave, paint its walls, fish and gather freshwater mollusks in the nearby streams and lakes, and hunt in the upland and lowland forests. Like Monte Verde, this site provides a wealth of data that strongly suggest Paleoindians could enter and survive in most, if not all, of the environments to be found at this early time on the South American continent.

Pedra Furada Rock Shelter

As with the preceding site, this one was discovered when the principal excava-tor, Nième Guidon, visited Pedra Furada and other nearby sites in 1973 to exam-ine the stunning prehistoric paintings done in red, yellow, black, gray, and white on their walls. Located some 1,400 kilometers to the southeast of Caverna da Pe-dra Pintada, Pedra Furada and neighboring rock shelters lie in the semiarid and faunally impoverished *caatinga* region, not a propitious environment today to support hunter-gatherers (see Figure 5.1). During the late Pleistocene, however, the pollen samples and faunal remains from several of these sites indicate that it was a lusher, more humid place that supported megatherium, horse, camel, and paleolama. Pedra Furada—whose full tongue-twisting name is Toca do Boqueirão do Sitio da Pedra Furada—is a large sandstone rock shelter that measures about 70 meters long and lies at the base of 90-meter cliffs overlooking the flatter plain of the *caatinga*.

By the end of the 1985 season, Guidon and her colleagues (Guidon 1984, 1987; Guidon and Delibrias 1986) had excavated a large area at the west end of the cave that extended about 4.6 meters down from the surface of the cave floor (Figure 5.20f, g). In the upper levels the excavators found numbers of well-made tools, including scrapers, knives, and bifaces fashioned out of materials such as flint, siltite, quartz, and quartzite. The upper strata, called Serra Talhada Phase (Figure 5.20a–e), also contained a number of well-defined living floors and hearths that were rich in ashes, charcoal, animal bone, wood, and plant remains such as fruit pits. In the original reports the excavators argued on the basis of the initial radiocarbon dates that the Serra Talhada Phase dated between 12,000 and 6000 B.P. Now, however, a suite of fourteen dates indicates that it extends from 10,400 ± 180 to 6150 ± 60 years B.P. (Meltzer, Adovasio, and Dillehay 1994). Taken in combination with the clear evidence of human occupation in the de-posits, this suggests that the initial period of Serra Talhada occupation is almost exactly coeval with that of Caverna da Pedra Pintada (if the Haynes average of 10,500 B.P. for the latter site is used).

Below a layer representing a substantial hiatus of occupation (dating between 14,000 and 10,400 B.P.) the excavators encountered what they argue is evidence for a human presence at Pedra Furada site extending between 48,000+ and 14,300 B.P. This phase they have labeled "Pedra Furada," after the site name it-self. If their arguments are correct, then this site clearly stands alone throughout the continent as a place of spectacularly early human occupation in the New World. Indeed, since there are literally no chronological antecedents anywhere to the north and northwest in South America, let alone in North America, one would probably have to argue for a transatlantic migration of these people from Africa—which is precisely what another researcher once did to get bottle gourds and early horticulture over from Africa at ~16,000 B.P. and introduced to the

166

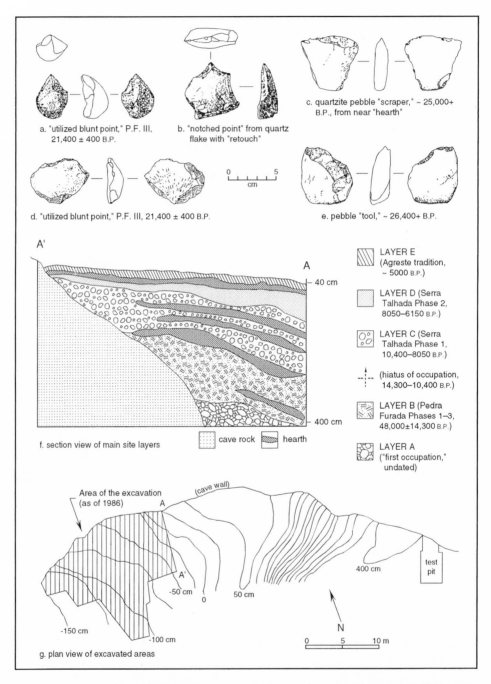

a. "utilized blunt point," P.F. III,
21,400 ± 400 B.P.

b. "notched point" from quartz
flake with "retouch"

c. quartzite pebble "scraper," ~ 25,000+
B.P., from near "hearth"

d. "utilized blunt point," P.F. III, 21,400 ± 400 B.P.

e. pebble "tool," ~ 26,400+ B.P.

0   5
cm

A'

A

— 40 cm

— 400 cm

f. section view of main site layers

cave rock   hearth

LAYER E
(Agreste tradition,
~ 5000 B.P.)

LAYER D (Serra
Talhada Phase 2,
8050–6150 B.P.)

LAYER C (Serra
Talhada Phase 1,
10,400–8050 B.P.)

(hiatus of occupation,
14,300–10,400 B.P.)

LAYER B (Pedra
Furada Phases 1–3,
48,000±14,300 B.P.)

LAYER A
("first occupation,"
undated)

Area of the excavation
(as of 1986)

(cave wall)

A

A'

-50 cm

0   50 cm

400 cm

test
pit

-150 cm

-100 cm

N

0   5   10 m

g. plan view of excavated areas

FIGURE 5.20   Lithics of reputed human manufacture dating to between ~14,300 and
48,000+ B.P. from Pedra Furada rock shelter, Brazil (a–e); a section view of the main layers at the site (f); and a plan view of the excavated areas (g). Redrawn and adapted from
figures in Guidon and Delibrias (1986) and Guidon (1984). Dates revised in accordance
with Meltzer, Adovasio, and Dillehay (1994).

"moist tropics" of the Amazon, thereby becoming the critically important progenitors of all later sociocultural evolutionary developments in South America (see Lathrap 1977).

Unfortunately the Pedra Furada phase contains dubious "hearths" and even more dubious "tools" (Figure 5.20). During a visit to the site by a large group of the PIP, it became clear at least to some of the visitors (see Meltzer et al. 1994; Meltzer 1995) that all of the 595 "tools" were suspiciously crude-looking in relation to the Serra Talhada phase materials, that the most (geologically) logical source of the quartz and quartzite materials of which they consisted was the cliff top directly above the site area, and that water action was highly likely to have been the cause of their "free fall" entry some 90 meters straight down into the cave—at which point a few bounces this way and that might well have produced modifications on the rocks that made them look like artifacts.

David Meltzer (1995) argues convincingly that over the thousands of years that the (nonhuman) Pedra Furada deposits were forming, nature surely might have produced a few tool-like geofacts (which, we may presume, were then picked out by the excavators from hundreds of other rocks that did not look like tools). In the context of some other site—such as Monte Verde or Caverna da Pedra Pintada—there would probably not be much difficulty in seeing some of the stones in Figure 5.20 as tools. Unfortunately, however, these deposits contain no other convincing evidence of a human presence, such as hearths, human bones, or animal bones with cut marks. It will take more work in better contexts (should any exist) at sites in this region to convince most archaeologists that the Paleoindian presence in South America dates any earlier than about thirteen thousand years ago.

CHAPTER 6

Amazonian Villages
and Chiefdoms

IN THIS CHAPTER WE DEAL WITH one of the most fascinating and controversial topics in the study of indigenous South American cultures, namely, the environmental constraints, evolutionary potentials, and societal regulatory features that have characterized recent and ancient adaptive systems all across the 6 million square kilometers of the vast Amazon Basin. Since the study of these indigenous systems has implications not just for theory construction and testing in anthropology but also for attempts by nation-states to "develop" the Amazon, there are few other areas in South America where ethnological and archaeological studies have such critical importance. Moreover, probably no other tropical rainforest ecosystem in the world has yielded as much ecologically related data, not to mention fruitful theorizing about those data, as has the study of the indigenous groups of Amazonia.

For example, Robert Carneiro's (1970) widely known "circumscription" theory—which attempts to account for the principal causal factors in the rise of all ancient civilizations around the world—originates in his 1950s study of the Kuikuru, an Amazonian village group located near the Kuluene River in the headwaters of the Xingú. The outline and critique carried out here of his arguments based on the Kuikuru study not only have narrower implications for the development of a reasonable perspective in understanding Amazonian adaptive systems, but also have broader implications for examining the validity of his theories about state origins in physically circumscribed environments such as that of northern coastal Peru, a subject taken up in Chapter 9.

In the overview of South American environments in Chapter 3, I described the general homogeneity of the Amazon Basin in terms of the high average temperatures, the mostly poor soils, and the rain forests found nearly everywhere throughout it. I also mentioned more specific heterogeneities, including the distinction in productivity between the *terra firme* and the *várzea* environments. The former area constitutes some 98 percent of the entire basin and is limited by ancient soils, a thinly developed humus layer, and heavy rainfall bringing about leaching of the nutrients from the soil. The latter constitutes about 2 percent of the basin and consists of that area adjacent to the main channel of the Amazon River and its Andean-derived tributaries where nutrient-rich soil is deposited on the levee banks and low islands every year almost without fail. Finally, standing in sharp contrast to the whitewater-*várzea* niche are the two other principal kinds of rivers in the basin—the blackwater and clearwater rivers. They are far more limited in productivity, thus making them roughly comparable in terms of their relative impoverishment to the *terra firme* (interriverine) environment.

In the discussion of subsistence productivity and its relationship to sociopolitical complexity in Chapter 4, I went on to describe the Amazonian *terra firme* as one of the moderately low productivity areas of the continent, where only nonintensive cultivation, or slash-and-burn horticulture, can be practiced. This subsistence strategy virtually everywhere produces plant foods that are rich in carbohydrates but poor in protein, thus requiring village-level populations of the *terra firme* to rely on other sources—mostly including game animals and fish—for the necessary protein in their diet. Following this discussion, in even briefer form, I characterized the *várzea* as a moderately high productivity area that provided a context within which chiefdom societies arose in the prehispanic time period.

With these preliminary characterizations of the Amazon Basin summarized and once again in mind, we can now proceed to investigate several key arguments and models that have been proposed in attempts to establish a predictive ecological paradigm for understanding human adaptive systems in the basin. Although the arguments of any number of Amazon researchers could be mentioned here, in the first section of this chapter I focus on those made by four of the most distinguished ones. Of these four researchers, two center their discussions on the environment and subsistence adaptations to it: Emilio Moran (1993), a sociocultural anthropologist who has advanced the best case for environmental diversity, or heterogeneity, in the *terra firme* area; and Betty Meggers (1971, 1996), an archaeologist whose elegant arguments about the differing subsistence potentials of the *terra firme* and the *várzea* still provide fundamental support for the sociopolitical distinctions that characterize the human adaptive systems of each of these environmental contexts. Of the remaining two, Carneiro (1961), like Marvin Harris, is one of the few sociocultural anthropologists truly engaged in an ecological and evolutionary argumentation that is informed by reference to both ethnological and archaeological knowledge. Donald Lathrap (1973), an archaeologist, proposes that we distinguish between the *várzea* and the *terra firme*, characterizing the former as the "true Amazonia" and the other as something else.

In presenting the arguments of these four researchers, I make the case for an overarching ecological paradigm that combines the best elements of their proposals in attempting to fairly and reasonably assess the cultural potentials and limitations of subsistence-settlement systems in the Amazon Basin. Then in light of this paradigm, I examine in the second section the data from three of the most interesting studies that have been carried out of indigenous *terra firme* groups: Robert and Yolanda Murphy's 1950s study of the Mundurucú of the upper Tapajós River (Murphy 1958, 1960; Murphy and Murphy 1985); Napoleon Chagnon's ongoing thirty-year study of the Yanomamö of the upper Orinoco River (Chagnon 1968, 1973, 1992, 1997); and Michael Harner's late 1950s–early 1960s study of the Jívaro, now usually called the Shuar, of the cloud forests of the eastern Ecuadorian Amazon (Harner 1984).

The third section presents an overview of Gerardo Reichel-Dolmatoff's (1971, 1972, 1976) data on the Desana of the eastern Colombian Amazon, who have a mixed hunting-fishing subsistence-settlement system. To anyone already aware of the vast store of knowledge that Amazonian people have of their environment, the stunning sophistication with which the Desana regulate and maintain their adaptation via enduring cosmological principles and ritual leadership probably comes as no surprise. But to those unfamiliar with Reichel-Dolmatoff's study, it may be illuminating to find out that the Desana's own *emic* appreciation of their adaptation not only squares extremely well with the model we will derive in the first section of this chapter but also is probably as good or better than any *etic* a scientist from the outside world could ever come up with to account for the functioning and regulation of their ecosystem!

Having dealt in the second and third sections with adaptations to the *terra firme* environment, I examine in the fourth section the ethnohistorical data on the Omagua chiefdoms that lived along the *várzea* niche of the main channel of the Amazon River, several hundred kilometers upstream from its confluence with the Río Negro. In contrast to the village-level societies exemplified by the Mundurucú, the Yanomamö, the Shuar-Jívaro, and the Desana (and, by extension, any other *terra firme* group in the basin), the *várzea* was capable of supporting the autocthonous development of chiefdom societies in the Amazon. That is, we do not need to invoke any sort of migrations from areas of the continent outside the basin to account for the complexity represented by the Omagua and other *várzea* chiefdoms (see Meggers and Evans 1973).

Finally, in the fifth section, I briefly discuss arguments by two anthropologists that take on substantial interest in light of the preceding discussions. The first is Anna Roosevelt's (1989, 1991) proposition that the Amazon Basin could and did support great sociopolitical complexity and that if there were no limitations on prehistoric sociopolitical developments anywhere in the basin, then the same should be true for Brazilian attempts to develop it today. The second, proposed by Pierre Clastres (1977), is similar to the first in implying that the basin is characterized by unlimited potential for prehistoric and recent indigenous sociopolitical development. However, Clastres differs in arguing that no complex societies ever occurred there (at least on the *terra firme*) because the traditional indigenous societies of the region devised mechanisms to keep them from developing. With respect to both of these arguments, we see that ultimately it is the indigenous people of this area who teach us about the potentials and limitations of the environment to which we now know they have been successfully adapted for more than eleven thousand years.

ENVIRONMENTS AND ADAPTATION

Moran's Argument

In *Through Amazonian Eyes*, which deals with environments and subsistence adaptations throughout the Amazon, Moran (1993) outlines his position that researchers have defined the basin in terms that are too homogeneous. He argues that there has been a tendency to rely on an oversimplified dichotomy that merely distinguishes between the *várzea* and the *terra firme* environments, with the latter uniformly characterized as possessing impoverished soils. Moran does not disagree, however, with making a basic distinction in productivity between the two environments. Instead, he argues that the characterization of the *terra firme* as uniformly impoverished overlooks the scientific evidence indicating that considerable variability of soil fertility is found across this vast area. Pointing to the obvious differences that exist among such far-flung *terra firme* environments as the central Brazilian savannas, the Xingú Basin, and the Río Negro Basin, Moran goes on to imply that what really lies behind such specious reasoning is an attempt to relegate *terra firme* adaptations strictly to levels of noncomplexity.

Figure 6.1 shows the principal habitats of the Amazon Basin, according to Moran. They comprise (1) the *várzea* floodplain and (2) the five main habitats of the *terra firme*: upland forests, lowland forests, the *caatinga*, upland savanna, and lowland savanna. In the same order, let us now briefly consider his discussions of the principal features of each of these environments.

The Várzea Floodplain

Moran divides the *várzea* floodplain into three separate microenvironments: the estuary, the lower floodplain, and the upper floodplain. The estuary is unlike any of the rivers in the Amazon proper in that under the force of the tides the river level here fluctuates twice a day rather than twice a year (i.e., as a function of the different rainy seasons to the north and south of the equator) and is influenced by massive influxes of saltwater. Although industrial-age agroforestry systems support high densities of people in the estuary, or some fifty persons per square kilometer, agriculture here is far "more difficult and less productive" (Moran 1993:27) than such extractive activities (see Figure 6.2b for the floodplain forest biome). Thus the estuary, which includes Marajó Island, was probably far less productive a niche than other parts of the *várzea* for aboriginal populations.

The lower floodplain, running from a point near the mouth of the Xingú River upstream to a point upriver from the Içá River, is the classic *várzea* niche. Annually, as mentioned earlier, the soils on river islands and the adjacent levee banks at the edge of the main channel are renewed by nutrient-rich alluvium brought down during flood stage by the Andean tributaries of the Amazon. In spite of the high productivity of the *várzea*, however, flood levels from year to year are variable and the timing of the flood itself varies. Both of these factors therefore had to be dealt with by the prehistoric inhabitants of the floodplain.

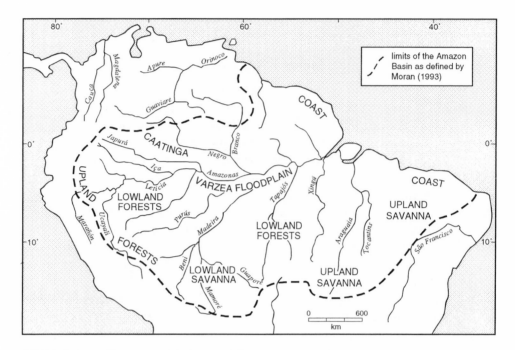

FIGURE 6.1 The principal habitats of the Amazon Basin. Redrawn and adapted from Moran (1993).

The upper floodplain is much like the estuary in having relatively more limitations than the classic *várzea* niche of the lower floodplain. For example, although alluvial soils in the Andean foothills of Peru and Ecuador are productive, those of the eastern Peruvian part of the Amazon Basin are highly acidic and saturated in aluminum, features that limit their productivity and thus make them inappropriate for higher population densities of the kind necessary to support a chiefdom society.

Upland Forests

As shown in Figures 6.1 and 6.2a, this habitat is limited to the extreme western periphery of the basin. According to Moran, it contains a wide variety of different microenvironments, all of them featuring anthropogenic, or human-influenced, vegetation, including palm, Brazil nut, bamboo, and liana forests. The soils of the liana forests, for example, have medium to high fertility. Such soils in the Amazon, also called *terra preta* ("black earth"), are generally the result of longer-term human occupation on a spot. Since they are richer than the natural, or nonanthropogenic, soils, one presumes they could sustain more than three years of cultivation (the upper limit for swidden, generally, in the Amazon)—if not for the fact that weed invasion ends up driving horticulturists on to new patches of soil before the nutrients in the old patch are completely used up.

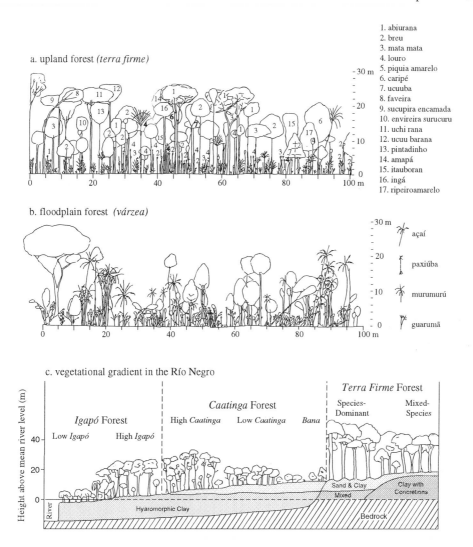

a. upland forest *(terra firme)*

-30 m

-20

-10

0

0   20   40   60   80   100 m

1. abiurana
2. breu
3. mata mata
4. louro
5. piquia amarelo
6. caripé
7. ucuuba
8. faveira
9. sucupira encamada
10. envireira surucuru
11. uchi rana
12. ucuu barana
13. pintadinho
14. amapá
15. itauboran
16. ingá
17. ripeiroamarelo

b. floodplain forest *(várzea)*

-30 m

-20

-10

0

0   20   40   60   80   100 m

açaí

paxiúba

murumurú

guarumã

c. vegetational gradient in the Río Negro

Terra Firme Forest

Species-Dominant   Mixed-Species

Caatinga Forest

High *Caatinga*   Low *Caatinga*   *Bana*

Igapó Forest

Low *Igapó*   High *Igapó*

Height above mean river level (m)

40

20

0

River

Hyaromorphic Clay

Sand & Clay

Mixed

Clay with Concretions

Bedrock

FIGURE 6.2   Cross-sections of (a) an upland *terra firme* forest, (b) a floodplain *várzea* forest, and (c) a blackwater forest on the Río Negro. Redrawn and adapted from Moran (1993).

Lowland Forests

The features of this habitat are mentioned only in passing by Moran, but they can be summed up as follows: Lowland forest soils are extremely poor, and as is the case nearly everywhere else in interriverine *terra firme* environments, most of the nutrients are locked up in the plant biomass, to which they are quickly recycled when leaffall occurs. Swidden cultivation in this area, then, presumably would be limited not by grass invasion, but by a massive falloff in soil nutrients by the third year of gardening on any particular spot in the forest.

The Caatinga

The Amazonian *caatinga* (of which a somewhat different version has already been described in Chapter 3 for the northern Brazilian highlands) is part of one of the least productive areas of the entire Amazon, namely, the so-called black-water ecosystems (see Figures 6.1 and 6.2c). In such areas *igapó* forests lie adjacent to the streams and rivers. These forests, by definition, are flooded annually for some months at a time and thus are avoided altogether for farming. Soils in the adjacent *caatinga* forest are composed of white, quartzitic sands that are extremely acidic and nearly devoid of nutrients, making these regions among the most fragile and unproductive of all habitats in the basin. Although patches of somewhat better soils are present in these areas as well, Moran notes that everywhere carbohydrate-rich manioc is the main source of calories and human settlements are accordingly very small.

Upland Savanna

As mentioned in the chapter on South American environments, a substantial portion of the Amazon Basin consists of extensive areas of upland savanna, especially in the southeastern part. Covering a total of 1.8 million square kilometers (Figure 6.3), upland savannas have soils that are acid, leached, and deficient in nutrients. Indigenous peoples of this area (including the Mundurucú) prefer to locate their villages in the savanna, near the gallery forests and not many kilometers from the rivers, in order to facilitate slash-and burn horticulture in the forests and hunting in both the savanna and forest habitats. Although some aboriginal villages here reached numbers as high as fifteen hundred inhabitants, Denevan (1976) estimates that overall population densities nonetheless are on the order of 0.5 person per square kilometer—that is, within the expected range of egalitarian village-level systems (Moran notes that Denevan's estimate for human population densities in the upland forests, the richest ecosystem of the *terra firme*, is even less than this).

Lowland Savanna

These savannas are inundated annually during the rainy season and are agriculturally limited because they feature highly acidic soils that are deficient in phosphorus, have excessive drainage, and are watered by very low amounts of rainfall in the growing season. Although some researchers have argued that chiefdom societies may have arisen here (e.g., in the Llanos de Mojos area; see Denevan 1966), Moran himself considers the constraints on productivity, and hence on population numbers, to have limited these societies to a level more consistent with the egalitarian village societies of the *terra firme*.

Summing up the data for the Amazon as a whole, Moran notes that 3 percent of the soils of the basin are extremely low in fertility, 75 percent are poor and

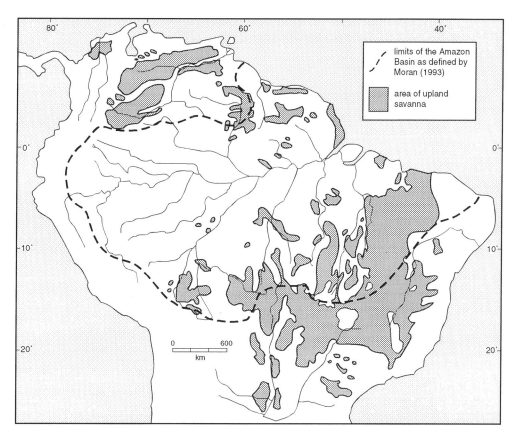

FIGURE 6.3 Map showing the upland savannas of the Amazon Basin and adjacent areas. Redrawn and adapted from Moran (1993).

acid, 14 percent are poorly drained alluvium of the *várzea* and *igapó,* and 7 percent are of medium to high fertility. Most tellingly, in light of these data, Moran does not argue that any single area of the *terra firme* could have sustained human adaptive systems at other than an egalitarian level of sociopolitical integration. Thus, the assertion of this book that a fundamental dichotomy exists between the *várzea* and the *terra firme* stands (but see Chernela 1993, who argues that the hierarchically ranked Wanano sibs of the Río Uaupés region of far northwestern Brazil were neither "fish nor fowl," that is, neither egalitarian nor chiefdom societies). In any case, Moran is perhaps the first ecologically oriented anthropologist to provide us with an appreciation of the environmental heterogeneity that characterizes this huge area. We should therefore expect nothing less of *terra firme* cultural systems; within the constraints of interriverine environments and related subsistence systems, they should exhibit a correspondingly high variability from place to place throughout the basin.

Meggers's Argument

In the two editions of *Amazonia*, Meggers (1971, 1996) constructs the definitive account of the environmental characteristics and subsistence potentials of the basin. In addition, in contrasting the principal features of the basin to those of temperate zone ecosystems, she warns us of the dangers of making assumptions about tropical ecosystems on a knowledge base (and related "developmentalist ideology") that often is narrowly restricted to a familiarity only with temperate ecosystems. If we assume that the classic twofold dichotomy between the *terra firme* and *várzea* is therefore fundamental to our understanding of the evolutionary potential of indigenous adaptive systems in the Amazon, then it is worth considering the main points she makes in comparing the subsistence potentials of each of these environments and in contrasting them to temperate systems.

Subsistence Potential of the Terra Firme

Meggers discusses the *terra firme* environment in terms of the following factors: (1) the physical and chemical absolutes that constitute the primary determinants of the *terra firme* biomass, (2) how the primary forest is adapted to these determinants, (3) how slash-and-burn horticulture cleverly mimics the adaptive features of the primary forest, (4) the dangers of temperate zone–style clear-cutting and intensive agriculture, and (5) the nutritional features of *terra firme* resources in relation to those of temperate zones.

Meggers argues that three physical and chemical factors are critically determinant for *terra firme* subsistence potential. The first is the antiquity of the soils, which over millions of years of chemical weathering have lost their soluble minerals and have been reduced to highly acidic sandy and clayey soils. The second is the fact that average temperatures in the basin are usually at or above 25°C, meaning that the humus layer, which accumulates only when temperatures are consistently below this level, is substantially impoverished. Since humus plays a vital role in enhancing nutrient absorption and moisture retention in sandy soils, as well as porosity and permeability in clayey soils, its near-total absence makes continuous agriculture impossible. Third, the heavy rainfall in the basin creates potential conditions of erosion and leaching that can remove vital substances, such as silica, kaolin, and phosphorus, that are necessary for plant growth.

That a luxuriant rain-forest vegetation is nevertheless characteristic of the basin—in spite of the severe constraints posed by these three determinants—provides a lesson in how well the forces of natural selection have operated to overcome them (see Figure 6.4a). First, the dense canopy reduces erosion by retaining fully 25 percent of the rainfall and converting the rest into a fine spray, while at the same time reducing insolation. The reduction of the impact of both these factors in turn permits the formation of a thin humus layer. Second, the canopy captures a substantial portion of the nutrients needed for growth and maintenance directly from the air. Third, the development of extensive shallow root systems and a rate of litter fall much greater than that of temperate forests

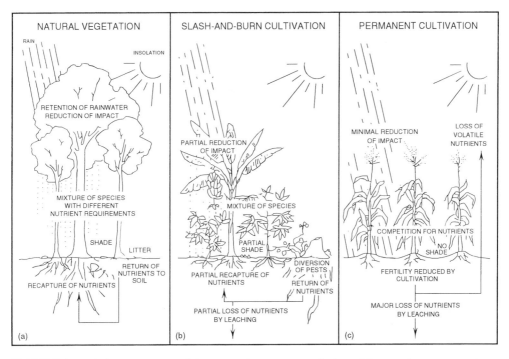

| NATURAL VEGETATION | SLASH-AND-BURN CULTIVATION | PERMANENT CULTIVATION |

FIGURE 6.4   Relative success of the natural vegetation, slash-and-burn cultivation, and permanent cultivation in minimizing the potentially detrimental effects of the tropical climate on *terra firme* soils of the Amazon Basin. Redrawn and adapted from Meggers (1971).

bring about a rapid recycling of nutrients back into the biomass, before they are lost to the local ecosystem through erosion. Fourth, the individuals of each plant species are widely scattered in favor of heterogeneous mixes of individuals of different species, each with somewhat different nutrient requirements. This widespread distribution is also an adaptation to the tendency for plant-specific diseases to spread quickly in the warm, humid setting.

Tropical forest slash-and-burn systems (Figure 6.4b) represent a viable way of overcoming the three primary limitations mentioned previously, while successfully mimicking the characteristics of the primary forest, as already suggested in Chapter 4. A section of forest is cut down to open an area of limited size to sunlight and rain, a necessary first step in permitting the survival and growth of the crops. At the same time, the slashed vegetation is left for some weeks to dry and then is burned on the spot to release the nutrients from the biomass directly to the soil. Larger-leafed trees that are planted in such plots become a substitute for the primary forest canopy—both by protecting the more delicate plants from excessive sun and rain and by reducing the danger of the permanent loss of nutrients through the leaching of the newly enriched soil. Since the "burn" usually does not destroy larger branches and tree trunks, the slash itself provides additional protection to the crop—never mind that to a neophyte Western observer it may appear to be lying about in total disorderliness, leading to the false conclusion that swidden horticulturists are not in "control" of their system when in fact they are (e.g., see the discussion of Bantu swidden plots of the Ituri rain forest in Turnbull 1961). Also, as shown in Figure 6.4, the individuals of each species of cultivar are scattered widely, which not only avoids overtaxing the nutrient supply but also keeps plant-specific diseases from easily spreading and killing the crop.

The adaptation has several limiting features, however, having to with the fact that slash and burn is not really a perfect imitation of the primary forest. First, as Meggers notes, swidden plots do not represent quite as "closed" (i.e., nutrient-retaining) a cycle as that represented by the primary forest. So, inevitably, nutrients are lost through leaching but, more significantly, through consumption as energy by humans. Second, the amount of nutrients in the burned biomass obviously is finite, with the limits usually reached by the third year of gardening everywhere in the Amazon (e.g., see Meggers 1996:Table 1). Although a fourth crop could sometimes be grown, the cost-benefit considerations of expending energy to open up a new plot nearby and massively increasing the yield compared even to that of the third year on the old plot outweigh any considerations of continuing the use of the old plot (except as a source of fruits from larger trees still growing there, as is the case with the Nukak, in Chapter 5). A final major limitation of swidden systems is that the old plots must be left fallow for at least twenty years before the forest regenerates. This means that each family needs roughly seven times the area for its garden than that needed by cultivators able to farm continuously on one spot. Hence, population densities must correspondingly be much lower than those where continuous farming is possible (e.g., the Andean highlands and coast, where irrigation waters continually provide an outside source of dissolved and suspended nutrients).

By this point it should be obvious that the clean-cutting systems employed in temperate zones would never work in a tropical forest setting (Figure 6.4c). First, the slash is cut and removed from the fields, a process that removes the principal (local) source of nutrients for the cultivars planted there. Second, exposing the ground surface to the sun and heavy rainfall of the tropics not only has disastrous effects on whatever nutrients might still be available, but also quickly erodes any soil that remains. Third, the monocropping strategy of temperate systems is doomed to quick failure in tropical environments given the rapidity with which diseases spread here. This is precisely what happened at the Fordlandia plantations in the Tapajós Basin in the early twentieth century, when Henry Ford attempted to monocrop rubber trees (*Hevea brasilensis*) over huge areas that had been cut out of the rain forest. Within six years of the inception of the project in 1926, a fungus had infested the trees; ultimately the costs of maintaining them by grafting on disease-resistant plants became too great to permit a profit (Moran 1981).

Finally, Meggers provides a telling comparison of the qualitatively differing productivities between *terra firme* swidden plots and primary forests, on the one hand, and temperate zone agriculture and vegetation, on the other. As shown in Figure 6.5a, temperate soils have high inorganic fertility. From W. B. Clapham (1983) we may add that in profile such soils always have thick, well-developed A

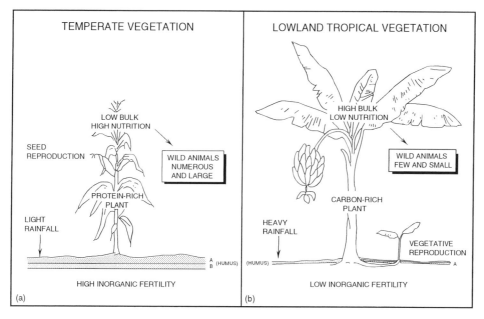

FIGURE 6.5   The effects of climate, soil, and rainfall on plant reproduction, nutritional content, and the size and numbers of wild animals in temperate (a) and lowland tropical (b) environments. Redrawn and adapted from Meggers (1971).

horizons consisting of humus-rich loam and often a humic B horizon as well. Rainfall in temperate zones is relatively light and temperatures are cool. When combined, all of these factors select for plants with low bulk that reproduce by means of protein-rich seeds. Such an environment not only favors the evolution of large populations of herbivores with large body size, but also permits relatively continuous cropping and high yields over the longer term.

Lowland tropical soils, in contrast, have low inorganic fertility (Figure 6.5b). Such soils have a very thin A horizon (that is, the humus layer is poorly developed). Rainfall is heavy and temperatures are warm. When combined, all of these factors select for plants with high bulk that reproduce vegetatively and are rich in carbon (carbohydrates) but very poor in protein. Wild animals are few and small in such environments as well as being widely scattered in low-density populations. In sum, there is no avoiding the fact that protein, not carbohydrates, is the critical limiting factor in tropical rain-forest environments.

Subsistence Potential of the Várzea

Although the *várzea* lies in the midst of the Amazon and thus is characterized by the same (limiting) determinants as the *terra firme*, as mentioned earlier it is qualitatively different from the *terra firme* in that its soils are renewed on an annual basis. Sustained yields are thus possible year after year on the same cultivated areas. However, the *várzea* also has its limitations, most obviously including the fact that during the months of the flood much of the land here is underwater and unavailable for human habitation. There are limitations as well with respect to which crops can be grown on the *várzea*. For example, manioc requires at least eight months to mature, so it cannot be grown on lower *várzea* ground, where there are fewer than eight months between inundations. Maize, however, which matures in 120 days, will yield one crop on the lower *várzea* and two crops on the upper elevations of the *várzea* year after year without any need to artificially fertilize the soil. Indeed, Meggers notes that yields on the *várzea* are often two or three times higher than even the first year on *terra firme* swiddens, primarily because each hectare of *várzea* annually receives some 9 tons of sediment containing all the essential nutrients for plant growth.

Although a rich animal biomass exists in the terrestrial environment, it is in the water where the almost incredible bounty of *várzea* animal life manifests itself. Fish are abundant in numbers and diverse in species, some of them like the piraibá, a catfish, reaching weights of over 135 kilograms. Water turtles are extremely abundant, one of the species, the tartaruga, measuring nearly 1 meter long and reaching weights of 35 kilograms. The largest creature of all is the manatee, which measures 3 meters long and attains a weight of 1,180 kilograms. The great abundance of smaller fish and wild seed grasses attracts a rich profusion of birds, including storks, herons, and ducks.

In spite of the much greater productivity of the *várzea* for hunting, fishing, and swidden horticulture, however, Meggers notes that a final major limiting factor is that at unpredictable intervals the Amazon flood rises higher than usual (as many as 2 meters higher), covering the *várzea* area more completely and for longer periods than normal. This creates a lean, or bottleneck, period that requires human populations to adapt at numbers more consistent with the *worst* of times rather than the best of times during normal years (see Figure 2.8b). That is, she implicitly invokes the principle of the limiting factor, or Liebig's law of the minimum, which states that organisms must adapt their numbers to that necessary resource or nutrient that is least plentifully available in relation to all other necessary resources or nutrients, or to that (unpredictable) year when all foods are available in quantities that are less than normal years (see Clapham 1983; Odum 1971).

Carneiro's Kuikuru Model

With the foregoing characterizations of the *terra firme* and *várzea* environments now in hand, let us proceed to briefly outline and critique Carneiro's model (1961) of the Kuikuru based on his study of this Amazonian village group in the early 1950s. Although Carneiro (1988) later amended his arguments about the unlimited nature of Kuikuru subsistence productivity—noting that "diminishing yields" usually lead to the abandonment of a swidden plot two or three years after it is opened in the forest—it is important to lay out his principal points here, not least because they are still cited by some researchers (e.g., Chagnon 1997:71–72) to support the assertion that virtually no environmental and subsistence limitations characterize *terra firme* adaptations. Moreover, as already mentioned in the introduction to this chapter, in spite of changes in his basic viewpoint over the years, as we see in Chapter 9 both Carneiro and the followers of his circumscription theory of state origins still cling to notions about the primary causality of circumscription that were based on the arguments of the Kuikuru paper.

The Model

The fundamental features of the Kuikuru adaptation are relatively easy to lay out in brief form. At the time Carneiro carried out his fieldwork in 1953 and 1954, the Kuikuru village was a fairly typical adaptive system of the *terra firme*. Located near the Kuluene River, one of the headwater tributaries of the Xingú River, some 145 people occupied a single settlement of nine thatched houses. Within a roughly 6.5-kilometer radius of the village—the distance people were willing to walk to open up a swidden plot—the Kuikuru had available about 5,463 hectares of land that could be used for horticulture. Of this land, only 39 hectares were in use at any one time, that is, a minuscule amount representing 0.007 percent of the 5,463 hectares. The main crop grown on their plots was manioc, which made up fully 80–85 percent of the diet. An additional 5 percent of their food came from other cultivars, such as maize, whereas fishing accounted for most of the rest of the diet. The hunting of game animals was not important, according to Carneiro, as it constituted less than 1 percent of the Kuikuru diet.

Although about one-half of the cultivated land was abandoned to long-term fallow each year, the Kuikuru apparently never had to move very far from one site to another in their 55-square-kilometer forest preserve. Indeed, they had lived in the same area for nearly one hundred years at the time of Carneiro's research. And with what appeared to be almost no effort on a daily basis (3.5 hours of gardening, 1.5 hours of hunting, and the remaining 10–12 waking hours spent "dancing, wrestling, and loafing" [Carneiro 1961:49]), the Kuikuru were able to produce roughly double the number of manioc calories (9,884,000 kcal/ha) that they actually needed to support the population of 145 persons—the rest of this amount being lost to wastage and to pests such as peccaries and ants. Furthermore, Carneiro estimated that if they had just elected to work harder, they could have produced enough food to support a population of at least 2,000 persons, or 13.8 times larger than the one they had in the early 1950s. In sum, it seemed to Carneiro that there were no limitations on subsistence productivity in tropical swidden systems that could account for why the Kuikuru had not evolved to some higher level of sociopolitical integration.

Using these data as a basis for his arguments, Carneiro concluded that the Kuikuru and other *terra firme* cultivators thus had nearly all of the requisite factors in place that would have permitted them to evolve to more complex societies—including (1) permanence of settlements, (2) potential for growth in settlement size, (3) potential for growth in subsistence productivity, (4) food surpluses to support full-time craftspersons, (5) more than enough leisure time to "create" such complexity, and (6) far richer soils than might be thought to be the case. As a matter of fact, Carneiro implied that there was no reason related to subsistence productivity that the Kuikuru and, by extension, other *terra firme* groups should not have evolved at least to the level represented by the Inca empire of the Andes. Arguing that a typical Inca *chacra* (plot) produced one maize crop of only 10.4 bushels per hectare per year, while an irrigated plot of the coast produced two crops, or double that amount, Carneiro estimated that Andean yields thus would have been at best 290,000 kilocalories per hectare per year on the coast—as opposed to the much higher yield of 830,000 kilocalories produced by Kuikuru manioc swidden after losses to wastage and pests. The demographic potential of manioc subsistence should therefore have been in a magnitude of at least three times greater per hectare than that of the Inca maize subsistence systems. Indeed, the question one might be led to ask here, then, was why a Kuikuru "empire" had not developed in the Amazon!

Given such an apparently productive subsistence base, Carneiro's answer to the question of why *terra firme* settlements never grew to the population numbers (not to mention site networks) characteristic of stratified societies was that village factionalism always occurred with too great an ease and frequency in the Amazon. The problem was that chieftainship (headmanship) was "notoriously weak" among Amazonian societies, so political leaders simply were not powerful enough to keep disputes among groups of people in a growing village from leading to its breakup into smaller settlements scattered across the landscape. Because of this, *terra firme* adaptive systems had never got to the point where they pressed hard against the carrying capacity of their subsistence system, a process that Carneiro presumed would lead to conflict over access to resources, the development of military leaders, and hence an increase in the overall complexity of local adaptive systems.

Put more bluntly, Carneiro's initial answer to the question of why tropical forest villages had never evolved beyond an egalitarian level was that they could not get their political act together. But he went beyond this (ostensibly biased) answer to argue that the real reason tropical forest villages had not evolved was because neither of the limitations on subsistence productivity or an inherent inability to develop the political power characteristic of complex societies; rather, this failure to evolve was due to a lack of pressure at the "external edge," or boundary, of the local system. *Terra firme* Amazonian societies had grown and fissioned at the local level, but in some "two thousand years" of human presence in the Amazon there simply had not been time for population growth to reach levels where one or another group was significantly circumscribed by other social systems that it adapted by evolving to a more complex level of integration.

In sum, failing to find evidence of any limitations inherent within the local *terra firme* adaptive system, Carneiro became convinced that the primary causal force leading to sociopolitical evolution must be pressures exerted on the system from without, namely, the pressures occurring because of circumscription. As we see later in Chapter 9, Carneiro eventually generalized his model beyond this narrower (social) definition of circumscription in an attempt to account for the rise of complex societies in a variety of environments (this involved distinguishing among three types of "pressures" at the external boundary of systems—social, resource, and environmental circumscription).

Figure 6.6 summarizes the principal data from Carneiro's Kuikuru study, as well as his reasoning about these data, in light of the systems-hierarchical model presented in Chapter 2. It also shows the three-step argument (from subsistence productivity through political leadership to social circumscription) by which Carneiro reached his conclusion about why *terra firme* swidden cultivators had failed to evolve beyond an autonomous-village level of sociopolitical integration.

A Critique of Carneiro's Model

Given the arguments made earlier in this chapter about the limitations of subsistence productivity in *terra firme* adaptive systems, there is no question about how Carneiro's model failed to take into account the internal constraints that characterized the Kuikuru system. Protein, not carbohydrates, is the critical limiting feature of these systems, irrespective of the presence of such potentially system-changing features as leisure time, sedentism, and pressures from other social groups. That is, even with an adaptive system characterized by social circumscription, competition for resources, all the free time in the world, and permanent occupation of a site, the constraints on protein availability in the *terra firme* would still have kept the Kuikuru at the village level of integration.

Indeed, to compare Kuikuru manioc-based swidden, which is rich in carbohydrates but nearly devoid of protein (see Food and Agriculture Organization 1954), to Inca maize-based horticulture, which included cultivars that provided a rich and well-balanced source of both proteins and carbohydrates, is equivalent to comparing apples to oranges—irrespective of the number of calories produced by the one in relation to the other. In other words, this is not a quantitative issue at all; rather, it is a qualitative one in which, in terms of the total protein produced by Central Andean "horticulture," the latter system comes out to be far superior in sustaining dense human populations. Moreover, Inca subsistence was far more intensive than would be suggested by Carneiro's use of the term *horticulture*, at least in contrast to the universally small-scale gardening that characterizes Amazonian swidden horticulture.

Given the arguments in Chapter 2 about the potential for massive population growth in light of growth rates and doubling times, it is also likely that if Amazonian populations ever grew at all—which Carneiro argues they did to the point of fissioning—then the presence of this tendency generally in the Amazon surely would have led to "sufficient" numbers of people somewhere in the basin so as to cause competitive pressures on resources that, in turn, would have led to evolutionary development toward complexity. Moreover, as we now know from Roosevelt's work at Caverna Pintada site (see Chapter 5), the time depth of occupation in the basin is not merely two thousand years but over ten thousand years. This, it almost goes without saying, is more than enough time for populations growing even at low rates to have reached the point where the pressures

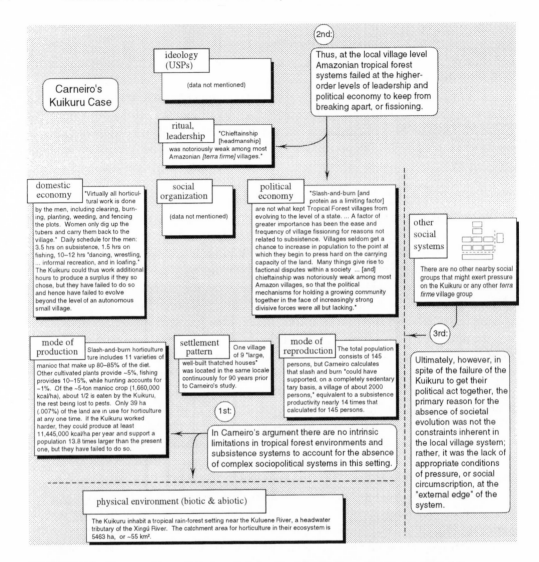

FIGURE 6.6   Systems-hierarchical model showing the Kuikuru data as described by Carneiro (1961).

Carneiro saw as essentially absent (at least with respect to the Kuikuru) would have manifested themselves. As a matter of fact, at least two of the groups discussed later in this chapter—the Yanomamö and the Jívaro—do exhibit this very kind of pressure, as indicated by a variety of features in their adaptive systems, including endemic warfare between local settlements. Yet even with decades, if not centuries, of such competition and conflict, neither of these village-level groups has ever exhibited any sign of evolving beyond small-scale egalitarian society.

Notwithstanding our critique of Carneiro's attempt at a single-factor explanation of swidden systems, in generalizing from our conclusions here, we must not overlook the probability that circumscription is indeed one among several factors—both internal and external—that could be important in assessing the potential of any adaptive system for evolution. However, to overlook, as Carneiro did, the internal constraints on a particular system—as if such constraints were irrelevant for assessing this potential—is tantamount to proposing that any preindustrial system anywhere could evolve to complexity regardless of the nature of the environment and the productivity of the subsistence strategies practiced within it. As should be clear from the arguments of this book, such a proposition is fundamentally an antiecological one.

Lathrap's Displaced Persons Argument

Having distinguished the productive potentials of the *várzea* and *terra firme* earlier in this chapter, we can now look at a different kind of argument proposed some years ago by Lathrap. In his paper on the hunting economies of the tropical forest zone, Lathrap (1973) begins with the reasonable assertion that the floodplains of the main Amazon channel not only were higher in subsistence productivity but also had far more sociopolitical complexity than the interriverine *terra firme* lands away from the channel. Following Carl Sauer and Julian Steward (see Steward 1963), among other "astute students of tropical forest culture," Lathrap (1973:88–89) also postulates that the cultures here in general represented less an adaptation to the rain forest, as such, than to the riverine environments of the basin.

In terms of an easier entry into the basin via watercraft that would have followed the main, highly productive lower and middle sectors of the Amazon River itself, this argument seems to make good sense—especially now that we have Roosevelt's recent finding of human occupation dating to ~10,500 B.P. at Caverna Pintada site. That is, it is not unreasonable to argue that the earliest occupation of the basin occurred first in the highly accessible and relatively more productive *várzea* niche. Given what we know about the heterogeneity of the *terra firme* environment from Moran, however, it is somewhat less reasonable to assert, as Lathrap (1973:84, 88, 90) does, that the *terra firme* (in relation to the *várzea*) had "laterized and heavily eroded soils," that the tropical forest was "far from [being] prime hunting territory," and that the "unproductive" swidden systems here were limited by "inefficiency." Lathrap's (1973:85–86) argument becomes even more unreasonable when he characterizes *terra firme* people as consisting of "primitive groups" in relation to the complex "slave raiding, head taking cannibals" of the *várzea*.

Thus implying that the only true Amazonia was the riverine part of the basin, Lathrap goes on to argue for a model of initial occupation of the prime *várzea* niche, followed by population growth beyond its carrying capacity, a concomitant rise of militaristic competition among the groups here, and, finally, the pushing away of militarily weaker groups off the *várzea* into the *terra firme* itself. The upshot was that "most of the primitive groups inhabiting the tropical forest uplands away from the major flood plains can be [seen] as the wreckage of evolved agricultural societies forced into an environment unsuitable to the basic economic pattern" (Lathrap 1973:94). In short, all indigenous *terra firme* groups were in essence displaced persons forced out of the *várzea* into a sort of bogus Amazonia.

Although the reader may well recognize more than just a couple of problems with Lathrap's argument, I want to refer here to two of the more obvious ones. The first is the proposition that any particular niche in the basin would be easier to penetrate and adapt to than any other. This is a problem I addressed earlier, in Chapter 5, in arguing that the environment in some areas of the basin was far less forested at 10,000 B.P. than it is now—and thus perhaps was more easily entered via land routes than would appear to be the case today. I also used the data from a number of Paleoindian sites to suggest that the earliest settlers of South America probably were far more able to adapt to its different environments, including the rain forests, than they have been given credit for by some researchers. Furthermore, hunter-gatherers entering the basin in relatively low numbers would have found the (pristine) *terra firme* environment to be just as attractive and productive as the *várzea*, since their numbers had not reached the ultimate carrying capacity of the traditional preindustrial adaptation. In sum, there is no reason that the peopling of the Amazon would have taken place only via the main river channel or other major tributaries, and it is not unlikely that interriverine areas were occupied in parts of the basin not long after the occupation of Caverna Pintada at ~10,500 B.P.

The second problem, a more serious one, is Lathrap's implication that the egalitarian societies that occupy less productive environments are "primitive" in relation to their (prehistoric) *várzea* neighbors. If we recall some of the earlier discussions of this book (e.g., in Chapter 2 on theory and in Chapter 5 on Steward's bands as marginals model), it becomes clear that his biased approach to distinguishing human adaptive systems is one that we have taken some pains to argue against. The point to make for the Amazon is simply the following: In reference to adaptive systems, the people of the *várzea* and *terra firme* niches are properly characterized only in terms of the greater or lesser productivity of their subsistence or the greater or lesser complexity of their overall system, not by a scale that equates the most productive environment of the basin, the *várzea*, with a high achievement that can become only a "degraded descendant" of the original when transferred to the *terra firme*.

THE MUNDURUCÚ, YANOMAMÖ, AND SHUAR-JÍVARO

As reference to Figure 1.1 shows, the *terra firme* groups discussed in this section live in three widely separate parts of the Amazon—the Mundurucú being situated in the south central part, the Yanomamö in the far north-central part, and the Shuar-Jívaro in the far western part of the basin. Although other well-studied Amazonian groups could be dealt with here—the Tapirapé (Wagley 1977), the Akwe-Shavante and Sherente (Maybury-Lewis 1974, 1988), the Bororo (Lévi-Strauss 1971, 1995), the Mehinaku (Gregor 1977, 1985), the Kalapalo (Basso 1988), the Mekranoti (Verswijver 1996), the Wanano (Chernela 1993), the

Campa (Weiss 1975), the Sharanahua (Siskind 1973), and the Cubeo (Goldman 1963)—the three groups chosen suit the purposes of this book well.

First, all three represent excellent examples of groups whose traditional adaptations are or were regulated by a variety of societal belief systems and behaviors that include higher-level superstructure (religion and cosmology), lower-level superstructure (shamanism and headmanship), political economy (warfare and trade), and varying population control practices (e.g., ritual abstinence from sex, long-term separation of the men and the women during raids, and general and preferential female infanticide). The researchers who carried out the work on these groups may or may not have been aware of (or even agree with) the connections we make among these and other variables, but all of them have written detailed studies that provide the kind of comprehensive data needed to make satisfactorily complete systemic arguments.

Second, although certainly not unique among Amazonian indigenous peoples in having an adaptation that is or was fiercely bellicose, each one of the three groups is of substantial interest (especially from a safe armchair perspective) for most of the following societal features: fortified settlements; chronic warfare with enemies located at varying distances from the attacking settlement(s); the raising of boys to be aggressive, demanding, and fierce to ensure they will be good warriors; alliance formation among separate settlements to create balances of power between enemy groups; complex trading networks that provide access to needed resources and enhance alliance formation; large gardens to provide food to guests invited over to be potential allies in war; treacherous feasts in which the guests are poisoned or otherwise violently killed by their hosts; the taking of trophy heads from killed enemy warriors that are imbued with awesome ritual power and, for a time, raise the warriors who take the heads to equally exalted levels of power and spirituality; shamans who hurl dangerous magical darts at the enemy; male chauvinist behavior, including physical abuse and gang rape of the women; the kidnapping of women and children from enemy villages; anxiety among men about their prowess as hunters, warriors, and lovers; sacred flutes (fraught with Freudian symbolism) that are guarded, viewed, and played only by the men; charter myths that justify the dominance of the men over the women; and, finally, cosmologies and female attitudes that appear in varying degrees to compensate for, or balance out, the dominance of men (e.g., *vagina dentata* myths postulating the danger of emasculation of the men by the women).

The Murphys' Mundurucú Data

Like other indigenous people located in the more remote parts of the Amazon, the Mundurucú remained unknown to the outside world for a long time after the arrival of the first European colonists in the mid-sixteenth century. In 1770 they made their presence known to the people in several recently established Portuguese settlements along the Amazon River by traveling over 700 kilometers from their upper Tapajós River fastness (Figure 6.7) to carry out a series of fierce attacks against the Portuguese settlers. The settlers finessed the situation by en-

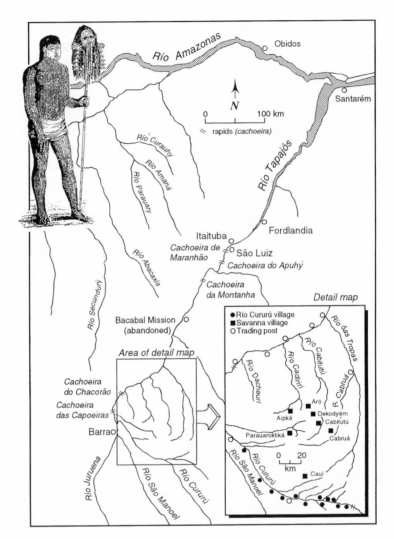

FIGURE 6.7   Map showing the location of the Mundurucú villages on the upper Tapajós River studied by Robert and Yolanda Murphy in the 1950s. Redrawn and adapted from figures in Murphy and Murphy (1985).

listing the aid of their attackers as mercenaries against other hostile indigenous groups of the central Amazon that had impeded European colonization of this area. This undoubtedly suited the Mundurucú, since it permitted them to continue a pattern of long-distance warfare against indigenous enemies that probably stretched well back into antiquity.

By the middle of the nineteenth century, the Mundurucú had begun producing surplus manioc (a historical fact cited by Carneiro [1961]) as a means of acquiring outside goods from itinerant traders called *regatões*. In the early twentieth century, as the need for rubber grew in the industrialized Northern Hemisphere, garden resources were increasingly replaced in this trade by rubber tapped in the gallery forests during the dry-season slack time in the agricultural cycle. As the trade continued, the Mundurucú began to move away from their savanna settlements to live permanently along the Cururú River to the south, where they could collect the rubber more efficiently. At about this time, or by the early 1920s, they had given up entirely their centuries-old practice of carrying out military expeditions against distant enemies.

By the 1950s, when Robert and Yolanda Murphy carried out their study of the traditional savanna villages, more Mundurucú lived along the European-influenced rivers of the upper Tapajós than lived in the savanna. Nevertheless, it is the traditional savanna adaptation on which the Murphys primarily concentrated, and that is the one we use as our touchstone for Mundurucú society—in other words, the recent ethnographic "present" of the 1950s. Moreover, some thirty years after the cessation of hostilities, many of the Mundurucú men still remembered in vivid detail their former raiding expeditions against distant enemies. Since the Murphys provide a wealth of data on the practice, politics, ritual, and cosmology of warfare, we also focus on this aspect of a somewhat more remote ethnographic "present."

Robert Murphy eventually produced two monographs, *Mundurucú Religion* (1958) and *Headhunter's Heritage* (1960), on his part of their joint research project and served as junior coauthor with his wife, Yolanda, on a third book, *Women of the Forest,* an anthropological classic published first in 1974 and then a decade later in an expanded second edition (Murphy and Murphy 1985). Aside from a more extensive series of publications than are usually produced by Amazonian researchers on a single group they have studied, it is notable that very few studies of indigenous South Americans have ever been carried out by a joint husband-wife team. Among the advantages of such a team are the greater ability of the female researcher to work comfortably with the women and the male researcher to work comfortably with the men—thus avoiding lacunae (not to mention biases) in the data resulting from the potential difficulty for one researcher, working alone in the field, to gain the confidence of members of the opposite sex. As we see, this was an especially fortunate aspect of the Murphys' research, since they chose a society where sex roles and gender-specific activities were kept rigidly separate, each forming a world that to a great degree was closed off to observers of the opposite sex.

Physical Environment

The traditional Mundurucú lived along the uppermost reaches of several tributaries of the upper Tapajós in gently rolling grasslands that begin about 40 kilometers to the east of the dense gallery forests that lie along the banks of the river. Although this windy, open location was a healthier one than the river because of the absence of malaria-bearing mosquitoes, there were two other more important advantages to locating settlements in the savanna at or near the edge of the gallery forests. First, it permitted greater diversity in the subsistence system by providing access both to the richer game resources of the savanna and to the nu-trients from burned slash for cultivating plots in the forested areas. Second, for defensive reasons the Mundurucú preferred to locate their villages on higher, open ground, where they had a better view of the surrounding terrain and more time to prepare a defense against an attacking enemy.

As is the case for other Amazonian savanna areas, the climate of the upper Tapajós is characterized by a distinct wet-dry cycle. The rainy season begins in September and lasts until late May, with the heaviest rains reaching a maximum of about 420 millimeters per month during the season's height between January and March. During the dry season, which lasts from June through August, rain-fall drops to as low as 6 millimeters per month. Although subsistence activities continued throughout the year, little or no horticulture was practiced during the dry season, and thus unburdened of the heavier tasks of gardening, a number of the men were essentially free to go on raiding expeditions at this time. Since the rivers rose and fell with the rains, becoming impassable at the height of the rainy season, long-distance travel was far easier at this time as well.

Mode of Production

Mundurucú subsistence was based primarily on horticulture and hunting, with a secondary reliance on fishing and gathering. Given the earlier arguments in this chapter about game as the critical limiting factor in *terra firme* adaptations, it is not surprising that the Mundurucú men defined themselves first and foremost as hunters of game, not as fishermen or gardeners. As we see shortly in discussing ritual and cosmology, even though gardening supplied the great bulk of caloric intake to the diet, it was hunters, not gardeners, who were honored in Mundurucú society and game animals, not manioc or other cultivars, that were closely linked to the spirit world.

Although tapirs, deer, pacas (*Cuniculus paca*, a large white-spotted rodent), monkeys, and birds were hunted, the most abundant source of game food con-sisted of two types of wild pig, the white-lipped peccary and the collared peccary, both of which are gregarious species usually found in larger herds of several dozen individuals. Thus, although hunters more frequently went out alone or in smaller groups, a major portion of the diet came from hunting carried out by all the men of a village, or sometimes by the men of several villages, joining together com-munally to surround a large herd of peccaries. In this manner game food suffi-cient to feed everyone in one or several villages for two or three days could be ob-tained in a single day's hunt. Nevertheless, the Murphys note that a village of eighty people could easily consume one tapir or two wild pigs in a day's time, and the men rarely were able to take more than a day or two off before they had to go out hunting again. Indeed, in light of our earlier discussion of protein as the crit-ical limiting factor of *terra firme* adaptations in general, it is particularly interest-ing to note that the supply of game was not superabundant in relation to the population size of the various Mundurucú villages. Occasional shortages in the meat supply were experienced, sometimes during the worst part of the rainy season when animal spoors were washed away, making the game difficult or impossible to track, and the Mundurucú could "be stuffed full on root crop dishes and still feel a terrible, almost indefinable hunger for meat" (Murphy and Murphy 1985:88).

Bitter manioc formed the dietary staple of the Mundurucú, although other tubers, including sweet manioc, yam, and sweet potato, were cultivated in swidden gardens along with pineapple, pepper, maize, beans, and squash. Early in the colonial period, probably, the Mundurucú adopted banana, rice, potato, and sugarcane and later, in the nineteenth century, cotton as well. The soil of the savannas is especially poor, so swidden plots were located mostly in forested areas. The Mundurucú subdivided the forest soils into three categories: clay, red, and black earth, this last soil type being by far the most productive but limited nevertheless in terms of its availability. In general, gardens would produce only for two years at most, with all of the crops mentioned here being planted during the first year of a new swidden plot but only manioc the second year. The second manioc crop took more than a year to mature, as opposed to the eight months for manioc growing in a newly opened plot. When all of the land in the immediate vicinity of a village had been farmed to the point of steadily diminishing yields, the Mundurucú would then move a short distance of several kilometers to an area with fresh soils. Since their moves were never carried out over greater distances than this and sufficient land always was available, it seems clear they had developed regulatory mechanisms that kept their numbers more or less in synchrony with the carrying capacity of the protein-rich game supply (a point we take up again shortly) and not with the more abundant supplies of carbohydrates produced in the gardens.

The gathering of wild plants was the least important source of food for the Mundurucú, with fishing next above gathering in its contribution to the diet, especially during the dry season when the rivers were lower or dried up to the point where *timbó* (barbasco) poison could be used to stun greater numbers of fish. Both the men and the women participated in these fishing expeditions, and on some occasions people from as many as four villages worked together to place the poison in a stream at several separate points, each lying about 300 meters apart. The yield from one of these larger "*timbó* parties" that took place during the Murphys' stay was estimated by them to be around 2 tons of fish. After part of the catch was consumed, the remainder was salted and dried, although it remained edible for a short period of less than two weeks.

Settlement Pattern

Seven savanna villages were in existence at the time of the Murphys' study, with nearly double that number located along the Río Cururú to the south. With the exception of the village of Cauí, six of the villages were scattered fairly widely over an area measuring roughly 30 × 40 kilometers, or 1,200 square kilometers (Figure 6.7). As shown in Figure 6.8, which is a schematic view based on textual description in the Murphys' book (1985), the traditional villages consisted of a

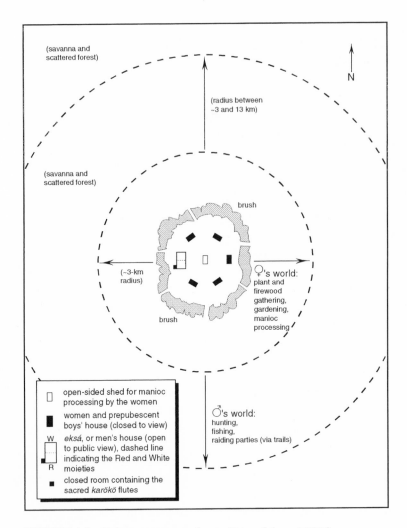

FIGURE 6.8   Schematic view of a traditional (pre-1960s)
Mundurucú village showing the areal divisions in men's and women's
daily activities. Based on textual description in Murphy and Murphy
(1985).

number of houses laid out in a circle around a cleared central plaza. The women
and prepubescent boys lived in a series of walled houses spaced around the north,
east, and south sides of the plaza, while all of the men lived in an open-sided
lean-to structure, called the *eksá*, that always was located on the west side of the
plaza so that the front of the structure faced east toward the sunrise. The differing
construction of the women's and men's houses was an indication of the nature of
Mundurucú society: The men were supposed to be public figures, dominant in
village life, whose activities were open to the scrutiny of all, whereas the women
were private figures who belonged in the home. In the traditional adaptation of
the 1950s, the women's houses were rectangular and measured about 6 × 12 me-

ters, whereas in the more populous past their houses had been elliptical in plan and were said to have measured at least 24 meters long. Similarly, the larger men's house of the 1950s was said to have been even larger in the past, when apparently it reached lengths of up to 30 meters.

Radiating out from the village in all directions was a series of paths that cut across the savanna grassland and scattered woodlands, running through two roughly concentrically defined areas in which the men and women carried out most of their activities on a separate basis. The first area, extending out in a 3-kilometer radius around the village, was the women's world, in which they drew water from streams for drinking and cooking, gathered firewood, and did the gardening. The second area—surrounding, protecting, and confining the world of the women and the life of the village to a distance of 3–13 kilometers away—was the world in which the men carried out most of the hunting. A series of trails, some leading to nearby villages and others used in the past for war expeditions, extended beyond the normal female and male activity spheres to the outside world and were used only by the men, except on those occasions when all the members of one village were visiting another for communal hunting, fishing, or ritual activities.

Mode of Reproduction

The total population of the seven savanna villages in 1950 was 360 people, a significant decline in numbers from the figures estimated by the Murphys for the nineteenth century, when there were at least 5,000 Mundurucú living in some twenty-five villages scattered over a much larger area. If we subtract the 25 persons of Cauí village (Figure 6.7), the population density for the 1,200-square-kilometer area occupied by the 335 persons living in the six other villages was ~0.30 person per square kilometer. The average size of a village in the 1950s was 50 persons, or one-quarter of the average size estimated by the Murphys for the nineteenth century. Given the indication of some pressure on game resources in the 1950s in spite of the lower numbers of people, it is probable that the twenty-five villages of nineteenth-century times were spaced more widely than the pattern of the 1950s, others things, such as the amount of game in the environment, being equal (i.e., the 1950s Mundurucú could possibly have been living in an environment degraded by overhunting, although, as we see in discussing the apparently "tight" control of ritual regulation over game resources, this is unlikely).

The Murphys provide no specific information on birth and death rates, but they do discuss in some detail the unequal sex ratios in many of the villages (e.g., thirteen men and eighteen women in the village of Cabrúa, or a sex ratio of 72) caused by the out-migration to the riverine villages of some of the men, always the more mobile sex in Mundurucú society. It does seem that couples usually had more than two children, although the population appears to have been kept in essential equilibrium by spontaneous and induced abortions as well as by occasional infanticide. Further demographic stability was achieved through the use of several birth control remedies, which consisted of drinking strong solutions produced by grating one of several kinds of roots (including ginger) into water and which, the women told Yolanda Murphy, would prevent a pregnancy for up to a year.

Domestic Economy

The local village economy was based on two fundamental institutions: first, the sharing of food and, second, cooperative behavior in carrying out daily activities of various kinds. In light of the varying luck the men had in hunting, the sharing of game was a means of balancing out access to this critical resource for as many people as possible. The Mundurucú had no means of storing game over a longer period of time, so when several men were successful in hunting several animals or one man killed a larger animal, the extra meat beyond the immediate needs of their families was divided up and distributed to the other households in the village. After the women in the various houses had cooked the meat, they each provided a portion to the *eksá* for the men's communal meal.

Almost all of the principal work in the village was carried out by communal groups consisting of either the men or the women separately, although men and women worked together to plant the manioc. The heavier work of clearing the forest for gardens and burning the slash was done by all-village male work groups, whereas the harvesting and processing of the manioc were done by all-village female groups. One group of women would be involved in digging up the tubers to transport them to the processing shed, while another was occupied with grating them and forcing the resulting pulp into the *tipití*, a long narrow basketry press similar to a Chinese finger squeezer, as the Murphys note, that when twisted would squeeze out most of the toxic prussic acid in the bitter manioc. The pulp was then toasted on clay (and, later, copper) griddles, producing a flat tortilla-like cake, called *beijú*, that could be stored over longer periods for consumption when needed.

Cooperative communal labor was so fundamental to Mundurucú society that no person could easily avoid participation in the men's and women's work groups without risking estrangement and accusations of witchcraft, a stance that if serious enough put him or her at substantial risk of being killed. The Murphys also stress the deep cleavage that existed between labor efforts considered proper for the women's groups and those considered proper for the men's groups. Although men's communal labor was structured at a more-inclusive level because of the common dwelling shared by all the men of the village, the minimal work unit for women's groups consisted of the females of one household. Indeed, unless engaged in a liaison with some man in the village, no woman ever went out alone onto the savanna, instead always going accompanied by other women. Not only was a lone person of either sex considered to be in danger of attack by malevolent supernatural beings, but also a woman found alone outside the village was subject to gang rape as a sanction by the men who found her there. The canons of proper behavior for Mundurucú women, then, were not taken lightly either in light of USPs or of male dominance.

Social Organization

Each person in Mundurucú society had a group of close relatives, including kin related both by blood (consanguineally) and by marriage (affinally). Aside from this, kinship was structured according to two principal categories: moieties and clans. Membership in the moieties (from *moieté*, the French for "half"), the more inclusive of the two categories, was inherited patrilineally by men and women alike, with everyone belonging either to the White or the Red moiety. Everyone had to marry outside of his or her moiety, as marrying inside it was considered incestuous. Although the moiety divisions did not involve a physical separation of the village into distinct residential halves, as was the case for the Bororo farther to the southwest (see Chapter 7), the men's house was divided—with the men of the White moiety in the northern half and the men of the Red in the southern half (Figure 6.8). The moieties were further divided into thirty-eight clans, with twenty-two clans in the White and sixteen in the Red moiety. These clans also were exogamic, and in fact it was considered more incestuous to marry someone from one's own clan than to marry someone from one's moiety. Although the moieties of a village engaged in both reciprocal and rivalrous relations, clans in Mundurucú society were never arrayed against each other, since this would weaken village ties. Intervillage ties were relatively strong, as fellow clansmen from different villages generally did not want to oppose each other.

Added to the rules of clan and moiety exogamy, one ideally married outside one's own village, and a substantial majority of marriages were matrilocal as well (e.g., 65 percent matrilocal and 35 percent patrilocal in the village of Cabruá). That is, the women tended to stay in their natal village and as a consequence had larger groups of female supporters around them than did the men, who might come from any of the other villages to join a particular *eksá*. In spite of the male-dominated society, the women thus appear to have had more solidarity, or more relationships of an "affective quality," than did the men. Tearing this solidarity somewhat asunder, however, was the fact that by the 1950s more men than women had migrated to the rivers, creating conditions in which the married women often were very suspicious of the single women, fearing that they were carrying on sexual liaisons with their husbands. However, little or no action ever was taken by a woman against a husband who had committed adultery, whereas more often than not a cuckolded husband would harangue, if not beat, his wife soundly for adulterous behavior.

In general, the sexes were very distinct and self-conscious social groupings, with men and women able to relax only when in the company of their own sex. The men often would laughingly recount a gang rape of a recalcitrant woman, causing an extremely uncomfortable reaction from the women and making them draw even closer together as a group. In every imaginable way the women took a back seat to the men—eating after the men did, walking at the rear of a file, never looking directly at the men, and covering their mouths when they laughed, since an open mouth was considered symbolic of an open vagina, or a sexual invitation to the men. Any woman who violated these rules was considered to be *yapö*, a nymphomaniac, the cure for which, predictably, was gang rape. Since the condition of being *yapö* was considered the result of bewitchery by a malevolent shaman, even female sexuality, according to the Murphys, was under the control of the men in Mundurucú society.

Indeed, the sexual act itself was a reflection of the subordination of women. A man paying a visit to his wife's household for the purpose of conjugal relations expected to receive sex from her on demand, usually with no foreplay, in an encounter characterized as much by its brevity as by the general lack of satisfaction on the part of the woman. As implied earlier, however, the women had ways of getting back at the men, balancing out to some degree, it appears, a male-dominated society. For example, since both the men and women went about nude, except for the penis sheath worn by the men, the women often found the men to be fair game for derisive comments aimed at their paltry male endowment. Such commentary, if followed by loud laughter and amused glances from the women, usually had the desired effect on the men.

Political Economy

I have already noted above that clan organization was one of the features that promoted intervillage integration and cooperative activities that included communal hunting and *timbó* fishing expeditions. In this regard, the Murphys point out that there were no fixed territories, since villages were located far enough apart that the areas habitually used for hunting did not overlap. I have also noted that the pre-twentieth-century time period was characterized by nearly four times as many villages (~twenty-five versus seven) and fourteen times as many people (~5,000 versus 360), but since intervillage cooperation was a significant feature of Mundurucú warfare, it is even more likely that these villages never engaged in open conflict among themselves, in spite of the probability of some occasional disruptions in social harmony. Traditional pre-1920s warfare thus always appears to have involved engagement with a non-Mundurucú enemy that often lived hundreds of kilometers away.

Every year during the months of the dry season, war parties from the Mundurucú area of the upper Tapajós would set out to attack groups within a radius of 800 kilometers from their homeland. Since the expeditions consisted of a fraction of the men from each one of a larger number of villages, a majority was able to remain home to hunt and provide a defense of the village if need be. After traveling great distances across intervening savannas and forests, the warriors would surround a village at night and attack it at dawn. Both the men and women of the village were killed and decapitated, with the heads thrown into baskets used to carry them back as trophies of war. The lives of the children were spared, and some were taken back to become part of Mundurucú society. If a warrior was killed or seriously wounded in the attack on the enemy, a member of his *iboiwatitit*, the clan to which his clan was linked in the opposite moiety, was responsible for bringing back his humerus, or upper arm bone, for ritual interment in lieu of his body—and the clansman would cut off his arm to obtain it, whether or not the fallen man was still alive.

According to the Murphys, the principal goal of warfare was to obtain trophy heads, which were prepared on the return march home in such a way as to keep the flesh of the victim intact for several years. The point of an arrow was inserted into the foramen magnum at the base of the skull to remove the brains. All the teeth were then knocked out and stored for later use, after which the head was briefly boiled and then dried near the heat of a fire. A cord was drawn through a hole knocked out of the hard palate of the mouth, so that its tassels would hang out of both the nostrils and the mouth. Finally, each eye socket was covered with beeswax and a paca tooth, and feather pendants were hung from each ear, which provided the "crowning glory" to the head.

Upon his return home, the taker of a head, who was called a *Dajeboiši*, and his wife were considered to be in an exalted ritual state that kept both of them isolated from normal social relations. In addition, they could not engage in sexual intercourse during a ceremonial period that lasted over two years after he had taken the trophy head. It almost goes without saying here that the result of carrying out such a ritualized and murderous act was the insurance of sexual abstinence among at least a substantial fraction of the Mundurucú population at any one time. A major (emic) function of the trophy head and its taker was that both were considered to be pleasing to the *putcha ši*, or Mother of the Game. The *Dajeboiši* could not hunt during the two-year period after he took the trophy head, but by bringing it with him as he accompanied other men to the edge of a hunting area, he and the trophy head were considered powerful ensurers of a good kill.

Thus warfare and the taking of heads were part of a complex politico-religious system that brought about abstention from sex, a reduction in the number of men who went out hunting game animals, and yet enhanced success for the men who did hunt. In an etic sense, there is little question that ritual abstention from sex for such a long period of time by a substantial minority of the population (all warriors who had been successful in taking trophy heads) helped in maintaining long-term regulatory control over the population size, especially since the supply of ritually sanctified warriors and trophy heads was continually renewed on a year-to-year basis. At the same time, the ritual reduction of the number of hunters had an equally real-world result in controlling human predation on the numbers and viability of game populations, the critical limiting factor in Amazonian adaptations, as I argued earlier in this chapter. Finally, although it is possible that the "blessing" of a *Dajeboiši* actually enhanced hunting success, it is far more likely to have been an expression of some anxiety about the (potentially precarious) relationship that existed between numbers of people and numbers of game animals—since any attempt by the hunters at overkill was considered a grievous offense against the spirits of the game.

In sharp contrast, the Murphys argue in a neofunctional but nonecological vein that the main point of warfare was that it enhanced social cohesion by serving as a "displacement device [for aggression] and as a rallying point for social cohesion" (Murphy 1960:130). Although this argument may account for the causal foundations of social cohesion in warfare (i.e., aspects of social organization that are causally linked to political economy), it does not account for the causal foundations of the warfare itself. That is, the Murphys appear to miss the overall ecological implications of the Mundurucú pattern of warfare and trophy head taking, namely, as one of the ways—in this case, political and ritual—of maintaining regulatory control over the size of the population and hence overall equilibrium in the adaptive system. Whether or not the Mundurucú knew this is what they were doing is irrelevant here (although we must always assume that the most astute among them indeed did). Nevertheless, the effective result was the exertion of control over the ever-present tendency of populations to rise against the critical limiting factor(s) characterizing a subsistence-settlement system.

Ritual and Leadership

There is no doubt, however, that the trophy-head rituals observed after a successful war promoted the intervillage social cohesion necessary to permit joint military expeditions against non-Mundurucú peoples. During a period of three years after each successful expedition, a series of rainy season rituals was held in which each village would host feasts to which other villages were invited. The ritual cycle began with the ceremony known as *Inyenborotaptam*, or Decorating the Ears, which inaugurated the head and its taker into high status. During the second rainy season after the inauguration of the cycle, the *Dajeboiši* would again invite the people of other villages to a ceremony known as the *Yašegon*, in which the skin was stripped from the head, its ornaments were removed, and the bare skull was hung up inside the men's house.

Also kept in the *eksá* was a set of three sacred trumpets, called *karökö*. These instruments, which measured about 1 meter long and less than 10 centimeters in diameter, were kept in an enclosed chamber (Figure 6.8) and could be viewed and played by any of the men, but not by the women, who were under penalty of gang rape if they even chanced to see the instruments. Although the *karökö* were played frequently and were not a part of any specific ritual, their music nevertheless was aimed at propitiating the spirits who owned the game and ensuring success in warfare and in obtaining trophy heads. The *karökö* themselves contained spirits that had to be ritually fed with an offering of food each night, else they would become displeased with their owners. Phallic in shape and owned by the men, the *karökö* clearly signified the dominance of the males in Mundurucú society, although the myth related to these musical instruments argued for a much different situation in primordial times.

Every village had in it one or two male shamans who were considered to have been born with supernatural powers passed on to them by their fathers. As with other South American indigenous groups, shamans in Mundurucú society used their powers both for curing the people in their village and occasionally for harming people who lived outside it, including those in nearby villages. In this latter case, the shaman cast small magical darts called *causi* to cause harm and disease, the Murphys noting that a particular type of *cauši* corresponded to each one of ten major kinds of diseases recognized by the Mundurucú. In curing ceremonies, the shaman would smoke tobacco to heighten his ability to find the *cauši* lodged in a patient's body, massaging the skin until it was coaxed to the surface and could be sucked out. In addition to performing cures as well as hexes, shamans were instrumental in propitiating the spirits of the game animals, ridding the village of evil forces, and inspecting the sites of new villages to ensure that no evil *cauši* were lying about.

Just as the Murphys see warfare as functioning to promote social cohesion, so do they view shamanism as a projection of latent antisocial tendencies that lay just below the surface of social relations—tendencies that were all the more powerful, perhaps, because of the pronounced emphasis in Mundurucú society on cooperation and social harmony. Shamans, in this sense, were an acceptable mechanism by which violence and aggressiveness could be expressed at the intervillage level, since if sickness and misfortune became too frequent in a village, people often blamed a shaman in some nearby village and conspired to kill him. Shamans thus clearly had rather ambivalent status in the eyes of non-shamans and were viewed in general as people who were "angry at everybody." In light of the relatively widespread dispersion of the Mundurucú settlement pattern, we also cannot overlook the possibility that shamanistic sorcery played an important role in regulating, or reducing, competition for game resources by promoting some distance among the villages in order to reduce any potential harm such magical malevolence might cause. That is, the fact that hunting territories rarely, if ever, overlapped would not at all be the result of random chance in such a ritually regulated system; rather, lack of overlap was the result (intentional or unintentional) of societal mechanisms—in this case sorcery—whose net result was the dispersal of people, or the lowering of population density on the land.

Aside from the ritual leadership and regulation carried out by shamans, the political leadership of each autonomous village was in the hands of a headman, who, like the shaman, inherited his position from his father. He also was exempt from the general rule of matrilocal residence after marriage. Although his opinion had considerable weight in decisions about village activities, including warfare, the headman was first among equals; in other words, his was merely one powerful voice among those of other senior adult males in the meetings conducted in the *eksá*. The rule of patrilineal inheritance did not always apply in the selection of a headman, since in the pre-1920 time period the choice would focus on a man who had especially distinguished himself by bravery in warfare and the taking of numerous trophy heads (in the post-1920 rubber-gathering era, the role shifted to one based on an ability to deal with traders and the outside world in general). Although the men were the predominant group in political decisionmaking, it is not surprising that they had less of a voice at the level of the individual matrifocal household, where a senior woman usually exerted prominent influence over day-to-day female group activities—another societal feature that tended to balance out to some degree the political and ritual dominance of the men.

Ideology (USPs)

The charter myth clearly lays out the origins of male dominance and chauvinism. At some time in the most distant past, the Mundurucú did not have sacred *karökö* trumpets. Then one day three women went into the forest, where they heard music coming from a lagoon. Returning with nets, they caught three fish, which turned into three *karökö*. The women kept this find a secret for a while, leaving the *karökö* in the forest, but the men found out and insisted that the women bring the trumpets to the village. The women complied but for their part insisted that the men permit them to occupy the *eksá*. Thus ensconced in the *eksá*, the gender roles and status of the men and women were completely reversed: The men were confined to the separate houses in the village and the area around it, where they drew water, gathered firewood, and gardened just as the women do today; the women lived in the *eksá* and demanded sex from the men just as the latter do today.

But all was not well because the men were also the hunters and the women, who were not, were unable to feed the *karökö* properly. In response, the men reoccupied the *eksá* and demanded that the *karökö* trumpets be given to them. Since that time the men have been in control—but an anxious one, at best. For example, the Murphys point out that the concept of the *vagina dentata* appears in a grim version of male humor, when this female sex organ is referred to as the "crocodile's mouth." At the same time, the men refer to their ability to discipline the women with the penis. It is noteworthy, however, that the women do not take very seriously the men's argument of innate superiority, nor are they particularly impressed by the *karökö*. (For some startling parallels and yet equally striking contrasts, see the role and function of sacred *molimo* trumpets in BamButi society in Turnbull 1961.)

The Murphys (1985:121) see all this as "a parable of phallic dominance . . . of male superiority based upon the possession of the penis." Women as mothers are the "center of love and affect . . . but swallower[s] of emergent [male] identity . . . and the vagina . . . is ambivalently conceived by the men as destructive" (Murphy and Murphy 1985:121). In this scenario everything about the men's house and male-dominated ritual is indicative of "the Oedipal transition and the transformation of the male child to man" (Murphy and Murphy 1985:121), with the men far more worried about emasculation by the women than the women envious of the men's possession of a penis. Although the Murphys' argument may well have merit as an adequate description of higher-order Mundurucú behavior, we do not have to search for the origins of such beliefs and behavior in the psyche of these or any other human groups. Instead, we can propose the counterargument that male chauvinist institutions are more likely to have their origins in the Mundurucú adaptive system, which clearly promoted warfare and other higher-order behaviors and ideology in order to regulate their numbers in relation to the human carrying capacity of protein in their environment. How else can we explain the regulation of population numbers and densities suggested both by trophy head–related prohibitions on sex and by the malevolent aspects of shamanism, as well as the consistent focus of ritual and ideology on the game animals? For example, if hunters did not observe proper etiquette in killing and disposing of game or made light of the animal they had killed, the Mother of the Game would punish them and Mundurucú society by robbing their souls, causing accidents such as snakebites, or sending malignant objects into their bodies that caused them to sicken or die.

Besides the game spirits, another important feature of Mundurucú cosmology was the belief in an underworld divided into three separate areas inhabited by the *kokeriwat,* a class of spirits that came forth to fight side by side with the Mundurucú in their wars. Visible only to the shamans, all the warriors nevertheless had to take precautions against the *kokeriwat,* since they could reduce the spiritual power of the trophy heads by stealing the teeth from them. The Mundurucú protected the teeth by extracting them from the killed warrior's head, stringing them on a cotton belt, and wearing them around the neck in a small box. The Mundurucú underworld itself was a sort of reverse version of the upper world, as people there had sexual intercourse standing up and the sun rose in the west. Up in "this world," however, the proper lifestyle was within-village communalism, intervillage cooperation and long-distance warfare, the taking of spiritually powerful trophy heads in warfare, male chauvinism, and a delicate balancing of gender relations that involved the downplaying of male ego and prowess by the women—in sum, an adaptive pattern that lasted for centuries until the inevitable forces of change during the twentieth century brought it to an abrupt halt.

Chagnon's Yanomamö Data

Unlike the Mundurucú, whose traditional cultural system is now gone, that of the Yanomamö has suffered far less at the hands of the outside world—although, as Chagnon, their principal ethnographer, has indicated in his recent publications, in the last thirty years they have begun to experience the more negative effects of encroachment by the developing nations, of which, as a result of historical serendipity, they are a part. With thousands more people in their tribal group than the Mundurucú, the Yanomamö have been the subject of more anthropological studies than the former group. Among the best or most fascinating of these studies, both earlier and recent, are William Smole's (1976) study of Yanomamö subsistence and settlement patterns; Brian Ferguson's (1995) massive cultural materialist study of the historical development of their warfare patterns; Judith Shapiro's (1972) doctoral dissertation, which provided independent confirmation of the male chauvinist nature, first reported by Chagnon, of Yanomamö society; Helena Valero's famous narrative (Biocca 1971) recounting her kidnapping in 1937 by the Yanomamö and her subsequent marriages to two headmen; Kenneth Good's (1991) cultural materialist and reflexive account of his fieldwork, which led, among other things, to his marriage to Yarima, a young Yanomamö woman; Jacques Lizot's (1985) book containing stories by the people themselves; and Alcida Ramos's (1995) recent study of their social organization and changing adaptation in the face of pressures exerted by the industrializing world around them.

Nevertheless, the most complete set of data published on all aspects of Yanomamö culture—from environment and subsistence to cosmology—has been produced by Chagnon himself. Since the beginning of his research in 1964, he has carried out what is certainly the most sustained long-term study of a single indigenous group anywhere in South America. In this section we rely on four of his key publications on this work: the first edition of his anthropological classic *Yanomamö: The Fierce People* (1968); the most recent (fifth) edition of this same classic, now simply entitled *Yanomamö* (1997), both for political (sensu strictu) and polemical reasons; another more popularized account of his studies, *Yanomamö: The Last Days of Eden* (1992); and, finally, an ecological paper entitled "The Culture-Ecology of Shifting (Pioneering) Cultivation Among the Yanomamö Indians" (1973). Both the first and fifth editions of his classic study are necessary sources here, since some of the information most pertinent to understanding the Yanomamö adaptation is contained only in the first edition. In any case, our discussion of the Yanomamö includes some data from the first edition that he now apparently rejects as irrelevant to understanding them—although these are the same sort of data related to environmental limitations and population control that characterize every other group we have studied to this point.

Physical Environment

The Yanomamö people occupy a vast area that extends over some 117,500 square kilometers of the upper Orinoco highlands of southeastern Venezuela and north-central Brazil (Figure 6.9). Although most of this area is covered with thick rain-forest vegetation, Chagnon notes the presence of some savannas—especially in the easternmost sector (compare Figure 6.3 to Figure 6.9)—that also are occupied by Yanomamö village groups. Aside from the savannas, the two principal microenvironments of the upper Orinoco jungle consist of extensive low-lying plains and adjacent rugged mountainous zones. The low-lying plains seem to be preferred over the more rugged zones because the rivers here are easier to cross during the dry season, gardens are easier to make, and game is more abundant, although numbers of villages are found in the mountains as well. Throughout both areas, however, the Yanomamö have traditionally focused their adaptation on gardening, hunting, and gathering in the interriverine zones, not on the resources of the riverine sector of their environment. As Chagnon puts it, the Yanomamö are "foot" people, not "canoe" people—a fact borne out by their construction of makeshift bark canoes that permit only the most precarious of river crossings or the occasional longer-distance trip along one of the streams of their area.

Mode of Production

Between 80 and 90 percent of Yanomamö subsistence is based on the produce of swidden plots, in which they cultivate plantains, avocados, papayas, chili pep-

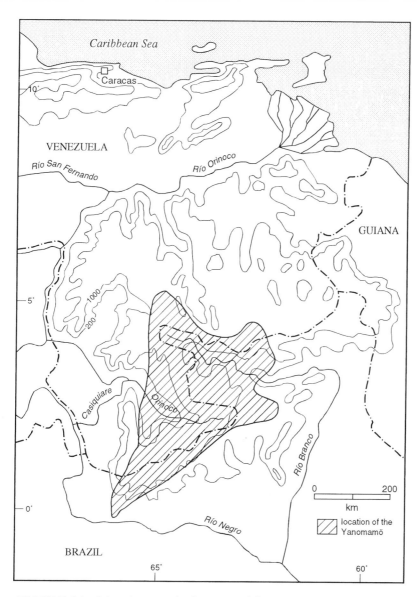

FIGURE 6.9   Map showing the location of the Yanomamö in the upper Orinoco Basin of southern Venezuela and northern Brazil.

pers, tobacco, and three varieties of tubers including the sweet potato—in other words, plants that are rich in carbohydrates, as well as various minerals and vitamins, but poor in protein. Wild plant foods gathered from the forest near the settlements supplement the diet and include palm fruits and hearts, hardwood fruits, tubers, several plants that are a source of products used to make hallucinogenic snuffs, and the Brazil nut—this last being one of the few plants available that is rich in protein. Although Chagnon does not argue that the carbohydrate-rich gardens are characterized by any limitations (e.g., the general absence of protein), he (1997:60) does note that if a Yanomamö group were to focus on wild plant resources alone, it would have to be "relatively small and chronically migratory."

With regard to the protein sources available to the hunters, Chagnon notes in the fifth edition of *Yanomamö* that a wide variety of animals is present—including two varieties of larger game birds, numbers of smaller bird species, white-lipped and collared peccaries, caimans, deer, tapirs, armadillos, anteaters, rodents, and several species of monkeys. Other sources of protein include palm larvae, caterpillars, tadpoles, freshwater crabs, and, during the dry season, fish from occasional stream-poisoning activities. Given all these foods, the Yanomamö subsistence system almost appears to be a "protein paradise," and indeed Chagnon (1997:60–61) asserts that they "enjoy a high standard of living by world health standards." Yet in the first edition of his book, Chagnon (1968:33) tells us—in passages that have been removed from the fifth edition—that "game animals are not abundant, and an area is rapidly hunted out, so that a group must keep constantly on the move." He (1968:33) goes on to say that on longer, five-day hunting trips in areas that had not been hunted for decades, he and the Yanomamö hunters he accompanied often would have been "extremely hungry" if they had not brought extra food along, since "we did not collect even enough meat to feed ourselves." Moreover, as is characteristic of some other *terra firme* groups, the Yanomamö distinguish between two kinds of hunger—having one word for regular hunger (Chagnon does not provide us with this word), which is satiated by any kind of food, and another word for meat hunger, *naiiki*.

A telling passage from the first edition indicates the seriousness with which the Yanomamö view the availability of meat in their diet. To drive home the point that Chagnon has excised all mention of data suggesting protein scarcity in the Yanomamö diet, let us look at the following passage, in which sentences set in roman type are still present in the fifth edition, whereas sentences set in italic type are in the first edition but removed from the fifth (cf. Chagnon 1968:91 to Chagnon 1997:132):

> The biggest meal of the day is prepared in the evening. The staple is plantains, but frequently other kinds of food are available after the day's activities. *Meat is always the most desirable food and is always considered to be in short supply.* It is a happy occasion when one of the hunters bags a tapir, for everyone gets a share of it. *It is good to share meat with others. This attitude is expressed in the sentiment that a hunter should give away most of the game he kills. One of the obligations men take very seriously is providing adequate quantities of meat for their wives and children. They genuinely abhor hearing their children cry for meat; this calls into question their abilities as hunters and marksmen, both of which are associated with prestige.*

As Chagnon (1997:91–97) implies in the fifth edition, the reason he has removed all of the preceding passages is that "protein-scarcity" researchers sifted through the first edition of his book, carefully searching for "suggestive statements about hunger, starvation, deprivations, or bad hunting luck that could, when stacked up in a pile, be used to make a circumstantial case for a 'theoretical' argument." Since Chagnon has seen no evidence among the Yanomamö of protein malnutrition, or kwashiorkor, he does not believe it is "fair" of such researchers (e.g., see Harris 1977, 1984) to use such off-the-cuff commentary to prove a case about why the Yanomamö do what they do in relation to protein (such as practice infanticide). The reader convinced otherwise, however, might well wonder why a well-adapted Amazonian population must necessarily exhibit malnutrition—in spite of the clear fact that tropical forests and the swidden systems adapted to them are indeed notoriously impoverished in protein (at least in relation to areas where intensive agriculture can be practiced). In other words, if regulatory institutions are working well, then there is no reason that a population cannot maintain itself quite healthily at or just below the protein carrying capacity.

Settlement Pattern

As we begin the discussion of settlement pattern, we must also address Yanomamö warfare, at least in a preliminary way, since the one cannot be understood without reference to the other. Indeed, as Chagnon points out in several of his publications, warfare as an institution or political phenomenon permeates all other features of Yanomamö society. One way warfare affects settlement is manifest in the size of the *shabono*, the round lean-to structure composed of adjoining family dwellings in which all traditional Yanomamö have lived (see Figure 6.10). First, in an area where warfare is occurring, the *shabono* must be large enough to accommodate a population that can adequately defend itself against any nearby enemy villages. Second, the *shabono* in such a situation must also be large enough to accommodate, even if temporarily, the members of any village invited over to engage in feasting and alliance formation. Autonomous villages often join in such alliances as the only means of defending themselves when their enemy is demographically superior. Chronic Yanomamö warfare also requires that the *shabono* be built with a log palisade around its exterior edge, a defensive feature that keeps arrows shot by an enemy force from easily penetrating the structure and killing or wounding its occupants. Finally, the location of a site for the *shabono* is selected not only with respect to the proximity of good garden land, but also in relation to the proximity of both enemies and allies.

With respect to the densities of Yanomamö villages on the landscape, Chagnon notes that sites are scattered rather thinly over the vast upper Orinoco area they occupy. Settlements thus are located at least several hours' walk away from each other, whether they are friends or foes, and villages can be as far as a ten days' walk apart. Given what we know about *terra firme* carrying capacity, such low site densities are not surprising, never mind that Chagnon does not think these densities have anything to do with protein scarcity in spite of his clear statements to the contrary in the first edition of *Yanomamö*. Moreover, he (1997:71–72) follows Carneiro—who "showed quite convincingly that Tropical Forest villages larger than 500 people were easily feasible [and even] that the

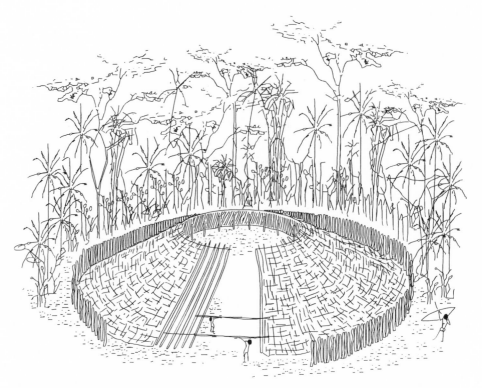

FIGURE 6.10   Drawing of a representative Yanomamö *shabono* under construction.
Based, in part, on Chagnon (1968).

Kuikuru produced more calories per acre than Inca farmers"—in asserting that
settlement moves have nothing at all to do with local carrying capacity, since villages often stay for decades in the same general vicinity. Instead, Yanomamö settlement moves come about entirely because of the nature of warfare and politics:
"The long moves made by the Yanomamö are not provoked by horticultural
techniques or the demands made on gardening. . . . They are motivated by politics and warfare and must be understood in this context. The most relevant 'ecological' variables here are human neighbors, not so much technology, economic
practices, or inherent features of the physical environment as such" (Chagnon
1997:75).
   Such an argument asks us to ignore everything having to do with the ecosystemic infrastructure (the *terra firme* environment, swidden subsistence, and human population numbers) and to pay attention only to the structural variables
(political economy) in our attempt to make sense of how the whole system works.
That is, it asks us to reduce our understanding of the system to just one variable,
as if what we knew about the infrastructure of Amazonian village groups simply
were irrelevant to understanding politics. Ultimately, as we have seen earlier in
addressing Carneiro's Kuikuru paper, this sort of proposition is simplistically reductionist and antiecological as well and would be acceptable only to those who
do not agree with Steward that cultural adaptations must be understood as much

in relation to their physical environmental context as they are in relation to their sociopolitical one. Putting the case another way, the approach taken in this book is that in the Amazonian case protein matters just as much as politics, so both of these variables are critical components of *terra firme* adaptations.

Mode of Reproduction

The Yanomamö population is thinly distributed across the 117,500-square-kilometer area it occupies. Within this area are some 200 to 250 villages, ranging in size between eighty and one hundred persons, and a total population estimated by Chagnon originally at about ten thousand people but more recently at twenty thousand people. If we assume this latter figure to be correct, the Yanomamö population density is 0.17 person per square kilometer (or 20,000 ÷ 117,500). Although this figure may appear to be low, it is nonetheless nearly twice the density of 0.10 person per square kilometer calculated in Chapter 5 for both the Ona of Tierra del Fuego and the Nukak of eastern Colombia. Some centuries ago it may well have been even lower, however, since, following the introduction of steel tools and plantains as early as the nineteenth century, the Yanomamö population has been growing at "explosive" rates, according to Chagnon, especially in the low-lying plains (he gives no actual growth rate figure, but based on our discussion of population growth potentials in Chapter 2, it would not have to be higher than between 1 and 2 percent per annum for nineteenth-century population numbers to have doubled every thirty-five to seventy years since that time).

We can therefore expect that lowland villages in particular would be characterized by population regulation measures, including infanticide, a practice that Chagnon (1968:74–75) discusses in some detail in the first edition. If a mother is already nursing a baby when another is born, she will kill the newborn irrespective of whether it is male or female. But Yanomamö parents prefer male babies to female babies, since this will enhance the number of people who grow up to be hunters and warriors—optimizing, in other words, protein capture and village defense. Thus, although Yanomamö mothers are not aware of it, Chagnon's data indicate that statistically speaking mothers tend to kill more female babies than male babies. The mothers are indeed aware, however, that their husbands may be very disappointed or disapproving if the first child born turns out to be female. In any case, the net result of the practice of preferential female infanticide is a skewing of the sex ratio, or the number of males to females, especially in the lowland villages.

For example, in a sample of seven traditional lowland villages the sex ratio ranged from 77 (Upper Bisaasi-teri) to 135 (Patanowä-teri), averaging a somewhat skewed figure of 114 (N = 449 males and 391 women). But since warfare among traditional Yanomamö villages results in the deaths of a substantial fraction of the adult male population, Chagnon surmises that the actual sex ratio probably was much more heavily skewed in favor of males—in other words, that it averaged much higher than 114. Whatever the case, under the assumption that a normal sex ratio is 105, or near parity between the sexes, the high inci-

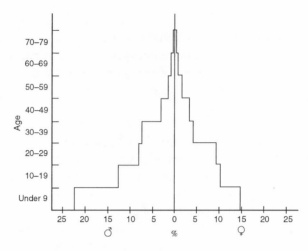

FIGURE 6.11   Age-sex pyramid of an undisturbed
Yanomamö population (N = 1,466). Redrawn and
adapted from Chagnon (1992).

dence of preferential female infanticide shows clearly in the age-sex pyramid of
Figure 6.11 (based on Chagnon 1997:Figure 4.15). In this figure, which represents a compilation from a number of traditional Yanomamö villages and a population total of 1,466, the sex ratio in the critical (immediately postnatal) 0–9 age
cohort is 150, that is, the males outnumber the females by a ratio of 1.5 to 1 (SR
= 22.5% × 1,466 ÷ 15% × 1,466 = 1.5 × 100, or 150).

Given his rejection of the effect of infrastructural behaviors—in this case,
both general and preferential female infanticide as a means of regulating population growth—on higher-order systemic variables, Chagnon, not surprisingly,
downplays this practice in the fifth edition, except for a footnote in which
Chagnon (1997:94) addresses why he has omitted the discussion of infanticide
that was included in the first edition. It turns out that he believes the Venezuelan
authorities, apparently after reading his book, would want to "mount an investigation" of any indigenous group murdering some of its babies (if so, let us hope
these authorities do not have access to the first edition, wherein Yanomamö
practices related to infanticide are laid out in some detail). In other words, the
omission of these data apparently has nothing to do with his rejection of infrastructure as one of the causal variables in adaptive systems. More tellingly from
our perspective, however, Chagnon (1997:94 n. 10) goes on to note that in any
case "it is inconceivable that human mothers would willfully destroy their newborn children in order to make the 'ecological niche' safe for monkeys, armadillos, and peccaries." To this we can respond that by making the environment
"safe" for game animals—by regulating hunting practices and by keeping population numbers tuned to the critical limiting factor of protein—the people constituting a local adaptive system make it possible for themselves to live healthily
there as well.

Domestic Economy

Like Mundurucú women, the Yanomamö women spend a great deal of their time engaged in a variety of laborious tasks that include collecting firewood, carrying water, gathering wild-food resources, and working in the gardens. Aside from hunting and warfare, the Yanomamö men are primarily responsible at the domestic level for the heavier work in constructing the *shabono* and in clearing the jungle to make the family garden. Although the gardens of most families are small, the headman of a village must clear a larger area than anyone else, since he takes on the primary responsibility of feeding allies when they are visiting his village. Cooking responsibilities are carried out by both the women and men of a village, with the women doing the day-to-day cooking and the men assuming this task during feasts and ceremonial occasions. In comparison to traditional Mundurucú society, where, as we have seen, men's and women's roles are sharply separated, those of Yanomamö society appear to be more overlapping in terms of the kinds of activities carried out at the village level. However, this should not be taken to imply that their society is any less male chauvinist than that of the Mundurucú.

Social Organization

Yanomamö villages are composed of at least two affinally related lineage groupings that provide a structured context within which both marriage and settlement fissioning take place. The principal rule governing the choice of a mate is that a man must marry a woman outside his own lineage who falls into the category of *suaböya*, or female cross-cousin—a daughter, in other words, of either his father's sister or his mother's brother. Although the Yanomamö have a strong rule of mother-in-law avoidance, men who are brothers-in-law, or *shoriwä*, develop an especially warm and affectionate relationship. Likewise, a man will usually have a warm relationship with his mother's brother, since he can marry his daughter. Whether he marries mother's brother's daughter or father's sister's daughter, each new son-in-law must carry out a period of bride service for his parents-in-law, hunting game and working in their garden for them. Since the general pattern is for local descent groups to pair with each other in exchanging women in marriage, when a village reaches a size at which increasing conflict occurs among the various paired lineages, it tends to fission into the smaller groups that have established these strong affective ties. As Chagnon (1997:139) points out, however, virtually everyone in a village is defined in terms of a kinship matrix, in other words, "all neighbors are some sort of kin." Since warfare is especially likely to occur between groups that have recently fissioned, it follows that Yanomamö war includes *internecine* war, or war among kin—unlike the Mundurucú, who carried out long-distance war with "foreign" enemies.

Yanomamö society is just as heavily male-biased as Mundurucú society—indeed, perhaps more so in terms of the way women are treated by their husbands. In comparison to the traditional Mundurucú, where often a group of males was involved in sanctioning a single female, male chauvinist behavior in the Yanomamö case usually is limited to the relationship between a man and his wife. She not only must anticipate his every wish but also must accede immediately to his demands, or she risks the probability of any one of a variety of painful punishments that will be meted out by her husband. These can include ripping the decorative sticks out of her perforated earlobes, hitting her with his hand, burning her skin with a glowing firestick, chopping her on the head with his machete, beating her on the head with a stick, and shooting her in a nonvital area of the body with an arrow. Since many Yanomamö men and women use a sharpened piece of bamboo to decoratively shave the tops of their heads in the form of a tonsure, the women whose heads have received such treatment often carry signs highly visible to everyone else in the village of just how much their husbands "care" for them. In the case of an especially abusive and cruel husband, a woman does have recourse to her brothers for protection against him, so in general Yanomamö women prefer to marry inside their own village rather than far away, where they will have little or no kinfolk protection should they marry such a man.

Political Economy

Because of the women's strong fear of being abducted by the men of a distant village, where they are certain to be treated even less well than in their own, the women sometimes goad the men into attacking an enemy village. When asked specifically why they engage in such continual warfare, however, the men invariably say that it is due to "fights over women." Given that the practice of preferential female infanticide results in a shortage of women, one strong cause of warfare is therefore the reduced number of marriageable women in many villages. But even though "fights over women" is the Yanomamö's stated reason, or emic, for going to war, they are not aware of the underlying reason—their tendency to kill more female babies than male babies—which is a primary mechanism of population control among people who do not have access to effective contraceptive devices.

Now disavowing his own earlier arguments, however, Chagnon apparently finds such an underlying etic explanation for Yanomamö warfare laughable. He has recounted such protein-scarcity arguments in detail to the Yanomamö, who find it equally absurd. In fact, in *Yanomamö: The Last Day's of Eden*, Chagnon (1992:115) says that conflict over sex and women "is also a major cause of fighting in our own culture. Some Saturday night just visit a hard-hat bar where fights are frequent. What are the fights usually about? Are they about the amount of meat in someone's hamburger? Or study the words of a dozen country-and-western songs. Do any of them say 'Don't take your cow to town'?"

Of course, we may note here that most people in American society have access to adequate contraceptive devices and therefore do not have to practice preferential female infanticide to keep their population numbers in check. Moreover, American society is characterized by an energy-intensive subsistence system and, if anything, an excess of protein in the diet of most of its inhabitants. In his argument about the "true cause" of Yanomamö warfare, then, Chagnon not only fails to take a truly systemic perspective—one in which cause involves a multiplicity of variables, including every critical feature related to a particular adaptation—he also implicitly assumes that he can treat American and Yanomamö cultures as if they have the same infrastructural features. But to compare an agroindustrial adaptive system to a swidden horticultural one is essentially to equate apples with oranges, just as with Carneiro's comparison of the (protein-rich) Inca system to the (protein-scarce) Kuikuru one.

In any case, as implied earlier, Yanomamö politics is far more complicated than merely going to war against an enemy. This politics involves not only actual conflict but also attempts to forge between-village alliances, as weaker villages try to create and maintain a political balance of power in relation to potential adversary villages of larger size. Complicating matters further is an aggressive ideology that requires each village, whatever its size, to behave as if it were strong enough to attack any other—even including potential allies—in order to coerce it out of its women. As a result, though weaker villages must seek out allies as a means of maintaining the balance of power, no village can ever totally trust any other during the period when the process of alliance formation is taking place.

As Chagnon indicates, the Yanomamö have created a unique economic system in adaptation to these political problems. In spite of environmental homogeneity and a universal availability of resources, each of the villages in a local region tends to specialize in different products—for example, hallucinogenic drugs, arrow points and shafts, hooks and lines for fishing, and cotton hammocks. This then sets up a context in which it becomes economically necessary for villages to get together for trading and feasting, processes that ultimately enhance each village's chances of survival in the hostile political environment. In the fifth edition Chagnon argues that the Yanomamö may not be aware that such an economic system "functions" to promote alliance formation, even though that is the actual result. That is, here, at least, he is willing to argue for a latent, or etic, function for a specific behavior, whereas he is not when it comes to the underlying causes of warfare.

In such a climate of distrust, the situation can often turn to violence when potential or actual allies get together for feasting and trading. To cope with this, the lowland Yanomamö have developed a graded series of levels in the escalation of violence that, when well controlled by the headmen and depending on their own political goals in such a situation, either keep a situation from escalating too fast to the point of no return or, on the contrary, permit it to escalate to the ultimate level of violence and killing. In order of least to most violent, these levels include (1) chest-pounding duels, (2) side-slapping duels, (3) club fights between two or more men, and (4) warfare proper. There is a fifth level, however, called *nomohori* ("dastardly trick"), which is the ultimate, most satisfying level of violence—namely, to invite one's enemies over on the pretense of a friendly social and economic exchange and, just when they are least expecting it, to kill as many of them as possible. Given the potential for a "treacherous feast," it is easy to see why the weaker of two potential allied villages always fears the worst when invited over for dinner and the exchange of a few gifts.

Ultimately, if a weaker village finds itself in increasing danger from all the surrounding settlements and can find no ally, it must move as far away from the threat as possible. Since subsistence support will be required immediately upon arrival at a new village site, however, villages have to plan their move many months in advance by selecting an area, opening up the jungle for new gardens, and beginning the cultivation of crops. The same will be true whenever increasing strife and factionalism in a growing village lead it to fission into two or more smaller settlements, at least one of which will have to establish a new *shabono* and gardens in order to survive in the new setting. Fissioning caused by population growth implies that the Yanomamö regulation of their numbers is not necessarily completely effective. But the fact that villages must always fission, as we saw in the case of the Kuikuru, clearly also implies that there are limitations on how many people can be sustained by swidden and hunting in the tropical rainforest setting. To argue otherwise is to accept the culture-bound and racist argument that some folks have what it takes to develop political mechanisms for staying together (and getting more complex) and some folks do not.

I have already mentioned the data from Chagnon's long-term study indicating the presence of two distinct environments in the Yanomamö area, including the wider-open lowlands and the more restrictive highlands, and that although Yanomamö villages are found throughout both of these environments, the greater part of the population has tended to inhabit the lowlands. In light of the higher numbers of people in the latter area, there are sharp differences in the sociopolitical features characterizing the adaptive systems of villages in the two environments as well. Table 6.1 has been constructed using data from the principal publications in which Chagnon (1973, 1997) discusses these distinctive systems. Although warfare and violence occur in both areas, it is clear from the table that much of the political economy described for the Yanomamö in this section is more characteristic of the lowland system than of the highland one.

Villages in the lowlands have larger gardens, more people, a higher incidence of preferential female infanticide, more abductions of women, a more elaborate series of levels in the escalation of violence, men who are more aggressive, more creation of artificial resource scarcities, and much more frequent warfare—in sum, more of the warlike male chauvinist behavior for which the Yanomamö are so well known. Given the higher numbers and greater population growth in the lowlands, we may conclude that much, if not all, of the sociopolitical system of the lowlands has developed as a result of the need to adapt to this demographic process. Rejecting such infrastructural causal forces, however, Chagnon believes that the larger size and greater bellicosity of lowland groups—not to mention other attendant systemic features such as preferential female infanticide and male chauvinist treatment of the women—have come about so that the Yanomamö can maintain control over their large, wide open environmental niche. In other words, he implies that people in such niches just turn out to be "meaner" than their counterparts in more restricted niches and that population control mechanisms involving the artificial reduction of the number of females have nothing to do with this at all.

TABLE 6.1   The Principal Differences in Societal Features Characterizing Yanomamö Villages in the Lowlands (Center) and Highlands (Periphery)

Societal Feature	Lowlands (center)	Highlands (periphery)
Headman's authority	More power and authority during times of warfare	Less power and authority
Incidence of warfare	Much more frequent and chronic	Less well developed
Patterns of political alliance	More elaborate, with large regular gatherings of allies for feasting and trading	Less elaborate and fewer gatherings of allies
Attitude of the men	Pushy and aggressive, more *unokais* (men who have killed other men), or 44% of all men	More sedate and gentle, fewer *unokais*, or 22% of all men
Extramarital liaisons	Trysts inevitably leading to fighting, killing, and village fissioning	Affairs tolerated, if not institutionalized
Graded levels of violence	Elaborately developed, graded forms of aggression: chest-pounding duels, club fights, and treacherous feasts	Less elaborately developed, with some of the forms of aggression entirely absent in the periphery
Abductions of women	More abductions, (17% of all women)	Fewer abductions (11% of all women)
Incidence of female infanticide	Intensity much greater, 30% excess of males (sex ratio = ~130)	Less intensity, 15% excess of males (sex ratio =~120)
Village size	Larger (upward of 300–400 people)	Much smaller (40–80 people)
Artificial resource scarcities	Deliberate specialization in dogs, bows, arrows, tobacco, cotton, hammocks, drugs, clay pots	Little or no creation of resource scarcities
Size of gardens	Larger, in order to feast allies	Smaller, since little or no need to feast allies

SOURCES: Chagnon (1973, 1997).

Ritual and Leadership

Even though headmen in the lowland villages have more power and authority in times of warfare, they are still like the leaders of other egalitarian village societies. They are usually among the most astute men in their village, experts at cajoling people into helping prepare for feasts, unflinchingly ready to leap into volatile interpersonal disputes to exert control over them, and braver warriors. They also are still merely first among equals, and although people always turn to them for guidance and leadership in difficult situations, villagers can choose to pay attention to a headman or ignore him as they wish. Sometimes headmen are shamans as well and experts at calling the *hekura* spirits—the small, magical entities that can be contacted and used for curing and causing ill only by taking the hallucinogenic snuffs blown by one man through a tube into the nostrils of another, as described in Chapter 3. But nearly all of the men of a village take hallucinogenic drugs on a daily basis and can beckon the *hekura* spirits.

Indeed, any man who wants to can become a shaman, thereby enhancing his ability to send the magical *hekura* darts against his or the village's enemies. It is thus often the case, as Chagnon notes, that a large proportion of the men in a given village become shamans. To do so, however, requires a long period of rigorous fasting and training that lasts a year or more. During this period the novice shaman must not engage in sexual intercourse, since the Yanomamö say that the *hekura* spirits find sex exceedingly distasteful. In the fifth edition Chagnon mentions that the observance of such a long period of sexual continence helps to reduce jealously among the men, although he no longer provides the data indicating the artificially created, severe shortage of women that would bring about such jealousy in a social system generally characterized by monogamous marriages. Given the nature of the lowland adaptation, we thus see more evidence here of the promotion of behaviors whose result is control over population growth.

Ideology (USPs)

Yanomamö origin myths, providing the ultimate justification for this male-dominated society, recount separate origins and inferior status for women. In a story about Moonblood, for example, one of the ancestors shot Moon in the stomach, whereupon his blood fell to earth and instantaneously turned into the male progenitors of the Yanomamö population. All of these men were *waiteri*, or "fierce," but where the blood of Moon had fallen on the earth in the most copious amounts, the men were even fiercer and more inclined to warfare. Yanomamö women in this origin myth are seen as having come from one original woman who had been created out of a kind of jungle fruit called *wabu*. This woman engaged in sex with all of the original population of men and became the ancestor of all Yanomamö women. The men thus existed prior to the women and are viewed not only as superior to them in some regards, but also as different from them in having been created to be fierce warriors.

The Yanomamö cosmos, like that of many other South American indigenous groups, is a multilayered one—consisting in this case of four thin and rigid layers, each of which lies close enough to the others for events in one sometimes to have effects on the others (Figure 6.12). The highest cosmic layer is *duku kä misi*, the "tender layer," which is now empty but is the place where many things now on earth were created. The next layer down, *hedu kä misi*, or "sky layer," contains most everything found on earth, including animals, plants, gardens, and *shabonos*. It is to this layer that the souls of dead Yanomamö go, where they do everything that humans on this earth do, including gardening, hunting, making love, making war, and throwing *hekura* darts at their enemies. Way out at the edge of this plane, the sun gets too close to its bottom surface and causes flames and smoke to appear. From this spot on the lower surface of *hedu*, at some time in

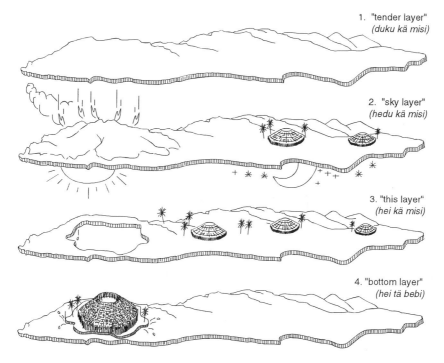

1. "tender layer"
   (duku kä misi)

2. "sky layer"
   (hedu kä misi)

3. "this layer"
   (hei kä misi)

4. "bottom layer"
   (hei tä bebi)

FIGURE 6.12   The four-layered cosmos of the Yanomamö. Redrawn and adapted from Chagnon (1973).

the distant past a piece of matter fell off and crashed right down through earth layer to the bottom layer, *ha tä bebi*, bringing a *shabono* village structure with it. Unfortunately for the people of this village, called Amahiri-teri, only their gardens were transported down with them, not the forest where they hunted. With no game animals available, these people turned into cannibals who prey on the spirits of Yanomamö children in "this layer," or *hei kä misi*. We may be not stretching matters too much here, then, to view this lower layer as equivalent to a Yanomamö Hades, a place in which there is a scarcity of the protein necessary for adequate survival and its inhabitants are turned into cannibalistic monsters.

A Summary Model

The principal features of the Yanomamö adaptation as described in Chagnon's key publications are shown in summary form in the systems-hierarchical model of Figure 6.13. The reader will note that no causal arrows are shown, not least because this keeps what is already a rather complex system from looking too counterintuitive. All of the key variables at every level in the Yanomamö adaptive system are shown nonetheless, including the limitations of the *terra firme* rainforest environment and the hostile neighboring village systems that lie around each village, especially in the lowland area. In summary form like this, in which all of the critical features from infrastructure to cosmology are shown, it may be

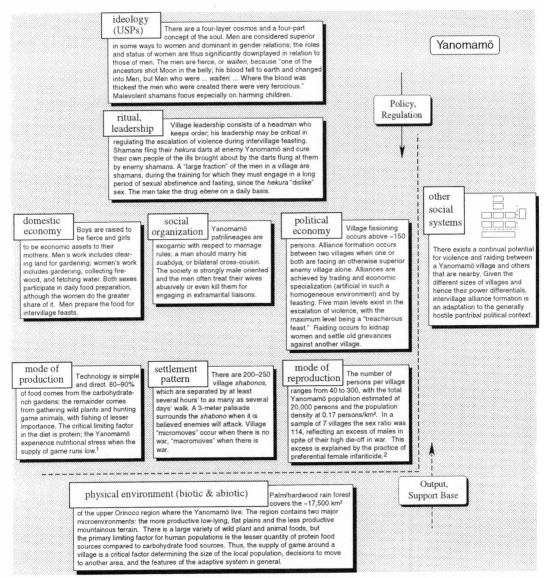

[1] "Game animals are not abundant, and an area is rapidly hunted out, so that a group must constantly keep on the move. ... I have gone on five-day hunting trips with the Yanomamö in areas that had not been hunted for decades, and ... we did not collect even enough meat to feed ourselves" (Chagnon 1968:33).

"The staple is plantains, but ... meat is always the most desirable food and is always considered to be in short supply. ... One of the obligations men take very seriously is providing adequate quantities of meat for their wives and children. They genuinely abhor hearing their children cry for meat; this calls into question their abilities as hunters and marksmen, both of which are associated with prestige" (Chagnon 1968:91).

"The silence was broken when a single man began singing ... 'I am meat hungry! I am meat hungry! Like the carrion-eating buzzard I hunger for flesh'" (Chagnon 1997: 196).

[2] "As is apparent ... there are more males in the Yanomamö population than females. This demographic fact results from the practice of selectively killing female babies: [preferential] female infanticide. The Yanomamö also practice male infanticide but because of the preference to have a male as their first child, they unknowingly kill more females than males. ... A child is killed at birth, irrespective of its sex, if the mother already has a nursing baby. ... Male babies are preferred because they will grow up to be warriors and hunters" (Chagnon 1968:74-75).

FIGURE 6.13   Systems-hierarchical model summarizing the principal features of the Yanomamö adaptive system. Based on textual data in Chagnon (1968, 1997).

harder to justify an approach to understanding the Yanomamö system that refers to just a single variable, such as politics, as a prime causal force (Chagnon's approach); refers to Yanomamö society as being the way it is primarily for inexplicable higher-order, ideological reasons ("just another example of a male-chauvinist society," as a symbolist might argue); or refers to Yanomamö society as being determined totally by infrastructural forces (Harris's approach). In the alternative approach suggested by this model, one must look at all the component variables of the system, forgetting none and invoking all in arriving at an explanation of why the Yanomamö system is the way it is.

Harner's Shuar-Jívaro Data

For the reader familiar with either the travel or anthropological literature of South America, there is probably no indigenous group that better evokes the image of the proud, indomitable Amerindian than the Shuar-Jívaro of the cloud forests and lowlands of eastern Ecuador (Figure 6.14). Because of their practice of cutting off and shrinking the heads of their enemies—to make a magical war trophy called a *tsantsa*—the very name *Jívaro* has come to represent the dangerous and mysterious savage lurking in jungle thickets to kill the hapless outsider, who, for whatever romantic, missionizing, or scientific reasons, might stray into their domain. Indeed, the Jivaroans were known to the outside world some years before even the first Europeans arrived on the western shores of the continent. As Harner (1984) mentions, in the early 1520s the Inca emperor Huayna Capac and part of his army attempted to penetrate a section of Jivaroan territory—presumably looking for sources of placer gold for state craft production—and were attacked by a large force of Jívaro, who banded together just long enough to drive away the foreign intruders coming out of the Andes. In 1599 the Jívaro again came together, out of their normal pattern of isolated autonomous households and loosely allied local household groupings, to handily repel Spanish settlers, who, like the Inca, coveted the placer gold found in the streams that run steeply down into the jungle lowlands off the mineral-rich Andean peaks to the west. Their means of getting it, however, involved as agents of extraction the Jívaro themselves, from whom the settlers had been attempting to require tribute payment in the form of gold dust.

The Jívaro response to this threat to their tribal autonomy established a reputation for bellicosity that effectively kept most outsiders from troubling them for the next three centuries. Uniting temporarily together in the thousands under the leadership of a great warrior named Quirruba, they attacked the Spanish border towns of Logroño and Sevilla del Oro, killing an estimated twelve thousand inhabitants in the one and three-quarters of the twenty-five thousand inhabitants in the other. To further drive home the point that foreign seekers of gold were not welcome in Jívaro territory, they sought out the Spanish governor to deliver a tax directly to his person that he, in his last moments of agony, must have found most unwelcome. Lounging semidressed in the confines of his home when they found him, the governor was taken outside, stripped naked, and tied up at

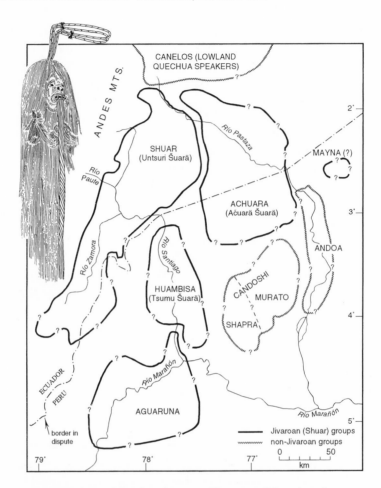

FIGURE 6.14   The distribution of Jivaroan (Shuar) and non-Jivaroan groups in eastern Ecuador and northern Peru. Map redrawn and adapted from Map 1 and the *tsantsa* traced from a photograph in Harner (1984).

the hands and feet, whereupon the Jívaro delivered the tax in the form of a quantity of molten gold that was poured down his throat. Finally, and for good measure, a number of young women were kidnapped from the two towns to be taken with the force as it retired back into the recesses of the vast forests lying to the east. The Spanish women apparently were never seen again, presumably remaining in Jívaro territory to become minor contributors to the gene pool that characterizes the Jívaro-Shuar population today.

By the late nineteenth century the Jívaro had established trading relations with their former enemies, the people of the town of Macas, who constituted the one Spanish-speaking community that had remained, however uneasily, in the Andean foothills bordering the western edge of their territory. In exchange for lard, salt, and *tsantsas*, the Jívaro received metal and other goods from the Ecuadorian national economy. Most recently, in the later twentieth century, the western Jívaro have reacted to the increasing encroachment of colonists, missionaries, and oil prospectors by forming the Shuar Federation—thereby indicating their intention both to defend the rights to their native land on a pantribal basis and to not be called "Jívaro," since in the highlands especially this name had come to take on a highly negative connotation. For this reason, in the following discussion of their adaptation I primarily use the term *Shuar*, although as their principal ethnographer, Harner (1984), points out the word is rather ambiguous in that they use it to describe other groups in this general area, not just the one we are dealing with here. Thus, as shown in Figure 6.14, there are at least three major groups that are part of the Shuar populations of eastern Ecuador—including the group studied by Harner in the 1950s, the Shuar proper, or in their language, Untsuri Šuarä; their enemy neighbors to the east, the Achuara, or Achuarä Šuarä, who have been brilliantly studied in a recent ethnography written by Phillipe Descola (1996b; see also 1996a), a student of Claude Lévi-Strauss; and their enemy neighbors to the south, the Huambisa, or Tsumu Šuarä.

Physical Environment

As shown in Figure 6.15, that part of the Shuar population studied by Harner is located primarily between the Río Pastaza and the Río Zamora, in an area of cloud forest that extends over roughly 9,600 square kilometers. The western edge of this rugged area begins just at the point where high waterfalls pouring off the Andes are replaced by rapids with steep gradients that run on down to the east; and the eastern edge ends where these fast-running streams give way to the meandering rivers that characterize Amazonia generally. Cutting north-south across the middle of the area is the Cordillera de Cutucú, a 2,000-meter-high outlier of the main Andean chain, which, interestingly enough, received its name from one Victor Oppenheim (personal communication), now a retired petroleum prospector residing in Dallas, Texas, and one of the first explorers from the outside world in the twentieth century to travel through Shuar territory and map it. Drenched with the rains from clouds of Amazonian origin that flow up against the high Andes, the entire area is covered with dense forests through which run swift streams that are generally unnavigable by canoe—both of these being factors that, in addition to the warlike nature of the Shuar, probably explain why European influences have been so slow in penetrating an area that lies just a scant 100 kilometers or so from the cities of highland Ecuador.

Mode of Production

As with other Amazonian groups, the principal source of carbohydrate calories in the Shuar adaptation is from the cultivation of small gardens, which prior to the 1950s or so were opened in the forest using stone axes; more recently they have been opened with steel machetes and double-headed axes traded in from the highlands. Harner estimates that the size of gardens ranges between about 0.5 and 1 hectare, depending on a host of interrelated factors, including the number

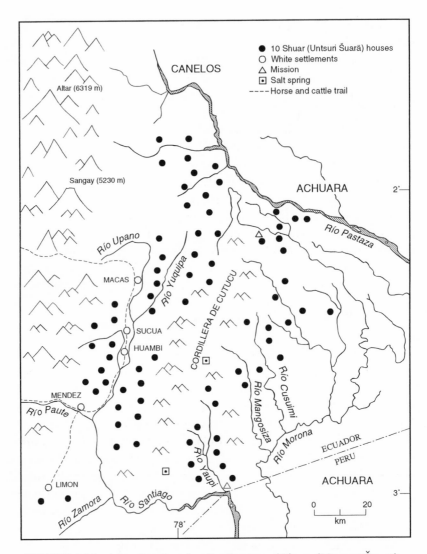

FIGURE 6.15   Map showing the distribution of Shuar (Untsuri Šuarä) household groupings in the area between the Río Zamora and the Río Pastaza, eastern Ecuador. Redrawn and adapted from Harner (1984).

of wives the head of household has, the feasting requirements of alliance formation with other local households, the prestige he wishes to acquire, his personal charisma and power, and the degree to which he is engaged in fighting with enemy households. Providing an estimated 65 percent of the diet, the crops grown in the gardens include tubers such as sweet manioc and sweet potato, as well as plantains, papaya, squash, tomato, maize, chili pepper, onions, sugarcane, cotton, gourds, tobacco, and achiote. In addition, other plants are cultivated that provide fish poisons, medicines, and hallucinogenic drugs, including *ayahuasca* and *Datura*. Although the head of household and any sons he has carry out the task of cutting down the vegetation necessary to open up the swidden plot, the women do the rest of the work, including gathering and burning the slash as well as planting and harvesting all of the crops except for maize, which is cultivated by the men. The gardens continually produce throughout the year, since there is little seasonality with respect to rainfall and temperature.

Sweet manioc is used by the Shuar to produce an alcoholic beverage called *ni-hamanchï*, which is prepared for interhousehold feasts as well as being drunk on a daily basis by most members of the household in quantities ranging between 3 and 4 gallons for the men, 1 and 2 gallons for the women, and a 0.5 gallon for the older children. The women prepare this drink by cooking and mashing up the manioc, masticating it, and then placing it in pottery vessels, where it is allowed to ferment under the influence of the enzymes that have been added from their saliva as they chewed it. Normally the fermentation process takes at least four days before the brew reaches its maximum potency, although for domestic use *ni-hamanchï* is usually consumed much sooner after its initial preparation, since it is much in demand. Indeed, Harner asserts that manioc beer is likely to have a healthful effect on all who consume it in that it enhances sweating and body cooling in a context of high heat and humidity.

The hunting of game animals, which provides about 20 percent of the diet, is generally undertaken by the male head of household, either alone or with one of his wives, who aids in handling the dogs, which are brought along when he is hunting peccaries, jaguars, or ocelots. Blowguns and curare-tipped darts are normally used to take arboreal creatures, such as monkeys and large birds, whereas muzzle-loading shotguns are used for ground-dwelling game. On occasion the men of various households will join together on a hunting expedition when they plan to go after a large troop of monkeys. As in the Yanomamö case, the area immediately around a settlement within half a day's walk rather quickly becomes characterized by a scarcity of game, and Harner notes that it was only in traveling with the Shuar through distant areas devoid of human inhabitants that he saw relatively great densities of game. When the hunting becomes markedly poor and several days have passed without meat being eaten in the household, a man may have to range so far that he does not return home until the end of the day. Nearly all Shuar families raise chickens, although a few have pigs, these latter usually being kept only when a *tsantsa* feast is being planned and they wish to augment the relatively meager supply of meat available from wild game.

The rest of the diet comes from fishing and gathering, the former activity not being of great significance to the Shuar given the difficulty of fishing the small, rapidly flowing streams that run through their area. As noted in the preceding chapter in discussion of the Nukak groups of eastern Colombia, fishing is of somewhat greater importance during the drier months of the year when fish are easier to trap and poison in receding, slower-moving waters. Gathering is not of great importance in the diet either, although a variety of fruits and insects is obtained by this means—insects in both the larval and adult stages being considered a special delicacy. Of substantial importance, however, to Shuar ritual is the use of a number of different hallucinogenic plants, which are sought out in the forest in addition to being grown in the gardens.

Settlement Pattern

As shown in Figure 6.15, Shuar settlements are scattered thinly across the landscape in isolated clusters consisting of roughly ten households, each cluster constituting a kindred composed of families with consanguineal and affinal ties to one another. Except for the dwellings of a man's sons-in-law, who live for several years after their marriage to his daughters a few hundred meters away from him, a household usually is located a minimum of 1 kilometer from any of the others. Quarrels among more distant relatives often erupt, however, not least because of conflicts over dwindling supplies of game, so the settlement pattern at any given point in time is highly volatile and subject to change as each household assesses its location in strategic relation to the others. A Shuar dwelling normally is built on higher ground near a stream and not far from a source of trees suitable for house construction, the commanding position being especially necessary, so that its inhabitants can look out over the surrounding garden to the edge of the forest in maintaining their vigilance against surprise attack.

In a context characterized by a continual threat of violence, Shuar dwellings are built as minifortifications to provide maximum protection to each family (see Figure 6.16). Sturdy sections of cut chonta palm are placed vertically in the ground in an oval plan, with each chonta stave placed just a few centimeters apart to permit light to enter but to keep the inhabitants protected from shots fired by an attacking enemy. Additional protection inside the structure is provided by sturdy crossbars used to lock the two entrances, an additional layer of chonta staves against the wall by each of the family's beds, the use of log breastworks and foxholes, and an escape tunnel permitting escape to a hidden spot in the garden—especially when conflict with other households, either faraway or nearby, has reached a point where the danger of attack is imminent. Outside the structure, booby traps, including covered holes containing sharpened sticks in upright positions (similar to the infamous excrement-covered *punji* sticks used by the indigenous combatants of the Vietnam War), may be placed either on trails or in the garden itself.

Although with an average size of nine to ten persons, Shuar families could easily accommodate themselves in a smaller structure, dwellings range between 7.5 and 11 meters in width and between 12 and 18 meters in length. This larger size is necessary because the head of household must often host visitors in order to maintain his political position in the local neighborhood cluster. The house must be large enough not only to enable drinking and dancing inside its walls, since during periods of heightened conflict it is not safe for the party to be held outdoors, but also to accommodate a number of additional people sleeping inside it during these gatherings. Moreover, as Descola points out for the Achuara, allied families sometimes must live together for weeks or months in the same household to protect themselves against attack from any large force that might overwhelm a single family.

Both the Shuar and the Achuara also divide the house conceptually and functionally into a men's and a women's side. In the Shuar case the men's side is

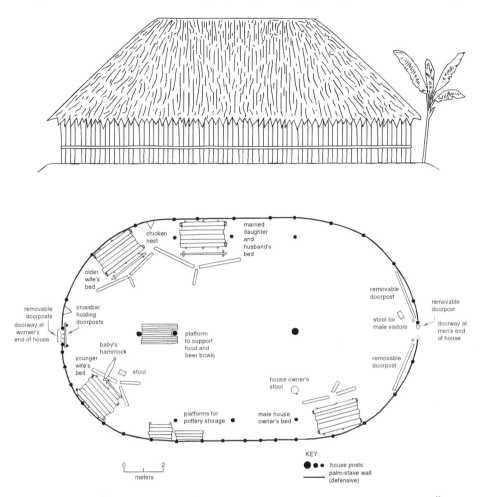

FIGURE 6.16 Elevation view and representative floor plan of a Shuar (Untsuri Šuarä) household. Floor plan redrawn and adapted from Harner (1984).

called the *tanamašä* and the women's side the *ekenta*. The male head of household may walk anywhere inside these two spaces he wishes, but his wives enter his side only when they are serving food to him and any other men who may happen to be visiting. If the head of household should die, he is buried seated on his stool in an upright position in a hole dug in the floor and the house is abandoned by the rest of the family. Otherwise dwellings are occupied for a period of nearly ten years, even though new gardens have to be opened up every three years or so as weed invasion and nutrient loss occur in the old plot. During this period any other person in the family who dies is buried in the floor and the house continues in use. A house site is maintained as long as there are enough game and palm logs in the immediate vicinity, but if the hunting gets poor, a family may have to move a distance of up to 15 kilometers away from the old site. Should nearby neighbors pose a clear threat of total annihilation of the family, then, as Harner notes, much longer moves of up to 130 kilometers may be required.

Mode of Reproduction

Harner estimates the population of Shuar in the area he studied to number a little over twenty-two hundred, based on an average number of nine persons per household and a total of 245 households—equivalent, in other words, to a population density of 0.46 person per square kilometer. Although this number may appear to be low, it is over double the figure of 0.17 person per square kilometer that we earlier estimated for the Yanomamö based on Chagnon's data. As with the Yanomamö, however, there is evidence around the turn of the twentieth century that the Shuar population began expanding as groups of warriors began making attacks on the Achuara and Huambisa that caused these two groups to retreat to the east and southeast, respectively, away from the Shuar threat. After a period during which no one apparently lived in the unoccupied zones, the Shuar moved in to claim them as they discovered that the supply of game animals there was far better than it had been in their own neighborhoods. At the same time, increasing expansion of Ecuadorian colonists into the western fringes of Shuar territory apparently caused an increase in population density as Shuar households were forced to move farther toward the interior. As this process occurred, the Shuar eventually turned increasingly to intratribal warfare—war among local households and household groupings—and away from the pattern of intertribal *tsantsa* raids they had carried out during the nineteenth century and (probably) earlier.

Not surprisingly for a warlike population, both men and women state that the preferred first child is a boy. But, ideally, after that the couple prefers that a girl be born. From the father's point of view, boys are needed not only to help him in hunting but also to aid in the defense of the household, whereas girls are needed for him and his sons to exchange in marriage, so that when his sons marry and move away, he will have one or more sons-in-law living near him to carry out the same subsistence and defensive tasks his sons did. Even though infanticide is rarely practiced, except in the case of children who are born deformed, the fact that the adult sex ratio is 50—i.e., with females outnumbering males roughly 2 to 1—clearly indicates a skewing that in this case comes about as a result of the deaths of many men in war. This has especially been true since the time when the warfare pattern evolved from intertribal raids in which all men, women, and children were killed to intratribal conflict in which the focus has been more on killing individual men for *tsantsas*.

Although a man may take his younger wife along on a hunting expedition, not only for helping with the dogs but also for enjoying a day or more of sexual activity in the absence of the rest of the family, it is considered dangerous for the success of the hunt to engage in sex during it. This rule obviously is not followed (or he would not take her with him), but since any small children she might have do interfere with her ability to accompany him, a man prefers to limit the frequency of sex with her to about once every six to eight days—a rule that he also attempts to follow with his other wives. This strictly followed rule of enforced abstinence from sex appears to be one way the Shuar population keeps its numbers in check, never mind that the population apparently was expanding slowly during the twentieth century. Another practice that probably restricts the number of births (by suppressing ovulation) is the observance of a long period of breast-feeding for each baby that lasts up to five or six years. As Harner (1984:87) rather wryly notes, "weaning is not emphasized."

Domestic Economy

In addition to clearing the area used for the garden, men's tasks in Shuar society most importantly include house construction and weaving, whereas women's tasks, as mentioned earlier, include the great bulk of the labor in burning slash and cultivating and harvesting the garden. Since the size and quality of the dwelling are a critically important indication of his personal power, or *kakarma*, a man puts a great deal of effort into its construction and is usually aided in this task by several male kinsmen from nearby households. Once the house is constructed, the women are more occupied than the men with domestic tasks, since on a daily basis they do the cooking and prepare the *nihamanchï* beer. The men are rarely idle, however, since they carry out all of the work of textile production—from the spinning of the cotton yarn to the dyeing and weaving of it into the material used to make the traditional clothing, which consists of kilts for the men and dresses for the women.

Aside from the adults and children, the other critical members of the household economy are the dogs, which are called *niawá*, the same name given to the fearsome jaguar, and which number at least one or two in each Shuar dwelling. As mentioned earlier, they are important in hunting especially the larger and more dangerous ground-dwelling species of game animals. They also act as guardians of the garden and, leashed to the women's beds at night, provide early warning by barking in the event of an approach by an enemy group. Their importance is so great that dogs are the object of several important rituals. For example, when a litter of puppies is born, one of the women of the household lies down with their mother to observe a form of couvade that is considered necessary to protect the litter from supernatural harm. Puppies also are breast-fed by the women along with their own children. Finally, dogs, as with Shuar of all ages, are given hallucinogenic drugs to help them acquire the supernatural power necessary to function properly in carrying out their daily activities.

Social Organization

Since a man's status in his neighborhood is directly dependent on the subsistence productivity of his gardens and his ability to provide large quantities of manioc beer and food to his guests during interhousehold feasts, the normal marriage pattern is polygyny, or marriage to at least two wives. And since he normally must go to live with his parents-in-law, a man prefers to marry sisters not only because they are reputed to get along better but also because he avoids the need to move to another new household following his second marriage. Although men often marry unrelated women from outside their neighborhood, the majority of marriages occurs between cross-cousins from either the father's or the mother's side of the family in the local kindred, not least because living outside it subjects him to the danger of being killed by someone with an earlier grudge against his family. In spite of the fact that females outnumber males by a 2:1 ratio in Shuar society, the pattern of sororal polygyny means that a man and his brother(s) usually are competing for the same restricted group of women in the local neighborhood and thus can become enemies. The potential for eventual hostilities between a man and his consanguineal relatives, including his brothers, is enhanced during the period following marriage when a man develops strong ties of mutual aid with his wife's family by performing tasks such as gathering firewood and helping his father-in-law with the hunting of game. Although he may substitute the gift of a shotgun for bride service in rare cases where neighbors of the parents-in-law are hostile to him, the new bridegroom and his wife usually live with them until the first child is born and then neolocally nearby her parents afterward.

Should either household be attacked by enemies, whether they are kinfolk with a grudge or not, both will join together in mutual defense. However, Shuar households in general are scattered and children usually grow up in relative isolation from other people outside their own nuclear polygynous family. Thus, in spite of the ties with nearby in-laws and shifting alliances with more far-flung families in the neighborhood, fathers, as Harner notes, often admonish their children with early morning lectures that warn them of the dangers of trusting anyone beyond the confines of their own household. Children who misbehave are first spanked with nettles and, if this does not work, are forced to remain over a small fire into which chili peppers have been thrown until they become unconscious (this latter punishment characterized childrearing practices in the ancient Mesoamerican Aztec state as well). At frequent intervals in their upbringing, children are given doses of hallucinogenic drugs not only to aid them in comprehending the righteousness of their parents' instructions but also to help them perform all the necessary tasks they will carry out during their lifetimes.

Between the age of two and eight years old, girls are given a hallucinogen mixed with a small amount of tobacco water to help them acquire a form of soul power called *arutam*, which enables them to be successful in having babies, working hard in their gardens, and raising domesticated animals. It is even more important for a boy to take hallucinogens and see an *arutam* soul—usually at a sacred waterfall—since the acquisition of this soul will be his only means of survival in an environment filled with potentially hostile enemies and shamans. Indeed, by the age of nine or so a young boy begins accompanying his father on *tsantsa* raids. When he reaches the age of sixteen, a boy goes into the forest to kill a tree sloth, from which he makes his first shrunken head. His father then gives two *tsantsa* feasts of celebration that are exactly the same as the feasts held for shrunken human heads, after which the young man formally takes on the status of an adult and is entitled to wear the headpiece, called *etsemat*, that all adult Jívaro men wear. A father also sponsors two feasts for his daughter when she reaches puberty, hallucinogenic drugs again being administered to her so that she will have dreams that augur success in gardening and taking care of other household tasks.

Political Economy

Hostilities among Shuar households arise for a variety of reasons, such as the competition for wives among brothers mentioned previously, but most importantly because most nonviolent deaths at the local household level are ascribed to the work either of bewitching shamans or of women who have poisoned the *nihamanchï* beer during a feast. Nearly all neighbors of a given household, whether relatively near or far from it, are thus potentially the targets of assassination raids carried out to avenge whatever ills may befall that household. Generally, however, killing at the local neighborhood or tribal level is carried out on a rather strictly observed one-to-one, or tit-for-tat, basis, as opposed to the earlier period, when the Shuar conducted raids against the Achuara or other enemies that involved mass murder of all the inhabitants of a household. In such a hostile sociopolitical environment, it thus comes as no surprise that most of the men Harner (1984:112) interviewed "expressed a strong desire to kill" and thus to establish or maintain their reputations as powerful men, or *kakaram*, who are not to be trifled with. The situation snowballs into ever-increasing danger for the man who is most successful at acquiring *arutam* soul power and killing, since he often is asked to lead revenge raids by weaker individuals in his neighborhood. This obviously leads to the creation of more enemies seeking to avenge his leadership of such a raid. Moreover, during the raid itself he always has to be on his guard, since he may well be the object of a treacherous killing by the very individuals who have enlisted his leadership and who, unbeknown to him, harbor some earlier grudge against him themselves.

At a point some weeks or months before a raid, a man goes out into the forest and takes a hallucinogenic drug that will permit him to acquire the *arutam* soul necessary for protection against any form of violent act, poisoning, or sorcery. He awakens in the night to find himself in the midst of a violent windstorm under a starless sky. Clinging to a tree to keep from being blown down and crushed by the trees falling all around him, he suddenly sees a vision consisting of a pair of giant jaguars or anacondas rolling toward him or, alternatively, a human head or a great ball of fire. He must then run forward and touch this Jerry Lee Lewis vision of magical reality, either with a stick or his hand, at which point he has acquired the *arutam* soul. Immediately, a surge of power and intelligence courses through his body, coupled with an overwhelming urge to go out and kill someone. Such a ritual system, of course, makes interhousehold violence and killing more or less a self-fulfilling prophecy on an ongoing basis.

The house of the intended victim of a raid is usually attacked just before dawn. On the afternoon of the day preceding the attack, the raiders stop somewhere nearby and each man declares what sort of *arutam* vision he has had, whereupon the *arutam* soul leaves his body as suddenly as it has entered, although the power to keep him inviolate will take several weeks to seep away from his body. Should a man die during the raid, it is taken as a sign that his *arutam* soul has accidentally escaped several weeks prior to the raid, leaving him unaware of the loss of his killer soul power. The man who successfully kills during the raid cuts off the head of his victim, taking it with him back into the forest as the raiders swiftly depart to escape any reprisals. During the return home he removes the skull and by a time-honored procedure shrinks the head of his victim down to about one-quarter of its original size. The lips of the *tsantsa* are pinned shut with three small sharpened sticks of chonta palm, and charcoal powder is rubbed into the skin to blacken it, a process that keeps the killed person's avenging soul, or *muisak*, from escaping to wreak vengeance on the man who assassinated him.

Upon the headtaker's return home, after about a year's time during which garden production is increased and pigs are raised, he holds a *tsantsa* feast to which all his neighbors are invited, sometimes in numbers of up to 150 persons. In this manner the headtaker is able to wine and dine his neighbors, impressing them with the productivity and power of his wives as gardeners and with his prowess as an acquirer of *arutam* soul power and killer of his enemies. As an added benefit, his wife and a sister hold on to him during the *tsantsa* dance to permit the power of the *muisak* soul to seep down into their bodies—giving them enhanced power over the productivity of both gardens and domestic animals (*tsantsas*, we might say, thus promoted "better homes and gardens" among the Jívaro). Finally, should he feel powerful and vengeful enough in relation to any of his guests against whom he harbors a grudge, one of his wives may well slip poison into the manioc beer and, undetected among all the other women serving the *nihamanchï*, serve it to yet another victim of his ire.

In a sociopolitical context characterized by chronic hostilities and no support from larger cooperative kin groups, the Shuar have nevertheless developed a series of ties to trading partners, called *amigri* (from the Spanish word for "friend"), that provide them not only with some social security but also with access to trading goods from the outside world. These ties are between a man and male neighbors to either side of him some kilometers away, and as shown in Figure 6.17a, they crosscut the hostile Shuar landscape on an east-west basis. Through the larger trading network thus created, industrial goods such as guns and steel machetes are acquired from highland Ecuador via the frontier Shuar living near the Spanish-speaking towns at the western edge of Shuar territory, and a large number of indigenous goods are acquired from the Achuara to the east. Although these ties are so strong that potentially hostile brothers sometimes become *amigri* primarily to ensure peaceful relations between them, no man feels safe traveling alone outside his own area for distances that exceed one to two days' travel away.

Ritual and Leadership

Given the increasing scarcity of game as a family continues living in one spot in the forest, men preparing to hunt engage in a ritual they hope will ensure its success. During a three-day period tobacco smoke is blown by one man into the lungs of another through a bamboo tube; the recipient must swallow every bit of

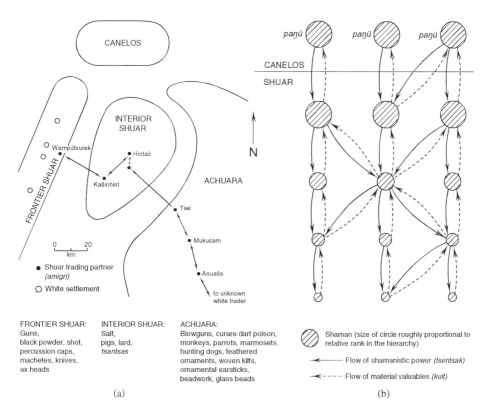

FRONTIER SHUAR:
Guns,
black powder, shot,
percussion caps,
machetes, knives,
ax heads

INTERIOR SHUAR:
Salt,
pigs, lard,
tsantsas

ACHUARA:
Blowguns, curare dart poison,
monkeys, parrots, marmosets,
hunting dogs, feathered
ornaments, woven kilts,
ornamental earsticks,
beadwork, glass beads

Shaman (size of circle roughly proportional to relative rank in the hierarchy)

Flow of shamanistic power *(tsentsak)*

Flow of material valuables *(kuit)*

(a)   (b)

FIGURE 6.17   Model of cross-cutting socioeconomic relations between local Shuar males and those of other groups: (a) east-west flow of material goods between *amigri* trading partners and (b) north-south flow of power and material goods between shamans. Redrawn and adapted from Harner (1984).

the smoke. Should the hunt fail to be productive, it is ascribed to the fact that the man did not swallow the smoke entirely. And given the scarcity of game resulting from an increasing Shuar population, a hostile, competitive environment characterizes both the political and ritual realms of their adaptation, and further regulation of population numbers is manifested especially in the case of ritual. Harner notes that fully one-quarter of all Jívaro men become shamans and that all who do so must go through at least a five-month period of fasting and strict sexual abstinence in order to achieve shamanic power.

As shown in Figure 6.17b, whereas trading relationships crosscut the Shuar area from east to west, shamanic power is acquired from a source lying to the north and moves down in ever-decreasing amounts as it is transmitted toward the southern part of the Shuar territory. The power itself, which is acquired from Canelos Quichua shamans (*paŋü*) who live in the eastern cloud forests just to the north of the Shuar, consists of tiny entities called *tsentsak,* or the same sort of magical darts used for bewitching enemies by the Yanomamö, Mundurucú, Ona, and Yahgan. Constantly flinging these darts around at their intended victims, the Shuar shamans are one of the primary features of the adaptation that not only "fan the flames" of internecine conflict but also keep people fairly thinly distributed across the landscape. With the danger of long-distance travel, a man who wishes to acquire shamanic power must establish contact with someone to the north who has access to someone else and so on. Interestingly enough, only magical darts come down from the north, whereas a substantial portion of the material goods available to the Shuar flow to the north.

Although the materialist observer might consider such an exchange a bad bargain for the Shuar—with only "objects of thin air" moving south and material goods moving north—we may note here that, if such magical reality keeps people from living too close to one another, then the ultimate effect is a very real-world one as well. That is, it helps maintain lower population densities in an environment that cannot sustain higher numbers of people. Furthermore, in what may be seen as a way of ensuring that no one "cheats" on the magical aspects of a ritual with such critically important real-world effects, there is a rule that a shaman returning home from the purchase of *tsentsak* power may dispense part of that power to no more than four men who live in his neighborhood or to the south of him. After that, and by using up his own power in bewitching his enemies, the shaman must seek out more *tsentsak* darts from his shamanic ally in the north. *Tsentsak* power, like the goods that are exchanged for it, is thus as scarce a commodity as any other in the Shuar political economy.

Ideology (USPs)

Shuar women are aided in their gardening by Nuŋuí, a fat little "earth mother" spirit about 1 meter tall who lives under the ground during the daytime and comes out to dance in the gardens at night. Since Nuŋuí is crucial in the growth of the plants, the women must attract her to the garden by keeping it weeded and providing her with "babies," consisting of three little chips of unworked jasper stone whose location is magically determined by the women when they take hallucinogens. Once Nuŋuí has been attracted to the garden, the women sing to her to push up the plants, to give their husband success in the hunt, to protect the family against snakebite, and to protect the household from attack by enemies. Indeed, as enemies are approaching a house through the garden, the manioc plants are viewed as able to suck the blood from anyone who touches them. To Nuŋuí the Shuar also owe their knowledge of pottery making and the gift of the dog, which helps protect the house against attack and aids them in hunting.

Shuar cosmology includes a belief in three kinds of souls, two of which have already been mentioned. The first is the *arutam wakani,* or "ancient specter soul," a vision that appears only occasionally to a man who has taken hallucinogenic drugs. Since it lasts only a minute or so, it must be touched immediately if he is to acquire security from violent death. If a man is lucky enough to acquire two *arutam* souls, which is the maximum he can have within him at any time, he becomes totally protected from death of any kind, whether violent or not. Although a man must lose his *arutam* soul before he engages in a killing his enemy, he can, according to Harner, "lock in" part of the remaining power by acquiring a new *arutam*. The second soul is the *muisak wakani,* or "avenging soul," which comes into existence precisely at the moment when a man who possessed an *arutam* soul at some earlier point in his life is killed by the enemy. This means, of course, that any killed man who has the misfortune of never having found an *arutam* soul dies without being able to spiritually avenge his death at a later time. The third soul is the *nekás wakani,* or "true soul," which is possessed by every living Shuar. Since it is represented primarily in a person's body by his or her blood, its gradual loss when a person is wounded is viewed as a form of soul loss. Otherwise, the *nekás wakani* is a passive soul that leaves the body at a person's death and then goes through a metamorphosis involving three stages: First, it returns to the house where the person was born and relives that individual's entire lifetime, always hungry and lurking in the shadows of the garden or house in the form of a deer or an owl; then, the *nekás wakani* changes into a "true demon," reliving the person's life again in this form but wandering hungry and solitary through the forest; finally, the *nekás wakani* changes into a giant butterfly, which lives a life of hunger before it drops dead to the ground and changes into water vapor.

As Harner points out, the Shuar dread the fate of their *nekás wakani* when they die, since it is so different from the real lifetime of its possessor. But here we may argue that such a soul would probably be created only in the cosmology of a people who to some degree feel that they live on the edge in terms of an adequate diet—as exemplified by the data suggesting a decrease in game as a family occupies a household over the years and the ritual aimed at hunting success and garden productivity. This is not to say that the traditional Shuar adaptation was not in equilibrium at the time of Harner's study in the 1950s—in other words, with the population regulated by a variety of cosmological, ritual, and sociopolitical mechanisms in light of the capacity of their rain-forest environment to sustain them. It does suggest, however, that the equilibrium was somewhat fragile and subject to disruption, especially given that the Shuar population was expanding during the earlier part of the twentieth century.

THE DESANA

As implied at the beginning of this chapter, Reichel-Dolmatoff's research (1971, 1972, 1976; see also 1996) on the Desana, of the far central-eastern Amazonian lowlands of Colombia, is one of the classic ecological studies of indigenous South American groups. Indeed, there are probably few examples anywhere in the world of a traditional society whose adaptive system involves such an explicit realization of the limitations, or constraints, on human population numbers and whose ecologically driven ideology is so much a part of daily life. Given the embeddedness of ideology in other component variables of the Desana adaptive structure, our neat categories, ranging from physical environment to ideological superstructure, become a bit more blurred than has heretofore been the case in this book. Thus, for example, along with the discussion of the more mundane details of Desana house layout and settlement pattern, it is necessary to begin the treatment of their complex ideological system.

Reichel-Dolmatoff's Desana Data

One potential drawback of Reichel-Dolmatoff's Desana study needs to be mentioned before we proceed: As he explicitly points out in the preface to his book *Amazonian Cosmos*, the majority of his data came from interviews with a single informant named Antonio Guzmán, who, although born and enculturated in Desana society, nevertheless had lived and worked a good part of his life in a highland urban Colombian setting. However, two aspects of Reichel-Dolmatoff's study go a long way toward mitigating the potential drawbacks of such an apparently limited sample of data. First, Guzmán clearly had an exceptionally good recollection and understanding of the key features of the Desana system. Second, after the interviews were completed, Reichel-Dolmatoff made several visits to the area of Guzmán's former residence in Desana territory, which enabled him to "ground-truth" his informant's statements by recording some fifty hours of material from a number of other Desana informants on every aspect of their society discussed in the book. In his preface the author notes not only that these informants corroborated what Guzmán had told him but also that the general ethnological literature on the area squared with his account.

Physical Environment

As shown in Figure 6.18, the Desana occupy an area that, judging from Reichel-Dolmatoff's textual description, encompasses about 4,000 square kilometers of rain forest delimited on the north by the Río Vaupés, on the south by the Río Papurí, and on the east and west, respectively, by the modern settlements of Mitú and Yavarete. The Desana do not occupy this large area uniformly, however, since settlements are concentrated along rivers—including the right bank of the Vaupés, the left bank of the Papurí, both banks of the Río Macú-Paraná, and several smaller watercourses that run across the area. Although the Vaupés is navigable, the Papurí features some thirty *cachoeiras*, or rapids, along its 280-kilometer length, making communication over longer distances along this river more difficult than along the Vaupés or other larger Amazonian rivers that flow through the flat terrain of the basin. Like the rest of the Amazon, however, temperatures are warm year-round, with little or no seasonal variation. Rain falls year-round as well, although during the months between January and March it tapers off enough so that indigenous inhabitants recognize this time of the year as the dry season.

Mode of Production

Desana men prefer to describe themselves in general as hunters, not as horticulturists or fisherfolk, even though only about one-quarter of subsistence is from

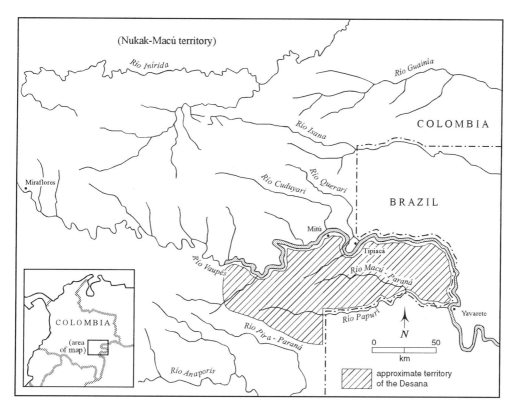

FIGURE 6.18   Map showing the location of the Desana of east-central Colombia. Redrawn and adapted from sketch map and textual descriptions in Reichel-Dolmatoff (1971, 1996).

hunting, whereas the remainder comes in more or less equal measure from swidden gardening and fishing. Although the bulk of caloric intake comes from manioc, the staple crop, the Desana define the capacity of the subsistence system to sustain their population numbers not in terms of brute calories, but in terms of the protein provided by fish and, especially, game animals. Moreover, the members of each local household (Figure 6.19) view their ecosystem as a bounded, confined area delineated by landmarks known to all and surrounded by the territories of other groups. Thus, each household has to be able to sustain itself over the longer term within this strictly limited area (see Figure 6.20). The adaptive problem the Desana have thus explicitly posed, not to mention solved, for themselves is to maintain their numbers rigorously in accordance with the protein supply in their local bounded environment, specifically by avoiding overhunting and scrupulously regulating the frequency of sexual relations.

Settlement Pattern

The Desana are organized into local kindreds called "sibs," that is, patrilineal groups consisting of four to eight nuclear families, all of whom occupy the same

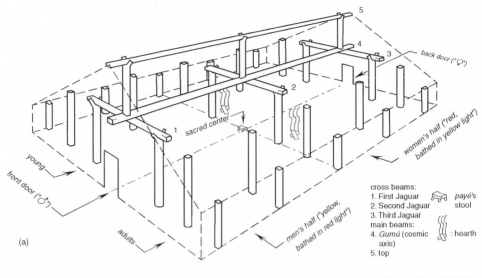

FIGURE 6.19 Hypothetical reconstruction of a Desana *maloca* of the upper Vaupés River (a) and depiction of the Yuruparí ceremony, during which the hallucinogen *Banisteriopsis caapi*, or yajé, is taken and the sacred flutes are played (b). Upper drawing based on textual description in Reichel-Dolmatoff (1971); lower redrawn and adapted from Schultes and Hoffman (1992).

dwelling and whose individual members marry exogamously. According to Reichel-Dolmatoff, sib households are spaced at considerable distance from each other along the rivers (although he does not give figures for this distance). The dwellings, called *malocas*, consist of long, low rectangular structures that are built using sturdy wooden logs and palm thatching (Figure 6.19). With the replacement of the thatching every four years or so and the even more occasional re-

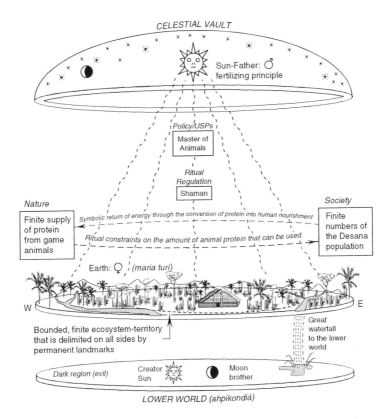

CELESTIAL VAULT

Sun-Father: ♂
fertilizing principle

Policy/USPs
Master of
Animals

*Ritual
Regulation*
Shaman

Nature

Finite supply
of protein
from game
animals

Symbolic return of energy through the conversion of protein into human nourishment

Ritual constraints on the amount of animal protein that can be used

Society

Finite
numbers of
the Desana
population

Earth: ♀ *(maria turí)*

W   E

Bounded, finite ecosystem-territory
that is delimited on all sides by
permanent landmarks

Great
waterfall
to the lower
world

Dark region (evil)   Creator
Sun   Moon
brother

LOWER WORLD (ahpikondiá)

FIGURE 6.20   Model of Desana cosmology showing a three-level cosmos: "lower world" *(ahpikondiá)*; earth, or "this world" *(maría turí)*; and "celestial vault." Based on textual description in Reichel-Dolmatoff (1976).

placement of the poles and beams on the interior of the structure, a *maloca* can last several decades. As with the Kuikuru case discussed earlier in this chapter, it thus appears that the Desana have achieved a stable adaptation in relation to the carrying capacity of their subsistence system that permits much longer residence in an area than might be predicted for a swidden horticulturist group in the Amazon.

Although the various families that occupy a *maloca* generally live in partitioned spaces along the rear half of the structure, as shown in Figure 6.19a, the front half is considered to be the male part of the structure; the rear half, the female part; the right half, the adult part; and the left half, the young part. The *maloca* is considered to be the uterus of the sib, enveloped in the protective placental thatching on the exterior of the structure, as well as a concrete manifestation of Desana cosmology. The most important parts of the interior in the cosmological sense are three smaller horizontal cross beams, called "jaguars," all of which are surmounted by poles and a long beam called the *gumú* that runs the length of the structure from the front door (male) to the back door (female). This beam is horizontal, but nevertheless the Desana view it as an axis mundi that *vertically* connects the three separate planes of the cosmos, which are indicated in Figure 6.20.

Another interesting symbolic complexity related to the interior of the *maloca* is that the male half is viewed as having the color yellow and the female half as having the color red, but each is considered to be bathed in the reflected light of the other. Furthermore, the yellow male half corresponds to the color seen as characterizing the top level of the cosmos, where the Sun-Father lives (Figure 6.20), whereas the red female half relates to the color of the earth, which is red (not green, as the outside observer might expect to be the case!). Finally, at the center of the interior, in the most sacred spot of the entire *maloca*, a small wooden stool is placed on which sits the *payé*, or shaman, who plays a critical role as the intermediary between the sib and the supernatural forces that created and continue to regulate the central plane of the cosmos, namely, "this world," or earth.

Mode of Reproduction

At the time the research was carried out in the 1960s, Reichel-Dolmatoff estimates that some thirty *malocas* were occupied in Desana territory, with an average of thirty-three persons inhabiting each (this latter figure may exclude younger children). In any case, these data suggest that the minimum population was about one thousand persons living in an area of 4,000 square kilometers, or a density of 0.25 person per square kilometer, with the possibility of somewhat higher densities if each *maloca* housed more than thirty-three persons. The rough density estimate of 0.25 person per square kilometer is not a true ecological density in any case, since it probably includes some interriverine areas that were not exploited even by hunters. If so, then the actual population density per unit of land used for subsistence was higher. Nevertheless, given the probability of fairly large catchment areas for the hunting of game, Desana densities probably did not exceed those characteristic of other areas of the Amazon Basin, which in general are much less than 1 person per square kilometer.

Although Reichel-Dolmatoff had the impression that the Desana population was growing "slightly," it was even clearer to him that the Desana kept their numbers tightly in check in two principal ways: first, through the use of oral contraceptives and, second, through control over the frequency of sexual relations. Desana women prepared concoctions from herbs available in the local environment that enabled them to space out the births of their children over several years longer than would otherwise have been the case. This method must not have been totally efficacious, however, given the strictness with which the Desana observed sexual abstinence. Indeed, Reichel-Dolmatoff notes that a strong puritanical streak characterized Desana society, and sex was thus considered to be the greatest of all dangers that humans faced in this life. The main ritual mechanism controlling sex was the requirement that all hunters—which, of course, included all males except the youngest boys and the oldest men—must observe general sexual abstinence, especially before and during the hunt. This mechanism was based on the idea that the humans and animals in a local ecosystem shared in the same, highly limited potential for procreation in light of its carrying capacity. If the human population increased at all beyond its equilibrium state, then, according to this view, both the game animals and the supernatural figure in control of their numbers (the Master of Animals) would become highly jealous. Such an increase would involve a misuse of part of the limited, shared sexual energy budget available to both populations in the local ecosystem, a portion of which the animals could claim quite rightly for themselves in order to maintain their own population levels (Figure 6.20).

In spite of these dual regulatory mechanisms, however, some Desana individuals apparently were either too highly sexed or too fecund to keep the number of children they had to a strict minimum and ended up having six or seven children who stayed alive to a marriageable age. The rest of the *maloca* group looked upon such unfortunate families with great scorn, considering them to be little better than a "family of dogs," which certainly suggests again that strong social controls generally were observed by the populace in order to keep their numbers in synchrony with the protein-carrying capacity of the environment.

Social Organization

Desana sibs, as mentioned earlier, are distributed along several major rivers and smaller watercourses in the Vaupés-Papurí region. In general, the sibs are ranked in accordance with their position along a particular river, with the lower-ranking sibs located in its higher reaches and the higher-ranking ones located in its lower reaches. Since the lower parts of a larger river generally are more navigable and afford more contact with other groups, the people living here are more acculturated than those who live in more remote parts of the river. Larger regional populations composed of twenty to thirty sibs are further organized into phratries. These phratry groupings are classified as being basically hunting, fishing, or horticulturist—seemingly in spite of what the exact subsistence mix of a particular phratry (or sib) might actually be. In light of this phratry structure, the general rule for marriage is that it should occur between individuals from different phratries and preferably between one kind of phratry group (e.g., hunting) and another (e.g., fishing), with virilocality being the normal residence pattern after marriage. Hunting-classified phratries are considered "male," and fishing-classified phratries are considered "female," and it is this sort of marriage that the Desana, who are classified as hunters, prefer. Reichel-Dolmatoff does not mention what the classificatory gender of horticulturist phratries is, although it was not a marriage sought after by the Desana at the time he was there.

Political Economy

Regional social harmony, exchange, and the control of political aggression are maintained between various groups at both the intersib and interphratry levels by frequent gatherings, which, especially at the latter level, permit reinforcement of the linkages that exist among Desana groups in the reciprocal exchange of women, religious ideology, and economic exchange. During these gatherings the visitors occupy the front (male) half of a *maloca*, while the residents occupy the back (female) half. However, during the performance of the rituals that accompany the gathering, which include a recitation of the creation myth, the adult men occupy the right front quarter of the *maloca*; the adult females, the right rear quarter; the male children, the left front quarter; and the female children, the left rear quarter. Reichel-Dolmatoff does not discuss the trade that occurs on these occasions in any detail, except to note that food, raw materials, and manufactured items are exchanged. He does note that harmonious relations are strongly promoted by these intergroup gatherings as well as by the reciprocal social and economic interactions; but he also points out that conflicts could occur between individuals, sibs, or even phratry groupings. The most common causes of such conflict are rape, the failure of a group to reciprocate in the exchange of women in marriage, and witchcraft. The concept of avenging one of these wrongs to the death is apparently a very strong part of Desana emotional and political life.

Relations with other groups most significantly involve a relationship with interriverine hunter-gatherer Makú groups, in which both parties to the interaction, Desana and Makú, see the latter group as subordinate to the former. Different in physical type, language, and subsistence technology, the Makú are viewed by the Desana as a sort of "slave class" that should serve their masters in any way they deem necessary. Thus, for example, during the intergroup gatherings mentioned previously, the Makú are also on hand to gather firewood, take care of the visitors' canoes, and care for the smaller children. And whereas the Desana call themselves *wira-porá*, or "sons of the wind," they call their Makú servants *wira-poyá*, meaning "spoiled Desana." Indeed, not surprisingly given the preceding discussions of cosmology and social organization, the Desana view themselves as "male" in relation to the "female" Makú, projecting a sort of ambivalent sexual image on them. Any Makú who maintain an independent life apart from the riverine Desana are viewed as evil cannibals. Given the fact, however, that even the "subservient" Makú apparently maintained their hunting-gathering adaptation apart from their dealings with the Desana, we may speculate that the relationship between the two groups was far more two-sided, or symbiotic, than that described by Reichel-Dolmatoff. If so, it would be rather similar to that characterizing BamButi hunter-gatherers and Bantu swidden horticulturists of the Ituri rain forest of central Africa. In this situation, each group attempts blatantly to exploit the other while more or less secretly downgrading it—but, as described by Colin Turnbull (1961), at the same time each not only benefits by obtaining resources from the other but also at least pays lip service to the other's cultural integrity.

Ritual and Leadership

Shamans, the primary leaders of the essentially peaceful Desana society, have access to pathogenic agents consisting of small black splinters or thorns that can cause great harm when magically ingested by an intended victim. Unfortunately, Reichel-Dolmatoff does not give us the name of these malign darts, which are similar to those used by almost every eastern South American group discussed to this point. It does appear that they could be and are used against potentially anyone who lives outside the boundaries of the local ecosystem. Although the Desana *payé* thus plays a central role in maintaining intergroup distance and low population densities, he is equally important in the maintenance of each local *maloca*'s subsistence adaptation in his role as an intermediary between the supernatural controllers of game animals and the Desana men who hunt these animals.

Just as the *gumú* beam is a symbolic connector of the separate cosmic levels, so can the *payé*, whose stool sits in the symbolic center of the cosmos in the *maloca*, take hallucinogens that enable him to leave this world and, by penetrating the celestial level above, achieve communication with Vihó-mahsë, minion of the Sun-Father and Master of Animals who jealously guards the number of game animals on earth. Without a specialist who has this ability, a Desana group would have no one to ensure that an optimum level of procreative energy and fertility was available to be tapped by their hunters. Upon encountering Vihó-mahsë on a spiritual journey to the Milky Way, the *payé* solicits a limited number of game animals by promising to cause the death of a certain number of people from neighboring groups and thus release their souls for use by the supernatural forces. Upon the *payé*'s return to earth, he engages in divinatory practices whose concrete result is Desana decisionmaking about the most propitious place and time to engage in hunting, fishing, and other subsistence activities. Moreover, as the main keeper of all animals and plants in the Desana ecosystem, the *payé* must be the main repository of knowledge about every one of these organisms—in other words, he must be as much of an expert lay naturalist as he is a practiced specialist in the esoteric activities that permit him to fly up into the cosmos. At the same time, the *payé* must serve as an exemplary role model representing ultimate sacred postulates such as continual abstinence from sexual activity. In sum, in maintaining a viable equilibrium and creating an ecologically based cosmos, the Desana have worked out an adaptation in which the primary regulatory functions of their society are not so much embedded in the day-to-day actions of individuals as in the person of the shaman.

Similar to the Mundurucú, the Desana use large hollow wooden musical instruments, or flutes, in an important ceremony called the "feast of Yuruparí," which usually takes place during a time of the year when there is an abundance of food from smaller fish and certain jungle fruits (Figure 6.19b). The Yuruparí is held when the number of pubescent girls in the *maloca* is sufficient enough for the local group to enter into a reciprocal arrangement with a sib from another phratry. With most of the women of the two sibs hiding in the brush, the men approach the *maloca* from the river landing playing pairs of "male" and "female" flutes and carrying the food for the ceremony. They enter the *maloca* still playing the instruments and deposit the food inside, after which they exit through the back door and return the flutes to a hiding place near the landing. All the men and women then return to the *maloca*, coming together in a playful union of the sexes. Although the younger premenopausal women are punished if they see the flutes, they are employed in a context that does not appear to involve any sort of general male chauvinism—unlike the Amazonian societies whose adaptive structure centers on warfare, the raising of fierce males, and maltreatment of women.

Ideology (USPs)

Figure 6.20 is a model of the Desana's myth of the origin, structure, and functioning of the cosmos. The Sun-Father, who presides over the cosmos, created its three levels: (1) the celestial vault (Reichel-Dolmatoff does not provide the Desana name for this level), where he now resides in command of his creation; (2) this earth, or *maría turí*; and (3) the lower world, or *ahpikondiá*, a place to which the souls of Desana who have lived their lives properly go. In placing the Desana on their part of the earth, the Sun-Father assigned to them a finite territorial space delimited everywhere by specific named landmarks, and he made available a limited amount of energy to which they must adapt by keeping their numbers in equilibrium. In other words, although the Desana people see their environment as an open system powered by the external light energy, or "yellow semen," emanating from the Sun-Father, they do not view it as capable of permitting any growth beyond the low number of people who currently inhabit it. Should they be tempted to disobey the laws governing their numbers and the use of energy in the environment, the need for the Sun-Father's continued presence in maintaining the viability of the ecosystem is incentive enough to obey his admonition to live conservatively. That is, he is not merely the creator but is the continuing sustainer of the Desana ecosystem; without him, chaos would quickly ensue. The Desana are reminded of these laws not only occasionally by the *payé* during formal rituals, but also every time they pass through the front door of the *maloca*, since symbols representing the most sacred socioecological principles governing their society are painted all across its front end (Figure 6.21).

In their observations of nature, the Desana have grasped the fact that they must continue to do battle against the natural force of entropy that tends to tear down and degrade their environment. In other words, they are explicitly aware of the second law of thermodynamics, wherein all energy transfers in an ecosystem tend to result in increasing disorder. Indeed, everything summarized to this point about the Desana adaptive system, from subsistence to ideology, is geared toward ensuring that energy is maintained and returned to the local environment by keeping population numbers strictly confined to sustainable numbers over the longer term. According to Reichel-Dolmatoff, ritual and the taking of drugs in the context of this cosmological scheme are overtly aimed at subverting entropy through the continual re-creation of the Desana universe, namely, by keeping all things in it—humans, plants, and game animals—exactly as they were placed here on earth by the Creator. In essence, then, there is no room beyond the autonomous village level for sociopolitical evolution in the Tukanoan part of the Amazon, which of course is the point we have been continually making in this

FIGURE 6.21 Selected Desana motifs symbolizing elements of society and cosmology, some of which are painted on the front of *malocas*. Redrawn and adapted from Reichel-Dolmatoff (1972).

chapter as we examined human adaptive systems in the broader *terra firme* environment of the basin.

THE OMAGUA

Many *terra firme* groups survived for a short time the initial onslaught of the European arrival in South America during the second quarter of the sixteenth century, and some groups, such as the Yanomamö and the Shuar, have survived more or less culturally intact up to the present day. The indigenous groups of the *várzea*, however, were exposed within a decade after the Spanish arrival in Peru and the Portuguese arrival in Brazil to a host of negative effects that brought about their disappearance by the early eighteenth century, or within a mere 175 years after the Conquest. That the first centuries of European occupation of the Amazon were much more devastating for *várzea* populations than for *terra firme* ones can be understood from an ecological perspective. Not only is the main channel of the river highly navigable, and therefore relatively easier to occupy than the remote interriverine forests, but also the richer *várzea* niche would become especially attractive to colonists looking for productive places to settle.

It is not the purpose of this section to discuss in detail what the negative effects of contact were, but we may note in passing that in the first decades after the European arrival they included the outright killing of indigenous people by Spanish conquistadors, who engaged in violent encounters with *várzea* groups as they sailed down the Amazon River on several voyages of exploration that began as early as 1541. By the late sixteenth century these effects also included the less violent but ultimately far more insidious effects of missionizing aimed both at capturing souls for Christianity and at acquiring indigenous lands, resources, and labor. Although these practices resulted in the destruction of native cultures, by far the more serious result of Contact was the inadvertent introduction from the outside world of diseases against which the *várzea* populations had no resistance. In a very real sense, then, the survival of *várzea* culture became a moot point in the face of the nearly total die-off of the human population necessary for its continued survival. By the early eighteenth century the *várzea* had been depopulated or abandoned, as a few surviving groups moved into more remote headwaters, such as the Río Napo, in a futile attempt to isolate themselves from European influence and control.

However negative the end result of Contact, the story of the first European voyage down the entire length of the Amazon by Francisco de Orellana's expedition of 1541–1542 is worth recounting here briefly, since it is one of the great tales of human exploration and discovery in a century known for almost unbelievable feats of courage and audacity, not to mention culture-bound arrogance and cruelty. The accounts of such expeditions are also, I might add, among our few sources of ethnohistoric information on indigenous *várzea* societies. Under the leadership of Gonzalo Pizarro, brother of the conqueror of the Inca state, Francisco Pizarro, an expedition of 220 Spaniards and 4,000 Andean porters left Quito in February 1541. They were in search of the mystical gold-rich lands of El Dorado, which they believed lay somewhere out to the east along the Amazon, a belief based on reports of what may well have been the Omagua culture located along the upper reaches of the river in what is now northeastern Brazil (Figure 6.22). Some ten months later, however, the expedition was mired in the rainy jungles of eastern Ecuador along the Río Napo, not all that far from their departure point.

Two crude brigantines were constructed from materials at hand, and it was decided that Orellana and fifty men would set off down the Napo to obtain help from nearby indigenous groups. Unfortunately for those remaining behind, who ended up having to struggle slowly back over the Andes to Quito, Orellana was unable to return upriver against the current and was pushed onto the main channel of the Amazon—becoming, in the process, the inadvertent discoverer of the Amazon River and its indigenous inhabitants. Unable to secure adequate food while proceeding downstream, the members of the expedition suffered continu-

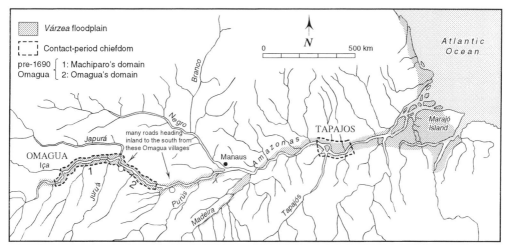

FIGURE 6.22   Map showing the approximate extent of the Omagua and Tapajós chiefdoms of the Amazonian *várzea*. Tapajós location based on a map in Meggers (1971) and that of the Omagua based on description in Acuña (1859 [1641]) and on Figure 1a in Carvajal (1934 [1535]).

ally from near starvation. As they began encountering the settlements of the Omagua in the domain of Machiparo, a *várzea* chief, the starving Spaniards used their guns in an attempt to capture some of the great wealth of food, including penned turtles, they saw in one settlement. From this point on in their voyage downriver, they were met with increasing hostility by canoe flotillas containing hundreds, if not thousands, of warriors who came out to pepper them with spears and darts as they floated slowly by. Near the mouth of the Amazon, eight months after the beginning of their voyage, they encountered large parties of warriors apparently led by women who fought even more fiercely against the invaders of their riverine territory. Seeing some of the men fleeing at the sight and sound of the Spanish arquebuses, their female war leaders shot them in the back with arrows for their cowardice. Recalling the classical legend from Asia Minor of female warriors called "Amazons," the members of the expedition dubbed this river the Río Amazonas; the rest, of course, is history.

Carvajal's, Acuña's, and Fritz's Omagua Data

In the remainder of this section, we rely on the report of Father Gaspar de Carvajal (1934 [1535]), who accompanied Orellana, and on the later accounts of Cristóbal Acuña (1859 [1641]) and Samuel Fritz's (1922) eighteenth-century manuscript to provide an overview of the Omagua, who were just one of the complex *várzea* societies encountered by the Spanish expeditionary forces of the mid-sixteenth century (see also Markham 1859; Hemming 1978). The Omagua people were organized in two separate polities, the upper one led by a chief named Machiparo and the lower one led by a chief named Omagua. Although the location of the boundary between the two polities is not known, it appears from the Spanish descriptions that each one comprised thousands of people living in hundreds of settlements that extended for a total of over 700 kilometers along the upper part of the Amazon. Information on both polities is included in the following discussion, although, where appropriate, specific characteristics of one or the other polity are pointed out (note that dual headings are used whenever the data for one societal variable are particularly scanty).

Physical Environment and Mode of Production

The early Spanish accounts describe the edges of the main river channel as being full of islands of varying sizes that were estimated to range from 4 to as many as 20 leagues in circumference (a Spanish league is equivalent to 5.6 kilometers). The Omagua fields, or garden plots, were situated on the banks at the edge of the Amazon and on the adjacent islands in areas that were subject to inundation by the yearly flood and thus to the annual renewal of the nutrient-rich silt brought down out of the Andes. Indeed, in light of the total destruction of the plots each year by the flood, Father Fritz, who worked in the area between 1686 and 1723, noted that it would have been better if they and the Omagua dwellings had been placed out away from the *várzea* on higher ground that was not flooded annually. What he did not understand, of course, was that to do so would have meant giving up the high year-to-year yields on *várzea* land as compared to the much more temporally limited productivity that could be gotten out of *terra firme* swidden plots. It thus follows that population numbers would have been much less and all other societal features would have been correspondingly far less complex. In other words, for the Omagua to have made such a shift would have entailed their becoming *terra firme* village societies rather than *várzea* chiefdom societies.

The staple crops, including maize and manioc, were planted immediately after the flood ended in June and harvested in January and February, just before the flood began again. Although the maize had to be stored in the houses during the flood, tuberous crops such as manioc could be stored without damage in special pits dug below ground level—even if they were underwater for some months on end. Both manioc flour alone and a mixture of maize and manioc flours were used to make "biscuits" that, when baked, would keep for months. In addition to the variety of plant foods, the dwellers of the *várzea* exploited the diverse species of riverine fish and animals that were available year-round, including turtles, manatees, tapirs, and deer. Just as manioc and maize were stored, so were the turtles trapped and kept penned up in thousands in pens and pools at the edge of the water. Indeed, the men of Orellana's expedition estimated that a force of one thousand men could have been fed for a year entirely on the resources that the Omagua had available in storage.

Settlement Pattern and Mode of Reproduction

Although the data on settlements are impressionistic at best, there is no question that they were larger and spaced far more closely than *terra firme* settlements. For example, the members of Orellana's expedition estimated that Machiparo's domain alone ran for at least 80 Spanish leagues and contained hundreds of settlements that ran nearly continuously (less than a "crossbow-shot" away from each other) along both sides of the river. One settlement alone stretched for 5 leagues, with its houses spaced very closely together, and in another the Spaniards counted a minimum of five hundred dwellings. Although it is likely that these settlements were not very wide in relation to their great length, one gets the impression that they had many more inhabitants than have characterized recent or historically known settlements of the interriverine areas of the basin. In spite of the presumed narrowness of the distribution of the *várzea* population along the Amazon, there may also have been settlements, fields, and other economically important sites out to the south away from the river, since the Spaniards saw and traveled on wide roads that ran out in the distance to the south (Figure 6.22).

Domestic Economy

Very little data are available in this category (see Figures 2.5 and 2.6), but we do know that the Omagua flattened their foreheads artificially, about which the men and women of this *várzea* group were proud and which they used to distinguish themselves from the indigenous peoples, whom they considered to be mere "savages," inhabiting the adjacent *terra firme* forests. Another feature of the domestic economy mentioned by Father Carvajal was the presence of great amounts of "porcelain" pottery, including large vessels with a storage capacity of some 25 *arrobas*, or 100 gallons. Given that the men of Orellana's force had seen the beautifully crafted pottery of the Inca state, it is even more noteworthy perhaps that they should remark on the beauty of Omagua pottery and the skill with which it was made.

Social Organization

Although most of the features of social organization are also unknown, we may presume that such a large-scale society organized under the leadership of a paramount chief included elites and commoners organized into two distinct, hierarchically ranked social groupings, with people in each of the two social categories having their status ascribed to them at birth. Father Fritz notes that many families had one or two slaves, or servants, who had been acquired either through capture during warfare with *terra firme* village societies or through barter of *várzea* resources with the mainland groups, which suggests yet a third level in the social hierarchy.

He also notes that both the boys and girls of Omagua's polity achieved the status of adulthood by going through different ordeals at the onset of puberty. He does not mention much about what the boys endured, except that they were scourged. But he describes the girls' ordeal in some detail. They were hung in a net located on the roof of the house for a period that often exceeded thirty days. During this time they were given spinning materials to keep themselves occupied (cotton, for example, was grown), but they were given almost no food other than a little water and manioc cakes each day. Following this, the girls were washed in the river, adorned with paint and feathers, and, accompanied by music and dancing, taken back to their homes, whereupon they were considered marriageable.

Political Economy

As implied by the taking of *terra firme* slaves, the Omagua chiefdoms appear to have engaged in continual conflict with the village societies that inhabited the rain forests to the north and south of the river. Although some prisoners of war remained alive for use as slaves, other more valiant prisoners eventually were killed, most likely for fear they would escape to engage in war with the Omagua again at a later date. Their bodies were thrown unceremoniously into the river, but their heads were kept as trophies on display in the houses, similar to the practice of the Mundurucú discussed earlier. As the Orellana expedition traveled through Machiparo's territory, it encountered on one occasion some 130 canoes containing an estimated eight thousand warriors. Given their apparent ability to field such maritime forces, the two Omagua polities may have engaged in conflict with other riverine groups, if not with each other from time to time.

These warriors used both spears and atlatls, or spear-throwers, as weapons, neither of which, to my knowledge, is known to be characteristic of *terra firme* rainforest groups (who use blowguns and the bow and arrow). Although none of the *várzea* chiefdoms turned out to be the fabled site of El Dorado, Carvajal does mention that gold and silver inlaid decorations were seen on some of the spear-throwers, and a copper hatchet was found as well, suggesting either that the Omagua trade networks were connected to Andean sources of metal or that more local sources of such minerals were available nearby.

Ritual and Leadership

Given the Amazonian context of the Omagua chiefdoms, shamans were an integral part of the social system. The Spaniards appear to have first seen shamans among the men in the 130 war canoes that came out to attack them from settlements in Machiparo's domain. However, from what we know of shamans in traditional present-day societies of *terra firme*, these shamans appear to have been a different sort of religious specialist in that they were all daubed in white paint and had their mouths full of ashes, which they spit out in the air as the canoes approached Orellana's brigantines. Then they began blowing on trumpets and beating drums as if to ensure victory for the *várzea* warriors or to scare the Spaniards, if not both. Unlike most shamans of *terra firme* societies, these appear to have lived apart from the rest of the populace in houses where the bones of dead shamans were kept as religious relics. Such practices are indeed more analogous to practices of some prehistoric Andean groups—such as the Inca, who kept the mummies of dead emperors as religious icons to be paraded before the populace on state ceremonial occasions (see Chapter 9). As for the appearance of

Machiparo and Omagua, there is no mention of the Spaniards having encountered either man during the voyage. We thus know almost nothing about the nature of chiefly institutions except that the individual settlements in each of the leader's domains apparently acknowledged the political control of the chief over them.

Ideology (USPs)

Another interesting distinction between *terra firme* and *várzea* groups is that the latter were seen by the Spaniards to have "idols" to which they ascribed powers over the productivity of the river and its fish, the garden plots, and victory in conflicts with their enemies. These idols apparently were not kept in any particularly noteworthy place, unlike the bones of the dead shamans, and were simply picked up from the corner of some dwelling to be used as weapons of magical power when placed in the prows of the war canoes. Carvajal mentions that in one house two idols of frightening appearance made out of palm leaves or feathers were seen—the Spaniards and others of this era, of course, thought that they were seeing the devil himself when beholding the religious icons of these and other indigenous American peoples. Each of the idols had large, perforated earlobes similar to those of the elite people of Cuzco, the Inca capital, although these perforations did not contain ear spools such as those worn by ancient Peruvians, including the Inca and many other earlier groups in the Central Andes.

ROOSEVELT'S AND CLASTRES'S MODELS

In the preceding sections of this chapter I have constructed a paradigmatic model of the Amazon Basin that views it as divided into two fundamental biomes: the *terra firme* and the *várzea*. In spite of the environmental variability that characterizes the *terra firme*, the data clearly support the argument that this vast area constituting about 98 percent of the basin is relatively limited in subsistence productivity compared to the *várzea*. *Terra firme* microenvironments do not generally have exogenous, or external, inputs of nutrients, and one way or another traditional human adaptive systems therefore have had to achieve equilibrium in light of this and other limiting factors of the Amazonian rain-forest ecosystem. Thus, in spite of the high degree of cultural variability from place to place in the *terra firme*, in our treatment of four widely spaced groups we have seen no evidence that interriverine sociopolitical integration exceeds an egalitarian level of organization. The *várzea* environment, in contrast, does have an exogenous source of nutrients—namely, from the annual flood—and in spite of its tropical forest setting and the employment of swidden agriculture, it could and did support the autochthonous development of stratified chiefdom societies. Although much more productive in general than the *terra firme* environments, the *várzea* nevertheless did not feature unlimited productivity, and it seems highly likely that its narrow configuration and limited size precluded the development of state societies.

In the introduction to this chapter I mentioned that two researchers, Roosevelt and Clastres, have proposed models related to indigenous developments in the Amazon that run directly counter to the model proposed here. In the remainder of this chapter, I deal briefly with each of these arguments.

Roosevelt's Model of Amazonian Complexity

With regard to Roosevelt's work in the Amazon, we have already seen in Chapter 5 that her excavations at the site of Caverna da Pedra Pintada, near Monte Alegre on the lower Amazon, have convincingly pushed human antiquity in the basin back to at least 10,500 B.P. In my discussion of Carneiro's Kuikuru model earlier in this chapter I alluded to Roosevelt's data from this Paleoindian site in arguing that, if chiefdoms and states ever were going to develop somewhere on the *terra firme*, .then more than ten thousand years of human occupation of the basin constituted plenty enough time for this to have happened, if indeed it could (which, according to the model presented in this chapter, it could not). During a number of seasons of fieldwork prior to the excavations at Caverna da Pedra Pintada, Roosevelt (1989, 1991) carried out excavations at Teso dos Bichos site, which is located in the eastern part of Marajó Island at the mouth of the Amazon. Based on her assertion that the archaeological remains represented at this site constitute a chiefdom whose complexity almost rivals that of any of the ancient states found in the Central Andes or elsewhere in the world, a claim that has been convincingly rebutted in several highly critical reviews by Betty Meggers (e.g., 1992a, 1992c), Roosevelt (e.g., 1991:xvii, 3) has gone on to argue that stratified societies could arise anywhere in the basin.

Given the model developed in this chapter, it would be impossible to dispute a claim that chiefdoms developed in a number of places in the *várzea* niche. However, as we have seen in discussing Moran's (1993) arguments, most, if not all, of Marajó Island consists of highly unproductive *terra firme* soils that are suitable for modern agroforestry but not for intensive agriculture. In a critique of Roosevelt's arguments, Meggers notes that eastern Marajó, where Teso dos Bichos site is found, is characterized by especially unproductive soils. It thus comes as no surprise, in spite of Roosevelt's grandiose claims, that the actual remains at this site consist of no more than thirty communal houses. If we assume, as Roosevelt's data suggest, that each contained an average number of eight hearths, or stoves, associated with an average of five persons, then the number of persons in each dwelling was forty and the overall population of the site probably did not far exceed one thousand persons (see Meggers 1992a:27). But this calculation is based on the assumption that all of the structures were indeed contemporaneous—a point that is unknown, since excavations were confined to limited areas in about one-half of the estimated thirty dwellings, whereas the rest were identified by "magnetic anomalies" registered in the soil. Even if these thirty dwellings were contemporaneous and the population estimate of one thousand persons (derived by Meggers following the logic of Roosevelt's arguments) is roughly correct, such numbers pale in comparison to the five hundred dwellings and eight thousand warriors seen by Orellana's force in the Omagua chiefdoms of the upper Brazilian Amazon.

Even more seriously, Roosevelt's claims have been picked up uncritically by the popular U.S. press. For example, a *New York Times* article (see Stevens 1990) implied that to find such complex chiefdoms (i.e., Teso dos Bichos site) means that, contrary to any argument that ancient Amazonian indigenous people were just a bunch of "primitive tribes living on the edge of existence," the entire Amazon Basin had been the scene for two thousand years of remarkable political developments that included the rise of "civilizations of chiefdoms." Most tellingly for such a specious argument, the article made no distinction at all between the higher productivity of the *várzea* niche and the lower productivity of the *terra firme* niche. Such a naïve proposition, when read by the Brazilian agencies attempting to bring industrial civilization to the Amazon and the world banks asked to fund such attempts, became tantamount to giving the outsiders a "green light" to proceed with the destruction of the indigenous people, animals, and vegetation found in this highly fragile ecosystem.

Clastres's Model of Amazonian Noncomplexity

Clastres's (1977) argument in *Society Against the State* is similar to that of Roosevelt, at least in its implication that the entire Amazon Basin was an appropriate context for the development of state-level societies. But in sharp contrast to Roosevelt, he argues that states never arose anywhere on the *terra firme* because its indigenous inhabitants knew in essence what a bad bargain the rise of the state would be—since they rest on the coercion of power from the populace and in the process become an impediment to the proper functioning of society. In a sense, then, Clastres is arguing against Carneiro's assertion that Amazonian *terra firme* societies never got their political act together, specifically in asserting that indeed they did. Somehow intuiting that the state would create an uncontrollable and oppressive power elite, these societies actively created institutions that severely limited a headman's power and ensured that he would deal humanely with all members of society.

Clastres's underlying rationale for such an argument is actually the same as the theoretical arguments made here in the chapter on theory. He wants to show that egalitarian societies were not "incomplete" or "barbarian" in lacking the institutions of statehood. I argue the same in this book, but for different reasons. Thus, although we can agree with Clastres that all societies—egalitarian or stratified—represent equally worthy adaptive solutions to the subsistence productivities of differing environments, it is unacceptably antiecological to imply that states could arise anywhere and thus that the people of places where they did not are somehow unworthy. Aside from arguing that environments and related subsistence systems can be compared and contrasted in terms of their productivity, I have also insisted that population numbers everywhere will tend to rise as people attempt to achieve the maximum intensification possible within the limits of the plants, animals, and environments at hand, given the general inability of preindustrial adaptive systems to keep their numbers in check when growth is (or becomes) possible. That is, all human adaptive systems can and will develop "oppressive" systems of government if the environment and subsistence system are capable of intensification. The development of chiefly complexity on the Amazon *várzea* is a good example of this process, but it is unrealistic to argue that all of the *terra firme* populations were aware of the nature of stratified society in this narrowly confined part of the basin, let alone that they could ever know what a chiefdom or state was like before such developments had occurred anywhere in South America. To argue otherwise, as Clastres does, is to promote the mystification of the lawful ecological processes that have characterized the development of indigenous systems on the continent.

CHAPTER 7

Northwest Villages
and Chiefdoms

ANUMBER OF PREHISTORIC AND RECENT indigenous cultures are reported in the archaeological and ethnographic literature for the northwestern area of the continent. In earlier chapters we have already dealt with several contemporary Amazonian groups located here, including the Shuar of eastern Ecuador, the Nukak and the Desana of southeastern Colombia, and the Yanomamö of southern Venezuela. The Andean highlands and Caribbean areas are less well known ethnographically and archaeologically than the Amazonian northwest, although a listing of the better-known prehistoric cultures of this part of South America would have to include, in rough chronological order, the Valdivia, Machalilla, Chorrera, Guangala, Jama-Coaque, Manteño, and Milagro cultures in Ecuador (~3400 B.C.–A.D. 1532; see Meggers 1969; Gartelmann 1985); the Calima, Tumaco, San Agustín, Quimbaya, Muisca/Chibcha, and Tairona cultures in Colombia (~500 B.C.–A.D. 1535; see Reichel-Dolmatoff 1965; Arciniegas, Plazas, and Echeverri 1990); and the Dabajuro, Barrancas, Valencia, Saladero, and Guayabita cultures in Venezuela (~3000 B.C.–A.D. 1300; see Rouse and Cruxent 1963).

However, no single area of the northwest is better understood than the northern slopes of the Sierra Nevada de Santa Marta (Figure 7.1), where, in spite of the disruptions brought about by the Spanish conquest in the early sixteenth century, an unbroken sequence of indigenous occupation runs from the Tairona of later prehistoric times through to the Kogi, their cultural descendants of colonial and modern times. This chapter accordingly begins with a discussion of these data, starting with the contemporaneous and thus better understood Kogi adaptation and going on to the prehistoric Tairona adaptation, which has become increasingly well known since the late 1970s as a result of the research in and around the famous "Lost City" of Buritaca conducted by Colombian archaeologist Alvaro Soto Holguín and his colleagues (Soto Holguín 1988; see also Reader's Digest Association 1986). Because of the intimate connection between

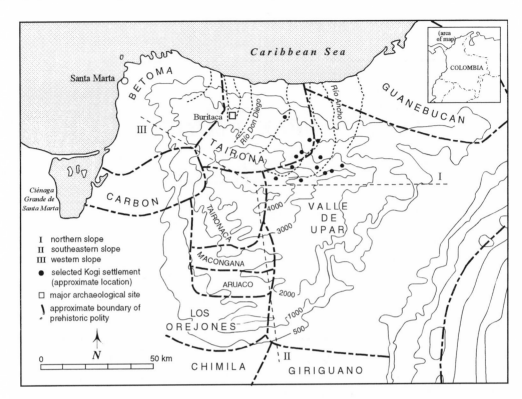

FIGURE 7.1   Map of the Sierra Nevada de Santa Marta showing the location of selected recent Kogi settlements, the Buritaca site, and the Tairona and neighboring polities dating to the period of the Spanish conquest. Redrawn and adapted from maps in Reichel-Dolmatoff (1950, 1951) and Soto Holguín (1988).

the vertical environment of the Sierra Nevada de Santa Marta and the adaptive systems of the Tairona and the Kogi, probably no other cultural area of the northwest is better known ecologically—at least in the sense that anthropological ecology has been defined earlier in this book—namely, as an approach that includes data on variables ranging from the physical environment through the modes of production and reproduction to leadership, ritual, and ideology.

The Kogi, in particular, recently came to worldwide attention when they invited representatives of the British Broadcasting Company (BBC) (Ereira 1992) up to their remote mountainside enclave to view and film their strongly traditional and enduring lifestyle. Describing themselves during the visit in a moral and ecological sense as "elder brothers" to the "younger brothers" of the outside industrialized world, they argued that the younger brothers are destroying the environment and taking everyone along with them "to hell in a handbasket" (my description of this reputed trend). Among the results of the BBC visit was Alan Ereira's film *From the Heart of the World,* in which, not surprisingly in light of the Kogi's own arguments to the BBC, their adaptation is presented as being perfectly well tuned to the local environment. But as we shortly see in dealing with the Kogi data, this (emic) argument does not necessarily square in all respects with the (etic) data presented by their principal ethnographer, Gerardo Reichel-Dolmatoff (1950).

Having dealt in the first sections of this chapter with the more recent Tairona and Kogi of the north of Colombia, I end with a discussion of the data from the ancient Valdivia Period site (~3400–1500 B.C.) of Real Alto, located on the southwest coast of Ecuador. The theme of village and chiefdom level societies is again relevant here because the work of Jorge Marcos, an Ecuadorian archaeologist, and the late Donald Lathrap has raised two critical evolutionary and ecological issues: the first being whether Real Alto represents the spectacularly early rise of a chiefdom at ~2700 B.C., which would be far earlier than such societies are thought to have occurred anywhere else in the Americas; and the second being whether this reputed development might have causal implications for the later rise of sociopolitical complexity in the nuclear areas of Mesoamerica and the Central Andes. With regard to the first issue, we have occasion to return to the Amazon, specifically in discussing the implications of the Real Alto researchers' argument (see Lathrap, Marcos, and Zeidler 1977) that the Bororo data from the southern Amazon Basin (see Lévi-Strauss 1971) constitute an ethnographically analogous case demonstrating the validity of their arguments that the Real Alto system represents a precocious example of chiefdom formation in the Americas.

THE KOGI

Although a number of anthropological studies of the Kogi were carried out in the earlier part of the twentieth century, the only trustworthy ethnography published to date on this group is that of Reichel-Dolmatoff (1950; see also 1990) following a total of ten months he spend in the Sierra Nevada during the years from 1946 to 1949. Except for a brief summary published in 1990, however, this monumental two-volume work has never been translated to English. Alan Ereira's recent book and film together constitute the best overview in English, but since they contain nothing about Kogi culture that is not present in much greater anthropological detail in Reichel-Dolmatoff's 1950 work, the following overview is based on the latter source. This does not detract in the least from Ereira's work as a remarkably sensitive account of Kogi culture and a rippingly good adventure tale as well, especially considering that we live in an age when most isolated traditional groups already seem to have been "discovered" by the outside world.

Reichel-Dolmatoff's Kogi Data

Physical Environment

As implied in the discussion of the Caribbean environmental zone in Chapter 3, the Sierra Nevada de Santa Marta is one of the most extraordinary geographic features of the world (Figure 7.1). Lying along the edge of the Caribbean coast and isolated by some 25 kilometers of intervening lower terrain from the main northern chain of the Andes, the Sierra Nevada rivals the highest peaks of the central and southern Andes in rising to an impressive 5,780 meters. What makes the Sierra Nevada particularly unique, however, is that this elevation rise occurs on a relatively small horizontal base and within a very short distance of 35 kilometers from the sea, making it the highest and most steeply ascending coastal massif in the world. The shape of the mountain is a trilateral pyramid—with a wider, more gradually sloping southeastern side; a steep, narrower northern side that plunges abruptly down to the Caribbean Sea; and a western side that falls somewhat less abruptly down to the Ciénaga Grande (Great Swamp) of Santa Marta.

Numerous rivers run off the three sides of the Sierra Nevada, most of them having their origins in lakes that form from snowmelt in the high *páramo*. The majority of these rivers, especially those of the northern slope, plunge steeply down to the jungle terrain that surrounds the mountain and thus have not formed broad alluvium-filled valleys that would provide a context for extensive irrigation subsistence systems. The principal positive factor for human adaptive systems here is the pronounced elevation of the Sierra Nevada itself, which, in ranging from the seacoast to the *páramo* over a relatively very short horizontal distance, provides a series of closely juxtaposed and vertically stacked climatic zones. These zones feature a broad variety of distinctive flora and fauna and the potential for an equally broad focus on plant domesticates adapted to every zone from the tropical through the temperate and alpine levels of the mountain.

Reichel-Dolmatoff divides the northern slope into five climatic zones (see Figure 7.2), the first four of which are of significant economic utility to the prehistoric and recent inhabitants of the mountain. The five climatic divisions are (1) the tropical zone, including the coastal plain and the lower slopes from sea level to ~1,300 meters elevation; (2) the subtropical zone, from ~1,300 to 2,500 meters; (3) the temperate zone, from ~2,500 to 3,500 meters; (4) the *páramo* zone, from ~3,500 to 4,500 meters; and (5) the snowline, between 4,500 and 5,780 meters. Given the broken topography of the mountain, however, land suitable for cultivation is scattered in small pockets throughout each of the main niches below the *páramo* zone, an environmental feature that throughout the sequence has set limits on population and settlement nucleation. (This is a feature of most, if not all, of the South American northwest, and it appears to have limited prehispanic societal development to either chiefdoms or village levels of sociopolitical integration.)

As is the case elsewhere to the south in the Andean chain, the great elevational range of the mountain generates an equally diverse range of climates and related vegetation types. Average temperatures in the coastal area are consistently above 24°C, and rainfall is from 1,000 to 2,100 millimeters per year, although lesser amounts of rainfall in the west near Santa Marta have created an extensive xerophytic desert quite unlike the area farther to the east, along the main northern slope of the Sierra Nevada, where humid tropical rain forests are found. Average temperatures in the next higher, or subtropical, zone range between 17° and 24° C, but rainfall is greater than in the coastal zone, ranging be-

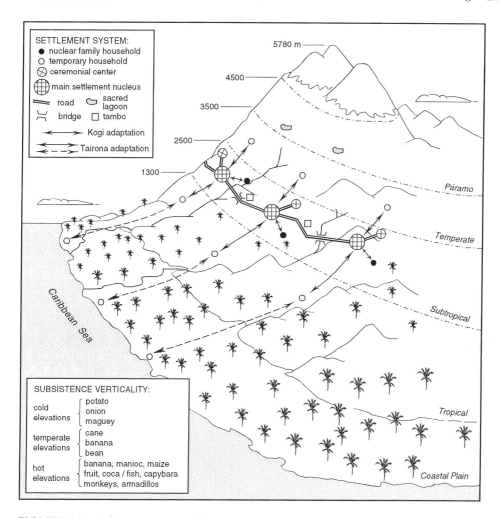

FIGURE 7.2   Schematic view of the Sierra Nevada de Santa Marta showing the main features of the Kogi-Tairona subsistence-settlement system and the main altitudinal zones and related resources available in the context of the traditional adaptation. Based on textual description in Reichel-Dolmatoff (1950).

tween 2,000 and 4,000 millimeters, which as a result produces more luxuriant forest cover than along the coast. In the temperate zone average temperatures drop even lower to between 11° and 15°C, although rainfall is as plentiful as in the subtropical zone and extensive forests grow here as well. Temperatures in the *páramo*, the final ecological zone, drop to rather frigid levels ranging between 3° and 13°C and hence disallow any vegetation beyond the short grasses that extend all the way up to the zone of perpetual snow at 4,500+ meters above sea level.

Throughout the northern slope there is a short "dry" season from the middle of December until late March, during which occasional cloudbursts are sufficient to maintain the lush vegetation found in the temperate and lower altitudinal zones of the Sierra Nevada. In sum, there is ample rainfall year-round on the northern side of the mountain but little flatter ground on which reasonably productive agriculture can be practiced. Not surprisingly, as we see in the case of the Amazon Basin, although the native fauna is quite varied, it is not particularly abundant with respect to the number of individuals of a given species. This fauna includes the jaguar, puma, tigrillo (gato pardo), tapir (danta), paca, peccary, capybara, armadillo, howler monkey, toucan, heron, pelican, crocodilians, and marine turtles and fish.

Mode of Production

As shown in Figure 7.2, the Kogi subsistence-settlement system is based on constant movement among the slash-and-burn plots located in the hot, temperate, and cold altitudinal zones of their environment. In each one of these zones (which correspond roughly to the climatic zones discussed previously), the Kogi focus on a limited set of crops that, taken by themselves, would not provide them with adequate nutrition. The principal foods are potato and onion in the higher temperate zone; bananas and beans in the lower temperate and upper subtropical zones; and bananas, manioc, fruit, and hunted animals in the lower subtropical and upper tropical zones. Maize is a part of the diet as well, but by the 1940s it had become an insignificant crop in most Kogi fields. In this regard, it is interesting that in the origin myth all foods except maize were made from the body of woman, whereas maize was made from the body of man.

Although Reichel-Dolmatoff characterizes the soils as being generally average in productivity, if not downright poor, the strategy of verticality provides the Kogi with an adequate diet as long as it is supplemented with marine fish traded or purchased from coastal markets. However, since the Kogi are not comfortable when they leave their mountain fastness to penetrate the hostile, European world of the coastal towns and cities, this important resource has become increasingly unavailable. Thus, the Kogi suffer at least periodically from inadequate nutrition. It is at this point that the first of several imponderables arises, for although Kogi subsistence appears barely adequate to sustain current low population numbers over the longer term, it turns out that in the areas that overlap with the Tairona occupation the Kogi are surrounded by ancient terraces on which the soil is at least better than that they currently farm. In some places, apparently, these terraces even contain black soil that would support reasonably intensive maize cultivation. However, for ritual reasons that are observed with great authority by the Kogi ritual leaders, or *mámas*, terraced lands created by the Tairona are today considered strictly off-limits for cultivation.

Instead, the ancient Tairona fields play an important role in Kogi religion as sacred places where offerings are made to the deities. As a matter of fact, if in tilling the soil on the lands of lesser quality that are currently used a Kogi comes across ancient artifacts such as potsherds, then the plot is abandoned, since it is considered to be potentially filled with evil spirits. Thus, for reasons apparently having nothing to do with "ecological good sense" and everything to do with sacred ritual, the Kogi have incorporated a belief system that limits their diet and subsistence productivity to levels that are less than they would be if the ancient terraces were used—in spite of the fact that they are completely "practical" when it comes to the vertical exploitation of their environment. (Here we may imagine a materialist wracking his or her brain to come up with an underlying, non-ideological cause of a subsistence strategy that avoids the use of rich lands cultivated in ancient times; however, until such a cause was proposed, we might remain convinced that a truly adequate ecological theory must therefore include nonmaterialist causes/explanations as well as materialist ones.)

Worse yet for Kogi subsistence productivity, Reichel-Dolmatoff notes that after centuries of slash-and-burn cultivation the hillsides and flatter alluvial areas are now mostly covered with eroded grassland featuring soils of highly reduced fertility. The only trees in these areas grow on the crests of ridges that are too steep and narrow to be farmed. Although the Kogi may characterize themselves as having treated their environment in a more ecologically sound way than the outside industrial world has treated its own, we nevertheless have grounds for arguing that their subsistence system has caused substantial deterioration of the local environment. This might explain in part why the Kogi express a great deal of anxiety about the adequacy of their system to provide enough food for everyone.

We come now to the second imponderable characterizing the Kogi diet. As shown in Figure 7.2, one of the principal crops of the tropical zone is coca. As is the case with Andean cultures all the way south into Bolivia and northwestern Argentina, it is chewed with lime to release narcotic alkaloids that help sustain people in carrying out hard work, traveling long distances, or dealing with hunger when food is not immediately available. But it turns out that the Kogi ideal is for the men to eat little food at all and to chew coca a great deal. And although Reichel-Dolmatoff states that the men, who are the only Kogi who chew coca, stoutly deny that it is a substitute for food, as we have seen in Chapter 4 chewing it does alleviate hunger pangs. From about the age of five years on, the Kogi boys join the men in experiencing a diet that is relatively inadequate in relation to that of the women and girls—not that the boys are permitted to chew the coca to stave off their hunger pangs, since they must wait until they pass through puberty rites in their middle teen years in order to chew it. The net result of such a diet is that the men tend to be skinny, while the women are plump and well-fed. Indeed, to be "beautiful" by Kogi standards is to be rather fat, and to be "ugly" is to be skinny; so the men consider themselves as being quite ugly and the women as being beautiful.

A third critical feature of the subsistence system is that during the time of Reichel-Dolmatoff's visits the Kogi experienced a series of a few years of good harvests followed by a number of bad ones. As shown in Figure 7.3, on a scale of subsistence productivity ranging from "very bad" through "very good," they characterized only two years over the twelve-year period from 1938 through 1949 as being "very good" (1942, 1943). Five years (1938, 1939, 1940, 1941, 1944) were described as "good," but starting in 1945 and lasting for four more years the subsistence system took a turn for the worse, either because of years of excessive rain

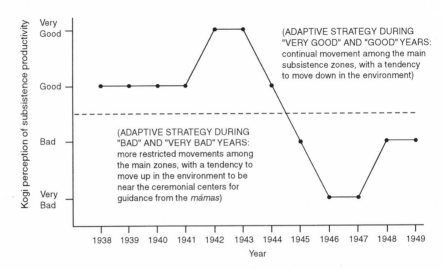

FIGURE 7.3   Graph showing the Kogi perception of varying subsistence productivity over a twelve-year period, from 1938 to 1949, and the corresponding adaptive strategies employed in light of this productivity. Data from Reichel-Dolmatoff (1950).

or years of inadequate rain. The Kogi described themselves as having suffered great nutritional deprivation during these lean years.

As Figure 7.3 indicates, the adaptive strategy during good years was continual movement among the fields throughout the altitudinal zones, with a tendency to move downward in the environment to be near the zones of greater productivity. Children born during these years were healthy, there was little illness, much trade occurred among the Kogi and between them and the coastal mestizos, many marriages occurred, and religious life was reduced to an indispensable minimum. The adaptive strategy during bad years was a relative restriction of movement among the altitudinal zones as people moved up toward the ceremonial centers inhabited by the *mámas,* to whom the Kogi always looked for spiritual guidance in times of suffering. All the Kogi experienced more hunger during these bad years, illness was more frequent, there were fewer marriages, no puberty rites were carried out, and the frequency of coca-caused impotence in the men increased. (The reader will have noted a potentially powerful population control mechanism in this last feature, not to mention the tendency toward impotence that is created by coca chewing in general.)

In light of the ritual taboos on using ancient terraces for horticulture, the deterioration of the lands that are used, and the cyclical downturns in subsistence productivity brought about by years of excessive rainfall and drought, it does not come as a surprise that the Kogi expressed a great deal of anxiety about the adequacy of future harvests to feed their population. Indeed, Reichel-Dolmatoff notes that at the end of the 1940s the Kogi thought that over the longer term of many decades they had experienced more bad years than good ones. Moreover, even during good years when there was more food on hand, they still had strong feelings of insecurity about subsistence productivity. Although this insecurity could arguably have been a feature restricted to the particularly bad times of the 1940s, such feelings extend to their general, more enduring views about the fragile continuity of the world and the entire cosmos.

Settlement Pattern

As shown in Figure 7.1, Kogi settlements are distributed at a wide range of elevations all across the eastern part of the Caribbean slope of the Sierra Nevada, overlapping partially with the core area of Tairona occupation, which extended across the central and western parts of the northern slope in prehistoric times. A primary reason for the different settlement distributions is that once the city of Santa Marta was founded in the sixteenth century, the Kogi appear to have migrated as far as they could to the east away from European influence. In spite of this migration, however, the European settlement of the coastline along the northern base of the Sierra Nevada has increasingly blocked the Kogi from direct access to the sea, thus cutting off the maritime sources of protein that provided a major part of the subsistence base for Tairona complexity in prehistoric times (direct access has also been cut off to sea shells, which are the principal source of the lime used in chewing coca).

Tairona and Kogi settlement patterns are depicted schematically in Figure 7.2. The thirty-five principal Kogi settlements are located between about 1,000 and 2,000 meters above sea level, usually in the bottom of a valley on the narrow alluvial terraces that overlook a river. Aside from a few small plots in which limited crops consisting of medicinal plants, coca, and tobacco are grown, farmland is limited in the area immediately around the principal settlements, and horticulture must be practiced in fields scattered around the settlements at some distance away. A few (generally unused) rectangular structures of European origin and function may be present (e.g., a small "Catholic" chapel), but all traditional Kogi structures are circular in plan, with a conical roof. Dwellings in the main settlements are scattered more or less randomly around a larger ceremonial structure. Although these settlements have a look of permanence and constant use, in fact they are occupied only a few days a week when families come in from the outlying fields. At this time all the men reside in the centrally located ceremonial structure, while the women, girls, and prepubescent boys occupy the family dwellings situated around it. Thus, one obvious feature of this residence pattern is that the married men and women do not get together for conjugal relations during the few days each week they spend in the main settlement.

During the rest of the week each family resides in its field houses, which are located at a distance ranging from a quarter hour's walk to as much as a full day's walk away from the main settlement. Each of these outlying settlements has two circular dwellings, which face each other across a small intervening open space where the wife cooks meals and the family comes together to eat. The husband slings his hammock in one of the structures, while the wife and children sleep in the other one; in this latter structure the women and prepubescent boys sleep on mats, while the older boys sleep in hammocks, just as their father does. Neither the husband nor the wife may enter the other's structure, even for conjugal relations, making the outside observer wonder when indeed they get together. Although Reichel-Dolmatoff notes that sexual relations do take place out in the fields during the occasional opportune moment, it appears that the frequency of conjugal relations is kept to a bare minimum by Kogi society. Beyond the excessive chewing of coca leaves mentioned earlier, this is obviously another mechanism of population regulation and control.

As we have already seen, the Kogi settlement pattern consists of more than the occupation of the field houses and the main settlement, since over the course of each year the families make trips to fields located above and below the zone of principal habitation. According to Reichel-Dolmatoff, the Kogi have no singular "home"; instead, each family ideally has at least three and usually four houses, which are occupied as needed as the family moves in and out of the main settlement each week and up and down the steep northern slope over the course of the year.

Mode of Reproduction

Reichel-Dolmatoff estimates that the Kogi population of the 1940s consisted of some two thousand persons. With the total area of occupation on the northern slope at this time roughly between 500 and 1,000 square kilometers (Figure 7.1), this suggests that population densities ranged between two and four persons per square kilometer. Although lower than the probable densities of the Tairona period occupation, they are still much higher than village-level adaptations in the Amazon Basin (see Chapter 6). In one community he studied the data indicate that 58 women had 195 births, 58 percent of which were males and 42 percent females, which is equivalent to a sex ratio of 138 (and thus strongly similar to the high Yanomamö ratios discussed in the preceding chapter). Of the 195 live births, 58 percent died before three months of age and 76 percent of the remaining children died before reaching one year.

Weaning was generally done at the time a baby was one year old, but infant mortality, especially that of males, went up even more at this point, since, according to Reichel-Dolmatoff, the babies were given dirty food and contracted intestinal problems that led to their death. Yet in spite of the fact that infant mortality was higher for male babies, in the Kogi population as a whole adult males outnumbered adult females 1.18 to 1, which is equivalent to a sex ratio of 118. Reichel-Dolmatoff also notes that infanticide occurred, even though the Kogi denied practicing it, but he does not mention the presence of any tendency toward female infanticide, which would explain the skewed sex ratio. Since the net result of fewer women in relation to men is indeed a factor to consider in the regulation of the birthrate, and hence population growth, it may well have been another feature of Kogi population maintenance in accordance with local long-term carrying capacity. Another possibly related factor in this maintenance is that Reichel-Dolmatoff notes that both male and female homosexuality were present in all villages.

Domestic Economy

As Figure 7.2 indicates schematically, the Kogi settlement pattern still includes ancient Tairona roads that run between the various villages, although apparently this feature of the landscape is most characteristic of the area where the two occupations overlap. On weekends when the families go into the ceremonial center, the *mámas* organize work groups that repair and maintain these roads and the log bridges that cross intervening streams along the road system. Each village devotes a number of weeks each year to the maintenance of the roads and bridges in its area as well as to the small *tambos* ("wayside stations") that provide shelter to travelers along longer sections that occur between some of the villages. Each *tambo* has cooking jars and firewood stored in it, as well as a small adjacent field from which a traveler can harvest the food needed to prepare a meal.

Kogi clothing is made from the cotton grown in fields in the middle and lower altitudinal zones. Both the men and women spin the cotton, but only the men carry out the task of weaving it into clothing. Only men make the pottery, and only men may plant and weed the sacred coca, although women take part in planting other crops and in harvesting the coca. Yet in spite of what appears to be a male-dominated division of labor, Reichel-Dolmatoff notes that in general the women work harder (possibly explaining why they must be better fed), and the net result is that the women are stronger and more muscular than the men. With respect to property, the men appear to have somewhat of a material edge in being considered the owners of houses, agricultural plots, and the domestic animals (which are few in number because of the difficulty of caring for them in light of the rugged environment and the transhumant adaptive strategy), whereas women are considered owners only of the household utensils. Inheritance is reckoned bilaterally, however, with women inheriting from their mothers and men from their fathers.

Social Organization

Since time immemorial Kogi society has been divided into two main social groups—one of them, called *Túxe*, composed of all the men, and the other, called *Dáke*, composed of all the women. These groups, in turn, are divided into many additional ones, with marriage possible between some of the groups and not between others. Since several dozen of these smaller groups exist, the determination of female partners who are eligible for marriage traditionally has been so complicated that the men have had to approach the *mámas*, who made it their business to know the details of eligibility, for guidance. By the 1940s, however, with far fewer women available for marriage than had formerly been the case, the general rule had become that a man could marry any women who was not related to him as mother, grandmother, aunt, sister, or daughter.

In the 1940s both men and women generally married between the ages of fourteen and eighteen, although for a first marriage a man preferred to marry an older woman of fifty to sixty who had recently been widowed, since he felt he could learn a "lot about life" from such a marriage partner. This preference was rarely achieved, however, not only because there were very few eligible women in this age category but also because older women were not interested in marrying a naïve younger man. The residence rule after marriage was a matrilocal one, with the groom required to work for his parents-in-law for one or two years until the *máma* decided that the couple could become independent and establish its own fields. If a man did not carry out his responsibilities to his in-laws to their liking, he was heavily criticized by everyone. If the case was more serious, not only could his wife be taken away from him by her family, but also the *máma* might threaten him with severe supernatural sanctions.

In spite of the clear indication of the importance of older unmarried girls to the family's subsistence efforts, as evidenced by the long service each man carried out for his bride's family, from an early age boys were taught by the older men that women were dangerous and represented cosmic forces of instability and chaos. Indeed, after marriage a man considered his wife to be the major stumbling block to his acquisition of knowledge through the chewing of coca and engaging in long conversations about Kogi cosmology and the "Ancient Ones" with the other men during their sojourns in the ceremonial structure. Not surprisingly, the antiaphrodisiac qualities of coca chewing and the long absences of the men during these sojourns were the cause of much tension with their wives (who apparently had little or no idea of what went on in the structure but could not have cared less!). Thus, married women considered the ceremonial house to be their greatest rival, while the men considered the greater sexual activity that they might have had to engage in to be simply too tiring to even think about. Worse yet, the men knew that the continued existence of the cosmos itself might be in jeopardy should they fail to acquire knowledge of the ancient wisdom, a knowledge that was attainable only if each man achieved the ideal of becoming "one" with the Universal Mother (see under ideology below).

Political Economy

It probably goes almost without saying that the Kogi represent one of the few South American groups about whom it can be said that there is no political economy, at least in the sense of their having any significant relations with either other nearby indigenous groups or with the outside industrial world. Indeed, the lack of such relations is the very reason the Kogi have been successful in maintaining their culture, located as it is in the "heart" of the (industrialized) modern world. This does not mean, however, that the Kogi have permitted themselves to become so divorced from the outside economy that they have cut off their access through Colombian markets to the seashells that provide the lime for coca chewing. For this reason, as direct access to the coastline has become increasingly difficult over the years, the Kogi have had to enter the modern cash economy in order to ensure access to the shells.

Ritual and Leadership

As implied by the plural use of the term earlier in this section, every village has two or more *mámas,* or ritual authorities who are in charge of all aspects of the secular and religious lives of the Kogi. Although the position is not hereditary, it is considered far easier for a *máma's* son to become one himself because of the arduous training that traditionally is necessary. As recently as the early twentieth century, a *máma* would divine whether a young male child would become such a ritual specialist. If it was deemed that he would be, then he was subjected to the following training: He had to sleep all day and be up all night, and thus for years he was not permitted to see the sun; he was rigorously controlled in terms of bodily functions, being taught to hold off any excretions until nightfall; at ten to twelve months old, when he could walk, he was taken to the ceremonial house of the *máma,* where he was taught by firelight, his hair grew long, and he was not permitted to play; at puberty he was given a *poporo,* a container made from a bottle gourd in which the lime for coca chewing is kept, and the *máma* spoke to him about sex, marriage, and rituals.

Finally, some eighteen years after beginning his training, the future *máma* was permitted to go outside into the world of light and people, where everyone greeted him but would not engage in conversation whenever he approached them. From that point onward he dealt with the world he had so recently confronted with the authority and knowledge his teacher had taught him. At the same time, he was restrained to a great degree, both by his training and by the respect people accorded him, from being truly an integral part of the mundane life whose existence he had only recently come to know. Indeed, because of this, he never failed to marvel at every one of its natural wonders in ways that no mere mortal ever would do. Similar to the Desana shaman, he had thus become the ultimate regulator/maintainer of the Kogi subsistence-settlement system.

Among other secular and ritual functions, the *máma's* authority extends to a variety of aspects of Kogi life that include deciding on the dates of communal celebrations, the rites of passage of each individual, the punishments for infractions of societal rules, how parents are to be treated, the dates of burials for the dead, the dates to plant and harvest the crops, when houses are to be built, how the ceremonial structures are to be built, and when communal labor groups are to come together to carry out their activities. Unlike other South American shamans, however, the *máma* does not cure illnesses. Rather, such misfortunes are seen as having been sent by disgruntled ancestors as punishment for a person's faults or misdeeds. Thus, illness is entirely the fault of the person because she or he has failed to live properly.

Anyone who does not participate in the communal work projects, including the maintenance and weeding of the walkways that run through the main village, can be punished by the *mámas*. Depending on the severity of the infraction, such punishment can include a period of fasting and penitence as well as several corporeal trials that involve having to sit nude on a pile of broken pottery or holding a large rock weighing 10–12 kilograms in each hand with the arms extended out to the front. At periodic intervals of roughly a month, each family must pay tribute to the *mámas*.

At puberty young men are given a *poporo* containing lime as well as a small stick to retrieve the lime from the gourd. During the puberty ceremony the *máma* says to the initiate that the gourd represents a "woman" whom the young man is now marrying, and the priest perforates the top of the gourd in an imitation of the ritual deflowering of women. The stick itself represents the male sexual organ. Whenever a Kogi man becomes nervous, which is something that both the film *From the Heart of the World* and Reichel-Dolmatoff's book suggest happens rather frequently, he introduces the stick (wetted by the saliva of his mouth) into the gourd and extracts the lime with rapid in and out movements. During the puberty ceremony the priest has already told the man that this symbolic sexual act is "good" and that it should be substituted as much as possible for the actual sexual act, which is "bad." At the risk of engaging in cracker-barrel psychological analysis, we thus see that in symbol and practice the chewing of coca is meant to be an alternative to sex.

Whether the ultimate effect of such a ritually charged practice is intended to act as a population control mechanism is, of course, irrelevant here. That is, its ultimate effect on the frequency of the sexual act is to keep it severely limited and therefore well regulated—in relation to a subsistence system that for material and cosmological reasons is apparently incapable of any further intensification. In spite of this feature, however, the Kogi system is not supremely well regulated, or else there would be no anxiety about the amount of food in relation to the number of people in each local system.

We have already discussed some of the effects of chewing coca, but it is worthwhile to review these and other effects at this juncture. First, coca chewing is important to the Kogi because it is thought to enhance mental lucidity during ceremonies and promote religiosity in general. Thus, a man who chews coca (and all of them do) becomes an animated, eloquent speaker whose memory for cosmological detail and verbal abilities to recount such detail are enhanced significantly. Second, coca reduces the effects of hunger, not only during ceremonies lasting several days but also during bad times when the men eat even less than they are accustomed to consuming. Third, coca helps men talk to the Ancient Ones. Fourth, although it is thought actually to enhance the sexuality of younger married men, in general coca chewing is viewed (and responded to) by the men as an inhibitor of the desire for and ability to have sex. This, cosmologically speaking, is considered a "good thing," as we have seen. Finally, coca is also viewed as causing insomnia, which is good, since the ceremonies often run day and night for hours on end, and a good participant will stay awake for every bit of the verbal activities that characterize them, each man reclining in his own hammock throughout the proceedings.

Ideology (USPs)

The Kogi have three fundamental sacred postulates about proper behavior. Interestingly, all of them involve behaviors that must not be engaged in rather than "positive" statements about what one must do. These postulates comprise abstention from physical aggression, abstention from food, and abstention from sex. Related to the behaviors from which one must abstain, the Kogi see themselves as facing a series of negatively charged "aggressions" throughout their life that include hunger, illness, societal persecution, and, worst of all, sex. Thus, as children grow up, they are taught to repress their sexual urges as much as possible; indeed, to do otherwise is considered the equivalent of what we might call a "mortal sin."

The Kogi also believe that nature is a "great screen" on which their culture and personalities are projected, so nature in this sense is defined by their own behaviors and feelings about the proper way to live. Everything in the universe is seen as related, since all things have a common origin in the Universal Mother. In the beginning, prior to her arrival on the scene, there was no order and all was chaos. Then nature in the form of the Universal Mother came to humans and asked them to feed her and praise her with song, with the warning that if they did not do as she asked, she would scorch and burn the earth in retribution. Thus browbeaten into submission by the Universal Mother, the Kogi have been singing to her and feeding her ever since the time of creation. It is their great preoccupation as the Universal Mother's chosen caretakers that, should they not do what she asks, the cosmos will dissolve into the chaos that originally characterized it.

The ceremonial house represents the uterus of the Universal Mother, and when the men go into it, they see themselves as returning to her womb. Moreover, when they enter their hammocks, they feel enveloped in her placenta, so when they pass the night chewing coca and talking about the Ancient Ones, they say, "We are inside the Mother herself." (Sigmund Freud would have loved the Kogi.) In fact, the men usually act gloomy and reserved when they are outside the ceremonial house but very animated and full of conversation when they are inside it. The ceremonial house also represents the universe itself, which is envisioned as a giant egg with its point at the top. Inside the egg, like giant round plates, are the nine levels of the cosmos, with the world we and the Kogi live in located in the middle (see Figure 7.4a, b).

The cosmic egg sits on two large wooden beams that are held up by four men, two on the east and two on the west. In a giant cosmic pool at the feet of these men sits the Universal Mother on a large flat-topped rock (Figure 7.4c). Her only task is to give food and water to the men, caring for them so that the cosmos will not fall off the wooden beams. Every once in a while, however, when one of them gets tired and shifts the load a little on his shoulder, the entire cosmos, including this world, shakes. This is the Kogi explanation for earthquakes and a potential harbinger of what could happen if they and the Universal Mother do not keep things on an even keel to maintain the cosmos. The Kogi have a rule that a woman must not move when she is having sex with her husband or else the cos-

266

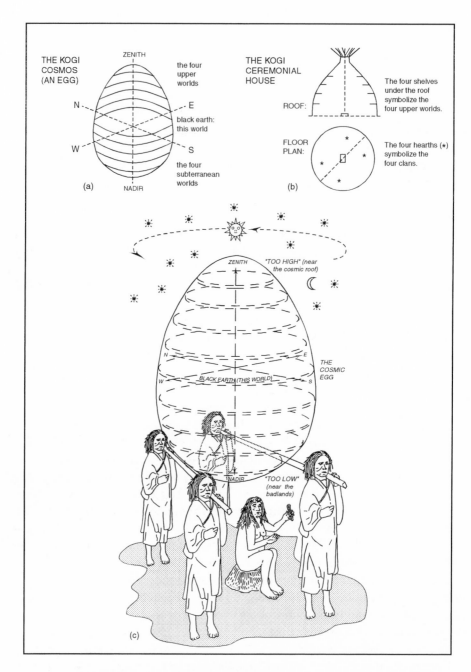

FIGURE 7.4 Drawings depicting the Kogi cosmos (a), its symbolic recreation in the roofs of dwellings (b), and the principle that the cosmic egg is supported by four men who are fed by the Universal Mother (c). Upper figures redrawn and adapted from Fundación Puntos Suspensivos (n.d.) and lower based on textual description in Reichel-Dolmatoff (1950).

mic egg will fall off the beams and destroy the universe. With the potential for such a disaster during conjugal relations, this certainly could be construed as a good means of ensuring that women will not enjoy sex very much; and thus it becomes yet another means the Kogi have developed of curbing such earthly delights and keeping their population numbers in check.

The sun lives in his circular house at the top of the cosmos (Figure 7.4c). He never leaves it, instead spending each day going from a door on one side of the house to a door on the other side—a pattern that he repeats nine times during the course of the day. Otherwise, he just sits there in the house chewing his coca or, occasionally when the need arises, toasting the leaves in preparation for chewing them, a procedure that explains why the earth becomes very hot at times. On the occasion of the solstices and equinoxes, the Kogi hold elaborate ceremonies to "make the sun turn around," imploring him to return once again to his house for yet another period of four months. According to Reichel-Dolmatoff, the Kogi do not exhibit any signs of joy during these ceremonies; instead, they are grimly and profoundly preoccupied to ensure the success of the ceremonies, so that the world will not end. Part of this success depends as well on a great number of ritual prerequisites that each man must observe—including fasting, abstinence from sex, insomnia, taking of baths, and exclusion of the women from the ceremonies.

Nevertheless, in spite of all this care in tinkering with the universe to ensure its continued existence, the Kogi predict that one day far in the future the four men will get overwhelmingly tired and will no longer be able to hold up the wooden beams that support the cosmos. The giant egg will then come crashing down right on top of the Universal Mother. She will remain unharmed, however; only humans will be destroyed in this ultimate of all apocalypses. The souls of a few "good" people will be saved, nonetheless, by their climbing up into the sky via a giant thread, in addition to the souls of those who have drowned or have been killed in falls and by snakebites. As for when the ultimate apocalypse will happen, at the time of Reichel-Dolmatoff's visit the Kogi saw themselves as having existed as a culture for the last nine hundred years, which includes the time of their ancestors, the prehistoric Tairona. They predicted that after another one hundred years have passed to end their first millennium on earth, yet another millennium would pass before the cosmos ends definitively (i.e., around the year A.D. 3050, in contrast to the Mesoamerican belief that the "Fifth World" would end around A.D. 2012; see Coe 1992).

The Kogi calendar is based on the observation of the solstices and the equinoxes, and according to constellations visible in the dawn sky, the year is divided into eighteen months of twenty days. The central ceremonial house is constructed in such a way that on the day of the spring and fall equinoxes (March 21 and September 21) a ray of sunlight shining down through a hole in the roof traces a line across the interior between the two opposing doors of the structure. The reader familiar with Mesoamerica will have noted a number of parallels between Kogi cosmology and that of various peoples of Mexico-Guatemala, including the Aztecs, who also had complex calendrical systems and similarly apocalyptic notions about the universe that required humans to tinker with it to ensure its continuity in great cycles of 365 days and 52 years, even though, similar to the Kogi, the universe—or "this world" we live in—was doomed to end at the completion of even greater time periods lasting 5,125 years.

The Kogi take as their signs of the Universal Mother's deteriorating health what they see in the physical environment around them; thus, every cloudburst, every drought, every glacier that melts, and every illness constitute signs that someone has not been following her laws. I might add here that, told by BBC visitors what modern industrial peoples are doing to destroy features of the world ecosystem, such as the damage to the ozone layer, and viewing for themselves the construction of smoke-belching factories on the Colombian coast as well as the destruction of their glaciers, the Kogi presentation of themselves to the outside world as the chosen, world-saving elder brothers is only logical. Worse yet, Colombian *huaqueros* (grave robbers) are digging up buried Tairona gold, which represents the Universal Mother's blood, her very essence, and this is substantial cause for Kogi alarm.

Ironically, however, although the Kogi are correct in their perception that industrial nations are badly damaging, if not destroying, parts of the world environment, this is not because the Kogi are "perfect ecologists" but because, fortuitously, their perception of this trend is an integral part of their (probably age-old) apocalyptic cosmology. For, as we have seen, when it comes to the materialist nuts and bolts of maintaining the integrity of their environment, the Kogi have been about as "bad" at handling this task as we have been, never mind that some of us might like to look (in our desperation) at their "teachings" and "warnings" as being capable of providing us with a guiding light to solve problems of a far larger scale than theirs.

A Summary Model

The principal features of the Kogi adaptive system are shown in the systems-hierarchical model in Figure 7.5. Recalling the complex ways in which ideology and ritual enter into all phases of Kogi life, from the selection of land appropriate for cultivation to the regulation of sexual relations, we should not be surprised that the two superstructural data sets require more text than the lower-order variables in the model. And let me make the point yet again that without the presentation of data on all ten variables in the model and corresponding arguments about their causal connections, it is highly unlikely that we could make adequate sense of the Kogi adaptive system in attempting to understand and explain its features. In light of what the model incorporates from Flannery and Rappaport's systems thinking, it is also useful to consider how the infrastructure *and* the superstructure are equally causal (or instrumental) in maintaining and regulating variables above and below them, respectively. For example, aspects of the Sierra Nevada environment and Kogi subsistence clearly determine the nature of a host of other variables—including the subsistence system, the settlement pattern, the mode of reproduction, ritual and leadership, and ideology/USPs. However, the fact that

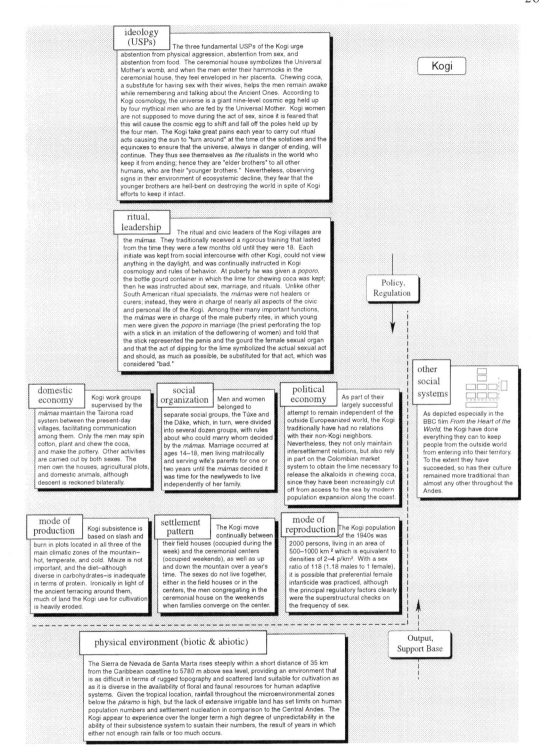

FIGURE 7.5 Systems-hierarchical model summarizing the principal features of the Kogi adaptive system. Based on textual data in Reichel-Dolmatoff (1950).

ideology and religion have developed historically in such a way that the Kogi are enjoined from using the good land on the terraces of the Ancient Ones clearly exerts a causal force on the infrastructure (e.g., in terms of the number of people that can be sustained by the subsistence system).

THE TAIRONA PREDECESSORS

As Reichel-Dolmatoff (1951) notes in his study of the ancient indigenous groups of the Santa Marta area of northern Colombia, the principal sources of ethnohistoric information on the Tairona predecessors of the Kogi include the Contact-period studies of Juan Castellanos (1847), Gonzalo Fernández de Oviedo y Valdés (1851–1855), and, especially, Pedro Simón (1892). This section first briefly summarizes the main ethnohistorical data on the Tairona from these Spanish documentary sources and then concludes with an overview of Soto Holguín's archaeological data from the area of the Lost City of Buritaca.

Ethnohistorical Data

On the basis of the documentary sources of the middle of the sixteenth century, the area of Tairona occupation of the Sierra Nevada was located, as mentioned earlier in this chapter, to the west of the current location of their descendants, the Kogi (Figure 7.1). Since the principal features of the environment are already outlined under the section on the Kogi, let us proceed to briefly review the other data on the Tairona that are discussed in the three principal sources just mentioned.

Mode of Production

Simón notes that the Tairona were outstanding cultivators who grew much maize, yuca, chili peppers, cotton, and many varieties of fruit trees, such as guayaba and guanábana. In strong contrast to the Kogi, the Tairona grew maize everywhere throughout the region, according to all three chroniclers, and indigenous agriculture was based on canal irrigation. The Tairona also kept bees for honey production, and Simón mentions that the number of hives in one small sector of the total area of Tairona occupation, the Caldera Valley, approached eighty thousand. Simón also writes that the Tairona never ate venison or other kinds of meat, instead basing their diet on the staple crops and on marine fish, to which they had direct access, since the Tairona area of occupation extended down to the edge of the sea.

Settlement Pattern

Among the most striking features of Tairona culture was the stonework found in the main centers (see Figure 7.6d). For example, in discussing the main ridgetop centers, Castellanos notes that they were approached by stone stairways with as

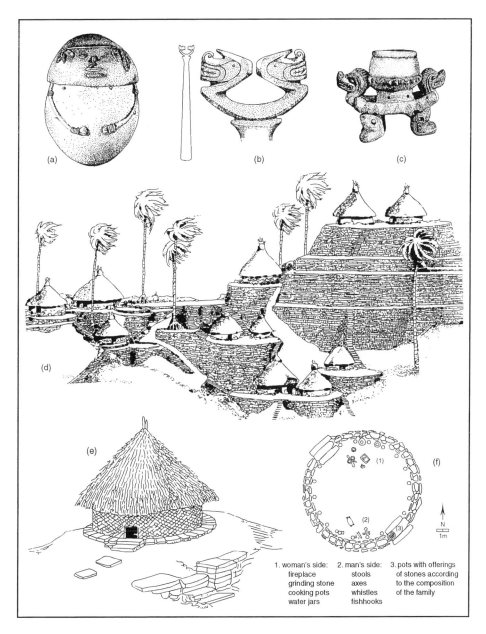

FIGURE 7.6   Selected examples of Tairona material culture, including artifacts
(a–c); a reconstruction view of part of Buritaca 200, or Ciudad Perdida, site (d); and
reconstruction and plan views of a dwelling (e–f). Top figures and lower left redrawn
from Reichel-Dolmatoff (1965), middle redrawn and adapted from Fundación Puntos
Suspensivos (n.d.), and lower right redrawn from Bray (1978).

many as nine hundred steps rising up the steep sides and spine of the ridge. There are few data in the documentary sources about the nature of the habitation structures in these settlements, other than the fact that they were circular. However, archaeological work prior to Soto Holguín's research indicates that both the husband and wife may have lived in the same circular structure. As shown in Figure 7.6f, there appears to have been a man's side in these structures (as evidenced by a restricted concentration of artifacts, including stools, axes, and fishhooks, on one side of the dwelling) and a woman's side (as evidenced by an equally confined hearth, grinding stones, and pottery vessels on the other side).

Mode of Reproduction

Although the Spanish chroniclers were not able to estimate overall population numbers with much accuracy, some regions within Tairona territory are described as having been very densely occupied with hundreds of settlements and tens of thousands of people. In the Caldera region alone, Simón notes that there were 250 settlements containing an estimated ten thousand dwellings—which suggests that, if all of these dwellings were contemporaneously occupied and each contained four to five persons, the population might have numbered as high as forty thousand to fifty thousand persons, or about twenty to twenty-five times greater than the population of the entire Kogi area today. It thus seems likely that the total Tairona population may have numbered in the several hundreds of thousands.

With regard to other aspects of reproduction, all the chroniclers are in accord in asserting that the Tairona were "abominable sodomites." Such "sinful" behavior was such a strong custom among them, notes Simón, that the ceremonies in the temples included public displays of sexual relations of various kinds. He is also shocked to note that the hooks on which they hung their clothing and other items were carved in a manner that would incite the inhabitants to commit even more of these abominations. Whatever the exact nature of Tairona sexual customs was, they certainly come across as highly different from their decidedly "prudish" Kogi descendants.

Domestic Economy

Little is said in the Spanish chronicles about the more mundane aspects of daily life, except for Simón's mention that the women spun the cotton and the men, like the Kogi of today, were in charge of the task of weaving it into clothing. Among other aspects of daily life that from the archaeological record we know characterized the Tairona, not to mention other groups of Colombia, was the use of the lost-wax technique of making hollow gold ornaments of exquisite artistry (e.g., see Arciniegas et al. 1990; Bray 1978) and the production of stone objects and large pottery vessels for storage and the burial of the dead (e.g., Figure 7.6a–c).

Social Organization

Whereas the recent and modern Kogi are organized at the level of an egalitarian village society, it is likely that local Tairona subsistence-settlement systems consisted of two classes of people, or elites and commoners, organized at the level of a chiefdom society. Oviedo, for example, notes that the elite were recognizably different from commoners by their manner and bearing, if not by their dress, and were shown great respect and deference by other Tairona (although his particular example deals with the manner in which a group of captives treated an elite woman).

Political Economy

As opposed to the modern Kogi, whose contacts with non-Kogi have been reduced to a bare minimum, the Tairona maintained strong trading ties not only among the various settlements in their own area but also with a number of other cultures located around the Sierra Nevada de Santa Marta. Among the items traded were cotton shawls, gold, emeralds, salt, and marine fish. Relations among the various groups included conflict as well, Castellanos noting that the Tairona were second to no other group in South America, including the famous warlike Araucanians of Chile, in their ability to wage war, with forces numbering as high as twenty thousand men. Although the Spaniards may have exaggerated the exact numbers (not least because they were under direct attack when the estimate was made!), the high population densities of the Sierra Nevada would have made the marshaling of such forces possible. Interestingly, however, it was only on the occasion of large battles that any war leaders were noticed by the Spaniards; otherwise, Tairona groups appear to have fought guerrilla style in smaller groups at the local level with no apparent leaders to guide them.

Ritual and Leadership

As for the possibility that the Tairona were characterized by a chiefdom level of organization, Oviedo notes that the communities in one area were divided into local political units, with each having its own leader, called a *naoma,* and the entire group of communities in a region was subject to a paramount chief whose name was Guacanaoma (it is interesting, in this regard, that the word *naoma* is similar in sound to the Kogi word *máma*). The *naomas* in each local settlement certainly had duties and authority similar to those of the *mámas.* They were responsible for punishing lazy persons and for organizing groups to carry out communal labor tasks that included the construction of ceremonial houses and the roads, bridges, and *tambos* that linked the various settlements in Tairona society.

The training of a priest, notes Simón, required a long period of teachings and periodic fasting that lasted sixteen to twenty years. Priestly initiates lived in caves and other remote places along the northern slope of the Sierra Nevada, so far away from the settlements that the only persons they ever saw during this time were those who took them food. Moreover, they were not supposed to see any woman during the period of training. In fact, if they did, whatever fasting they had been doing up to that point had to be ritually started all over again. Thus, some features of Kogi society, including the celibacy required of priests in training, clearly do have their origins in the practices of prehispanic times. Inside the ceremonial houses were storage areas for gold jewelry, shawls, and feathers, and here also the Tairona carried out their festivals and dances. In contrast to the rather drably dressed Kogi of today, all Tairona men, women, and children apparently were adorned with various items of jewelry made of gold and precious stones, including labrets, ear spools, and necklaces. Capes made from the feathers of macaws, parrots, and humming birds also were worn, as were costumes made of jaguar skins.

Ideology (USPs)

Castellanos, in speaking generally about Tairona religion, mentions that the Tairona worshiped the planets from high mountaintops rising above the coastal plain—which at least implies that Kogi knowledge about the seasonal movements of celestial bodies has its origins in prehispanic times. He also notes that divinatory practices existed as well, yielding many predictions about the future, which suggests that the Tairona were as cosmologically uncertain and anxious about the future of their society as are their descendants, the Kogi.

Soto Holguin's Buritaca Data

The site of Buritaca 200 is located at an elevation of 1,130 meters above sea level in the dense rain forest of the uppermost part of the tropical zone of the Sierra Nevada. Although the site lies only a scant 50 kilometers to the southeast of the modern port city of Santa Marta (see Figure 7.7), in light of the dense vegetation and rugged slopes it is not surprising that the Lost City was unknown to the outside world until 1975, when word was received by Soto Holguín of a Tairona city that was in danger of destruction at the hands of *huaquero* looters. Since that time the Colombian archaeological team headed by him has carried out extensive excavations at Buritaca and has surveyed a substantial area of nearly 28 square kilometers around it as well (Soto Holguín 1988). Although the gold and other artifacts of the Tairona were of worldwide renown prior to the work at Buritaca, this research has thrown the first scientific light on the nature of Tairona sites and settlement patterns.

The main part of the site lies on the top and steep upper sides of a ridgetop situated high above the Río Buritaca and extends over an area of 20 hectares. In this highly vertical setting the Tairona made such an extensive site possible by constructing curving rock-faced terraces on which they built their circular dwellings and ceremonial houses. Although some of these terraces have a relatively modest height of about 50 centimeters, others reach heights of 30 meters,

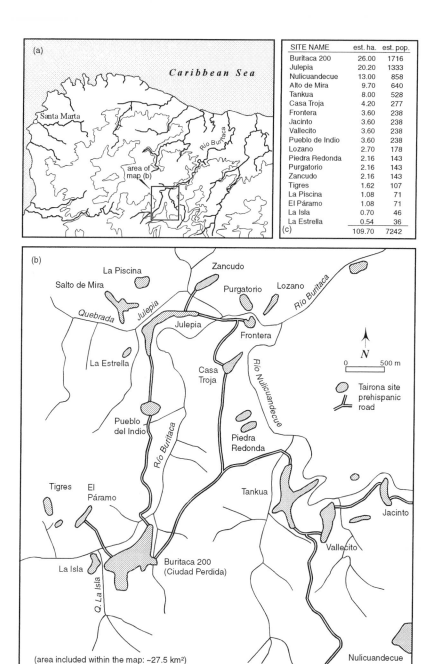

FIGURE 7.7   Location maps (a, b) and a chart (c) showing site names, area in hectares, and the estimated population size of Tairona occupations in the area of Buritaca 200 site. Redrawn and adapted from figures in Soto Holguín (1988).

which is higher than any of the famous stone-faced terraces of the Inca and other cultures to the south in the Central Andes (see Figure 7.6d). As shown in the plan view (Figure 7.8), the urban part of Buritaca consisted of both forested sectors containing fruit trees and cultivated fields and sectors containing residences, religious structures, and open areas where work activities of various kinds were carried out. Since Buritaca includes a number of residential structures of larger size, measuring ~12 meters diameter, in contrast to the majority of dwellings, which measure ~5 meters or a little more in diameter, Soto Holguín suggests that they housed the Tairona elite. Like the houses of the Kogi, however, all dwellings large and small have two opposing entrances. The typical house is divided into male and female areas, each of which is characterized by its own unique set of features and artifacts (e.g., as in Figure 7.6f).

Both utilitarian and ceremonial pottery is present in various parts of the site, including bowls, cups, and jars with a highly burnished black finish containing modeled representations of human faces and of snakes, turtles, and jaguars. A jaguar skull was found near the entrance to one of the ceremonial houses, and ethnographic analogy based on similar Kogi practices suggests that the structure was dedicated to a jaguar god in the Tairona pantheon. Gold artifacts were found in the excavation of cemetery areas on the site, showing that the lost-wax and hammered techniques of gold working were present. Artisans worked with both pure gold and (more frequently) *tumbaga*, an alloy of copper and gold treated with acidic solutions on the surface of an object to give it the appearance of pure gold while permitting the conservation of the supplies of the precious metal.

The oldest radiocarbon date obtained from Buritaca site is A.D. 1000 ± 70 years (not too far off the Kogi cosmologically based estimate of their antiquity as a culture). Although C-14 dates are not reported from the twenty other Tairona sites that lie to the north and east, the similar pottery and other artifacts characterizing them suggest that most, if not all, of those shown in Figure 7.7 date to the same period of occupation. Support for this assertion comes from the formal network of roads, some of them measuring up to 4 meters in width, that connects many of the sites. Soto Holguín and his team have measured the area of nineteen of the sites, including Buritaca 200, at a total of 109.7 hectares. With an average population density estimated at 66 persons per hectare, the overall population of the 27.5-square-kilometer study area was ~7200 persons. If such densities (equivalent to about 260 persons per square kilometer) characterized the entire 1,500-square-kilometer area of Tairona occupation shown in Figure 7.1, then the total population would have been a little over 390,000, a figure that squares rather well with the statements about Tairona population size made by the sixteenth-century Spanish chroniclers.

VALDIVIA CULTURE

Although located far away in space and time from the Tairona-Kogi adaptation of the Sierra Nevada de Santa Marta, the Valdivia site of Real Alto, located on the southwest coast of Ecuador (see Figure 7.9), presents an interesting case for at

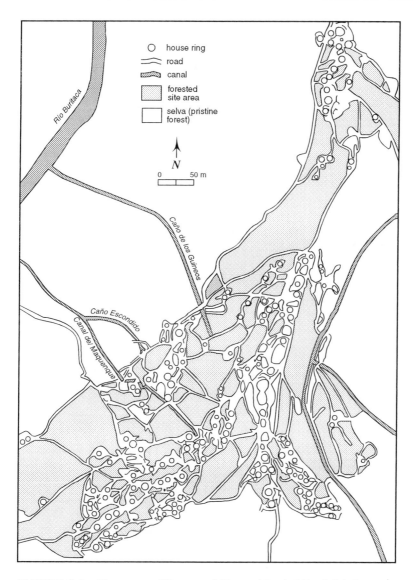

FIGURE 7.8   Plan view of Buritaca 200 site (Ciudad Perdida) showing house rings and the forested areas of the site. Redrawn and adapted from Soto Holguín (1988).

least two reasons that grow out of the arguments of this book. First, we have just looked at two adaptive systems that can be characterized rather straightforwardly within an ecological/evolutionary framework—in other words, a number of related variables from the mode of production through ritual and leadership permit the characterization of the Kogi as a village society and the Tairona as a chiefdom society. The same should be true of the Real Alto system, especially since there is little reason to suppose that either its subsistence productivity or its overall complexity was any greater than that of the current Kogi adaptation. I thus

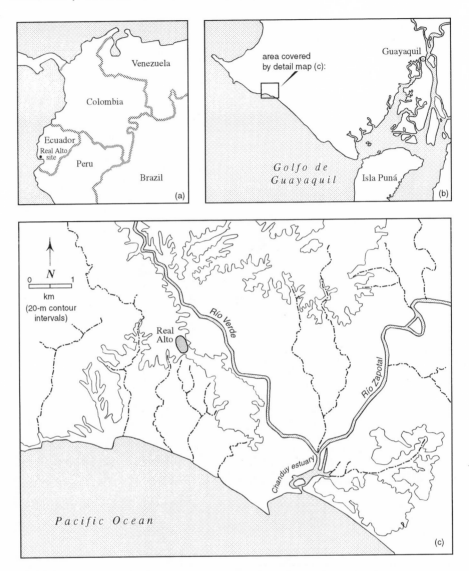

FIGURE 7.9   Maps showing the location of the Valdivia Period (~3550–1500 B.C.) site of Real Alto, on the southwest coast of Ecuador.

take issue with the Real Alto researchers' argument that the Valdivia Period society at this site represents the development of a chiefdom level of integration.

Second, we examine the implications of Lathrap's diffusionist argument that complex sociopolitical systems, including material features such as large public spaces (e.g., plazas), do not arise in the context of local need as populations grow. Rather, they are phenomena that probably are invented somewhere only once (or in a geographically restricted area), and thus their appearance elsewhere at later time periods must mean they "diffused" from some external point of origin. The coast of Ecuador, long considered to be a part of the "intermediate area" that lay between the "high civilizations" of the Central Andes and Mesoamerica, turns out according to Lathrap's argument to have had critical developments of its own far earlier (beginning at ~3400 B.C.) than any such developments in the two nuclear areas. Therefore, according to the antiecological illogic of this argument, the coast of Ecuador must have been causal in any subsequent developments in the two areas to the north and south.

Lathrap, Marcos, and Zeidler's Arguments

Let me begin by noting that the limited, marginal climate that currently characterizes the southwest coast of Ecuador would a priori suggest support for an argument against sociopolitical complexity at Real Alto. Nevertheless, there is some evidence that conditions during the Valdivia Period (~3400–1500 B.C.) were more favorable for the kind of subsistence productivity that might support such complexity. Bathed by the same cold Peru Coast Current that creates conditions of nearly total aridity to the south, the southwest coast is today so scarce in water that modern inhabitants sometimes have to truck it in during the dry season (Paulsen 1970). Although small amounts of rainfall occur on a yearly basis during the time the equatorial countercurrent penetrates the normally cool, upwelling waters along the coast, at ~200 millimeters per year (see Cañadas Cruz 1983) there is not enough rainfall to support productive agriculture, nor do the normally dry riverbeds run with a volume of water sufficient for intensive canal irrigation.

Although these arid conditions have been generally constant throughout the past millennia, research cited by Allison Paulsen (1970) suggests that the presence of substantial numbers of riverine mollusks, especially *Anadara tuberculosa*, in Valdivia middens indicates that during this period the rivers of the southwest coast, including the Río Verde (Figure 7.9), were running with greater volume than now. We may thus speculate that canal irrigation agriculture of sufficient productivity to support a chiefdom was a feature of local adaptive systems during this period. Real Alto site itself is located a little over 2 kilometers inland from the ocean, on a low ridge overlooking the Río Verde (Figure 7.9c). This implies, to the Real Alto researchers, that the subsistence system was based primarily on the "fertile agricultural lands of the Río Verde" (Lathrap, Marcos, and Zeidler 1977:5). In this regard, although no remains of maize or maize pollen were present on the site, the analysis of phytoliths from the midden debris by Deborah Pearsall (1978), not to mention the presence of apparent impressions of maize kernels on the rims of Valdivia Phase III pottery (~3100 B.C.), suggest to the researchers that this productive crop was part of the subsistence system.

The occupation of the site extends back into the pre–3400 B.C. period, when it was first occupied by a small hunter-gatherer group that focused its subsistence system primarily on the gathering of mollusks from coastal mangrove swamps and made a crude, heavily sand-tempered pottery that is quite unlike the later Valdivia pottery (e.g., Figure 7.10a). The creation of an open public space did not begin until the later part of Valdivia I period (~3400 B.C.), however, at which point the construction of two long mounds containing long lines of dwellings

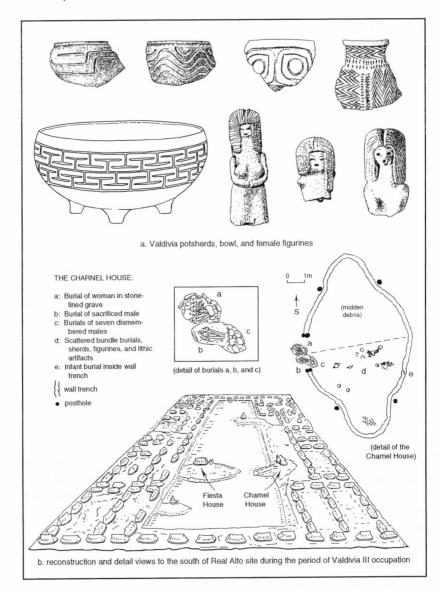

a. Valdivia potsherds, bowl, and female figurines

THE CHARNEL HOUSE:

a: Burial of woman in stone-lined grave
b: Burial of sacrificed male
c: Burials of seven dismem-bered males
d: Scattered bundle burials, sherds, figurines, and lithic artifacts
e: Infant burial inside wall trench

⟨⟨ wall trench

• posthole

(detail of burials a, b, and c)

(midden debris)

(detail of the Charnel House)

Fiesta House   Charnel House

b. reconstruction and detail views to the south of Real Alto site during the period of Valdivia III occupation

FIGURE 7.10   Selected Valdivia Period artifacts (a) and reconstruction and detail views of the Valdivia III remains at Real Alto site (b). Pottery redrawn and adapted from Willey (1971) and site from Lathrap, Marcos, and Zeidler (1977).

that flanked a large plaza was under way. By Valdivia III, Real Alto had reached its maximum size of 12 hectares and contained an estimated population of fifteen hundred persons, with a charnel (burial) house located along the west edge of the plaza and a fiesta house on a low mounded area that extended out beyond the east edge (Figure 7.10b). Although a tomb adjacent to the Charnel House contains the burial of what the Real Alto researchers consider to be a high-status woman, adjacent to a pit containing seven sacrificed males (whose disarticulated bones may well represent secondary burial), neither the Charnel nor the Fiesta House (which appears to about the same size as a Kogi ceremonial house) appears to be outside the scale of complexity that characterizes many village-level societies of the Amazon Basin (e.g., the Mundurucú).

Interestingly enough, judging from the much smaller extent of Valdivia VI–VIII occupation, the Real Alto excavations suggest that the on-site population was correspondingly much smaller as well after the Phase III occupation. By Valdivia VI a number of outlying settlements apparently had been established, and Lathrap and his colleagues think that this indicates the development of the two-level hierarchy of site size and function that characterizes a chiefdom society. However, aside from indicating that the closest site lies fully 20 kilometers away from Real Alto, they provide no data on the size, location, and internal nature of these sites (perhaps because no systematic and comprehensive settlement pattern survey has ever been done on the southwest coast in the area near Real Alto site). This lack of data does not, however, deter them (Lathrap, Marcos, and Zeidler 1977:12) from arguing that there existed a "distinction between rural hamlets and a central ceremonial center manned by full-time specialists in religion."

Arguing that without exception all of the "civilizations" (i.e., chiefdoms, states) of the New World featured ceremonial centers containing sacred public spaces where rituals important to the health and maintenance of the polity were carried out, Lathrap and his colleagues see one of two basic kinds of public spaces as having been present in these centers. The first type is characteristic of Peru and consists of single large platform structures with arms in the form of long, low mounds that extend out from the main structure. The second type consists of plazas bounded by flanking mounds. Although the second type is found in the southeastern United States and Mesoamerica, they note that the earliest public spaces in Mesoamerica, such as the Olmec site of La Venta, are constructed in the Peruvian form.

Since public spaces obviously indicate the presence of a corresponding ideology, the Real Alto researchers ask whether the ideology of such far-flung, yet similar, centers could possibly have arisen independently in North and South America or, conversely, whether it happened only once in some suitably earlier development. They conclude that similar ideologies and their corresponding material correlates could not possibly have arisen so far away from each other without some singular, earlier achievement in the intermediate area, namely, the one at Real Alto—never mind that Real Alto is located so far "south" in the intermediate area that it is just about as far away from Mesoamerica as the north coast of Peru, where, as we see in Chapter 9, some of these early developments took place.

We might attempt to "win" a debate against the Real Alto researchers' diffusionist point of view—for example, by arguing that there are too many differences among the public structures and open plaza areas of the many chiefdoms and states of North and South America for such phenomena to have anything other than local evolutionary origins. However, as the reader might well already have surmised, such a debate is probably in the realm of a no-win exercise: The diffusionists will always tend to give more weight to the structural similarities between cultural artifacts, and the ecologists will always tend to discount apparent similarities in favor of local evolutionary processes based on functional need. (In this regard, this debate is similar to the one evolutionary ecologists have with equally recalcitrant archaeologists whose atheoretical, inductivist-historical focus makes them unwilling to use "band, village, chiefdom, and state" categories to engage in meaningful discussion about the relationship between environment and levels of sociopolitical integration and between intensification and sociopolitical evolution.)

However, at the very least let us assume that if the people of the New World were "clever" enough to come up with sociopolitical complexity, as we know without question they surely were, then those of South America and North America (not to mention those of Ecuador and Peru) were equally capable of the independent development of ideologies and public spaces that helped in the coordination, management, and regulation of both noncomplex and complex societies whenever and wherever they developed. Real Alto, in this sense, becomes important not for the impulse it gave to the Americas, but for the very early example it gives of the developments in ideology and public architecture that occur along with the rise of sedentary society. If this argument is plausible, then we should be placing far greater weight on local ecological contexts and far less on stimulus diffusion.

Lévi-Strauss's Data on the Bororo

The Real Alto researchers cite the Bororo data of the Brazilian highlands not so much as proof of their argument that the Ecuadorian coastal site was a chiefdom, but as an indication through ethnographic analogy of what kinds of data are available from studies of recent groups of the myriad connections between the physical layout of an indigenous center and the ideology of the culture in question. However, by invoking the data from the southern Amazon, where the environment is characterized by a strong wet-dry seasonal cycle, they end up inadvertently showing that Bororo settlements can quite handily accommodate as many as one thousand inhabitants or more during the rainy season, when horticultural subsistence productivity is at its highest, in a complex social system that nevertheless is completely egalitarian.

During the lean dry season, when subsistence depends on scattered wild-food resources, the Bororo break up into much smaller mobile groups, which forage across the vast landscape around their settlements in a highly dispersed fashion. Were the overall settlement pattern to be studied, however, it might end up appearing to consist of a two-level hierarchy of site size and function, but it nevertheless would exclude all the other critical features of a chiefdom society, including monumental architecture at the main center (indicating its religious, political, and economic primacy) and a social division into commoners and elites based on ascribed status. As a matter of fact, we have no reason to suppose that during the drier part of the year the same process of a seasonal division into small mobile band groups was not a part of the Real Alto adaptation, especially given the reestablishment of marginal climatic conditions toward the end of the Valdivia Period.

As Claude Lévi-Strauss (1971) states, included among the Gê linguistic group of the southern Brazilian highlands are the Kayapó, the Apinayé, the Sherente, the Canella, and the Bororo—all of whom have a complex subsistence-settlement pattern involving complicated village layouts that contain the entire group during the more productive times of the year, but that remain essentially empty when the larger, egalitarian group breaks up during the dry period to go trekking. The Bororo village of Kejara, shown in Figure 7.11, provides an example of such a society. Lying along the left bank of the Río Vermelho, the village is arranged in a circle of twenty-six huts, with a larger men's hut, where both married and single adult males live, located in the center of the village. As in the case of the Mundurucú, the women are forbidden to enter the men's hut.

The village is divided into two basic moieties by a line that cuts across the center of the village parallel to the river. The people to the north of the line are called the Cera, and those to the south are called the Tugaré. Each individual in the village belongs to the moiety of his mother and must marry a woman from the other group. Since marriage is matrilocal, essentially what a man must do is move from one side of the men's hut to the other when he gets married. Two doors are present in the men's hut, the one on the Tugaré side called the "Cera" door and the one on the Cera side called the "Tugaré" door. The functions of the basic moiety division go far beyond the marriage rule, however; for example, the members of one moiety are responsible for carrying out the funeral when someone in their "partner" moiety dies.

The Kejara social system is more complicated than described to this point, however, since a second imaginary line crosses the center of the village roughly at a right angle to the river, further dividing the Cera and the Tugaré into upstream and downstream moieties (no one was able to tell Lévi-Strauss what the precise function of this second line was, except that people on one side were called "upstreamers" and people on the other side were called "downstreamers"). The Kejara population, which in the 1940s consisted of a mere 150 people but had earlier been as large as 1,000+ people, is further divided into a number of clans, the females and prepubescent boys of each clan living in their own separate dwelling. Each clan is in turn divided into "upper," "middle," and "lower" families, with each of these three groups apparently marrying endogamously within its own "class." Otherwise, one clan from the Cera group will ally itself with one from the Tugaré group, with the different clans varying in their social standing and some being considered "rich" and others "poor." Each clan, in addition, emblazons its religious and other material objects with symbols peculiar to that clan (e.g., see the club and bull-roarer in Figure 7.11).

The mythical heroes of the Tugaré are responsible for the existence of the things of this world, including water, rivers, fish, vegetation, and artifacts. It was the Cera heroes who assisted in ordering the relations among living beings at the time of the Creation. Paradoxically, despite the creative vigor of the Cera, it is the Tugaré who are considered "strong" and the Cera who are considered "weak,"

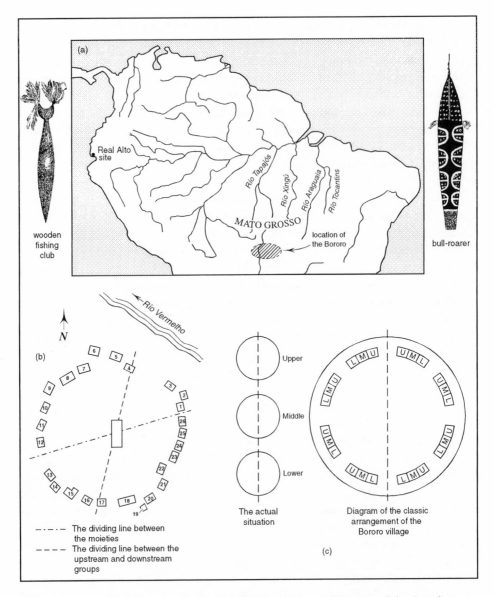

FIGURE 7.11   Map showing the location of the traditional Bororo of the Brazilian Mato Grosso in relation to Real Alto site (a); a plan view of the Bororo village of Kejara (b); and diagrams showing the real and apparent social structure of the village (c). Bororo figures redrawn and adapted from Lévi-Strauss (1971).

just the opposite characteristic of what they are known to be. But the Tugaré are closer to the physical universe and the Cera to the universe of humans, and the natural hierarchy of things requires the Tugaré to take precedence. As Lévi-Strauss puts it, the social order of humans cannot "cheat" the hierarchy of the cosmos and get away with it.

What Lévi-Strauss ended up seeing as he lived in this highly complicated social system—one in which people seem to delight in making things in a small-scale, 150-person society exceedingly more complex than one would think they need to be—is that the Bororo live a marvelously well-choreographed "ballet." Like dance partners engaged in a pas de deux, each of the two primary moieties lives and breathes for the other as it engages in numerous reciprocal behaviors, including the exchange of women in marriage and the burial of the other side's dead. Both the Bororo's grandiose cosmology and their more mundane social system seemed to Lévi-Strauss (1971:230) to bear witness to the eternal truths of Bororo life, namely, in resolving the inevitable contradictions of social life: "Every opposition was rebutted in favor of another. Groups were divided and redivided, both vertically and horizontally, until their lives, both spiritual and temporal, became an escutcheon in which symmetry and asymmetry were in equilibrium . . . in a society whose complexities seem to spring from a delight in complication for its own sake."

CHAPTER 8

Contemporary Central Andean Villages

W E COME NOW, IN THIS and the following chapter, to a consideration of
some of the more exemplary indigenous adaptive systems that have characterized
the Central Andes in recent and ancient times. In light of our earlier argument
that the productivity of traditional subsistence was greatest in this part of South
America—ultimately leading to the development of the most complex prehispanic societies anywhere on the continent—it is appropriate to begin with a discussion of specific quantitative figures that lend further support to this argument.
Since the focus later in this chapter is on two recent sierra groups, the Q'eros
Quechua and the Kaata Aymara/Quechua, for the moment we confine the treatment of subsistence productivity and related cultural features (including population densities) to the Andean highlands, leaving the discussion of human adaptation to the coastal part of the Central Andes until the next chapter.

Following a quantitative overview based on David Robinson's (1971) excellent discussion in *Peru in Four Dimensions*, the first section presents the main features of the Andean altitudinal zones between the elevations of 2,300 meters and
4,800 meters, following the model proposed by the Peruvian geographer Javier
Pulgar Vidal (1996). Compared to the environment of the Sierra Nevada de
Santa Marta, discussed in the preceding chapter, the sierra of Peru and Bolivia is
far more complex by virtue of its much greater extent and remarkable geographic
variability. The reader will recall from our discussion in Chapter 3 that the pronounced variability of the Central Andean region is due to several factors: its
wide elevational range, from ~2,000 to 7,000 meters above sea level; its equally
broad latitudinal range, from 5° to 18° south latitude over a distance of 2,000
kilometers; and the presence of highly variable weather patterns to the east and
west of the main mountain chain (see Figure 8.1). However, since no geographer
has ever dealt satisfactorily with the full range of this variability, I attempt here
only to suggest what some of its principal component features are as they relate

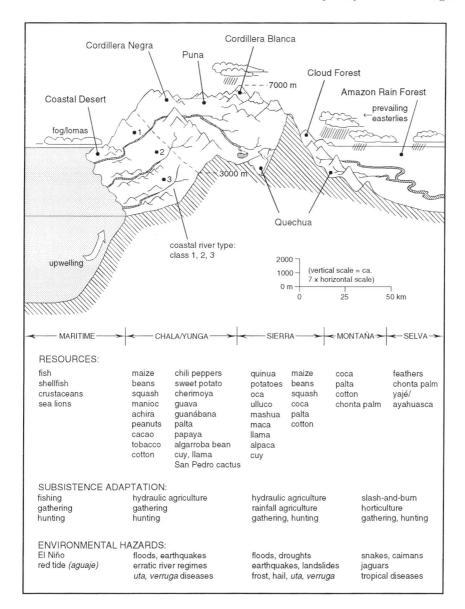

FIGURE 8.1   Profile view to the north of the main microenvironments of the Central Andes and listings of the resources, subsistence adaptation, and environmental hazards of each.

to local Andean adaptive systems (e.g., rainfall and temperature as a function of location, elevation, and latitude).

Following this, based on Bernard Mishkin's (1963) discussion of the Quechua, I proceed to a consideration at an equally general level of some of the main sociocultural features that characterize these adaptive systems. A generic approach is necessary here simply because, as in the case of the geographic literature, no anthropologist has yet produced an overview that deals adequately with all of the variability—from subsistence to cosmology—that must characterize Central Andean Quechua- and Aymara-speaking groups in light of the great diversity of local environments they inhabit. The first section ends with a presentation and brief critique of the five cases of vertical control of a maximum of ecological zones, proposed some years ago by Andeanist scholar John Murra (1975) in an attempt to account for the range of adaptive diversity in the Central Andes during the later prehispanic and early Colonial periods (~A.D. 1100–1600).

In spite of the foregoing implication that we still know all too little about traditional Quechua and Aymara adaptive systems across the length and breadth of the Central Andes, mention of the more outstanding ethnographies that have been published in the past quarter century indicates the contributions that are now being made toward understanding this variability. Proceeding from the Cajamarca area in the north to the Lake Titicaca area in the south, a minimal list would include the following nine ethnographies: Stephen Brush's (1977) study of Uchucmarca, a farming community that lies about 200 kilometers to the east of Cajamarca; Kent Flannery, Joyce Marcus, and Robert Reynolds's (1989) study of five communities of llama herders near Ayacucho; Billie Jean Isbell's (1978) study of the farming town of Chuschi, located some 50 kilometers south of Ayacucho; Gary Urton's (1981) study of Andean cosmology and ecology in Misminay, near Cuzco; Michael Sallnow's (1987) study of communities that carry out pilgrimages in the Cuzco area; Steven Webster's (1972) study of the Q'eros communities, located in the Andes 80 kilometers to the northeast of Cuzco; Lawrence Kuznar's (1995) ethnoarchaeological study of Awatimarka, a herding community located in the Andes southwest of Lake Titicaca; Hans and Judith-Maria Buechler's (1971) study of the Bolivian farming village of Compi, located immediately to the east of the Copacabana area of Lake Titicaca; and Joseph Bastien's (1985) study of Ayllu Kaata, which is located to the northeast of Lake Titicaca in the *yungas*, or deep valleys, lying along the eastern cordillera of the Bolivian Andes.

Obviously, it would be impossible to deal adequately with all nine of these studies here—never mind that some of them are more interesting and useful to read than others in view of their completeness, or lack thereof, in dealing with the principal features of a community's adaptive system. For example, Brush's otherwise excellent study of Uchucmarca is almost Stewardian in its consistent focus on lower-order variables, including the land, the subsistence technology used, and the social relations of those who farm it, while virtually ignoring the cosmologies and rituals that we might want to examine in light of their potential connectedness to aspects of the material adaptive system he describes so well. Sallnow's study in the Cuzco area does not ignore geography, but it nevertheless focuses essentially on higher-order variables, including cults, pilgrimages to cult centers, and the social relations of those who participate in the cults, without revealing much about the connections between these belief and ritual systems and the day-to-day lives and subsistence activities of the participants.

Among the studies that stand out as truly "complete" in our sense—that is, they not only describe all or most of the critical systemic variables, from subsistence to cosmology, but also propose arguments about the adaptive significance of both higher-order and lower-order features in the system—are Webster's ethnography of the Q'eros community and Bastien's ethnography of Ayllu Kaata. For this reason, they are the focus of the middle and last sections of this chapter. In addition to Webster's study, the Q'eros people have been the subject recently of a particularly excellent film entitled *Qeros: The Shape of Survival*, produced in 1979 through Mystic Fire Videos by John Cohen, an ethnographic filmmaker. Thus, although no published book is available on the Q'eros people, the interested reader can at least opt to view this film to supplement the information from Webster's study that is summarized in the middle section of this chapter. Bastien's study is remarkable for several reasons, not the least of them being that (1) he is a former priest who worked with indigenous groups of the Titicaca area and during his experience there became sensitive to the importance of both the traditional and Catholic religious traditions in the maintenance of local adaptive systems; (2) he received his doctorate from Cornell University under the tutelage of John Murra; and (3) the Ayllu Kaata people themselves view the mountain they live on in terms of the metaphor of a human body, to mention just one of several complexities that must be described in understanding the system they have devised in adapting to the vertical levels of the mountain that provides both their sustenance and cosmological raison d'être.

ADAPTATION TO THE SIERRA
Robinson's Data on Land and Population

Of the total land area of 1,285,216 square kilometers encompassed within the boundaries of Peru, Robinson calculates that only 26,600 square kilometers (2,660,000 hectares) were in cultivation in the early 1960s, or a minuscule 2 percent of the land surface of the country. In terms of the distribution of these cultivated lands throughout the three main environmental regions, 8.5 percent (2,261 square kilometers) were located in the *montaña*, 28.5 percent (7,851 square kilometers) on the coast, and 63 percent (16,758 square kilometers) in the sierra, with an additional 5,000 square kilometers estimated to have been lying fallow at any one time in this last region. Robinson also estimates that the supply of natural, or uncultivated, pastureland in Peru covered some 400,000 square kilometers (40 million hectares), of which we must assume that something approaching 100 percent of the total was present in the sierra alone, given that nearly all of the land in coastal valleys is (and has been) used for intensive irrigation agriculture and that very little land in the Amazon part of the country was then used for grazing animals.

Taking all of these figures into consideration for the sierra alone, we may summarize the situation in the early 1960s as follows: 16,758 square kilometers were in active use for crop production, an additional 5,000 square kilometers of crop-land were lying fallow, and 40,000 square kilometers were used as pastureland—which adds up to a combined subsistence area of 61,758 square kilometers. If we estimate the total area covered by the Central Andean sierra to be about 411,000 square kilometers (Instituto Geográfico Militar 1989), then the area used for traditional subsistence agriculture constituted about 15 percent of that total, or 7.5 times more than the average figure for the entire country. Thus, although at first glance the figure of 2 percent mentioned at the outset of this section appears to contradict any argument that the Central Andean area was capable, at least in prehispanic times, of supporting the rise of the most complex societies ever to develop anywhere on the continent, the Peruvian sierra is a relative "breadbasket" compared to either the *montaña* or the coast (and, as we shortly see, compared to any other area in South America as well).

The Peruvian census figures for 1961 presented by Robinson include an estimated total of 9,925,986 persons, with 58.6 percent of this number, or 5,816,627 persons, living at elevations between 2,000 and 4,500 meters in the sierra. If we assume that everyone who lived here at this time was reliant for food on the sierra alone, then we may calculate the ecological density of this population as follows: 5,816,627 persons ÷ 61,758 square kilometers = 94 persons per square kilometer (or 0.94 person per hectare). Of course, we may also calculate a "crude" population density for the sierra by dividing 5,816,627 persons by the total land area of 411,000 square kilometers, which results in a figure of 14 persons per square kilometer (or 0.14 person per hectare). This density figure, however, also includes all of the uncultivated land (85 percent) as well as the small amount of land used for traditional subsistence (15 percent) and thus is not meaningful for comparison with other areas of the South American continent, where, as we have seen, nearly all of the environment was indeed used in carrying out slash-and-burn cultivation as well as for hunting and foraging activities.

We are now in a position to compare the traditional subsistence-based demographic potential of the Central Andes, estimated above at 94 persons per square kilometer, to the average potential of some of the adaptive systems we have discussed earlier in this book. They include the Ona of Tierra del Fuego, at ~0.10 person square kilometer; the Amazon overall (Denevan 1976), at 0.50 person per square kilometer; the Mundurucú, at 0.30 person per square kilometer; the Yanomamö, at 0.17 person per square kilometer; the Shuar-Jívaro, at 0.46 person per square kilometer; the Kogi, at a maximum of 4 persons per square kilometer; and, finally, the Tairona, at 260 persons per square kilometer. The reader will note that, except for the Tairona case, the maximum estimated population density for traditional Andean subsistence ranges from 940 times greater (94 persons versus 0.1 person per square kilometer) to about 23.5 times greater (94 persons versus 4 persons per square kilometer) than any other adaptive system we have examined outside the Central Andes. However, the estimated population density for the Tairona is about 2.8 times greater than that estimated here for the Central Andes. But even if we assume the density figure of 260 persons per square kilometer for the Tairona adaptation to be correct, there is a single significant difference between the Sierra Nevada de Santa Marta and the Peruvian sierra: The total area potentially usable by the Tairona for subsistence is estimated to have been about 1,500 square kilometers (thus indicating a maximum population potential of 390,000), whereas the total subsistence area that can be utilized by traditional groups of the Andean sierra of Peru is about 62,000 square kilometers (indicating a population potential of nearly 6 million persons).

Pulgar Vidal's Model of Andean Environmental Zones

Compared to the Sierra Nevada de Santa Marta, where today there are low numbers of inhabitants and the knowledge of the potentials and limitations of the different altitudinal levels is restricted entirely to the Kogi and a few anthropologists, the vertically stacked environmental zones of the Central Andes are quite widely known not only by the inhabitants of the sierra itself but also by most ecologically literate Peruvians who occupy the two other principal regions of the country. This is not particularly surprising, since such knowledge is an integral aspect of successful survival, not least for all of the sierra individuals and groups that are engaged in one or another aspect of agriculture.

Indeed, given the geographic complexity of the Central Andes, it also is not surprising that a number of different scholars have come up with various classificatory schemes designating the most significant of these environmental zones. Putting my own gloss on the case, the number of zones identified in these schemes (see Pulgar Vidal 1996) may be viewed as ranging from the "acceptable" through the "rather dreary" to the "impossibly complex" in terms of their meaningfulness and utility for most students of the area—as exemplified by Joseph Tosi's (1960) seven *altitudinal floors* (tropical, subtropical, lower montane, upper montane, subalpine, alpine, and nival); Leslie Holdridge's (cited in Tosi 1960) eight *humidity provinces* (superarid, arid, semiarid, subhumid, humid, perhumid, superhumid, and nival); and Tosi's thirty-four *vegetational provinces* (from humid tropical forest to montane desert, with thirty-two other provinces in between!).

In recent years Pulgar Vidal's model based on "eight natural zones" has come increasingly into acceptance by anthropologists (e.g., Flannery et al. 1989; Richardson 1994) and geographers alike—not least because it is fairly easy to remember and therefore to understand, but also because it is based in large part on the terms the indigenous people themselves have used for these zones. From today's perspective it may be said that, although the local inhabitants of the sierra may not know the exact elevations that are now used to delimit each zone, they certainly know far better than any outsider what the potentials and limitations of the zones they live in are. Although I am speculating, since the Andes often feature a close geographic juxtaposition of two or more zones, it is highly likely that as vertical strategies of exploitation developed early in prehispanic times, indigenous groups designated each zone with a distinct name rather than always having to mention a multitude of its unique characteristics.

To proceed with Pulgar Vidal's classification, he identifies the following eight natural zones from west to east (i.e., from coast to Amazon) based on their elevation above sea level and on the complex of climatic, floral, and faunal features that characterizes each: *chala*, or coast (0–500 meters); *yunga* (500–2,300 meters); *quechua* (2,300–3,500 meters); *jalca*, or *suni* (3,500–4,000 meters); *puna* (4,000–4,800 meters), cordillera, or *janca* (4,800–6,768 meters); *ruparupa*, or high selva (400–1,000 meters); and *omagua*, or low selva (80–400 meters). Of these eight zones, we are concerned here with the three that provide the main context for human habitation in the sierra above 2,300 meters elevation: the *quechua*, the *jalca*, and the *puna*.

All of Pulgar Vidal's zones for the coastal and sierra regions are employed in Figure 8.1, although cloud forest/*montaña* and Amazon rain forest are substituted for his *ruparupa* and *omagua*. Figure 8.1 also shows some of the material resources that are characteristic of the main zones as well as the nature of subsistence adaptations and environmental hazards in each. It thus attempts to show both the potentials and the principal limiting factors that characterize the zones. Another important point to be drawn from the figure, in anticipation especially of our discussion of Murra's cases, is the proximity of distinct environmental zones over relatively short horizontal distances. In the Andes, unlike in nonvertical environments of the world, any given human group has at its potential disposal the resources of all or nearly all of the climatic zones known to humankind—although, in this case, these resources obviously are South American and Andean in nature. A final point to make is that the figure is a decidedly simplified version of Andean environmental reality, since any given zone (e.g., the *quechua*) can be found anywhere on either side of the two cordilleras where the defining features of elevation and associated climate (e.g., 2,300–3,500 meters and seasonal rainfall) are present.

The Quechua Zone

This environment is located along both the western and eastern slopes of the cordilleras and extends in long strips throughout the Andes between 2,300 and 3,500 meters above sea level. Pulgar Vidal describes a typical *quechua* setting as occurring just above the upper reaches of the *yungas* (coastal valleys, in Peru) and the *montaña* at the point where a section of the mountains opens into a broad amphitheater characterized by steep ridges and equally steep-sided hill slopes. Much of this landscape has been occupied for centuries by the Andean people, and everywhere here one sees canals, rock-walled terracing, scattered households, and small communities. Rainfall is neither excessive nor light in this zone, although occasional heavier rains can cause massive landslides, called *huaycos*, in spite of the fact that the land has usually been heavily modified with rock walls and terracing to avoid erosion of the hill slopes and to retain the soil in the fields. Average annual temperatures fluctuate fairly narrowly, and temperature swings between daytime and nighttime can be markedly greater, or as much as a difference of 10°C. Fogs and mists are quite common, especially during the rainy summer months from October to March. In the highest reaches of the *quechua* zone, one encounters the lower limit of winter frosts, especially on cloudless nights—a factor that makes agriculture less predictable here. However, of all the sierra environmental zones, the largest number of cultigens can be grown in the *quechua*, including maize, squash, wheat (a European introduction), and a host of other Andean crops, such as arracacha, caigua, granadilla, llacón, and pashullo.

The Jalca Zone

Like the *quechua*, the *jalca* zone extends in long strips along the western and eastern sides of both cordilleras. It is more compressed vertically, however, in that it ranges narrowly between 3,500 and 4,000 meters above sea level. It is also less suitable for agriculture not only because temperatures are cooler, averaging between 7° and 10°C and dropping as low as −1° to −16°C in winter, but also because the *jalca* is defined as consisting of (1) narrow rolling strips of floodland along mountain streams, (2) very steep areas with limited amounts of soil, and (3) sharp ridges covered with scattered outcrops of rocks. Vegetation in this zone varies from spiny xerophytic plants along the drier western cordillera to occasional dense forests along the well-watered eastern cordillera and, finally, to scattered grass and dwarf trees in the enclosed basins that occur between the cordilleras. Because of the lower temperatures, maize and squash generally cannot be cultivated, although hardier cold-adapted Andean crops, such as mashua, quinua, cañigua, achis, tarhui, oca, and olluco, thrive here.

The Puna Zone

The *puna* lies between 4,000 and 4,800 meters above sea level, although its upper limit, immediately below the permanent snowline, is higher in the northern Andes near the equator and lower in the southern Andes as a function of increasing distance away from the equator. The most general aspect of the *puna* is great expanses of grassy tundra that vary in width as a function of the distance between the cordilleras but reach their greatest extent in the Lake Titicaca area, where the cordilleras are as much as 100 kilometers apart. In the central and southern sectors, especially, days are cold and nights are even colder. Summer daytime temperatures may reach as high as 22°C, however, which, combined with the heavier rainfall that occurs during this time of year, provide conditions suitable for a single growing season from October to May. Although hardy grains such as quinua and barley can grow in the more temperate parts of the *puna* that lie around the larger lakes, and sheep, a European introduction, also do well in the lower reaches of this zone, in general the main resources consist of the cold-/altitude-adapted complex of Andean tubers and camelids.

Variability in Rainfall Patterns and Temperature

Figure 8.2 shows data on rainfall and temperature recorded over nearly a century for six cities in the Central Andean sierra (from north to south, Cajamarca,

	Jan	Feb	Mar	Apr	May	Jun	Jul	Aug	Sep	Oct	Nov	Dec	Year
CAJAMARCA (2620 m)													
mm of rainfall	95	103	121	92	39	12	5	9	32	79	61	77	725 mm
temperature °C	*15*	*15*	*15*	*15*	*14*	*15*	*14*	*15*	*15*	*15*	*15*	*16*	*15°C*
HUANUCO (1859 m)													
mm of rainfall	51	65	64	29	10	4	3	6	14	32	43	59	375 mm
temperature °C	*21*	*21*	*21*	*21*	*21*	*20*	*19*	*20*	*21*	*22*	*22*	*22*	*21°C*
JAUJA (3410 m)													
mm of rainfall	115	118	106	46	13	10	4	7	28	62	63	97	663 mm
temperature °C	*11*	*11*	*11*	*11*	*11*	*11*	*10*	*11*	*12*	*12*	*12*	*12*	*11°C*
AYACUCHO (2740 m)													
mm of rainfall	107	118	81	39	11	42	7	12	45	34	62	62	610 mm
temperature °C	*18*	*18*	*17*	*18*	*17*	*16*	*16*	*17*	*18*	*19*	*19*	*1*	*18°C*
CUZCO (3248 m)													
mm of rainfall	149	115	97	38	7	3	4	6	24	47	70	109	671 mm
temperature °C	*13*	*13*	*13*	*13*	*12*	*10*	*10*	*11*	*13*	*14*	*14*	*1*	*12°C*
JULIACA/PUNA (3826 m)													
mm of rainfall	131	109	96	38	9	3	2	6	21	37	52	90	577 mm
temperature °C	*11*	*11*	*11*	*10*	*9*	*7*	*7*	*8*	*10*	*12*	*12*	*12*	*10°C*
TINGO MARIA[a] (664 m)													
mm of rainfall	430	418	367	285	219	150	141	119	171	303	314	362	3277 mm
temperature °C	*24*	*24*	*24*	*25*	*25*	*24*	*24*	*25*	*25*	*25*	*25*	*24*	*24°C*
AREQUIPA[b] (2524 m)													
mm of rainfall	29	42	18	2	0	0	0	1	0	0	1	6	100 mm
temperature °C	*15*	*15*	*15*	*15*	*15*	*14*	*14*	*14*	*15*	*15*	*16*	*16*	*15°C*
LIMA/CALLAO[b] (13 m)													
mm of rainfall	1	1	1	0	1	2	4	3	3	2	1	1	20 mm
temperature °C	*22*	*23*	*22*	*21*	*19*	*17*	*16*	*16*	*16*	*17*	*19*	*21*	*19°C*

NOTES: Data in general are for the years 1900–1990; figures are rounded to the nearest millimeter and the nearest degree; rainfall in the Year column is expressed as an average yearly total, and temperature is expressed as the monthly average for the years in the data set; elevation is in meters above sea level.

[a]Tingo María is located in the eastern *montaña*.

[b]Arequipa and Lima/Callao are located on the western, or coastal, side of the Andes Mountains.

SOURCE: www.worldclimate.com.

FIGURE 8.2   Average annual rainfall (in mm) and temperature (in C°) for selected cities of the Peruvian sierra in comparison to cities located in the Amazon *montaña* and the Pacific coast, with a detail map showing the location of the cities included in the table (shaded area indicates mountains above 2,000 m elevation).

Huánuco, Jauja, Ayacucho, Cuzco, and Juliaca/Puno) compared to data recorded for one city located in the eastern *montaña* (Tingo María) and two located on the western side of the Andes (Arequipa and Lima/Callao). At various earlier points I have mentioned the strong seasonality that characterizes rainfall patterns in the sierra. Going from left to right in the columns, or from January to February, the start of the "summer" dry season is clearly evident in the sharp reduction in rainfall in all six sierra cities that begins in May and reaches its full expression in June, with rainfall beginning to pick up again in September.

Note also that Lima-Callao is typical of all sectors of the coast in receiving relatively no rainfall at all in comparison to the sierra cities, whereas Tingo María, located in the eastern *montaña*, receives a minimum of four times more rainfall than any sierra city. In comparison to the *montaña* and the Amazon proper, then, areas throughout the sierra annually receive adequate or moderate amounts of rainfall ranging between averages of 375 millimeters (Huánuco, located in the deep desert canyon of the Huallaga River) and 725 millimeters (Cajamarca, located in the northern highlands just to the south of the rainy *páramo* area of Ecuador). As a result, rainfall agriculture can be employed as a consistent strategy, although irrigation often is necessary as well—especially in drier areas or on the western slopes of deep canyons, where the "rain shadow" effect comes into play as the prevailing easterlies dump most of their precipitation on east-facing slopes.

Although data on more cities would show the full dynamic of the relationship between temperature and elevation and latitude the figure provides at least some indication of how temperature in the Andes drops to cooler levels as a function of increasing elevation and latitude. Both of these factors, then, must be taken into consideration, with rainfall, in assessments of the agricultural potential of any given part of the Central Andean sierra. The other significant point to make about the temperature data in Figure 8.2 is that each area of the Andes, no matter whether it lies to the north or south, exhibits strikingly little month-to-month variation in temperature. However, given the greater southern latitude, the most variation in month-to-month temperature in the sierra occurs in the Juliaca/Puno area on the northwestern shore of Lake Titicaca. Temperatures there average a cool 10°C annually at an elevation of 3,826 meters above sea level, whereas temperatures in the *punas* of the Jauja area average about the same (11°C), but at a lower elevation. Temperatures, of course, would be cooler in the Juliaca/Puno area were it not for the temporizing effect of the lake.

Mishkin's Model of Quechua Adaptive Systems

The term *quechua* is employed here both to describe a particular environmental *zone* in the Central Andes and to designate the *people* who speak the language of the same name and inhabit the sierra from Ecuador south to central Bolivia (a pocket of Aymara-speaking people live in the northern part of Bolivia). We rely here on Mishkin's 1963 paper on the Quechua people as a basis for commenting on selected general features of adaptive systems in the southern Andes, the geographic focus of the middle and last sections of this chapter. Although written a half century ago, Mishkin's paper deals more effectively with these features than anything published since that time. This does not mean, however, that a book-length overview of sierra adaptive systems is not urgently needed or that more research should not be carried out in areas where little or none has been done to date (e.g., the far northern sierra) or where incomplete data are available (e.g., studies that have taken the Stewardian materialist approach mentioned earlier).

Mode of Production

Given the rugged Andean topography and the remoteness of settlements, traditional Quechua agriculture even today in the late twentieth century is based on a labor-intensive, nonmechanized subsistence system. Although cultivation is practiced virtually throughout the Peruvian sierra, herding becomes increasingly important, and usually the dominant system, anywhere above 4,000 meters as well as in the colder southern latitudes of the Cuzco and Lake Titicaca areas. Except for the extensive *altiplano* area around the lake, however, most groups are located close enough to other altitudinal zones to obtain access to the resources of these zones. The two main seasons, as we have seen, are the dry season (late May–late September) and the wet season (early October–early May), although the exact timing of planting in spring and harvesting in early fall varies significantly as a result of the diversity of local conditions from east to west and from north to south throughout the sierra.

Although Mishkin describes the land as "poor and exhausted," the Quechua practice careful rotation of crops (e.g., potatoes the first year, ocas the second, barley the third, and back to potatoes the fourth) and in general seem quite firmly in command of the techniques (e.g., fallowing) necessary to ensure continued use of their land over the longer term. In addition, Peruvian census figures from 1940 to the present show that population numbers have not gotten lower in the sierra. Instead, they have gone from a figure of about 3,511,000 in 1940, to 5,816,627 in 1961, to about 6,569,350 in the 1986 census (see Instituto Geográfico Militar 1989). This suggests, if anything, that sierra agriculture has been capable of continuing intensification—although this may be due more to modernization near the cities and to the construction of additional roads to remote areas than to changes in traditional practices in the remoter areas. Nevertheless, it is likely that the sierra has increasingly approached the upper limits of its agricultural carrying capacity in the past few decades, since, as anyone who follows events in Peru knows, as the population of the country has risen to a point that is now above 20 million, the percentages of people in the sierra versus the coast have been nearly exactly reversed—not only because of the attractive economic force posed by the capital city of Lima, but also because the land in the sierra has been increasingly unable to absorb the burgeoning population of that area (e.g., see Isbell 1978). Thus, although in 1940 only 31 percent of Peru's population was on the coast and 63 percent was in the sierra, by 1986 some 52 percent of the population was on the coast and 37 percent was in the sierra (with only minor changes in the selva figures).

Traditional subsistence agriculture in the Andes relies either (1) on the European-derived complex of yoked oxen teams and steel-tipped wooden plows, used in larger fields and near the cities; or (2) on the Andean-derived patterns related to the *chaquitaclla*, the traditional foot plow that is still used in steeper or smaller fields and in the more remote locations of the sierra. As shown in Figure 8.3, the *chaquitaclla* is a digging stick to which a handhold and a footrest are attached and (since the Colonial period) a steel blade as well. Although the *chaquitaclla* is widely utilized in the central and southern Peruvian Andes, its greatest use is confined to the southern Andes between Cuzco and Lake Titicaca, making it likely that it originated here in the prehispanic period. Grimaldo Rengifo Vásquez (1987) estimates that one man with a digging stick can plow an area of about 200 square meters a day and needs about 415 hours of work to complete a hectare-sized area (10,000 square meters). He also notes that the rate of coverage per unit of time is dependent upon a number of factors, including the weight, strength, and skill of the man; the moisture content and texture of the soil; the steepness of the hill slope; and the social context in which the work is carried out.

Domestic Economy

A traditional agricultural work party, or *masa*, consists of the field's owner, the immediate family of the owner, and several nearby relations or neighbors who are invited to carry out the initial preparation of a field for planting. Each day the group convenes at the owner's house for a session of coca chewing, the coca being supplied by him, followed by a number of hours of work, which are interrupted frequently for more coca chewing and, halfway through the day's effort, for a lunch of potatoes and cheese (also often supplied by the owner of the plot). Depending on the size of the group, work parties break into smaller groups of three persons, with two men using *chaquitacllas* while a third member of the group, usually a woman or a boy, breaks the clods with a steel-tipped wooden adze called a *taclla*. The whole group works in rhythmic unison, often breaking into song, and the preparation of a small field for planting can be carried out in this communal fashion with impressive efficiency and speed. Sowing is also carried out in groups of three, with one person using a *chaquitaclla* to push down a hole, another casting pulverized manure in and around the hole, and a third putting the seeds into the ground before covering them with dirt.

The lending of labor for group efforts in working a family's fields and the owner's provision of coca and food to those who lend this labor are based on *ayni*, the Quechua word for a sierrawide institution that Mishkin (1963:419) notes "is the most significant factor in the division of labor, running through all currents of Andean economic life." Ayni is a form of generalized reciprocity (see Sahlins 1972) in that those who lend their labor not only can expect immediate recompense in the form of a hospitable offering of food and coca, but also can expect help in their own fields when the time comes for plowing and sowing. In work

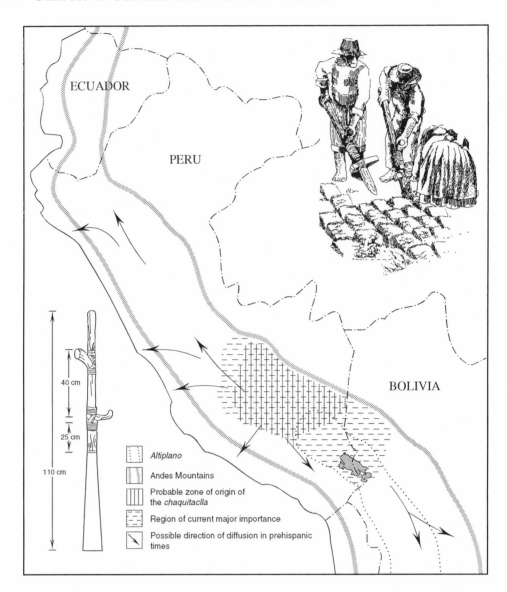

FIGURE 8.3   Map showing the possible zone of origin of the *chaquitaclla*, the Andean foot plow; its principal distribution in the Central Andes; and detail drawings of its features and use in traditional agriculture. Redrawn and adapted from Rengifo Vásquez (1987).

carried out in *ayni*, then, everyone is always inviting neighbors over for help with some task and giving them food and coca for lending a hand. Knowing that their hospitality will be reciprocated with more food and coca, they are always glad to return the favor. *Ayni* is thus similar to the neighborly lending of help on American farms, where, in carrying out a barn raising, the family that owns the barn "puts on a feed" for all those who come over to help.

Ritual and Religion

Rituals are a significant part of the agricultural cycle of the southern Andes. In August prior to the preparation of the fields for planting, offerings of coca and *aguardiente* (cane alcohol, or, literally, "firewater") are made to ensure a successful harvest and the well-being of the family. Incense is burned whenever hail appears to threaten the crops, and bonfires are lit as a magical means of warding off frost. However, the bonfires are not viewed in any practical sense as a means of warming up the crops on a frosty night. Instead, they are employed to engage the frost in mortal combat. Unfortunately, "Frost" sometimes becomes highly aggravated by the lighting of these fires and responds by destroying every plant in the fields.

Both the Sun (Inti Huayna Capac) and Christ, to the extent a Quechua group has been affected by the outside world, are important deities, but both are considered to be so far above the mundane aspects of life—such as the agricultural cycle and human survival—that they play a very minor role in day-to-day affairs. It is the Aukis and Apus, lesser deities who inhabit the interiors of mountains, who are invariably called upon when any sort of trouble strikes that threatens the well-being of the families and their communities. These mountain deities are thought to live in underground palaces together with great herds of livestock, including condors, which are their "chickens"; vicuñas, which are their "llamas"; and a ferocious cat called the Ccoa, which carries out any nasty acts they may wish to wreak on the humans who live on the slopes below. It is thus the Ccoa who ultimately brings hail and frost to destroy the crops or who kills people with lightning during thunderstorms (which are frequent during the rainy season). Throughout the southern Andes there are two classes of shamans: good ones who fight the Ccoa and bad ones who use the Ccoa's power for their own malevolent ends. Bad shamans always are rich and their fields are never damaged by the elements, whereas the good ones are poor, with low-yielding fields.

Putting our own gloss on the Quechua adaptation, we can see that ritual and cosmology clearly indicate that the practice of agriculture in the Andes is subject to the vagaries of a highly unpredictable climate. When hail, frost, or other natural phenomena destroy a crop that has nevertheless been protected with ritual and magic, it is because some person has carried out a malevolent act against the family or community. Indeed, any person known to be a shaman whose fields always seem to remain inviolate is probably in some danger of being killed by those who have been experiencing misfortune. Since it is ultimately the Ccoa who is in charge of such an act, however, great care must be taken to propitiate this malevolent feline with offerings such as cane alcohol, incense, bits of gold and silver tinsel, llama fat, and the seeds of certain plants. But if the Ccoa thinks the offerings are unsatisfactory or the people have fought off too vigorously the hail he brings to "steal" the harvest crop, then he will do his worst. In sum, Quechua ritual and religion are aimed, among other things, at ensuring survival in an environmental context subject to significant, and often disastrous, climatic swings.

Murra's Five Cases of Vertical Control

The vertical exploitation of resources located at multiple environmental levels is a strategy characteristic of most, if not all, indigenous groups of the Central Andean sierra. Thus, it is worthwhile to discuss five cases of this adaptive strategy discussed by Murra (1975) for the prehistoric and early colonial periods not only to establish some sense of its variability in time and place, but also to act as a prelude to discussion of Andean archaeology in Chapter 9. His landmark paper has appeared in two Spanish-language publications but has never been published in English and therefore has not been readily available to readers in the Northern Hemisphere.

Murra's five cases occurred approximately from the years 1460 to 1560, that is, immediately before and after the Spanish Conquest (see Figure 8.4). He is talking about "islands" of vertical control—namely, situations where a local community or a set of communities or a polity directly controlled isolated resources in places that lay at a substantial distance of more than a two days' walk from the main settlement nucleus, with intervening territory that presumably was under the control of other groups. The five cases thus do not apply to an imperial polity (e.g., the Inca) whose political boundaries embraced a series of adjacent, vertically stacked resource zones. Nevertheless, they presumably would indeed apply to a situation where a local community within the boundaries of such a polity continued to exert direct control of the kind envisaged by Murra over far-flung resources. Indeed, as we see later, this case also applies to present-day situations within the modern nation-state of Peru, where a local community such as the Q'eros Quechua exerts vertical control over isolated "islands" of resources.

Murra never intends that his research in Central Andean ethnohistory and archaeology, on which the five cases are based, has established every possible type of the vertical control of multiple resource zones that might have characterized either the prehispanic or Colonial periods. He does imply, however, that vertical adaptive strategies of one kind or another were not just characteristic of the (vertical) Andean sierra but also that they should have been characteristic of the adjacent (horizontal) Pacific coast. Although we can certainly agree that there is strong evidence that they apply universally to the sierra, the assertion that they apply equally broadly to the prehispanic coast is still open to question and will remain so for the near future, or at least until more archaeological projects have been done that attempt to link a given area of the coast with neighboring populations in the adjacent sierra.

Case 1: Small Sierra Communities of the Chaupiwaranqa Area

This case deals with small ethnic groups that inhabited the Chaupiwaranqa area, located in the *quechua* environmental zone of the upper reaches of the Marañón and Huallaga Rivers (Figure 8.4). Employing a strategy of permanent settlements inhabited by people who were from the nucleus and maintained an allegiance to it as well as their own household in it, the Chaupiwaranqa nucleus exploited re-

301

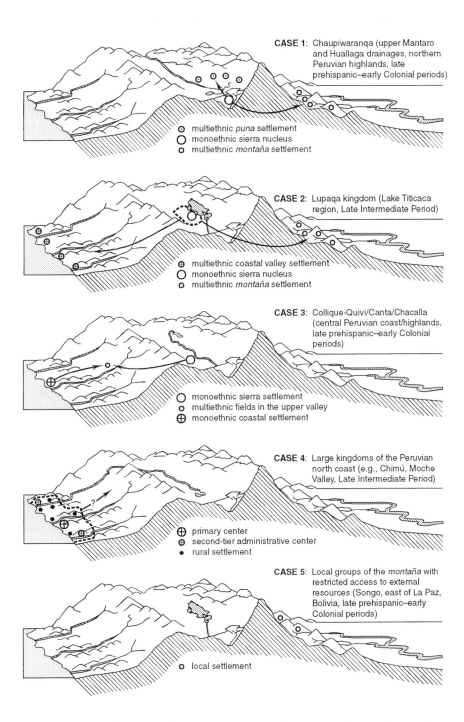

FIGURE 8.4   Schematic illustrations of Murra's five cases of vertical control of multiple environmental zones in the Central Andes. Based on Murra (1975).

sources lying in the *puna* (herds, salt) at some three days' walk away as well as resources lying in the *montaña* (coca, cotton) between two and four days' walk away. Making matters more complex, various Chaupiwaranqa nuclei apparently had developed this strategy of vertical control, since Murra mentions that the *puna* and *montaña* settlements were "multiethnic." Each of the small "ethnic groups," or polities, including the people in all three vertically stacked resource zones, numbered between five hundred and three thousand people.

Case 2: The Lupaqa Kingdom of the Lake Titicaca Area

This case deals with a far larger polity, the Lupaqa kingdom of the immediately pre-Inca Late Intermediate Period (Figure 8.4; see Chapter 9, Figure 9.2, for prehistoric Central Andean chronology). Located along the southwestern shores of Lake Titicaca, the Lupaqa consisted of about twenty thousand household units with a total population estimated at 100,000 to 150,000 persons. Located many days' walk away, or at far greater distances than those characterizing case 1, the Lupaqa established "archipelagos" in the southern coastal valleys of Arica, Sama, and Moquegua, where they cultivated maize and cotton and exploited marine resources from the Pacific. At equally great distances away to the east, in the *montaña* and Amazonian lowlands, they established other archipelagos where they cultivated coca and collected resources of the selva forests. The central site, along Lake Titicaca, was located at about 4,000 meters above sea level, whereas the peripheral archipelagic sites were located at elevations just above sea level far below to the west and east, respectively, of the central nucleus of control. In spite of the great distances between the two islands of resources and their sierra nucleus, the inhabitants considered themselves to be Lupaqa in both a political and cultural sense.

Case 3: Small Coastal Communities of the Canta Valley

This case came to light in the sixteenth century when the people of the community of Collique, located in the central coast valley of Canta, got involved in litigation with the people of the two adjacent sierra communities of Canta and Chacalla over rights of access to fields located in the intervening area of the upper Canta valley at an elevation of "below 1,000 meters." These fields had originally been used by the coastal Collique people to cultivate coca, chili peppers, manioc, peanuts, sweet potatoes, and several kinds of Andean fruit, but they were taken over in late prehispanic times when the two sierra groups marched down with a military force into the upper Canta and laid claim to them. The point here is not that the sierra people were practicing verticality because indeed they were, and moreover, we know from cases 1 and 2 that they did so elsewhere. Instead, to Murra it appears to be a possible case of a coastal group, or Collique, practicing verticality in the period prior to the sierra takeover of the fields.

However, let us note that there is a real question here as to whether fields located at a mere 1,000 meters, or below, in the upper coastal reaches of a Peruvian valley truly qualify as an island of exploitation that was separated by intervening, uncontrolled territory from the nucleus lying downvalley nearer to the ocean. One could answer this question by carrying out a settlement pattern survey aimed, among other things, at looking at prehispanic occupations in the intervening area—to see, for example, if settlements in that area were (or were not) characterized by the same pottery and other cultural diagnostics that characterized occupations near the sea and those near the fields that were in dispute. If they were not, then Murra's case would appear to hold true in arguing for coastal verticality; if, however, they were characterized by such diagnostics, then settlements located at ~1,000 meters above sea level in the upper part of a coastal valley would be defined as part of the same geographically continuous polity whose nucleus lay downstream.

Case 4: Kingdoms of the Peruvian North Coast

The fourth case is actually an apparent "negative" one, since, as shown in Figure 8.4, it deals with the archaeologically known Chimú of the north coast. As far as is known to date, this polity never exerted any direct control over archipelagic islands in the adjacent sierra in spite of the fact that it had ties to the Cajamarca area during the pre-Inca period. However, there is much archaeological evidence (e.g., Moseley and Day 1982; Willey 1953; Wilson 1988) to suggest that the Chimú polity extended its control *horizontally* over at least twelve main north coast valleys in the 425-kilometer distance between Lambayeque and Huarmey prior to A.D. 1475, the year of the Inca conquest of the Chimú.

Both of Murra's coastal cases of verticality are open to strong question—one (case 3) because it has not been tested archaeologically and the other (case 4) because there appears to be no archaeological support for it, although both cases nevertheless present important hypotheses for future research on the possibility that coastal nuclei controlled islands of resources in the sierra.

Case 5: Small Sierra Communities of the Songo Area of Bolivia

Interestingly enough, in light of our critique that Murra's cases 3 and 4 do not stand up to initial scrutiny, Murra straightforwardly presents his case 5 as a negative example. That is, although he includes it in a paper that purportedly presents five cases of verticality, he actually sees it as an example of nonverticality. In the Songo area, located in the upper *montaña* to the east of La Paz (Figure 8.4), there were small ethnic groups that Murra sees as not having had control over archipelagic islands, since in the immediate vicinity of their settlements they apparently cultivated a wide variety of crops, including yuca, maize, arracacha, beans, and fruit trees. Nevertheless—and somewhat enigmatically—Murra mentions that they also cultivated coca at lower elevations down to the east, apparently at distances of one to two days away. Since by definition they did not control the intervening territory between their settlements and the coca fields, the Songo case actually appears to be as good an example of verticality as are cases 1 and 2. That is, it is the third good example of the direct vertical control of multiple resource zones from the late prehispanic and early Colonial periods in the Central Andes. We do not yet have any good evidence, to repeat, of the vertical control of the sierra by ancient coastal communities or polities.

THE Q'EROS QUECHUA

Although located only 160 kilometers due east of Cuzco, the Q'eros are among the most isolated groups of the Andes primarily because the rugged 1,700-square-kilometer area they occupy on the Amazon side of the eastern cordillera has not permitted the construction of roads that would facilitate easy entry and exploitation by the outside world (see Figure 8.5). Since their adaptive system includes the entire range of Andean microenvironments lying between the *puna* and the *montaña* over a very short distance of 35 kilometers, they have been of interest to Andeanist anthropologists ever since they were first studied by Oscar Núñez del Prado, of the University of Cuzco, in the 1950s. The most complete study of the Q'eros was carried out by Webster (1972) over a thirteen-month period from October 1969 to November 1970, and it is the one this section is based on.

Interestingly, in some contrast to an earlier impression that their adaptation extends back in time some hundreds of years, based on historical evidence of ties between them and local haciendas Webster now thinks (personal communication) that the adaptive system I describe here dates only as recently as the 1930s. Just prior to this time, he argues, the Q'eros were in fact "small 'capitalist' farmers" who apparently were a part of the Peruvian national economy. However, there are two lines of evidence that suggest this is not the case—in other words, that the Q'eros represent an enduring and probably centuries-old adaptive system. First, in the film *Qeros: The Shape of Survival,* the Q'eros themselves characterize their vertically adapted system as extending back at least to the Inca state in late prehispanic times. Moreover, they recount in some detail several significant elements of traditional Andean cosmology, including Inti Huayna Capac as a major deity and the Auki's wrath in sending hail to destroy crops. It is hard to believe that Q'eros who were so recently "capitalist farmers" would remember cosmological traditions that presumably dated back to traditional "precapitalist" times, but at the same time would forget that only fifty years earlier they had not practiced traditional Andean subsistence verticality at all. Second, that no modern routes of travel—including even the roughest of dirt roads—had yet penetrated the Q'eros territory during the time period in question suggests that it would have been exceedingly difficult, if not impossible, for them to have been integrated enough into the national economy to warrant calling them "capitalist farmers."

But as we know that Webster is the principal authority on the Q'eros people, let us assume that his argument is correct—namely, that the Q'eros adaptation is not a traditional aboriginal one at all but instead dates back a very short fifty years from the time the film was made. If this is so, then the adaptation we describe here—which fits any imaginable model for evaluating a system of classic

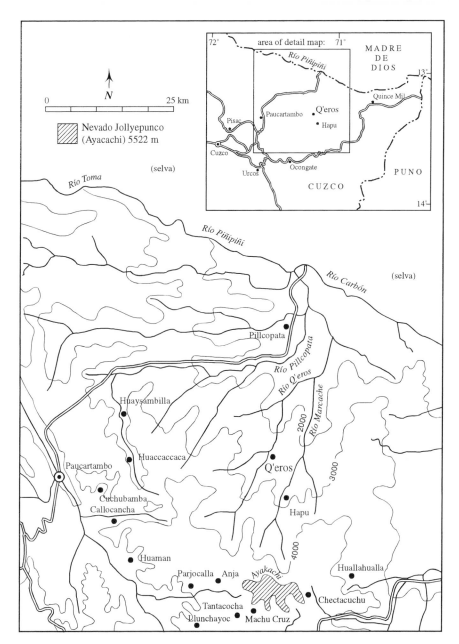

FIGURE 8.5 Map showing the Q'eros area, located in the Andes to the northeast of Cuzco. Redrawn and adapted from a map in Webster (1972).

Andean verticality—had emerged fully blown in the short space of forty years, or from the early 1930s to the time of Webster's study in 1969–1970! Assuming the correctness of his argument, we have presented no better example in this book of how an environment and a related subsistence complex (consisting, in this case, of Andean tubers, camelids, and maize) can bring about in very short order the adaptive response of a classic Andean subsistence-settlement system. The time depth of the Q'eros system we describe here therefore probably does not matter at all; it is an ideal model of the efficient vertical exploitation of multiple resource zones that has characterized Andean systems since prehispanic times.

Webster's Q'eros Quechua Data

Physical Environment

The Q'eros adaptive system is spectacularly situated between the high, snow-capped peaks of the Ayakachi range that rise to 5,400 meters and the mist-shrouded *montaña* that lies below to the north at an elevation of 1,800 meters above sea level (see Figure 8.6). The southern edge of their subsistence range consists of high *puna* pastures located immediately below the peaks of the Ayakachi range at elevations between 4,700 and 4,100 meters. As shown in Figure 8.6, several deep gorges run steeply down to the north off the *puna*, converging at the level of the *qeshwa* (*quechua*) zone, some 1,200 meters lower, in a narrow valley where limited agriculture appropriate to that zone is carried out. From this point on to the north runs a single steep, narrow canyon down through which the Q'eros must travel to reach their *montaña* fields, which are located at the far northern edge of their subsistence territory. Thus, the overall elevational range they cover in carrying out their herding and agricultural activities runs between 4,700 and 1,800 meters above sea level, or the equivalent of an astonishing 2.9 kilometers of vertical drop over the relatively short distance of 35 kilometers mentioned earlier.

Webster notes that throughout their extensive but narrowly constricted territory the Q'eros have assigned numerous place-names to the natural and cultural features that define and delimit it. Given the nature of the environment, no place is described without explicit reference to its location "up" and "down" (*wichay* and *uray*) in the environment and "inside" and "outside" (*uxu* and *hawa*) the canyons that become increasingly narrow as one proceeds from the *puna* down toward the *montaña*. Thus, for example, the *puna* is *wichay* and *hawa* because it is high and outside the narrowly constricted canyons of the gorges that lie below it, whereas the *montaña* is *uray* and *uxu* because it is low and boxed in by the walls of the main canyon.

As we have seen earlier in this chapter in general for the Andes, average ambient temperatures and rainfall in the Q'eros area are a function both of elevation and seasonality. For example, at 4,100 meters on the lower fringes of the *puna* the average daytime temperature in the summer months between November and April ranges between 10° and 15°C. But since temperatures can drop to below freezing at night and this is the time of the rainy season, sleet is frequent as well. At the same time, because the mean temperature throughout Q'eros territory also normally rises by a little over a half degree Celsius for each 100-meter drop in elevation, average temperatures are substantially higher in the *montaña*. Thus, when the temperature is 15°C in the *puna*, it will be about 30°C at elevations

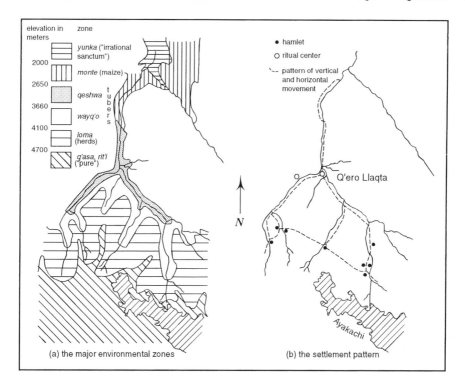

FIGURE 8.6   Maps showing (a) the principal environmental zones of the
Q'eros area and (b) the patterning of settlement during the seasonal round.
Adapted from maps in Webster (1972).

that are 2,900 meters lower in the *montaña*. Complicating climatic matters further is the fact that, whereas rainfall is seasonal in the sierra part of Q'eros territory, it occurs throughout the year in the *montaña* part. For this reason, thick mists form at night in the *montaña* and ascend in the early morning hours toward the *quechua* and *puna* levels at all times of the year, although during the dry season the mists are usually burned off quickly by the sun as the day wears on.

Mode of Production

Interestingly, in comparing the Q'eros to similar Old World adaptations, Webster notes that the typical subsistence pattern of Old World groups that have mixed subsistence regimes involving agriculture and herding is to focus primarily on the former and only secondarily on the latter. However, since in the Q'eros case *puna* pastures are focused in one area and productive throughout the year, whereas agricultural fields are dispersed throughout the rest of the territory and only seasonally productive, the situation for the Q'eros is more or less exactly reversed: They are primarily pastoralists who must focus constant attention on the care of the herds but who nevertheless spend a great deal of time caring for the fields at lower elevations. Indeed, Webster estimates that fully 80 percent of the Q'eros diet comes from tubers grown in the middle altitudes. Moreover, as with many other groups in the Andes, maize and maize beer, or *chicha*, are critically important not only for rituals and exchange with other groups but also for nutritional considerations, so the *montaña* fields where maize is cultivated are a constantly attractive and necessary subsistence focus—in spite of the difficulty of getting down through and back up the canyon to get to the altitudes where it can be grown.

The Q'eros, like other sierra groups, are well aware of the potentials and limitations of each of the principal altitudinal zones that make up their adaptive range between the high *puna* and the *montaña*. As shown in Figure 8.7, the highest zone (4,000 to 4,700 meters), where the herds are pastured, is called the *loma*, whereas the zone above it (4,700+ meters), which is too frigid and barren to have any economic use, is called the *q'asa* or *rit'i*, meaning "pure." Below the *loma* lies the *wayq'o* zone (3,660 to 4,000 meters), where scattered fields located on the slopes adjacent to the gorges are the focus of bitter potato cultivation. Below this is the *qeshwa* zone (2,650 to 3,660 meters), the upper level of which is appropriate for growing nonbitter varieties of potatoes as well as a number of other Andean tubers, including oca and ulluco. Here, also, in a few protected places of limited size that are provided by ruined house walls and abandoned corrals the Q'eros cultivate several Andean grains, such as tarwi and kañiwa. Below the *qeshwa* zone is the *monte* (~1,800 to 2,650 meters), where maize is grown along with other temperate/subtropical crops such as sweet potato, unkucha (*Xanthosoma saggittifolium*, a New World taro), yacón, arracacha, several varieties of squash, and chili peppers. Finally, lurking like a sort of terra incognita at the very edge of the selva to the east comes the *yunqa waqo*, meaning "irrational sanctum." The Q'eros also call it *sacha-sacha* ("endless trees") and *tuta* ("darkness"), indicating their reluctance to step out beyond the *montaña* transitional zone into the selva proper not only because they fear the insects and other animals that inhabit the selva, but also because they view it as the home of great numbers of dangerous spirits.

Every Q'eros family without exception owns alpacas and llamas, although there is a substantial difference among families in terms of the number of animals, which ranges from herds as small as ten to ones as large as a hundred head. Both alpacas and llamas are a source of wool, meat, hides, fertilizer, and fuel, although of the two animals the alpacas provide the finer wool for clothing and the llamas serve as beasts of burden in carrying the harvested crops between the *wayq'o*, *qeshwa*, and *monte* zones and the primary domiciles located in the *loma* and upper *wayq'o* zones. The alpacas, which constitute roughly three-quarters of each herd, are far more restricted than the llamas in terms of their habitat requirements. They are highly dependent for pasturage upon a type of alpine moor called *waylla* that grows only in the *loma* zone and, compared to the llama, have relatively tender feet that do well only in the softer, moist soils present in this zone. Having become adapted over the centuries to the conditions characteristic of this high elevation, they also suffer from pulmonary problems and *sarna* (or pelt itch) when they are moved out of the *loma* zone to lower elevations. The op-

Weberbauer (S.E. Peru)	Elevation (in meters)	Q'eros Natural	Q'eros Domesticated
cold desert (rock oases)	5300 4700	q'asa rit'i (limp'u)	none ("pure")
puna mat (Distichia moor, cushion rosette) (grasses)	4400 4000	loma (hamlets)	herds
tola heath (ichu mat)	3660	wayq'o	bitter papa
	3300	upper	Andean tubers
		— qeshwa —	
ceja (ferns, sphognum)	2650	lower (ritual center)	(collecting only)
	2000	monte	maize (temperate and subtropical crops)
montaña (palms, subtropical forest	1800	yunka yanqa wako	none ("irrational sanctum")

SOURCE: Webster (1972:94).

FIGURE 8.7   Major ecological zones and related resources of the Q'eros adaptive system in comparison to Weberbauer's (1945) classificatory scheme for southeastern Peru. Redrawn and adapted from Webster (1972).

timum adaptive range of the llamas, in contrast, is broader. They can be pastured either in the *loma* or the *wayq'o* zones and can spend long periods of time in the *qeshwa* and the *monte* zones without experiencing any difficulties. Moreover, their tougher feet and physical agility permit them to traverse with far greater ease the treacherous trails and narrow bridges that lie between the primary settlements and the *monte* fields located far below.

Given the focus on three main altitudinal levels characterized by different climatic regimes, a family must coordinate and time its subsistence efforts carefully throughout the year. The care and pasturing of the herds are a constant necessity, but when the time comes for planting and cultivation, between August and November, and for harvesting, between February and June, then limited family labor resources must be assigned for some weeks to the fields of the *qeshwa* and *monte* zones. Agricultural plots are not farmed by slash-and-burn techniques; instead, the vegetation covering an area in which a field is being prepared is cut down and simply left to dry and decompose on the surface. Thus, in the *monte*, where no fertilizer is added to the fields, the productivity of the soil is limited to two to three years of cultivation before decreasing returns make it necessary for the family to move to a new location. Even in the *qeshwa* zone, however, where camelid dung is employed, the soil is so poor that a field must be left fallow for six years after each year of use. Fields in both the *qeshwa* and the *monte* zones are tilled and cultivated with the *chaquitaclla* digging stick. Unlike some other areas of the sierra, however, no irrigation is practiced, and the Q'eros are thus reliant on rainfall to sustain the growing crops.

Although seasonal and year-to-year variability in rainfall and temperature patterns affects the subsistence efforts of all families in more or less the same way, disruptions nevertheless can occur in a given family's cyclical routine, at which point that family must rely on stopgap, or compensatory, strategies in hopes of mitigating any problems created by these disruptions. For example, if a family has fallen behind in its preparation of tuber fields in the upper *qeshwa* zone, it can speed up the stages of field preparation—which include fertilization, aeration, hilling, and cultivation—although this ultimately can bring about a less than optimum harvest. By the same token, if a family falls behind in preparing a new *monte* field, it can always rely on an old field that, while nearly depleted of nutrients, will still produce at least a meager crop—which is, of course, better than no crop for that year. Finally, an even more radical strategy is to suspend totally the family's activities in one of the altitudinal zones (usually the *monte*, since it is most remote from the primary domiciles). The result of such a decision, however, will be that for the coming year the family has no maize beer, a critically important feature if it must undertake feasting responsibilities for the Q'eros community.

Settlement Pattern

At the risk of some redundancy, let us emphasize again that the Q'eros settlement pattern is a dispersed, transhumant one—that is, the kind of subsistence-settlement system that occurs everywhere in the Andes where a local group of people is able to develop an adaptive strategy that permits the group to exploit the diverse resources of closely juxtaposed, vertically stacked microenvironmental zones. Webster notes that the Q'eros settlement pattern consists essentially of the following four altitudinal components: (1) the hamlets of the uppermost *wayq'o*; (2) the main ceremonial center located in the *qeshwa*; (3) the maize fields of the *monte*; and (4) more ephemerally occupied sites located in the intermediate zone between the hamlets and the ceremonial center.

As shown in the perspective view of Figure 8.8, the hamlets that form the primary domiciles of the Q'eros are located in the upper reaches of the deep gorges that run down to the north off the edge of the high *puna* pastures. All lie more or less at the same distance of 10 kilometers, or a maximum of three hours' walk, away from the ceremonial center at elevations of about 800 meters above it. Each hamlet consists of a number of households dispersed in extended family

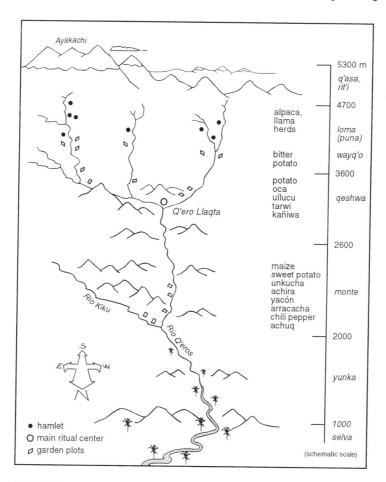

Ayakachi

| | 5300 m |
| q'asa, rit'i |
| 4700 |
| alpaca, llama herds | loma (puna) |
| bitter potato | wayq'o |
| 3600 |
| potato oca ullucu tarwi kañiwa | qeshwa |
| Q'ero Llaqta |
| 2600 |
| maize sweet potato unkucha achira yacón arracacha chili pepper achuq | monte |
| 2000 |
| yunka |
| Río Kiku |
| Río Q'eros |
| 1000 |
| selva |

• hamlet
O main ritual center
◻ garden plots

(schematic scale)

FIGURE 8.8   Perspective sketch to the south indicating the entire range of environmental zones and settlement patterns in the Q'eros adaptive system. Based on maps and textual account in Webster (1972).

groupings over an area that usually measures less than 1 kilometer in length. The location of the hamlet is determined with respect to the proximity of water, pastures for the animals, and the passes that connect the separate gorges. The extended family household groupings usually are connected by the walls of stone corrals, which are used to protect the alpaca and llama herds at night. Not surprisingly, then, the primary domiciles are called *tiyana wasi* ("living houses") or *paqocha rikuh wasi* ("alpaca-watching houses") and each extended family grouping is called *kuska wasi* ("together houses").

The main ceremonial settlement, called Q'ero Llaqta, is located at about 3,400 meters elevation, precisely at the point of convergence of the three principal gorges where the main canyon of the Río Q'eros runs down toward the *montaña*. Although this settlement is larger and more nucleated than any of the hamlets, and its houses are larger than those constituting the primary domiciles in the *puna*, Q'ero Llaqta is essentially deserted throughout the year except for brief periods when the entire community comes together to celebrate feast days and rituals. All but five of the fifty-six buildings here are secondary domiciles that are called *hatun llaqta wasi* ("main town houses"). Although hardly ever occupied, these houses must be big enough to accommodate an entire extended family when it comes down from the *puna* to participate in the festivals. The doors of most of the *hatun llaqta wasi* face toward the direction of the sunrise, which on cloudless days occurs directly over the edge of a huge cliff called Anka Wachana ("Incubator of Eagles") that looms high above and directly across the canyon to the east of Q'ero Llaqta. The other five buildings of the ceremonial center are a Catholic chapel, three ex-hacienda structures, and a (then) new but unused schoolhouse.

Although Webster does not discuss the exact nature of the dwellings located adjacent to the fields of the *monte*, they are decidedly more temporary, and thus far less formally constructed, than those in either the hamlets or Q'ero Llaqta. Indeed, the Q'eros sometimes call the *monte* itself *yunqa waqo*, or "irrational sanctum," because they enjoy neither their trip down through the canyon nor their stay there while they cultivate and harvest the maize and other crops. The journey down the canyon is a difficult one involving a steep descent of 2,200 meters over a distance of 25 kilometers and takes about six hours, with occasional stops being made at spiritually significant places to eat, chew coca, and rest. As shown in Figure 8.8, the fields themselves are located on the interior edges of the "V" formed by the confluence of the Río Q'eros and the Río Kiku. Just as temporary as the *monte* field dwellings are those of the *astana* camps, which are maintained by the Q'eros near the scattered tuber plots of the *wayq'o* and upper *qeshwa*.

In light of our earlier discussion of the time depth of the Q'eros subsistence-settlement pattern, it is relevant to comment that Webster's oldest informants in 1969–1970 told him that it had existed as described here "since even the beginning dawn of this world," or *kay pacha illiriymantarah*. Since time immemorial, in other words, the hamlets had been located in the heads of the gorges; the maize fields, however difficult they were to reach, had existed in the *monte*; and the ritual center of Q'ero Llaqta had been situated at the confluence of the gorges to integrate the activities of the far-flung hamlet groups throughout the entire horizontal and vertical range of their adaptive system.

Mode of Reproduction

With families rarely congregating in one spot at the same time, and the Q'eros dispersed throughout the different altitudinal zones across an area 35 kilometers in length, it is not surprising that Webster is not certain of the ultimate accuracy of his census figures. Nevertheless, he was on the scene throughout an entire year and was able to obtain figures that he thought were reasonably precise. Based on his 1970 genealogical data, he counted a total of 376 people living in eighty-two conjugal families, which were dispersed in fifty-two domestic groupings among the hamlets scattered across upper *wayq'o* along the edge of the Ayakachi *puna*.

In contrast, the census made by Oscar Núñez del Prado in 1955 tallied 240 people in sixty-six conjugal families, which were dispersed across the *puna* in forty-six groupings. Thus, it appears that the Q'eros population had grown by a substantial 156 percent in the intervening period. Birthrates are indeed high, with seven or eight living children reported by families in several cases and most women probably having at least four or more children during their childbearing years. However, the birthrate is balanced out by an equally high infant mortality rate of 40–60 percent, which brings the number of children who survive to reproduce down to two or three per family.

Although Webster does not calculate human carrying capacity figures, nor does he give us a precise estimate of the area occupied by the specific Q'eros communities he studied (some fraction, presumably, of the total area of 1,700 square kilometers occupied by his study group and their neighbors), he does argue that in the 1960s the study area population appears to have been pushing against the limits of the carrying capacity of the subsistence-settlement system. He also concludes that a substantial amount of emigration had occurred during the time of pronounced population growth as a function of the inability of the Q'eros system to sustain many more than the estimated 376 people. In this regard, we may note that if emigration were the principal means of adapting to such growth, then it would not have been necessary to practice infanticide (e.g., in contrast to several Amazonian groups discussed in Chapter 6). Indeed, given the rigors of climate and lifestyle in the Q'eros area and the correspondingly high infant mortality rate, it is highly likely that a maximum amount of nurturance is lavished on all babies, since, in spite of this care, mothers are well aware that half or more of their children will die at an early age. Webster also notes that limitations in habitat carrying capacity at the local level—in each of the gorges, or valley-heads, occupied by the various hamlets—are mentioned by the Q'eros in at least one-third of all cases of the translocation of individuals and families from one area to another. These limitations are manifested, for example, in the competition that occurs over access to local pasture lands.

Domestic Economy

The Q'eros' isolation from the outside world of Peru is evident in the severe austerity and generally homemade items that characterize each household. Aside from the rock-walled and thatch-roofed structure itself, the items inside usually include only a clay hearth, a grinding stone for processing food, pottery vessels for cooking and eating, homespun blankets and hides for sleeping on, and a few wooden tools, such as the *chaquitaclla* with steel blades attached to them. Other items that occasionally are present include large pottery cooking vessels used to prepare *chicha*, or *axa*, and carved wooden goblets called *q'eros*, vessels that are used to drink the maize beer and from which the Q'eros region gets its name. Clothing is usually homespun, although everyone wears the traditional automobile tire-tread sandals that are purchased in nearby market towns such as Ocongate (see Figure 8.5). Such sandals are ubiquitous in Andean South America, and a visitor from the outside world walking along a trail may be quite surprised at first to encounter the foot-shaped "tire tracks" left by people wearing this sort of gear.

Whatever the size of a family, its ability to allocate labor efficiently can be stretched to the limits in light of the extensive territory and rugged topography that characterize the Q'eros subsistence-settlement system. In general, it is considered normal for women, children, and elderly people to be responsible for herding activities in the *puna* area immediately above the primary domiciles. Adult males are considered to have greater travel and labor potential, and it is they who do most of the heavier work in the scattered fields of the *qeshwa* and *monte* zones that lie far below the hamlets.

Social Organization

The general pattern of marriage among the 376 people who constitute the adaptive group studied by Webster is an endogamous one, not least because of their geographic isolation from other vertically adapted indigenous groups of the region. Fully 60 percent of the marriages within the study area are exogamous with respect to a given valley-head. Marriage is normally patrilocal, with a young woman going to live with her husband and his family in one of the other two major valleys. However, if a young man lives in an area that is experiencing a downturn in its ability to support the local population, or where for political or other reasons he has acquired enemies, then he may seek a spouse in another valley-head and settle with her and her family there. Conversely, married sons who have stayed in their father's household will move their families when pressures are experienced with respect to the availability of critical resources. This is done in order of seniority, with the eldest son removing himself and his family first from the area of the local household grouping, followed by the next eldest son and his family, until the youngest son is the only one left to inherit the bulk of the family's lands and other resources at the death of his father.

Beyond the level of the immediate nuclear family, the adaptive unit that shares its labor in *ayni* is the household grouping composed of several conjugal families linked by actual and expressed consanguineal or affinal ties. The houses in these groupings, notes Webster, are never located more than a few paces from each other, and although individual families are the basic adaptive units that move up and down the mountain among the three main altitudinal zones, each family can also count on the relationship of reciprocity that it has with its nearest neighbors should help be needed in a given subsistence task.

Childhood rituals include the *ch'uxcha rutusqa* ("mowing of the hair"), which is carried out for both boys and girls between the ages of three and six years. From this point onward, instead of being called by the gender-free term *wawa*, or "child," a boy is called *irqe* and a girl *p'asna*, and each is considered to be a contributing member of family subsistence and household activities. Both boys and girls learn essentially the same tasks, although by their early teen years they are guided toward those they will be primarily responsible for as adults, including heavier labor and long-distance travel for the boys and lighter labor and herding for the girls. At the onset of puberty, girls are elevated to the status of *sipas* and boys to the status of *maqt'a*. In their late teens and early twenties their status changes yet again to indicate the achievement of the maturity necessary for marriage, at which point the girls are called *warmi*, or "women," and the boys *wayna*, or "men."

Political Economy

As described to this point, since at least the early 1930s the Q'eros adaptive system appears to have functioned essentially independently of the economy of the developing Peruvian nation, in spite of the occasional contacts between the Q'eros and the outside world that bring in limited numbers of industrially produced goods, such as the steel employed in making agricultural implements. Nevertheless, the Q'eros have had trade relations involving the exchange of native staples (e.g., wool, tubers, maize) with indigenous people of the *puna* of Vilcanota and Lake Titicaca, located 150 kilometers to the south, for a period that probably extends back over five hundred years, or into late prehispanic times prior to A.D. 1532. These contacts are usually not direct ones, however, that entail long-distance trips on the part of the Q'eros; instead, the resources of these two far-flung areas are exchanged via itinerant merchants who are received with great enthusiasm and respect by both parties to the exchange. The Q'eros call these merchants *runa*, or Quechua for "people"—that is, visitors who are not received with the suspicion, distrust, and downright hostility reserved for almost anyone else who happens to enter the Q'eros area from the outside world.

Outsiders of the latter kind include urban mestizos, Anglo foreigners, and all other Quechua who inhabit the sierra to the immediate south, west, and north of Q'eros. These folks, called *misti*, are not made to feel welcome at all. Indeed, Webster notes that because of his outsider status throughout his year-long stay in Qeros

> I was confronted by the vague fear and confusion characteristic of an isolated tribal people, but grown impenetrable and hostile through a millennium of accommodations to highland colonial regimes. . . . The evasiveness and suspicion characteristic of the Q'eros . . . is certainly based on a long habituated strategy of anonymity and obscurity which has been successful in protecting them from the incursions of militant religions and exploitative colonial economies.

And to his later chagrin Webster discovered that one "Marianu Akarapi" who figured prominently in his genealogical data actually did not exist at all, that the name "Akarapi" meant "really in the shit." This little way of dismissing the anthropologist's earnest endeavors at recording the intricacies of an indigenous kinship system echoes Napoleon Chagnon's attempts to record such data for the Yanomamö. Chagnon (1968, 1977) was given names by supposedly trustworthy and earnest informants for other individuals that he later found out meant such deprecatory appellations as "hairy vagina," "feces of harpy eagle," and "dirty rectum"—which, when used directly in speaking to the individuals so named, got him into a great deal of trouble and occasioned no little amusement on the part of his informants.

Such hostile behavior to outsiders on the part of the Q'eros can be attributed in large measure to the fact that the people of the region have been subjected to long-term exploitation and control by at least two outside forces in the past. The more recent of these began during the early Colonial period and culminated in the establishment of several haciendas in the Q'eros region; this exploitation is still manifested in the remains of the hacienda houses in Q'ero Llaqta itself. The other was the Inca state of the late prehispanic period. The capital of Cuzco lay just over 100 kilometers due west, and it probably exercised relatively direct and firm control over the Q'eros region, especially considering that the remains of ramps and roads built in the Inca style are found in the vicinity of Q'ero Llaqta. In addition, the men of the Q'eros area still dress in the sleeveless tunic, called an unku, that was an item of clothing during the time of Inca influence in this and other parts of the Andes. That the Q'eros people may have attempted to re-sist the Inca encroachment for a time is indicated by a pre-Inca settlement pat-tern in which most habitation sites are located on steeper, defensible ridges and sometimes in association with fortresses, in contrast to the pattern of recent times in which sites are located in open, less defensible positions. The Q'eros people appear not to have submitted readily to Inca control, however, as their myths express hatred and contempt of their prehispanic conquerors.

Ritual and Ideology

All four of the principal community feasts of the Q'eros area are held in Q'ero Llaqta during the months before the maize and tuber harvests have begun, or be-tween January and March, which is also the period when families experience in-creasing depletion of the stored food from the previous year's harvest. Each of these feasts is held under the auspices of one or several *karguyoh*, men selected at the end of the previous year's festivals to work with their kinfolk and affinal rela-tions in amassing a large quantity of food and entertainment to present to the en-tire Q'eros community over the two-to-five day period during which each feast lasts. The *karguyoh* and his relations have to carefully marshal their resources during the harvest period and must resist the temptation to consume them dur-ing the months following harvesting and planting, so that they will be prepared to feed everyone for the brief period of the festival.

The Q'eros festival system is therefore geared toward ensuring not only that some families will work a little harder than others in amassing surplus resources, but also that the burden of doing this will be cyclically distributed more or less equally among all geographic areas over the longer term on a year-to-year basis. As a result, the adaptive benefits are that (1) everyone has access to a predictable source of food during the lean period, (2) only a fraction of the population has to deny itself each year as the onerous burden of the *karguyoh* is assumed, (3) the *karguyoh* and their families receive prestige in return for their efforts, and (4) the potentially negative effects of subsistence intensification in a given locale are minimized. Andean systems of delayed reciprocity also are manifest in the Q'eros festival cycle, wherein those who are guests and accord prestige to their hosts during this year's feast will be hosts the next year, or shortly thereafter, and will have an expectation of receiving enhanced prestige themselves.

Twice a year rituals are observed at the extended family level that are aimed specifically at ensuring the fertility of the alpaca and llama herds. They include the use of libations of *axa* maize beer or cane alcohol, which are poured upon small stones called *kuy'a* whose origin on the slopes of high mountains relates them to the Auki mountain deities and gives them extraordinary powers in maintaining and enhancing the fertility of the herds. Ritual libations are also poured on the ground inside the corrals and over *kuy'a* stones placed on a special piece of sod, called a *ch'ampa*, cut from the *puna* soil, which is considered to represent the power of the Pacha Mama, or Earth Mother. In addition, during the fertility ritual called *Axata Uxuchichis*, which literally means "our causing to drink maize beer," the llamas are forced to drink substantial quantities of maize beer, which is believed to enhance not only their fertility but also that of the alpacas and the agricultural fields .

Most Q'eros festivals, both community and familial, involve the sacrifice of one or more llamas and alpacas, since the provision of meat to the assembled guests is considered to be as important in prestige acquisition as is a plentiful supply of other kinds of foods. The sacrifice of camelids takes place in the earlier morning hours, with the animals sprawled out in such a manner that their heads are aimed toward the rising sun. Each animal's spinal cord is then cut, followed quickly by a cutting of its throat, so that the still-beating heart will efficiently pump out the blood into a waiting receptacle. Some of this blood may be flicked by the fingers of the hand in the direction of the mountain deities, the Aukis, as a propitiatory offering in attempting to ensure the fertility of the herds and the land. Any subsequent problems, not surprisingly, will be blamed on a failure to carry out properly one or another aspect of these rituals. Although Webster does not specifically mention a belief in the Ccoa, the mythical feline who serves the Aukis in carrying out destructive acts, the Q'eros do call on benevolent Aukis via divinatory rituals to enlist their aid in stopping the destruction of crops and herds by the malevolent Aukis who send hail and lightning. Every several years or so when such destruction is particularly severe, the Q'eros ascend Wanaripa, a 5,140-meter peak that is considered the dominant Apu of the entire region, and make offerings directly to it.

THE KALLAWAYA

Some 300 kilometers to the southeast of the Q'eros area, along the rugged eastern side of the Andes, lies the territory of the Kallawaya. Like the Q'eros, the Kallawaya, who number some fifteen thousand people, live in an area that is sufficiently remote from the outside developing world that they have been able to maintain their traditional culture during a period of over one thousand years. In spite of their isolation, however, during the late prehispanic period they were affected by the extension of Inca imperial control over the entire Central Andes. But unlike their neighbors to the northwest, the Kallawaya were incorporated into the state with a considerable and long-held renown as superior curers and coca diviners. As a result, the Inca extended the Kallawaya special privileges that included acting as favored religious specialists and as official bearers of the Inca's litter whenever he traveled anywhere throughout the land (see Figure 8.9). Not surprisingly, then, the Kallawaya have more positive memories of their relationship with the Inca state than do the Q'eros.

The coca diviners of the community of Kaata, which lies on a mountainside by the same name in the heart of the Kallawaya area about 150 kilometers to the northwest of Lake Titicaca (see inset map in Figure 8.10), are particularly renowned for their ability as soothsayers, and they still receive visits from Andean people who come from hundreds of kilometers around to have their fortunes read. Fully one-fifth of Kaata's adult population, including sixty-one women and forty-six men, is engaged as part-time specialists in attending to these visitors, making it one of the most heavily ritually focused and specialized communities in the entire Andes. Following Bastien's studies in Kaata and other nearby communities located on Mount Kaata, we know that the Quechua/Aymara people who live on the mountain have one of the most complex cosmologically regulated societies anywhere in western South America. They view the entire mountain and the communities integrated into their supravillage adaptive system both metaphorically and concretely as representing a giant human body whose health and continuity they must be ever vigilant in maintaining.

As mentioned in the introduction to this chapter, Bastien received his doctoral degree at Cornell University, where he studied with Murra and also was influenced by the writings of symbolic anthropologist Victor Turner. In the course of study, Bastien combined the economic and materialistic perspectives of Murra with the symbolic dimensions of Turner, producing an approach to anthropological research and theory construction that is quite similar to the one taken in this book. His background includes more than just an intensive career focus on anthropology, however. Bastien (1985:xv) worked as a Maryknoll priest among the Aymara of Bolivia for six years and came to the realization that "my endeavors had failed because I was oblivious to an ancient Andean religion, rich in symbolism and ritual. Deeper symbolic patterns governed the lives of these Indians who preferred to worship land instead of spirits. It appeared to me that anthropologists had been successful in interpreting these patterns, so I decided to become an anthropologist to better understand the Aymaras."

Bastien's Ayllu Kaata Data

Physical Environment

As shown in the schematic illustration of Mount Kaata in Figure 8.10, the physical context within which the community of Kaata and its immediate neighbors of Niñokorin and Apacheta have established their integrated system can be

FIGURE 8.9   Felipe Guáman Poma de Ayala's sixteenth-century drawing showing Kallawaya men carrying the litter of the Inca emperor Topa Inca Yupanqui and his queen, Mama Ocllo. Redrawn and adapted from Guáman Poma de Ayala (1978 [~1567–1615]).

straightforwardly described as a classic Andean setting consisting of three main vertically stacked microenvironmental zones: the *yunga*, the *kichwa (quechua)*, and the *puna*. In some contrast to the preceding Q'eros case, however, the elevational breadth of the Ayllu Kaata system is more vertically restricted in that it ranges from 3,200 to 5,200 meters (or a total of 2,000 meters), whereas that of the Q'eros ranges from 1,800 to 4,700 (or a total of 2,900 meters). The horizontal range of the Ayllu Kaata system is 25 kilometers, which, although extensive, is still less than the 35-kilometer range of the Q'eros. Nevertheless, although the Ayllu Kaata system does not extend its direct control below an elevation of 3,200 meters, land suitable for the cultivation of midelevation grains (as opposed to higher-elevation grains, such as quinua) is available in the Niñokorin area (Figure 8.10). All in all, then, Ayllu Kaata has access to the same broad series of resource zones that are available in the Q'eros case.

Bastien estimates that the Ayllu Kaata area receives about 760 millimeters of rain annually, indicating that it is well watered in comparison to most other areas of the Andean sierra (see Figure 8.2). Each morning humid air blows up the deep *yunga* canyons from the *montaña* and, upon mixing with the descending cooler dry air of the *puna,* often leaves the general Kallawaya region drenched in thick

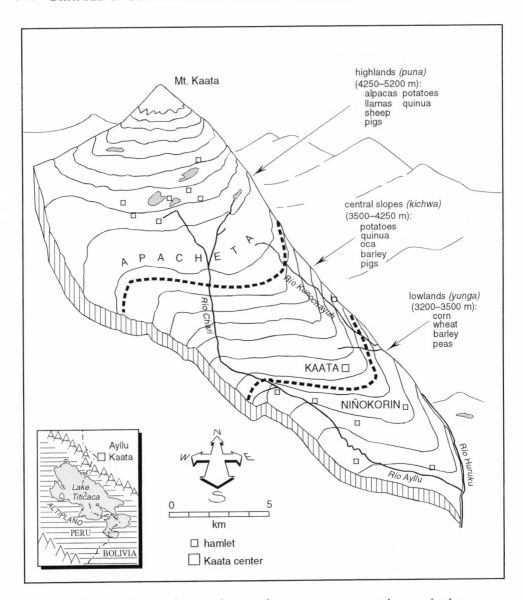

FIGURE 8.10   Perspective drawing showing the main environmental zones, food resources, and settlements of the Kaata adaptive system. Based on textual account and maps in Bastien (1985).

fog, not to mention creating gale-force winds capable of moving small stones. As is the case elsewhere in the sierra, there is greater temperature variation between the daytime and nighttime hours than there is seasonally between summer and winter, with the temperature dropping a full 15 °C in the several hours after the sun sets. Even in the summer temperatures in the high *puna* often drop to below freezing at night; nighttime frost can occur during the winter in both the *kichwa* and higher *yunga* zones.

Mode of Production and Settlement Pattern

Although each of the main communities throughout the three altitudinal zones consists of a politically autonomous settlement or settlements—including Kaata itself, Niñokorin and surrounding hamlets, and the scattered hamlets of Apacheta—the entire system is tightly integrated economically, socially, and ritually. For this reason, it is appropriate here to discuss subsistence and settlement at the same time. Then, immediately following the description of the main features of the subsistence-settlement system, a section is included that discusses how Mount Kaata itself serves as a geographic metaphor for the integration of the socioeconomic system. In other words, we leap directly to the levels of social organization and abstract but adaptively significant ideology, escaping momentarily from the bounds of the bottom-up, variable-by-variable, and level-by-level discussion that has generally characterized the presentation of data heretofore in this book.

Niñokorin is located in the *yunga* zone (3,200–3,500 meters) not far above the base of the mountain and at a point about two hours' walk below the settlement of Kaata. Although maize, wheat, and barley grow here, their cultivation is limited to narrow riverine strips along the Río Huruku, which runs around the northern and eastern base of the mountain, and the Río Ayllu, which runs off the *puna* along the southwestern side of Ayllu Kaata. This is the upper altitudinal limit for growing wheat and maize in this part of the Andes, since lower temperatures, a shorter growing season, and unpredictable frosts in the *kichwa* zone make it impossible to cultivate them there. Quinua and barley, however, are hardier and more cold resistant, and thus both can be grown in the *kichwa* zone (3,500–4,250 meters) where the central community of Kaata is located. Potatoes and oca grow in abundance on the extensive lands above Kaata, with fields being cultivated rotatively (potatoes, oca, barley) during three successive rainy seasons before they are put to rest for some years, slowly regaining their lost nutrients primarily as a function of droppings left by sheep pastured on the fallowed fields. Finally, the *puna* zone (4,250–5,200 meters) is occupied by scattered herders who comprise the hamlets of Apacheta, which lies a full day's walk up the mountain from Kaata. Although some bitter potatoes and quinua are grown in protected places here, this altitudinal level is generally too cold for anything other than pasturing alpacas, llamas, sheep, and pigs.

Up to this point the adaptive system of the people of Mount Kaata appears to be much like that of the Q'eros, with scattered smaller settlements located in the highest and lowest zones and a single central community located in the middle zone. However, unlike Q'eros, all of the Ayllu Kaata settlements are permanently occupied and sedentary—that is, instead of accessing the diverse resources of the three environmental zones by means of a strategy of continual movement up and down the mountain, the people of Ayllu Kaata have integrated themselves in such a way as to ensure permanent exchange of resources among all three zones. Indeed, a most interesting aspect of the overall adaptive system of Ayllu Kaata is that the Apachetan people, who are as integrally a part of the system as the two lower-level groups, speak Aymara, whereas the people of Kaata itself and the Niñokorin area speak Quechua. How such language and cultural diversity, as well as geographic distance in the case of Apacheta, could nevertheless be overcome to create the socioeconomic interaction sphere called "Ayllu Kaata" is one of the most fascinating aspects of Bastien's study, and it requires us briefly to enter into the realm of social organization, ritual, and cosmology.

Mount Kaata as a Corporeal Metaphor for Ayllu Kaata

The integration that characterizes the people living in the three vertically stacked environmental levels of Mount Kaata can be understood first and foremost by reference to the *ayllu*, which is the overarching unit of socioeconomic organization that links the disparate, politically autonomous settlements of the mountain. *Ayllu*, here and elsewhere in the Andes, refers to a group of people who live in a defined territory (*llahta* or *llacta*) and tend to marry endogamously within it. Membership in the *ayllu* is constantly reaffirmed not only by social interaction and economic exchange but also, in the case of Ayllu Kaata, by the feeding of "earth shrines" scattered throughout the three altitudinal zones. Moreover, the people of Mount Kaata see their *ayllu* as having a vertical pyramidal shape, with Apacheta at the closed apex of the ascending generation; Niñokorin at the broad, open base of the descending generation; and Kaata in the middle. In both their languages (which are otherwise essentially mutually unintelligible) Apacheta means "ancestor" or "leader" (from *Apu*) and Niñokorin means "lower child."

Just as the mountain is a metaphor for the generational aspect of social organization, so is it a metaphor for the *ayllu* itself: Mount Kaata *is* Ayllu Kaata, and if everyone traces his or her putative descent from one ancestor, *huh yayayuh*, then so does the mountain trace its descent from this apical ancestor. But since Ayllu Kaata consists of people and the mountain is a metaphor for the *ayllu*, Mount Kaata is also viewed as a human body whose various parts are maintained in integral form by the continuity of the members of the *ayllu* in their territory (see Figure 8.11). The *puna* highlands of Apacheta are the head, or *uma* in Quechua. Moreover, *uma* also means "water" in Aymara, and since there are numerous small lakes in Apacheta, the metaphor works well in either language. The grass that grows in the *puna* and the wool on the llamas that graze on this grass are metaphors for the "hair" on the head of the body. But the metaphor goes even farther: Two of the larger lakes in the *puna* are the "eyes," the dispersed hamlets of this zone are the "differentiated features" of the face, and a larger lower lake forms the "mouth."

The central ceremonial site of Kaata constitutes the vital organs of the mountain body, and just as the tubers that grow underground in the fields around it provide energy to the people, so do the viscera and rituals carried out here sustain the *ayllu* body. Kaatapata, the oldest hamlet in the immediate vicinity of Kaata, contains the central chapel of the *ayllu*, and this chapel is the liver, whereas the political leaders ("secretaries") who meet in it constitute the heart. The eight strips of fields that fold around this part of the mountain are the layers

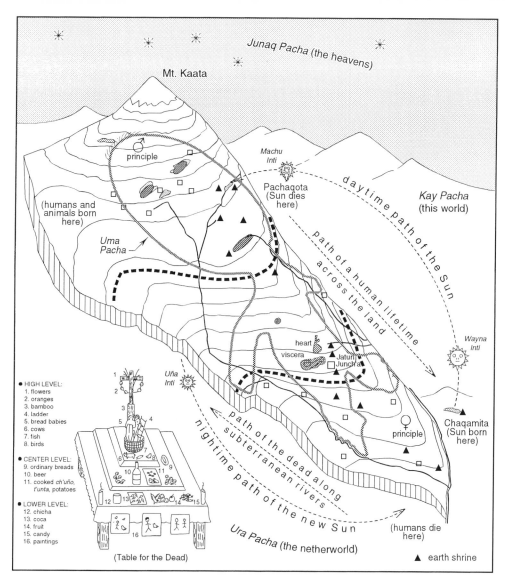

FIGURE 8.11 The Kaata cosmological system in relation to the Mountain of the Condor and the conceptualization of this system in the Table for the Dead. Based on textual account and figures in Bastien (1985).

of fat on its belly. Kaata's location in the central, visceral part of the metaphorical mountain body qualifies its inhabitants geographically to serve as the principal curers and coca diviners not only for the Ayllu Kaata body but also for the Kallawaya area and the entire Central Andes.

Finally, the Niñokorin area forms the lower extremities of the mountain body, with the right leg located near the edge of the Río Ayllu and the left leg opposite it on the northern edge of the mountain's lower slopes. To indicate the time depth of the mountain body metaphor, Bastien notes that in the early seventeenth century, when the Spanish governor of the nearby town of Charazani had taken over the land where the left leg is located for his hacienda, the people of Ayllu Kaata resisted this encroachment on their territory by insisting that the governor had stolen the "left leg" of their mountain—thus threatening the very survival of the *ayllu* socioeconomic body. Bastien also mentions, somewhat wryly, that they did not get the left leg back until the end of the Colonial era.

Mode of Reproduction

Bastien's study does not give population figures for Ayllu Kaata, but he has recently noted (personal communication) that he estimates there to be a total of 500 adult inhabitants in Kaata, with Niñokorin and Apacheta each having an estimated 125 additional adults. Assuming that there are roughly equal numbers of men and women (a sex ratio of approximately 100), that all the men and women are married, and that there is an average of two children per family, he estimates the total population of Ayllu Kaata at 1,500 persons—in other words, there are about 1,000 people in Kaata, 250 in Niñokorin, and 250 in Apacheta.

For the entire Kallawaya area, he gives an estimate of 15,000 persons living in an area that covers 2,525 square kilometers. If we divide 15,000 persons by 2525 square kilometers, this results in a crude population density figure of about 6 persons per square kilometer. This is not far from the crude population density of 14 persons per square kilometer we calculated for the Andean sierra at the beginning of this chapter, but it is substantially below the 94 persons per square kilometer we calculated as an average ecological population density for the Peruvian Andes to the north of here. Although Bastien does not give an estimate of the area covered by the Ayllu Kaata adaptive system, using his maps and associated scales, we can calculate this area at about 250 square kilometers. Thus, somewhat coincidentally, the ecological population density figure for Ayllu Kaata alone turns out to be 6 persons per square kilometer (1,500 persons ÷ 250 square kilometers), or the same as the crude density figure for the entire Kallawaya area. Perhaps the point to make in this regard, considering how low the Ayllu Kaata population density is in relation to the average for the Central Andes in general, is that it exemplifies well the difference in subsistence potential between areas of the sierra where states arose in contrast to those, like Ayllu Kaata, where village societies represent the maximum potential long-term equilibrium adaptation.

Domestic Economy

Few data germane to this particular societal variable are included in Bastien's monograph, although from his study it is clear that the division of labor is typical of that of other Andean groups mentioned earlier in this chapter—with men, women, and older children working together in the fields and in pasturing the flocks, depending on where they live on the mountain. Bastien also notes that the people of Ayllu Kaata see the mountain not only as feeding them but also as providing them with the wool for their clothes. Their clothes and the symbols woven into them are thus constant visual reminders of how the mountain feeds and clothes them, just as they feed the earth shrines to keep the mountain (as a metaphor for the *ayllu*) alive. By virtue of this mutually beneficial interaction, "they become the mountain and the mountain becomes them" (Bastien 1978:xxv). Men's and women's clothing also becomes more elaborate as social status rises during their lifetimes, and cloth itself, as is the case elsewhere in the Andes, is considered such an important symbol of society and its integration that each woman must present a symbolic dowry of cloth to her husband when they marry.

Social Organization

As opposed to the bifurcate-merging kinship systems of many Amazonian groups—where a distinction is made in the ascending generation between parent's siblings of the same and opposite sex in determining who is a nonmarriageable parallel cousin (the offspring of mother's sister and father's brother) and who is a marriageable cross-cousin (the offspring of mother's brother and father's sister)—the people of Ayllu Kaata, to make a long story short, blur this distinction entirely. That is, all aunts are called "Mother" and all uncles are called "Father," and all their offspring are called "Brother" or "Sister." Nevertheless, they know who their true, or lineal, siblings are and who their fictive, or collateral, siblings are and often add the word *dueño* in front of a sibling term to distinguish lineal from collateral siblings. For example, although *wawqui* in general means "brother," *dueño wawqui* is used to indicate one's consanguineal brother; *wawqui* can be understood in the same conversational context to mean one's cousin.

Although there still may be plenty of marriageable people living in or near one's settlement who are neither lineal nor collateral relatives, the marriage rule in Ayllu Kaata is that a person living in one of the altitudinal levels must choose a spouse from either one of the other two levels. For example, someone from Kaata must marry someone from Apacheta or Niñokorin. Since there is also a patrilocal rule following marriage, women, in marrying, cross from one level to the other and create solidarity and integration among the people of the entire *ayllu*. Marriage, in addition to economics, ritual, and cosmology, thus continually reinforces and emphasizes reciprocal exchange among the three levels of human occupation of the mountain. Of equal importance in this exchange is that no altitudinal level—high, middle, or low—is seen as being dominant or subordinate in relation to the other two. All people, whether Aymara speakers engaged in herding in the *puna* or Quechua speakers engaged in farming in the *kichwa* and the *yunga*, are equal. Interestingly, although there is a patri-bias in the residence rule after marriage, descent with respect to inheritance is bilateral and both women and men can own the land—in other words, daughters inherit from their mothers and boys inherit from their fathers. For example, although once a woman marries she leaves her land to go to another altitudinal level, a daughter may well marry someone from her mother's level and hence return to work the land she inherited from her mother.

Political Economy

The adaptive system I have described to this point for Ayllu Kaata is not unique among the Kallawaya. Scattered along the eastern side of the Andes throughout their territory of 2,525 square kilometers are eight other *ayllus*, each of which is vertically adapted to a particular mountainside that is characterized by the three main altitudinal levels of *puna*, *kichwa*, and *yunga*. The other *ayllus*, like Ayllu Kaata, are called by the name of the mountain on which they are located: Amarete, Chajaya, Chari, Chullina, Curva, Inca, Kaalaya, and Upinhuaya. Although Bastien notes that each *ayllu* is essentially self-sufficient with respect to basic subsistence resources, the areal extent and productivity of each of the main altitudinal levels vary from place to place. For example, Ayllu Chullina includes an area that borders on the *montaña* rain forest, and oranges and apples do well on its warm, humid lower slopes. Ayllu Chari includes an extensive area of *puna* and thus can specialize in animal grazing to a greater extent than other *ayllus*. Both Ayllu Inca and Ayllu Kaata have extensive tuber-producing *kichwa* and wheat-producing upper *yunga* slopes. In light of this resource variability, a system of exchange has developed among all nine *ayllus* that permits each one to have access to resources that are less plentifully available in its own area.

In addition, in spite of the fact that the Kallawaya territory is more or less homogeneous with respect to local environments and resources, each of the nine *ayllus* also has particular craft specialties that it focuses on (this, it will be recalled from Chapter 6, is analogous to the Yanomamö situation where villages specialize in different craft specialties in spite of the homogeneous environment in which all are found). For example, Ayllu Amarete produces pottery vessels and wooden tools, and Ayllu Upinhuayas produces the pressed sheep's wool hats with wide brims and rounded crowns that are worn by all Kallawaya men and women on ritual and other social occasions. The people of Ayllu Chajaya are the only ones who specialize in jewelry making, a tradition that goes back at least five hundred years to the time of the Inca state when they made ornaments for the ruling elite of Cuzco. As is the case, then, with the Yanomamö of Venezuela, specialization in particular crafts that are desired by other *ayllus* promotes continual socioeconomic interaction among the villages and hamlets throughout the Kallawaya area and beyond.

Access by the nine *ayllus* to resources outside the territory is facilitated by trips made into nearby areas by the people of the *ayllus* located on the territory's peripheries. Ayllu Upinhuaya, for example, is located three days' walk from the lower *yungas* where incense can be harvested. Coca leaves, which are critical in Andean divinatory practices, are obtained from Ayllu Kaalaya, which is located in a central position in the territory adjacent to excellent coca-growing land. Just as the people of Ayllu Kaata are famous as diviners, so are the men of Ayllus Curva and Chari well known for their ability as curers. They periodically descend to the lower *yungas* to collect minerals and gather herbal remedies of various kinds from the rain forest. Upon returning home, they make trips up to the central *puna* of the Lake Titicaca area where they have long had reputations as outstanding curers. The Kallawaya pharmacopoeia, as discussed in Chapter 4, includes over one thousand remedies, and although most are still unknown to modern medical science, some are known to be natural sources of the same drugs found in penicillin, quinine, and aspirin.

Although the Kallawaya appear to have an enduring tradition of peaceful exchange among themselves, their relations with Colonial and modern regimes have been a somewhat different story, as implied earlier. For example, Bastien notes that during the period of governmental reforms instituted in the 1950s, surveyors came out to Ayllu Kaata from La Paz and decided that each of the three levels of the mountain should be designated as a politically bounded entity that would henceforth compete economically with the other two. That is, the surveyors were able to perceive the environmental and resource diversity of the mountain but did not realize that, in spite of these differences and the political autonomy of its various community members, the *ayllu* functioned as a highly integrated, ritually maintained socioeconomic entity. This created great problems for a time for the settlements in Ayllu Kaata, but their overarching ritual and cosmological principles eventually served them well in overcoming this well-meaning but ecologically naïve meddling from the outside world (given our discussion of theory in Chapter 2, the reader will not have missed the point here that this case provides an excellent example of the causal force of mental, or ideological, phenomena in *re-creating* an economic infrastructure, arguing therefore against perspectives characterized by the reductionistic approach of Harrisian infrastructural determinism).

Ritual and Leadership

Every adult male of Ayllu Kaata is required to hold a series of consecutively higher posts from the time he is sixteen until his late forties, whether or not he has outstanding leadership qualities. Together with other leaders and community elders, he will be instrumental in making decisions about all important community matters, including rituals and fiestas. Husbands and wives often work together in sponsoring community feasts. For example, Bastien mentions Carmen and Marcelino Yanahuaya, who sponsored a series of four major separate feasts, each of which cost them a whole year's supply of food. Once a person has gone through the succession of leadership posts and feast sponsorships, he or she becomes a community elder, or *pasado runa,* and from that point on does not have to carry out further responsibilities aside from participating in making decisions about matters of concern to the integrity and maintenance of the *ayllu.*

The diviners of Kaata, located in the visceral heart of the community, are responsible for ritually pumping energy into each one of the thirteen earth shrines distributed throughout the three altitudinal levels (see Figure 8.11). To do this, they obtain blood and fat from Kaata, llama fat and fetuses from Apacheta, and *chicha* beer from Niñokorin. In this way the body of the mountain is able to eat produce from all three levels and in turn provide sustenance to its human inhabitants. The Kaata ritualists acquire their power from the tombs of ancestors, called *chullpa machulas*, from which in earlier times the mummified remains of ancient Ayllu Kaatans were brought out to be carried around the fields during fertility rituals. One such tomb, which represents the probable burial of an ancient shaman, was excavated by Swedish archaeologist Stig Rydén (1957) in the early 1950s. The contents of the tomb (see Figure 8.12), illustrations of which were later published by S. Henry Wassén (1972), included reed tubes and lids used as paraphernalia in ritual enemas; various spatulas and sticks with animal effigies carved on them, wooden tablets with bird head carvings and other iconographic features depicting ancient Kaatan deities, bundles of holly leaves (*Ilex guayasa*) used in curing practices, and, finally, several subsistence-related artifacts, such as arrows and three-stone bolas.

The cranium of the occupant of the tomb had been artificially deformed early in his life and also exhibited the characteristic hole and cut marks left by trephination surgery at some later point during his lifetime. Radiocarbon analysis of the contents of the tomb indicated that it dated sometime around A.D. 800, or to ~1200 B.P., suggesting that the Kallawaya people had developed their skill as curers and diviners at least this early. Indeed, evidence of human occupation in the area goes back at least to ~1000 B.C. (Bastien 1985), and there seems every reason to suppose that Kallawaya culture as described here already was developing three thousand years ago in this part of the Andes.

The traditional importance of ritual diviners in Ayllu Kaata became clear to Bastien upon his arrival to carry out research on the mountain. A man named Sarito Quispe, who was regarded by all the other ritual specialists in Kaata as the best and most powerful diviner among them, made the sign of the cross and then took into his hands fourteen coca leaves to see if the auguries were favorable for Bastien to be permitted to stay in Kaata and carry out his study. Three brown-colored leaves were chosen representing "bad luck," three shiny green ones were chosen representing "good luck," and the remaining eight, all of them marked with distinctive bites from Sarito Quispe's teeth, represented the family with whom he would stay, Marcelino and Carmen Yanahuaya; the settlement of Kaata; Joseph Bastien and his wife, Judy (he had earlier quit the priesthood as he embarked upon his anthropology studies); the book he hoped to write from his study; and the road up to Kaata. Manipulating the leaves during the reading, Quispe examined them to see how each of the teeth-marked leaves matched up with the good luck and bad luck leaves. Of course, the auguries were favorable; otherwise this section could not have been included in the present chapter.

Sarito is the ritual principal, as Lord of the Seasons, who is responsible during a major ceremony called New Earth for circulating the blood and fat via the earth shrines that maintain the lives of all the people, crops, and animals of the *ayllu*. If he cannot do this well—that is, if problems arise that affect the living features of the environment—then the other ritualists will meet and designate someone else to do the job. Sarito is also able to wave his staff of office at hail when it occurs, sending it off to bother neighboring (unidentified) enemies. He inherited certain paraphernalia from his father that help him to carry out his divinatory tasks, including receptacles of seashell (*mullu*) in which he places coca.

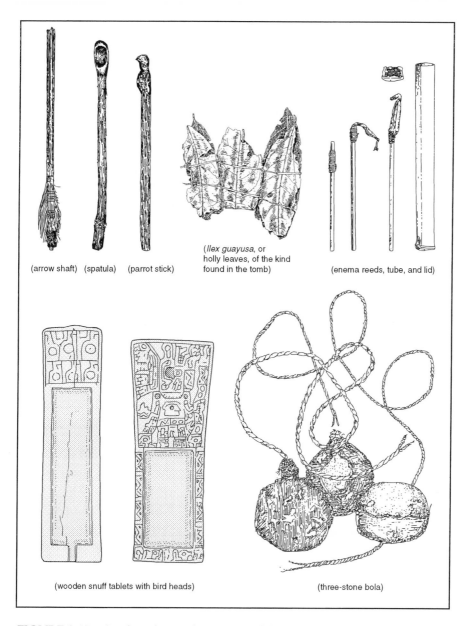

(arrow shaft) (spatula) (parrot stick)

(*Ilex guayusa*, or holly leaves, of the kind found in the tomb)

(enema reeds, tube, and lid)

(wooden snuff tablets with bird heads)

(three-stone bola)

FIGURE 8.12 Artifacts from a shaman's tomb located near Niñokorin. Redrawn and adapted from illustrations in Wassén (1972).

Bastien notes that the people of Ayllu Kaata place great importance on the magical power of exotic paired items brought from separate places—in this case the coastline and the *yungas*—to be used in divination.

Earth shrines are assigned gender depending on their nature and where they are located in the environment. Male earth shrines include rocks, hills, and high elevations, all of which are metaphors for male permanence in settling in one place on the mountain and staying there. Female earth shrines include lakes and low places, indicating their fertile aspect and the fact that they cross environmental levels when they marry. Although rivers cannot become earth shrines, they are nevertheless a metaphor for women, since they cross different altitudinal levels and bind them together.

During a sequence of three rituals—"Chosen Field" (*Chacrata Qukuy*), New Earth, and "Potato Planting" (*Kallay Papa Tarpuna*)—the members of Ayllu Kaata come together from Apacheta, Kaata, and Niñokorin to bring about the rebirth of the mountain in preparation for growing the crops. During *Chacrata Qukuy*, about a year before planting begins, the elders and other community leaders visit each of the fallow fields to determine which of them are ready to be used for yet another cycle of growing potatoes, oca, and barley. During New Earth, the men open up the earth with their plows, symbolizing a vertical aspect, while women throw the seed into the opening from their laps, symbolizing a horizontal spreading aspect. At this time divination involving the sacrifice of a guinea pig may be carried out, with white spots on the liver taken to mean that hail and snow will come to destroy the harvest if the earth shrines are not fed more blood and fat.

At the same time, llama sacrifices are carried out with specially chosen animals called *qochu* brought from the *puna*. Llamas are important because they cross levels in carrying produce from one place to another, and with the sacrifice of their blood, they unite the mountain. The *qochu* llama is forced to kneel down, with his head facing the place of the sun's birth, and those who are about to sacrifice him embrace him and shed tears as he is made ready to depart for Ura Pacha, the underworld. Quickly making a slash across his throat and down onto his chest, a community leader plunges his hand into the chest to remove the heart. Blood from the animal flows to all parts of the *ayllu* to revitalize living things, and the heart (*sonqo*), the seat of thought and emotions to the Kaatans, is read to see when the rains will come and thus when planting should start. Potato planting is the last of the three rituals, celebrated just after the Feast with the Dead, who are instrumental (like the Shuar earth mother, Nuŋuí) for pushing up the growing plants from inside the earth.

Ideology (USPs)

Unlike some other religions, according to Bastien's study, the Kallawaya religion is focused neither on conceptual abstractions nor on a complex world of spirits. Instead, as we have seen in the case of Ayllu Kaata, it involves a metaphorical relationship between the mountain as deity and the people who inhabit the mountain. Indeed, since the *ayllu* communities and the land they farm are integral parts of the mountain deity itself, it may be asserted that they and the mountain are one and the same. Kaatan myth, like that of many other Andean communities, identifies the deity Wiraqocha ("Sea of Fat") not only as the creator of the cosmos and all the things in it but also as a prototype of the Inca emperor. Thus, when the Kallawaya make offerings of llama fat to the earth shrines to feed the mountain, they are making them ultimately to Wiraqocha (Viracocha), the Lord of the Earth.

In addition to indicating the parts of the mountain that make up its giant metaphorical human body and that of Ayllu Kaata, Figure 8.11 shows the principal features of Kaatan ideology in relation to the mountain setting. First, Kaatan cosmology is constructed in accordance with the spatial model provided by the three environmental levels of the mountain: The universe is divided into the heavens (*Junaq Pacha*), this world (*Kay Pacha*), and the netherworld (*Ura Pacha*). Like each of the three levels of the mountain, each of the three cosmological levels has three temporal dimensions: ancient, or beginning, time; past time; and present time. These dimensions are symbolized, respectively, by the *chullpa* tombs (≈ ancestral mummies), the cross (≈ Christ), and the graveyard (≈ the recent dead). The earth shrines themselves embody all these ideas about space (the verticality of the mountain), time (the mountain's present and past), and existence, or being (feeding them ensures the continuity of the mountain and thus of the *ayllu*).

Kaatan cosmology expresses the belief that the sun is born each morning in Chaqamita Lake at the foot of the mountain (Figure 8.11). This "young sun," or *wayna inti*, then rises up all day long from east to west, dying as "old sun," or *machu inti*, near the top of the mountain in Pachaqota Lake, which swallows it, puts out its fire, and shrinks it down to almost nothing. Sinking during the early evening hours to the bottom of the lake, this sun is reborn from the interior of the old sun as miniature sun (*uña inti*) and, making its way down the mountain during the night through the three altitudinal levels, is born once again in the morning as *wayna inti*. The Kaatans argue that the young sun has fewer rays than the old sun, which is shown in pictographs with twenty-eight rays around its head as opposed to the forty-four shown for old sun. In contrast to the upward daily and downward nightly path of the sun, humans and animals are viewed as being born at the head of the mountain. The living emerge from the mountain's eyes and spend their lifetime traversing down through the three altitudinal levels, finally dying at the very bottom of the mountain. Here they enter the underground to travel upward under the mountain's surface toward Uma Pacha, the mountain's head from whose lacustrine eyes they may emerge once again. Since the Apachetans live here, they are qualified to be the ritualists of lakes and the dead.

Each year during the Feast with the Dead, the souls of the Ayllu Kaatans who have died within the past three years are invited back for the annual transition from the dry to the wet season, which is the time between resting and growing. Inside household kitchens, the whole constellation of Kaatan cosmological postulates is metaphorically represented by a Table for the Dead (Figure 8.11), which contains the products of the *yunga* on its lowest level, the products of the *kichwa* on its central level, and the products of the *puna* on its highest level. The legs of the table represent the netherworld. The Kaatans have no wish to go to any sort of Christian heaven; instead, when they die they want to stay intimately associated with their mountain, forever remaining an integral part of the cycles of life and death that formed part of their existence as living members of the *ayllu*.

In sum, the people of Ayllu Kaata are characterized by a ritual system that integrates ecologically the different altitudinal levels on which they grow their crops and pasture their flocks. The Kaatan earth shrines pertain to these levels, representing the communities of Niñokorin, Kaata, and Apacheta as well as the parts of their inhabitants' bodies. In feeding the earth shrines, the people continually reflect upon the production of the crops and the exchange of resources among the inhabitants of the three altitudinal levels of the mountain. At the same time, in feeding the shrines of the mountain, the people feel that their bodies will be complete. In other words, in caring for the mountain, they will be cared for by its resources—including the protein from the highest level of Apacheta, where the alpacas are pastured; the carbohydrates from the central level of Kaata, where the tubers grow; and additional nutritional requirements such as vitamins and minerals from the lowest level of Niñokorin, where grains, fruits, and vegetables grow. Bastien has provided a definitive study of how Andeans put environment, subsistence, and intervillage relations together with the more abstract world of symbols and ritual—showing, in the process, how the lives of the mountain's inhabitants are integrated, maintained, and regulated by ritual.

A Summary Model

A summary systems-hierarchical model of the Ayllu Kaata adaptive system is presented in Figure 8.13. Comparing this figure to the ones used to summarize earlier data sets in this book (e.g., see Figures 5.6, 6.13, and 7.5, on the Ona, Yanomamö, and Kogi, respectively), the reader will note that the model of the Ayllu Kaata system requires the inclusion of more data on the features of the superstructure than any other earlier one except the Kogi. This should not be taken to imply, however, that the superstructural subsystem (ideology/USPs and ritual/leadership considered in their entirety) of Ayllu Kaata is more complex than that of the Ona and Yanomamö. Nevertheless, this case is an example of how important it is to take the qualitative, higher-order superstructural data into account in our attempting to understand all aspects of the functioning, maintenance, and regulation of a system. For example, the inclusion of such data in the Kuikuru case (Chapter 6) might well have been instructive in our attempting to understand how they regulate their numbers in a situation that is probably far less productive, and therefore more constraining, than the ethnographer might have realized. Furthermore, and returning now to the Ayllu Kaata case, once we contemplate a summary of the full data set gathered by Bastien, we can easily see that most of the truly interesting aspects of the Kaatan system do not lie in the mundane realm of the infrastructure. Rather, aside from the physical environment—which is interesting, of course, for its own sake as an example of a spectacular Andean setting—we see that the more compelling features are the *integrative* ones that lie in the realm of social organization, political economy, ritual and leadership, and ideology.

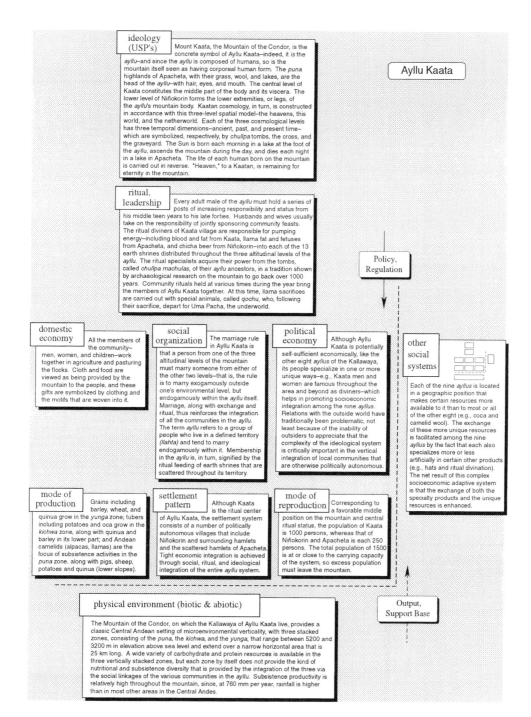

ideology (USP's)
Mount Kaata, the Mountain of the Condor, is the concrete symbol of Ayllu Kaata—indeed, it *is* the *ayllu*—and since the *ayllu* is composed of humans, so is the mountain itself seen as having corporeal human form. The *puna* highlands of Apacheta, with their grass, wool, and lakes, are the head of the *ayllu*—with hair, eyes, and mouth. The central level of Kaata constitutes the middle part of the body and its viscera. The lower level of Niñokorin forms the lower extremities, or legs, of the *ayllu*'s mountain body. Kaatan cosmology, in turn, is constructed in accordance with this three-level spatial model—the heavens, this world, and the netherworld. Each of the three cosmological levels has three temporal dimensions—ancient, past, and present time—which are symbolized, respectively, by *chullpa* tombs, the cross, and the graveyard. The Sun is born each morning in a lake at the foot of the *ayllu*, ascends the mountain during the day, and dies each night in a lake in Apacheta. The life of each human born on the mountain is carried out in reverse. "Heaven," to a Kaatan, is remaining for eternity in the mountain.

ritual, leadership
Every adult male of the *ayllu* must hold a series of posts of increasing responsibility and status from his middle teen years to his late forties. Husbands and wives usually take on the responsibility of jointly sponsoring community feasts. The ritual diviners of Kaata village are responsible for pumping energy—including blood and fat from Kaata, llama fat and fetuses from Apacheta, and chicha beer from Niñokorin—into each of the 13 earth shrines distributed throughout the three altitudinal levels of the *ayllu*. The ritual specialists acquire their power from the tombs, called *chullpa machulas*, of their *ayllu* ancestors, in a tradition shown by archaeological research on the mountain to go back over 1000 years. Community rituals held at various times during the year bring the members of Ayllu Kaata together. At this time, llama sacrifices are carried out with special animals, called *qochu*, who, following their sacrifice, depart for Uma Pacha, the underworld.

Ayllu Kaata

Policy, Regulation

domestic economy
All the members of the community—men, women, and children—work together in agriculture and pasturing the flocks. Cloth and food are viewed as being provided by the mountain to the people, and these gifts are symbolized by clothing and the motifs that are woven into it.

social organization
The marriage rule in Ayllu Kaata is that a person from one of the three altitudinal levels of the mountain must marry someone from either of the other two levels—that is, the rule is to marry exogamously outside one's environmental level, but endogamously within the *ayllu* itself. Marriage, along with exchange and ritual, thus reinforces the integration of all the communities in the *ayllu*. The term *ayllu* refers to a group of people who live in a defined territory (*llahta*) and tend to marry endogamously within it. Membership in the *ayllu* is, in turn, signified by the ritual feeding of earth shrines that are scattered throughout its territory.

political economy
Although Ayllu Kaata is potentially self-sufficient economically, like the other eight *ayllus* of the Kallawaya, its people specialize in one or more unique ways—e.g., Kaata men and women are famous throughout the area and beyond as diviners—which helps in promoting socioeconomic integration among the nine *ayllus*. Relations with the outside world have traditionally been problematic, not least because of the inability of outsiders to appreciate that the complexity of the ideological system is critically important in the vertical integration of local communities that are otherwise politically autonomous.

other social systems
Each of the nine *ayllus* is located in a geographic position that makes certain resources more available to it than to most or all of the other eight (e.g., coca and camelid wool). The exchange of these more unique resources is facilitated among the nine *ayllus* by the fact that each also specializes more or less artificially in certain other products (e.g., hats and ritual divination). The net result of this complex socioeconomic adaptive system is that the exchange of both the specialty products and the unique resources is enhanced.

mode of production
Grains including barley, wheat, and quinua grow in the *yunga* zone; tubers including potatoes and oca grow in the *kichwa* zone, along with quinua and barley in its lower part; and Andean camelids (alpacas, llamas) are the focus of subsistence activities in the *puna* zone, along with pigs, sheep, potatoes and quinua (lower slopes).

settlement pattern
Although Kaata is the ritual center of Ayllu Kaata, the settlement system consists of a number of politically autonomous villages that include Niñokorin and surrounding hamlets and the scattered hamlets of Apacheta. Tight economic integration is achieved through social, ritual, and ideological integration of the entire *ayllu* system.

mode of reproduction
Corresponding to a favorable middle position on the mountain and central ritual status, the population of Kaata is 1000 persons, whereas that of Niñokorin and Apacheta is each 250 persons. The total population of 1500 is at or close to the carrying capacity of the system, so excess population must leave the mountain.

physical environment (biotic & abiotic)
The Mountain of the Condor, on which the Kallawaya of Ayllu Kaata live, provides a classic Central Andean setting of microenvironmental verticality, with three stacked zones, consisting of the *puna*, the *kichwa*, and the *yunga*, that range between 5200 and 3200 m in elevation above sea level and extend over a narrow horizontal area that is 25 km long. A wide variety of carbohydrate and protein resources is available in the three vertically stacked zones, but each zone by itself does not provide the kind of nutritional and subsistence diversity that is provided by the integration of the three via the social linkages of the various communities in the *ayllu*. Subsistence productivity is relatively high throughout the mountain, since, at 760 mm per year, rainfall is higher than in most other areas in the Central Andes.

Output, Support Base

FIGURE 8.13 Systems-hierarchical model summarizing the principal features of the Ayllu Kaata adaptive system. Based on textual account in Bastien (1985).

CHAPTER 9

Prehistoric
Central Andean States

Having looked in detail at the range of prehispanic and recent traditional human adaptive systems throughout the rest of South America, we come finally to an examination of the environmental features and sociopolitical developments that suggest why the Central Andean area experienced levels of societal complexity in the prehispanic period that did not occur anywhere else on the continent. The sierra region has already been discussed in the preceding chapter, so to complete our picture of the overall context within which highland and coastal states of this area arose, we now proceed to examine the main features of the two principal microenvironments of the coast: the fifty-odd river valleys that run down out of the Andes across the coastal desert and the rich marine waters that lie adjacent to these rivers along the central western part of the continent (Figure 9.1). This, as it turns out, is a particularly appropriate beginning for our treatment of Central Andean prehistory, since current archaeological evidence indicates that the rise of the earliest stratified societies in South America took place on the Peruvian coast.

A lively debate has been occurring, however, during the past twenty years or so about whether this development occurred first (before ~1800 B.C.) on a marine subsistence base or whether, in accordance with cross-cultural evidence from elsewhere in the world, it occurred somewhat later (during or after the Initial Period; see Figure 9.2) in a river-valley setting characterized by the presence of Andean cultigens and irrigation-based subsistence technology. Once we have looked at the nature of these two environmental contexts, the second section goes on to outline and critique the argument proposed by Michael Moseley (1975) in the 1970s that an essentially marine-focused system gave rise to state-level complexity in the late preceramic period, or sometime just prior to 1800 B.C. If his argument were acceptable, this would be an astonishingly early date for such a development anywhere in the Americas. However, an evaluation of the

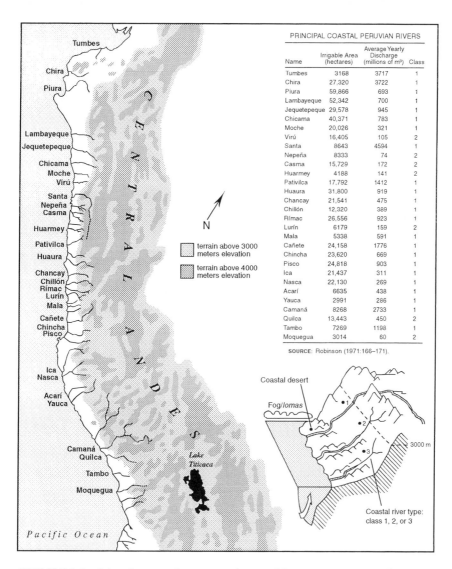

PRINCIPAL COASTAL PERUVIAN RIVERS

Name	Irrigable Area (hectares)	Average Yearly Discharge (millions of m³)	Class
Tumbes	3168	3717	1
Chira	27,320	3722	1
Piura	59,866	693	1
Lambayeque	52,342	700	1
Jequetepeque	29,578	945	1
Chicama	40,371	783	1
Moche	20,026	321	1
Virú	16,405	105	2
Santa	8643	4594	1
Nepeña	8333	74	2
Casma	15,729	172	2
Huarmey	4188	141	2
Pativilca	17,792	1412	1
Huaura	31,800	919	1
Chancay	21,541	475	1
Chillón	12,320	389	1
Rímac	26,556	923	1
Lurín	6179	159	2
Mala	5338	591	1
Cañete	24,158	1776	1
Chincha	23,620	669	1
Pisco	24,818	903	1
Ica	21,437	311	1
Nasca	22,130	269	1
Acarí	6635	438	1
Yauca	2991	286	1
Camaná	8268	2733	1
Quilca	13,443	450	2
Tambo	7269	1198	1
Moquegua	3014	60	2

SOURCE: Robinson (1971:166–171).

FIGURE 9.1   Map showing the principal coastal Peruvian rivers in relation to the adjacent Andes, with an inset drawing showing the three classes of rivers and a table indicating their irrigable area, average yearly discharge, and class.

maritime argument in light of the environmental and archaeological data shows that the argument has a number of problems, the overwhelming weight of which make it a highly unlikely scenario. In the third section we "move onto the land," so to speak, to examine Robert Carneiro's (1961, 1970) arguments about the rise of state societies as a function of circumscribed environmental contexts and internecine war.

Although it is far more likely that state-level society in the Central Andes arose in a river-valley context rather than a marine one, there are equally lively arguments about the precise timing and nature of the sociopolitical develop-

Estimated Absolute Date	Period	Major Culture/ Polity	Coastal Valley Polity	Selected Sites
1532 1470	LATE HORIZON	**INCA**		**Cuzco Huánuco Pampa**
	LATE INTERMEDIATE	Chimú		
1000				
	MIDDLE HORIZON	Wari Tiwanaku		
600				
		MOCHE	**GUADALUPITO**[a]	**Moche, Sipán, Huaca Tembladera**
	EARLY INTERMEDIATE		**LATE SUCHIMANCILLO**[a]	
A.D.				
B.C.			**PATAZCA**[b]	**Pampa Rosario**
350				
	EARLY HORIZON	**CHAVIN**	**CAYHUAMARCA**[a]	**Chavín de Huántar**
800				
	INITIAL		**MOXEKE**[b]	**Pampa de la Llama–Moxeke, Cerro Sechín, Taukachi–Konkán**
1800				
	LATE PRECERAMIC			**Las Haldas, Aspero, El Paraíso**
3000				

NOTE: Cultures/sites discussed in the text are shown in **bold letters**.
[a] Santa Valley polity.
[b] Casma Valley polity.

FIGURE 9.2   Central Andean chronology.

ments that followed the rise of agriculture. Since in my own research on the Peruvian coast I have had occasion to deal for some years with the theoretical implications and data related to both Moseley's and Carneiro's models, the beginning sections of this chapter deal with issues that have formed a direct inspiration for my career to date in this geographic area. However, even though I therefore am standing on the shoulders of my distinguished predecessors here, this does not mean that I do not aim a few sparks at their heads (to mangle the metaphor in the interest of propriety). With the goal of resolving several major issues related to the timing and nature of state formation on the Peruvian coast, then, we unleash our ecologically based theoretical "guns" as we attempt to throw light on the processes leading to the development of societal complexity and the state.

The remaining sections of this chapter go beyond the evaluation of theories of state formation to deal with three Central Andean cultures that stand as particularly spectacular and noteworthy developments of relevance to the theoretical and substantive focus of this book. The first of these is Chavín (~900–200 B.C.), which developed in the highlands and coast of north-central Peru. Chavín represents the first appearance in the Central Andes of an extensive interregional interaction sphere that, although most probably not a state, at the very least involved the widespread sharing of a religious-ceremonial complex that focused on animals of rain-forest origin. Associated with this exotic focus was the development of what is perhaps the most stunning art style of any time period in the Central Andean sequence. The second culture is Moche (~A.D. 200–750), which developed entirely on the north coast, although it overlaps to a degree with the prior Chavín sphere of interaction and indeed appears to have grown in part out of Chavín influences on iconography and related cosmology. Although local-valley state formation may well have occurred earlier, it is nonetheless the best-documented candidate we have to date for pristine state formation at the regional level in the Central Andes. Like Chavín, Moche is characterized by the creation of an art style with highly distinctive features, especially in pottery forms and iconography, that have made it well known to students of art history and archaeology alike. The third culture is the Inca (~A.D. 1200–1532), whose initial development occurred locally in the Cuzco area of the southern Peruvian highlands. Ultimately, however, it spread throughout the Andes to cover most of the sierra and coast from Ecuador south to central Chile, making it by far the largest state ever to develop in the Central Andes or, for that matter, anywhere else in North and South America. As impressive as its political and economic achievements were, the Inca art style is equally interesting—not only for the decidedly sober, geometric iconography on the pottery, but also for the fact that many of its diagnostic characteristics in both pottery and architecture appear to arise nearly without evolutionary precedent in the Andes.

ADAPTATION TO COASTAL PERU

Just as the human carrying capacity of the Andean sierra is a function of the amount of land suitable for grazing animals as well as for practicing rainfall and irrigation agriculture, so is that of the neighboring coast desert and Pacific littoral based first and foremost on several crucial environmental factors. For adaptive systems focused on the river valleys the factors would have included (1) in the earliest time period, the densities and extent of faunal and floral resources that were available to hunter-gatherers; and (2) in later time periods, the average yearly discharge of water carried by a given river and the amount of land available on or near the valley floor that was suitable for cultivation by traditional contour irrigation canals. For adaptive systems focused on the adjacent marine waters, the critical environmental factors would have included the location, numbers, areal extent, and accessibility of marine fauna in relation to the coastline.

This section presents selected data on the coastal valley setting as one of the contexts appropriate for the rise of prehispanic sociopolitical complexity, followed by an overview of the unique features that characterize the adjacent waters of the Pacific Ocean. It ends with a discussion of the implications of the environmental data for the complexity of prehispanic fishing and agricultural groups, specifically in terms of both the productivity potentials and the limiting factors that must be taken into consideration in our understanding of each of these distinct adaptive systems. This is a necessary prelude to critiquing the model of maritime complexity proposed by Moseley.

Coastal River Valleys

The coastal rivers of Peru are classified in three categories based on the nature of their drainage system and the degree to which they penetrate the sierra to an altitude near or beyond 3,000 meters, the point above which limited annual precipitation occurs on the western edge of the Andes (Figure 9.1). Class 1 rivers are those that extend up into the adjacent Andes well to the east of the 3,000-meter level, thereby capturing more than enough water from precipitation and snowmelt to flow year-round. In the continuously temperate setting of the littoral, these rivers thus permit year-round irrigation agriculture on the valley floor alluvium at the point where the river widens out in its coastal sector. Class 2 streams are those that penetrate less deeply into the sierra, but sufficiently beyond the 3,000-meter level to capture precipitation during the rainy season between October and March. Such rivers permit irrigation cultivation most of the year. Class 3 streams occur wherever the Andean topography permits only a limited headwater system, so they capture far less water and flow intermittently from year to year. Although they may nevertheless permit year-to-year irrigation cultivation, their human carrying capacity and potential for the development of sociopolitical complexity are far less than those of the other two classes.

Another important variable is the amount of land available in a given coastal valley. As shown in the table in Figure 9.1, the supply of land available to the class 1 and class 2 rivers of the coast varies dramatically between about 3,000 hectares (30 square kilometers) for valleys such as Tumbes, Yauca, and Moquegua and 40,000–60,000 hectares (400 square kilometers) for valleys such as Piura, Lambayeque, and Chicama. Moreover, the valleys at each end of this size range vary even more dramatically in terms of their average yearly discharge of water in millions of cubic meters (or 10^6 cubic meters). Thus, whereas Tumbes has a yearly flow estimated at $3,717 \times 10^6$ cubic meters, Yauca and Moquegua have relatively more reduced flows of 286×10^6 cubic meters and 60×10^6 cubic meters, respectively. Even more strikingly, the three valleys at the upper end of the size range are characterized by average yearly discharges that are far less than that of Tumbes, or 693×10^6 cubic meters for Piura, 700×10^6 cubic meters for Lambayeque, and 783×10^6 cubic meters for Chicama. We return momentarily to the implications of these data on the areal extent of valleys and volume of discharge of their rivers.

The Maritime Setting

All of the streams along the littoral contribute nutrients in the form of dissolved salts to the waters of the adjacent Pacific. In combination with the continual upwelling that keeps them near the surface, the rich inflow of salts from these streams creates conditions of high productivity in the *pelagic* zone, or the uppermost layer of the ocean where photosynthesis is possible as a result of the penetration of sunlight. Indeed, pelagic invertebrates, including zooplankton and phytoplankton, are so plentiful in the Peru Coastal Current that the sea here has been likened by Jean Dorst (1967:224) to a "thick soup." With the highest natural densities of such invertebrates anywhere in the world, the plankton form the basis as primary producers for a rich marine food chain that runs up through various trophic (or feeding) levels—including anchovies at the herbivore level, a huge variety of larger fish including bonitos and tuna at the primary carnivore level, and such animals as sea lions at the secondary carnivore level. Scavengers such as the Andean condor, if feeding on dead sea lions, form an additional, or tertiary, carnivore level at the top of the food chain. To give an example at just one of these trophic levels of the massive productivity that characterizes the current, the total number of anchovies during normal times has been estimated to approach 10,000 billion ($10^4 \times 10^9$) individuals, which represents a biomass of about 20 million tons, other things being equal, such as the amount taken by human predators in the form of the annual fisheries catch.

Every year around Christmastime the warm countercurrent called El Niño, or "The Christ Child"—which flows clockwise against the central west coast of South America out of the equatorial maritimes—extends a little farther down to the south along the northernmost part of Peru than it normally does during the rest of the year. As this happens, modest amounts of rainfall occur for a few weeks in areas that do not otherwise receive measurable precipitation (including the southwest coast of Ecuador, as mentioned earlier). The countercurrent, like all tropical oceanic waters, is far lower in saline content and is therefore much less productive in terms of marine biota than the Peru Coastal Current.

But every ten years or so on average (estimates range from seven to thirteen years), with essentially no advance warning, El Niño countercurrent extends much farther south along the Peruvian littoral than it does in its normal yearly cycle. When this happens, the marine and terrestrial ecosystems of the littoral are thrown disastrously out of kilter. For example, temperatures in the arid terrestrial environment rise to abnormal highs that are accompanied by heavy rainfall and flooding for periods that range from several weeks to many months. In terms of the effects on the organic biomass of the littoral, what El Niño does to the marine ecosystem is far more disastrous than the more visible short-term damage it does on the normally bone-dry land. Cold-water species, finely tuned to unvarying conditions of temperature and salinity (i.e., they are stenothermal and stenohaline species), perish in great numbers starting with the plankton at the primary producer trophic level and reaching up through the rest of the marine food chain. As Dorst (1967:233) puts it, "The whole complex life cycle is thus disrupted and the only recourse for those thriving on the riches of the sea is to seek nourishment elsewhere." In sum, El Niño is a malevolent "child" if ever there was one.

Implications for Prehispanic Adaptive Systems

Theoretically speaking, there are two approaches to assessing the human carrying capacity of the marine and terrestrial environments of the Peruvian littoral and hence the potential for the development of sociopolitical complexity. One of these is to estimate the relative numbers of people that could have been sustained by each of the environments by focusing on (1) the nature of each microenvironment, (2) fishing and agricultural subsistence productivity in relation to each microenvironment, and (3) population numbers in relation to the physical environment and the mode of production (i.e., on three of the four infrastructural variables in our systems-hierarchical model, excluding settlement patterns). This is, however, the more difficult of the two approaches, since it involves assessing such potential imponderables as the nature of ancient subsistence technology, not to mention estimating more or less precisely the caloric requirements of a given human group, the catchment area it exploited, and the intensity of its labor input in carrying out subsistence efforts.

The other approach is to focus on the settlement pattern of the adaptive system in question (i.e., the fourth critical infrastructural variable in our model) in estimating not only the numbers of sites and related numbers of people that characterize the system in question but also its sociopolitical complexity. These data, combined with an assessment of the nature of the subsistence system (e.g., to determine whether it was focused primarily on fishing or on agriculture), can then be compared to the assessment of human carrying capacity carried out by means of the first approach. Although this second approach is less challenging than the first, especially in light of the superb preservation of ancient sites dating as early as pre–1800 B.C. (i.e., back into the preceramic period; Figure 9.2), nonetheless it obviously involves assumptions about our ability to obtain a complete, or nearly complete, sample of the sites in any one system for the period in question.

In sum, we see that there are two ways of approaching an understanding of the two main subsistence-settlement systems—marine and agricultural—that characterized the prehispanic Peruvian coast. One involves looking at the potential productivity of the subsistence system to gain some sense of the expected numbers of people it might have produced, whereas the other involves looking at the nature of the settlement system to see how many people and how much complexity actually were produced by that subsistence system irrespective of any theoretical attempt to estimate its carrying capacity. However, neither approach has to be carried out alone; it may be more effective to attack the problem from both sides—including a focus on both subsistence productivity (carrying capacity) and the related settlement system.

Although all this preparatory commentary may seem, theoretically speaking, somewhat akin to "counting anchovies and maize cobs on the heads of pins," it is a serious matter to archaeologists interested in understanding cross-culturally the kinds of environments and subsistence systems that gave rise to state-level societies around the world. For example, any scholar who has studied prehistoric cultures on a worldwide basis is aware that the overwhelming consensus of evolutionary anthropologists is that states arose in environments that were particularly suited to relatively high subsistence productivity and that the kind of subsistence practiced everywhere they arose appears to have been agriculture. It follows as a corollary to this argument that states probably could not arise on a wild-food-gathering subsistence base both because of its relatively limited productivity and the difficulty of intensifying such an adaptation.

Agriculturally Based Systems

The reader who has perused the table in Figure 9.1 undoubtedly will have already concluded that the subsistence productivity—and hence the demographic potential and sociopolitical complexity—of a given coastal river valley would involve an optimum combination of both land and water rather than just one or the other of these two crucial variables. Thus, other factors, such as the timing of the introduction of cultigens and irrigation technology, being equal, it is theoretically predictable that the centers of the first major states might well be focused in valleys where optimum combinations of water and land gave them relative demographic, and hence military, superiority over nearby valleys characterized by lesser carrying capacities.

As we see later in discussing Carneiro's state origins theory, the fact that adjacent valleys in one section of the Peruvian north coast (see Virú, Santa, Nepeña, and Casma in Figure 9.1) are characterized by roughly the same amount of land but relatively quite different water regimes may well provide us with the material underpinnings of a model that attempts to explain the origins of intervalley warfare and societal complexity in this area. Furthermore, given models that include the potential for both intervalley conflict (war) and cooperation (trade and/or alliance formation), it becomes interesting to compare contemporaneous cultural diagnostics from valley to valley in an attempt to construct arguments about the complex mix of trade and warfare that might have characterized regional interaction spheres. In this regard, as the map in Figure 9.1 indicates, although each Peruvian coastal river valley is to some degree an environmental isolate, most are not located at greater distances than one-half to a full day's walk from their neighbors to the north and south. Therefore, both war and trade in exotic resources occurring as a result of locally experienced pressures/needs would have been potential adaptive solutions that lay as close at hand as the next river valley to the north or south. Moreover, although the climb up into the adjacent Andes was more difficult and probably took somewhat more time (a full day's walk or more), Andean resources such as llamas, grains, tubers, and minerals not as readily available on the coast theoretically would have made the adjacent sierra an attractive focus of exchange for coastal inhabitants.

Marine-Based Systems

With respect to the marine microenvironment, if we are to assess properly the nature of the maritime-focused human adaptive systems that characterized the late preceramic and Initial Period on the coast of Peru, then it should be done not only in light of the normally high biological productivity that characterizes the Peru Coastal Current but also in terms of the lean periods created by the El Niño countercurrent. This is an approach entirely in accord with Mark Cohen's (1977) "continual population pressure" model (Figure 2.8b is a version of this model), which argues that we must view the carrying capacity of a subsistence system in terms that include the best of times and the lean, or bottleneck, periods. Furthermore, if these latter bottleneck periods occur unpredictably over the longer year-to-year term and are of sufficient duration, then they may provide a lower limit above which a human population cannot rise.

Another complication arises from the probability that prehispanic and modern traditional human fishing groups could enter this chain as primary, secondary, or tertiary carnivores (if not any combination of these levels) depending on their access to the marine species at a particular level (below them) in the food chain. The trophic level (or levels) a group occupied would thus have significant consequences in terms of total energy capture and hence in terms of numbers of people and the overall sociopolitical complexity of their adaptive systems. A final critical limiting factor on the Peruvian coast is the availability of nearby water sources to any fishing settlement located on the desert shoreline to the north or south of a given coastal valley. Since the distance between the fifty valleys of the Peruvian littoral ranges between 15 and 50 kilometers, any settlement located along the coastline more than a few kilometers away from the closest valley would probably be demographically constrained simply as a function of the difficulty of transporting water from the closest source(s) in nearby valleys.

MOSELEY'S MARITIME COMPLEXITY MODEL

Two key assertions of the systems-hierarchical model are that human adaptive systems are best understood by reference to as many of the ten variables in the model as the data will permit and that our understanding must be based on demonstrably logical relationships among the critical variables that constitute the system—including the physical environment, the mode of production, the settlement pattern, the mode of reproduction, social organization, the political economy, leadership/ritual, and so on. I have insisted that an explicit model of levels of sociopolitical integration is critically necessary in any attempt to resolve arguments about the kind of society that is presumed to have arisen in the context of a particular environment and related subsistence base.

From the chapter on subsistence types and productivity, it follows that an attempt to argue for state formation in the Central Andes—or, indeed, anywhere else in South America—should be based on the clear demonstration that a given environment and related subsistence system were among the highest in productivity to be found anywhere on the continent. Moreover, in light of the rather simple and direct technologies that characterize the lower productivity systems of the eastern lowlands of South America, theoretically we expect to find more complexities characterizing the subsistence system of a state. In other words, as part of our argument about the systemic reasons for the rise of a state-level society, we wish to demonstrate that a critical function, if not raison d'être, of the ruler and other higher-level officials was to manage, coordinate, and maintain the middle- and lower-level economic features of that society. In light of our earlier discussions of band societies, however, this statement should not be taken to mean that many aspects of hunter-gatherer systems are not exceedingly complex (e.g., recall the challenge of survival in Tierra del Fuego), but that state societies, by definition, consist of subsistence-settlement systems whose complexities far surpass those of egalitarian societies in terms of scale. Among other things, then, to the extent state societies are effectively integrated on a vastly larger territorial and systemic scale, they require not just a ruler but also a substantial class of hierarchically organized underlings engaged in the societywide management of the economic subsystem, not to mention the political and religious subsystems of the state as well.

A (Re)statement of the Issue

In the foreword to Moseley's (1975) book *The Maritime Foundations of Andean Civilization,* Jeremy Sabloff and C. Lamberg-Karlovsky appear to take strong issue with the archaeological "consensus" that the rise of civilization must necessarily follow the rise of agriculture and settled village life—namely, they explicitly accept his argument that such a process occurred on the coast of Peru "without the benefit of agriculture." In his Introduction Moseley makes the same assertion—using as his model of a "civilization" not the kind of *level heuristic* for a state that I have proposed earlier in this book, but the stratified society that arose on the north coast of Peru several centuries before the arrival of the Spaniards led by Francisco Pizarro in A.D. 1532. Since here he is specifically referring to the Chimú (e.g., see Moseley and Day 1982), we must hasten to agree that this was indeed a society that most archaeologists would characterize as a state.

For example, Chimú culture embraced at least eleven north coast valleys, with its primary center in the Moche Valley at the site of Chan Chán, a vast complex of adobe compounds and structures that sprawled over an area of at least 16 square kilometers. Below Chan Chán in the state hierarchy, most, if not all, of these valleys contained a provincial center as well as several widely scattered local centers and many dozens of rural habitation sites (e.g., see Willey 1953; Wilson 1988). Linking a population whose size probably substantially exceeded one hundred thousand was a complex interdesert road system and a state-imposed set of artistic canons that determined how pottery was to be made (mold-made redware and grayware in a specific, limited set of vessel forms) as well as how architectural construction was to be carried out (e.g., employing *tapia* walls, or walls consisting of mud packed into wooden forms in discrete sections). Finally, to mention one other feature, when the rulers of Chan Chán died, they were buried in elaborate monumental platforms along with dozens of sacrificed female retainers and a wealth of gold, silver, and other elite goods—all of which was aimed at providing an enduring material indication of their vast power at the head of a complex polity whose control extended over several hundred kilometers of the north coast.

It is precisely this kind of society that Moseley (1975:5) had in mind when, working at late preceramic sites on the Peruvian coast in the early 1970s, he came to the realization that compared to later coastal states such as Chimú, "the social organization of *the maritime population was, in fact, very complex*, highly evolved, and a majority of the behavioral characteristics associated with later coastal civilization had emerged independently of any significant agricultural input." In light of the theoretical perspective of this book, his assertion raises a number of questions about the nature of subsistence-settlement systems of the late preceramic period. First, what is his basis for assessing the productivity of the marine environment, and does he take perturbations such as El Niño into account in his model of this productivity? Second, how large an area of ocean does he see the preceramic populations as having utilized, and hence what inferences does he make about the productivity of the maritime subsistence base? Third, how complex was subsistence technology, and, in a related vein, was fishing a group or an individual activity? Fourth, what are the features of late preceramic sites—such as size, monumentality of architecture, and burial remains—that lend support to his assertion that complex society indeed arose on an essentially maritime subsistence base? Fifth, what evidence is there for late preceramic populations comparable in size to the Chimú? Sixth, and finally, what social evidence (e.g., differential burial treatment) does he put forth to show that stratified society had developed?

Before presenting Moseley's case, let me mention that the great majority of late preceramic sites on the Peruvian coast, from Huaca Prieta to Asia (see Figure 9.3), are too small and noncomplex to support his argument. The principal exceptions to this pattern are the sites of El Paraíso, located at the mouth of the Chillón Valley; Aspero, located at the mouth of the Supe Valley; and Las Haldas, located on the desert shoreline some 25 kilometers south of the Casma Valley. Not surprisingly, it is the data from these sites that Moseley most relies on in support of his case. Let us now proceed briefly to outline the main elements of Moseley's maritime model before going on to critique it.

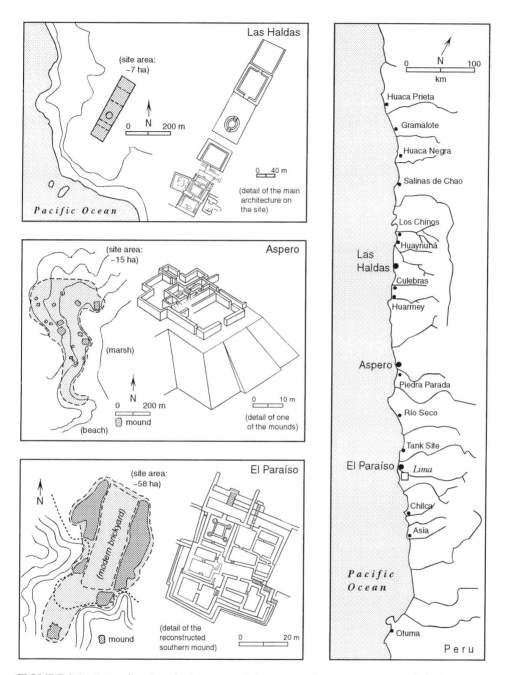

FIGURE 9.3   Map showing the location of the principal preceramic sites of the Peruvian central and north coasts and detail views of the three most complex sites. Detail views redrawn and adapted from illustrations in Moseley (1975).

The Model

Physical Environment

Since the near-shore waters of coastal Peru are among the most productive any-where in the world—such as measured by the fact that the modern fisheries har-vest constitutes fully one-fifth of the world's entire commercial catch—Moseley believes there is little reason to suppose that this area could not have been in late preceramic times an exception to the general rule that civilizations arise on an agricultural base. Indeed, he argues that the distribution of the complex ancient sites, including Las Haldas, Aspero, and El Paraíso, corresponds exactly with the area of the greatest modern fisheries productivity, which lies to the south of the Santa Valley (Figure 9.3). He knows that the fertility of the sea is severely af-fected aperiodically, but fairly frequently (e.g., in 1891, 1925, 1953, 1957, 1965, and 1997–1998), by El Niño phenomena. Thus, El Niño clearly would have had a significant impact on late preceramic populations by reducing the amount of food, although in Moseley's opinion it would be difficult, if not impossible, to calculate quantitatively what its effect would have been.

But this difficulty is of little importance in his model, since Moseley ends up rejecting totally the importance of El Niño as an aperiodic limiting factor. Al-though it is true that El Niño would kill off the fish (including anchovies) at the base of the marine food chain, he suggests that fish-eating sea birds, in "weak-ened condition" from the loss of their normal source of food, would alight in great numbers on the beaches and be easy pickings as a dietary stopgap for the ancient fisherfolk. However, in spite of his rejection of El Niño as a quantifiable limiting factor, Moseley clearly realizes that the restoration of the lost marine biomass would take significantly longer than the actual duration of severe events, which last several months at most. For example, he (1975:11) states that "nature can take several years to hone the blade of her great double-edged sword and bring sea and shore life back to sharpened balance."

Mode of Production

Moseley sees marine subsistence, including shellfish gathering and fishing, as having been of overwhelming significance in the diet of the late preceramic complex societies. However, the associated technology was "remarkably simple" and "unelaborate"—consisting, in other words, of cotton nets, hook and line, basketry, and so on. Indeed, he (1975:54) argues that the "archaeological record does not reveal any sort of drive by the preceramic population to get more return from the sea by means of technological refinement or adoption of new innova-tions." For example, there is no evidence that late preceramic populations had any sort of watercraft such as the small one-man reed rafts that appear on the coast a little later in the sequence. In his model the late preceramic "civilization" therefore must have been confined strictly to the exploitation of "marine resources . . . localized in a narrow belt stretching along the littoral zone" (Moseley 1975:43).

And lest it be thought that agriculture played an important role in sustaining the late preceramic "civilization," Moseley downplays its importance in the subsistence system of such sites as Las Haldas, Aspero, and El Paraíso. He argues that, although other cultigens are present (e.g., a small cache of maize at Aspero), these remains principally include "industrial" crops, such as cotton and gourds, which were used in making netting, line, and net floats for exploiting marine resources. Nevertheless, since there is no evidence for the storage of marine products in the late preceramic, Moseley does recognize that the presence of storable cultigens such as maize would have provided a means of sustaining a population when a "macrocyclic variation" in oceanic waters (El Niño) brought about food shortages that could not be mitigated by the population eating dead and dying birds on the beaches.

Settlement Pattern and Demography

Moseley's model does not rest entirely, however, on an evaluation of the precise mix of the marine and agricultural contributions to the late preceramic diet. As implied earlier, it also rests on the argument that the late preceramic occupations at El Paraíso, Aspero, and Las Haldas were of such size and internal complexity that they strongly support the assertion that civilization had emerged at each of these sites. Of the three, it is El Paraíso that especially stands as an anomaly that must be explained by any counterargument to Moseley's model. As shown in Figure 9.3, El Paraíso extends over an area of 58 hectares and contains as many as nine separate constructions built of stone masonry, making it the largest and most complex preceramic period site anywhere in the Americas (Moseley 1975). Unfortunately for any argument about its precise internal nature, however, much of the site has been destroyed by workers digging clay for a modern brickyard. Nevertheless, two long mounds measuring 250 × 50 meters still flank this recently quarried area and contain most of the estimated 100,000 tons of rock used in constructing the site. Based on size alone, Frederic Engel (1967), the site's original excavator, suggested that the number of inhabitants ranged between fifteen hundred and three thousand. But more recent excavations (Quilter 1985) show little evidence of habitation debris, which makes it likely that far fewer people lived on the site. Since its monumentality nevertheless indicates that a sizable number of workers would have been required to build it, Moseley suggests that these workers must have lived in sites elsewhere in the valley. Unfortunately for such an argument, we do not yet have anything approaching a complete picture of contemporaneous late preceramic settlements in the Chillón Valley.

In any case, Jeffrey Quilter's excavations at El Paraíso turned up substantial evidence not only for marine resources, including "small fish" (the site lies only 2 kilometers from the ocean), but also for the presence of agriculture, including the aforementioned industrial cultigens as well as various fruits, achira, possibly squash, and jícama. Located on the valley floor adjacent to the site are 90 hectares of land that could have been farmed using floodwaters from the Chillón River and an additional 150 hectares of land suitable for farming by short canals. Given the complexity of the labor effort at El Paraíso, the late preceramic population in this area of the valley clearly was capable of carrying out small-scale irrigation agriculture of the kind necessary to grow the crops found at the site.

The other two sites in question, Aspero and Las Haldas, are substantially smaller than El Paraíso. Aspero site extends over an area estimated at 15 hectares (Figure 9.3) and contains six larger platform mounds and an additional eleven smaller ones. None of these mounds stands much higher than 1.5 meters (the highest is Huaca de los Idolos, at 4 meters, which is shown in Figure 9.3), their superficiality thus suggesting that the labor effort at this site was substantially less than that expended at El Paraíso. Although Moseley attaches little importance to this finding, a cache of forty-nine maize cobs was excavated at Aspero in 1941. In addition, cotton, gourds, fruits, and several legumes were found at the site, all of which could have been cultivated in the ample valley-floor area that lies adjacent to the site at the mouth of the Supe Valley. In spite of the smaller size of the site, Moseley estimates that the population at Aspero ranged between fifteen hundred and three thousand persons, or about the same as Engel's suggested numbers for El Paraíso.

Compared to Aspero, the central architectural complex at Las Haldas site, which lies near Casma Valley in the north, covers an even smaller area of about 7 hectares (Figure 9.3). This suggests to Moseley that its population was substantially smaller than his estimates for the other two sites. Indeed, the site is characterized by very shallow midden deposits dating mostly to the early ceramic periods—as does much of the architecture, including the circular sunken court, that lies on the surface of the site. Excavations carried out in late 1979–1980 by archaeologists Thomas and Shelia Pozorski (1987) show that the preceramic occupation at the site actually was relatively minor, which appears to take Las Haldas completely out of the picture in supporting Moseley's model of late preceramic sociopolitical complexity (see also Matsuzawa 1978).

Social Organization

Moseley's support for social stratification in the late preceramic does not come from any of the three principal sites just mentioned. Instead, he cites data from Engel's 1963 work at the preceramic site of Asia to show that among the forty-nine burials excavated there, several stood out as having two to three times more goods than the rest. Since one of the burials was of a young male (whose age is not mentioned), Moseley (1975:76) argues that this indicates "maritime society was neither homogeneous nor egalitarian in terms of the distribution of mortuary wealth." (The reader will not have missed the point here, however, that the Asia subsistence-settlement system is not touted as a candidate for state-level complexity in Moseley's model.)

Ritual and Leadership

Moseley also has some difficulty providing evidence that would suggest why societies whose purported level of sociopolitical integration was that of a state should have needed the higher-order leadership that such societies are commonly assumed to have. Indeed, just as we have seen that the technology itself was simple and direct, he (1975:55) argues that

> the technology of the . . . Preceramic . . . is related to an unelaborate subsistence labor organization. Collecting . . . along the littoral zone was basically an individual undertaking. Some hunting activities no doubt required group activity, and fishing with float nets along the sand beach also necessitated small groups of people working together. Yet, in overview, the early subsistence technology seems neither to have called for nor to have benefited from large-scale coordinated activity. This suggests that the efficient use of labor was a relatively passive factor in the process of economic change at least until the advent of canal irrigation.

Epilogue

Moseley, like all those familiar with the Peruvian sequence, knows that the primarily marine-oriented systems of the late preceramic period were replaced during the Initial Period (after 1800 B.C.) by irrigation-based systems that ultimately provided the material subsistence base for developments such as the Chimú state. But since he argues for a great abundance of marine resources in relation to the somewhat limited populations of even the largest sites, such as El Paraíso, he finds it difficult to explain what sorts of material pressures might have led to the development of agricultural societies. Late preceramic populations presumably carried out their subsistence activities on an individual or small-group basis, and "their availability in time and space was not subject to human manipulation" (Moseley 1975:106). However, as becomes clear in the following statement, he (1975:119) has a nonmaterialist card up his sleeve to explain this evolutionary development:

> Why the maritime folk ever made the shift to farming is not clear, and several models can be put forward. If the population level reached the carrying capacity of marine resources then a demographic commitment to a reliance on plant foods could have arisen. Thus, population pressure might have pushed people into a new subsistence pattern. Yet, refining of the simple maritime subsistence technology could easily have channeled off demographic pressures for economic change. . . . Alternatively, the change to farming as a way of life may lie in cultural institutions that cannot be explained in terms of subsistence or demography. [Or] perhaps a political model is applicable. In Peru the first "states" grew out of a maritime economy not susceptible to control by corporate authority. Like civilization in general, continued development of corporate authority rested on the furthering of institutions which allowed a few to organize and many to labor. Fishing was a dead end for the emerg-

ing state, but farming and irrigation agriculture were the avenues to totalitarian control.

Thus, ironically enough, he *can* find substantial reason for higher-level management in the infrastructure of the later agricultural systems, since the availability of domesticates in these systems was far more predictable than wild-food resources and hence more subject to manipulation and control. Moreover, far larger labor groups working together en masse would have brought about the need for complex higher-level management.

A Critique of the Model

What Moseley does not seem to realize is that he has provided the perfect materialist explanation of why such leadership did arise on an agricultural subsistence base from the Initial Period on and why, by the same reasoning, this is unlikely to have happened on the wild-food resource base that he sees as characterizing the late preceramic period. Yet unable to construct a similarly materialist explanation for the earlier shift from marine to agricultural systems, he opts for an argument that sees the rise of the state as having been a cagey plot constructed by a despotic elite seeking to create an infrastructure (i.e., irrigation agriculture) that would permit it to gain total control over the laboring masses—never mind that he offers no evidence from the late preceramic archaeological record for the existence of such an elite and such a plot.

The main arguments of Moseley's model of late preceramic maritime "complexity" are summarized in Figure 9.4. With regard to the physical environment, the model rests on the assertion not only that the Peru Coastal Current is—and would have been in preceramic times—the richest fishing ground in the world, but also that one can discount entirely the effects of El Niño downturns in marine biological productivity. With regard to the mode of production, the model argues that ancient fisherfolk were confined entirely to the shoreline, that fishing-gathering technology was simple and direct, and that subsistence effort was individual or small group. With regard to the preceramic settlement pattern, the model argues for sites that at best were no larger than three thousand persons and for a rural supporting population whose existence—in the absence of any hard evidence—is at best hypothetical. Moreover, in spite of his initial assertion of a maritime civilization, even the more limited data available to Moseley in the early 1970s strongly indicate that the complexity of sites such as El Paraíso, Aspero, and Las Haldas can be seen as resting on both agricultural and marine foods. With regard to the presumed elite that provided the leadership for these complex late preceramic societies, Moseley offers neither strong evidence for its existence nor any practical reasons as to what its systemic functions or overall raison d'être would have been. Finally, since Moseley sees no possible infrastructural reason that maritime civilizations were replaced by agricultural ones, he is forced to offer up a Marxist model of agricultural state formation—one in which the elite, fully conscious of what it was about, made a decision to shift to agricul-

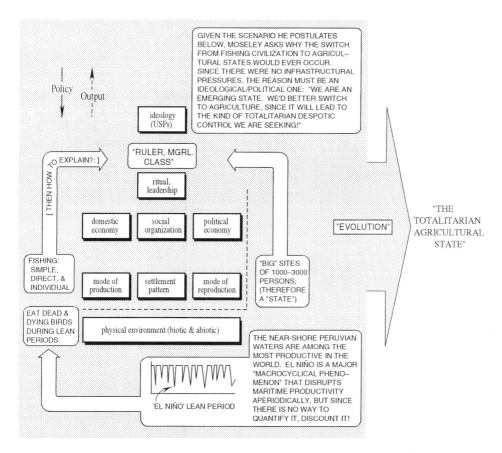

GIVEN THE SCENARIO HE POSTULATES BELOW, MOSELEY ASKS WHY THE SWITCH FROM FISHING CIVILIZATION TO AGRICULTURAL STATES WOULD EVER OCCUR. SINCE THERE WERE NO INFRASTRUCTURAL PRESSURES, THE REASON MUST BE AN IDEOLOGICAL/POLITICAL ONE: "WE ARE AN EMERGING STATE. WE'D BETTER SWITCH TO AGRICULTURE, SINCE IT WILL LEAD TO THE KIND OF TOTALITARIAN DESPOTIC CONTROL WE ARE SEEKING!"

Policy Output

ideology (USPs)

[TO EXPLAIN?:]

[THEN HOW

"RULER, MGRL. CLASS"

ritual, leadership

domestic economy   social organization   political economy

FISHING: SIMPLE, DIRECT, & INDIVIDUAL

mode of production   settlement pattern   mode of reproduction

"BIG" SITES OF 1000–3000 PERSONS; (THEREFORE A "STATE")

"EVOLUTION"

"THE TOTALITARIAN AGRICULTURAL STATE"

EAT DEAD & DYING BIRDS DURING LEAN PERIODS

physical environment (biotic & abiotic)

'EL NIÑO' LEAN PERIOD

THE NEAR-SHORE PERUVIAN WATERS ARE AMONG THE MOST PRODUCTIVE IN THE WORLD. EL NIÑO IS A MAJOR "MACROCYCLICAL PHENOMENON" THAT DISRUPTS MARITIME PRODUCTIVITY APERIODICALLY, BUT SINCE THERE IS NO WAY TO QUANTIFY IT, DISCOUNT IT!

FIGURE 9.4   Systems-hierarchical model showing the key features of Moseley's argument about the nature of late preceramic polities and their evolution to totalitarian agricultural states.

ture as a political ploy to complete the process of wresting power and autonomy from the masses.

In 1981 I published a paper entitled "Of Maize and Men: A Critique of the Maritime Hypothesis of State Origins on the Coast of Peru" in which I criticized Moseley's model more from an ecological and archaeological perspective (e.g., taking El Niño into account as a significant limiting factor) than from the perspective of the procedure carried out here. That is, here I have critiqued the maritime model in light of its inability to provide a convincing and logical overview that significantly relates all aspects of the Peruvian maritime environment (including its normal and aperiodic features) to a human adaptive system whose elements (including ancient sites and their constituent features) make sense in light of that environment. I do not intend to repeat the main elements of the argument developed in the 1981 paper, but it is nevertheless useful to summarize briefly some of the ecological implications that I have been developing in the years since its publication.

The main thrust of the paper was that human adaptive systems must be understood as much or more in light of the aperiodic limiting factors (El Niño) that characterize the environments of which they are a part than in light of normal conditions (the roughly twelve out of thirteen years during which El Niño does not occur). Although it would clearly be impossible, as Moseley rightly argues, to estimate "actual" ancient human carrying capacity in light of the productivity of the current and El Niño as a limiting factor, the paper argues that it would indeed be possible to characterize with some accuracy the limitations of the current by using estimates of primary productivity at the primary consumer level (or herbivore level, in that anchovies feed both on zooplankton and phytoplankton) based on *modern fisheries productivity*. That is, if it could be shown on the basis of a *best-case* estimate of ancient carrying capacity that maritime adaptive systems still would not be productive enough to support a complex society, then Moseley's maritime model of state origins could be rejected in favor of the alternative agricultural model. This could be done, however, only if one had a good theoretical notion of the overall systemic nature of ancient states such as has been outlined in this book (see Figure 2.7).

The approach taken in the 1981 paper was to make every effort, first and foremost, to be fair to Moseley's assertions of extremely high fisheries productivity. My best-case estimate of ancient fisheries was thus based on the modern fisheries catch, which clearly would be much greater than the ancient one considering (1) that we are comparing one-man *caballito* rafts, hook-and-line, and small throw nets to the catch taken by large industrial boats with huge holds to store tons of fish; (2) the much broader area fished by modern boats; and (3) the availability of fish at different levels in the maritime food chain to ancient versus modern fisheries. With regard to this third point, for example, modern fisheries data showed that anchovies would not be available to shoreline- or near-shoreline–restricted fisherfolk because most schools are located many kilometers out to sea and in the deeper pelagic zone (they rise toward the surface around 4:00 P.M. and 10:00 P.M. only).

Second, the paper attempted at the same time to take El Niño rationally into account as an unpredictable phenomenon (one that ancient fisherfolk could not store up food against because they could not predict it) that was of sufficient duration to have grave nutritional, and hence survival, consequences for populations that were an integral part of the maritime food chain. Thus, whatever the productivity of the current might then turn out to be, one also had to take El Niño bottleneck periods into account to provide a realistic appraisal of marine productivity. To summarize this part of the paper succinctly, the effects of El Niño were assumed to bring bottleneck, or lean-period, productivity down to one-sixth that of normal (this was based on a comparison of the amount of carbon fixed by photosynthesis in the current versus that of the open tropical Pacific Ocean, which is a relative marine "desert" compared to the upwelling area along the Peruvian littoral).

Figure 9.5 summarizes some of the data used to construct the argument in the 1981 paper and their implications for productivity: (1) if El Niño is taken into

A Comparison of Secondary Productivity as Measured in Fish Production
from Selected Freshwater and Marine Ecosystems (after Odum 1971:71)

ECOSYSTEM	HUMAN HARVEST	
	Kg/ha/year	Kcal/m²/year
I. Unfertilized Natural Waters		
World marine fishery (average)	1.7	0.3
Great Lakes	1–8	0.2–1.6
U.S. small lakes	2–252	0.4–36
II. Peru Current Upwelling Area (Anchovies)		
Heavy natural fertilization	1681.0	335.0

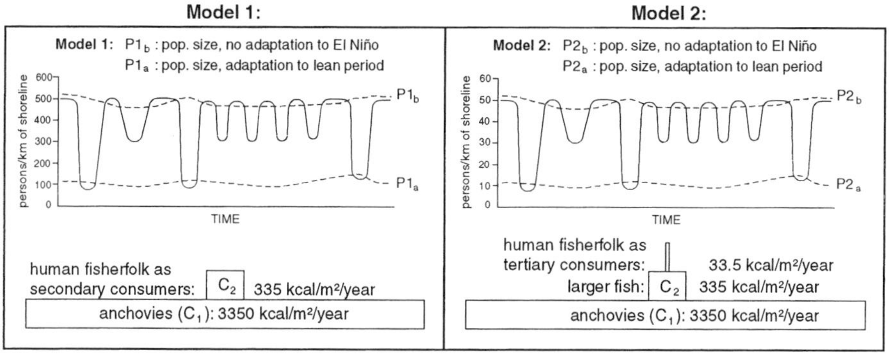

Model 1:

Model 1: $P1_b$: pop. size, no adaptation to El Niño
$P1_a$: pop. size, adaptation to lean period

persons/km of shoreline — 600, 500, 400, 300, 200, 100, 0 — TIME — $P1_b$, $P1_a$

human fisherfolk as secondary consumers: C_2 335 kcal/m²/year
anchovies (C_1): 3350 kcal/m²/year

Model 2:

Model 2: $P2_b$: pop. size, no adaptation to El Niño
$P2_a$: pop. size, adaptation to lean period

persons/km of shoreline — 60, 50, 40, 30, 20, 10, 0 — TIME — $P2_b$, $P2_a$

human fisherfolk as tertiary consumers: 33.5 kcal/m²/year
larger fish: C_2 335 kcal/m²/year
anchovies (C_1): 3350 kcal/m²/year

Note: Models 1 and 2 assume exploitation of each km² adjacent to the shoreline at a "best-case" level equivalent to the modern fisheries catch of 335 kcal/m²/year and caloric requirements of 2023 kcal/person/year on average.

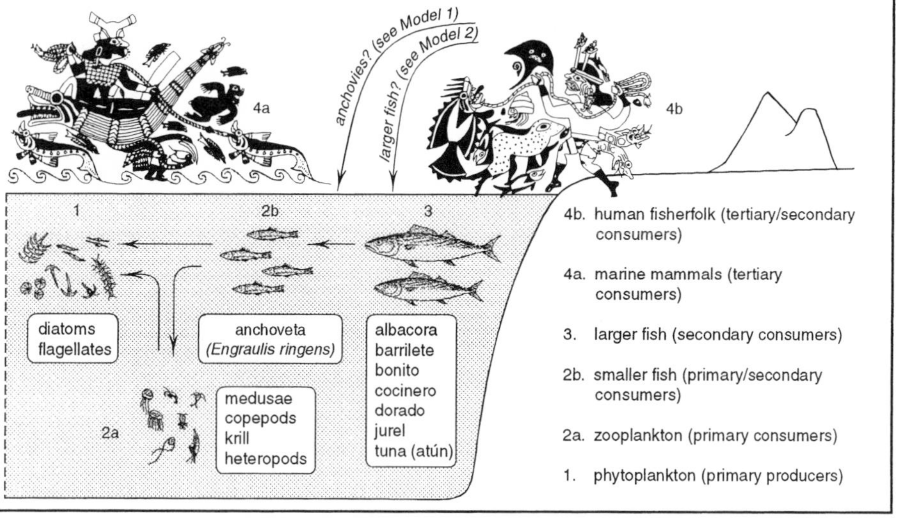

4a

anchovies? (see Model 1)
larger fish? (see Model 2)

4b

1   2b   3

diatoms flagellates

anchoveta (Engraulis ringens)

albacora barrilete bonito cocinero dorado jurel tuna (atún)

2a

medusae copepods krill heteropods

4b. human fisherfolk (tertiary/secondary consumers)

4a. marine mammals (tertiary consumers)

3. larger fish (secondary consumers)

2b. smaller fish (primary/secondary consumers)

2a. zooplankton (primary consumers)

1. phytoplankton (primary producers)

FIGURE 9.5   Data on the modern fisheries catch at the level of anchovies in the Peru Coastal Current in comparison to selected ecosystems elsewhere and two models of the ancient fisheries catch used to critique Moseley's maritime model of the origins of state-level society.

account as a limiting factor (my approach) or, alternatively, if El Niño is not taken into account (Moseley's approach); and (2) if humans were at least at the tertiary level in the food chain, that is, they were eating the larger fish that ate the anchovies (my approach, based on the inaccessibility of anchovies to shore-line-restricted folk as well as the fact that bones of larger fish appear to outnumber those of smaller fish, such as anchovies, in ancient midden debris), or, alternatively, if they were eating the anchovies themselves (an approach favorable to Moseley's case, since, based on the *law of energy transfer efficiency*, it means that fully 10×, or one order of magnitude, greater amount of calories would be available to ancient fisherfolk; see Odum 1971).

The law of energy transfer efficiency states simply that for every quantity of calories available per unit area per unit of time at one level in the food chain, only one-tenth will be available at the next level up (see Odum 1971:37–85 for an excellent discussion of energy budgets at different trophic levels). The upshot of this law is that the lower an organism eats in the food chain, the more numbers (e.g., as measured in terms of kilocalories per unit of area per unit of time) there will be of that organism. For ancient fisherfolk on the coast of Peru, it means that groups that could eat anchovies would outnumber groups that "ate the fish that ate the anchovies" by fully ten times!

If we assume, as the 1981 paper does, that the average weight of ancient males was 50 kilograms and that of ancient females was 40 kilograms, and if we take as an average a temperature of 25°C, using Food and Agricultural Organization (1957a, b) charts, we can calculate the average food intake of all people in a particular maritime group (men, women, and children) at 2,023 kilocalories per person per day, or 738,395 kilocalories per person per year. Then, assuming that ancient fisherfolk actually had *caballito* rafts and could get out 1 kilometer from the shoreline (this is best case, since Moseley restricts them to the shoreline itself!), we can calculate how much area of ocean each person would need to survive over a year's time—or, alternatively, how many people 1 square kilometer of ocean would sustain over a year's time—given the carrying capacity of normal times and the carrying capacity during El Niño events when productivity is reduced to one-sixth of normal.

To begin a series of calculations using these data and concepts, I assumed in the paper (best case) that the productivity of ancient fisheries was equivalent to that of modern times, or a productivity equivalent to 335 kilocalories per square meter per year (note in the table in Figure 9.5 how much more productive the Peru Coastal Current indeed is in comparison to all other natural waters of the world). That is, the energy budget at the level of anchovies is actually 3,350 kilocalories per square meter per year, and without losing viability, the anchovy population can "give up" 335 kilocalories per square meter per year to the next higher level (i.e., the "sustainable" productivity, presumably, of modern fisheries if overfishing is not occurring, which, unfortunately, actually has been the case in the twentieth century). To summarize the results of more recent analysis (again, the reader is referred for basic details to Wilson 1981), the best-case estimates of human carrying capacity for fisherfolk who used *caballitos* to fish a square kilometer adjacent to the shoreline are as follows: (1) Model 1/P1$_a$ (humans as secondary consumers eating anchovies and El Niño taken into account): one hundred persons per square kilometer of shoreline waters; (2) Model 1/P1$_b$ (humans as secondary consumers and El Niño not taken into account): five hundred persons per square kilometer of shoreline waters; (3) Model 2/P1$_a$ (humans as tertiary consumers eating the fish that eat the anchovies and El Niño taken into account): about eight persons per square kilometer of shoreline waters; and (4) Model 2/P1$_b$ (humans as tertiary consumers and El Niño not taken into account): fifty persons per square kilometer of shoreline waters.

Note that the approach of this book (and that of the 1981 paper) is that we must take El Niño lean periods into account; therefore Model 1/P1$_b$ and Model 2/P2$_b$ are not realistic and may be rejected. Note, also, that in the paper I argued that Model 1/P1$_a$ is not appropriate because the archaeological evidence strongly suggests that ancient fisherfolk were not consuming anchovies directly but were eating the larger fish that ate the anchovies (this, again, is based on actual anchovy distributions along the coast and on the types of fish bones found in ancient sites). Therefore, the only acceptable model is Model 2/P2$_b$—in other words, the one that argues that the best-case carrying capacity of 1 square kilometer of shoreline, with an adaptation to the unpredictable El Niño lean period, was in a magnitude of eight persons per square kilometer.

Obviously, the "actual" carrying capacity of 1 square kilometer of shoreline would have been lower than this—although perhaps not all that much lower if reasonably effective traditional techniques were used in exploiting the shallow waters along the beaches. But to test Moseley's model of "maritime statehood," let us again hasten to be fair and assume a mere ten thousand persons in the ancient "complex" maritime state society of a given coastal valley area (we assume these people needed the river water for drinking and the land for growing "industrial" crops). If we employ Moseley's model, which confines these inhabitants to the shoreline alone, it is hard to imagine how the rich Coastal Current could support such vast numbers. However, if we employ Model 2/P2$_a$, even assuming the effective use of each square kilometer adjacent to the shoreline, the ancient maritime society in question would need fully 1,250 kilometers of shoreline, or 625 kilometers to the north and 625 kilometers to the south of its central site—way too extensive a length of shoreline for one relatively small-scale state to control and effectively utilize (e.g., cost-benefit considerations would come into play here). Obviously, an ancient society might have achieved an equivalent maritime subsistence carrying capacity by extending its adaptation out into the ocean (e.g., an area that was 10 kilometers wide along the shoreline and 125 kilometers deep out to sea). But we take Moseley at his (theoretical) word here and assume that such intensification (or *extensification*, in this case) of the maritime adaptation never occurred.

To take the implications of the quantitative analysis carried out here one step further, with Model 2/P2$_a$ we have proposed a way out of the nonmaterialist dilemma posed by Moseley's nonpressure model. For if it were the case, as I have argued theoretically in Chapter 2, that maritime populations tended to rise against the carrying capacity of the current as measured by lean period productivity and, second, that such demographic pressure were experienced at least once a human generation (i.e., here we invoke Cohen's continual population pressure model), then it is possible to see how primarily maritime-oriented folk would accept agriculture as an alternative strategy to relieve (at least for a time) such pressure. Farming could be done in the relatively confined and cohesive area of a narrow river valley, and it was by definition capable of intensification in a way that, apparently by historical happenstance, the maritime adaptation was not— or we would not see such heavily populated states as the Moche and the Chimú arising on an agricultural base.

CARNEIRO'S COERCIVE MODEL

We have already seen in Chapter 6 that the theoretical underpinning of Carneiro's circumscription model of the origins of societal complexity lies in his work with the Kuikuru group of the upper Xingú River, in the Amazon Basin. There I critiqued as ecologically unrealistic his model, which argues that the "failure" of *terra firme* groups to reach complexity (i.e., sociopolitical stratification) was due strictly to a lack of pressure at the boundary, or external edge, of those societies. I argued that equally important, if not exceedingly more so, is the fact that the *terra firme* is restricted relative to the *várzea* (and the Central Andes) by the greater limitation on protein availability that characterizes human adaptive systems there. That is, even though societies such as the Yanomamö and the Shuar-Jívaro have experienced the pressures exerted by hostile neighboring settlements for decades (and probably centuries), neither they nor any other *terra firme* Amazonian group is yet known to have experienced a concomitant rise of state-level society as a result of such demographic and political processes.

In spite of the problems with Carneiro's Kuikuru model, I took pains to argue that his circumscription concept is important because it points out the need to take external edge pressures into account in modeling a particular adaptive system. But I also argued that single-factor arguments (circumscription) cannot possibly account either for all the complexities of a system or its evolution to a more complex level of sociopolitical integration. In other words, any realistic model of an adaptive system must potentially include a multiplicity of factors that are both *internal* (environment, diet, settlement pattern, population, social organization, cosmology, etc.) and *external* (encroachment, war, trade, etc.) with respect to that system and both *higher order* (leadership, cosmology, etc.) and *lower order* (environment, population, social organization, war) in the adaptive milieu of that system. As Kent Flannery (1972) puts the matter, although such an approach may be messier and more circular, ultimately it turns out to be far more satisfactory in attempts to construct adequate descriptive and explanatory models of the real-world systems we study as anthropologists.

In the classic "A Theory of the Origin of the State" paper published in 1970, Carneiro went on to develop a universal model of state origins based in part on his earlier work with the Kuikuru. At first glance this model appears to be adequately systemic in that it takes a number of variables into account, including the physical environment, irrigation agriculture, population growth and pressure, warfare, and political leadership. Nevertheless, Carneiro ends up arguing that the single most important, temporally antecedent cause of state formation in all environments characterized by narrow valley floors surrounded by absolute deserts (coastal Peru, the Nile Valley, the Tigris-Euphrates Basin, the Indus Valley, and the Hwang Ho Basin) was *warfare*—never mind that he sees this conflict as having been preceded by such processes as the development of agriculture and population growth. In a very real sense, then, Carneiro's model is actually a prime-mover, rather than a systemic, one in that it sees warfare as the single most critical cause that immediately precedes the rise of the state. Another way of putting the case is that, even though it invokes a number of variables as causal factors, nevertheless it strings them out over time in linear, flowchart fashion (valley-floor environment → irrigation agriculture → population growth → competition over resources → warfare and rise of military leaders → the state). My approach in this book, in contrast, has been to view all of these variables and more (e.g., cooperative trade, not just war) as potentially critical *at one and the same time* in any given system.

But Carneiro does not argue merely that warfare is the inevitable result of these processes in circumscribed environments; he also insists that in all such environments of the world where states arose this warfare must have been *internecine*—consisting, in other words, of warfare at the local level (e.g., within a single coastal Peruvian valley) among neighboring kinfolk. Indeed, in spite of evidence to the contrary, he and his theoretical followers have clung stubbornly to internecine warfare as the single, or prime-mover, cause of state formation anywhere and everywhere it occurred in the world (e.g., Roscoe and Graber 1988).

The Model

Carneiro begins the development of his model by arguing that prior to the rise of the state all human groups lived in band or village societies that were "completely autonomous." The stratified societies that developed with the rise of agriculture consisted by definition of networks of sites that were integrated economically and politically. That is, to the extent that lower-level settlements (second order, third order, and so on) were effectively integrated into the system, so had they handed over most, if not all, of the autonomy that had characterized village settlements during the prestate stage. Given this evolutionary scenario, Carneiro postulates that only two general theories can account for the origins of the state: voluntaristic and coercive. In the *voluntaristic*, or consensual, theory village-level people willingly set aside their individual autonomies to become part of the larger integrated networks of sites that constitute chiefdoms and states. But this theory, Carneiro (1970:734) asserts, cannot possibly be valid because of the "demonstrated inability of autonomous political units to relinquish their sovereignty in the absence of overriding external constraints." Having set up a rigidly dichotomous set of possible scenarios, he (1970:734) thus finds that the only acceptable theory is the *coercive* one, in which "force, and not enlightened self-interest, is the mechanism by which political evolution . . . led . . . from autonomous villages to the state."

After discussing the three possible kinds of circumscription (social, resource, and physical) that produce pressure on an adaptive system at its external edge (see Chapter 6), Carneiro lays out a detailed evolutionary scenario using coastal Peruvian valleys as his example of how military force and internecine conflict created the state within an environmentally circumscribed setting. Most importantly, he (1970:735) makes it clear that he has deduced this scenario from the logic of his model rather than from the available archaeological data: "The reconstruction of these events that I present is admittedly inferential, but I think it is consistent with the archaeological evidence." Since his argument is about the evolution of entire subsistence-settlement systems—groups/networks of sites in a given coastal valley—only temporally and spatially comprehensive settlement pattern data would provide an adequate test of Carneiro's theory. That is, a proper test of the coercive theory could not be carried out by the excavation of one or several sites employing the more traditional approach to the archaeological retrieval of knowledge that is still followed by most (nonsystemically oriented) researchers.

In this regard, the first problem-oriented settlement pattern survey anywhere in the world was carried out by Gordon Willey (1953) as an integral part of the Virú Valley Project of 1946. Evidently, however, Carneiro did not think the Virú settlement data were supportive of his model (one later analyst nevertheless has thought so; see Webb 1968), the central problem with the Virú data being that Willey did not carry out a truly comprehensive survey; clearly, a partial data set would not be appropriate for convincingly testing the detailed scenario that accompanies Carneiro's theory.

The first stage in the evolutionary sequence Carneiro deduces from his model begins at an early time when only small, dispersed, autonomous agricultural villages are present in a coastal Peruvian valley. Eventually during this stage the populations of the settlements begin to grow. The villagers adapt to the resulting excess numbers by intensifying the agricultural subsistence base and by fissioning, in which excess people move off some distance away to establish their own autonomous villages. The second stage begins at a point when intensification and the opening up of new land in the valley have failed to keep pace with the burgeoning population. Confined by the desert lying to the north, south, and east, but now presumably experiencing nutritional stress, the autonomous villages of the valley begin fighting with their nearby neighbors and kinfolk over access to land. By the third stage in the sequence, egalitarian society is no longer present in the valley as several chiefdoms consisting of a central site and numbers of rural sites have formed. But led by an increasingly powerful military elite, the fighting continues among these chiefdoms. By the fourth stage in Carneiro's evolutionary scenario, a valleywide state has emerged. Conflict does not end with this stage, however, as it now begins to occur at the regional level between the separate valleys. It is no longer internecine warfare in any case, as conflict is now taking place between the relative "foreigners" of neighboring valleys. The final evolutionary stage, of course, would be (as we see in the Moche case later in this chapter) the creation of a multivalley state as a larger and more demographically powerful valley takes over a number of the neighboring valleys to its north and south.

Figure 9.6 lays out in a hypothetical coastal valley my graphic version of the settlement patterns predicted by Carneiro for the first four stages in his model. In period 1 the model predicts that a only a few widely dispersed settlements will be present in the valley and that there will be no sign yet that internecine warfare has begun to occur. In period 2 the model predicts that more settlements will be present but that they will still be widely distributed. With increased competition for land, however, internecine war will now be occurring—as evidenced both by the widespread site distribution itself and, presumably in the best of all data sets, by the presence of small fortifications protecting each of the autonomous villages. By period 3 nucleated aggregations of sites exhibiting at least a twofold hierarchy of site size and function will be present as several chiefdom societies emerge. The indication that warfare is occurring between these aggregations will be present in the form of fortresses poised against the neighboring enemy chiefdom (or chiefdoms) within the valley. Given the enhanced power of societal leaders and the rise of corporate labor groups, we may expect both that monumental architecture will be present at the chiefly centers and that fortresses will be larger and more complex. As rural sites are incorporated into the several chiefdom systems, we also would expect that pottery and architectural styles will be far more homogeneous within these aggregations than they had been earlier when village-level societies determined for themselves what their artistic styles would be. Finally, by period 4 at least a threefold hierarchy of site size and function will have emerged in the valley. Architecture at the primary site will now be even more monumental, a panvalley pottery style will have emerged, and a series of fortresses will be poised on the desert margins to the north and south against the possibility of attack by foreign groups in other nearby valleys.

A Critique Based on the Santa Valley Data

In the late 1970s while I was planning my doctoral research project in the Santa Valley (Figures 9.1 and 9.2), I studied in detail the elegant and convincing scenario that Carneiro lays out about state origins. My research aimed, among other things, at testing Carneiro's coercive theory in a valley that had long been known for the presence of a whole series of spectacular fortresses dating to the earlier periods in the sequence (e.g., see Shippee 1932, 1933). Indeed, in the early stages of the research I fully expected that the comprehensive settlement pattern survey I was carrying out might provide the first convincing evidence of the validity of the coercive model in accounting for the origins of societal complexity in that area of the Peruvian coast.

As it turned out, however, the research supports only a part of Carneiro's argument, namely, that warfare had indeed been an integral part of the processes leading to the formation of increasingly complex societies in the Santa Valley.

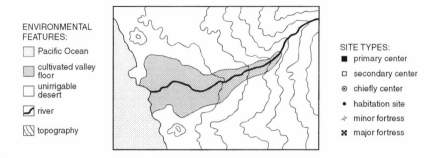

ENVIRONMENTAL
FEATURES:

▨ Pacific Ocean

▨ cultivated valley
floor

☐ unirrigable
desert

☑ river

▧ topography

SITE TYPES:

■ primary center

☐ secondary center

◉ chiefly center

• habitation site

�⳾ minor fortress

✖ major fortress

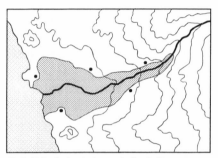

Period I–the first sedentary agricultural villages occur in the valley, each of which is politically autonomous in relation to the others, although marriage and exchange probably link the villages.

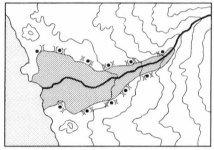

Period II–population growth in relation to the limited subsistence potential of early agriculture creates resource competition and between-kin warfare among the villages at the local-valley level.

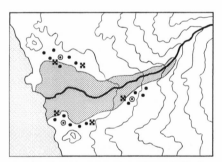

Period III–continuing internecine warfare at the local-valley level leads to the conquest of the weaker settlements by the stronger ones, ultimately bringing about the formation of competing chiefdom societies.

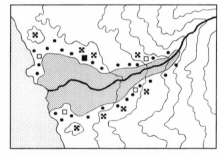

Period IV–continuing warfare among the chiefdoms of Period III leads to the conquest of the weaker polities by the stronger ones, ultimately bringing about the formation of a single integrated state in the valley.

FIGURE 9.6   Maps of a hypothetical Peruvian coastal valley showing the on-the-ground implications of Carneiro's (1970) circumscription/coercive theory.

But the data do not square with the predictions of Carneiro's coercive model either in terms of the overall nature of the settlement patterns in the early prestate periods of the sequence or in terms of the kind of warfare that clearly seems to have been occurring in the valley. Herein lie several empirically derived lessons relevant not only for theory construction but also for our understanding of the very different kinds of adaptive systems that arose in prehispanic times on the

Central Andean coast and in more recent times in the Amazon Basin. The Santa Valley settlement data make rather clear that a model of warfare deduced by an ethnographer (Carneiro) from his knowledge of the Amazonian data does not necessarily apply to ancient irrigation-focused systems on the Peruvian coast.

In several earlier publications, I have presented a full account of the research methods and results of the Santa Valley settlement pattern survey (Wilson 1983, 1987, 1988, 1989, 1997). Therefore, here I discuss only briefly the principal results of the survey and their implications for Carneiro's coercive theory, including the Cayhuamarca and the Late Suchimancillo Periods—the earliest and latest periods in the prestate sequence, respectively. Figure 9.7 shows the settlement patterns of the two periods accompanied, in the case of Cayhuamarca Period (~1000–350 B.C.), by perspective drawings of three of the twenty citadels of the period and, in the case of Late Suchimancillo (~A.D. 200–400), by drawings of selected pottery diagnostics and of one of the spiny oyster shells (*Spondylus* sp.) that we frequently found in looted graves dating to this period.

A comparison of the Cayhuamarca settlement pattern with that generated for the earliest period in Carneiro's model (period 1 in Figure 9.6) shows that the earliest agricultural system in the Santa Valley does not square at all with Carneiro's deductive reasoning about what the earliest farming society in an environmentally circumscribed valley should look like. Instead of being widely and thinly distributed throughout the valley, sites are grouped in substantial numbers in four major settlement clusters, or aggregations, in the upper and middle parts of the valley. Each of these clusters is separated by a distance of several kilometers from neighboring clusters, and each contains one or more of the main site types of the period—including habitations, ceremonial-civic centers, and citadels. That each cluster contains a full contingent of site types suggests that each probably was characterized by some autonomy in relation to other clusters, an assertion that also follows from the fact that most sites in each cluster are located within only a few hundred meters of each other. However, it is far more likely that none of the clusters was politically and economically autonomous with respect to the others. First, there is a disparity in the estimated populations of each (see Table 9.1)—with cluster 1 having ~950 persons, cluster 2 having ~3,000, cluster 3 having ~1,050, and cluster 4 having ~950. Second, a best-case estimate of human carrying capacity based on the amount of irrigable land available to each cluster and the assumption of three crops a year (the Santa River runs year-round in this temperate climate) indicates that neither cluster 1 nor cluster 2 had enough land available to support its estimated populations (see Table 9.1).

We are now in a position to evaluate the nature of warfare, which clearly was occurring *processually*—in other words, over the longer term as a continual threat, since people had invested a great deal of time and effort in the construction of fortresses on high hilltops and remote ridges throughout the settled area. Theoretically, we could think of three kinds of warfare that might have been occurring in a coastal valley: (1) between-site warfare, which would support Carneiro's theory; (2) between-cluster warfare, which would support his idea of

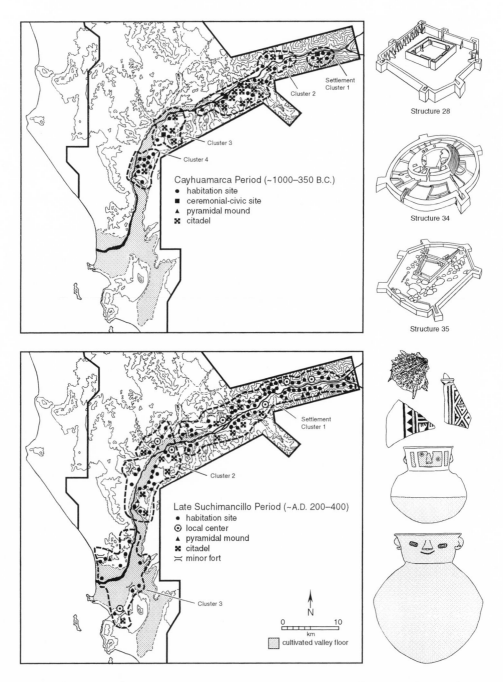

FIGURE 9.7 Settlement pattern maps of the Cayhuamarca and Late Suchimancillo systems of the lower Santa Valley and illustrations of selected cultural diagnostics. Redrawn and adapted from figures in Wilson (1988).

TABLE 9.1 Intracluster Subsistence Analysis for the Early Ceramic Periods in the Santa Valley

Period Name and Estimated Dates	Clusters				
	1	2	3	4	5
Late Suchimancillo					
Maximum irrigable land (ha)	381	1432	3603		
Triple-crop human carrying capacity	2880	10,835	27,260	–	–
Estimated population size	18,835	7645	3285		
Early Suchimancillo					
Maximum irrigable land (ha)	11	1890	2995		
Triple-crop human carrying capacity	80	13,900	22,020	–	–
Estimated population size	1070	15,030	4010		
Vinzos					
Maximum irrigable land (ha)	11	82	237	866	350
Triple-crop human carrying capacity	75	570	1645	6110	2430
Estimated population size	1180	825	955	995	1310
Cayhuamarca					
Maximum irrigable land (ha)	11	368	380	275	
Triple-crop human carrying capacity	75	2510	2590	1875	–
Estimated population size	950	3005	1040	950	

internecine war but in a somewhat modified form; and (3) between-valley warfare, assuming that an argument for internecine, or within-valley, war cannot be sustained. For at least two major reasons, we could not imagine that *between-site warfare* was occurring in Cayhuamarca Period. First, the sites in each cluster are located in such immediate proximity to each other that all-out warfare would have created an impossibly chaotic context for continued survival. Second, the fact that longer canals were found along both sides of the valley, and that these are the only way people in even the earliest periods could have farmed the valley floor, strongly suggests that the people of each cluster existed in reasonably cooperative harmony. It also is hardly likely, again for two principal reasons, that between-cluster warfare was occurring as a continual process within the valley. First, the clusters did not have the requisite demographic balance of power to sustain such warfare (i.e., cluster 2 would have won any war with the other clusters in reasonably short order). Second, since not enough land was available, clusters 1 and 2 had to have access to irrigable valley floor located downstream not only in the gap between clusters 2 and 3, but also farther down. This clearly would have required cooperation among the clusters, not just among the sites that constituted them.

It follows from this reasoning that the only warfare that could have been occurring during the Cayhuamarca Period was between the Santa and other neighboring valleys. Since the pottery style of this period is quite similar to that of valleys to the north (including Virú) and different from styles of valleys to the south (including Nepeña and Casma), I have argued that the likelier source of conflict was from the south. Comparing the water regimes of the valleys to the south with that of Santa, I have suggested that differing environmental contexts provide a likely reason for the continual attacks carried out against it. For example, although Casma has more than double the irrigable land that Santa has, it has a paltry second-class water regime in comparison to the huge flow of water in the Santa. Assuming an early population that was rising against an erratic year-to-year flow in the Casma Valley, I have argued that such continual pressure would require either strict attention to population control (e.g., similar to those of Amazonia discussed in Chapter 6) or an attack on a valley blessed with far more water in an attempt to incorporate it as part of an early polity. Evidently, the people of either the Nepeña or Casma Valley, if not both, continually chose the second course of action.

The scenario of between-valley warfare applies equally to the Late Suchimancillo Period. Three clusters of settlements are present, and sites are especially tightly distributed in clusters 1 and 2 located in the upper and middle sectors of the Santa Valley (Figure 9.7). The populations of the three clusters are estimated at ~18,800, ~7,650, and ~3,300, respectively, indicating a distinct lack of the demographic balance of power that would theoretically be necessary to sustain intercluster warfare as a long-term process. And as in the case of all the preceding periods including Cayhuamarca, the pottery of the Late Suchimancillo Period exhibits strong similarities to that of Virú Valley, two valleys to the north, and equally strong differences from the pottery styles of Nepeña and Casma, to the south. Moreover, as indicated by the presence of substantial quantities of sierra-derived kaolin ware (e.g., black-on-white resist-decorated; see the two top sherds in Figure 9.7), at the same time warfare was occurring between Santa and valleys to the south, so were the people of the Santa Valley probably engaging in intensive trade with the adjacent highlands (llama drawings and ancient corrals further corroborate this assertion). The *Spondylus* shells in graves of this period indicate that trade was occurring with valleys to the north that were connected to sources in Ecuador, from which this warm-water species comes.

The subsistence-settlement systems of the prestate Santa Valley periods are depicted in the generalized systems-hierarchical model of Figure 9.8. As in the case of the earlier models in this book, the reader will note that contrary to most systems models currently in vogue in the literature (e.g., see Chapter 14 in Fagan 1998), Figure 9.8 does not depict any "causal arrows" among the variables. Thus, although it summarizes the data and arguments just discussed, it also requires active participation by the reader to consider not only the possible causal relationships that exist among the various variables, but also the improbability of any argument that would deny such causal relationships. Although based on the results of an intensive and comprehensive settlement pattern survey, the model is nothing more or less than a working hypothesis for further research. Thus, the validity of the model can be tested both by further research in the Santa Valley and by settlement pattern data from the presumed "enemy" valleys to the south. This is precisely what my current research project in the Casma Valley has been attempting, among other things, to do.

Before proceeding, however, I conclude this section by mentioning two of the more important implications of the Santa Valley survey for Carneiro's coercive

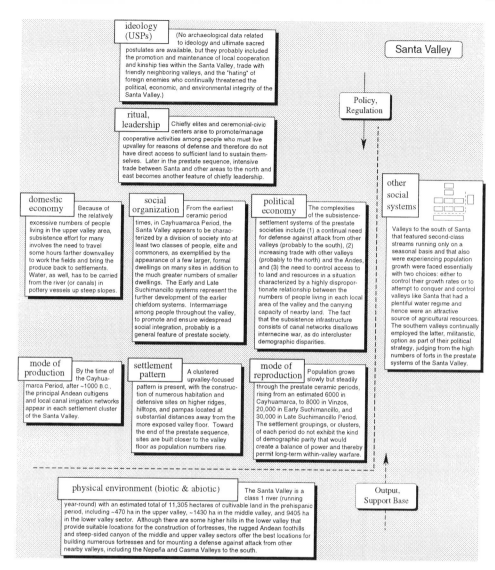

Santa Valley

ideology (USPs) (No archaeological data related to ideology and ultimate sacred postulates are available, but they probably included the promotion and maintenance of local cooperation and kinship ties within the Santa Valley, trade with friendly neighboring valleys, and the "hating" of foreign enemies who continually threatened the political, economic, and environmental integrity of the Santa Valley.)

Policy, Regulation

ritual, leadership Chiefly elites and ceremonial-civic centers arise to promote/manage cooperative activities among people who must live upvalley for reasons of defense and therefore do not have direct access to sufficient land to sustain themselves. Later in the prestate sequence, intensive trade between Santa and other areas to the north and east becomes another feature of chiefly leadership.

domestic economy Because of the relatively excessive numbers of people living in the upper valley area, subsistence effort for many involves the need to travel some hours farther downvalley to work the fields and bring the produce back to settlements. Water, as well, has to be carried from the river (or canals) in pottery vessels up steep slopes.

social organization From the earliest ceramic period times, in Cayhuamarca Period, the Santa Valley appears to be characterized by a division of society into at least two classes of people, elite and commoners, as exemplified by the appearance of a few larger, formal dwellings on many sites in addition to the much greater numbers of smaller dwellings. The Early and Late Suchimancillo systems represent the further development of the earlier chiefdom systems. Intermarriage among people throughout the valley, to promote and ensure widespread social integration, probably is a general feature of prestate society.

political economy The complexities of the subsistence-settlement systems of the prestate societies include (1) a continual need for defense against attack from other valleys (probably to the south), (2) increasing trade with other valleys (probably to the north) and the Andes, and (3) the need to control access to to land and resources in a situation characterized by a highly disproportionate relationship between the numbers of people living in each local area of the valley and the carrying capacity of nearby land. The fact that the subsistence infrastructure consists of canal networks disallows internecine war, as do intercluster demographic disparities.

other social systems Valleys to the south of Santa that featured second-class streams running only on a seasonal basis and that also were experiencing population growth were faced essentially with two choices: either to control their growth rates or to attempt to conquer and control valleys like Santa that had a plentiful water regime and hence were an attractive source of agricultural resources. The southern valleys continually employed the latter, militaristic, option as part of their political strategy, judging from the high numbers of forts in the prestate systems of the Santa Valley.

mode of production By the time of the Cayhuamarca Period, after ~1000 B.C., the principal Andean cultigens and local canal irrigation networks appear in each settlement cluster of the Santa Valley.

settlement pattern A clustered upvalley-focused pattern is present, with the construction of numerous habitation and defensive sites on higher ridges, hilltops, and pampas located at substantial distances away from the more exposed valley floor. Toward the end of the prestate sequence, sites are built closer to the valley floor as population numbers rise.

mode of reproduction Population grows slowly but steadily through the prestate ceramic periods, rising from an estimated 6000 in Cayhuamarca, to 8000 in Vinzos, 20,000 in Early Suchimancillo, and 30,000 in Late Suchimancillo Period. The settlement groupings, or clusters, of each period do not exhibit the kind of demographic parity that would create a balance of power and thereby permit long-term within-valley warfare.

physical environment (biotic & abiotic) The Santa Valley is a class 1 river (running year-round) with an estimated total of 11,305 hectares of cultivable land in the prehispanic period, including ~470 ha in the upper valley, ~1430 ha in the middle valley, and 9405 ha in the lower valley sector. Although there are some higher hills in the lower valley that provide suitable locations for the construction of fortresses, the rugged Andean foothills and steep-sided canyon of the middle and upper valley sectors offer the best locations for building numerous fortresses and for mounting a defense against attack from other nearby valleys, including the Nepeña and Casma Valleys to the south.

Output, Support Base

FIGURE 9.8   Systems-hierarchical model of the prestate system of the Santa Valley indicating the main features of the argument about how sociopolitical complexity arose in a complex adaptive context that included intervalley militarism and trade. Based on data from Wilson (1988).

theory. First, I consider the Santa Valley data to have provided a definitive test of the theory. The results of the analysis indicate that, although warfare was an important processual variable in the rise of sociopolitical complexity in this area, it was not the kind of warfare that Carneiro predicted, namely, internecine war. This sort of war is indeed present in the Amazon—as we have seen in the Yanomamö and the Shuar-Jívaro cases, where settlement autonomy is universally present and where, in deciding on adaptive strategies, the people of these settlements appear often to engage in conflict with other settlements in which their kinfolk are present. Small-scale autonomous villages are the norm, it appears, in environmental contexts where slash-and-burn horticulture and hunting are practiced and where protein scarcity is a principal limiting factor. However, in Peruvian coastal valleys economically and politically integrated aggregations of settlements appear to have been the norm in a context where networks of irrigation canals are the primary adaptation and where other factors, such as land and water availability, are the main limiting factors. In light of Stewardian theory, which asserts that there are significant connections among a specific environment, the kind of subsistence practiced in it, and the overall nature of the adaptive system, we must see as inescapable the conclusion that the Amazon Basin and coastal Peruvian valleys would of (ecologically lawful) adaptive necessity produce different kinds of systems characterized by very distinct kinds of variables, including war.

Second, even though I invoke the Santa Valley data we currently have in arguing forcefully against the universality of Carneiro's theory, this does not necessarily mean that warfare could not occur among sites or settlement aggregations in other coastal valley contexts. For example, it seems likely in a situation where a valley was of greater length and more uniform width—with equal amounts of land available to a series of several settlement aggregations—that population growth and pressure could indeed lead to within-valley internecine conflict between these aggregations. However, most coastal Peruvian valleys are no longer than Santa and most generally are wider at the mouth and narrow down significantly as they approach the Andes, so such a context may or may not be present here.

Preliminary Data from the Casma Valley

In 1989, with funding from the National Geographic Society, I began a settlement pattern survey of the Casma Valley, located two valleys to the south of the Santa Valley (Figure 9.1). Over the course of six seasons of work, the survey, completed in 1997, has produced a total of 1,343 prehispanic occupations dating to nine periods in the sequence, from the late preceramic through the Late Horizon period (pre–1800 B.C.–A.D. 1532). In light of the theoretical issues dealt with to this point in the chapter, the subsistence-settlement systems of two of the earliest periods in the sequence are most relevant here. They are the Moxeke Period (equivalent to the Central Andean Initial Period), dating between ~1800 and 900 B.C., and the Patazca Period (equivalent to late Early Horizon/beginning Early Intermediate), dating between ~350 B.C. and A.D. 0 (the intervening period, Pallka, is not dealt with here).

The earlier of the two periods has become well known in the popular American press in recent years (e.g., Stevens 1989), primarily because of the pioneering excavations of the Pozorskis in some of the precociously large sites with monumental architecture located near the confluence of the Casma and Sechín Rivers, which form the two main branches of the Casma Valley. Although earlier than the Cayhuamarca Period (ca. 1000–350 B.C.) in Santa, the Moxeke Period is relevant to our examination of the nature and timing of state formation in the Central Andes not least because these excavators (e.g., Pozorski and Pozorski 1994) claim that the period represents the rise of the earliest state anywhere in the Americas. By the same token, the Patazca Period becomes relevant as an alternate, if not second, period of state formation in the valley. Irrespective of which case seems the better candidate for state formation in Casma, the origins of complex society did occur here far earlier than the current best candidate for the rise of a pristine Central Andean state, or the Moche polity at ~A.D. 400. Although I have just finished the Casma Valley survey and final analysis of the settlement pattern data remains to be completed, I can outline here several tentative models of early warfare in the valley that, once analysis is done, will undoubtedly have implications for Carneiro's theory.

The Moxeke Period (~1800–900 B.C.)

Both the settlement pattern and the plan and detail views of the main site, Pampa de la Llama-Moxeke, of this period are shown in Figure 9.9. Interestingly enough, again in contrast to the predictions of Carneiro's model, the settlement pattern does not consist of a series of widely scattered sites; rather, like the Cayhuamarca Period, sites are aggregated in a series of clusters (five), with an additional small number of isolated sites scattered in between the clusters. Although the estimated population is a relatively small 18,500 persons (i.e., more than 10,000 fewer people than the Late Suchimancillo system of Santa, which I have suggested elsewhere represents a chiefdom level of integration), the large site of Pampa de la Llama-Moxeke provides support for any assertion that an urban primary center at the head of a small state arose during the Moxeke Period. My measurement from the aerial photographs showed that it extends over a huge area of 1.1 square kilometers, and on-site evaluation, in conjunction with a photographic enlargement of the site, indicated that it contains two long lines of major public structures flanking the large mound called Huaca "A" and its associated plazas. Although only 20 hectares of the 111.8-hectare site area contain residential structures, a preliminary population estimate for the site is about 2,000 persons.

Elsewhere in the system my survey found fifty-one other habitation sites covering a total area of 165 hectares; if we assume an average population density of 100 persons per hectare, a rough preliminary estimate of the rural population is about 16,500 persons—bringing the overall population estimate for Moxeke Period to 18,500 persons. Although the settlement clusters are widely scattered in the valley, some of them farther than 20 kilometers and nearly a day's walk away from Pampa de la Llama-Moxeke, the monumental size of the site and its low population size rather strongly suggest that the rural population played a significant role in the construction of the site. Pronounced similarities between the pottery assemblages of Pampa de la Llama-Moxeke and the rural sites lend further support to the assertion that these sites were an integral part of the Moxeke system. Thus, although the survey found nine small-scale fortresses scattered

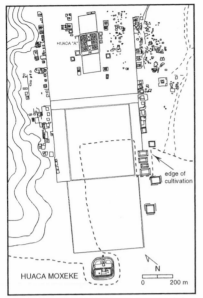

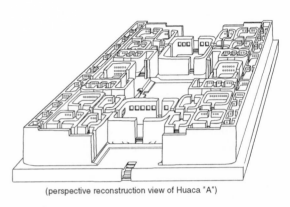

(perspective reconstruction view of Huaca "A")

(plan view of Pampa de la Llama–Moxeke site)

(Moxeke Period settlement pattern)

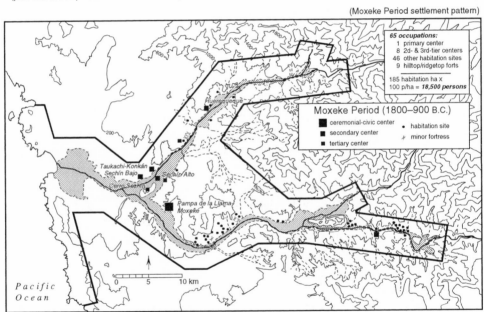

FIGURE 9.9 Settlement pattern map of the Moxeke Period system of the Casma Valley and plan and detail views of the primary site of Pampa de la Llama-Moxeke. Based on data from the Casma Valley Project, 1989–1997. Huaca "A" redrawn from Stevens (1989).

throughout the system, it seems unlikely—in spite of the substantial distance between some of the clusters—that any between-cluster warfare was occurring. However, until subsistence analysis aimed at testing the self-sufficiency of each of the clusters is completed (in general the valley does not narrow down in its upper reaches as dramatically as the Santa Valley does), the possibility that some intercluster warfare—for example, between the uppermost Casma, or southern, branch and sites farther downstream—was occurring in the system remains open.

The Patazca Period (~350 B.C.–A.D. 0)

The settlement pattern of this period and plan views of two of its principal sites, Chanquillo fortress and the Sechín Alto ceremonial-civic complex, are illustrated in Figure 9.10. As the settlement map shows, the number of sites in the valley now rises to 196 occupations, which, compared to the two preceding periods including Moxeke, clearly represents the emergence of a tightly integrated polity in the Casma Valley. Sites are distributed nearly continuously throughout both branches of the valley from near the ocean to a point 40 kilometers inland in the northern Sechín branch and 50 kilometers inland in the southern Casma branch. Moreover, there is at least a four-tier hierarchy of site size and function in the valley—with the probable primary center located at Pampa Rosario site, precisely at the confluence of the two branches, and with secondary centers (including the huge pyramidal complex of Sechín Alto, which reaches its developmental apogee in this period) and tertiary centers widely and evenly distributed across the system. Although some question remains about whether Moxeke Period represents an integrated system, there is little doubt that the Patazca system marks the rise of state-level society sometime prior to A.D. 0 in the valley. The rough population estimate, as shown in Figure 9.10, is over fifty-four thousand persons, compared to fewer than twenty-thousand in the Moxeke system—numbers that are sufficient enough to define such an integrated system as a state.

At the same time, the widespread distribution of minor and major fortresses (of which Chanquillo is the most complex example) suggests that warfare was a significant processual phenomenon affecting the adaptive system of this period. Since, by definition, an integrated system extends throughout the valley (e.g., we see none of the clustering that characterizes contemporaneous systems in the Santa Valley, which is not to say that those of Santa are not clearly integrated as well), this warfare must have been occurring with other nearby valleys—perhaps including Santa. Patazca Period could, of course, represent our period/stage 4 derived from Carneiro's model, a period during which valleywide integration has developed. The question of whether such integration was preceded in earlier periods—including Moxeke—by *dis*integrated settlement systems will, of course, have to await final analysis of the Casma Valley settlement data.

Recalling Moseley's arguments about complex maritime sites, we might want to compare the size of Sechín Alto complex—which appears to be a candidate for a second-tier ceremonial-civic complex in the Patazca system—to that of Las Haldas, one of the three earlier sites he touts as examples of the presumed sociopolitical complexity of the late preceramic. As the inset plan view of Las Haldas in Figure 9.10 shows, it is relatively minuscule in comparison to Sechín Alto. Indeed, a comparison of the 50-hectare site of El Paraíso with either Pampa de la Llama-Moxeke (110 hectares) or Sechín Alto (56 hectares) indicates that both of these early Casma sites are far more complex and monumental architecturally

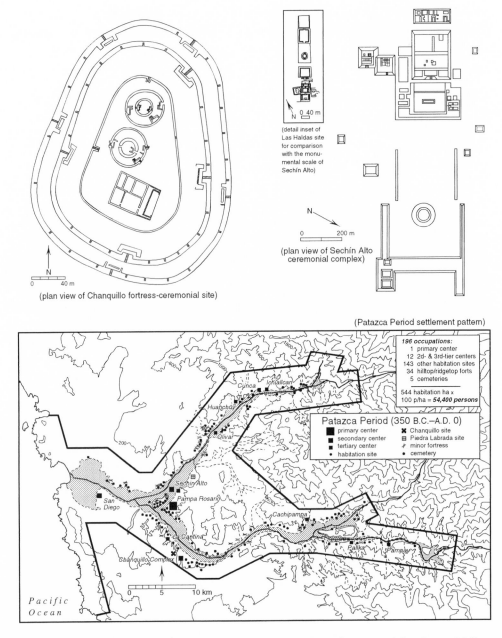

(detail inset of
Las Haldas site
for comparison
with the monu-
mental scale of
Sechín Alto)

(plan view of Sechín Alto
ceremonial complex)

(plan view of Chanquillo fortress-ceremonial site)

(Patazca Period settlement pattern)

196 occupations:
  1 primary center
 12 2d- & 3rd-tier centers
143 other habitation sites
 34 hilltop/ridgetop forts
  5 cemeteries

544 habitation ha x
100 p/ha = 54,400 persons

Patazca Period (350 B.C.–A.D. 0)
■ primary center   ✕ Chanquillo site
■ secondary center   ⊞ Piedra Labrada site
■ tertiary center   ⚡ minor fortress
• habitation site   • cemetery

FIGURE 9.10   Settlement pattern map of the Patazca Period system of the Casma Valley and plan views of two of the principal sites of this period. (Detail inset shows the contemporaneous site of Las Haldas, located 25 km south of Casma, at the same scale as Sechín Alto site.) Based on data from the Casma Valley Project, 1989–1997.

than El Paraíso. One of the points I have made earlier about arguments for the presence of complex systems is that it helps to have a comprehensive settlement pattern survey data set available to corroborate such claims. Thus, in the case of Patazca, we do not merely have one or a few spectacular sites in the database; rather, if we assume a nearly 100 percent sample because of the comprehensive survey methodology and the spectacular preservation of ancient sites in this arid setting, we can actually refer to the extensive geographic integration of the system to support such a claim. Returning momentarily to Moseley's model, since no such data are yet available for the late preceramic, we see that arguments about sociopolitical complexity for this earlier period elsewhere on the coast are thus more difficult to accept—never mind that El Paraíso, Aspero, and Las Haldas are likely to represent the centers of chiefdom-level societies that were based on mixed maritime and agricultural subsistence.

THE CHAVÍN CULT

The conclusion implied by the preceding sections is that we are armed with an ecologically based theory of no little power in addressing the inconsistencies of arguments such as those proposed in the maritime and coercive models. But this conclusion does not imply that the model serves as a flawless *retro*dictive tool leaving no room for surprises (or a sense of mystery and wonder) as we confront the data related to a particular archaeological *phenomenon*, a word that is defined in my dictionary as "something that impresses the observer as extraordinary, a remarkable thing." If we take this definition to mean that the "something" observed cannot be explained entirely by reference either to mundane data or the models derived from the ecological theory outlined earlier in this book, then prehistoric Chavín culture clearly qualifies as a phenomenon. For example, there is nothing particularly special about the subsistence productivity of the small valley where it was located that explains the architectural complexity of Chavín de Huántar site, although its position on the eastern side of the Cordillera Blanca, roughly equidistant from the coast and the Amazon, would have enhanced its development as a "nodal locus" of communication with both of these regions. If we assume that the location of Chavín was indeed a strategic one, then part of the reason for the complexity of its architecture as well as the spread of its equally complex iconographic style surely lies in the realm of the environmental infrastructure.

But as Richard Burger (1992) argues persuasively in his recent state-of-the-art book on Chavín, an adequate explanation of the appearance and spread of Chavín culture must also be based on reference to the prestige of a religious cult that was focused on awesome, if not terrifying, deities characterized by iconographic features (crocodilians, harpy eagles, jaguars, anacondas) derived not from the local environment, but from the Amazonian rain forest. The Amazon, as we have seen in the Q'eros case (Chapter 8), is a region that has traditionally been outside the normal purview of indigenous Andean folk. If so, then neither ethnographic analogy (reference to ethnographies of traditional Andean groups) nor ecological models would necessarily lead us to predict the strong tropical deriva-tion of Chavín culture. Confronted with the archaeological data indicating such a derivation, we may thus find ourselves somewhat at a loss to explain in scien-tific terms why this should be so—other than seeing this as a good example of how important inductively derived empirical observations are in the construc-tion and refinement of deductively derived theory.

In any case, although Burger's book presents the most convincing argument to date about the role of both infrastructure and superstructure (not to mention po-litical economy at the level of structure) in the rise and spread of the Chavín sys-tem, and I have therefore relied heavily on it in preparing the account that fol-lows, a minimal list of the scholarly literature on Chavín that precedes his synthesis should also make mention of the following works (including his own) that provide the underpinning to the arguments he makes: Burger (1984, 1988), Donald Lathrap (1971, 1985), Luis Lumbreras (1971, 1989), John Rowe (1962, 1971), and Julio Tello (1960).

Burger's Account of the Chavín

Physical Environment and Subsistence

Chavín de Huántar, the type site of the Chavín sphere of influence, lies at an ele-vation of 3,150 meters along the Mosna River at the point of its juncture with the Huachesca River, just below the precipitous eastern slopes of the Cordillera Blanca. It is strategically situated almost exactly at the midway point between the Amazon rain forest and the coastal desert, or at a distance that Burger estimates would have involved a six-day walk either way in preindustrial times (Figure 9.11). Anyone who has made just the western leg of this trip, up from the Casma Valley to Chavín, knows that this is a tortuous enough journey by motor vehicle in the modern era. It involves a steep climb up the canyon of the Upper Casma River, a crossing of a pass over the Cordillera Negra at 4,300 meters, a drop steeply down to 3,000 meters into the Callejón de Huaylas canyon, and then an-other climb to cross the *puna* and, finally, the snowy Cordillera Blanca at eleva-tions of over 4,600 meters, before the traveler makes a steep descent into the Chavín area. Nevertheless, Chavín clearly was as much in contact with the peo-ple of valleys like Casma as it was with the people of the selva down to the east.

Like most deep valleys located along the eastern slopes of the Andes, the Chavín area offers opportunities for the exploitation of resources in multiple, vertically stacked microenvironmental zones over very short distances that can be climbed in two to three hours. Camelid herding occurs in the adjacent area of the *puna* above 3,800 meters; both herding and the rainfall cultivation of An-dean tubers and grains are practiced on steep hillsides in the area within a 10-kilometer radius immediately around the site. Subsistence strategies in the Chavín area are relatively nonintensive, however, in that canal irrigation can be carried out only on the narrow valley floor over an area that constitutes about 4 percent of the land within this radius. In short, the local environment is no dif-

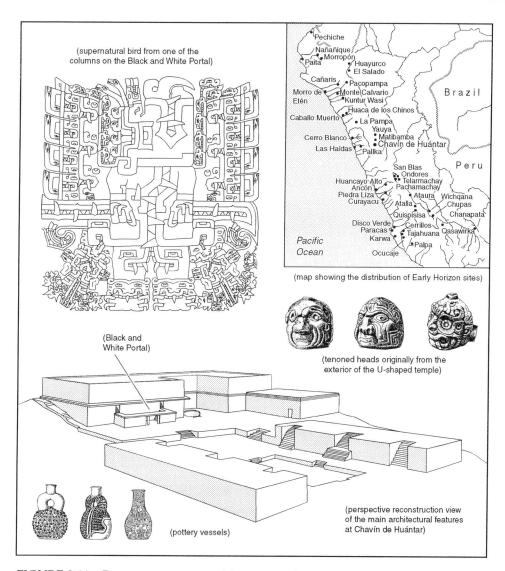

(supernatural bird from one of the columns on the Black and White Portal)

(map showing the distribution of Early Horizon sites)

(tenoned heads originally from the exterior of the U-shaped temple)

(Black and White Portal)

(perspective reconstruction view of the main architectural features at Chavín de Huántar)

(pottery vessels)

FIGURE 9.11   Reconstruction view of the main architectural features at Chavín de Huántar site, an example of Chavín iconography, and an inset map showing the principal sites of the Early Horizon. Bottom figure redrawn and adapted from Reader's Digest Association (1986), lowermost left and middle right from Kauffman Doig (1978), upper left from Lumbreras (1974), and upper right from Burger (1992).

ferent from dozens of other valleys of the eastern cordillera that have traditionally supported village-level societies.

Settlement Pattern, Demography, and Social Organization

Based on excavations at the small residential settlement that lies nearby the principal architectural remains at Chavín de Huántar, Burger divides the sequence of occupation of the entire site into three phases that extend chronologically between the late Initial Period and the later Early Horizon: Urabarriu (~1000–500 B.C.), Chakinani (~500–400 B.C.), and Janabarriu (~400–200 B.C.). During the Urabarriu phase the residential sector covered an area of ~7.5 hectares and contained a population estimated at about five hundred persons, a very small number of people considering that the northern two-thirds part of the main structure, the Old Temple, was constructed during this period. In the Chakinani phase the residential sector grew to be twice as large and contained a population that is estimated at one thousand persons. During Janabarriu, the final phase, Chavín became one of the largest sites in late Early Horizon Peru, covering an area Burger estimates at 42 hectares and containing a population of between two thousand and three thousand persons.

However, as large as it was by this time in relation to most other Central Andean sites, Chavín still does not qualify at the local level of the upper Mosna Valley as a society whose sociopolitical complexity was any greater than that of a chiefdom. Indeed, Burger has located a series of dispersed sites of smaller size around Chavín de Huántar, thus indicating that the classic two-tier hierarchy of site function that characterizes a chiefdom had probably developed. Certainly, compared to the Patazca system of the Casma Valley discussed earlier, even during Janabarriu phase the local subsistence-settlement system of Chavín and its environs appears to have been substantially less complex than that of coeval coastal valley systems a six-day walk down to the west—never mind that there is no Patazca Period site in Casma (including Sechín Alto) with the exquisite architectural complexity that characterizes Janabarriu phase Chavín de Huántar. So although Burger sees the elite priests that he argues were present at Chavín as having had substantial economic, political, and religious power over the nearby surrounding commoner populace, we must look to reasons other than politics for Chavín's enduring influence on a great number of sites that stretched throughout the Central Andes from Chanapata in the south to Pechiche in the north, over an area measuring roughly 250 × 1,100 kilometers, or 275,000 square kilometers (see the map in Figure 9.11).

During the Urabarriu phase construction began on the main U-shaped temple, which, as shown in Figure 9.11, encloses a semisubterranean circular court that is 2.5 meters deep and 21 meters in diameter and is entered by two narrow wedge-shaped stairways that face each other across the court. Around the exterior facade of the temple, at a height of about 10 meters above its base, was a series of huge anthropomorphic and zoomorphic tenoned stone heads, each weighing up to a half ton (see Figure 9.11). (I return to these heads later to discuss Burger's hypothesis about the possible emic viewpoint toward hallucinogenic drug-taking at Chavín.) In the interior of the temple itself is a complex network of subterranean galleries and small rectangular rooms that constitutes one of the most remarkable features of any building in prehispanic Peru. Constructed as the temple was being built, the galleries consist of long stone-walled passages measuring about 1 meter wide and 2 meters high that are surmounted by heavy stone lintels and stacked in several vertical levels sometimes connected by stairways. As they turn on 90° angles to the right or left, the passages ultimately create a labyrinthine maze that even today would be utterly dark and intimidating, if not downright terrifying, for any person who should have the misfortune to get lost in them without a source of artificial light.

Political Economy

The Gallery of the Offerings, located to the north of the circular sunken court and excavated in the mid-1960s, has produced some of the best evidence that Chavín de Huántar played a central role in the extensive Central Andean interaction sphere that developed during the late Initial and Early Horizon. The main passageway of the gallery extends for almost 25 meters through the interior of the northern section of the temple (on the right in the drawing in Figure 9.11). In the middle of this passageway the excavators discovered the skull of a middle-aged woman surrounded by a circle of forty infant teeth. Strewn about elsewhere along the passageway were fragments of an estimated eight hundred pottery vessels, which, judging from surrounding bones, had once been filled with the remains of Andean camelids, cuys, deer, and fish. Along with these remains were mussel shells from the Peruvian coast and *Spondylus* shells from Ecuador. Finally, the partial skeletal remains of twenty-one people of varying age, from children to mature adults, were discovered as well. Adjoining the passageway were nine doorways providing access into small rectangular rooms. Each of these rooms seems to have had a storage function related to a certain kind of item, since, for example, the first contained pottery bottles; the third, pottery bowls and plates; and the ninth, stone artifacts. Some of these artifacts have been identified as coming from a number of far-flung areas in the Chavín interaction sphere, including Kuntur Wasi site in the far northern highlands, the Chicama Valley on the north coast, and the Casma Valley and, possibly, the central coast.

It is difficult to determine whether the remains in the Gallery of the Offerings represent (1) "offerings" per se (if so, then they were presumably made to the deities of Chavín), (2) stored objects that were used in ritual or other activities at the site, or (3) stored objects that were redistributed to other nearby sites—if not a combination of two or more of these possible uses. In any case, Burger notes that the system of air ducts present in the main temple keeps temperatures and humidity levels constant throughout the gallery system, and we may therefore assume that the temple could easily have served as a storage center for pottery and other nonperishable goods and for such perishable items as food and textiles.

Following the arguments of others, Burger makes a good case that the site served as a center of ritual and worship for Andean pilgrims who might have come from a variety of places in the known sphere of interaction shown in the map in Figure 9.11. If so, then Chavín may have served a function similar to that of Contact-period Pachacámac site, in the Lurin Valley on the central coast, in having an oracle present who answered questions about pilgrims' concerns, including weather, agricultural productivity, threats of attack by enemies, and health and longevity.

Burger's excavation data from the residential sector of Chavín support the assertion that during the earlier two periods, from the Urabarriu phase through the end of the following Chakinani phase, the site's relationship with sites outside its local area changed. For example, in the first phase of occupation the flesh of wild animals is predominant in the diet. By Chakinani times fully 95 percent of the faunal assemblage in this sector consist of camelids, with llamas far more predominant than alpacas. The predominance of pack animals among these remains suggests that Chavín had intensified its relationship with the people of the nearby *puna*, partly for obtaining meat but also perhaps for carrying trade items between the site and other places in the Chavín sphere. The signs of connections with these other places show up in the Chakinani midden materials in the form of shellfish of various kinds from the Pacific coast, obsidian from Quispisisa in the southern part of the interaction sphere, and pottery vessels from the Casma Valley (Isabel Druc, personal communication) and other sites in the far northern highlands. By the Janabarriu phase, Burger notes, one part of the residential sector contains far more of these exotic items than do the others—from which we can hypothesize that some people had more access to these resources than did others and hence that stratified society had emerged.

The Chavín Art Style

The drawing of the supernatural bird in Figure 9.11, one of the low-relief engravings placed around the circular columns that support the lintel over the black and white portal along the eastern side of the main temple, shows essentially all of the elements of the complex Chavín art style. As Burger notes, the figures of mythical anthropomorphized animals—in this case a harpy eagle, judging from the beak (*Harpia harpyja*; see Lathrap 1971)—were portrayed through the use of a limited set of conventional elements, including parallel straight or curvilinear lines (called *guilloche*), scrolls, and the heads of smaller figures with dual canine teeth and eccentric pupils in the eyes. All of these elements were organized according to several principles, which include modular width (the various elements are drawn across a figure at comparable sizes within a series of imaginary parallel lines), rough bilateral symmetry in relation to the vertical axis, and anatropic organization (some of the smaller figures within a larger figure can be appreciated only when the whole figure is viewed upside down).

A series of snake heads, themselves depicted with eccentric-pupil eyes, is used metaphorically to represent hair, Rowe (1962) having called such visual metaphors in Chavín art *kennings*, after the Old Icelandic term for a verbal metaphor. The talons of a raptorial creature are shown on both the hands and the feet, probably depicting another aspect of the harpy eagle. The profile of an Amazonian crocodilian emanates from the taloned hand to either side of the supernatural bird, and the heads of a feline creature, probably depicting a jaguar, are found along both sides of the head of the supernatural bird. In sum, the more the viewer attempts to appreciate the main figure, the more it seems to have been obscured, if not mythicized, by the inclusion of all the numerous repeated, smaller elements. The overall effect on the viewer is not only intimidation and awe but also astonishment at the control the artists had over their medium, which often consists of hard, white, crystalline granite from a quarry that lies 18 kilometers from Chavín de Huántar itself. Indeed, it is easy to conclude that such carvings could have been done only by well-trained, full-time craftspeople—another characteristic of a stratified society.

Other well-known carvings, all of Chavín de Huántar provenience, are shown in Figure 9.12. The carvings comprise

A. a smaller carved tablet that is located in a frieze around the circular sunken court and that depicts a zoomorphized man carrying what is probably a stalk of San Pedro (*Trichocereus* sp.), the cactus mentioned in Chapter 4 that indigenous Andean peoples have used for thousands of years to induce hallucinogenic visions
B. the so-called Medusa figure of Chavín, which is carved on a stone tablet of comparable size and holds a *Strombus galeatus* shell in the right hand and a *Spondylus* shell in the other, both shells of western coast origin
C. a winged and tusked man holding a severed human trophy head
D. the Raimondi stela, which depicts the principal deity of Chavín, the Staff God, carved on a piece of thin, hard granite measuring 198 × 74 × 17 centimeters and part of whose iconographic elements are organized anatropically
E. the Tello obelisk, whose central figure consists of a rain-forest crocodilian (for a complex—if occasionally implausible—interpretation of its other features, see Lathrap 1971)
F. the principal deity of the Old Temple, the Lanzón, which is located in the center of the "+"-shaped terminus of a passageway in the subterranean galleries to the west above the circular sunken court, at the place where an oracle could have spoken to pilgrims through a hole in the ceiling from a room located immediately above it.

Ritual and Leadership

Given the artifactual evidence of Chavín's far-flung trade with other regions and their influence on its iconography, as well as the strategic geographic position of the site, Burger (1992:156) concludes that "the Chavín cult was created by fusing tropical forest and coastal elements to forge a unique local highland religion. The end product was a cosmopolitan ideology consonant with Chavín de Huántar's position at the crossroads of long-distance trade routes linking the highlands with the coast and eastern lowlands."

A significant part of the ritual power of the priests at Chavín, in Burger's opinion, may well have been related to the belief that by taking psychotropic drugs such as San Pedro and vilca, or huilca (*Anadenanthera* sp.; see Chapter 4), they were able to transform themselves into mythic creatures, including jaguars and eagles, much as we have seen at various points earlier in this book for the

FIGURE 9.12   Examples of Chavín iconography carved on stone. Figures (a–c) and (f) redrawn and adapted from Burger (1992); (d, e) redrawn from Kauffman Doig (1978).

shamans of the Amazonian lowlands to the east. Indeed, an analysis of the features of the several dozens of tenoned heads still present at the site indicates that different heads may well represent the stages through which this mythical transformation took place. For example, of the three heads in Figure 9.11, the one on the left appears to show a man before the transformational process has begun, the middle one shows the human face beginning to change into that of a feline, and the one on the right shows the transformation completed. Although the nose, eyes, and ears of the right figure appear to still be human, the mouth has been transformed into a jaguar's jaws with fearsome double canines and the head bristles with feline fur depicted metaphorically in the form of snake kennings with eccentric-pupil eyes.

Other figures, not shown here, depict strands of mucous dripping down from the nostrils of the apparent drug takers, much like the green mucous that hangs from the nostrils of Yanomamö shamans when they have taken ebene. Using the Desana case discussed in Chapter 6 as an analog, we can speculate that the religious functionaries of Chavín may also have employed hallucinogens to rise beyond their material world to speak directly to the gods about environmental and social issues of concern to the pilgrims who visited Chavín (we are assuming here that the data on settlement patterns, architecture, iconography, and artifacts and ethnohistorical analogue based on the Contact-period case at Pachacámac site support the assertion that a priestly class was present and that pilgrims visited the site).

The Rise and Collapse of the Chavín Cult

A question that remains to be answered, of course, is why Chavín de Huántar appears to have become the ritual focus of sites scattered throughout such a large area of the Peruvian highlands. Based on the assertion that during the later Initial Period many coastal societies began to experience environmentally caused economic decline, coupled with a resulting disintegration of their societies, Burger argues that they were attracted to the exotic religion developing in the adjacent highlands at Chavín de Huántar because it provided them with an ideological coping mechanism. Although this is obviously not a testable hypothesis, there is indeed substantial evidence in the Casma Valley for a sociopolitical decline during the Pallka Period, when, for example, the number of sites drops from 65 to 45 and the overall complexity of the subsistence-settlement system appears to be far less than that of the preceding period. However, with 196 sites, a four-tier hierarchy of site size and function, and an estimated population of 54,500, the following Patazca Period system (Figure 9.10) is substantially more complex than either of the preceding systems, not to mention that of the contemporary Janabarriu system at Chavín. Even though the people of Casma may have needed the exotic Chavín cult as a coping device earlier, this is likely to have become unnecessary by 350 B.C. Indeed, the Casma Valley went on to develop some of the most complex subsistence-settlement systems anywhere on the north coast during the Middle Horizon and later.

Chavín de Huántar, in contrast, was abandoned as an active ritual center by the end of the later Early Horizon for reasons that are not yet clear. Its apparent influence on the development of Central Andean culture did not wane, however, with the formal end of the cult. As shown in Figure 9.13, both the Staff deity and a variant with pronounced canines appeared shortly thereafter on the north coast in the art of the Moche culture, which also adopted the basic stirrup spout vessel form of Chavín (Figure 9.11, lower left). At about the same time along the southern edge of Lake Titicaca in Bolivia, the Staff God appeared as the central figure

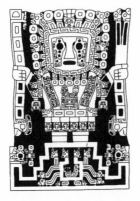

a. Staff Deity from the Gateway of the Sun at Tiwanaku Site, Bolivia (~A.D. 300–1000).

b. Tusked Deity, or the Decapitator, from jewelry in the tomb of the Lord of Sipán, Lambayeque Valley, Peru (~A.D. 450–650).

c. Chavinoid staff goddess painted on a cotton textile, from a tomb at Karwa site, Ica Valley, Peru (~400–200 B.C.). Note the depiction of *vagina dentata*.

FIGURE 9.13 Representations of the Staff/Tusked Deity showing the probable influence of the Chavín art style on the cultures of other regions and periods in the Central Andean sequence. Bottom figure redrawn and adapted from Roe (1974) and upper left from Proulx (1983); upper right traced from a photograph in Alva and Donnan (1993).

over the Gateway of the Sun at Tiwanaku site. Later, in the Middle Horizon, the Staff God once again appeared as a prominent deity in the iconography of the Wari culture, which was centered in the Ayacucho area of the south-central highlands of Peru.

THE MOCHE

Although the pottery, metalwork, and architectural remains have been known to the outside world since the time of the Spanish Conquest, it was not until the 1950s that the "Mochica" people of the Peruvian north coast were given a name that distinguishes them culturally and temporally from their Late Intermediate Period descendants, the Chimú. Since then, the term *Moche*—a variant derived from the Moche Valley, where the primary center is located—has been increasingly used by Central Andean archaeologists and the literate public alike to refer to the culture that gives us the best candidate we currently have for pristine multivalley state formation along the western littoral of South America (see Figure 9.14). Throughout the first eight decades of the twentieth century, excavations and settlement pattern surveys threw much scientific light on the origins and development of this Early Intermediate culture, which endured for some 650 years, or from about A.D. 100 to 750 (in order of publication date, see, for example, Uhle 1915; Kroeber 1925, 1926, 1930; Strong and Evans 1952; Willey 1953; Proulx 1968; Wilson 1988).

The chronology universally used to assess the development of Moche culture is the scheme first proposed by Peruvian scholar Rafael Larco Hoyle. On the basis of pottery stirrup spout vessels found in burial lots, he postulated that this development could be viewed in terms of five discrete phases, beginning with Moche I and ending with Moche V. Among the most pronounced diagnostic features on these vessels are changes over time in the morphology of the spouts that protrude from the upper central part of the circular stirrup—including the shape of the spout, its height, and the presence/absence of a lip at its rim. Thus, as shown in Figure 9.14 (right), Moche I is characterized by a shorter spout with a pronounced lip at the rim (very similar to the spouts on earlier Chavín vessels, from which this Moche vessel form is undoubtedly derived); Moche II, by a similar spout with a somewhat less pronounced lip; Moche III, by a flaring spout with no lip at the rim; Moche IV, by a taller, straight-sided spout with no lip; and Moche V, by a shorter spout that narrows toward the top and, like those of Phases III and IV, has no lip at the rim. Presumably these phases run between A.D. 100 and 750, although questions remain about the precise timing of each.

Garth Bawden, whom we follow here, sees Moche I and II as dating prior to ~A.D. 400 (i.e., A.D. 100–400), Moche III and IV as dating between ~A.D. 400 and 600, and Moche V as dating between ~A.D. 600 and 750. Phase I and II, in his scheme, constitute the Early Period, Phases III and IV the Middle Period, and Phase V the Late Period. It is on this basis, as well as by reference to radiocarbon dates from stratigraphic excavations, that it is possible to make arguments about the timing of the development of the Moche state in the areas to the north and south of the "core" valley of Moche itself.

In spite of the continual research conducted since the 1920s, Moche archaeology could be considered almost to have languished prior to 1987, the year that the illicit activities of *huaquero* grave robbers brought to light the spectacular "royal tombs" of Sipán site. Here, in the interior of a rather unprepossessing mud

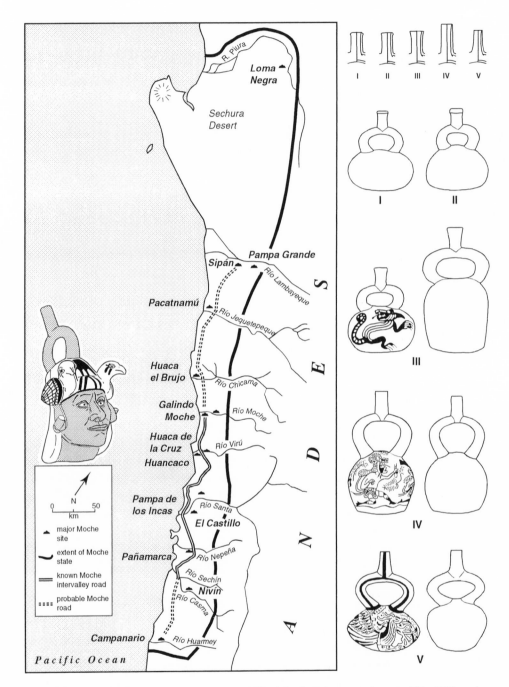

FIGURE 9.14   Map showing the boundaries of the Moche state (~A.D. 450–650) and illustrations of Moche spout and vessel diagnostics of Phases I–V. Map redrawn and adapted from Alva (1988), vessels to the right from Donnan and Mackey (1978), and male portraiture vessel from a photograph in Lavalle (1985).

brick platform mound lying alongside several larger mounds in cultivated fields in the middle Lambayeque Valley, local *huaqueros* uncovered the tomb of a Moche elite personage that contained a wealth of gold, silver, shell, and pottery artifacts—some of which began making their way via the illegal antiquities market to art collectors in the United States and elsewhere. Informed by the local police of what was going on, Peruvian archaeologists Walter Alva and Susana Meneses, his wife, began excavating a series of these tombs with the aid of Christopher Donnan, one of the foremost Moche scholars in the United States, and grants from the National Geographic Society. Ultimately, they found the undisturbed tombs of a number of individuals whose accompanying dress and paraphernalia indicated they were the principal functionaries in Moche sacrifice and blood ceremonies. Prior to Alva and Meneses's work, such ceremonies had been thought by archaeologists (e.g., see Donnan 1976) merely to represent mythical scenes painted on the sides of stirrup spout vessels. In the short period of ten years since the Sipán discovery (see Alva 1988), a number of other significant projects have begun—most of them carried out by archaeologists of the University of Trujillo—that undoubtedly will continue to modify our understanding of the rise, development, and ultimate collapse of the Moche polity.

Along with the increase in the research on Moche archaeology there has been a correspondingly impressive rise in publications on this culture and the polity it created. In chronological order, among the more outstanding books on the Moche since the early 1970s are Elizabeth Benson's *The Mochica* (1972); Donnan's *Moche Art and Iconography* (1976) and *Moche Art of Peru* (1978); José Antonio de Lavalle's *Moche* (1985); Sidney Kirkpatrick's *Lords of Sipán* (1992); Alva and Donnan's *Royal Tombs of Sipán* (1993); Santiago Uceda and Elías Mujica's *Moche* (1994); and Bawden's *The Moche* (1996). Since this last work is the most recent general synthesis of research to date, parts of the following section (as indicated at the appropriate points) are based on arguments Bawden presents about the principal systemic features of the Moche state. Where relevant, I also refer to my own research on the Moche periods of occupation in the Santa and Casma Valleys, located in the southern part of the Moche sphere of influence and political control.

The Moche Polity

Physical Environment

As Figures 9.1 and 9.14 show, although each of the ten principal valleys that made up the Moche polity was highly suitable for the practice of large-scale irrigation agriculture, these valleys differ significantly from north to south in terms of the amount of available land and water. Thus, the four northernmost valleys (Piura, Lambayeque, Jequetepeque, and Chicama) all have class 1 river regimes and at least 30,000 hectares of irrigable land. In some contrast, the five southernmost valleys (Virú, Santa, Nepeña, Casma, and Huarmey) represent a mix of class 1 and class 2 regimes and have at most 15,000 hectares of land, if not substantially less. With about 20,000 hectares of irrigable land, the centrally located Moche Valley, a class 1 river and the presumed center of the state during the Middle Period, is therefore intermediate not only in a geographic sense but also with regard to the land it has available. If we assume that all ten valleys were developing at more or less the same pace prior to the rise of the Moche polity—an argument that is clearly substantiated by the settlement pattern surveys in Virú, Santa, and Casma—it follows that the valleys to the north should have been characterized by greater demographic and military potential than the valleys to the south. It also follows that we must come up with a reasonable explanation of how the Moche Valley—which appears to have been the scene, along with neighboring Chicama Valley to the north, of the earliest developments of Moche culture in Phases I and II—could have conquered the demographically superior valleys farther to the north. We return to these points under political economy as we consider possible scenarios for the rise and consolidation of the Moche state.

Aside from issues about the nature of political consolidation, however, part of the attraction for the development of socioeconomic ties between the northern and southern valleys may well have been the resources available from their distinctive climatic regimes. Bawden notes that Lambayeque and Piura constitute a transitional ecological zone between the temperate valleys farther to the south and the rainy, tropical forests of the southern coast of Ecuador. Both valleys are characterized by semitropical environments that feature animals, such as parrots, toucans, pumas, iguanas, and boa constrictors, that are not found in valleys to the south. Since these animals sometimes figure prominently in the iconography of the pottery vessels that accompanied human burials in all of the valleys in the Moche sphere, a desire for access to such resources may have promoted trade and hence socioeconomic integration between these two valleys and the other eight to the south.

Mode of Production

In spite of the climatic and faunal variation from north to south, however, by Moche times the agricultural subsistence system in all ten valleys is likely to have been based on the full contingent of Andean crops that had been domesticated by 1800 B.C., the beginning of the ceramic part of the sequence. On the coast these crops included one major grain (maize); a number of roots and tubers (manioc, achira, sweet potato, jícama, oca, ulluco); several pulses or legumes (jack bean, lima bean, peanut); several fruits (guava, avocado, cherimoya, pacay); two cucurbits (squash, the bottle gourd); a condiment (chili pepper); and cotton (see Chapter 4). Supplementing the agricultural resources were freshwater shrimp from the canals and river channels, shellfish from the beaches and shallow bays, sea lions from rookeries along the coastline, and a large variety of marine fish. Thus, in spite of the differences in natural resources between the semitropical far north and the more temperate south, the valleys constituting the Moche interaction sphere were characterized by a pronounced redundancy of agricultural and marine resources from valley to valley throughout the 700-kilometer distance between Piura and Huarmey. Given the essential lack of resource variability, other than items such as parrot and toucan feathers, we must therefore look beyond the kinds of resources that were available in identifying the possible forces that led to state formation by the beginning of Moche IV, at ~A.D. 500. Put another way, the north coast of the Moche period does not appear to have been characterized by sufficient valley-to-valley variability of resources for trade, or exchange, in exotics to have led to political integration.

By the time of the Moche, it is also probable that the first large-scale irrigation networks were being constructed in most or all of these valleys. Such networks in modern times consist of two main types of canals—primary ones that bring the water down along the sides of a valley and secondary ones that carry it out onto the valley floor. The primary canals begin at intake points in the upper reaches of a valley and may run along its north and south edges for many kilometers, snaking across the lowermost slopes of desert hills and the mouths of dry washes, or *quebradas*, that lie just above the flatter cultivable valley floor. At various points along these main canals, smaller secondary canals run down off the edge of the desert to distribute the water among the cultivated fields that occupy both sides of the floor between the river and the edge of the desert. Unfortunately, because the valley floors have been occupied more or less continuously in the centuries since the Moche period of occupation, all or most of the secondary canal network has been obliterated, if not totally buried, under aggrading alluvium—a process resulting from the continual introduction of silts carried in to the fields by the canals.

Nevertheless, it is possible to detect and date to the Moche or other periods of occupation sections of ancient primary canals as long as several kilometers (e.g., in the Santa Valley; see Wilson 1988). This is usually because more recent ones have been built on the hillsides a few meters downslope from the ancient ones (thus preserving the older canals), and because prehistoric habitation sites with datable remains such as pottery are found immediately adjacent to the ancient canal. Even where both primary and secondary prehispanic canals have been destroyed, however, their probable (ancient) presence in a given sector of a valley is often strongly indicated by the finding of a continuous distribution of ancient sites dating to one period (e.g., Moche) located along desert hills at the edge of the cultivated area. We return to this point in discussing the settlement pattern of provincial valleys.

Settlement Pattern

To understand the nature of the Moche state and its influence on other north coast valleys, it is useful first to examine the architectural features of the presumed primary center at Cerro Blanco site, which lies along the south desert margin of the Moche Valley 6 kilometers inland from the ocean (Figure 9.15). Until recently the site has been known mainly for its two huge adobe-brick pyra-

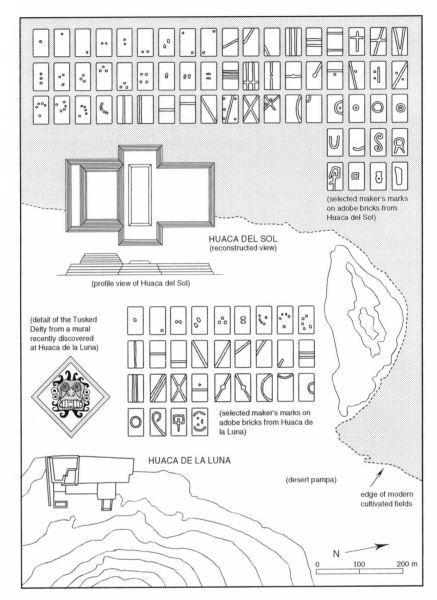

FIGURE 9.15   Plan view of Cerro Blanco site showing the main pyramidal mounds and detail views of a recently discovered mural and adobe bricks with maker's marks found at the two structures. Site plan redrawn and adapted from Stierlin (1984) and adobe bricks from Moseley and Hastings (1975); Tusked Deity traced from a photograph taken by the author.

midal platforms, the Huaca del Sol and the Huaca de la Luna, not as an urban center of substantial size. However, excavations carried out in the 1990s have begun to show that the remains of dense urban habitation extend over at least 1 square kilometer in the area between the two platform mounds. The argument that Cerro Blanco was indeed the capital of the Moche polity is based on comparative data indicating that, in relation to other contemporaneous sites in the Moche sphere of interaction, it is larger in both the area it covers and the monumentality of its mounds. However, since Moche Phase I is barely represented at the site (nor is it significantly present elsewhere in the system for that matter), it appears that Cerro Blanco was begun in Moche Phase II (~A.D. 300–400) with construction continuing on through at least Phase III (~A.D. 400 and 500), that is, to a time dating to a century or less prior to panvalley state formation.

The Huaca del Sol, the larger of the two platform mounds at Cerro Blanco site, has huge basal dimensions of 340 × 160 meters and, at its higher southern end, stands 40 meters tall—making it one of the largest prehispanic adobe brick structures in South America. Alfred Kroeber, an earlier-twentieth-century anthropologist and a renaissance scholar who conducted ethnographic and archaeological research in both North and South America, visited Cerro Blanco site in the 1920s and discovered that the Huaca del Sol had been built using an unusual construction technique that involved placing the bricks in a series of discrete, mud-jointed columns that rise vertically from the pampa right up to its maximum height. In light of this construction technique, Kroeber (1930:61) suggested that the structure had been built as a single unit—rather than being added to by gradual accretion over time—and that the discrete columns may well have been constructed by different social groups, "each contingent of a community building its own wall or column." Later studies by members of the Harvard Chan Chan–Moche Valley project (see Moseley and Hastings 1975) added strength to Kroeber's theory in their finding that the adobe bricks composing each of the columns are imprinted with "maker's marks" that to a large degree are unique from column to column (Figure 9.15). This suggests that separate groups did indeed contribute their labor to the construction of the *huaca* (mound), in return for which they were permitted, if not required, to add a lasting (if hidden) set of symbols that commemorated their work on the project.

If we project a similar Inca model called *mit'a* back on Moche times, the state may also have reciprocally provided food and drink to people whose labor involved a "command performance" they could not easily refuse. In other words, by the time of the Moche the relationship between the state and its citizens had become a coercive one based on asymmetrical power and a sort of "fictive reciprocity," as opposed to the balanced reciprocity that has probably characterized more localized, egalitarian Andean groups such as the Q'ero and Ayllu Kaata for centuries (see Chapter 8).

More recent excavations on the summit of the smaller Huaca de la Luna have shown that similar segmentary construction techniques were used in building it as well. Extensive polychrome-colored murals, most of them beautifully well preserved, have been discovered along the walls that cover the summit of this mound. As indicated in the detail drawing in Figure 9.15, the central figure portrayed in these murals is a tusked deity whose features, like those of Moche stirrup spout vessels, appear to represent a strong continuity of Chavín-derived tradition and ideology. In addition to the murals, the excavations on the Luna summit resulted in the discovery of the skeletal remains of at least thirty-five individuals, the majority of whose necks showed signs of having been traumatically sliced open—a probable indication of the practice on this mound of the Moche sacrifice ceremony, about which we have more to say under ritual.

Although the Huaca del Sol and the Huaca de la Luna are similarly constructed, the excavations carried out to date on their summits suggest that they served somewhat distinct roles as the central architectural features of Cerro Blanco site and the Moche state. Based on the finding of extensive habitation debris across the top and a number of elite burials on the lower terraces, Huaca del Sol appears to have been the residence of higher-status state functionaries. Since it is by far the more impressive and commanding of the two *huacas*, Sol may also have been the scene of various civic-ceremonial activities, including the presentation of prisoners captured in war and tribute from provinces conquered by the Moche and incorporated as part of the expansionist state (e.g., see the scenes that appear to represent these two state activities in Figure 9.16c, d). Luna has some evidence of habitation debris, although in much lesser amounts, and the finding of even fancier tombs and accompanying grave goods on this mound suggests that it may have been the residence of a limited number of royal persons of the highest status. The remains of platforms and courts surrounded by high walls on its summit lend further support to this argument, although the finding of the remains of sacrificed individuals indicates that Luna may well have played a role both as a royal residence and as the supreme focus of the sacrifice ceremony. Both the Huaca del Sol and the Huaca de la Luna, in sum, served multiple functions as places of elite residence, elite burial, state civic and ceremonial activities, and, in the case of Luna, the burial of sacrificial victims.

Mode of Reproduction

The best evidence on population numbers comes from spatially and temporally comprehensive settlement pattern surveys—in other words, from surveys aimed at retrieving all sites dating to all periods over the entire area of each coastal valley. Although the first survey anywhere in the world that attempted such coverage was done during the Virú Valley Project of 1946 (see Willey 1953), no truly comprehensive settlement study was conducted anywhere on the Peruvian coast until the Santa Valley Project of 1979–1980 (see Wilson 1988). Nevertheless, we now have at hand well-published survey data not only from Virú and Santa but also from the Nepeña Valley (see Proulx 1968). Other surveys have been done in several other valleys—for example, by Izumi Shimada in Lambayeque, Glenn Russell and others in Chicama, and me in Casma—but they are either not yet completely published (Casma, Chicama) or were incomplete in their coverage of all periods in the entire coastal valley ecosystem (Lambayeque). In spite of the paucity of demographic data for the entire Moche polity, however, it is fair to assert that the consensus of north coast archaeologists is that population numbers rose steadily upward in each of the ten valleys from Initial Period times on through the end of the Early Intermediate Period (1800 B.C.–A.D. 750). This is certainly the case in the Santa Valley, where the population rose from about five

FIGURE 9.16 Iconography of the Moche state: (a) a battle between Moche and non-Moche warriors; (b) the transport of prisoners across the desert; (c) the presentation of prisoners of war to a state administrator; and (d) the possible presentation of tribute from conquered areas. All illustrations redrawn and adapted from Wilson (1988).

thousand persons in the earliest ceramic periods to at least four times that number by the time of Moche state formation.

If we assume that the 22,000 persons estimated for the Moche period population of the Santa Valley is a reasonable guide to populations elsewhere, then, in relation to David Robinson's (1971) estimate of the irrigable area in Santa (8,643 hectares, as shown in Figure 9.1; but see Wilson 1988 for an estimate of 11,307 hectares), we can proportionally estimate, on the basis of available irrigable land, the optimum population of each of the ten valleys from Piura to Huarmey. In other words, with ~22,000 persons supported by 8,643 hectares of land in Santa, the population estimates for the other nine valleys, from north to south, are the following: for Piura (59,866 hectares), ~152,000 persons; for Lambayeque (52,342 hectares), ~133,000 persons; for Jequetepeque (29,578 hectares), ~75,000 persons; for Chicama (40,371 hectares), ~102,000 persons; for Moche (20,026 hectares), ~51,000 persons; for Virú (16,405 hectares), ~42,000 persons; for Nepeña (8,333 hectares), ~19,000 persons; for Casma (15,729 hectares), ~40,000 persons; and for Huarmey (4,188 hectares), ~11,000 persons. The estimated total population of the Moche sphere would therefore have been in a magnitude of nearly 650,000 persons, which represents a population density of 254 persons per square kilometer on the total of 2,554 square kilometers (255,400 hectares; see Figure 9.1) of irrigable land in the ten valleys.

These figures are very likely to change once comprehensive surveys have been done in all the other valleys. For example, although the data from Casma Valley have not yet been worked up for final publication, my survey found only thirty-one sites dating to the Moche Period—of which twenty-one had habitation extending over a small total area of about 34 hectares. Based on an average of 100 persons per hectare of habitation area, the resulting population estimate is 3,400 persons for the valley, or 36,600 persons *fewer* than the 40,000-persons estimate for Casma based on the Santa data. But Casma, like Huarmey, was located at the relatively remote southern end of the state, and there may well have been reasons that the population was so low there (such as the forced transfer of people to other valleys, similar to the Inca institution of *mitmacuna* colonists, discussed later in this chapter). If so, then the populations of the valleys to the north of Santa may well have been roughly in line with the numbers estimated here. In any case, the main implication of these calculations is that the population of the first multivalley, or interregional, state in South America is likely to have consisted of at least several hundred thousand people, if not over a half million.

Domestic Economy and Social Organization

Based on well-preserved surface remains as well as excavations in habitation sites, the basic Moche residential dwelling was quite similar to the wattle-and-daub *quincha* structures that are still used as rural houses on the north coast today. Such structures consist of four vertically placed wooden poles that support horizontal cross beams and are covered on all four sides and the roof with totora reed matting. Ancient structures were built in this fashion, although they frequently differ from modern ones in having low surrounding rock walls about 50 centimeters high that probably provided additional support. Roofs in both ancient and modern times are usually flat, or slightly sloping at most, since with little or no rainfall there is no need to gable them.

Bawden notes that the dwellings of rural nuclear families in the Moche period consisted of two main spaces: (1) an ample room with surrounding sleeping benches where the entire family slept and, in light of the remains of copper needles, spindles, and other weaving implements, the production of cloth took place; and (2) an adjacent food preparation area in a formal open space at the side of the structure. At the larger sites of Cerro Blanco, Galindo, and Pampa Grande that are thought to have served in succession as the capitals of the Moche state (see Figure 9.14 for their location), residences vary in size and the quality of their artifactual remains, most probably as a function of the different social classes that lived in them.

The superb quality of Moche weavings, pottery vessels, and metallurgy strongly suggests that state artisans were engaged full-time in carrying out their respective craft specialties. For example, the famous scene painted on the interior rim of a flaring funerary bowl (see Figure 9.17a) depicts a number of women engaged in the production of textiles. They employ backstrap looms that hang from the forked poles supporting several larger *quincha* structures, apparently using decorated pottery vessels that hang on nearby walls as models for the designs they are weaving into the textiles. That so many women are shown working together in the scene strongly suggests that weaving was carried out in special areas of the principal sites devoted to that particular craft activity. The scene also depicts several elaborately dressed men, probably representing state overseers, who are seated in formal positions nearby the weavers. Other male functionaries may either be handing food in pottery bowls to the overseers or, alternatively, may be bringing more vessels whose designs will be used as models for later weavings. In any case, the overseers are the only people in the scene who are not engaged in physical labor, and they are shown at least four to five times larger than the women and the other male functionaries. Their relatively much greater size and elaborate garb suggest that they are higher-status individuals and hence that in this weaving scene we are looking not only at the specialized craft production that occurs as states arise but also at the socioeconomic stratification that characterizes them.

Political Economy

Prior to the expansion of the Moche polity beyond the confines of the core area of Moche and Chicama, most of the valleys to the north and south of the central area had probably experienced the rise of chiefdom or state polities at the local-valley level. Although all of the valleys from Santa north to Lambayeque were influenced in varying degrees by the pre-Moche Gallinazo culture, thus suggesting that strong socioeconomic interaction was occurring among them, the relatively high degree of variability in cultural diagnostics—especially including pot-

(a)

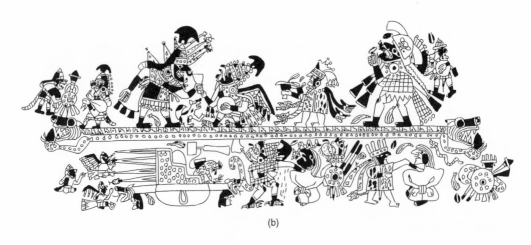

(b)

FIGURE 9.17   Iconography of the Moche state: (a) funerary bowl showing a craft production workshop in which weavers use the designs on pottery vessels as models for the textiles they are producing and (b) a depiction of the Sacrifice Ceremony, in which the throats of bound prisoners are cut (bottom register) and their blood is drunk by a royal priest (top). Redrawn and adapted from Donnan (1978) and Alva and Donnan (1993).

tery styles—suggests that panregional state formation had not yet occurred. Indeed, as we have seen in the discussion of Late Suchimancillo Period Santa earlier in this chapter, the valleys from there to the south appear to have been engaged for almost a millennium in continual conflict with each other. Because presentation of a united front against other valleys was probably the best adaptation to such confrontations, meaning that there was nearly total valleywide sociopolitical integration, we may presume that the ideological correlates of regional conflict included a strong sense of local-valley environmental and cultural integrity. If this was the case in the northernmost valleys as well, then we may presume that all (or most) of the valleys to the north and south of the Moche-Chicama core would have employed military force in attempting to resist incorporation into the developing Moche state.

Such strategies may well have worked for a time, but, for reasons that are not yet clear in the archaeological record, in Moche Phase III the core area began a military expansion into the southern valleys that by Phase IV times had resulted in the total subjugation and incorporation of Virú, Santa, Nepeña, Casma, and Huarmey Valleys into what had become a huge multivalley state. Since comprehensive settlement pattern surveys have not been done in the northernmost valleys specifically to provide data on valleywide systems immediately prior to and contemporaneous with the Moche Middle and Late Periods, it is not yet clear whether the valleys from Jequetepeque north were militarily subjugated by the core area. In the well-studied southern valleys, however, there is excellent evidence for Moche conquest—for example, in the Virú Valley, where there was an abrupt and total replacement of Late Gallinazo architectural and pottery diagnostics by the Moche style (Strong and Evans 1952). However, nowhere do we have better evidence to date of the far-reaching effects of this incorporation than in the Santa Valley. As a comparison of Figures 9.7 and 9.18 shows, from prestate systems characterized by a strong upvalley focus and rampant warfare, the subsistence-settlement system of the Moche period of occupation in Santa changes to a strong middle- and (especially) downvalley focus. Instead of being located in high, remote, defensible positions away from the valley floor, as was the case earlier, sites in Guadalupito (Moche) period Santa are now universally located on or immediately adjacent to the valley floor and there are no fortresses anywhere in the system.

Moreover, for the first (and only) time in the sequence, sites and canals are located all along both the mouth of the Santa Valley proper and the mouth of the Quebrada de Lacramarca, which lies immediately to the south. This suggests that the Moche state completely reordered the subsistence-settlement priorities of the local Santa folk, essentially by requiring them to settle in the most productive downvalley areas where intensive agriculture most probably resulted in significant food surpluses that could be channeled via the provincial center of Huaca Tembladera on to the Moche capital at Cerro Blanco. This center (Figure 9.18 upper) sprawls over a huge area that, at ~1.5 square kilometers, is nearly as large as Cerro Blanco site itself. Much of the site, however, was devoted to agricultural fields, and its habitation area and two main pyramids are much smaller than

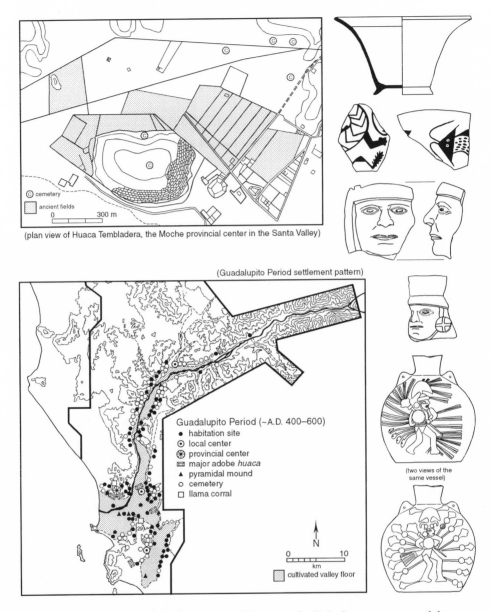

(plan view of Huaca Tembladera, the Moche provincial center in the Santa Valley)

(Guadalupito Period settlement pattern)

Guadalupito Period (~A.D. 400–600)
- ● habitation site
- ⊙ local center
- ✳ provincial center
- ▱ major adobe *huaca*
- ▲ pyramidal mound
- ○ cemetery
- ☐ llama corral

cultivated valley floor

(two views of the same vessel)

FIGURE 9.18   Settlement pattern map of the period of Moche occupation of the lower Santa Valley, a plan view of the principal sites of this period, and drawings of selected pottery diagnostics. Redrawn and adapted from Wilson (1988).

those at the primary center of the state. On the lower slopes at the western end of the hill where the habitation area is located, in direct sight of the main pyramidal mound, my survey found a number of pottery molds used for mass-producing ceramic vessels in the Moche style. Since such molds were essentially absent at the other 204 sites in the system, it seems likely that Huaca Tembladera was the main center of ceramic production in the valley. It is thus not surprising that the survey found a great deal of homogeneity in pottery vessels and decoration from site to site throughout the system, a situation that contrasts sharply with the heterogeneity in the distribution of pottery types in the four prestate systems of the valley. This in turn suggests that, however much the prestate systems had been integrated at the valleywide level in their continuing attempts to resist outside military encroachment, the Moche were able to integrate settlements effectively and tightly into their polity in a way heretofore unknown in this area of the north coast.

In light of the columns with maker's-marked adobe bricks at Cerro Blanco, it is highly significant that the survey found adobes with similar marks on them on the main pyramidal mound at Huaca Tembladera. In addition, similar to the findings at the Huaca del Sol, the survey found habitation debris on the summit of the principal mound and on terraces along its sides. Among other ancient roads that still remain well preserved on the site, over fourteen hundred years since their construction, is an elevated causeway that was designed to approach the main mound directly out of the desert to the northeast. Since it then proceeds to climb via a ramp in zigzag fashion directly up to the summit of the main mound, it is not difficult to imagine that, similar to the main *huacas* at Cerro Blanco, Moche administrators and other elite lived atop both of the Huaca Tembladera mounds, carrying out state activities from the heights overlooking the rest of the provincial center. In sum, in addition to reorganizing the entire subsistence-settlement system of Santa, the Moche state imposed its own canons of pottery making, pyramid construction, and administrative policies on a system that had formerly been characterized by regional autonomy and a fierce resistance to such outside control over its local environment and sociopolitical affairs.

The iconography on the Moche pottery vessels depicted in Figure 9.16 can be utilized to hypothesize about the nature of the processes that led to the incorporation of provincial valleys into South America's first large-scale state. In Figure 9.16a we see a number of fancily garbed Moche warriors—on the right in the upper register and on the left in lower—engaged in hand-to-hand combat with less well-dressed warriors, who, presumably, are from a north coast valley outside the core area. The prickly-pear cactus (*Opuntia* sp.) and the epiphytic dune-clinging plant *Tillandsia* shown in the scene indicate that this battle occurred somewhere out in the intervalley desert away from the area of cultivation. Given nearly a millennium of resistance to military encroachment in valleys such as Santa, it is not hard to imagine that what we are viewing here is another attempt by a valley to keep outsiders from taking it over. In Figure 9.16b, a scene painted on the inside rim of a flaring funerary vessel from the Santa Valley area, the Moche army has overcome a group of warriors who, in defeat, have had their clothing removed and have been tied with ropes. The prisoners are being escorted across the desert, as indicated by low cactus-covered hills in the background.

Their probable destination is shown in the scene in Figure 9.16c, already discussed as we considered the probability that elite Moche administrators lived and carried out state activities on top of the main pyramidal mounds at Cerro Blanco site. In the scene prisoners of two statuses (the higher-status ones being carried in litters) are presented to a state administrator who sits under a low *quincha* structure on the summit of a pyramidal platform. Other prisoners are shown consulting with Moche women (shamans?) in another structure, and yet others are shown dead or dying on the sandy plain in front of the platform. Finally, in Figure 9.16d we see elaborately garbed individuals and llamas laden with various goods (some of which "float" in the air immediately above) ascending a stairway to the summit of a platform to be presented to a state administrator who, similar to the preceding scene, is seated inside a small roofed structure. Given the evidence from valleys such as Santa and Virú, we may hypothesize that this scene depicts the payment of tribute to the Moche polity by the people of a conquered province.

With a thousand-year period of prestate warfare in the southern valleys and the likelihood that the Moche polity achieved its ends by warfare, conquest, and coercive control over provincial populations, it is somewhat ironic to note that in the process it created a climate of panvalley peace on the Peruvian north coast. In other words, it brought about what I (Wilson 1988) have elsewhere called a *Pax Moche* similar to the *Pax Romana* created by the rise of the Roman Empire in the Old World. In this context intervalley socioeconomic interaction and goodwill were probably more intense than they ever had been before.

But in spite of the "momentary" panvalley integration, each valley was separated by a day's walk or more from its neighbors, and in spite of the Moche attempt to subvert local-valley autonomy, an ideology of local-valley ecosystemic and sociopolitical integrity most likely persevered through the period of integration. In this environmental and ideological context, then, we can see the inevitability of the ultimate disintegration of the state. I therefore take issue with Bawden's (1996) structuralist assertion that the state fell apart because of the internal "contradictions" brought about by its failure to create complex administrative controls and a coercive infrastructure, focusing instead, in his opinion, merely on the construction of an ideology that supported a ritually powerful elite. In light of the material-world evidence from Santa Valley, at least, the state was nearly 100 percent effective in coercing local valley populations to its own ends and in putting an administrative structure in place to ensure the continuity of these ends. That is, it completely altered settlement locations to maximize the production of food surpluses and established a valleywide control hierarchy consisting of the provincial center at Huaca Tembladera and a series of evenly distributed lower-level rural centers (Figure 9.18 lower).

Ritual, Leadership, and State Ideology

In spite of these arguments, however, there is no question that Bawden is correct in asserting that the Moche created a powerful ideology and related set of rituals that permeated the state from the far northern valleys to at least the Nepeña Valley in the south. At Pañamarca site in this last valley, for example, the Moche constructed one of the largest adobe pyramidal mounds ever built there and placed on it a series of large polychrome murals, one of which depicts a scene that includes an elaborately dressed priest carrying an offering cup, several priestly attendants carrying similar cups and dressed in feline masks, a warrior capturing a prisoner and getting set to use a whip on him, and several prisoners bound with ropes (see Bonavía 1985). The entire scene is flanked prominently by large club-and-shield drawings that seem to emphasize further the element of war in Moche iconography. When we put all the components of the scene together, it is now clear that prisoners taken in war were not just sacrificed, as discussed earlier, but also that their blood was taken from their slit throats by attendants to be handed to priestly specialists as offerings in the Moche sacrifice ceremony.

My survey found a similarly large mural at El Castillo site, Santa Valley (located on the valley floor immediately to the east of Huaca Tembladera; see Figure 9.18), although all that it depicted was a series of club-and-shield motifs. Since murals like those in Nepeña and Santa were highly visible to anyone visiting Moche centers, their symbolic message probably included a plainly advertised statement about (1) the fait accompli of the Moche conquest of the valley, (2) the imposition of the sacrifice ceremony on the local system, and (3) the danger of military reprisal should the valley's inhabitants harbor thoughts of engaging in rebellion against the state.

The most elaborate depiction of the Moche sacrifice ceremony is the one shown in Figure 9.17b. Standing at left center on a platform decorated at each end with feline heads is the central figure in the scene. He has been called the Warrior Priest by archaeologists because he is wearing the typical military gear shown on warriors in battle scenes—gear that includes both a metal backflap and a conical helmet crowned with an inverted sacrificial knife called a *tumi* (e.g., compare to Figure 9.16a, b). At the same time, he is getting set to drink from a cup proffered to him by an attendant, who, because of the mask he is wearing, is called the Bird Priest. Standing immediately behind the two men is a priestess who is holding a cup and whose long braids are tipped with snake heads. To her right, at the far end of the upper register, is yet another priest from whose feathered helmet emanates an anthropomorphized club-and-shield motif (note the human legs).

In the lower register are two nude bound prisoners together with club-and-shield bundles that probably represent their captured war gear. The prisoner at the right is about to have his throat cut by a priestly attendant, while blood already flows in copious amounts from the throat of the prisoner at the left and will soon be picked up by the cup shown in the right hand of the attendant who has sacrificed him. At the left end of the lower register is a parked litter, probably belonging to the Warrior Priest, the handles of which are decorated with snake heads and severed trophy heads presumably taken in war. It takes but a slight leap of the imagination to conclude that the Warrior Priest is drinking the blood of the war captives. Given that floating here and there in the scene are depictions of the ulluchu fruit, a plant with known anticoagulant properties, Alva and Donnan (1993) argue that the juice of this plant was added to the sacrificial cups to keep the blood from coagulating before it was drunk by the main priest.

As mentioned earlier, at Sipán site in the Lambayeque Valley archaeological evidence has been found indicating that such state ritual functionaries actually existed. The pyramid complex at Sipán lies in the midst of cultivated fields on the south side of the valley, a little over 30 kilometers inland from the ocean. Because some annual rain occurs in the far northern valleys, the mud-brick structures here have been heavily eroded on their outermost surfaces, which gives them a decidedly unpromising appearance when we consider the well-preserved and spectacularly furnished elite tombs that at least one of them—the platform in the left foreground in Figure 9.19c—is now known to have contained deep in its interior. The first intact tomb found and scientifically excavated by Alva and Meneses's team is Tomb I, the tomb of the so-called Lord of Sipán (see the location and cutaway views in Figure 9.19a, b).

To begin the excavations, the team focused on a 10 × 10-meter area on the summit that, by sheer chance, turned out to be more than just a little productive. Within a few centimeters below the surface, for example, team members came upon a small rectangular chamber measuring 3 × 2 meters in area that contained what may be the largest offering of prehispanic vessels ever found in the New World. It consisted of a cache of 1,137 human effigy vessels that included depictions of warriors holding clubs and shields, nude prisoners with ropes tied around their necks, musicians with drums, and seated figures wearing beaded chest ornaments. Associated with this offering was the skeleton of a man who probably had been sacrificed to accompany it. Not far below, the excavators found the remains of a man wrapped in a cotton shroud (upper right in Figure 9.19) both of whose feet were missing—indicating perhaps that he was sacrificed and placed there to guard the main tomb.

Below him lay the occupants of the main part of the tomb, including the Lord of Sipán himself, whose cane coffin had essentially decomposed except for eight clusters of copper straps (four on top and four on the bottom) that had originally held the coffin together (Figure 9.19b). The drawing of the lord's body in the figure does little justice to the wealth of grave goods and ornaments that accompanied him (for colored photographs and detailed descriptions, see especially Alva 1989; Alva and Donnan 1993). Among many other items, they include

- three sets of exquisitely crafted gold-and-turquoise ear ornaments
- several gold nose ornaments
- three sets of gold-bead necklaces (double-strung through dual perforations to keep them facing forward while worn around the lord's neck)
- a gold mask placed over the lord's face
- bracelets of turquoise, shell, and gold
- large gold and silver scepters (both of which depicted military paraphernalia, battle scenes, and the treatment of prisoners)
- a set of silver sandals on the lord's feet
- a large gold headdress
- gilded copper bells

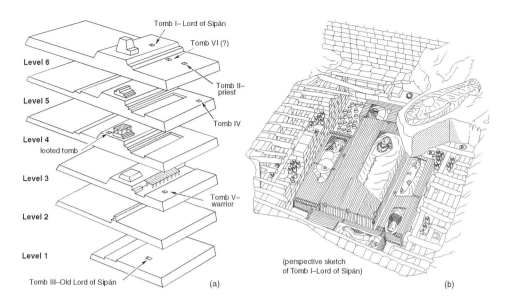

Tomb I– Lord of Sipán
Tomb VI (?)
Level 6
Tomb II–priest
Level 5
Tomb IV
Level 4
looted tomb
Level 3
Tomb V–warrior
Level 2
Level 1
Tomb III–Old Lord of Sipán
(a)

(perspective sketch of Tomb I–Lord of Sipán)
(b)

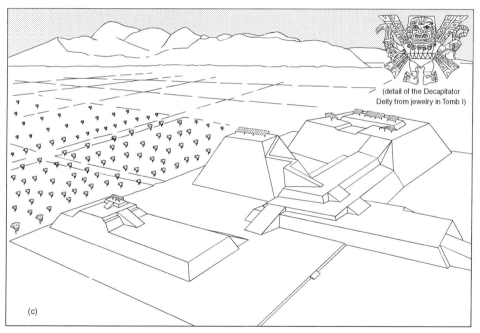

(detail of the Decapitator Deity from jewelry in Tomb I)

(c)

FIGURE 9.19   Perspective reconstruction views of Sipán showing (a) the sequence of construction and placement of the royal tombs in the excavated mound; (b) the tomb of the Lord of Sipán; and (c) the principal mounds, including the one in the left foreground, where Alva conducted his excavations. Figure in (a) from Alva (1988), (b) from Schuster (1992), and (c) redrawn and adapted from Alva and Donnan (1993); Decapitator Deity inset drawn from a photograph in Alva and Donnan (1993).

- gold and silver backflaps similar to those depicted iconographically on pottery vessels showing warriors, battles, and the sacrifice ceremony.

Both the copper bells and the backflaps were decorated with the figure of the Decapitator Deity, who holds a sacrificial *tumi* knife in his left hand and a severed human head in his right and whose dual canine teeth recall Chavín iconography (Figure 9.19c upper right).

The remainder of the contents of the tomb include the following (some of which are shown, in Figure 9.19b): (1) hundreds of crudely produced mold-made pottery vessels; (2) two sacrificed llamas, one on each side of the foot of the Lord of Sipán's cane coffin (not shown in the figure); (3) the body of a small child perhaps ten years of age seated with its back against the side of the tomb wall (not shown); and (4) five additional coffins containing a man dressed as a warrior, with one of his feet missing, located at the lord's right; the body of another man accompanied by a dog, located at his left; two women in separate coffins, lying at the head of the lord; and a woman whose coffin lay on the feet of the small boy, at the foot of the main coffin. All of the women represent secondary burials taken from elsewhere rather than individuals sacrificed at the death of the Lord of Sipán.

The accouterments and offerings placed in his coffin seem to suggest that this individual was none other than one of the Warrior Priests depicted in the left-central upper register in the sacrifice scene discussed previously. Other lesser tombs were found at deeper levels in the platform mound, and since then Donnan has excavated the tomb of a woman at San José de Moro, in the Jequetepeque Valley to the south, who was accompanied by all of the clothing and gear worn by the priestess in the sacrifice ceremony scene.

In sum, the Sipán finds, in combination with over seventy-five years of scientific archaeological work, have demonstrated fairly clearly that the Moche culture represents a multivalley conquest polity that itself grew out of prior evolutionary trends, including the development of the complex of Andean cultigens, population growth, and the associated rise on this infrastructural base of local-level chiefdoms and states. Although much more corroborative research needs to be done, we can hypothesize that both the rise and collapse of Andean multivalley states such as Moche were predictable outcomes of the processes we have focused on in this and earlier chapters. These processes include

- the tendency of populations to grow
- the corresponding ability of Andean agriculturists to adapt by developing new means of intensifying their subsistence base
- continuing population growth that in some valleys led to nutritional pressure in light of unpredictable and/or limited water regimes
- the eventual conquest, as populations and local-valley complexity developed further, by an alliance of valleys (Moche-Chicama) of other valleys to the north and south, perhaps as a means of mitigating these local pressures

- effective incorporation for a time of provincial populations into the newly enlarged polity via the development of both an effective state infrastructure and a corresponding state-oriented ideology
- the eventual collapse of the multivalley polity, since such integration seems bound to have broken down in a context where people in each local valley defined themselves, over the long term, more as a singular "inviolate" ecosystemic entity than as a subordinate province in a state whose ultimate material goals and ideology did not mesh with their own.

A Summary Model

Figure 9.20 includes both textual and graphic systems-hierarchical models of the Moche state, together with a map of the main valleys included within it. The textual model at the top summarizes the main descriptive data that can be inferred, on the basis of archaeological research, about the nature of state policy at the provincial level. With settlement pattern at the level of the infrastructure, two kinds of evidence are available indicating the material changes that occurred as the state expanded into a valley: first, the construction of monuments featuring Moche diagnostics (characteristic of nearly all the provincial valleys) and, second, abrupt changes in the settlement pattern in relation to the prestate periods (e.g., the Santa Valley). Based on changes in the settlement pattern (e.g., Santa) and the construction of Moche period canals, inferences can be made, in turn, about state policy related to the maximization of agricultural production. At the level of structure we can make a number of inferences about the political economy based on archaeological evidence that, for example, includes the imposition of *mit'a*-type labor (as evidenced by the construction of monuments using adobe bricks with maker's marks) and the mass production of pottery (as evidenced by the appearance of standardized Moche forms and motifs). The appearance of various statuses in the iconography on murals and pottery vessels strongly suggests the rise of the pronounced social stratification that follows state formation. At the level of ritual, in the superstructure, that same iconography supports the inference that the Sacrifice Ceremony was imposed on the provincial systems of the state. Finally, at the highest-order level of state ideology, the material remains of the state (from pyramid construction and settlement patterns through the iconography on various state media, including murals and pottery) suggest that it attempted to effect changes in the ideology of its subjects at the local, provincial level—or, at the very least, attempted to "broadcast" the nature of that ideology by displaying its symbols in a prominent way here and there throughout the conquered provincial system.

The graphic model in Figure 9.20 (middle) attempts to indicate systemically just how complex the state was in relation even to the provincial polities that had preceded it in many north coast valleys. At the time of the state's inception, the Moche successfully imposed some, if not most, of the features of their own local-valley adaptive system on the conquered areas. If we recall theoretical arguments made by Flannery (see 1972), the Moche elite was thus *promoting* itself to

402

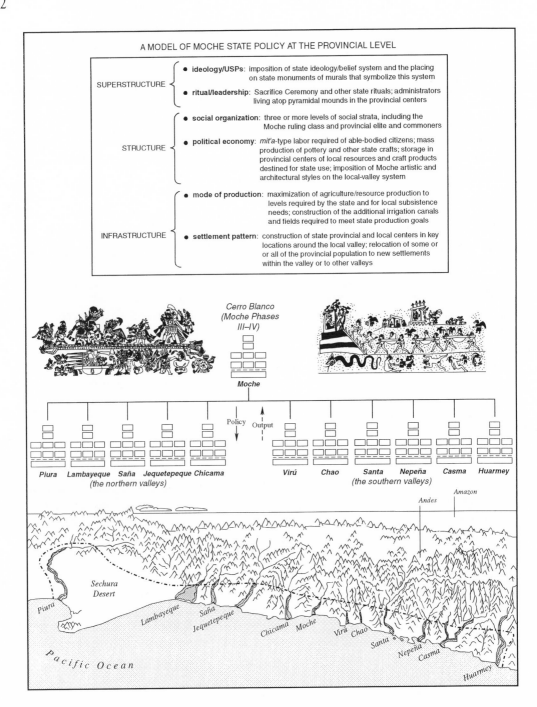

FIGURE 9.20 Systems-hierarchical models of Moche state policy at the provincial level (top) and of the political control hierarchy of the state (middle), accompanied by a perspective map of the north coast area showing the principal valleys encompassed within the state.

a paramount level in the newly created hierarchy—with the elite and Moche Valley at the top and everyone else at the bottom. However, as time went on, the elite must have had to adapt to the real-world problems posed by its own creation. In other words, having founded an extensive multivalley polity—a unique form heretofore unseen in this part of South America—the Moche leaders probably also had to create new strategies of integration on an equally unprecedented scale. But in spite of the imposition of a state ideology as a means of controlling and maintaining their creation, we can be reasonably certain that they did not root out completely, if at all, the local (prestate) ideologies that would have continually provoked behaviors (such as insurrection) guaranteed to return to each valley its ecosystemic integrity.

THE INCA

In contrast to the Moche, who have achieved their identity as a prehistoric culture only in the past seventy-five years or so, the Inca have been known since "history" began with the arrival of their conqueror, the Spaniard Pizarro, in A.D. 1532. Indeed, because of the richly detailed Spanish documentary sources and nearly a century of scientific archaeology, we probably know more about this prehistoric state than about any other ancient polity on the continent. Even a minimally adequate list of the principal recent publications on the Inca state is therefore longer than a corresponding one for the Moche. Among the most outstanding papers on the Inca, and one that still provides a useful and accurate summary of the materials from the Spanish documentary sources, is Rowe's "Inca Culture at the Time of the Spanish Conquest" (1963). Among the better general monographs written on Inca culture and statecraft since Rowe's paper was published are Burr Cartwright Brundage's *Empire of the Inca* (1963) and *Lords of Cuzco* (1967), Ann Kendall's *Everyday Life of the Incas* (1973), and Thomas Patterson's *The Inca Empire* (1991). In part as a means of redressing the Cuzco-specific focus of much of the ethnohistoric and general literature, studies have been increasingly carried out at the provincial level in an attempt to throw light on the actual relationship of local populations to the empire as opposed to the official Inca emic regarding the empire's effect on these populations. The three most outstanding studies from this provincial perspective are Craig Morris and Donald Thompson's *Huánuco Pampa* (1985), Brian Bauer's *The Development of the Inca State* (1992), and Ramiro Matos Mendieta's *Pumpú* (1994).

As those who have visited the Andes and Cuzco know, Inca culture is as renowned for the stunning beauty of its architecture as it is for its statecraft and the extent of its empire. In the twentieth century only one study has truly captured the essence of its buildings and stonework: *Inca Architecture*, by Graziano Gasparini and Luise Margolies (1980). The Inca are also equally well known for their road system, which, although preceded by complex earlier networks in places such as the Peruvian north coast, reached so extensively throughout the 1,835,000-square-kilometer area of the empire that it represents an engineering achievement perhaps unequaled anywhere else in the world, except for the Great Wall of China. The outstanding student of the road system and the settlements along it, John Hyslop, wrote two books, *The Inka Road System* (1984) and *Inka Settlement Planning* (1990), culminating some years of study and travel throughout the Andes. His recent death has robbed us all too prematurely of the benefits of his dedication and insights about the communications infrastructure of the Inca state. Among the key recent publications on the highly complex economic and social organization of the Inca are John Murra's *La organización económica del estado inca* (1978), R. Tom Zuidema's *Inca Civilization in Cuzco* (1986), and Terry LeVine's *Inka Storage Systems* (1992).

Probably the "hottest" new topic in Inca studies, from the perspective of many archaeologists and the informed lay public alike, is the studies carried out by Johann Reinhard, and others, of Inca high-altitude burial sites where sacrificial children, called *capac hucha,* were offered up to the mountain deities. To date only a few publications have appeared on this research, including two papers published by Reinhard in *National Geographic*—"Sacred Peaks of the Andes" (1992) and "Peru's Ice Maidens" (1996)—and one by Colin McEwan and Maarten Van de Guchte, "Ancestral Time and Sacred Space in Inka State Ritual" (1992).

Before beginning our treatment of the Inca, let me mention the key sixteenth- and seventeenth-century Spanish documentary sources, most of them currently available in English translation, that provide a wealth of eyewitness data on the rich complexity of Inca culture and daily life. These sources include Inca Garcilaso de la Vega's *Royal Commentaries of the Incas and General History of Peru* (1966 [1609, 1616–1617]), Pedro de Cieza de León's *The Incas of Pedro Cieza de León* (1959 [1553]), Father Bernabé Cobo's *History of the Inca Empire* (1979 [1653]) and *Inca Religion and Customs* (1990 [1653]), Juan de Betanzos's *Narrative of the Incas* (1996 [1557]), Felipe Guamán Poma de Ayala's *Letter to a King* (1978 [1567–1615]), and Joan de Santa Cruz Pachacuti Yamqui Salcamaygua's *Relación de antigüedades deste reyno del Piru* (Pachacuti Yamqui Salcamaygua 1993 [1613]).

Ethnohistorical Background and Chronology

The development of Inca cultural identity and the rise of empire are thought to have occurred in the relatively brief time between A.D. 1200 and 1532, the date of the Spanish Conquest of the Inca state. This 332-year period is, in turn, usually divided into Early Inca (A.D. 1200–1438) and Late Inca (1438–1532). The Early period begins with the legendary founding of the capital city of Cuzco by Manco Capac. Arriving there with his wife, Mama Ocllo, from their origin spot on the Island of the Sun in Lake Titicaca (or, in an alternative myth, from a cave near Paccaritampu in the Cuzco area), Manco tested the richness of the soil with a golden rod as the deity Viracocha had instructed him to do. Seeing that the rod sank rapidly as Viracocha had prescribed, Manco Capac founded Cuzco on the spot.

The other eight emperors who succeeded him during the rest of the Early period are equally obscured in the mists of Inca legend, although as time goes on they become increasingly acceptable as historical figures. According to the myths, the second, third, and fourth emperors—Sinchi Roca, Lloqui Yupanqui, and Mayta Capac—are not credited with any state-building at all. Cuzco, we thus may presume, was at this time a society of no greater complexity than a localized chiefdom. Following this, during the reigns of the fifth, sixth, and seventh emperors—Capac Yupanqui, Inca Roca, and Yahuar Huacac—the Inca began a series of conquests in the region immediately surrounding Cuzco. Even by this point, however, they still had not created a polity any larger than the area encompassed within the province of Cuzco (see Figure 9.21).

By the end of the Early period Cuzco was merely one of a series of local kingdoms in the area, all of whom were sizing each other up for conquest in a context that, from a materialist point of view, fairly reeks of local population growth and pressure similar to what we found in relation to the Moche. To ensure survival in this bellicose milieu, the eighth emperor, Viracocha Inca, formed an alliance with nearby Anta and the neighboring Quechua kingdom, with the aim of presenting a united posture against their traditional enemies, the Chanca, whose kingdom lay to the west. By the end of his reign the Incas not only had conquered the Chanca but also found themselves at the head of a territory that included all the other kingdoms in the area immediately around Cuzco. They had become, in other words, a regional state of the kind we have seen in the case of the earlier Moche. Given their success at state-building beyond the local level of Cuzco, it is not surprising that Viracocha Inca was the first ruler to title himself Sapa Inca, or Supreme Inca (see the detail drawing in Figure 9.21).

The Late period, which marks the beginning of empire, starts with the reign of Viracocha's son, Pachacuti (Earth Shaker, or Cataclysm), in A.D. 1438. However, according to the ethnohistoric sources, Pachacuti himself stayed home in Cuzco developing the policies that would ensure effective incorporation of conquered provincial areas into the growing empire, while his own son, Topa Inca, carried out the actual campaigns that led to the extension of Inca territory beyond the relatively narrow confines of the southern part of what is now Peru. Topa Inca began by conquering north in the Andean highlands toward Ecuador, returning from there to conquer all of the north and central coast as far south as the Lurín Valley; next he conquered the remaining principal coastal valleys between Mala and Nasca; then he carried out a successful military campaign against the Colla and the Lupaqa kingdoms of the Lake Titicaca region; and, finally, he extended Inca control farther south in Bolivia as well as into Chile to the Maule River.

By the time Topa Inca himself became the Sapa Inca around A.D. 1471, the state had grown in three short decades from a petty local state to an empire of unprecedented size. After Topa Inca's death in 1493 his son, Huayna Capac, succeeded him and extended the empire north to the border between modern Ecuador and Colombia. Huayna Capac contracted a strange pestilential disease in 1525 (possibly smallpox, introduced to South America when Christopher Columbus made landfall in the early 1500s on the Colombian coast) and died so suddenly that he was unable to name his successor. As a result, during the ensuing seven years before the arrival of the Spaniards, the empire was torn by civil

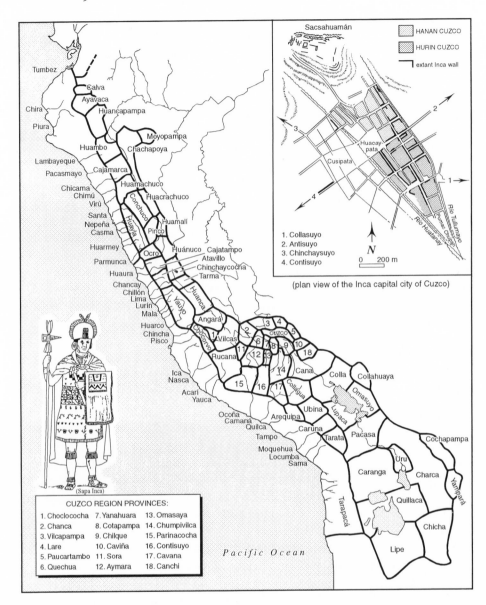

FIGURE 9.21 Central Andean provinces of the Inca state and a plan view of the capital city of Cuzco. Redrawn and adapted from illustrations in Rowe (1963), Gasparini and Margolies (1980), and Kauffman Doig (1978).

war as his two sons, Huascar (Cuzco faction) and Atahuallpa (Quito faction), fought for the imperial supremacy previously enjoyed by their father and his immediate predecessors. Although Atahuallpa was winning the war by the time of Pizarro's arrival in 1532, the chaotic political situation undoubtedly enhanced the ability of a relative handful of European outsiders to turn it to their own advantage. In any event, the New World's largest prehistoric empire was thus essentially created and consolidated in the brief period of eighty-seven years, from A.D. 1438 to 1525.

At its maximum the empire stretched for an astonishing 4,300 kilometers from north to south, although it measured an average of only 350 kilometers wide, since the Inca never were able to incorporate the environmentally "foreign" Amazon that bordered the empire along its entire eastern side. Nonetheless, to have gained military and political control over an area of 1,835,000 square kilometers was no small achievement, since at the empire's height it was larger than any single modern Andean nation-state from Chile to Colombia. Although the recent literature has increasingly attributed aspects of Inca statecraft to Andean predecessors (e.g., the probable development of *mit'a* labor control as early as the Moche and certainly no later than the Chimú and road-settlement networks in both the Andes and on the coast), much of the Inca's achievement appears almost de novo on the Andean scene.

This is not to suggest, however, that there were not ample evolutionary-ecological precedents for the rise of an extensive imperial system. These included, for example, the much earlier development of hunter-gatherer adaptations in the Andes; the rise of population numbers; the subsequent development of agriculture as an adaptive response; a corresponding further rise in population; and, ultimately, the development of states such as the Moche (not to mention the Nazca, the Wari, the Tiwanaku, and the Chimú) whose architectural achievements, road networks, and principles of corporate labor organization provided part of the material and nonmaterial bases that were incorporated into the Inca system.

The Imperial Inca System

Physical Environment

At various earlier points I have dealt in detail with the highly variable and challenging physical environment contained within the territorial boundaries of the Inca state—including, in Chapter 3, the overall Andean sierra and coastal environment and, in Chapter 8 and the beginning of this chapter, a detailed consideration of the sierra and coastal sectors of the Central Andes. It is unnecessary to summarize those discussions here, although the reader who again peruses the relevant sections will find grounds for astonishment at the Inca achievement in incorporating such a vast and topographically rugged environment into their empire. Even today, aside from a few modern travelers, probably very few people have traveled by land in one fell swoop from the southernmost part of the empire, at the Maule River in central Chile, to the northernmost part, which lies at the Ancasmayo River on the border between Colombia and Ecuador.

To get a sense of what this sort of trip might have been like on foot, as it was in prehistoric times for the Inca, one should read *Vagabonding Down the Andes,* written by Harry Franck and published in 1917. Having graduated from the University of Michigan earlier in the century, around the time that Hiram Bingham discovered the fabled Inca site of Machu Picchu, Franck traveled by steamship to

Panama, where he worked for a time in the canal zone. Shortly after that he traveled by ship to the port of Cartagena and by train up to Bogotá, in the central Colombian highlands, from whence he proceeded to walk 1,900 kilometers through the Andes of southern Colombia, Ecuador, and northern Peru until he reached Cerro de Pasco, a sierra mining camp located to the northeast of Lima. After a short trip by train from Cerro de Pasco to Huancavelica, Franck walked an additional 350 kilometers through the mountains to Cuzco. Suffering at times from illnesses contracted along the way and often harboring a highly misanthropic attitude toward the people he encountered on the trail, Franck nevertheless was awestruck by the remains of the Inca road system and sites that he saw on his journey. Eventually, after taking various forms of land transportation from Cuzco to Cochabamba, a large town in the central Bolivian highlands, Franck walked across the rest of Bolivia to the border with Paraguay, before proceeding by bus on down to Buenos Aires.

But to get a real sense of the Inca achievement in linking the vast area from northwestern Argentina to Colombia, one should read Franck's book accompanied by large-scale topographic maps (e.g., the 1:1,000,000-scale Operational Navigation Charts). It then becomes possible to proceed step by arduous step with him over the many months his trip took to complete—across vast sections of grassy *punas* and frequent plunges via tortuous trails hundreds of meters down one side of gorges nearly as deep as the Grand Canyon before a climb back up the other side to proceed on with his journey. It is then, and only then, that one begins to appreciate the relatively much greater efficiency and speed the Incas achieved in getting messages by *chasqui* couriers, for example, from Cuzco to Quito in a mere fourteen days or so—a long trip that, although aided by the Inca road system, involved the couriers climbing continually up and down between frigid *punas* and jungle-filled canyons, not to mention crossing high over rivers on treacherously swinging grass-rope suspension bridges. The total distance from Cuzco to Quito is some 1,850 kilometers, and yet it still represents a mere 45 percent of the 4,300-kilometer length of the empire.

Mode of Production

Like the subsistence systems of more localized Andean groups before and since, Inca subsistence in the sierra was based on the practice of agriculture and pastoralism at the two main altitudinal levels of the *quechua* and the *puna*. Although maize had earlier been a staple crop of most Andeans, who gained access to it either through the inclusion of lower-elevation lands within their boundaries or through trade, in the Inca state it became a high-status food related both to religion and to the elite. Because of this twofold importance, it was a major state policy to extend the amount of lands in the *quechua* zone to the maximum possible in order to ensure adequate supplies of maize. For example, in the steep Urubamba canyon to the north of Cuzco additional agricultural land was created essentially through the "flattening" of the hill slopes in the form of huge rock-faced terrace systems that extended for hundreds of meters up and down both sides of the canyon walls.

These systems, many of which still remain in an excellent state of preservation throughout various parts of the Andes, were built by *mit'a* laborers, or able-bodied individuals between the ages of twenty and fifty who, on a yearly basis, were required to leave their own local communities and carry out state projects for a relatively brief period of time. Each terrace face itself consisted of a well-constructed rock wall that leaned slightly inward toward the hill slope. The interior side of the wall was then filled in its lower part with rock rubble and in its upper part with good soil. As with terracing systems elsewhere in the world, once such a project was completed, steeper mountainsides of little economic value were transformed into an extensive series of juxtaposed horizontal units that, with intensive additional labor effort including the addition of fertilizer and canal building, could be made to produce crops at continuously higher levels.

Similar to the coastal irrigation networks, the Inca built primary canals that channeled water from intake points located many kilometers upstream from the fields to be irrigated. Since nearly horizontal gradients were maintained in constructing each canal, by the time it reached the fields located farther down the canyon, the canal usually lay hundreds of meters above the valley bottom itself and in this fashion could be used to irrigate the huge expanses of terraced fields that lay between it and the river far below. The construction of rock-faced terraces and irrigation canals, in combination with an ample supply of nutrient-rich runoff during the rainy season, thus transformed the *quechua* zone in many parts of the Andes into breadbaskets whose productivity compared favorably with that of the coastal valleys.

The state subsistence system in the higher *puna* elevations was focused on camelid pastoralism and the cultivation of the Andean complex of tubers, thus continuing more or less unchanged a tradition that had begun with the rise of domestication centuries earlier. However, the difference from earlier times was that the Inca now required able-bodied citizens to provide *mit'a* labor on state lands at this altitudinal level as well. In addition, the chewing of coca leaves in the time-honored Andean tradition came under state control. Coca was grown in the humid *montaña*, on the eastern edge of the Andes, and its use was now controlled by the state. Elite folks were permitted to use it, as were elderly citizens, and all who chewed it carried the leaves in a small textile bag called a *chuspa*. The state also expropriated some land from local communities to be used in support of the official state religion, focused on the sun god Inti, and of various governmental activities. The latter included the provision of food to *mit'a* labor groups, the army, and others such as the *aqllacuna* women who served the state in perpetuity. As in the case of the road system, the use of which was prohibited to anyone not involved in state business, the Inca carefully controlled fields set aside to support religion and the state by measuring the land in units called *topos*, setting up boundary markers, estimating the size of the harvest, and storing it for later use in groups of small rock-walled chambers called *collca*.

Settlement Pattern

The population of Cuzco (Figure 9.21) is estimated to have been about one hundred thousand persons at the time of the Spanish Conquest in 1532, making it the largest city anywhere in South America, even though it covered a relatively small area of about 5 square kilometers. It was divided into two main sectors: (1) a central sector covering about 40 hectares that lay between two canalized rivers, the Río Huatanay and the Río Tullumayo, and contained the houses of Inca royalty and priests as well as important religious structures such as the *Qori Cancha*, the ideological heart of the empire; and (2) a larger outlying sector comprising a dozen residential districts that housed Incas "by birth," or people who traced their heritage back to the founding of the state, and elite representatives of the conquered provinces who were required to spend at least four months each year living in the capital. The central sector of Cuzco itself was further divided into two "halves," or moieties, Hanan Cuzco (Upper Cuzco) and Hurin Cuzco (Lower Cuzco), each of which was associated with five of the ten royal *ayllus*, or *panacas*, of the Inca elite. Each *panaca* in Hanan Cuzco, in turn, was paired with one of the *panacas* in Hurin Cuzco, producing a dyadically based structure whose complexity probably far exceeded that of the Amazonian Bororo discussed in Chapter 6.

The public heart of the city was the Huacaypata ("Wailing Terrace") (Figure 9.21), an immense plaza that covered an area measuring about 175 × 175 meters, or slightly over 3 hectares. The most important ceremonies of the Inca state were held here, and on such occasions the mummified bodies of deceased Inca rulers were brought to the Huacaypata both to witness these events and to be revered as the empire's most sacred human relics. According to the chroniclers, the earth dug up from this plaza as it was being built was carried out to the four corners of the empire to be revered by people in all of the provinces. The plaza was then covered deeply with sand brought from the beaches of the Pacific Ocean, located 400 kilometers to the west, in which offerings of gold and silver artifacts were buried during the ceremonies. Among the huge stone-walled compounds that faced the main plaza was the Amarucancha ("Serpent Enclosure"). Inside its walls was the Aqllahuasi, or the "House of the Chosen Women." Its inhabitants, called *aqllacuna*, were chaste women who served the Inca state in perpetuity by carrying out important ritually related craft activities such as the production of *chicha*, the sacred maize beer used to grease social wheels on important state occasions, and textiles, used, among other things, to reward those who had loyally served the state in all its complex activities.

As shown in the plan view of Cuzco in Figure 9.21, the entire city contained between the Huatanay and Tullumayo Rivers was laid out in the shape of a puma whose belly and paws lay along the southwest side of the central sector and whose head was formed by the great military-religious structure of Sacsahuamán located high above the city directly to its northwest. Here the Inca rulers constructed a three-tiered set of terraces composed of diorite porphyry stones from a quarry located near the site. Carved in polygonal fashion to mesh perfectly with one another, some of the stones in the main walls at Sacsahuamán stand as high as 8 meters and weigh up to 200 tons. Compared to the stones used in most other constructions elsewhere in the empire, they are gargantuan in size. According to the chroniclers, some twenty thousand men were involved in working in the nearby quarries, hauling the great stones hundreds of meters to the site, and erecting these walls.

Emanating from the back and belly of the puma in the city below were roads leading out to each of the four quarters of Tahuantinsuyu ("Land of the Four Quarters"), the Inca name for their empire. As described by Hyslop, the road system itself (see Figure 9.22), called the *Capac Ñan* ("Royal Road"), formed a complicated lattice that extended for at least 23,000 kilometers throughout much of the 1,835,000-square-kilometer area contained within the empire. Two principal roads formed the backbone of this vast network: the coastal road that ran from Tumbes down into northern Chile, and the sierra road that ran the entire length of empire between Guaca, in northern Ecuador, and Santiago. As alluded to earlier, Inca roads served as major communication routes for transmitting state information via the *chasqui* couriers. These couriers carried messages in the form of decimally knotted strings, called *quipus,* whose different colors represented such items as food, llamas, and people. The roads also were used to facilitate the travel of functionaries carrying out state business, people from the provinces on their way to and from Cuzco, and the Inca army. Indeed, without the road system the Inca could never have effectively integrated such a large and diverse area as that contained within its boundaries.

The integration of the empire was further served by the hundreds of state settlements that were built along its roads, including (1) smaller way stations called *tampu,* which lay at distances that have been estimated as being roughly 20 kilometers apart (see Hyslop 1984, 1990); and (2) larger administrative centers, which have been estimated as being roughly four to five days' travel apart (see Morris and Thompson 1985). The *tampu* were the mainstay of *chasqui* communication in the state—with each courier traveling as quickly as possible from one *tampu* to the next, there to hand over in relay fashion whatever items or information he was carrying to the next courier, who, in turn, would carry them to the next way station, and so on. The administrative centers had more complex functions that included not only the provision of storage and housing for individuals and large groups traveling long distance from one part of the empire to another, but also the integration of local conquered populations into the socioeconomic and religious system of the state. Hyslop estimates that roughly two thousand *tampu* settlements of varying smaller size were constructed throughout the Inca road network in addition to several dozen administrative centers (some of the latter are shown in Figure 9.22).

Mode of Reproduction

Unfortunately, despite the Inca propensity to keep censuses of nearly everything important to the state, including people, any population estimates they might have been made for Tahuantinsuyu as a whole were irrevocably lost during the

412

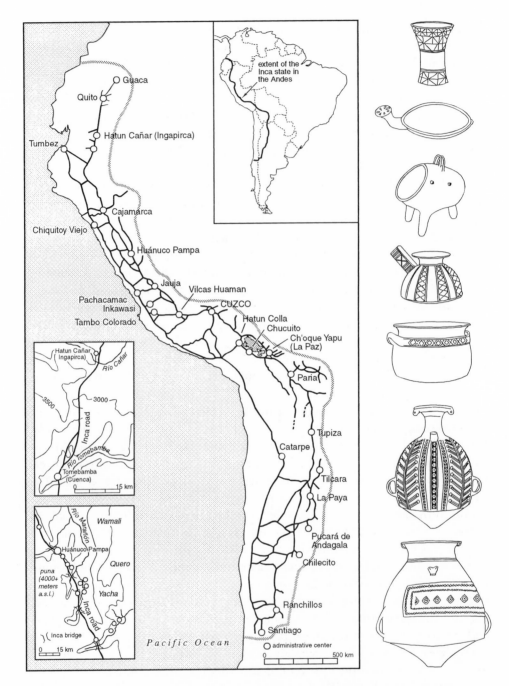

FIGURE 9.22 Map showing the extent of the Inca state and its road system, with drawings of selected state pottery diagnostics. Map redrawn and adapted from illustrations in Hyslop (1984) and pottery from illustrations in Kauffman Doig (1978).

Spanish Conquest. At the time Rowe wrote his account of the Inca in the late 1940s, the modern population of the entire Andean area that had been included within the empire numbered about 14 million people. With the industrialization and urbanization that had occurred by then, however, he argued reasonably that the population of the Inca state would probably have been smaller than the modern figure. Basing his estimate on limited census data from certain Inca provinces in 1525 in comparison to figures for those same areas in 1571, Rowe produced a conservative figure of 6 million persons for Tahuantinsuyu. But if we consider our earlier estimate (in Chapter 8) of 6 million persons sustainable by traditional agriculture in the Peruvian sierra alone, Rowe's figure appears some-what low, since the Peruvian sierra represents only about half the area covered by the empire. A more realistic estimate, perhaps, would be that it contained at least 10 million people. If we assume, in any case, a population that numbered between 6 and 10 million living within the 1,835,000-square-kilometer area of the state, this represents crude population density figures ranging between 3.2 and 5.4 persons per square kilometer. If, however, only about 15 percent of all this area was actually cultivated (as we assumed for the sierra alone in Chapter 8), the ecological density of the state would have ranged between about 20 and 35 persons per square kilometer (i.e., 6 million and 10 million persons $\div$ 0.15 $\times$ 1,835,000 km^2).

Domestic Economy and Social Organization

Family life at the provincial level probably went on much as it had before and in-deed has continued since the time of the Inca, as we have seen in discussing the Q'eros and Ayllu Kaata in Chapter 8. Children were given their names between the ages of one and two during a special haircutting ceremony called *Rutuchico*. As soon as they were able to carry out domestic tasks responsibly, both boys and girls were incorporated into the daily routines of tending to the flocks and the fields and engaging in household activities. In Cuzco the sons of elite families were required to attend the *Yachahuasi* ("Teaching House"), where men of wisdom called *amauta* were entrusted with teaching them the arts of Inca statecraft and warfare, matters related to agriculture and the seasons, and how to record and read the information on the *quipu* strings. Both girls and boys were initiated into adult-hood by formal puberty rites. Those for girls, called *Quicochico*, were restricted to a private ceremony in their homes following their first menses. A girl would re-main fasting at home for three days, at the end of which she was given a new out-fit woven by her mother at a ceremony attended by all of her relatives, whom she was expected to serve until her marriage. Those for boys, called *Huarochico*, were carried out in collective public ceremonies and, depending on the status of the participants, were held in the local villages for commoners, at the local provincial level for the sons of local elite, and in Cuzco for Incas by blood and royalty.

Marriage for young men usually took place by the time they were twenty-five and for young women between the ages of sixteen and twenty. Although after marriage young women were not required normally to serve the state, they worked with their husbands at all levels, from the household at the most restricted level to the administrative centers at the most general. Each family also was required to weave one garment a year for the state, and since it is the women who traditionally have used backstrap looms in the Andes, presumably it was they who carried out this activity (Figure 9.23g). Once a man married, in contrast, he was considered an adult citizen responsible to the state for the payment of labor in tribute. Thus, he not only had to engage in the time-honored tradition of participating in labor tasks at the local community level in the form of *ayni* reciprocity, as we have discussed for recent sierra villages in Chapter 8, but he also owed a portion of his yearly labor to the lands of the local *curaca* leader as well as to state religion and the Inca in the form of *mit'a* labor (Figure 9.23a, b, c). Male taxpayers also were required through the institution of *mit'a* to provide labor service in repairing the state suspension bridges (Figure 9.23e), manning the *tampu* way stations, working in the mines, and serving in the imperial army (Figure 9.23h).

The organization of *mit'a* taxpayers in each province was hierarchical and pyramidal. The system began at the provincial base with groups of 5 individual male taxpayers; each of these groups, in turn, was paired with another group to constitute a group of 10 individuals. The 10 were organized in five groups that made up 50, the 50 in two groups that made up 100, and, so on, through 100, 500, 1,000, 5,000, and 10,000 taxpayers. Each group of 5, 10, 50, 100, etc., *mit'a* taxpayers was led by men of increasingly higher rank in the organizational hierarchy up to the provincial level itself, which, interestingly enough, was seen by the state as (ideally) constituting 40,000 male taxpayers, no matter what the size of the province actually was.

Also in time-honored Andean tradition, the commoners at the local level were organized in territorially based endogamously marrying groups called *ayllu*, an institution we have discussed for the Q'ero in Chapter 8. With the rise of empire, a hierarchical social structure developed with local leaders and their families situated at an intermediate level between the rural commoners and the Inca elite in the provincial capitals and Cuzco. The local leaders, called *sinchi* ("headman") prior to the rise of the empire, were given the formal title of *curaca* by the Inca, and their position was made hereditary. Although they therefore came to enjoy special privileges much beyond those characterizing the pre-imperial *sinchi*, they were never accorded the privilege of calling themselves *Inca*, a designation that was reserved for the descendants of the original inhabitants of Cuzco and its immediate environs and that became synonymous with the highest social stratum in the state. The Inca himself, like royalty in some other parts of the world, such as the pre-Contact Hawaiian Islands, took as his principal wife, or *Coya*, his own full sister, a precedent established by Pachacuti Inca after A.D. 1438. In this manner the royal blood was kept 100 percent pure at best, should the *Coya* prove to be faithful to her husband, and 50 percent pure at worst, should she have a child out of wedlock with someone other than the emperor or other royalty.

a. preparation of the fields for planting using *chaquitacllas*

b. carrying of the harvest to the *collca* storage structures

c. Topa Inca Yupanqui and his administrator of the *collcas*

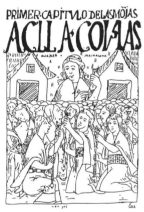

d. the *acllacuna* spinning thread under state supervision

e. the administrator in charge of suspension bridges

f. the administrator in charge of state *quipu* string records

g. a weaver carrying out her *mit'a* labor service to the state

h. the Inca army battling with an indigenous army from Chile

i. a *chasqui* messenger announcing his arrival with a shell trumpet

FIGURE 9.23   Drawings from Guamán Poma de Ayala's seventeenth-century manuscript showing selected aspects of Inca state organization. Redrawn from Guamán Poma de Ayala (1956 [1567–1615]).

The Inca royalty in Cuzco viewed itself as directly descended from Inti, the Sun God, and thus ruled the empire and its inhabitants by divine right. Members of the highest-level elite set themselves off not only by the finery of the textiles they wore but also by the privilege of wearing large fancy earplugs (Figure 9.23c, e, h) similar to those we have discussed earlier in the case of the Moche state. Since this practice resulted in a significant elongation of the earlobe, which was perforated and gradually enlarged by earplugs of increasing size, these elite members were called *orejones*, or "large ears," by the Spaniards at the time of the Conquest. Those in the elite of Cuzco were members of one of the ten royal *ayllus*, or *panaca*, that constituted the Hanan and Hurin moieties. All of imperial society, including everyone from the elite of Cuzco to the commoners of rural settlements, was divided into three basic groups: royalty and legal kin of the Inca, called *Collana*; servants and other retainers to the Inca, called *Payan*; and all the rest of the people in the state not related to royalty, called *Cayao*.

There were two groups of people who served the state in perpetuity. The first group, about which little is known, was called the *Yanacuna*. It consisted of men who had been born into the class and had no choice but to serve the state in caring for the royal herds of llamas and alpacas. But although they apparently did as they were told on a year-round basis, they were not "slaves" in the sense that they could be alienated from the state according to imperial whim or defined as property belonging to it. The other group was the *aqllacuna* (also called *mamacuna*), women who had been chosen when young from their local communities and trained to serve the state from that point on to the end of their lives. They remained unmarried, lived in cloistered buildings, were guarded by eunuchs, and were the principal spinners and weavers in the production of state cloth and the principal preparers of the sacred *chicha* beer. Among other tasks they carried out in Cuzco were religious functions related to the cult of Inti.

Political Economy

As discussed earlier, the origins of the Inca state can be pinpointed with reasonable accuracy to the period of Viracocha Inca's reign, just prior to A.D. 1438, when Cuzco formed an alliance with the Anta and Quechua people against the Chanca kingdom. From this point on, the state grew to imperial proportions in less than thirty years. Although I have argued that the regional wars that led to the rise of the Inca polity may well have originated in a context of population pressure, the potential validity of this hypothesis has yet to be tested by means of comprehensive settlement pattern surveys in the Cuzco basin and its environs. Indeed, a competing nonmaterialist hypothesis proposed by Geoffrey Conrad (1981) is that the political expansion of the Inca state had nothing at all to do with a materialist, or infrastructural, cause. Conrad suggests instead that the Inca system of split inheritance explains the expansion. In this system, at the death of a ruler he relinquished only the office of emperor itself to his successor, not his rights to the people and resources of the land he had conquered during his reign, which were destined to serve his mummy (or the retainers who served it) in perpetuity. Thus, each new ruler was forced to expand the imperial boundaries so as to include new lands and people who would provide him with the specific revenue necessary to support his person.

Although the issue of cause in Inca state origins can be resolved only with more problem-oriented field research, we may nevertheless suggest that the split inheritance hypothesis does not explain how Pachacuti Inca would rely on his son and named successor, Topa Inca, to incorporate lands that would not end up serving Topa Inca at all. Moreover, since the empire had nearly reached its maximum territorial size by the time Topa ascended to the imperial throne, the increasingly diminishing returns to later emperors would have created a huge temptation to overturn such an institution. Finally, in light of the fact that the chroniclers describe the resources of the state as being generally available to each emperor from Pachacuti on through the end of Huayna Capac's reign in A.D. 1525, split inheritance seems far more likely to have been an idealized structural principle rather than a practical policy governing each emperor's access to the resources he needed to maintain and expand the state. Whatever the role of split inheritance, the official policy justifying the continuing expansion of the state was that all Andean peoples beyond its boundaries were mere barbarians who could only benefit from their incorporation into the civilized Inca system.

Since the army was charged with the daunting task of conquering provincial populations with centuries of military experience, it may seem paradoxical that its permanent membership consisted of a relatively small group of several thousand professional soldiers who acted as the emperor's personal bodyguard. Even as early as Topa's successful northern campaign, however, the state was able to marshal a force of some 250,000 warriors from the area around Cuzco to accompany him on his sweep north to Ecuador and back south along the north and central coasts of Peru. Similar to the citizenry in general, Inca soldiers were organized on a provincial basis in groups of 10, 50, 100, 500 individuals, and so on, the groups at each level in the chain of command being led by men with the most experience in battle. For example, a group of 10 warriors was led by a *Chungacamayoc* ("Guardian of Ten") and a group of 50 was led by a *Picha Chungacamayoc* ("Guardian of Fifty"). Since the majority of adult males carried out their *mit'a* service on local labor projects, however, only a fraction of the taxpayer population actually was engaged in military service at any one time.

Before a military campaign the emperor consulted both with his supreme council and with an oracle who performed a divination ritual called *calpa*, which entailed observing the markings on the lung of a sacrificed llama to determine the outcome of the upcoming campaign. Soldiers from the nearby provinces were summoned with their leaders to Cuzco, where they camped until the royal commanders of the force felt ready to begin the campaign. Provincial squadrons located at greater distances from Cuzco along the path of the army's march waited to join its growing numbers as it moved into their area. Given the size of the force and the need to move efficiently through the rugged Andean terrain, the army met its logistical requirements by traveling along the Inca road system from *tampu* to *tampu*, at which were stored quantities of food and other supplies. Once at the scene of an impending battle and failing initial attempts to resolve matters by means of diplomacy, the army proceeded to carry out its attack in a systematic way that began with the use of slings while still at some distance from the enemy, was followed by the shooting of arrows and darts as the armies came closer together, and ended with hand-to-hand combat using maces and short swords as the two forces met (see Figure 9.23h).

Following the conquest of a province, the state dispatched various administrators, including the *Quipucamayocs* ("Guardians of the Quipu Strings") to make a detailed assessment of its population and resources. Clay models were made of important settlements and their environmental contexts, and a census was carried out that included a count of each adult male head of household and all of his dependents categorized by sex and by age groups, as well as an estimate of the amount of agricultural land, the crops grown on it, and any other resources that would be useful to the state. All of this information was then taken to Cuzco to provide the emperor with a detailed overview of the province's situation. From among the ranks of Inca royalty, he then appointed a provincial governor who oversaw state projects and the enforcement of imperial policy. To ensure compliance by the provincial population and its conformity to Inca standards, the state required that both local deities and *curaca*'s sons be sent to Cuzco as hostages and instituted a standardized dress code. Although permitted to continue the worship of local deities, including the Auki mountain gods, provincial populations were required to accept Inti as their supreme deity.

Whenever they carried out their *mit'a* labor tasks in producing pottery or elite-related formal architecture for the state, taxpayers also were required to adhere closely to state canons, or rules, of form and design. Imperial pottery forms were relatively restricted in number and, with the exception of *kero* goblets (Figure 9.22 right top), which have precedents in Wari forms, appear essentially de novo on the Andean cultural scene. And although the repetitive geometric motifs that decorated the surfaces of these forms have more precedents (e.g., in Wari), they also are easily distinguishable from anything that came before both by a more unvarying rigidity of line and by the use of more somber colors. As a result, it is usually a very straightforward task to distinguish imperial vessels from those of antecedent ceramic styles throughout the area included within state control. But the state did not require rural provincial populations to change either their pottery or architectural styles. Thus, although the presence of Inca pottery and architecture at many widespread sites throughout the Andes (e.g., Tomebamba, Huánuco Pampa, and Ranchillos) clearly indicates a strong formal imperial presence, the absence of such diagnostics in nearby rural settlements does not usually imply a lack of imperial control over those settlements.

One important means of this control, other than *mit'a*, which regulated the labor of individuals and families, was the institution of *mitmac* (settlers, or colonists, usually spelled *mitmaq* by neo-*Inka* scholars), which involved the relocation of whole communities of individuals and families and as such is more properly called *mitmacuna*, or "people who are moved." There were three kinds of *mitmacuna*. First, there were people whom the state moved to occupy a distinct environmental zone located relatively near their original community—with the intent of making a wider variety of resources available to all the members of the community, especially those who remained in the main center. It will be recalled that we have already dealt with a sixteenth-century case of this kind in Chapter 8 in discussing Murra's Chaupiwaranqa case of vertical control. Second, there were populations who were Incas by privilege (i.e., from settlements nearby Cuzco) and whose unquestioned loyalty to the empire made it useful to send them into areas where newly incorporated and potentially recalcitrant populations were located. There they served as examples of Inca customs, languages, and loyalty to state policy, not to mention keeping watch over state projects. The third kind involved the real recalcitrants, who, in spite of Inca conquest and the subsequent intrusion of the second type of *mitmacuna*, remained a strong security risk to state policies and goals. Rather than killing them en masse, the state instead sent them off to live in unpopulated areas that needed development or to live in fragmented groups among people it deemed more loyal.

A final critically important means of control was the establishment of larger administrative centers throughout the highway network of the empire. One of the most complex, well-preserved, and best-studied of these centers is the site of Huánuco Pampa, located in the north-central highlands of Peru (see Figure 9.22). Although thoroughly excavated and mapped in the 1960s and 1970s by its principal investigator, Craig Morris of the American Museum of Natural History, Huánuco Pampa was a part of a larger-scale regional project devised by Morris and his colleague Donald Thompson, of the University of Wisconsin, aimed at studying not just the center itself but also outlying rural settlements and *tampu* sites (see Morris and Thompson 1985). As should be obvious, the goal of the two researchers was to throw light on Huánuco Pampa's imperial role as an administrative center by placing it within its regional context as a probable critical node for effectively incorporating the surrounding rural population. The results of their research are too varied and complex to report on in detail here, although a brief summary of the principal findings is useful nonetheless—not least for the light it throws on the relationship between the Inca state and the people it conquered.

Before proceeding, however, I want to emphasize again (see Chapter 8) that the adaptation of local communities in the Andean sierra is far more vertical than horizontal, although throughout prehistoric and historic times sierra polities have indeed extended their control horizontally over broad areas of varying territorial extent. The Inca, of course, are the example par excellence of such a horizontal, or geographically extensive, adaptation. However, in the specific case of the Huánuco Pampa area the local adaptation today is, and most likely was in pre-Inca times as well, a vertical one—with the majority of the local community practicing agriculture in the warmer *quechua* zone on the steeper slopes and valley bottom of the nearby Marañón and Orqomayu Rivers and lesser numbers of people growing tubers and pasturing flocks in the higher and colder *puna* zone. Yet it is precisely in this latter area, at an elevation of some 3,800 meters, where the Inca located Huánuco Pampa, their principal center for the entire province of Huánuco.

As shown in Figure 9.24, the site covers a large area of 2 square kilometers and contains the remains of at least four thousand separate buildings. With a population size estimated at between ten thousand and fifteen thousand people, it was the largest Late Horizon settlement anywhere in the region. Morris and Thompson suggest two reasons that Huánuco Pampa was located on the relatively unpopulated *puna* rather than at lower elevations. The first has to do with the nature of the main sierra road system in this and most other areas, namely, that it was built across flatter ground to connect the far-flung provinces in as straight a manner as possible. Since by definition most of the flatter ground in the sierra is in the higher *puna*, the state chose to keep the road system there rather than having to construct frequent detours down into the more heavily populated lower canyons of the *quechua* zone. The second reason has to do with the fact that one of Huánuco Pampa's most important functions was storage. Since this involved such perishable foodstuffs as potatoes and maize, it would have been easier to achieve long-term storage by locating the site at the highest elevations possible. That Huánuco Pampa was clearly located in what might be termed an *ecologically artificial* position with respect to traditional subsistence-settlement systems in the area is exemplified by the abrupt abandonment of the site immediately following the capture and killing of the Inca emperor Atahuallpa by Pizarro and his group of *conquistadores*.

Another indication of the culturally intrusive nature of the site is that its architecture and pottery are for the most part very close copies of the Inca imperial style of Cuzco and thus stand in sharp contrast to local styles. The formal Inca residences at Huánuco Pampa are rectangular structures with gabled roofs built of carefully worked stones laid in regular horizontal courses (Figure 9.24). Most local dwelling structures in the surrounding region are circular and built of rough fieldstone. Nevertheless, the Inca buildings at most are only close approximations of the Cuzco style, which suggests to Morris that their construction was actually carried out by local laborers under the supervision of state functionaries. Indeed, the presence in the southern sector of Huánuco Pampa of a great number of circular structures built in the local provincial style suggests that *mit'a* laborers lived in them temporarily while they carried out construction activities in and around the site. Judging both from the large open spaces present in the plaza and several other architectural sectors immediately around it, as well as from the presence of high percentages of serving vessels in these latter sectors, Morris makes a strong case that one of the principal functions of Huánuco Pampa was to carry out feasting ceremonies for the local population. That is, in spite of coercing the local population into a command performance of labor at the site, the state nevertheless reciprocated via the *mit'a* institution by wining and dining the laborers and probably the local *curacas* as well.

Among the provincial laborers who worked at the site most probably were *aqllacuna* women. As shown in Figure 9.24, the likely candidate for an *Aqllahuasi*, or "House of the Chosen Women," is situated along the north-central edge of the plaza. It has a single entrance flanked on the interior by a small rectangular structure, suggesting that access to the compound was restricted and guarded. Inside

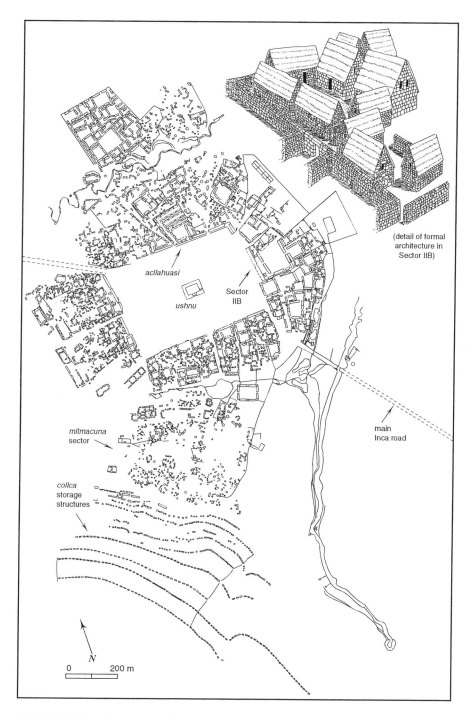

(detail of formal
architecture in
Sector IIB)

acllahuasi

ushnu

Sector
IIB

mitmacuna
sector

main
Inca road

collca
storage
structures

N

0   200 m

FIGURE 9.24   Plan view of the Inca provincial center of Huánuco Pampa, with
a detail view of selected structures in the administrative sector (IIB) of the site.
Redrawn and adapted from illustrations in Morris and Thompson (1985).

the compound is a series of fifty small rectangular dwellings of standardized size built in the imperial style, in and around which were found numerous remains of brewing jars as well as bone weaving tools and ceramic spindle whorls. Taken together, the architectural and artifactual data lend strong support to the hypothesis that the compound served as a place where *aqllacuna* worked in producing *chicha* and cloth for state functions.

Ritual and Leadership

The Inca emperor, or Sapa Inca, was the supreme head of the civil, religious, and military branches of the state. Serving as his council of advisers in Cuzco were the *Apu*, or the governors of each of the *suyu*, or geographic, quarters of the state. Under the Sapa Inca and his council were the governors of each of the provinces, which numbered over one hundred—including fifty provinces in the Peruvian-Bolivian area, roughly forty major coastal valleys in the same area, and several dozen more in the far northern and southern regions of Tahuantinsuyu. At the fourth-tier, or provincial, level in the imperial hierarchy were the *curaca* leaders of the various polities that had existed at the time of the Inca conquest.

Although the Sapa Inca was the sole head of government and religion, his main wife, the *Coya*, played a role that in many ways put her on an equal footing with him. For example, when the Inca was engaged in a military campaign away from the Cuzco area, she acted as his regent in Cuzco for the duration of the campaign. And just as he was the head of the religion of the Sun, so did she play a complementary role as the head of the religion of the Moon Goddess, Quilla. Aside from the Sapa Inca, the *Coya*, and the Supreme Council, also living in Cuzco was the *Uillac Uma* ("Highest Priest"), the head of all other priests in the empire, including those of the conquered populations.

In the preceding section we have seen how the road system, the *tampu*, and the provincial administrative centers provided the infrastructure that facilitated imperial integration via such institutions as *mit'a* and the *aqllacuna*. In addition to these integrative mechanisms, many rituals were carried out both in Cuzco and the far-flung secondary centers that further enhanced the coherence of the empire. Thus, just as *mit'a* itself was a form that may have developed out of traditional egalitarian Andean institutions based on *ayni* reciprocity (see Chapter 8), so did the state carry out a series of ceremonies in accordance with the pan-Andean agricultural calendar (see especially Cobo 1990 [1653]). One of the most spectacular of these Inca integrative rituals, about which much more has become known in the latter half of the twentieth century, was the *Capac Hucha*.

To stage the *Capac Hucha*, the provinces would send each year young boys and girls, aged six to ten years old, traveling with local officials along the road system to Cuzco. Once they all had convened in the capital, the Sapa Inca and the *Uillac Uma* would receive the children in the name of the state and the Sun religion, whereupon the boys and girls were symbolically married. Following this, the children, their provincial companions, and priests from the capital assigned to accompany them all walked back to the provinces. However, instead of following the roads on the return trip, they were required to take as absolutely a straight-line course as they possibly could, a route on which presumably the travelers encountered many hardships. Once they had returned to their home areas, the boys and girls were taken up on the highest mountaintops, wherein the *Apu*, or *Wamani*, dwelled, and sacrificed to these deities. The chronicles indicate that the *Capac Hucha* sacrifices were carried out for several reasons, including the observance of important festivals in the agricultural round and the promotion of the health and well-being of the Sapa Inca and the empire in general. Perhaps most importantly, however, they served to ensure the fertility of the land and an abundant harvest in each provincial area where the sacrifices were carried out.

In a sense, then, out of an ancient Andean tradition of mountain worship—itself probably an expression of uncertainty about subsistence productivity in light of local populations that were pushing against the carrying capacity of their area—the Incas created an overarching institution based on human sacrifice to the gods that promoted a positive relationship with the provinces and strengthened their ties to Cuzco. It was as if the state were saying to its citizenry: "Are you anxious about the ability of your local subsistence system to sustain your population? Then send some children to Cuzco for the *Capac Hucha*, and we'll consecrate them and sacrifice them on your mountains to ensure that next year will be a good one for you!"

The first find of a *Capac Hucha* sacrificial site in modern times occurred in 1954 when a local cobbler climbed to 5,394 meters elevation, high on the slopes of Mt. Plomo in central Chile, and discovered the remains of a boy who, before he was killed, had been given *chicha* to inebriate him, and then he was strangled. Almost perfectly preserved after some five hundred years of burial in a formal stone crypt on the mountain, the boy's remains were quickly taken down to Santiago, where nearly a half century later they are still preserved in cold storage in a museum. In the years since the Mt. Plomo find, many more high-altitude sites have been located and studied by a new breed of alpinist archaeologists who specialize in the difficult task of exploring the peaks of southern Peru and northern Chile, where the *Capac Hucha* sites are located. The best-known recent discovery was of a young girl dubbed "Juanita," made by Johann Reinhard and his Peruvian colleagues at a point just below the summit of 6,320-meter-high Mt. Ampato, located north of the city of Arequipa (see inset map in Figure 9.25).

The discovery had an element of serendipity to it, since ash from nearby erupting Sabancaya volcano had blanketed the highest slopes of Ampato. Warmed by the greater amount of sunlight being absorbed by the ashfall, the ice surrounding Juanita's tomb melted away and caused her body to fall many dozens of meters down the side of the peak, where it was spotted by Reinhard and his team. He (1996:66) describes their find as follows:

> Near the mummy, strewn about on the ice, were pieces of cloth, a miniature female figurine of Spondylus shell, llama bones, sherds of pottery, and two cloth bags containing corn kernels and a corncob. . . . When we stepped onto the lower summit, we were amazed to see that the whole area was covered with grass—hundreds of

424

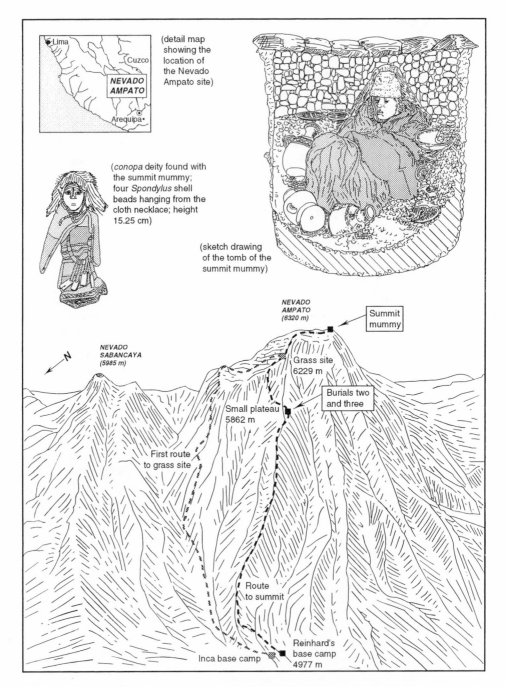

FIGURE 9.25   Perspective sketch of Nevado Ampato, where "Juanita, the Ice Mummy" and others were sacrificed by representatives of the Inca state, with detail drawings showing the location of the site and the contents of the tomb. Redrawn and adapted from illustrations in Reinhard (1996).

square yards of it. Exploring the site, we saw pieces of Inca pottery and textiles, bits of rope, chunks of wood, even leather and wool sandals. The Inca must have used this spot as a resting-place before attempting to climb the final steep ridge to the summit proper. The remains of wooden posts suggest that tentlike structures once stood here. The next morning we moved our camp up to a small plateau at 19,200 feet . . . [and] found the remains of other Inca structures . . . and an elevated stone-walled platform about two and a half feet high and five hundred square feet in area. This was probably a place where ritual offerings of food and drink were made.

A month later, after carrying Juanita's body down off the mountain, the team returned to a small plateau at 5,850 meters on the summit of Mt. Ampato and made additional discoveries, including the remains of two other Inca children who had accompanied Juanita in sacrifice to the mountain deities. Both bodies had been struck by lightning at some point after their burial, and as a result both were badly charred. However, the presence of shawl pins on one of the bodies and their absence on the other suggested that they were the remains of a girl and a boy, respectively, and hence as the chronicles state, that "married" children were indeed sometimes buried together in the *Capac Hucha* ceremony.

Ideology (USPs)

A number of related aspects of Inca cosmology are depicted in the three diagrams in Figure 9.26, each of which shows features of the division of the spatial and temporal order in the Inca understanding of their universe. Figure 9.26b is an adaptation of Pachacuti Yamqui's drawing, published in 1613, of the model he asserted was painted on an end wall of a structure inside the Coricancha, the ritual center of Cuzco and the empire. It shows the origins, structure, and social principles by which the Inca, and to a great degree all Andeans, ordered the cosmos. Figure 9.26c is a diagram of the sacred *ceque* lines that were viewed as emanating out from the Coricancha to the surrounding Andean world of Tahuantinsuyu. Among the several functions of these lines was the representation of the social order of Cuzco and the empire in general. Figure 9.26a brings together the most important elements of the other two diagrams, showing how the Inca viewed their cosmos in terms of its principal spatial features and the great yearly cycles in the movement of celestial phenomena across the Andean sky.

As interpreted by Constance Classen (1993), Pachacuti Yamqui's diagram represents a charter model for the dualistic concepts that structured the world of the Inca, including the relationship between earth and sky and between men and women. To understand the vertical relationship, one can imagine the model to be divided in two parts by a central horizontal line separating earth and sky. Things of the sky are shown in its upper half—including Viracocha (the Creator), Inti, Quilla, Venus as Morning Star, Venus as Evening Star, and the Summer and Winter Pleiades. Things of the earth are shown in its lower half—including Lightning (Thunder); Rainbow; the Pachamama (Earth Mother); the sacred Pilcomayo River; *Huacas* (sacred places); Man and Woman; Mamacocha

426

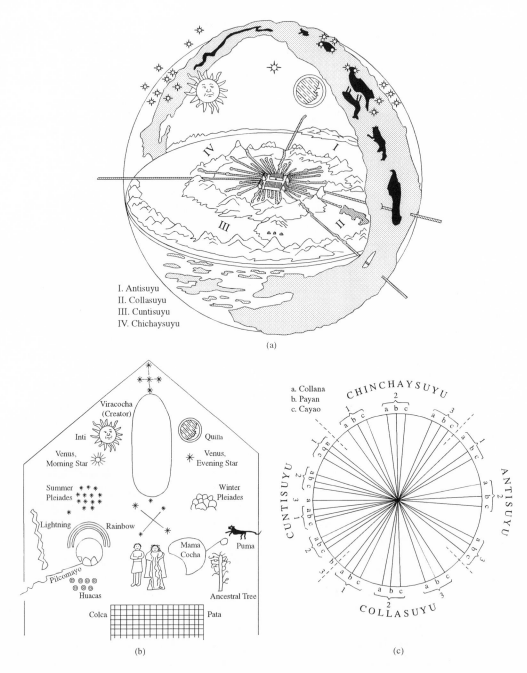

I. Antisuyu
II. Collasuyu
III. Cuntisuyu
IV. Chichaysuyu

(a)

Viracocha
(Creator)

Inti

Quilla

Venus,
Morning Star

Venus,
Evening Star

Summer
Pleiades

Winter
Pleiades

Lightning

Rainbow

Mama
Cocha

Puma

Pilcomayo

Huacas

Ancestral Tree

Colca

Pata

(b)

a. Collana
b. Payan
c. Cayao

CHINCHAYSUYU

CUNTISUYU

ANTISUYU

COLLASUYU

(c)

FIGURE 9.26   Inca cosmological concepts: (a) a three-dimensional view of the cosmos
showing Cuzco at the center of the empire, Tahuantinsuyu, (b) Pachacuti Yamqui's diagram
of the cosmos as it appeared on a wall in the Coricancha in Cuzco, and (c) Zuidema's diagram of the *ceque* system of Cuzco. Redrawn and adapted as follows: (a) Carlson (1990),
(b) Silverblatt (1987) and Kendall (1973), and (c) Kendall (1973).

(the Sea); the *choquechinchay* puma/cat (or *Ccoa*; see Chapter 8), which spits hail; the Ancestral Tree; and, farthest down in the diagram, terraced agricultural fields *(Colca Pata)*. Centrally shown in the upper half is Viracocha, the Creator deity; Man and Woman are shown not only as the central feature of this world but also as the mediating element between the sky and the earth. To understand the horizontal relationship, one can imagine the model to be divided into a left and a right part by a central vertical line that runs straight down from the peak of the roof. All things on the right side of the model are female—beginning with Mama Quilla, the patroness deity of women, and ending with Mother Sea and Woman herself. All things on the left side of the model are male, beginning with Tata Inti and ending with Pachamama (here seen as "male" in order to contrast Earth with Sea) and Man himself.

If we consider that the Inca state was one of the most stratified societies ever to exist in South America, perhaps the most important feature of Pachacuti Yamqui's drawing of Inca cosmological concepts is what the model says about the relations between men and women on this earth. It clearly indicates not only that Man and Woman are independent of each other, but also that they form complementary and cooperative halves of a singular unity, or whole, as exemplified in the case of the Sapa Inca and the *Coya*. There was no hierarchy between men and women, with one dominant and the other subordinate; instead, each part of the world, the male and the female, was characterized by its own hierarchical structure. Under the patronage of the Sun the Sapa Inca was head of all men and male institutions, whereas under the patronage of the Moon the *Coya* was head of all women and female institutions. Classen remarks that this parallel complementarity is also expressed in traditional Andean society in the custom of women inheriting from their mothers and men inheriting from their fathers.

We have also seen such complementarity in our earlier discussion of the cooperative roles men and women play in carrying out household and agricultural tasks in traditional Andean communities. If we recall some of the societies discussed earlier in this book (e.g., the Mundurucú and the Yanomamö), the Andean case (e.g., the Moche and the Inca) suggests that gender inequalities are not inevitable features of sociopolitical evolution and the rise of state but rather occur in specific adaptive circumstances as a function of how people work out their relationship to critical features of their physical and social environments.

Although Pachacuti Yamqui's diagram depicts dualistic concepts that are both vertical (the division between earth and sky) and horizontal (the division between male and female on this earth), it is essentially a vertical model of the hierarchical order that the Inca saw as existing between earth and sky, humans and deities, and the parallel lines of descent between men and women, their ancestors, and Viracocha, who created the material cosmos. In contrast, the *ceque* lines formed an on-the-ground horizontal model that the Inca utilized to conceptualize and distinguish the social hierarchy characterizing the relations of humans on this earth. Although the lines themselves were imaginary, they were formed by a series of 328 *huacas*—including, among many other topographical features, hills, stones, fountains, bridges, and houses—that lay in and around Cuzco. The alignments formed by groups of these *huacas* were seen as creating 41 separate lines that radiated out in a highly organized fashion from the Coricancha. Although published interpretations of the lines are complicated almost beyond comprehension (e.g., see Zuidema 1964, 1986), basically the 41 *ceques* were divided in terms of the four quarters, or *suyu*, of Tahuantinsuyu: Chinchaysuyu, Antisuyu, Collasuyu, and Cuntisuyu. In turn, each *suyu* contained a minimum of nine lines in three groups—with a line in each group that represented the three main hierarchically ranked social groupings of the state: *Collana* (Inca royalty), *Payan* (servants and retainers), and *Cayao* (the rest of the population). The complexities of current analyses do not end there, however, as the *ceque* system is now seen as also having regulated Inca irrigation, rituals, astronomy, and the calendar.

Having briefly discussed the *ceques*, let us return to the relatively more intelligible abstractions of Pachacuti Yamqui's diagram. In addition to its indications about the nature of gender relations, it also has much to say about the importance of the agricultural subsistence system and the relationship of men and women to nature. Not only are agricultural fields shown at the (environmental) base of the diagram, but also the alternating seasons are indicated by the Summer and Winter Pleiades and other stars whose cycles of movement across the sky constitute cosmic features marking the times to sow and harvest. The cosmic diagram in Figure 9.26a shows that the central feature of these cycles is the Milky Way, which is viewed by Andeans as flowing into the underworld, from which it brings patches of fertile mud to the sky to form various animals, including snake, toad, mother and baby llama, and fox. Returning yet again to Pachacuti Yamqui's drawing, we see that the rainfall that is critical to earthly productivity is shown in the form of Lightning and the Rainbow, as is the flow of water in the form of the Pilcomayo River. Human anxiety about the productivity of the harvest is implied by the depiction of the hail-spitting *choquechinchay*, or *Ccoa*. In sum, we might suggest that the Inca knew what Julian Steward knew: namely, that no state, however large and complex it may be, is freed of a concern about the environment and the subsistence system that support it.

CHAPTER 10

Toward a Scientific Paradigm in South Americanist Studies

Sᴛᴀɴᴅɪɴɢ ᴏɴ ᴛʜᴇ ᴛʜᴇᴏʀᴇᴛɪᴄᴀʟ ꜱʜᴏᴜʟᴅᴇʀꜱ of a number of distinguished predecessors and colleagues—including Julian Steward, Marvin Harris, Roy Rappaport, Kent Flannery, Jeffrey Parsons, Gordon Willey, Betty Meggers, and Gerardo Reichel-Dolmatoff—the preceding chapters have presented within an explicit environmental, ecosystemic, and evolutionary framework the archaeological and ethnographic data on a number of Amerindian groups across the vast geographic space of the South American continent through thirteen thousand years of time. Building especially on Steward's theoretical arguments and work, I have had two main goals in writing this book, the first of which is theoretical and the second empirical. With regard to the first goal, I critiqued the paradigmatic strategies of the first four of these predecessors and, then, leaving the less useful features of these strategies aside, attempted to construct out of their positive features a more reasonable overarching paradigm for the study of human adaptive systems. With regard to the second goal, following an extended discussion of the various environmental zones of the continent and their variable subsistence productivity, I proceeded to apply the updated paradigm consistently in presenting the data (and arguments about those data) on a variety of exemplary indigenous adaptive systems. In the process, I have discussed several groups in each one of the principal environmental zones that, taken in their entirety, represent the full range of levels of sociopolitical integration from bands through states.

Instead of reiterating the main details of the arguments and data presented in earlier chapters, the three sections of this brief concluding chapter deal with the most general theoretical implications of this book. After a short introductory discussion related to my ongoing attempt at paradigm construction, the first section consists of an explicit statement of the evolutionary and ecological theoretical structure—the systems-hierarchical evolutionary paradigm—presented at the end of Chapter 2. Aside from providing what purports to be a useful summary of the paradigm, I intend here to suggest an implied counterargument to the assertions of some anthropologists that we either have, at worst, no "theory" at all in our discipline or we have, at best, just a lot of little competing theories and no "paradigm." The second section then goes on to present brief critiques of several current paradigmatic approaches that have not been dealt with earlier in this book. Not surprisingly, here I wish to provide further support for the paradigm presented in the first section by arguing that these approaches do not represent a satisfactorily complete or logically supportable "paradigmatic hat" to put on one's head and attempt to think with. Finally, the third section summarizes some of the main theoretical conclusions that can be drawn from the data on the four main levels of sociopolitical integration that were discussed in Chapters 5 through 9.

THE SYSTEMS-HIERARCHICAL
EVOLUTIONARY PARADIGM

In Chapter 2 I implied that the theoretical models presented in the last part of that chapter have evolved rather substantially out of the crude initial structures that I used to "think with" some years ago. Since the time I wrote that chapter a number of months ago, I have continued thinking about improvements that might be made to the systems-hierarchical model with regard both to its adequacy in dealing with all aspects of human adaptive systems and to the issue of infrastructural versus mental cause in sociopolitical evolution that we dealt with there. The two principal results of this continuing process of paradigm construction are shown in Figure 10.1. First, and more importantly, the human biogram has been added to the model. Simply stated, this addition represents an acknowledgment that the human genotype and phenotype constitute a critical biological "adaptive interface" between human groups and their physical environment. Second, given the validity of this argument, the figure argues for the causal primacy of human genetics in the mental expression of the sex drive (viewed here as a constant characterizing all human groups), which, in turn, leads to population growth.

I incorporated within the systems-hierarchical evolutionary paradigm in Chapter 2 the argument that *reproductive pressure* is indeed a critical engine of sociocultural evolution, but I attempted to finesse Harris's materialist argument that such pressure represents an independent variable—in other words, that it is not, in turn, caused by some other, perhaps higher-order, variable. Given the assertion that humans are highly sexed and fecund and thus that human populations always tend to grow, I argued that the *mental stress* created, first, by such regulatory practices as sexual abstinence, abortion, and infanticide and, second, by the continual potential for nutritional pressure is an equally plausible candi-

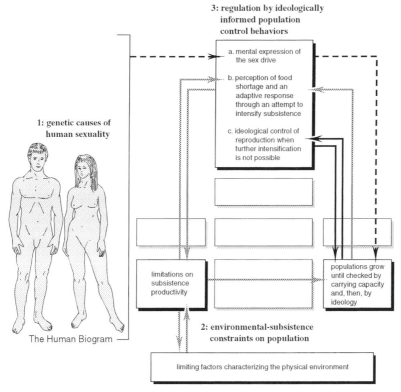

3: regulation by ideologically
informed population
control behaviors

a. mental expression of
the sex drive

b. perception of food
shortage and an
adaptive response
through an attempt to
intensify subsistence

c. ideological control of
reproduction when
further intensification
is not possible

1: genetic causes of
human sexuality

limitations on
subsistence
productivity

populations grow
until checked by
carrying capacity
and, then, by
ideology

The Human Biogram

2: environmental-subsistence
constraints on population

limiting factors characterizing the physical environment

The Human Adaptive System

FIGURE 10.1   A diagram showing (1) the causal primacy of the human
biogram in the mental expression of the sex drive and its effect on population growth, (2) the checks on this growth by environmental-subsistence constraints, and (3) the resulting causal nexus between ideology
and population in the attempt by the members of an adaptive system to
control the strong tendency for population to grow nonetheless. Figures
at left redrawn and adapted from Sagan (1977).

date as the primary engine of human adaptation leading to sociocultural evolution (e.g., intensification leading to irrigation agriculture in appropriate contexts). After this argument was completed, however, I retained a nagging uncertainty about whether the issue had really been firmly settled, since I still had not
addressed the issue of what, ultimately, makes population grow. I therefore reasoned that if indeed I had not resolved it, then Harris might well be correct in his
insistence that population growth is the independent causal variable in sociocultural evolution.

This problem is precisely what Figure 10.1 attempts to resolve in arguing that
the chain of causation proceeds in the following manner: genetic causation of
human sexuality → mental expression of the sex drive → population growth →
perception of food shortage → attempts to intensify → ideological control of reproduction (→ abstinence, abortion, infanticide, etc.) when the constraints of

environment/subsistence are reached. (Of course, although not shown in the figure, we may continue the chain here as follows: . . . mental stress → opportunistic behavior → further intensification and sociocultural evolution, when these are permitted by adaptive changes to the subsistence system in a particular environmental context.) In light of this causal chain, the model also shows a systemic feedback relationship, or a causal nexus, between the superstructure and the mode of reproduction in light of the constraints posed by environment and subsistence. Within the realm of culture as viewed in light of the systems-hierarchical model, we may thus conclude that *first cause* may be assigned to superstructure, since the upper level of superstructure is viewed in the model as consisting of mental phenomena. Perhaps now, and only now, have we actually finessed Harris's Marxist-derived (and therefore materialist) argument for unvarying infrastructural cause. But frankly, I think anyone who studies Figure 10.1 closely could just as easily end up deciding that cause really lies everywhere, since causation is truly a complex circular process. That, to a great degree, is what the systemic arguments of this book have been all about.

Let me now confess that, having developed the model in Figure 10.1, I was sorely tempted to insert it in Chapter 2 and then rewrite the last section of the chapter, as if there had never existed the slightest doubt in my mind that the issue of mental versus material causation could be easily resolved. Obviously, I resisted the temptation. My reason for doing so is a simple and straightforward one: namely, to make clear that theory construction, in my opinion, never involves any sort of absolute, or immutable, truths; instead, it is a never-ending process of critical thought, modification, and ultimate refinement of paradigms, related theories, and the graphic models derived therefrom.

A final point with regard to Figure 10.1 is that I do not see the addition of the human biogram to the paradigm as requiring a return to the discussions of Chapter 5 through 9 to bring biology into play in relation to one or more of the groups with which we have dealt. The reason is simply that this book, in large part for reasons of brevity, has taken the human biogram to be a *constant* of all the groups discussed here, not a variable to be explained, as are the features of adaptive systems from environment through infrastructure and structure to superstructure. This should not be taken to imply, however, that at least the phenotype of indigenous South Americans is not a variable. For example, people who are born at high altitude in the Andes develop shorter stature and barrel-chestedness as a function of the rigorous environment and the relative lack of oxygen and are therefore characterized by a phenotype that is quite distinct from that of other indigenous groups of the continent.

The Three Elements of the Paradigm

Human Adaptive Systems

Human societies consist of adaptive systems that exist in a more or less bounded region and in the course of time change or stay the same as a function of the interaction of a basic series of discrete, yet interrelated and hierarchically organized, variables. Any meaningful description or explanatory account of a human adaptive system must begin by breaking that system down into the series of component parts that together make up the whole. These component parts, or variables, include (1) the physical environmental context, both biotic and abiotic; (2) the social environmental context, or other systems with which it interacts; (3) a series of cultural variables internal to the system itself, including (a) lower-order infrastructural variables (subsistence, settlement pattern, demography), (b) middle-order structural variables (domestic economy, social organization, political economy), and (c) higher-order superstructural variables that are both behavioral (leadership, ritual) and abstract (ideology/cosmology); and, potentially, (4) the human biogram (genotype, phenotype). Once data are available on these variables and depending on the descriptive/explanatory problem at hand, any meaningful description or account of the system must then proceed by constructing arguments about the interactions among variables at any and all levels in terms of both policy-down and output-up as well as maintenance/support considerations involving circular, multivariate causality. Such a description or account must also potentially include considerations of both higher-order and lower-order cause as well as environmental and (external) social cause.

Levels of Sociopolitical Integration

Utilizing the systems-hierarchical model as a guide for determining the broadest possible set of criteria by which different human adaptive systems can be compared and contrasted, the researcher employing the paradigm asserts a priori that human adaptive systems at a continentwide (if not worldwide) level can be meaningfully categorized in terms of their level of sociopolitical integration by reference to the following variables: (1) the nature of the habitats that form their environmental, or geographic, context (e.g., grasslands, semitropical uplands, tropical rain forests, mountains, coastal deserts, to name the most important South American ones); (2) the latitude, longitude, rainfall and ambient temperature patterns, nature of soils, seasonality, and other specific geographic features that are critical not only in determining the overall productivity of each habitat but also in comparing different habitats; (3) the nature of subsistence productivity as determined by reference to such strategies as hunting, gathering, horticulture, and intensive agriculture and how this productivity differs from habitat to habitat; and, finally (4) all the cultural variables internal to the system (i.e., infrastructure, structure, and superstructure), including the nature of the on-the-ground settlement pattern.

The Role of Population

The continual potential for population pressure, given the tendency of human numbers to rise against predictable short-term and unpredictable long-term fluctuations of the subsistence carrying capacity in all adaptive systems, makes it one of the prime causal variables internal to those systems that explain evolutionary change over time from simpler to more complex societies. In light of the different productivities of the full range of habitats suitable for human occupation at a continentwide (if not worldwide) level, the paradigm therefore asserts a priori that populations will tend to grow to the highest levels in those subsistence-environment contexts where productivity—given reference to all possible strategies of food-getting—is determined to be the highest. The reason for the rise of stratified societies therefore is a function of the universal ability of all human groups to adapt to environments where relatively unlimited subsistence intensification is possible.

Theoretical Basis of the Paradigm

In the broadest sense the systems-hierarchical evolutionary paradigm builds on the best features of paradigmatic construction and theoretical arguments about human adaptive systems and sociocultural evolution that go back to the nineteenth-century work of Herbert Spencer and Lewis Henry Morgan. However, as stated earlier, the paradigm's immediate historical roots go back no farther than the work of Julian Steward in the 1940s. From this point on in time, it is indebted to the work of many scholars, including those already mentioned in the introduction to this chapter and others such as Elman Service, Morton Fried, and Robert Carneiro. In general, the theoretical underpinning of the paradigm lies in the following areas: (1) cultural evolutionary science and theory; (2) the theory, laws, and methods of ecological science; (3) ethnological science; (4) archaeological science; and (5) neo-Darwinian evolutionary science (the biological component).

Intellectual Benefits of the Paradigm

Among the benefits and advantages of the paradigm are the following:

1. It resolves the issue of the mental versus the material in the causation and functioning of human adaptive systems, since both are potentially critical.
2. It resolves the issue of internal versus external cause, seeing both as critical.
3. It does not ignore higher-order variables, such as ritual, religion, ideology, cosmology, symbols, and psychology, as has been done by cultural ecologists.
4. In light of Odum's (1971:3) definition of ecology as "the study of organisms in their home," it sees *human* ecology as the study of every aspect of human adaptive systems from infrastructure through superstructure. (The corollary here is that ecological anthropology therefore consists of much more than "counting kilocalories," since it also involves higher-order control/maintenance/regulatory phenomena such as ritual and ideology.)
5. It thus focuses both on quantitative data, at the infrastructural and other levels where such data are obtainable, and on qualitative data, at the su-

perstructural and other levels where such data are appropriately viewed in this manner. The paradigm argues that both kinds of data are equally important in anthropological science, contrary to any researchers who, wrapping themselves in the cloak of science, think that only countable, weighable, siftable phenomena are relevant to our science.

6. It focuses on the multivariate maintenance, regulation, and change of systems, not on single-variable linear causation.

7. It does not view the ten principal groups of variables (eleven, counting the human biogram in cases where it is relevant) as "black boxes," since each of these groups is explicitly seen as containing numbers of subvariables.

8. It applies across the board to all of the societies that traditionally have been the focus of anthropological research, both archaeological and ethnographic (bands, villages, chiefdoms, states), and most probably to cases of semi- or fully industrialized societies as well.

9. It does not rely just on anthropological science in theory formulation, data gathering, and methods; rather, it permits the researcher to address relevant theories, data, models, and insights from outside the discipline.

OTHER PARADIGMS, OTHER MODELS

Perhaps it is the case, as Harris (1979) has argued, that a scholar incorporates a paradigmatic approach into her or his thinking by accepting its validity in making better sense out of complex data sets than other competing strategies and by referring to its ability to answer more questions than other strategies. This has certainly been one of my goals in taking the best elements of the theories of Steward, Harris, Rappaport, and Flannery in constructing the systems-hierarchical evolutionary paradigm. It may also be the case that an approach such as the one developed in this book is best learned through its application to a number of cases, as we have done in looking at the Ona and the Yahgan of Tierra del Fuego, the Nukak of eastern Colombia, the Mundurucú of the south Amazon, the Yanomamö of the north Amazon, the Shuar-Jívaro of eastern Ecuador, the Desana of eastern Colombia, the Kogi and the Tairona of northwestern Colombia, Real Alto site of southwest Ecuador and the related Bororo data, the Q'eros of southern Peru, the Ayllu Kaata people of northern Bolivia, the Chavín and the Moche of north Peru, and the Inca. The systems-hierarchical paradigm has also provided a frame of reference as we examined and critiqued Steward's bands-as-marginals argument, Carneiro's Kuikuru case, Lathrap's displaced persons argument, Roosevelt's argument for sociopolitical complexity in the Amazon, Clastres's case for Amazonian societies against the state, Moseley's case for Peruvian maritime complexity, and Carneiro's argument about the roles of circumscription, agriculture, population, and warfare in ancient state origins.

However, a paradigm also is made more acceptable through demonstration that its overall approach and basic tenets are superior to or more all-encompassing than those of other ones. Harris, as anyone who has read him knows, has certainly argued that one of the principal features of anthropology is the (not infrequently hostile) clash that occurs between advocates of the various paradigmatic approaches in our still-nascent discipline. In other words, for Harris the different approaches to anthropological explanation are anything but ships passing in the night whose captains have little or no concern for what else is on the water. Harris, for his part at least, has armed his cultural materialist boat with an impressive array of gunnery so as to be able to sink every other ship, no matter how close or far it may be from his own. This sort of game in anthropological science is unquestionably a deadly serious one, to be engaged in only by those who would observe the rules of scientific argumentation in a rigorously logical manner. But it is still a game that can be played for the sheer intellectual delight of it, a delight produced only by encounters with the most truly noteworthy opponents. Certainly every person mentioned in this book, from Carneiro and Clastres, through Lévi-Strauss and Meggers, and on to Moseley and Zuidema, is an equally worthy and interesting player, although I do not intend to suggest that those who have been left unmentioned here are not.

Having implied that current competitors are at least fair game, however, let me now proceed to briefly examine three different graphic models and the accompanying arguments of the researchers who developed them—to see not only where we stand with the systems-hierarchical evolutionary paradigm, but also what other captains are out there in the night who might be lighting argumentative beacons to attract the minds of those who aspire to engage in paradigm construction and theory testing. The question to be decided by the reader, of course, is whether we have approached these other paradigmatic ships with sufficient gunnery to at least shoot out their beacon, if not sink them in the muddy depths.

Johnson and Earle's Paradigm

In *The Evolution of Human Societies,* which is dedicated to Marvin Harris and Marshall Sahlins "for their inspiration and disputation," Allen Johnson and Timothy Earle (1987) have developed the model shown in Figure 10.2. Since it is used throughout the book, obviously they take it to be an adequate representation of all the systemic variables that need to be invoked in understanding the evolution of states out of their less complex predecessors. Their typology of sociopolitical levels includes the *family-level group* (bands), the *local group* (villages), and the *regional polity* (chiefdoms and states). A comparison of their model with the systems-hierarchical model quickly indicates which of all potential societal variables they see as critical in sociopolitical evolution, which variables they do not see as critical, and how they view cause in this process.

Comparing theirs and the systems-hierarchical model, one notes first that, as in Harris's cultural materialist paradigm, the physical environment is not specifically included as an important variable in the differences among the several levels of societal integration. Instead, only "population growth under economic constraints" is shown at the base of the model, and in a one-way causal path from the bottom to the top, population is seen as the independent variable that pur-

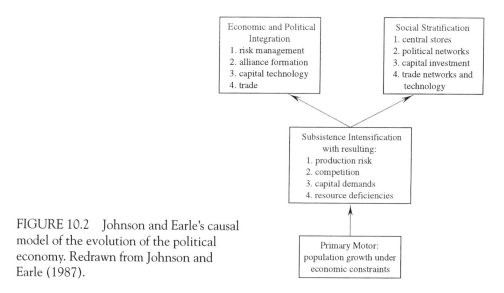

FIGURE 10.2   Johnson and Earle's causal model of the evolution of the political economy. Redrawn from Johnson and Earle (1987).

portedly has been singularly causal in the whole process of sociocultural evolution. Moreover, as in Steward's cultural ecology model, everything above the level of population and subsistence—including the variables subsumed under economic and political integration and social stratification—seems directly related, in the sense of Steward's "cultural core," to population and subsistence. We may be forgiven for asking, almost rhetorically at this point, What else in addition to the physical environment has been left out of the model that other researchers might consider important? The answer, of course, is everything having to do with social organization, ritual, ideology, and cosmology at the levels of structure and superstructure.

My critique can be summed up with the assertion that the authors do not appear to be indebted primarily to Harris, who at least includes the higher-order superstructure in his cultural materialist model. Instead, they appear to rely far more on the mid-twentieth-century arguments of Steward, who saw causation as a strictly one-way, bottom-up process based on demographic and technological influences—with ritual, cosmology, and so on relegated to the status of mere epiphenomenal variables. In some fairness to Johnson and Earle, however, the model appears to have been constructed less in the interest of talking about all the important features of systems at one point in time and more in the interest of focusing on the evolutionary process, or the origins of societal change. But they take a very Stewardian perspective on the material causes of this change. In contrast, as I have argued in this book, sociopolitical evolution from the systems-hierarchical perspective is seen as occurring in a context of more variables than just the ones assigned importance in Johnson and Earle's model—including both higher-order ones, such as social organization, rituals, and ideologies, and lower-order ones having to do with environmental differences from zone to zone across a continent. We may thus conclude that their paradigmatic strategy does not get us much farther than Steward's 1950s cultural ecological focus.

Two Systems Models of Prehistoric Process

In taking a quick initial glance at the models shown in Figures 10.3 and 10.4, the reader might be forgiven for wishing to retreat back to the apparently simpler argument of Johnson and Earle's paradigm. As is often the case with models that are currently taken by some researchers to represent the most realistic, all-encompassing, and "sophisticated" accounts of cause in sociopolitical evolution, both of them are replete with little boxes as well as arrows running every which way. So, again briefly as in the preceding case, let us take a look at the two models to see how they differ in subtler ways from the systems-hierarchical evolutionary strategy.

The model in Figure 10.3 comes from the concluding chapter in Paul Bahn and John Flenley's (1992) excellent account of the rise and ultimate *devolution* of human adaptive systems on Easter Island. Following the arrival of pioneering groups and the introduction of agriculture, the population rose to levels that approached ten thousand persons, a series of small competing chiefdoms arose around the island, hundreds of giant stone statues were constructed, and a related cult of agricultural fertility and chiefly power arose. At the same time or shortly thereafter, however, the primeval forests were being cut down, the environmental context for practicing productive agriculture was being increasingly degraded, the island erupted in chronic internecine strife, and, ultimately, the entire chiefly system, including its productive base, "crashed" to a lower level of sociopolitical integration. This is admittedly a very brief overview of the processes of evolutionary change on the island, but it clearly indicates that a complex set of variables, from environment and subsistence to ritual and cosmology, was involved at every step of the way throughout the prehistoric Easter Island sequence, from the rise of chiefdoms to their ultimate devolution (see also Van Tilburg 1994).

There is no question that Bahn and Flenley provide a model that can be understood through some minutes of study and thought. But at least four problems arise as one begins a perusal of the model. First, where does one indeed *begin*? Bahn and Flenley (1992:211) see the center of their model—the first causes that get the evolutionary process going—as "human population growth" and "forest clearance for agriculture and firewood," although these starting points are not, in my mind, all that obvious. Second, the more one looks at the model, the more the arrows and boxes begin to swim around before one's eyes in a way that approaches virtual chaos. Third, the more one looks, the more one realizes that even with twenty-four "little boxes" the model still makes little or no room for social organization (e.g., chiefly elites, commoners), the ancient statues themselves, and related ritual and ideology. It is therefore systemically incomplete. Fourth, after some additional contemplation, the observer (recalling Rappaport's Tsembaga Maring model, discussed in Chapter 2) realizes that the model is an ad hoc one; in other words, it was constructed solely for the case at hand. Thus, one would be hard-pressed to apply it to other cases—especially since its paradigmatic organizational principles are not at all obvious (in fact, we might conclude

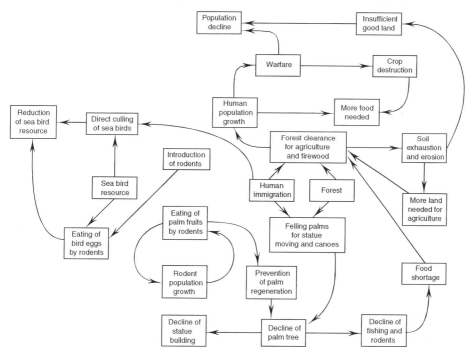

FIGURE 10.3   Bahn and Flenley's model of the processes leading to population de-cline on prehistoric Easter Island. Redrawn from Bahn and Flenley (1992).

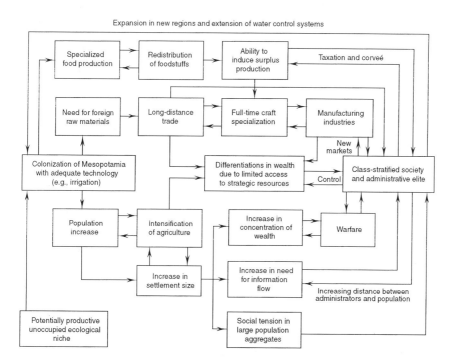

FIGURE 10.4   Redman's model of state origins in Mesopotamia. Redrawn from Fagan (1998).

that the authors do not possess an explicit working paradigm other than attempting to do "good archaeology" and summing up the materialistic aspects of their argument with a supercomplicated but systemically incomplete graphic).

"Well, okay," the reader might say, "but how about your graphic, Wilson?" (I knew you would ask.) All I can say about it in comparison to Bahn and Flenley's graphic is that the same model is applied again and again to all cases, and it therefore becomes a working mnemonic device that, like an old shoe, is easily recognizable when one sees it. As to where to start with our model, I leave that up to the preferences of the reader. For my part, depending on the points I wish to make as I present data in classes or seminars, I usually start either with the highest-order variables (always interesting) to then show how they relate adaptively to lower-order ones or with the infrastructural ones (always necessary) to show how they relate adaptively to higher-order ones. And, of course, our model always makes room for cosmology, symbols, rituals, and so on—indeed, anything of a higher-order nature that the researcher wants to include in systemic argumentation. Okay, I concede that our model causes *big* boxes, not to mention the textual and quantitative data contained within them, to swim round in one's mind as well, but ultimately it still is possible for the observer to get an easier grip on the model, since it is used across the board for all cases.

The model in Figure 10.4 comes from the latest (ninth) edition of Brian Fagan's *People of the Earth* (1998), which without a doubt is the most popular text used in the United States to teach prehistoric cultures to undergraduate students. Fagan's model comes originally, however, from Charles Redman (1978), who devised it some years ago in an attempt to account for the origins and development of the most ancient state societies in the world, the Mesopotamian city-states of the Tigris-Euphrates Basin. But even though the model contains fewer boxes, it more than makes up for this diminution by including more causal arrows. Notice, too, that, although everything but the proverbial kitchen sink seems to be thrown into the model, it nonetheless lacks any mention of the highest-order superstructural features of these city-states, even though we know plenty about these features from the cuneiform texts.

Now, taking into consideration that the model proceeds from early times, at left, to later times and the rise of the state, at right, note that it mostly includes infrastructural variables at the far left and structural variables in the middle and at the far right. What might we be falsely led to conclude from serious contemplation of the model? I hope that this question is a rhetorical one at this point and that the conclusion is obvious to the reader: namely, that the early egalitarian folks of ancient Mesopotamia did not really have adaptive systems that included structural and superstructural variables, whereas the later stratified folks no longer had an infrastructural base. More naïve students of the data and this model could thus be forgiven for concluding that the early folks were really quite "vulgar" (i.e., they just migrated and farmed) and that the later folks were quite "effete" and above all such considerations (i.e., they just sat around in palaces and carried out trade and wars).

Finally, since this model is included in Fagan's text as a representation of the "latest" developments in systems thinking—never mind that it actually dates back to the systems dark ages of the 1970s!—the undergraduate student who even takes time to study the model ("Will this thing be on the exam?") might well be forgiven for changing his or her major to economics, where they truly know how to model, or to geology, where no one cares because "rocks don't exhibit the kind of truly interesting and complex behavior that requires systems modeling, anyway!" However, with the proper training in theory the undergraduate student who sticks with anthropology might just be convinced to opt for the systems-hierarchical evolutionary model—standing as it does on the shoulders of many worthy predecessors—as opposed to the truly dark-age thinking of some current researchers who represent a sort of throwback to the antievolutionary thinking of Boasian historical particularist times. We truly do have a worthy paradigm and many testable theories in light of it!

INDIGENOUS ADAPTIVE SYSTEMS

By between about 14,000 and 10,500 years ago the first human inhabitants of South America had established themselves across much of the length and breadth of the continent—from the Caribbean Sea in the north to the Fuegian archipelago in the south, and from the Andean cordillera in the west to the eastern lowlands of the lower Amazon River and northwest Brazil in the east. The data from such far-flung sites as Fell's Cave, Monte Verde, Pikimachay Cave, Tibitó, Taima-Taima, Caverna da Pedra Pintada, and Pedra Furada Rock Shelter indicate that Paleoindian adaptive systems were as highly variable in terms of their material and nonmaterial constituents as were the environments that sustained these systems.

Everywhere the Paleoindians migrated and established themselves across the continent, they made successful use of the wide variety of plant and animal resources available in these different environments. The very success of their adaptive systems meant not only that population numbers began slowly to rise, but also that very early on in the South American sequence, as was the case elsewhere in the world, people were faced with the problem of devising a variety of cultural mechanisms that would maintain continuing regulatory control over their numbers, so that they could maintain themselves within the long-term carrying capacity of their subsistence-environmental contexts. At the same time, continuing a tradition that must surely have characterized indigenous ancestors to the north, the indigenous populations of the continent gradually established themselves as experts in the use and manipulation of the fauna and flora of their environments. Thus, as populations rose against the longer-term sustainability of their particular hunting and gathering contexts, everywhere across the central and northern environmental zones of South America people came into interaction with the wild progenitors of the huge variety of plants, as well as the few animals, whose domestication was virtually completed by around 5000 B.P., or roughly nine thousand years after the first Paleoindian inhabitants appear to have arrived on the continent.

Aside from the differences in productivity of the main environmental zones themselves, the two principal processes that explain the overall nature of indigenous adaptation therefore clearly are, first, the tendency of populations to grow and, second, the corresponding ability of humans to adapt in a variety of ways to the constraints and potentials of their environmental contexts by developing regulatory controls and/or intensifying subsistence. By the time of the European intrusion in the early sixteenth century, these prehistoric evolutionary processes had resulted in the appearance of four principal levels of sociopolitical integration across South America. Band-level adaptive systems were present throughout most, if not all, of the south-central and far southern zones of the continent—including Patagonia, the Pampas, and the Gran Chaco—and in isolated pockets of relatively low productivity found scattered here and there elsewhere across the continent. Village-level systems were present across much of the Brazilian Highlands, virtually everywhere across the vast *terra firme* environment of the Amazon Basin, and in scattered pockets of moderately low productivity throughout the Andes and the adjacent Pacific littoral. Chiefdom-level systems were found in every area of moderately high productivity, including the *várzea* niche of the Amazon River and the rugged highlands of the northern Andes. Finally, a single state-level system, the Inca, was present throughout the Andes, from Ecuador in the north to central Chile and northwestern Argentina in the south. Since a close correspondence exists between the productivity of the main environmental zones and the variable complexity of the systems that evolved within them, we may therefore conclude that the sociocultural evolutionary processes that characterized the continent were the inevitable result of lawful demographic and adaptive tendencies that characterize *all* human adaptive systems.

Band-Level Systems

In addition to a review of Paleoindian sites and Richard MacNeish's data on the development of agriculture out of early Andean band-level adaptations of the Ayacucho Basin in Peru, we have looked at three band systems: the Ona, the Yahgan, and the Nukak. The first two of these latter societies are especially excellent examples of the close adaptive relationship between environments and the cultures that develop within them. The Ona recognized three principal environments on Tierra del Fuego Island: the northern plains where cururos were hunted, the southern plains and woods where guanacos were hunted, and the far eastern area where maritime resources were hunted and collected. These environments and subsistence systems correlated exactly with the cultural divisions that the Ona saw as existing at the most general level on the island: the P'ámica, the Hámška, and the Aush. Although economic interaction occurred among the three groups, very little social interaction took place. At the more local level the entire island was viewed as being divided into thirty-eight territorial units whose boundaries were well delineated and continually defended against the intrusion of other band groups within each of the three main divisions. Although inter-marriage continually took place among the people of the territorial units in each division, warfare and hostile shamanism employing the use of deadly magical darts called *kwáke* were also continual. Aside from these density controls, the Ona data are incomplete, however, in that they do not provide a clear indication of how population numbers were maintained in such a way as to result in the low densities (~0.1 person/km^2) that characterized their adaptive systems. Subsistence throughout Tierra del Fuego island was almost entirely in the hands of the men, which meant, predictably, that only the boys were taken through puberty rites and that the men saw themselves as dominant in Ona society. Nevertheless, this dominance was balanced by reference to a mythical time when the women were in control, but only precariously and briefly, since even at that time the men were viewed as having been the main source of food. Based on reference to subsistence, then, the only "right" system for the Ona apparently had to be one in which the men were dominant in behavior and myth, in spite of the essential egalitarianism of their society in general and gender relations in particular.

The Ona were separated from the Yahgan by the high, nearly impenetrable mountain barrier that lies between the southern edge of Tierra del Fuego and the island archipelago to the south. Given this barrier and the distinctive nature of the Yahgan subsistence system, which throughout the southern archipelago was almost entirely reliant on the use of canoes and localized shoreline gathering, it is predictable that highly distinct cultural adaptations characterized by mutually unintelligible languages would arise in such geographic proximity to each other. The Yahgan recognized five main territorial divisions, in addition to a number of localized areas occupied by kindreds. Primary importance was assigned to the women in the ownership and maintenance of canoes and to the men in the acquisition of food. This division was somewhat blurred, however, as the men built the canoes and the women were important in food-getting activities. Since both males and females had critically important roles to play in subsistence, Yahgan gender relations were predictably much more egalitarian than those of the Ona; thus both the boys and girls went through puberty rites. Nevertheless, the fact that the Yahgan men still saw themselves as dominant—which nevertheless appears to have been balanced out in myth by reference to a time when the women had been dominant—is a feature of their society I have left unexplained in this book. That the Yahgan had risen against the longer-term carrying capacity of their environment, and hence must have had to control their numbers rigorously, is suggested by the specific delineation of subsistence-settlement boundaries, the defense of habitually used territories, and the continual hostilities that occurred between people at the local level. These hostilities included continual interpersonal and intergroup conflict as well as malevolent shamans who flung magical darts called *yékuš*.

The Nukak, like other scattered band groups in the Amazon, provide us with an example of the complex subsistence-settlement strategies that can characterize stable, longer-term migratory adaptations. From the data gathered by Gustavo Politis and his colleagues we know their environment has been made user-friendly by constant disruption of the natural processes of forest succession as clearings are made for temporary campsites throughout the 10,000-square-kilometer area occupied by the Nukak. Contrary to descriptions of hunter-gatherers as never engaging in the cultivation of plants, we now know that Nukak bands have long had a secondary focus on horticulture, in addition to their collecting-hunting focus—a fact that has substantial importance for models of the prehistoric domestication process in the Amazon. However, the published data from the first pioneering studies carried out in the 1990s by Politis and his colleagues are incomplete. We need to know more about social organization, intergroup relations, shamanism, and the maintenance and regulation of the Nukak adaptive system in relation to its environment, and we can only look forward to a continuation of this outstanding research project.

This is an age in which traditional, "pristine" indigenous adaptive systems are fast coming into contact with the outside world and anthropology as a discipline is changing as a result (e.g., in the development of a Marxist political-economy perspective that purports to look at the "world" system rather than the "local" systems we have looked at in this book—if, indeed, such systems as the Chavín, the Moche, and the Inca can be considered all that local). But the still-enduring Nukak band societies indicate that the process, thankfully, is not yet complete and that much more research in localized adaptive contexts will be possible, at least in the near future.

Village-Level Systems

The village-level societies we looked at in this book are, in order of geographical area, (1) six groups in the Amazon Basin—the Kuikuru, the Mundurucú, the Yanomamö, the Shuar-Jívaro, the Desana, and the Bororo; (2) one group in the far Andean north, the Kogi; (3) an archaeological site in Ecuador, Real Alto; and (4) two groups in the Central Andes, the Q'eros and Ayllu Kaata. In dealing with the environment of the Amazon and indigenous adaptations to it, systems across the entire terra firme area are limited by the availability of protein in their environment (just as the limiting factor characterizing hunting-gathering adaptive systems in the far south of the continent was the inapplicability of horticultural and agricultural subsistence to the entire area). As we conclude this book, let me mention that the protein-limiting argument is a far more controversial one than I have indicated earlier. I have intentionally avoided getting embroiled in this argument, not least because much, if not all, of the argumentation is carried on by researchers who take a decidedly unsophisticated approach to ecology (e.g., see Descola, 1996b, who "rails" unconvincingly against what he views as the scientific inadequacy of Meggers's division of the basin into terra firme and várzea environments).

In fact, to paraphrase a comment made earlier in this book, to those who would deny the ecological validity of the protein argument I direct the following challenge: Go out in the terra firme and find a place where either chiefdoms or states existed in the recent or ancient past. (Until such data are available, and certainly one can reject out of hand here Anna Roosevelt's specious arguments for Marajó Island "complexity," I take Meggers's argument to be valid.) If someone wishes to take up this challenge, she or he must play this game only in accordance with the rules of the evolutionary paradigm: by articulating a complete set of criteria for distinguishing different levels of sociopolitical integration. In other words, this player must make her or his paradigm explicit in order to test the protein theory!

But whether or not one takes as valid the assertion of this book that protein availability is the critical limiting factor of the basin, we have seen ample evidence for the regulation of human population numbers in each of the Amazon adaptive systems we have looked at. To summarize one example from the data we discussed in Chapter 6, the entire Mundurucú subsistence system prior to the 1960s was oriented around the limited availability of meat from game and the ritual regulation of the number of hunters who could engage in hunting. The Mundurucú maintained their numbers in light of the protein constraint by practicing a form of warfare that is unique in South America, with the men going out on long-distance military expeditions that took many of them away from their villages each year for several months on end. Those who successfully took a trophy head on these expeditions became *Dajeboiši* upon their return, men who could neither engage in sexual relations with their wives for two years nor hunt game, although their presence on the hunt was viewed as enhancing the ability of the other, nonritually restricted men to bring home the necessary game to feed a village. In accordance with this ritually and militarily regulated system, the Mundurucú also downplayed the importance of women in a variety of ways in their society, including the sanction of gang rape for any woman who cast her eyes on the sacred (phallus-charged) *karökö* trumpets. But like the Ona, the subordination of women was balanced out by reference to a mythical time when the women had been in control of society, although things had not been "right" because men had carried out the hunting even then. Finally, although intervillage relations among the Mundurucú essentially were peaceful, we have seen that the invisible darts called *causi* were hurled by the shamans at neighboring villages in the Mundurucú area itself. The maintenance of the adaptation thus clearly required that villages be distributed in densities low enough to keep the population attuned to the protein carrying capacity of their ecosystem.

In dealing with each of the other Amazonian groups (the Yanomamö, the Shuar-Jívaro, the Kuikuru, the Desana), we have seen that the *only* predictability about *terra firme* adaptive systems is that protein is universally the critical limiting factor. Otherwise, there is a tremendous amount of variability in how each group works out its adaptation so as to restrict its numbers and densities. The fundamental differences between the Yanomamö and the Shuar-Jívaro systems provide an example of this variability. Whereas the former group practices preferential female infanticide and has high sex ratios, the latter apparently does not practice any form of infanticide, yet has low sex ratios. The Shuar regulate their numbers by ritual abstinence from sex whenever a man is going out to hunt game and when he is training to become a shaman. As in the case of the Yanomamö, however, population densities are regulated by the occurrence of continual inter-settlement hostilities. In addition, the Shuar-Jívaro have one of the most complex cosmologies in relation to souls and soul power that we have seen: They obtain killer, or *arutam*, souls by taking hallucinogenic drugs; control the avenging, or *muisak*, soul of a killed warrior by sewing up the lips and eyes of the *tsantsa*; and then use this soul power in a magically charged but ritually practical way as a continual source of power in women's gardening, which is in itself critical for alliance formation and human survival in the hostile Shuar-Jívaro political milieu.

Apart from the systems of the eastern lowlands, localized Andean groups represent the other major type of village-level adaptive system in South America. Each group we have dealt with—the Kogi, the Q'eros, Ayllu Kaata—represents a variation of the general Andean adaptive strategy of verticality, although the limiting factors that characterize each of the three systems are variable from north to south. For example, the Kogi are constrained by three main factors. First, they have been cut off from direct access to the sea and its protein resources by the intrusion of Europeans onto the coastal plain; second, over the past several centuries there appears to have been a substantial degradation of their environment; third, they have developed an ideology that sees the (apparently) still-rich terraced lands of their Tairona ancestors as being ritually off-limits for modern use. The Kogi have maintained a good part of the vertical strategy that characterized their prehistoric ancestors, but the impact of these three (historical, environmental, and cosmological) constraints is that their adaptation is restricted to an egalitarian-village level of integration. In response, they have developed regulatory mechanisms that include the constant promotion of coca-produced male impotence, a rigorously maintained residential and ritual segregation of the sexes, and the removal of any pleasure in the sexual act by the confinement of women to a rigid position in order to ensure that the cosmic egg does not fall off the two logs that are held up by the four mythical men who sustain the universe. In spite of the well-integrated features of this system, the Kogi do not appear to see it as resulting from the severe constraints that have emerged at least since the beginning of European Contact in the sixteenth century. Instead, adopting the view that they have been chosen to regulate the precarious balance of the universe by ritual restraint, they see themselves as elder brothers to the ecologically misguided younger brothers of the outside world.

Although we have characterized the Andes overall as providing the most productivity of traditional (preindustrial) subsistence systems anywhere in South America, many Central Andean groups are limited by their confinement to smaller amounts of useable land circumscribed by high mountains. Both the Q'eros system, which is located only a relatively short distance to the northeast of the Cuzco Basin, and the Ayllu Kaata system, located east of Lake Titicaca, are examples of such environmental constraints, and each provides us with further evidence of the variability that characterizes the basic strategy of verticality throughout the Andes. Unlike the Kogi, who live near their ceremonial nuclei in the middle elevations of their geographic range, the Q'eros have established small permanent settlements in the highest elevations of their range, using Q'ero

Llacta, their ceremonial nucleus in the middle elevations, only infrequently on the occasion of (integrative) festivals. Nonetheless, all groups that participate effectively in the system must move continually throughout each year among the three elevation zones that characterize the range. The people of Ayllu Kaata have achieved access to the resources of the vertically stacked environmental zones in their area by integrating the various settlements in a single socioeconomic grouping, the *ayllu*. The mountain on which they live has been assigned cosmological status as a human body, whose various parts extend throughout the *ayllu* and whose integration is ritually maintained by specialists who live in the settlement nearest the viscera of the *ayllu* body.

In sum, although we see that the constraints characterizing both eastern lowland and Andean systems are predictable features of the study of human ecosystems, a great deal of variability characterizes village-level societies from place to place across the continent. If for no other reason than achieving further understanding of this variation, all those interested in South America surely will welcome research focused on the systems that still remain to be studied. It is thus not only in the similar problems that characterize these systems (e.g., protein or other social/physical environmental constraints) but also in the variable ways they have adapted to the constraints inherent in their subsistence-settlement systems that we find the data truly of interest to the student of ecological anthropology.

Chiefdom-Level Systems

As the reader is aware by this point, South American chiefdom systems either were totally extinguished shortly after the period of European Contact or disappeared earlier in the prehistoric period as part of normal evolutionary processes. The chiefdoms we have examined, either in detail or in brief in relation to a theoretical argument, are (1) the Omagua, of the Amazon *várzea*; (2) the Tairona, of the Sierra Nevada de Santa Marta; (3) Chavín de Huántar site, of the north central Peruvian Andes; and (4) the late preceramic and early ceramic period sites/systems of the central and north coastal areas of Peru (El Paraíso site, the Moxeke Period system of Casma Valley, and the prestate systems of Santa Valley).

The first three in this list are systems that for their location and time period represent the maximum level of sociopolitical integration that probably could be achieved within their adaptive contexts. For example, although the *várzea* niche of the main Amazon River channel is characterized by a sustainable year-to-year productivity that is substantially greater than that of the adjacent *terra firme*, nevertheless it is limited not only by its areal extent but also by the yearly inundation that covers most of it. And although the Tairona provide an example of the complexity that could occur with the extension of Andean verticality down onto the Caribbean shoreline to effectively incorporate marine resources in the overall subsistence system, the geographic extent of this system was highly limited in comparison to the Central Andean subsistence-environment systems that supported the development of state societies. However, in spite of the limitations of a small and sharply circumscribed local environment, the cult centered on

Chavín de Huántar rose spectacularly (and rather unexpectedly) above these constraints to influence ideologically a huge geographic area of the north-central Peruvian highlands and coast.

Of the archaeological data we have looked at, the late preceramic maritime site of El Paraíso appears to qualify as the center of a chiefdom society, irrespective of arguments about the precise nature of the mix of maritime and agricultural subsistence resources at the site. However, as is often the case with larger, architecturally complex sites in coastal Peruvian valleys, no published settlement pattern data are yet available from Chillón, the valley in which it is located, that would provide some understanding of the rural sites and demographic base that supported it. But a significant part of the site's subsistence base was indeed agricultural, and furthermore, the architectural remains at the site are not nearly as monumental as those characterizing any of the clearer candidates for statehood that have been discussed here (e.g., Sechín Alto, in the Patazca Period system of the Casma Valley; Cerro Blanco site, in the Moche multivalley system; and Cuzco, the Inca primary center). Given El Paraíso's relative noncomplexity in comparison to these clearer candidates, its status as the center of a two-level chiefdom society thus remains secure.

Indeed, the later, Initial Period Moxeke system of the Casma Valley features Pampa de la Llama-Moxeke, a site that is far more extensive than El Paraíso and substantially more complex architecturally. Yet in light of the preliminary estimate of fewer than twenty thousand persons in the system and its rather dispersed (nonintegrated) nature, the Initial Period Moxeke candidacy as a state-level system is doubtful. The Late Suchimancillo system, which is the most complex in the prestate sequence of the Santa Valley, does feature a larger population (estimated at around thirty thousand persons) than that estimated for the Moxeke Period, but there is no evidence of the architectural monumentality that characterizes societies that are clearly at a state level of integration. In fact, in comparison to the main temple at Chavín de Huántar—which hardly qualifies as an urban center by anyone's definition of a state—none of the architecture in late preceramic Chillón Valley, Moxeke Period Casma Valley, or Late Suchimancillo Santa Valley is nearly as complex.

In sum, the main conclusion to be drawn here is quite simply a comparative one: Whatever the level of stratification (i.e., chiefdom or state) to which one wants to assign these central Andean systems, they clearly were far more complex than any of the band- and village-level societies elsewhere in South America. That, of course, is one of the central Stewardian-derived arguments of this book.

State-Level Systems

In this book we have restricted the designation of a state level of sociopolitical integration to (1) single coastal Peruvian valley settings, in relation to anywhere else in Peru, for the earliest evidence of pristine state formation (i.e., the Patazca Period system of the Casma Valley, dating ~350 B.C.–A.D. 0); (2) the north Peruvian coast, in relation to anywhere else in the Central Andes, for the earliest evidence of multivalley state formation (i.e., the Moche system, dating ~A.D. 100–750); and (3) the Andes from Ecuador to northwest Argentina and central Chile, in relation to anywhere else in South America, for evidence of the maximum imperial polity that ever developed on the continent (i.e., the Inca system, dating ~A.D. 1200–1532). Since these states have been discussed in the preceding chapter, I shall not tax the reader's patience with a litany of the features suggesting that each is an example of the maximum complexity that could occur at the appropriate place and time—early on, in a localized context, the Patazca valleywide state appears; later on, in a regional context, the Moche multivalley state develops; and even later on, in a pan-Andean context, the Inca state expands to the level of an empire. Even in the one area of South America where states could evolve, then, there were still a rhyme and a reason to the development of the maximum complexity that could characterize indigenous adaptive systems of the continent.

A continuing process of the rise and fall of complex societies led to state societies of ever-increasing complexity in the Central Andes. This, in turn, was a process driven by the continuing tendency of populations to rise and human adaptive systems to respond by intensifying their subsistence base and, failing this, by expanding militarily and encroaching on other systems. That such processes—still driven by population, intensification, politics, and systemic expansion—continue to occur at an ever-expanding scale in the modern world seems to be, at the least, one of the principal lessons we can draw from our study of indigenous adaptive systems in South America, not to mention elsewhere as well.

Glossary

abiotic environment   the part of the physical environment that contains its inorganic features and elements.

achieved status   the form of status acquired by an individual over a lifetime of good works in relation to other individuals and the only kind of status that generally is characteristic of an egalitarian society. Compare *ascribed status*.

affines   kin related to an individual by marriage (as in "affinal kin"). Compare *consanguines*.

altiplano   the microenvironmental zone that lies at elevations of about 4,000 meters around Lake Titicaca and points south in central highland Bolivia. Like the Peruvian *puna*, the *altiplano* features seasonal rainfall and expanses of grassy tundra suitable for camelid pasturing and tuber cultivation but is increasingly colder and drier than the *puna* as it extends south into the higher latitudes. Compare *páramo, puna*.

ascribed status   the form of status assigned to an individual at birth, usually of a higher or lower sort in relation to other individuals, in a context that generally involves a stratified society. Compare *achieved status*.

ayni   a form of generalized reciprocity that has characterized traditional Central Andean egalitarian communities for centuries, in which people lend labor to their neighbors (often kinfolk), who, in return, provide them with food and coca.

band   the level of sociopolitical integration that refers to the less complex of the two forms of egalitarian society. Compare *village*.

biotic environment   the part of the physical environment that contains its organic features and elements.

bottom-up causation   a theory about the functioning and/or evolution of an adaptive system that includes reference to the effect that lower-order variables have on higher-order variables. Compare *multivariate causation, top-down causation*. See also *cause (causation), cultural materialism*.

carrying capacity   the productivity of a human adaptive system as expressed in terms of the number of people that can be sustained at a given point in time by the subsistence system and the relevant physical environment.

cause (causation)   the arguments that a researcher or theoretician makes in deciding which variable (e.g., mode of reproduction) or set of variables (e.g., the infrastructure) should be assigned primary responsibility either in the maintenance of equilibrium or in evolutionary change in a system. See also *multivariate causation*.

chief   the leader of a chiefdom.

chiefdom   the level of sociopolitical integration that refers to the less complex of the two forms of stratified society. Compare *state*.

consanguines   kin related to an individual by blood (as in "consanguineal kin"). Compare *affines*.

cordillera   a mountain chain in South America.

cosmology   belief systems about the meaning of the world. Compare *ideology*.

cultural ecology   the theoretical field of anthropology developed in the 1940s by Julian Steward. He proposed that a human adaptive system be understood primarily in reference to its environmental context and the culture core, or the material features that include the subsistence system, settlement pattern, and demography. See also *bottom-up causation*.

cultural materialism   the theoretical field of anthropology developed in the 1960s and 1970s by Marvin Harris. He proposes that a human adaptive system be understood as composed of five principal groupings of variables organized hierarchically in three levels. These levels (with the five variable groups shown in parentheses) are infrastructure (mode of production, mode of reproduction), structure (domestic economy, political economy), and superstructure (which is also a variable). Harris argues that cause (or causation) in the evolution and maintenance of the systems lies strictly in the infrastructure. Compare *multivariate causation*. See also *bottom-up causation*.

demography   the features of a human adaptive system that have to do with population numbers and densities, population controls and regulation, fertility, birthrates, and death rates. See also *mode of reproduction*.

domestic economy   the organization of the mode of production and the mode of reproduction at the structural level of the household and the local settlement.

doubling time (DT)   the number of years it takes for a population to double in size. The doubling time is computed by the following simple formula: $DT = 70/r$, where r = the growth rate of the population (e.g., if the growth rate is 2 percent, then $DT = 70/2$, or a 35-year doubling time).

ecological anthropology   the theoretical field of anthropology developed in the 1960s and 1970s by Roy Rappaport and others. Its adherents propose that a human adaptive system be understood as composed of hierarchically stacked sets of variables. The higher-order variables of the system (including ideology, ritual, and leadership) are critical in controlling, regulating, and maintaining the lower-order variables (including the physical environment, the subsistence system, the settlement pattern, and demography). The lower-order variables are critical in providing the productive output and the support base of the system. See also *multivariate causation, systems-hierarchical evolutionary paradigm*.

egalitarian society   the form of society, comprising the band and the village, whose members are essentially equal to one another except as a function of the achieved status acquired by certain individuals over their lifetime. Compare *stratified society*.

emic   the perspective about a human adaptive system that involves statements, beliefs, and explanations about its nature and functioning made by an individual or individuals who are part of that system—in other words, the indigenous viewpoint. Compare *etic*.

environmental zone   one of the eight geographic areas—Patagonia, the Pampas, the Gran Chaco, the Brazilian Highlands, the Amazon Basin, the Orinoco Basin, the Caribbean, and the Andes—identified for the continent of South America in this book.

etic   the perspective about a human adaptive system that involves statements, explanations, and beliefs about its nature and functioning made by individuals who study that system as anthropologically trained observers. This perspective not only takes into account the emic viewpoint of the participants (especially with regard to superstructure and general rules about behavior), but also relies on the researcher's own observations, data gathering, and knowledge base (e.g., with regard to cross-cultural data). Compare *emic*.

grand unifying theory   an approach, borrowed from theoretical physics, that proposes the unification of what appear to be disparate subfields in a discipline (e.g., anthropology) by reference to an overarching paradigm under which all of the subfields are subsumed (e.g., the systems-hierarchical evolutionary paradigm).

headman/headwoman   the male and female leaders of activities, specific or general, in an egalitarian society. See also *band*, *village*.

higher-order variable(s)   a variable (or variables) located in the upper levels of an adaptive system whose functions involve either the regulation and maintenance of that system (e.g., ritual and leadership) or beliefs and statements about its nature (e.g., cosmology, ideology, and ultimate sacred postulates). See also *lower-order variable*.

huaca   an adobe pyramidal platform construction dating to the prehispanic time period.

human adaptive system   the cultural (and biological) system by which a human group adapts to its physical context, including the biotic and abiotic environment, and the social environment. The ten variables of the systems-hierarchical model represent the graphic representation of this system. See also *systems-hierarchical evolutionary paradigm*.

ideology   the more abstract, higher-order features of the superstructure, including belief systems, that promote and maintain a society, inform its members about appropriate behaviors, and reinforce the behaviors necessary for systemic survival. Compare *cosmology*.

infrastructure   the lowest of the three levels of a human adaptive system. It comprises the mode of production, the settlement pattern, the mode of reproduction, and the physical environment. Compare *structure*, *superstructure*.

kichwa   an alternate pronunciation of the microenvironmental zone *quechua*, reflecting the variability of the Quechua language throughout the Central Andes.

levels of sociopolitical integration   an alternative term to "types" and "stages" for discussing the four main kinds of societies—band, village, chiefdom, and state—that are part of the systems-hierarchical evolutionary paradigm.

leadership   along with ritual, one of the more concrete aspects of the superstructure involving collective and individual behaviors at the level of policy that maintain, regulate, and change the human adaptive system. For purposes of the systems-hierarchical evolutionary paradigm, leadership includes the charisma, power, coordinative skills, and related directive actions of a headman, headwoman, chief, ruler, or other societal functionary.

Liebig's law of the minimum   the ecological principle that organisms must adapt their numbers to that necessary resource or nutrient that is least plentifully available in relation to all other necessary resources or nutrients or to that (unpredictable) year when all foods are available in quantities that are less than normal years. See also *ecological anthropology*.

limiting factor   a focus, related to Liebig's law of the minimum, on the factor (or factors) most parsimoniously accounting for the constraints on the productivity of an environment that, in turn, explain the number of individuals in a particular population that is adapted to that environment. Examples of limiting factors discussed here are the colder southerly latitudes (bands of Tierra del Fuego), protein availability (villages of the Amazonian *terra firme*), size of the agricultural niche and flooding (chiefdoms of the Amazonian *várzea*), El Niño countercurrent (chiefdoms of the ancient Peruvian maritime), and the size of the cultivable valley floor and volume of water flow (states of coastal Peruvian valleys).

littoral   the narrow microenvironmental zone that lies immediately to the west of the Andes Mountains along the far western edge of the South American continent and includes the coastal landmass itself and adjacent Pacific waters.

lower-order variable(s)   a variable (or variables) located in the lower levels of an adaptive system whose functions involve the productive output that provides the support base of that system (including the physical environment, the mode of production, the settlement pattern, and the mode of reproduction). See also *higher-order variable*.

microenvironmental zone   any of the subzones within one of the eight major environmental zones of South America—the *páramo, puna, altiplanto, quechua, montaña*, and littoral of the Andes; the *várzea* and *terra firme* of the Amazon Basin—identified in this book.

mit'a   the prehispanic Central Andean state-level institution involving the requirement that able-bodied individuals provide labor service to state construction projects each year on a short-term basis, in return for which they were provisioned with food and drink during the time of their service.

mode of production   the behaviors and technology involved in the production and consumption of the energy base, whose productive potential (or carrying capacity) is determined by the nature of both the subsistence system and the relevant physical environment.

mode of reproduction   the behaviors involved in regulating population size and density in the area occupied by the adaptive system.

montaña   the microenvironmental zone located at elevations between 1,500 and 3,000 meters above sea level along the eastern slopes of the Andes in which heavy rainfall and dense tropical vegetation occur.

multivariate causation   a theory about the functioning and/or evolution of a human adaptive system that includes reference to a multiple set of variables—potentially including ones in the superstructure, structure, and infrastructure—in explaining and understanding the nature of that system. Such a theory is the one employed in the systems-hierarchical evolutionary paradigm, and it can invoke both top-down causation and bottom-up causation. See also *ecological anthropology*.

other social systems   social systems outside the boundaries of a human adaptive system with which it interacts, either in a cooperative (e.g., trade) or a hostile (e.g., war) manner.

páramo   the Andean microenvironmental zone that lies at elevations of 3,000 meters above sea level between the two cordilleras of Ecuador and extends northward into Colombia. It is characterized by a cold climate, despite the equatorial latitudes, and abundant amounts of rainfall. Compare *puna, altiplano*.

physical environment   the relevant features of the abiotic and biotic environment, including energy resources and such systemic maintenance features as settlement spacing and defense, that provide for the survival of the human population with respect to other social systems.

political economy   the organization of the infrastructure and the local human adaptive system in general in relation to other social systems.

puna   the Andean microenvironmental zone that lies between about 4,000 and 4,800 meters above sea level and features cooler temperatures and seasonal rainfall and consists of expanses of grassy tundra on which the main subsistence adaptations have traditionally been camelid pasturing and tuber cultivation. Compare *altiplano, páramo*.

qeshwa   an alternate pronunciation of the microenvironmental zone *quechua*, reflecting the variability of the Quechua language throughout the Central Andes.

quechua   the temperate microenvironmental zone located along both sides of the Andes at elevations between about 2,300 and 3,500 meters above sea level that has traditionally been the principal focus of population, agricultural subsistence, and the cultivation of maize, quinoa, and other protein-rich cereals and crops in the Andes. See also *kichwa, qeshwa*. Compare *Quechua*.

Quechua   the language and name of one of the principal indigenous groups of the Central Andean highlands. Compare *quechua*.

rain forest   the humid tropical lowlands of the Amazon Basin.

ritual   along with leadership, one of the more concrete aspects of the superstructure involving centralized collective and individual behaviors at the level of policy that maintain, regulate, and change the human adaptive system. For purposes of the systems-hierarchical evolutionary paradigm, ritual includes ceremonies and shamanic activities that have an effect on the mind-set and behaviors of the participants or onlookers.

ruler   the leader of a state.

settlement pattern   the number, density, permanence, size, and function of settlements across the landscape within the area occupied by the human adaptive system.

sex ratio (SR)   the arithmetic ratio indicating the relative numbers of males and females in a population, obtained by dividing the number of males by the number of females and multiplying by 100. Since the normal sex ratio around the world is 105, one that is well above this number is male biased (e.g., the Yanomamö), and one that is well below it is female biased (e.g., the Shuar-Jívaro). In the systems-hierarchical evolutionary paradigm any sex ratio (normal, high, or low) requires explanation by reference to the features of the human adaptive system.

social environment   the aspects of neighboring systems that affect the local human adaptive system in terms of its own regulation, functioning, and survival. See also *other social systems*.

social organization   the central adaptive institutions at the level of structure that involve rules, patterns, and behaviors related to kinship and marriage and their role in organizing the domestic economy, the political economy, and the infrastructure.

state   the level of sociopolitical integration that refers to the more complex of the two forms of stratified society. Compare *chiefdom*.

stratified society   the form of society, comprising the chiefdom and the state, whose members are essentially unequal in relation to one another as a function of ascribed status. Compare *egalitarian society*.

structure   the middle of the three levels of a human adaptive system. It comprises the domestic economy, the social organization, the political economy, and, by extension, other social systems. Compare *infrastructure, superstructure*.

subsistence system   the way in which people obtain their food and other necessary resources in a traditional human adaptive system. See also *mode of production*.

superstructure the top of the three levels of a human adaptive system. It comprises ritual and leadership at the lower level of concrete, or material, behaviors and ideology/USPs at the higher level of the abstract, or nonmaterial, features of a human society. Compare *infrastructure, structure*.

systems theory the field of science that proposes that human adaptive systems (and other systems) be studied by breaking them down into a series of component variables whose maintenance, regulation, and evolution be understood and explained in terms of the causal relationships among those variables.

systems-hierarchical evolutionary paradigm a specific paradigmatic approach in ecological anthropology (developed in this book) that proposes human adaptive systems be studied in terms of (1) the four levels of sociopolitical integration (band, village, chiefdom, and state) and (2) ten variables organized hierarchically in three levels: infrastructure (the physical environment, the mode of production, the settlement pattern, the mode of reproduction), structure (the domestic economy, the social organization, the political economy, other social systems), and superstructure (ritual and leadership, ideology/ultimate sacred postulates). See also *ecological anthropology*.

systems-hierarchical model the graphic (and textual) representation of a human adaptive system that consists of ten major variable groups organized hierarchically in three main levels. See also *ecological anthropology, systems-hierarchical evolutionary paradigm*.

terra firme the area constituting about 98 percent of the Amazon Basin. Relative to the *várzea*, the *terra firme* is more limited in terms of energy productivity (e.g., protein) because of its ancient soils, a thinly developed humus layer, and heavy rainfall bringing about leaching of the nutrients from the soil.

top-down causation a theory about the functioning and/or evolution of an adaptive system that includes reference to the effect that higher-order variables have on lower-order variables. Compare *bottom-up causation, multivariate causation*.

ultimate sacred postulate (USP) from a term proposed by Roy Rappaport signifying the most sacred kinds of ideological/cosmological propositions and statements made by the members of a society about their adaptive system. USPs serve to inform or guide the thoughts and behaviors of a society's members.

várzea the area constituting about 2 percent of the Amazon Basin that consists of the main channel of the Amazon River and its Andean-derived tributaries. In comparison to the *terra firme*, the *várzea* is less limited in terms of subsistence productivity because of the nutrient-rich soil deposited on levee banks and low islands every year almost without fail.

village the level of sociopolitical integration that refers to the more complex of the two forms of egalitarian society. Compare *band*.

References

Acuña, Cristóbal de. 1859 [1641]. A New Discovery of the Great River of the Amazons. In *Expeditions into the Valley of the Amazons*, ed. Clements Markham, 41–134. London: Hakluyt Society.

Alva, Walter. 1988. Discovering the New World's Richest Tomb. *National Geographic* 174(4):510-523.

Alva, Walter, and Christopher Donnan. 1993. *Royal Tombs of Sipán*. Los Angeles: UCLA Fowler Museum of Cultural History.

Arciniegas, Germán, Clemencia Plazas, and Jaime Echeverri. 1990. *Secrets of El Dorado, Colombia*. Bogotá: El Sello Editorial.

Bahn, Paul, and John Flenley. 1992. *Easter Island, Earth Island*. New York: Thames and Hudson.

Basso, Ellen. 1988. *The Kalapalo Indians of Central Brazil*. Prospect Heights, Ill.: Waveland Press.

Bastien, Joseph. 1985. *Mountain of the Condor: Metaphor and Ritual in an Andean Ayllu*. Prospect Heights, Ill.: Waveland Press.

_____. 1987. *Healers of the Andes: Kallawaya Herbalists and Their Medicinal Plants*. Salt Lake City: University of Utah Press.

Bates, Henry Walter. 1975 [1876]. *The Naturalist on the River Amazons*. Reprint, New York: Dover.

Bauer, Brian. 1992. *The Development of the Inca State*. Austin: University of Texas Press.

Bawden, Garth. 1989. The Andean State as a State of Mind. Review of *The Origins and Development of the Andean State*, edited by Jonathan Haas, Sheila Pozorski, and Thomas Pozorski. *Journal of Anthropological Research* 45:327–332.

_____. 1996. *The Moche*. Cambridge, Mass.: Blackwell.

Benson, Elizabeth. 1972. *The Mochica: A Culture of Peru*. New York: Praeger.

Betanzos, Juan de. 1996 [1557]. *Narrative of the Incas*. Austin: University of Texas Press.

Biocca, Ettore. 1971. *Yanoáma: The Narrative of a White Girl Kidnapped by Amazonian Indians*. Trans. Dennis Rhodes. New York: Dutton.

Bird, Junius. 1988. *Travels and Archaeology in South Chile, with Travel Segments by Margaret Bird*. Ed. John Hyslop. Iowa City: University of Iowa Press.

Bode, Barbara. 1989. *No Bells to Toll: Destruction and Creation in the Andes*. New York: Scribner's.

Bonavía, Duccio. 1985. *Mural Paintings in Ancient Peru.* Trans. Patricia Lyon. Bloomington: Indiana University Press.

Bray, Warwick. 1978. *The Gold of El Dorado.* London: Royal Academy of Arts.

Bridges, E. Lucas. 1950. *Uttermost Part of the Earth.* New York: Dutton.

Brundage, Burr Cartwright. 1963. *Empire of the Inca.* Norman: University of Oklahoma Press.

_____. 1967. *Lords of Cuzco.* Norman: University of Oklahoma Press.

Brush, Stephen. 1977. *Mountain, Field, and Family: The Economy and Human Ecology of an Andean Valley.* Philadelphia: University of Pennsylvania Press.

Bryan, Alan. 1987. Points of Order. *Natural History* 6:6–11.

Bryan, Alan, Rodolfo Casamiquela, José Cruxent, Ruth Gruhn, and Claudio Ochsenius. 1978. An El Jobo Mastodon Kill at Taima-Taima, Venezuela. *Science* 200:1275–1277.

Buechler, Hans, and Judith-Maria Buechler. 1971. *The Bolivian Aymara.* New York: Holt, Rinehart and Winston.

Burger, Richard. 1984. *The Prehistoric Occupation of Chavín de Huántar, Peru.* University of California Publications in Anthropology, vol. 14. Berkeley and Los Angeles: University of California Press.

_____. 1988. Unity and Heterogeneity Within the Chavín Horizon. In *Peruvian Prehistory*, ed. Richard Keatinge, 99–144. New York: Cambridge University Press.

_____. 1992. *Chavín and the Origins of Andean Civilization.* New York: Thames and Hudson.

Byers, Douglas S., and Richard S. MacNeish. 1966–1977. *The Prehistory of the Tehuacán Valley.* 5 vols. Austin: University of Texas Press.

Cañadas Cruz, Luis. 1983. *El mapa bioclimático y ecológico del Ecuador.* Quito: Banco Central del Ecuador.

Carlson, John. 1990. America's Ancient Skywatchers. *National Geographic* 177(3): 76–107.

Carneiro, Robert. 1961. Slash-and-Burn Cultivation Among the Kuikuru and Its Implications for Cultural Development in the Amazon Basin. In *The Evolution of Horticultural Systems in Native South America, Causes and Consequences: A Symposium*, ed. Johannes Wilbert, 47–67. Caracas: Sociedad de Ciencias Naturales La Salle.

_____. 1970. A Theory of the Origin of the State. *Science* 169:733–738.

_____. 1988. Indians of the Amazonian Forest. In *People of the Tropical Rain Forest*, ed. Julie Denslow and Christine Padoch, 73–86. Berkeley and Los Angeles: University of California Press.

Carvajal, Gaspar de. 1934 [1535]. *The Discovery of the Amazon, According to the Account of Friar Gaspar de Carvajal and Other Documents.* Ed. José Toribio Medina. Special Publication no. 17. New York: American Geographical Society.

Castellanos, Juan. 1847. *Elegías de varones ilustres de Indias.* Madrid: Biblioteca de Autores Españoles.

Chagnon, Napoleon. 1968. *Yanomamö: The Fierce People.* New York: Holt, Rinehart and Winston.

_____. 1973. The Culture-Ecology of Shifting (Pioneering) Cultivation Among the Yanomamö Indians. In *Peoples and Cultures of Native South America*, ed. Daniel Gross, 124–142. Garden City, N.Y.: Natural History Press.

_____. 1992. *Yanomamö: The Last Days of Eden.* New York: Harcourt Brace Jovanovich.

_____. 1997. *Yanamamö.* 5th ed. New York: Harcourt Brace Jovanovich.

Chernela, Janet. 1993. *The Wanano Indians of the Brazilian Amazon*. Austin: University of Texas Press.

Cieza de León, Pedro de. 1959 [1553]. *The Incas of Pedro de Cieza de León*. Trans. Harriet de Onis. Ed. Victor Wolfgang von Hagen. Norman: University of Oklahoma Press.

Clapham Jr., W. B. 1983. *Natural Ecosystems*. 2d ed. New York: Macmillan.

Classen, Constance. 1993. *Inca Cosmology and the Human Body*. Salt Lake City: University of Utah Press.

Clastres, Pierre. 1977. *Society Against the State: The Leader as Servant and the Humane Use of Power Among the Indians of the Americas*. Trans. Robert Hurley. New York: Urizen Books.

Cobo, Bernabé. 1979 [1653]. *History of the Inca Empire*. Austin: University of Texas Press.

_____. 1990 [1653]. *Inca Religion and Customs*. Austin: University of Texas Press.

Coe, Michael. 1992. *Breaking the Maya Code*. New York: Thames and Hudson.

Cohen, Mark Nathan. 1977. *The Food Crisis in Prehistory: Overpopulation and the Origins of Agriculture*. New Haven: Yale University Press.

Conrad, Geoffrey. 1981. Cultural Materialism, Split Inheritance, and the Expansion of Ancient Peruvian Empires. *American Antiquity* 46(1):2–26.

Correal Urrego, Gonzalo. 1986. Apuntes sobre el medio ambiente pleistocénico y el hombre prehistórico en Colombia. In *New Evidence for the Pleistocene Peopling of the Americas*, ed. Alan Bryan, 115–131. Orono, Maine: Center for the Study of Early Man.

Darwin, Charles. 1962 [1860]. *The Voyage of the Beagle*. Garden City, N.Y.: Doubleday.

Denevan, William. 1966. *The Aboriginal Cultural Geography of the Llanos de Mojos, Bolivia*. Berkeley and Los Angeles: University of California Press.

_____. 1976. The Aboriginal Population of Amazonia. In *The Native Population of the Americas in 1492*, ed. William Denevan, 205–234. Madison: University of Wisconsin Press.

Descola, Philippe. 1996a. *In the Society of Nature: A Native Ecology in Amazonia*. Trans. Nora Scott. New York: Cambridge University Press.

_____. 1996b. *The Spears of Twilight: Life and Death in the Amazon Jungle*. Trans. Janet Lloyd. New York: New Press.

Dillehay, Tom. 1984. A Late Ice-Age Settlement in Southern Chile. *Scientific American* 251(4):106–112, 117.

_____. 1987. By the Banks of the Chinchihuapi. *Natural History* 4:8–12.

Donnan, Christopher. 1976. *Moche Art and Iconography*. Los Angeles: UCLA Latin American Center Publications.

_____. 1978. *Moche Art of Peru: Pre-Columbian Symbolic Communication*. Los Angeles: UCLA Museum of Cultural History.

Donnan, Christopher, and Carol Mackey. 1978. *Ancient Burial Patterns of the Moche Valley, Peru*. Austin: University of Texas Press.

Dorst, Jean. 1967. *South America and Central America: A Natural History*. New York: Random House.

Engel, Frederic. 1967. Le Complexe Preceramique d'El Paraiso (Perou). *Journal de la Société des Américanistes* 55(1):43–96.

Ereira, Alan. 1992. *The Elder Brothers: A Lost South American People and Their Message About the Fate of the Earth*. New York: Knopf.

Fagan, Brian. 1998. *People of the Earth: An Introduction to World Prehistory*. 9th ed. New York: HarperCollins.

Ferguson, R. Brian. 1995. *Yanomami Warfare: A Political History*. Santa Fe: School of American Research Press.

Flannery, Kent. 1968. Archaeological Systems Theory and Early Mesoamerica. In *Anthropological Archaeology in the Americas*, ed. Betty J. Meggers, 67–87. Washington, D.C.: Anthropological Society of Washington.

———. 1972. The Cultural Evolution of Civilizations. *Annual Review of Ecology and Systematics* 3:399–426.

Flannery, Kent, Joyce Marcus, and Robert Reynolds. 1989. *The Flocks of the Wamani: A Study of Llama Herders on the Punas of Ayacucho, Peru*. New York: Academic Press.

Food and Agricultural Organization of the United Nations. 1954. *Food Composition Tables—Minerals and Vitamins*. FAO Nutritional Studies no. 11. Rome: FAO.

———. 1957a. *Calorie Requirements. Report of the Second Committee on Calorie Requirements*. FAO Nutritional Studies no. 15. Rome: FAO.

———. 1957b. *Protein Requirements*. FAO Nutritional Studies no. 16. Rome: FAO.

Franck, Harry. 1917. *Vagabonding Down the Andes*. New York: Garden City Publishing.

Franklin, William L. 1981. Living with Guanacos: Wild Camels of South America. *National Geographic* 160(1):63–75.

Fritz, Samuel. 1922. *Journal of the Travels and Labours of Father Samuel Fritz in the River of the Amazons Between 1686 and 1723*. Trans. (from the Evora manuscript) George Edmundson. London: Hakluyt Society.

Fundación Puntos Suspensivos. N.d. *Colombia precolombina, Tairona*. Bogotá: Fundación Puntos Suspensivos.

Garcilaso de la Vega, Inca. 1966 [1609, 1616–1617]. *Royal Commentaries of the Incas and General History of Peru*. Trans. Harold Livermore. Austin: University of Texas Press.

Gartelmann, Karl Dieter. 1985. *Las huellas del jaguar: La arqueología en el Ecuador*. Quito: Imprenta Mariscal.

Gasparini, Graziano, and Luise Margolies. 1980. *Inca Architecture*. Trans. Patricia Lyon. Bloomington: Indiana University Press.

Gibbons, Ann. 1996. First Americans: Not Mammoth Hunters, but Forest Dwellers? *Science* 272(5260):346–347.

———. 1997. Monte Verde: Blessed but Not Confirmed. *Science* 275(5304):1256–1257.

Goldman, Irving. 1963. *The Cubeo Indians of the Northwest Amazon*. Urbana: University of Illinois Press.

Good, Kenneth. 1991. *Into the Heart: One Man's Pursuit of Love and Knowledge Among the Yanomama*. New York: Simon and Schuster.

Gregor, Thomas. 1977. *Mehinaku: The Drama of Daily Life in a Brazilian Indian Village*. Chicago: University of Chicago Press.

———. 1985. *Anxious Pleasures: The Sexual Lives of an Amazonian People*. Chicago: University of Chicago Press.

Gross, Daniel, ed. 1973. *Peoples and Cultures of Native South America*. Garden City, N.Y.: Natural History Press.

Guamán [Huamán] Poma de Ayala, Felipe. 1956 [1567–1615]. *La nueva crónica y buen gobierno*. 3 vols. Lima: Editorial Cultura.

———. 1978 [1567–1615]. *Letter to a King: A Peruvian Chief's Account of Life Under the Incas and Under Spanish Rule*. Trans. Christopher Dilke. New York: Dutton.

Guidon, Niède. 1984. Les premières occupations humaines de l'aire archéologique de São Raimundo Nonato, Piauí, Brésil. *L'Antropologie* 88(2):263–271.

———. 1987. Cliff Notes. *Natural History* 8:6–12.

Guidon, Nième, and G. Delibrias. 1986. Carbon-14 Dates Point to Man in the Americas 32,000 Years Ago. *Nature* 321(6072):769–771.

Gumilla, Joseph. 1791. *Historia natural civil y geográfica de las naciones situadas en las riveras del Río Orinoco*. Barcelona: C. Gilbert y Tuto.

Gusinde, Martín. 1986. *Los indios de Tierra del Fuego: Los Yámana*. 3 vols. Trans. Werner Hoffman. Buenos Aires: Centro Argentino de Etnología Americana.

_____. 1990. *Los indios de Tierra del Fuego: Los Selk'nam*. 2 vols. Trans. Werner Hoffman. Buenos Aires: Centro Argentino de Etnología Americana.

Harner, Michael. 1984. *The Jívaro: People of the Sacred Waterfall*. 2d ed., with new preface. Berkeley and Los Angeles: University of California Press.

Harris, Marvin. 1968. *The Rise of Anthropological Theory: A History of Theories of Culture*. New York: Crowell.

_____. 1974. *Cows, Pigs, Wars, and Witches: The Riddles of Culture*. New York: Vintage Books.

_____. 1977. *Cannibals and Kings: The Origins of Cultures*. New York: Vintage Books.

_____. 1979. *Cultural Materialism: The Struggle for a Science of Culture*. New York: Vintage Books.

_____. 1984. A Cultural Materialist Theory of Band and Village Warfare: The Yanomamo Test. In *Warfare, Culture, and Environment*, ed. R. Brian Ferguson, 111–140. New York: Academic Press.

Haynes, C. Vance. 1997. Dating a Paleoindian Site in the Amazon in Comparison with Clovis Culture. *Science* 275(5308):1948.

Hemming, John. 1978. *Red Gold: The Conquest of the Brazilian Indians*. Hong Kong: Papermac.

Hyslop, John. 1984. *The Inka Road System*. New York: Academic Press.

_____. 1990. *Inka Settlement Planning*. Austin: University of Texas Press.

Instituto Geográfico Militar. 1989. *Atlas del Perú*. Lima: Instituto Geográfico Militar.

Isbell, Billie Jean. 1978. *To Defend Ourselves: Ecology and Ritual in an Andean Village*. Prospect Heights, Ill.: Waveland Press.

James, David. 1973. The Evolution of the Andes. *Scientific American* 229(2):61–69.

Jennings, Jesse, ed. 1978. *Ancient South Americans*. San Francisco: Freeman.

Johnson, Allen, and Timothy Earle. 1987. *The Evolution of Human Societies: From Foraging Group to Agrarian State*. Stanford: Stanford University Press.

Kauffman Doig, Federico. 1978. *Manual de arqueología peruana*. Lima: Iberia.

Kendall, Ann. 1973. *Everyday Life of the Incas*. New York: Dorset Press.

Kirkpatrick, Sidney. 1992. *Lords of Sipán: A True Story of Pre-Inca Tombs, Archaeology, and Crime*. New York: Morrow.

Kroeber, Alfred. 1925. The Uhle Pottery Collections from Moche. *University of California Publications in American Archaeology and Ethnology* 21(5):191–234.

_____. 1926. Archaeological Explorations in Peru, Part I: Ancient Pottery from Trujillo. *Field Museum of Natural History, Anthropology Memoirs* 2(1).

_____. 1930. Archaeological Explorations in Peru, Part II: The Northern Coast. *Field Museum of Natural History, Anthropology Memoirs* 2(2).

Kuznar, Lawrence. 1995. *Awatimarka: The Ethnoarchaeology of an Andean Herding Community*. New York: Harcourt Brace.

Lathrap, Donald. 1970. *The Upper Amazon*. New York: Praeger.

_____. 1971. The Tropical Forest and the Cultural Context of Chavín. In *Dumbarton Oaks Conference on Chavín*, ed. Elizabeth Benson, 73–100. Washington, D.C.: Dumbarton Oaks.

_____. 1973. The "Hunting" Economies of the Tropical Forest Zone of South America: An Attempt at Historical Perspective. In *Peoples and Cultures of Native South America*, ed. Daniel Gross, 83–95. Garden City, N.Y.: Natural History Press.

_____. 1977. Our Father the Cayman, Our Mother the Gourd: Spinden Revisited, or a Unitary Model for the Emergence of Agriculture. In *Origins of Agriculture*, ed. Charles Reed, 712–791. The Hague: Mouton.

_____. 1985. Jaws: The Control of Power in the Early Nuclear American Ceremonial Center. In *Early Ceremonial Architecture in the Andes*, ed. Christopher Donnan, 241–267. Washington, D.C.: Dumbarton Oaks.

Lathrap, Donald, Jorge Marcos, and James Zeidler. 1977. Real Alto: An Ancient Ceremonial Center. *Archaeology* 30:2–13.

Lavalle, José Antonio de, ed. 1985. *Moche*. Colección Arte y Tesoros del Perú. Lima: Banco del Crédito del Perú.

Leonard, Robert, and George Jones. 1987. Elements of an Inclusive Evolutionary Model for Archaeology. *Journal of Anthropological Research* 6:199–219.

LeVine, Terry, ed. 1992. *Inka Storage Systems*. Norman: University of Oklahoma Press.

Lévi-Strauss, Claude. 1971. *Tristes Tropiques: An Anthropological Study of Primitive Societies in Brazil*. Trans. John Russell. New York: Atheneum.

_____. 1995. *Saudades do Brasil*. Seattle: University of Washington Press.

Lewin, Roger. 1982. *Thread of Life: The Smithsonian Looks at Evolution*. Washington, D.C.: Smithsonian Institution Press.

Lizot, Jacques. 1985. *Tales of the Yanomami: Daily Life in the Venezuelan Forest*. New York: Cambridge University Press.

Lumbreras, Luis. 1971. Towards a Re-evaluation of Chavín. In *Dumbarton Oaks Conference on Chavín*, ed. Elizabeth Benson, 1–28. Washington, D.C.: Dumbarton Oaks.

_____. 1974. *The Peoples and Cultures of Ancient Peru*. Trans. Betty Meggers. Washington, D.C.: Smithsonian Institution Press.

_____. 1989. *Chavín de Huántar en el nacimiento de la civilización andina*. Lima: INDEA.

Lynch, Thomas. 1983. The Paleo-Indians. In *Ancient South Americans*, ed. Jesse Jennings, 87–137. San Francisco: Freeman.

_____. 1990. Glacial Age Man in South America? *American Antiquity* 55(1):12–36.

_____, ed. 1980. *Guitarrero Cave: Early Man in the Andes*. New York: Academic Press.

Lyon, Patricia. 1974. *Native South Americans: Ethnology of the Least-Known Continent*. Boston: Little, Brown.

MacNeish, Richard. 1971. Early Man in the Andes. *Scientific American* 224(4):36–46.

_____. 1992. *The Origins of Agriculture and Settled Life*. Norman: University of Oklahoma Press.

Markham, Clements, ed. 1859. *Expeditions into the Valley of the Amazons, 1539, 1540, 1639*. London: Hakluyt Society.

Matos Mendieta, Ramiro. 1994. *Pumpú: Centro administrativo Inka de la Puna de Junín*. Lima: Editorial Horizonte.

Matsuzawa, Tsugio. 1978. The Formative Site of Las Haldas, Peru: Architecture, Chronology, and Economy. *American Antiquity* 43(4):652–672.

Maybury-Lewis, David. 1974. *Akwe-Shavante Society*. New York: Oxford University Press.

_____. 1988. *The Savage and the Innocent*. Boston: Beacon Press.

McEwan, Colin, and Maarten Van de Guchte. 1992. Ancestral Time and Sacred Space in Inka State Ritual. In *The Ancient Americas: Art from Sacred Landscapes*, ed. Richard Townsend, 359–371. Chicago: Art Institute of Chicago.

Meadows, Donella H., Dennis L. Meadows, and Jørgen Randers. 1992. *Beyond the Limits: Confronting Global Collapse, Envisioning a Sustainable Future*. Post Hills, Vt.: Chelsea Green.

Meadows, Donella H., Dennis L. Meadows, Jørgen Randers, and William W. Behrens III. 1972. *The Limits to Growth: A Report for the Club of Rome's Project on the Predicament of Mankind*. New York: Signet Books.

Meggers, Betty. 1969. *Ecuador*. New York: Praeger.

_____. 1971. *Amazonia: Man and Culture in a Counterfeit Paradise*. Arlington Heights, Ill.: Harlan Davidson.

_____. 1992a. Amazonia: Real or Counterfeit Paradise? Review of *Moundbuilders of the Amazon: Geophysical Archaeology on Marajó Island, Brazil*, by Anna Roosevelt. *Review of Archaeology* 13(2):25–40.

_____. 1992b. *Prehistoric America*. New York: Aldine.

_____. 1992c. Review of *Moundbuilders of the Amazon: Geophysical Archaeology on Marajó Island, Brazil*, by Anna Roosevelt. *Journal of Field Archaeology* 19:399–404.

_____. 1996. *Amazonia: Man and Culture in a Counterfeit Paradise*. Rev. ed. Washington, D.C.: Smithsonian Institution Press.

Meggers, Betty, and Clifford Evans. 1973. An Interpretation of the Cultures of Marajó Island. In *Peoples and Cultures of Native South America*, ed. Daniel Gross, ed. 39–47. Garden City, N.Y.: Natural History Press.

Meltzer, David. 1995. Stones of Contention. *New Scientist* 146(1983):31–35.

Meltzer, David, James Adovasio, and Tom Dillehay. 1994. On a Pleistocene Human Occupation at Pedra Furada, Brazil. *Antiquity* 68:695–714.

Mishkin, Bernard. 1963. The Contemporary Quechua. In *Handbook of South American Indians*, ed. Julian Steward, 2:411–470. New York: Cooper Square.

Moore, Ruth. 1964. *Evolution*. New York: Time.

Morales, Edmundo. 1995. *The Guinea Pig: Healing, Food, and Ritual in the Andes*. Tucson: University of Arizona Press.

Moran, Emilio. 1981. *Developing the Amazon*. Bloomington: Indiana University Press.

_____. 1993. *Through Amazonian Eyes: The Human Ecology of Amazonian Populations*. Iowa City: University of Iowa Press.

Morris, Craig, and Donald Thompson. 1985. *Huánuco Pampa: An Inca City and Its Hinterland*. New York: Thames and Hudson.

Moseley, Michael. 1975. *The Maritime Foundations of Andean Civilization*. Menlo Park, Calif.: Cummings.

Moseley, Michael, and Kent Day. 1982. *Chan Chan: Andean Desert City*. Albuquerque: University of New Mexico Press.

Moseley, Michael, and Charles Hastings. 1975. The Adobes of Huaca del Sol and Huaca de la Luna. *American Antiquity* 40(2):196–202.

Murphy, Robert. 1958. *Mundurucú Religion*. University of California Publications in American Archaeology and Ethnology, vol. 1, no. 1. Berkeley and Los Angeles: University of California Press.

_____. 1960. *Headhunter's Heritage: Social and Economic Change Among the Mundurucú Indians*. Berkeley and Los Angeles: University of California Press.

Murphy, Yolanda, and Robert Murphy. 1985. *Women of the Forest*. 2d ed. New York: Columbia University Press.

Murra, John. 1975. El control vertical de un máximo de pisos ecológicos en la economía de las sociedades andinas. In *Formaciones económicas y políticas del mundo andino*, ed. John Murra, 59–115. Lima: Instituto de Estudios Peruanos.

———. 1978. *La organización económica del estado inca*. México, D.F.: Siglo Veintiuno.

National Research Council. 1989. *Lost Crops of the Incas: Little-Known Plants of the Andes with Promise for Worldwide Cultivation*. Washington, D.C.: National Academy Press.

Netting, Robert. 1968. *Hill Farmers of Nigeria: Cultural Ecology of the Kofyar of the Jos Plateau*. Seattle: University of Washington Press.

Odum, Eugene. 1971. *Fundamentals of Ecology*. 3d ed. Philadelphia: Saunders.

Oviedo y Valdés, Gonzalo Fernández de. 1851–1855. *Historia general y natural de las Indias islas de tierra firme del Mar Océano*. Madrid: Biblioteca de Autores Españoles.

Pachacuti Yamqui Salcamaygua, Joan de Santa Cruz. 1993 [1613]. *Relación de antigüedades deste reyno del Piru*. Lima: Institut Français D'Études Andines.

Patterson, Thomas. 1991. *The Inca Empire: The Formation and Disintegration of a Pre-Capitalist State*. New York: Berg.

Paulsen, Allison. 1970. A Chronology of Guangala and Libertad Ceramics of the Santa Elena Peninsula in South Coastal Ecuador. Ph.D. diss., Columbia University.

Pearsall, Deborah. 1978. Phytolith Analysis of Archaeological Soils: Evidence for Maize Cultivation in Formative Ecuador. *Science* 199(4325):177–178.

———. 1992. The Origins of Plant Cultivation in South America. In *The Origins of Agriculture: An International Perspective*, ed. C. Wesley Cowan and Patty Jo Watson, 173–205. Washington, D.C.: Smithsonian Institution Press.

Politis, Gustavo. 1995. *Mundo de los Nükák: Amazonía colombiana*. Bogotá: Fondo de la Promoción de la Cultura.

Politis, Gustavo, and Julián Rodríguez. 1994. Algunos aspectos de subsistencia de los Nukak de la amazonía colombiana. *Colombia Amazónica* 7(1–2):169–207.

Pozorski, Shelia, and Thomas Pozorski. 1987. *Early Settlement and Subsistence in the Casma Valley, Peru*. Iowa City: University of Iowa Press.

———. 1994. Early Andean Cities. *Scientific American* 270(6):66–72.

Proulx, Donald. 1968. *An Archaeological Survey of the Nepeña Valley, Peru*. Research Report no. 2. Amherst: University of Massachusetts, Department of Anthropology.

———. 1983. Tiahuanaco and Huari. In *Art of the Andes: Pre-Columbian Sculptured and Painted Ceramics from the Arthur M. Sackler Collection*, ed. Lois Katz, 87–106. Washington: Arthur M. Sackler Foundation.

Pulgar Vidal, Javier. 1996. *Geografía del Perú*. 10th ed. Lima: Peisa.

Quilter, Jeffrey. 1985. Architecture and Chronology at El Paraíso, Peru. *Journal of Field Archaeology* 12(3):279–297.

Ramos, Alcida Rita. 1995. *Sanumá Memories: Yanomami Ethnography in Times of Crisis*. Madison: University of Wisconsin Press.

Rappaport, Roy. 1968. *Pigs for the Ancestors: Ritual in the Ecology of a New Guinea People*. New Haven: Yale University Press.

———. 1971. Nature, Culture, and Ecological Anthropology. In *Man, Culture, and Society*, ed. Harry Shapiro, 237–267. Rev. ed. New York: Oxford University Press.

Ravines, Rogger. 1978. Recursos naturales de los Andes. In *Tecnología andina*, ed. Rogger Ravines, 1–74. Lima: Instituto de Estudios Peruanos.

Reader's Digest Association. 1986. *Mysteries of the Ancient Americas: The New World Before Columbus.* Pleasantville, N.Y.: Reader's Digest Association.

Redman, Charles. 1978. *The Rise of Civilization: From Early Farmers to Urban Society in the Ancient Near East.* San Francisco: Freeman.

Reichel-Dolmatoff, Gerardo. 1950. *Los Kogi: Una tribu de la Sierra Nevada de Santa Marta, Colombia.* 2 vols. Bogotá: Editorial Iqueima.

———. 1951. *Datos histórico-culturales sobre las tribus de la antigua gobernación de Santa Marta.* Instituto Etnológico del Magdalena, Santa Marta. Bogotá: Banco de la República.

———. 1965. *Colombia.* London: Thames and Hudson.

———. 1971. *Amazonian Cosmos: The Sexual and Religious Symbolism of the Tukano Indians.* Chicago: University of Chicago Press.

———. 1972. The Cultural Context of an Aboriginal Hallucinogen: *Banisteriopsis caapi.* In *Flesh of the Gods: The Ritual Use of Hallucinogens,* ed. Peter Furst, 84–113. New York: Praeger.

———. 1976. Cosmology as Ecological Analysis. *Man* 11:307–318.

———. 1990. *The Sacred Mountain of Colombia's Kogi Indians.* New York: Brill.

———. 1996. *The Forest Within: The World View of the Tukano Amazonian Indians.* Tulsa: Council Oak Books.

Reinhard, Johan. 1992. Sacred Peaks of the Andes. *National Geographic* 185(3):84–111.

———. 1996. Peru's Ice Maidens: Unwrapping the Secrets. *National Geographic* 189(6):62-81.

Rengifo Vásquez, Grimaldo. 1987. *La agricultura tradicional en los Andes: Manejo de suelos, sistemas de labranza y herramientas agrícolas.* Lima: Editorial Horizonte.

Richardson III, James. 1994. *People of the Andes.* Washington, D.C.: Smithsonian Institution Press.

Rick, John. 1980. *Prehistoric Hunters of the High Andes.* New York: Academic Press.

Robinson, David. 1971. *Peru in Four Dimensions.* Detroit: Blaine Ethridge.

Roe, Peter. 1974. *A Further Exploration of the Rowe Chavín Seriation and Its Implications for North-Central Coast Chronology.* Studies in Precolumbian Art and Archaeology no. 13. Washington, D.C.: Dumbarton Oaks.

Roosevelt, Anna. 1989. Lost Civilizations of the Lower Amazon. *Natural History* (February):76–82.

———. 1991. *Moundbuilders of the Amazon: Geophysical Archaeology on Marajó Island, Brazil.* San Diego: Academic Press.

Roosevelt, Anna, C. M. Lima da Costa, C. Lopes Machado et al. 1996. Paleoindian Cave Dwellers in the Amazon: The Peopling of the Americas. *Science* 272(5260):373–384.

Roscoe, Paul, and Robert Graber, eds. 1988. Circumscription and the Evolution of Society. *American Behavioral Scientist* 31(4):405–511.

Rouse, Irving, and José Cruxent. 1963. *Venezuelan Archaeology.* New Haven: Yale University Press.

Rowe, John. 1962. *Chavín Art: An Inquiry into Its Form and Meaning.* New York: Museum of Primitive Art.

———. 1963. Inca Culture at the Time of the Spanish Conquest. In *Handbook of South American Indians,* ed. Julian Steward, 2:183–330. New York: Cooper Square.

———. 1971. The Influence of Chavín Art on Later Styles. In *Dumbarton Oaks Conference on Chavín,* ed. Elizabeth Benson, 101–124. Washington, D.C.: Dumbarton Oaks.

Russo, Raymond, and Paul Silver. 1995. The Andes' Deep Origins. *Natural History* (February):53–58.

Rydén, Stig. 1957. *Andean Excavations*. Vol. 1: *The Tiahuanaco Era East of Lake Titicaca*. Publication no. 4. Stockholm: Ethnographical Museum of Sweden.

Sagan, Carl. 1977. *The Dragons of Eden: Speculations on the Evolution of Human Intelligence*. New York: Ballantine Books.

Sahlins, Marshall. 1972. *Stone Age Economics*. Chicago: Aldine-Atherton.

Sallnow, Michael. 1987. *Pilgrims of the Andes: Regional Cults in Cusco*. Washington, D.C.: Smithsonian Institution Press.

Sauer, Carl. 1963. Geography of South America. In *Handbook of South American Indians*, ed. Julian Steward, 6:319–344. New York: Cooper Square.

Schultes, Richard Evans, and Albert Hofmann. 1992. *Plants of the Gods: Their Sacred, Healing, and Hallucinogenic Powers*. Rochester, Vt.: Healing Arts Press.

Schuster, Angela. 1992. Inside the Royal Tombs of the Moche. *Archaeology* 45(6):30–37.

Service, Elman. 1962. *Primitive Social Organization: An Evolutionary Perspective*. New York: Random House.

Shapiro, Judith. 1972. Sex Roles and Social Structure Among the Yanomama Indians of Northern Brazil. Ph.D. diss., Columbia University.

Shippee, Robert. 1932. The "Great Wall of Peru" and Other Aerial Photographic Studies by the Shippee-Johnson Peruvian Expedition. *Geographical Review* 22(1):1–29.

_____. 1933. Air Adventures in Peru. *National Geographic* 63:81–120.

Shoumatoff, Alex. 1978. *The Rivers Amazon*. San Francisco: Sierra Club Books.

Silverblatt, Irene. 1987. *Moon, Sun, and Witches: Gender Ideologies and Class in Inca and Colonial Peru*. Princeton: Princeton University Press.

Simón, Pedro. 1892. *Noticias historiales de las conquistas de tierra firme en las Indias Occidentales*. 5 vols. Bogotá: Casa Editorial de Medardo Rivas.

Simpson, George Gaylord. 1967. *The Meaning of Evolution*. Rev. ed. New York: Bantam Books.

Siskind, Janet. 1973. *To Hunt in the Morning*. New York: Oxford University Press.

Smith, Bruce. 1995. *The Emergence of Agriculture*. New York: Freeman.

Smole, William. 1976. *The Yanoama Indians: A Cultural Geography*. Austin: University of Texas Press.

Soto Holguín, Alvaro. 1988. *La ciudad perdida de los Tayrona: Historia de su hallazgo y descubrimiento*. Colombia: Centro de Estudios del Neotrópico.

Stevens, William. 1989. Andean Culture Found to Be as Old as the Great Pyramids. *New York Times*, October 3.

_____. 1990. Research in "Virgin" Amazon Uncovers Complex Farming. *New York Times*, April 3.

Steward, Julian. 1955. *Theory of Culture Change: The Methodology of Multilinear Evolution*. Urbana: University of Illinois Press.

_____. 1977. *Evolution and Ecology: Essays on Social Transformation*. Ed. Jane Steward and Robert Murphy. Urbana: University of Illinois Press.

_____, ed. 1963. *Handbook of South American Indians*. 7 vols. New York: Cooper Square.

Steward, Julian, and Louis Faron. 1959. *Native Peoples of South America*. New York: McGraw-Hill.

Stierlin, Henri. 1984. *Art of the Incas and Its Origins*. New York: Rizzoli.

Strong, William, and Clifford Evans Jr. 1952. *Cultural Stratigraphy in the Virú Valley, Northern Peru: The Formative and Florescent Epochs*. New York: Columbia University Press.

Sullivan, Lawrence. 1988. *Icanchu's Drum: An Orientation to Meaning in South American Religions.* New York: Macmillan.

Tello, Julio. 1960. *Chavín: Cultura matriz de la civilización andina.* Lima: Archivo "Julio C. Tello" de la Universidad Nacional Mayor de San Marcos.

Tosi Jr., Joseph A. 1960. Zonas de vida natural en el Perú: Memoria explicativa del *Mapa Ecológico del Perú.* Lima: Instituto Interamericano de Ciencias Agrícolas.

Towle, Margaret. 1961. *The Ethnobotany of Pre-Columbian Peru.* Viking Fund Publications in Anthropology no. 30. New York: Wenner-Gren Foundation for Anthropological Research.

Turnbull, Colin. 1961. *The Forest People.* New York: Simon and Schuster.

Uceda, Santiago, and Elías Mujica, eds. 1994. *Moche: Propuestas y perspectivas.* Trujillo, Peru: Universidad Nacional de La Libertad.

Uhle, Max. 1915. Las ruinas de Moche. *Boletín de la Sociedad Geográfica de Lima* 30(3–4):57–71.

Urton, Gary. 1981. *At the Crossroads of the Earth and the Sky: An Andean Cosmology.* Austin: University of Texas Press.

Van Tilburg, Jo Anne. 1994. *Easter Island: Archaeology, Ecology, and Culture.* Washington, D.C.: Smithsonian Institution Press.

Verswijver, Gustaaf. 1996. *Mekranoti: Living Among the Painted People of the Amazon.* New York: Prestel.

Wagley, Charles. 1977. *Welcome of Tears: The Tapirapé Indians of Central Brazil.* New York: Oxford University Press.

Wallace, Alfred Russell. 1972 [1889]. *A Narrative of Travels on the Amazon and Rio Negro.* Reprint, New York: Dover.

Wassén, S. Henry. 1972. *A Medicine-Man's Implements and Plants in a Tiahuanacoid Tomb in Highland Bolivia.* Ethnology Study 32. Göteborg, Sweden: Etnografiska Museum.

Weberbauer, August. 1945. *El mundo vegetal de los Andes Peruanos.* Lima: Die Pflanzenwelt der peruanischen Anden.

Webb, Malcolm. 1968. Carneiro's Hypothesis of Limited Land Resources and the Origins of the State: A Latin Americanist's Approach to an Old Problem. *South Eastern Latin Americanist* 12(3):1–8.

Webster, Steven. 1972. *The Social Organization of a Native Andean Community.* Ann Arbor, Mich.: University Microfilms.

Weiss, Gerald. 1975. *The World of a Forest Tribe in South America.* Anthropological Papers, vol. 52, pt. 5. New York: American Museum of Natural History.

Whitmore, T., and G. Prance, eds. 1987. *Biogeography and Quaternary History in Tropical America.* Oxford: Clarendon Press.

Willey, Gordon. 1953. *Prehistoric Settlement Patterns in the Virú Valley, Peru.* Bulletin no. 155. Washington, D.C.: Smithsonian Institution, Bureau of American Ethnology.

———. 1971. *An Introduction to American Archaeology: South America.* Englewood Cliffs, N.J.: Prentice-Hall.

Wilson, David. 1981. Of Maize and Men: A Critique of the Maritime Hypothesis of State Origins on the Coast of Peru. *American Anthropologist* 83:93–120.

———. 1983. The Origins and Development of Complex Prehispanic Society in the Lower Santa Valley: Implications for Theories of State Origins. *Journal of Anthropological Archaeology* 2:209–276.

———. 1987. Reconstructing Patterns of Early Warfare in the Lower Santa Valley: New Data on the Role of Conflict in the Origins of Complex North Coast Society. In *Ori-*

gins and Development of the Andean State, ed. Jonathan Haas, Sheila Pozorski, and Thomas Pozorski, 56–69. New York: Cambridge University Press.

———. 1988. *Prehispanic Settlement Patterns in the Lower Santa Valley, Peru: A Regional Perspective on the Origins and Development of Complex North Coast Society.* Washington, D.C.: Smithsonian Institution Press.

———. 1989. Full-Coverage Survey in the Lower Santa Valley: Implications for Regional Settlement Pattern Studies on the Peruvian Coast. In *The Archaeology of Regions: The Case for Full-Coverage Regional Survey,* ed. Suzanne Fish and Steven Kowalewski, 117–145. Washington, D.C.: Smithsonian Institution Press.

———. 1997. Early State Formation on the North Coast of Peru: A Critique of the City-State Model. In *The Archaeology of City-States: Cross-Cultural Approaches,* ed. Deborah Nichols and Thomas Charlton, 229–244. Washington, D.C.: Smithsonian Institution Press.

Zuidema, R. Tom. 1964. *The Ceque System of Cuzco: The Social Organization of the Capital of the Inca.* Leiden: Brill.

———. 1986. *Inca Civilization in Cuzco.* Trans. Jean-Jacques Decoster. Austin: University of Texas Press.

Index